KIKI
DE MONTPARNASSE
CATEL & BOCQUET

KIKI
DE MONTPARNASSE

CATEL & BOCQUET

SELF MADE HERO

To Christiane and Jean
Danielle and Michel

Thank you
for their active participation to Laetitia Lehmann, Laetitia Bocquet and Line Sheibling, for their support
and their help to Agnès Aittouares, Sophie Blainvillain, Brigitte Boujassy, Sylvie Buisson, Christine Cam,
Laurence Caracalla, Elsa Daillencourt, Kathy Degreef, Jean Digne, Alexandre Fillon, Pascal Gauthier,
Philippe Ghielmetti, Héloïse Guerrier, Anne Lacour, Jacques Loustal, Martine Marchand, Hanifa Melhenas,
Marion Meyer, Jesus Moreno, Françoise Navailh, Christian Parisot, Jean-Marc Pau, Niki Picalitos, Jean
Pieffort, Philippe Pierre-Adolphe, Julie Schleibling, Sir Guigui, Gilles Surirey, Lili Sztajn, Marie-Thèrése
Vierira, Jeanine Warnod & Steve Cuzor, for translations into English to Manon Manœuvre and into
German to Jean Muller. Thanks for the warm welcome at the Welcome hotel in Villefranche-sur-mer on the
Mediterranean at Saint-Tropez and to the Île-Bouchard Commandery.

First published in English in 2011 by SelfMadeHero, a division of
Metro Media Ltd, of 5 Upper Wimpole Street London W1G 6BP.

Illustrated by Catel
Written by José-Louis Bocquet

Translated from the Belgian edition by Nora Mahony
c/o Parkbench Publishing Services
Editorial & Lettering: Lizzie Kaye
Marketing Director: Doug Wallace
Publishing Director: Emma Hayley
With thanks to: Jane Laporte and Nick de Somogyi

Published with the financial assistance of the Centre National du Livre
Ouvrage publié avec le soutien du Centre National du livre

First published in French by Casterman in 2007 as:
KIKI de Montparnasse
Copyright text and illustrations © 2007 by Casterman

10 9 8 7 6 5 4 3

ISBN: 978-1-906838-25-6

Printed and bound in China

1901 - Châtillon-sur-Seine

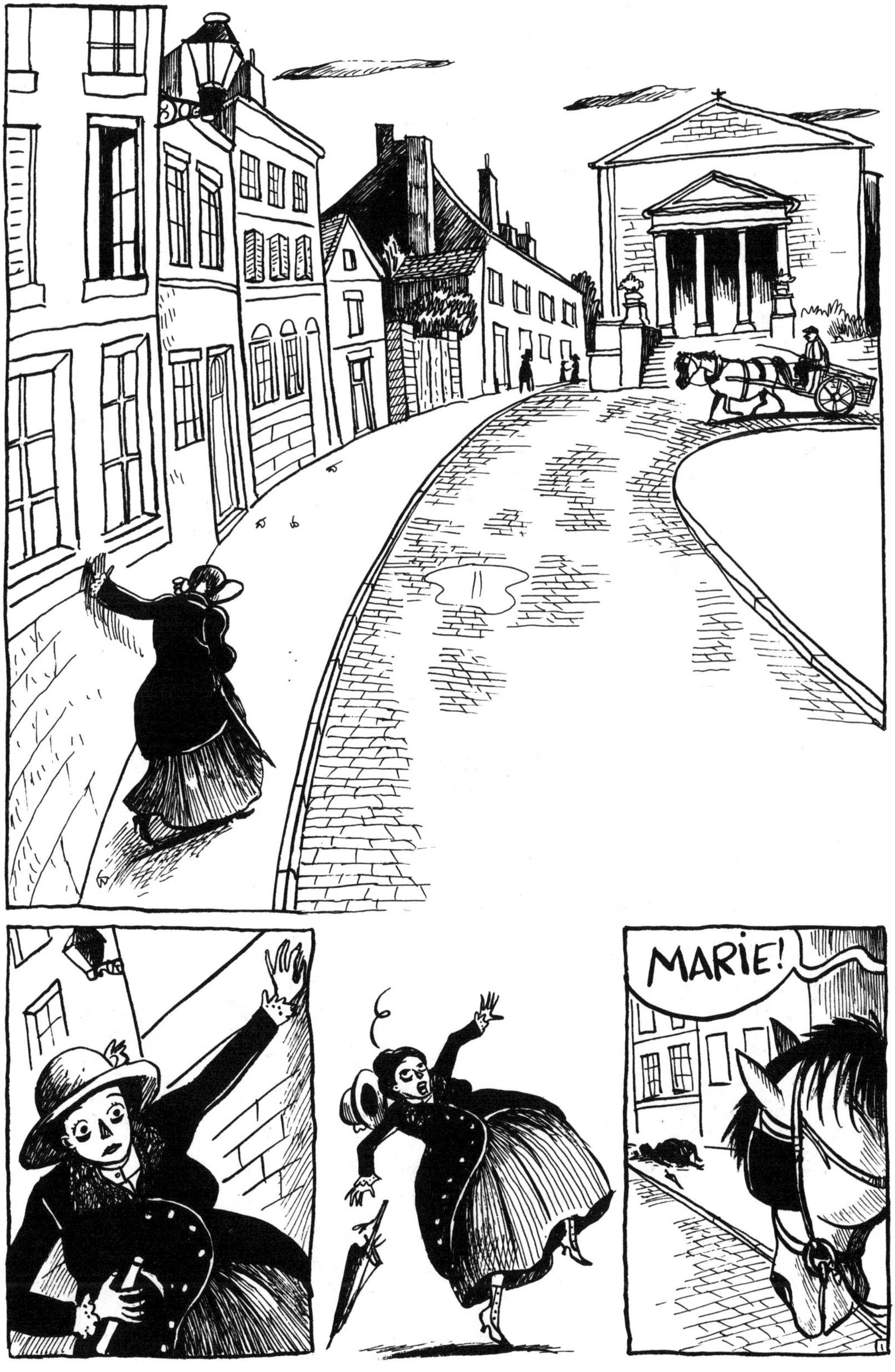
MARIE!

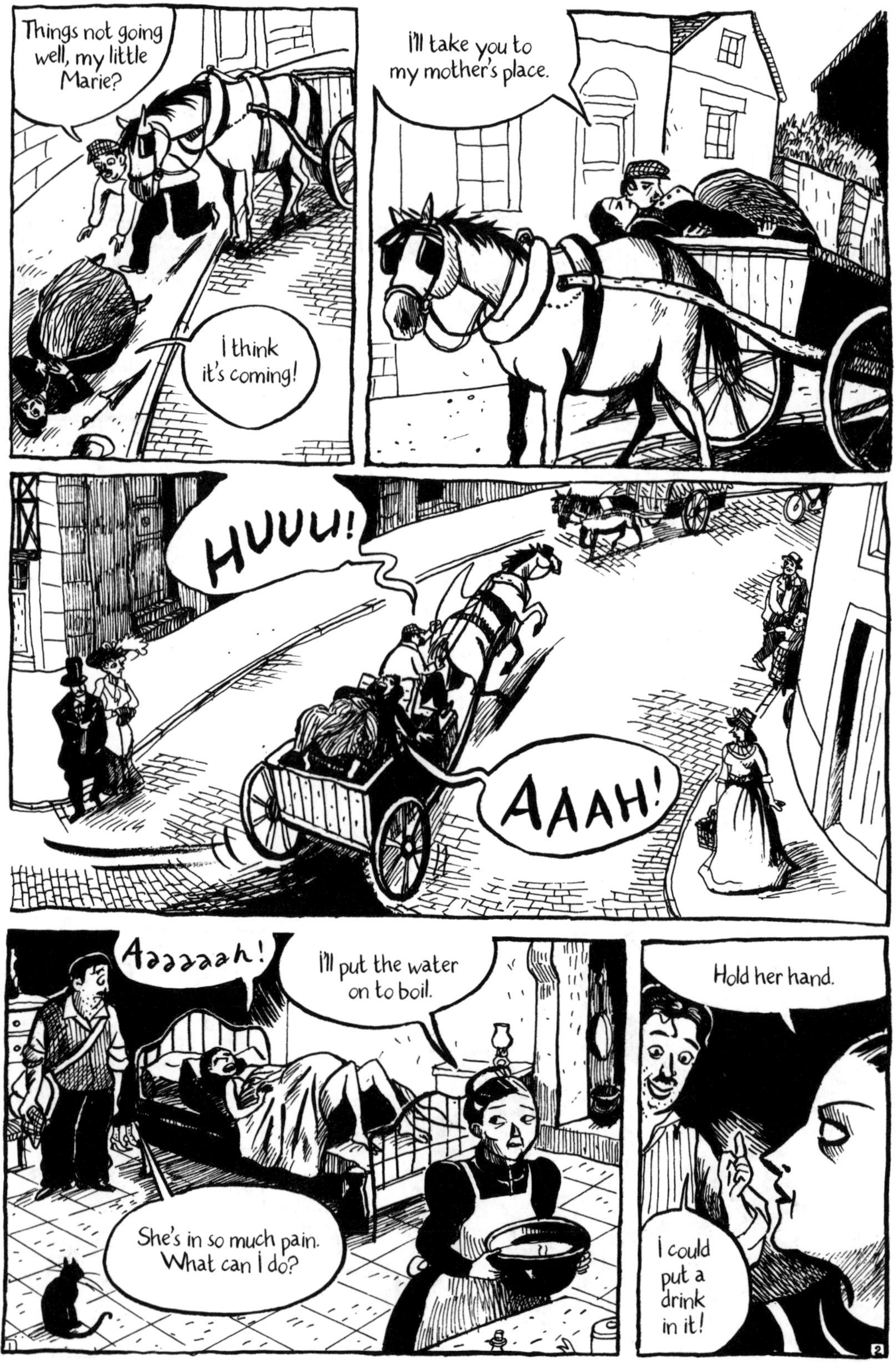

Things not going well, my little Marie?
I think it's coming!
I'll take you to my mother's place.
HUUU!
AAAH!
Aaaaaah!
I'll put the water on to boil.
She's in so much pain. What can I do?
Hold her hand.
I could put a drink in it!

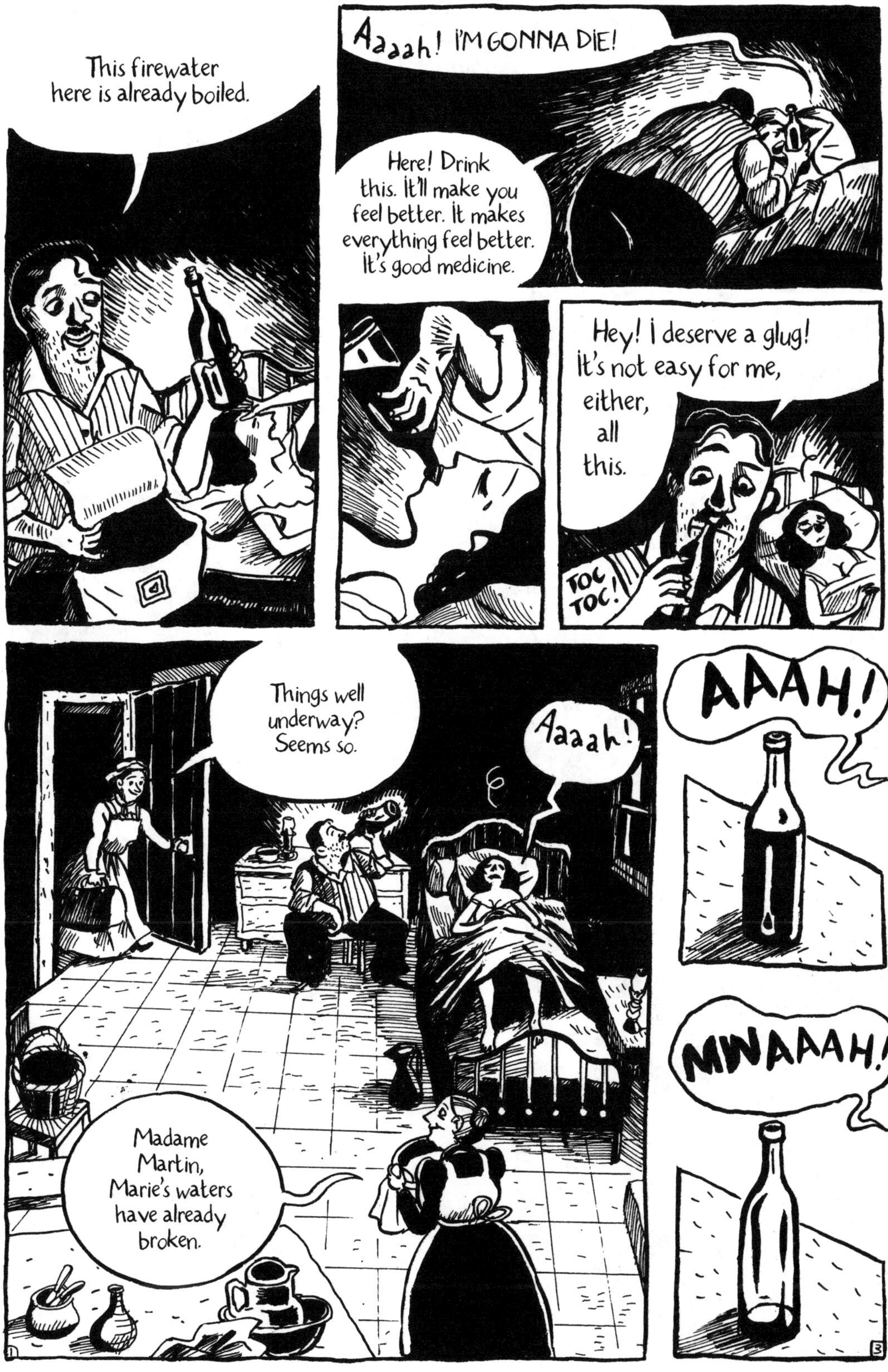
This firewater here is already boiled.
Aaaah! I'M GONNA DIE!
Here! Drink this. It'll make you feel better. It makes everything feel better. It's good medicine.
Hey! I deserve a glug! It's not easy for me, either, all this.
TOC TOC!
Things well underway? Seems so.
Aaaah!
Madame Martin, Marie's waters have already broken.
AAAH!
MWAAAH!

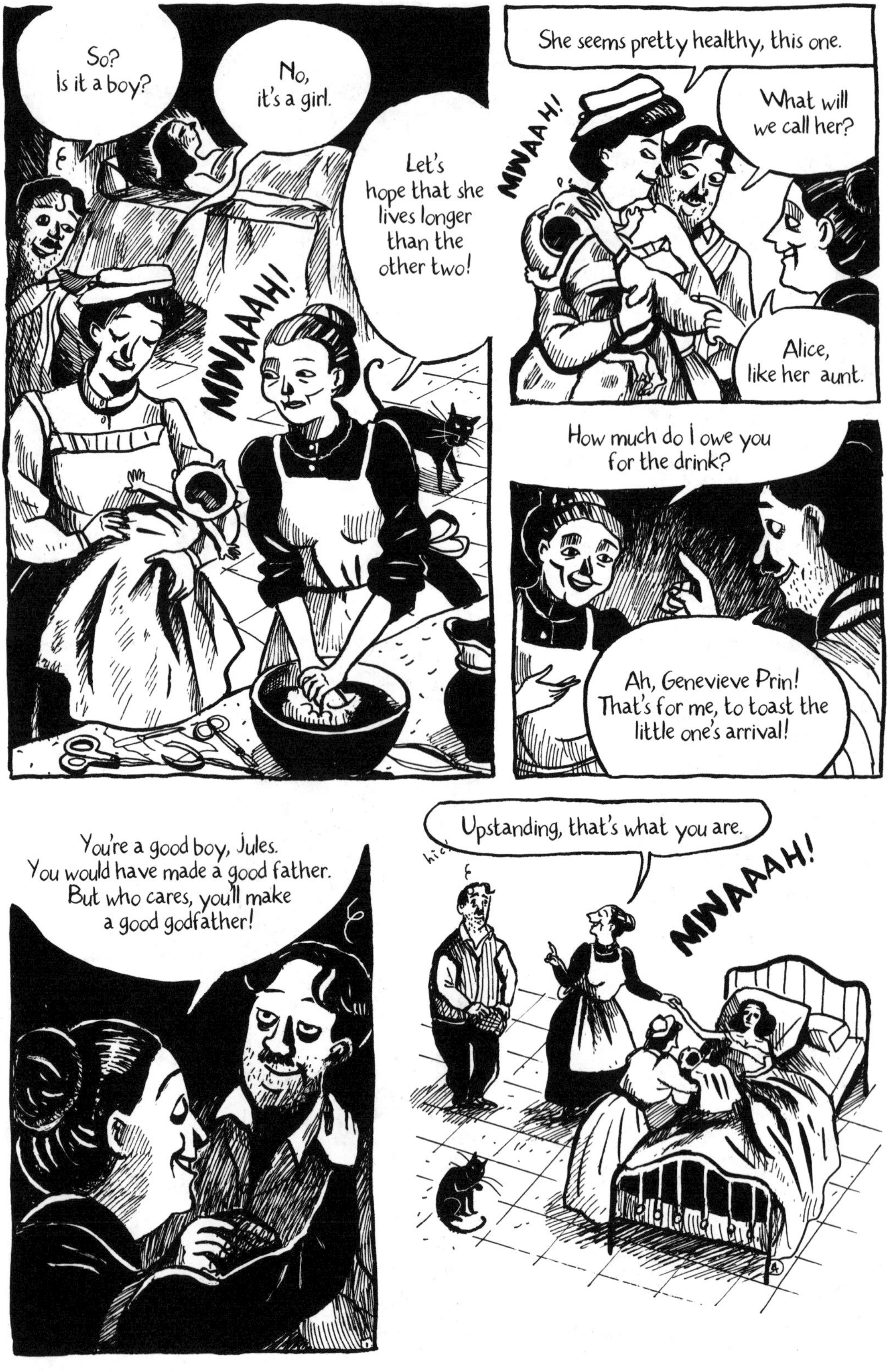

So? Is it a boy?
No, it's a girl.
Let's hope that she lives longer than the other two!
MWAAAAH!
She seems pretty healthy, this one.
MWAAAH!
What will we call her?
Alice, like her aunt.
How much do I owe you for the drink?
Ah, Genevieve Prin! That's for me, to toast the little one's arrival!
You're a good boy, Jules. You would have made a good father. But who cares, you'll make a good godfather!
Upstanding, that's what you are.
hic!
MWAAAH!

1911 - 11, rue du Cygne

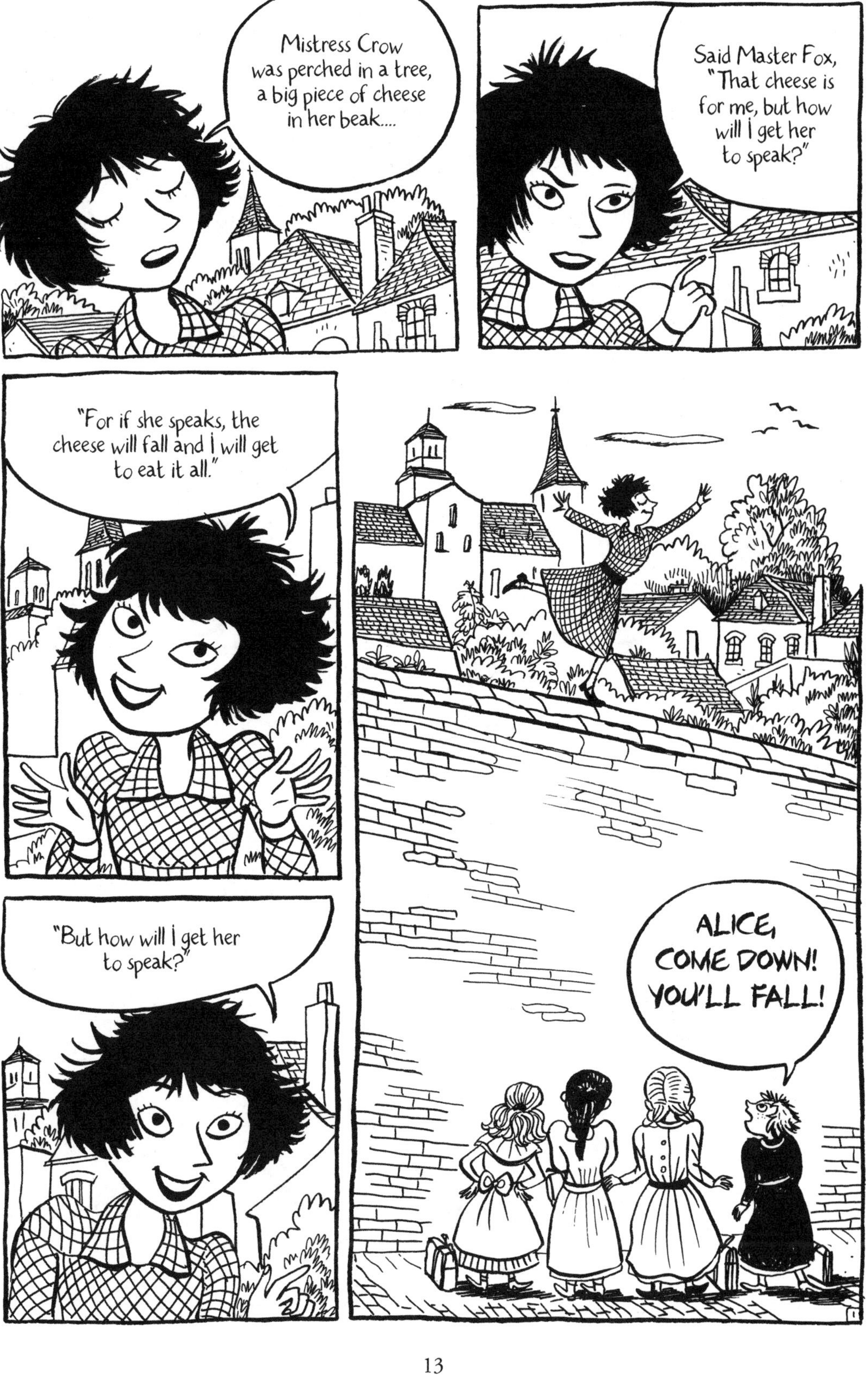
Mistress Crow was perched in a tree, a big piece of cheese in her beak....
Said Master Fox, "That cheese is for me, but how will I get her to speak?"
"For if she speaks, the cheese will fall and I will get to eat it all."
"But how will I get her to speak?"
ALICE, COME DOWN! YOU'LL FALL!

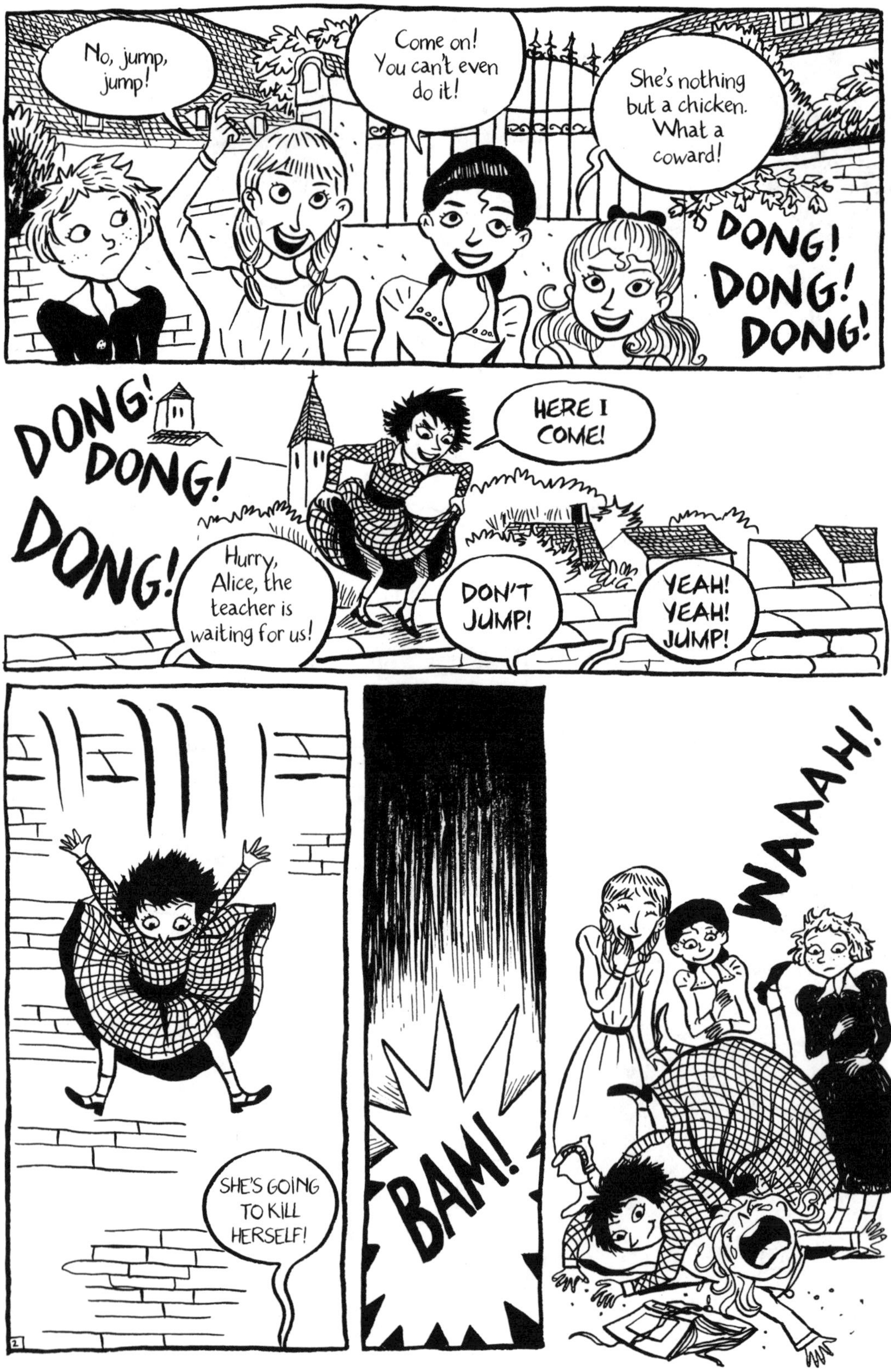
No, jump, jump!
Come on! You can't even do it!
She's nothing but a chicken. What a coward!
DONG! DONG! DONG!
DONG! DONG! DONG!
HERE I COME!
Hurry, Alice, the teacher is waiting for us!
DON'T JUMP!
YEAH! YEAH! JUMP!
SHE'S GOING TO KILL HERSELF!
BAM!
WAAAH!

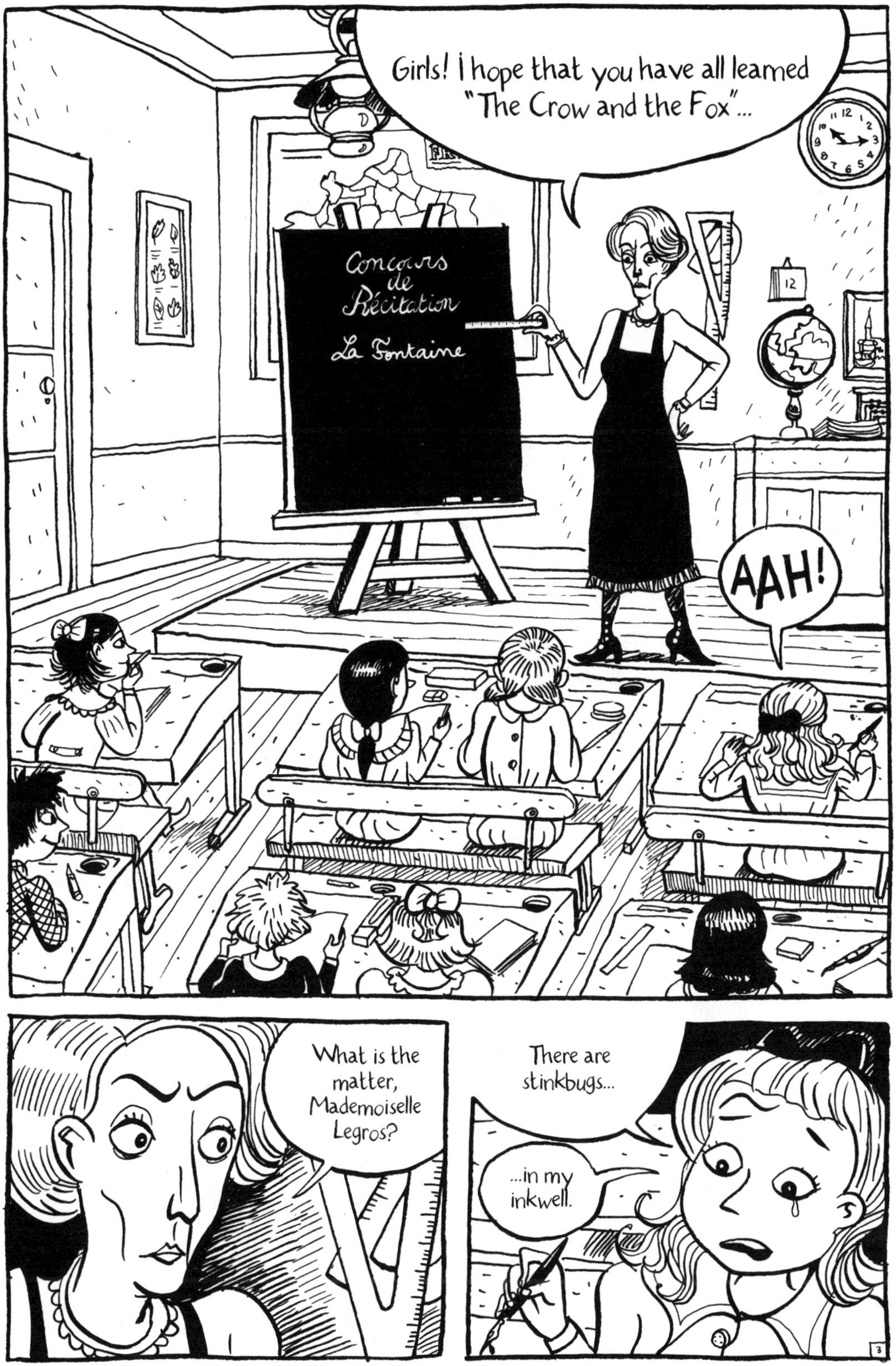
Girls! I hope that you have all learned "The Crow and the Fox"...
Concours de Récitation
La Fontaine
AAH!
What is the matter, Mademoiselle Legros?
There are stinkbugs...
...in my inkwell.

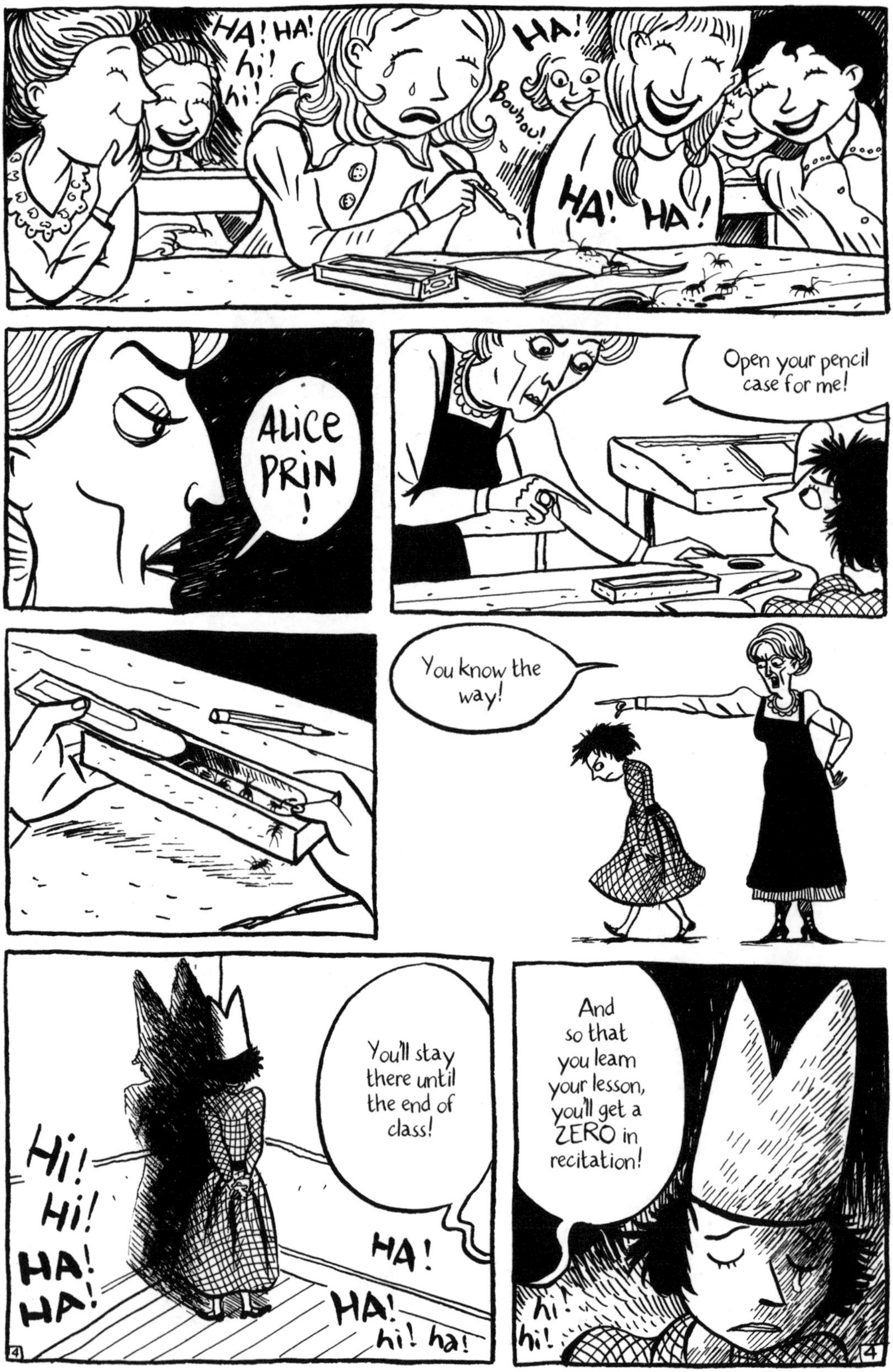
HA! HA!
hi! hi!
Bouhou!
HA!
HA! HA!
ALICE PRIN!
Open your pencil case for me!
You know the way!
Hi! Hi! HA! HA!
You'll stay there until the end of class!
HA!
HA! hi! ha!
And so that you learn your lesson, you'll get a ZERO in recitation!
hi! hi!

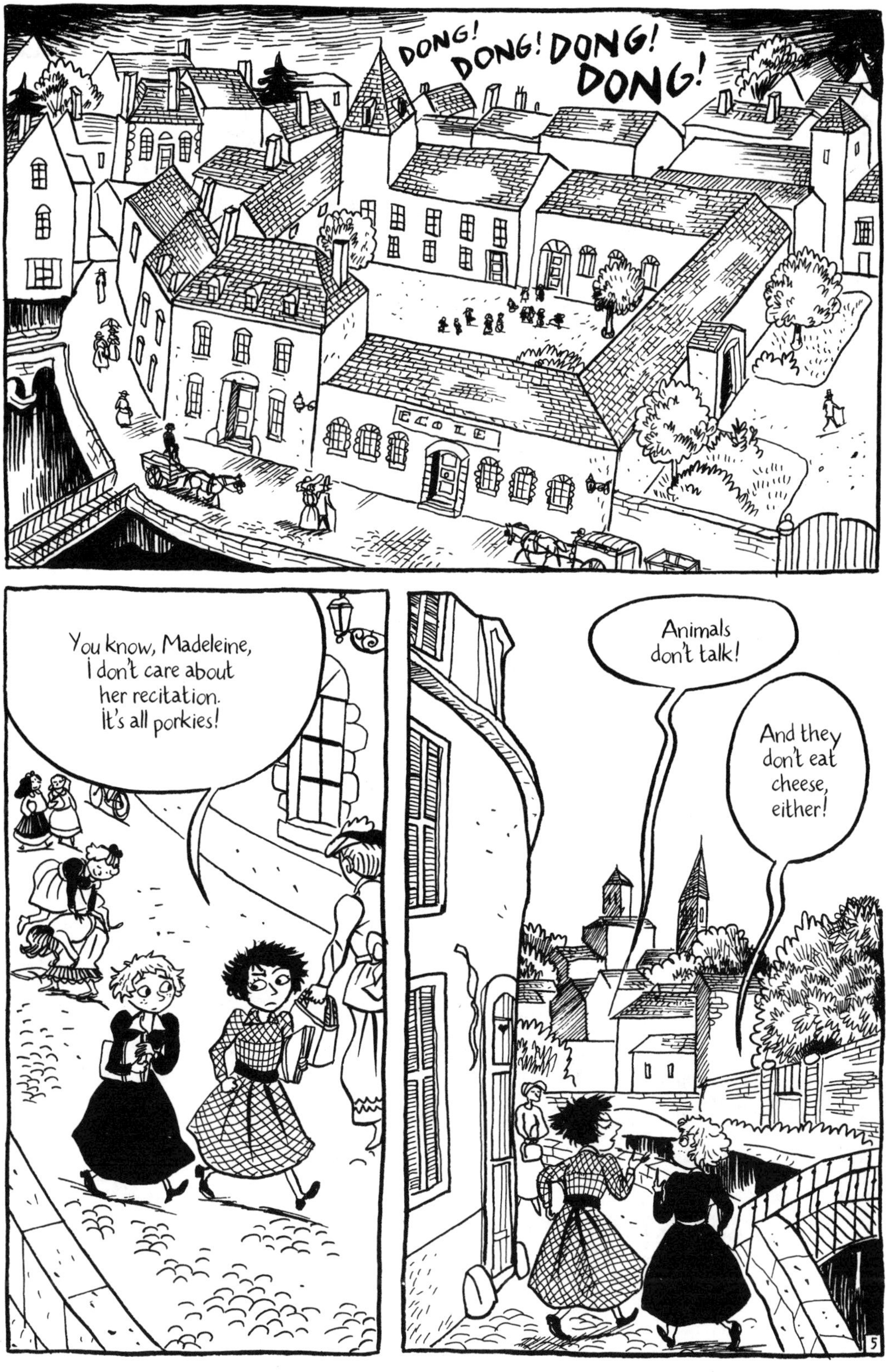
DONG! DONG! DONG! DONG!
ECOLE
You know, Madeleine, I don't care about her recitation. It's all porkies!
Animals don't talk!
And they don't eat cheese, either!
5

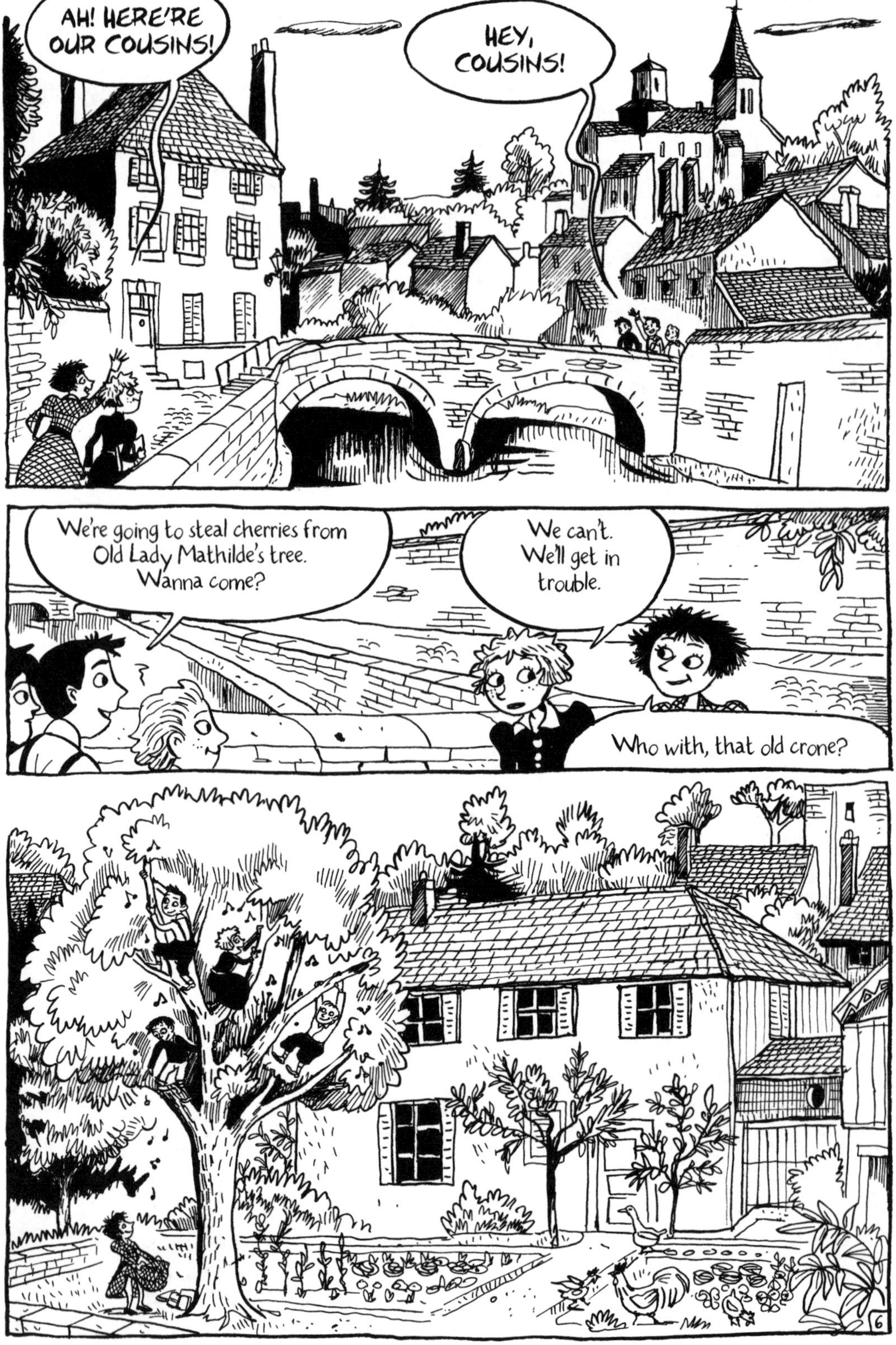
AH! HERE'RE OUR COUSINS!
HEY, COUSINS!
We're going to steal cherries from Old Lady Mathilde's tree. Wanna come?
We can't. We'll get in trouble.
Who with, that old crone?
6

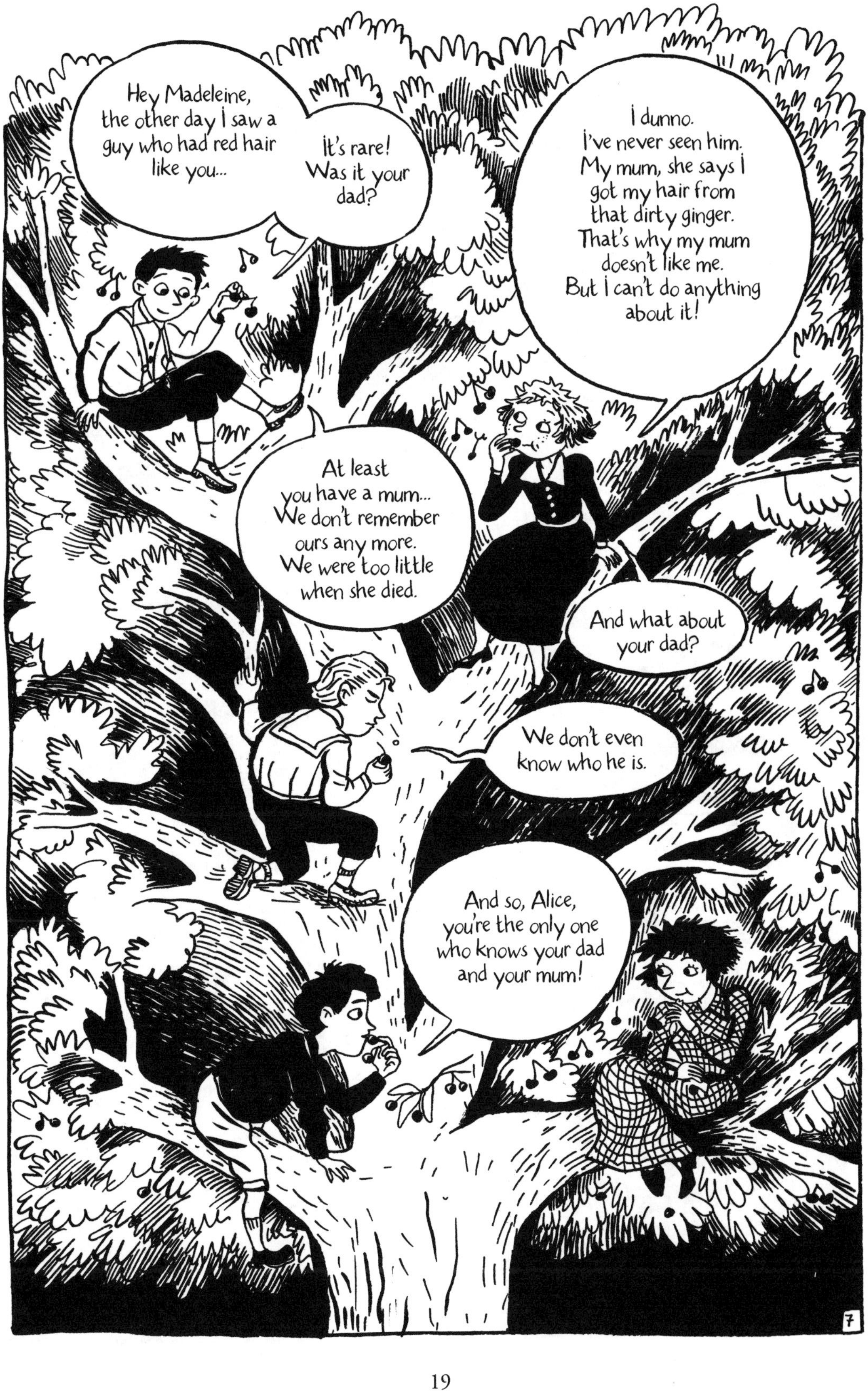
Hey Madeleine, the other day I saw a guy who had red hair like you...
It's rare! Was it your dad?
I dunno. I've never seen him. My mum, she says I got my hair from that dirty ginger. That's why my mum doesn't like me. But I can't do anything about it!
At least you have a mum... We don't remember ours any more. We were too little when she died.
And what about your dad?
We don't even know who he is.
And so, Alice, you're the only one who knows your dad and your mum!
7

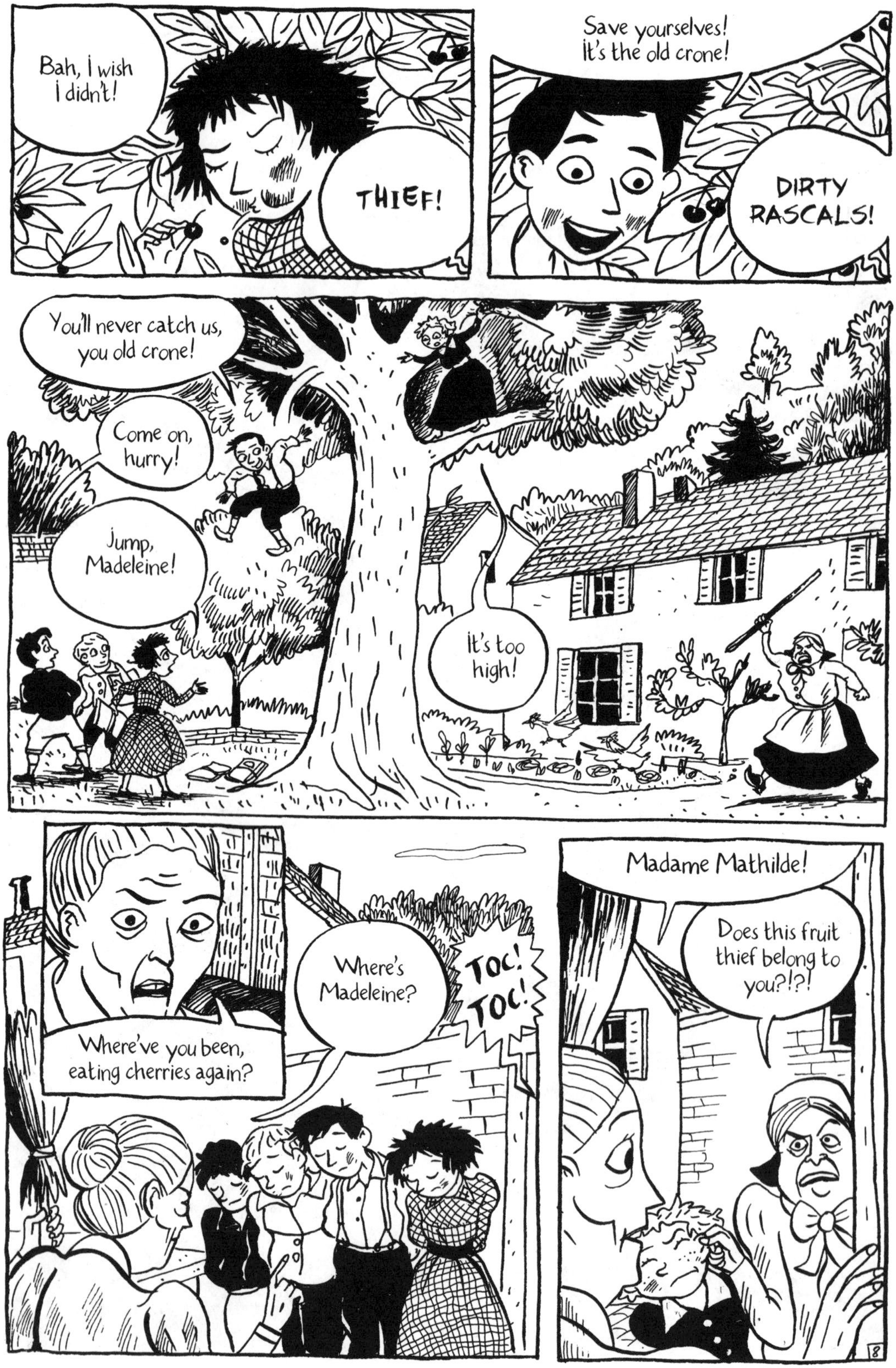
Bah, I wish I didn't!
THIEF!
Save yourselves! It's the old crone!
DIRTY RASCALS!
You'll never catch us, you old crone!
Come on, hurry!
Jump, Madeleine!
It's too high!
Where've you been, eating cherries again?
Where's Madeleine?
TOC! TOC!
Madame Mathilde!
Does this fruit thief belong to you?!?!
8

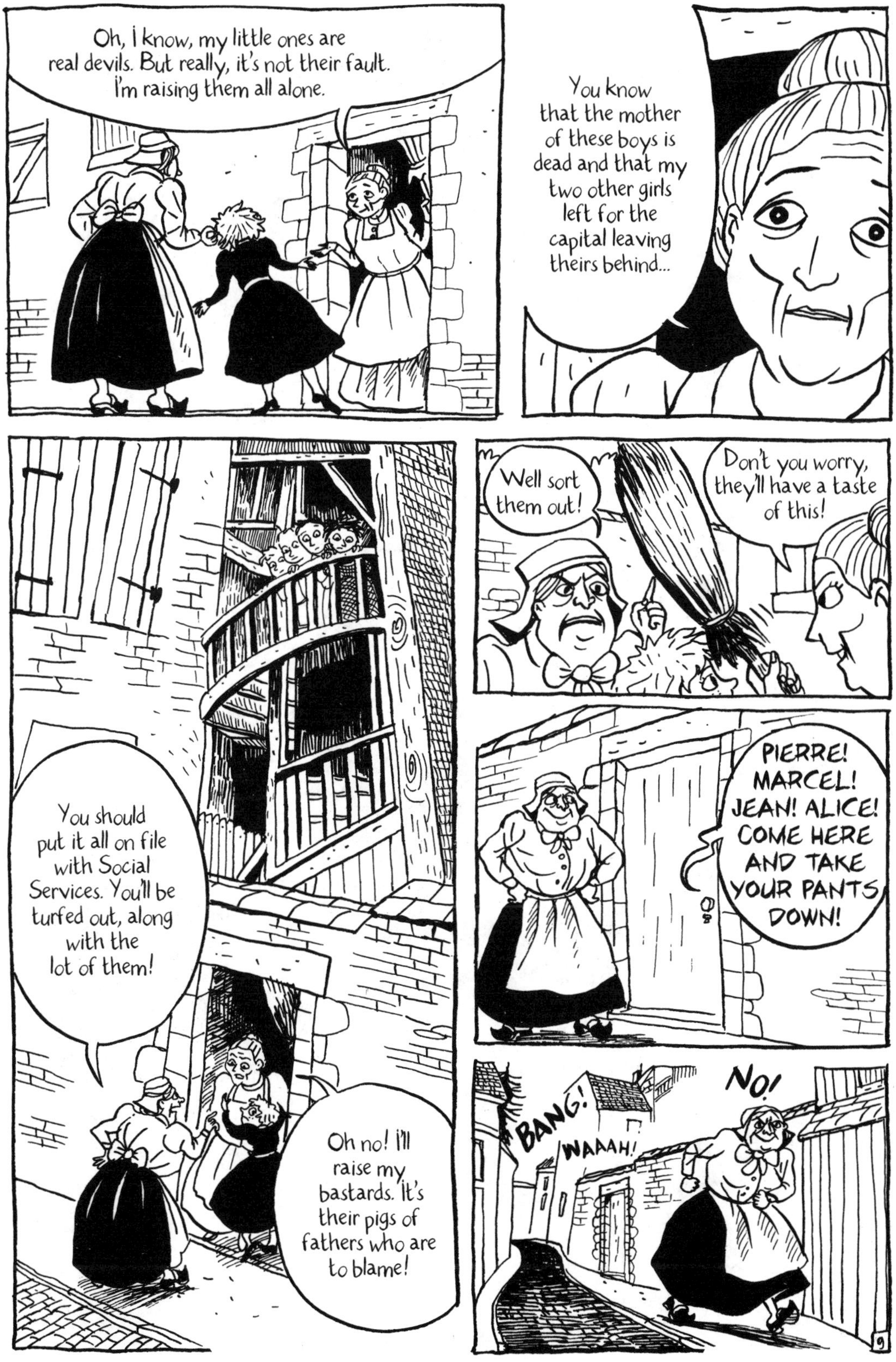

Oh, I know, my little ones are real devils. But really, it's not their fault. I'm raising them all alone.
You know that the mother of these boys is dead and that my two other girls left for the capital leaving theirs behind...
You should put it all on file with Social Services. You'll be turfed out, along with the lot of them!
Oh no! I'll raise my bastards. It's their pigs of fathers who are to blame!
Well sort them out!
Don't you worry, they'll have a taste of this!
PIERRE! MARCEL! JEAN! ALICE! COME HERE AND TAKE YOUR PANTS DOWN!
NO!
BANG!
WAAAH!

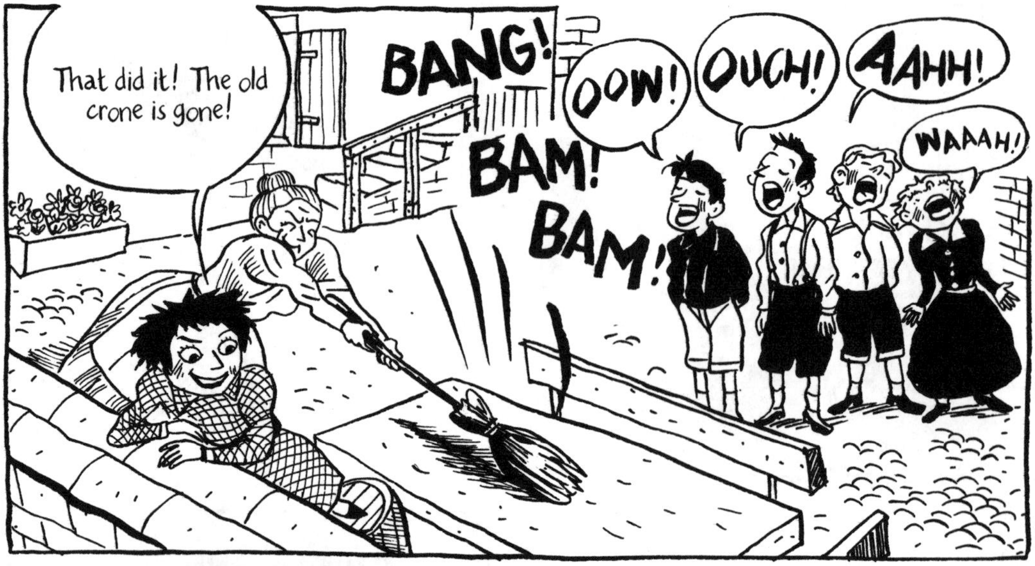
That did it! The old crone is gone!
BANG!
BAM!
BAM!
OOW!
OUCH!
AAHH!
WAAAH!

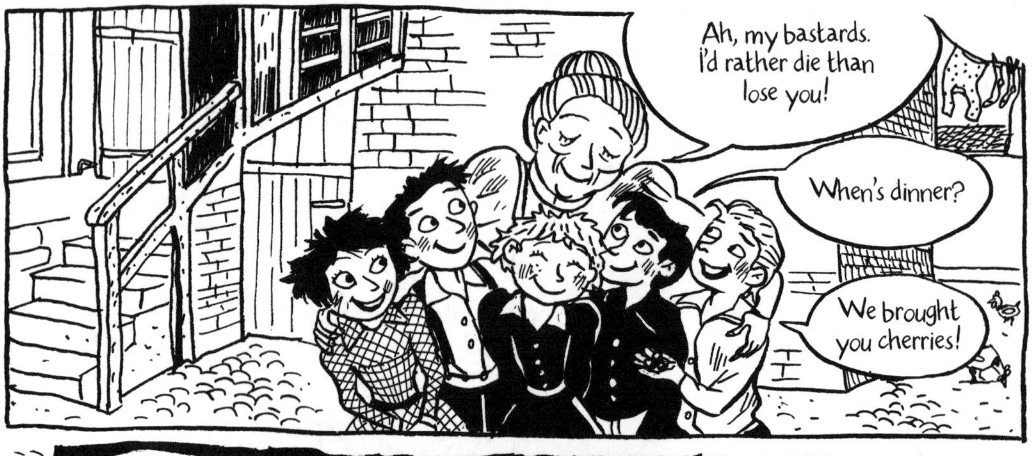
Ah, my bastards. I'd rather die than lose you!
When's dinner?
We brought you cherries!

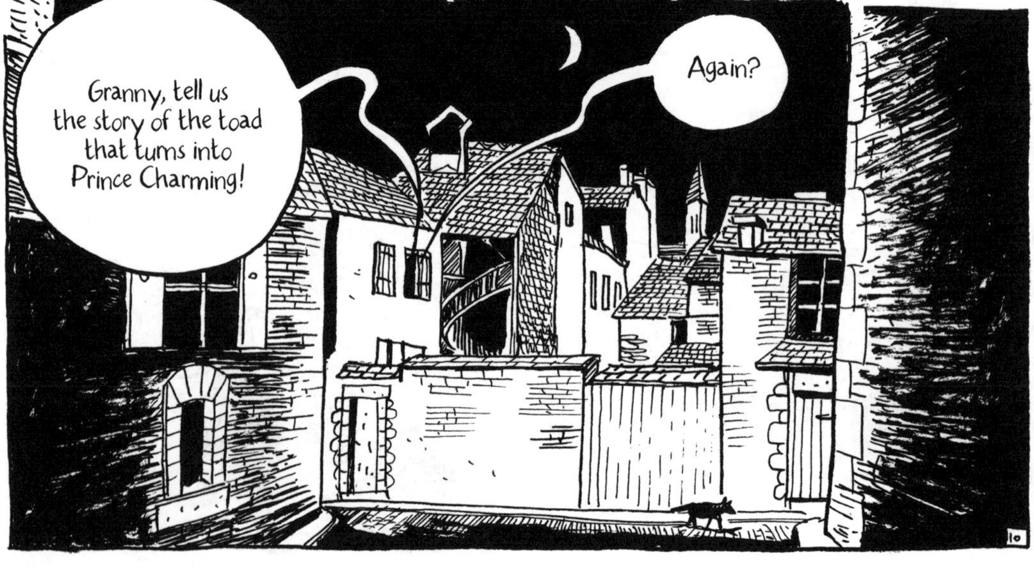
Granny, tell us the story of the toad that turns into Prince Charming!
Again?
10

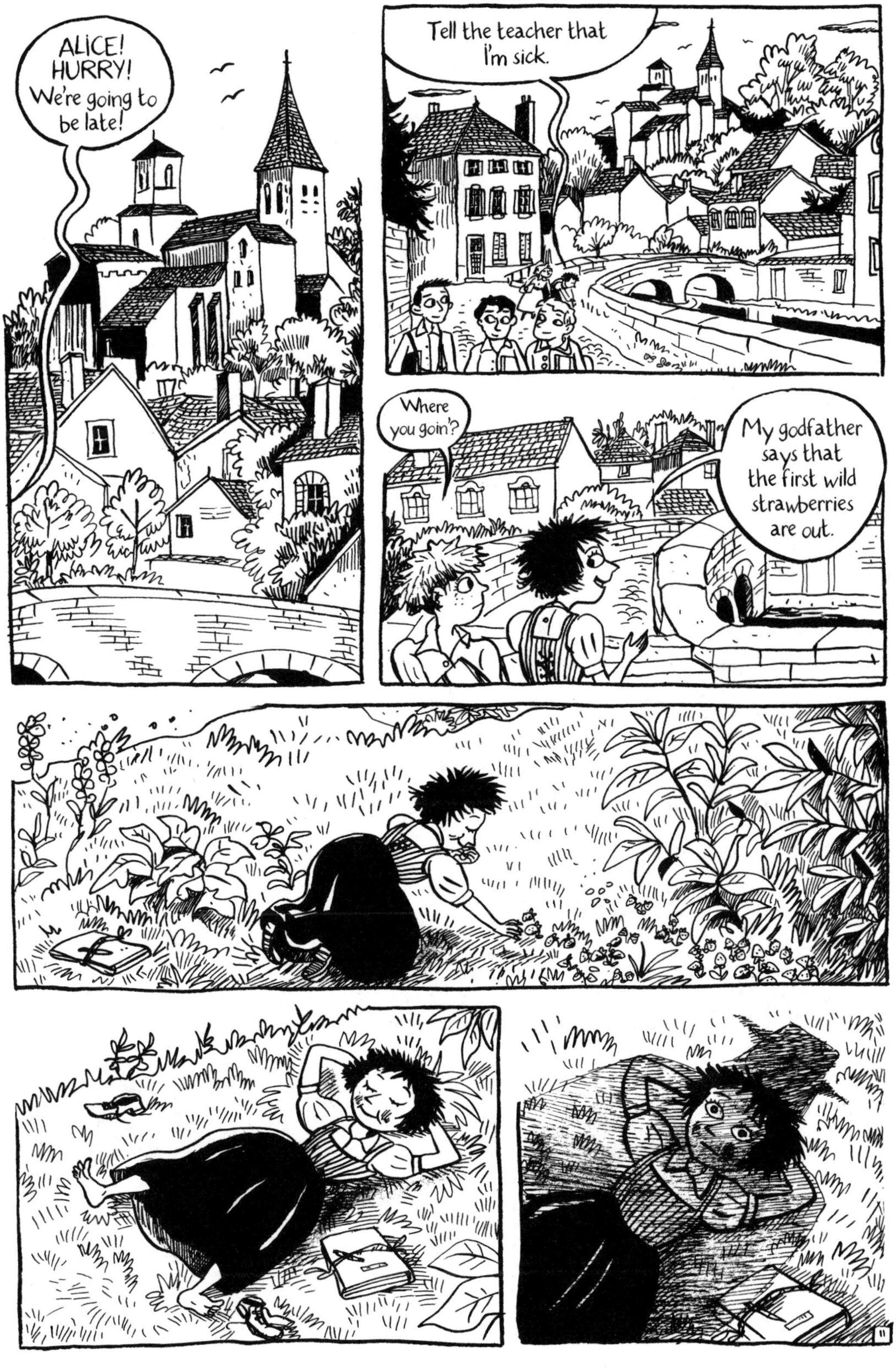
ALICE! HURRY! We're going to be late!
Tell the teacher that I'm sick.
Where you goin'?
My godfather says that the first wild strawberries are out.

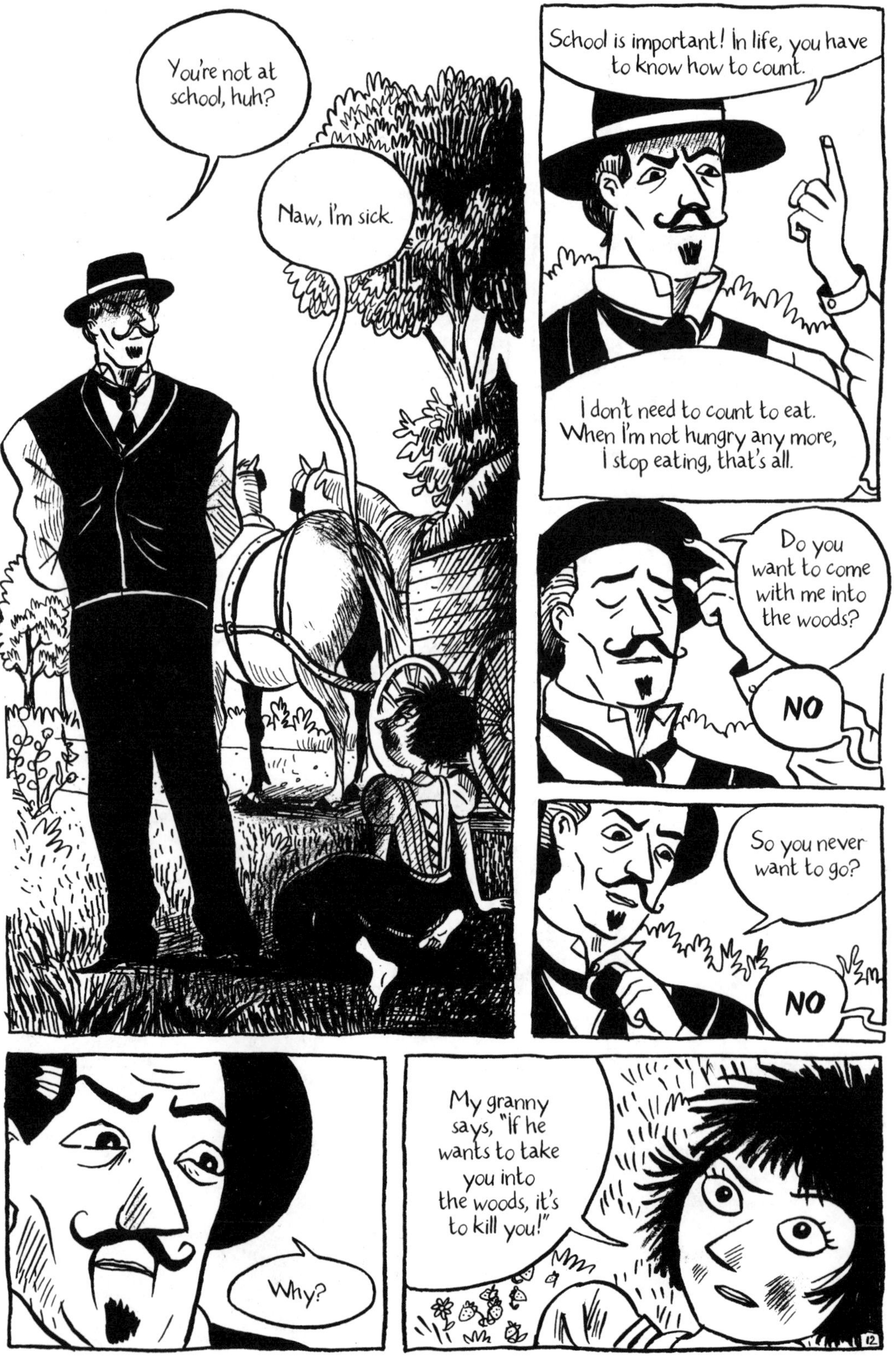
You're not at school, huh?
Naw, I'm sick.
School is important! In life, you have to know how to count.
I don't need to count to eat. When I'm not hungry any more, I stop eating, that's all.
Do you want to come with me into the woods?
NO
So you never want to go?
NO
Why?
My granny says, "If he wants to take you into the woods, it's to kill you!"
12

HA!
HA!

Do you want to know why I'm going down there?

NO

It's to bum some nice wood to make some good charcoal that I can go to sell later.

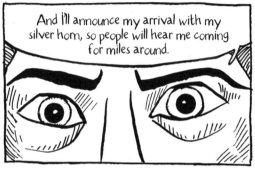

And I'll announce my arrival with my silver horn, so people will hear me coming for miles around.

Do you want to hear it?

NO!

You're stubborn as a mule.

Just like your mother!

MAXIME
LEGRO
Bois et Char

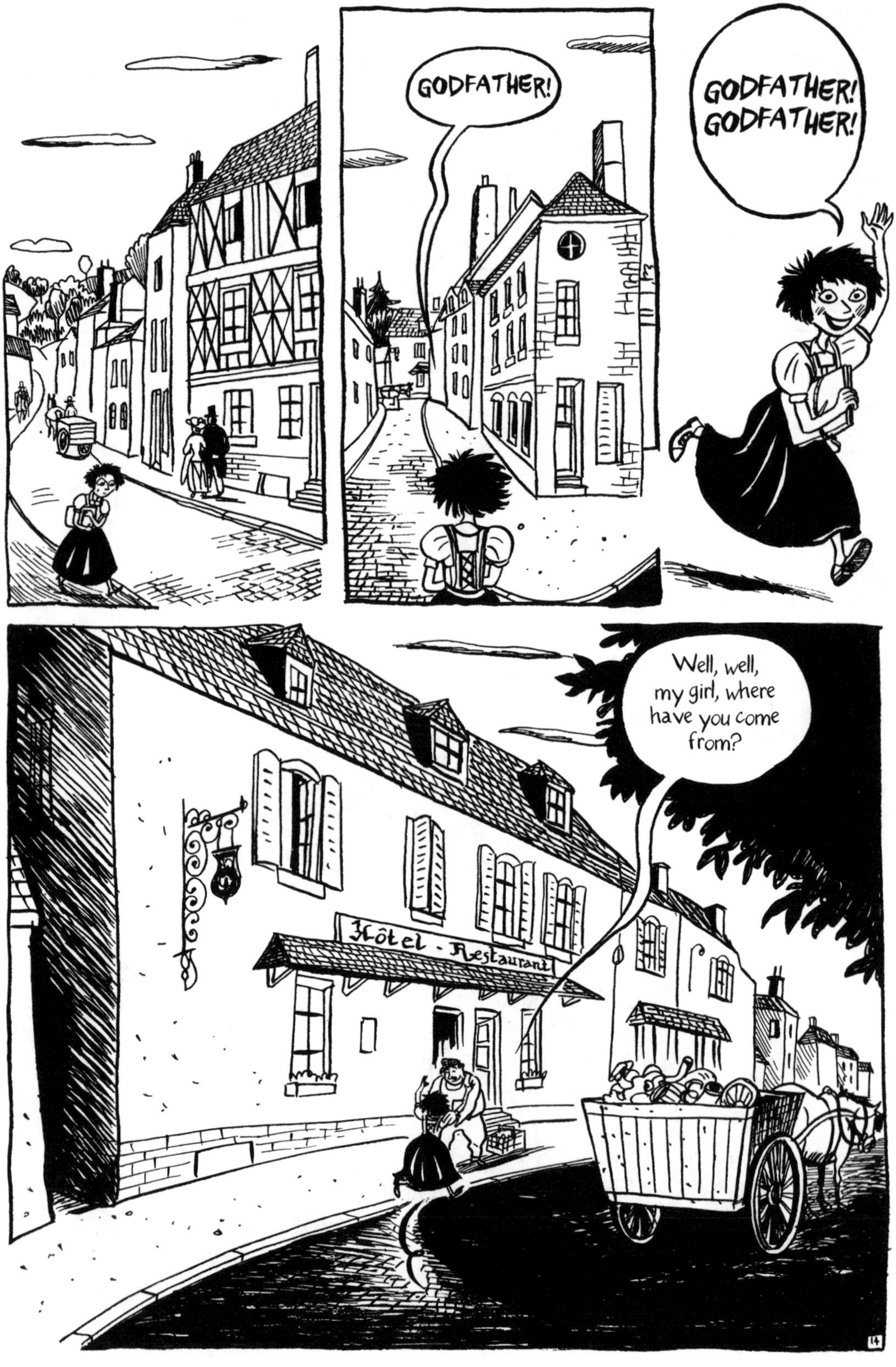
GODFATHER!
GODFATHER! GODFATHER!
Well, well, my girl, where have you come from?
Hôtel - Restaurant
14

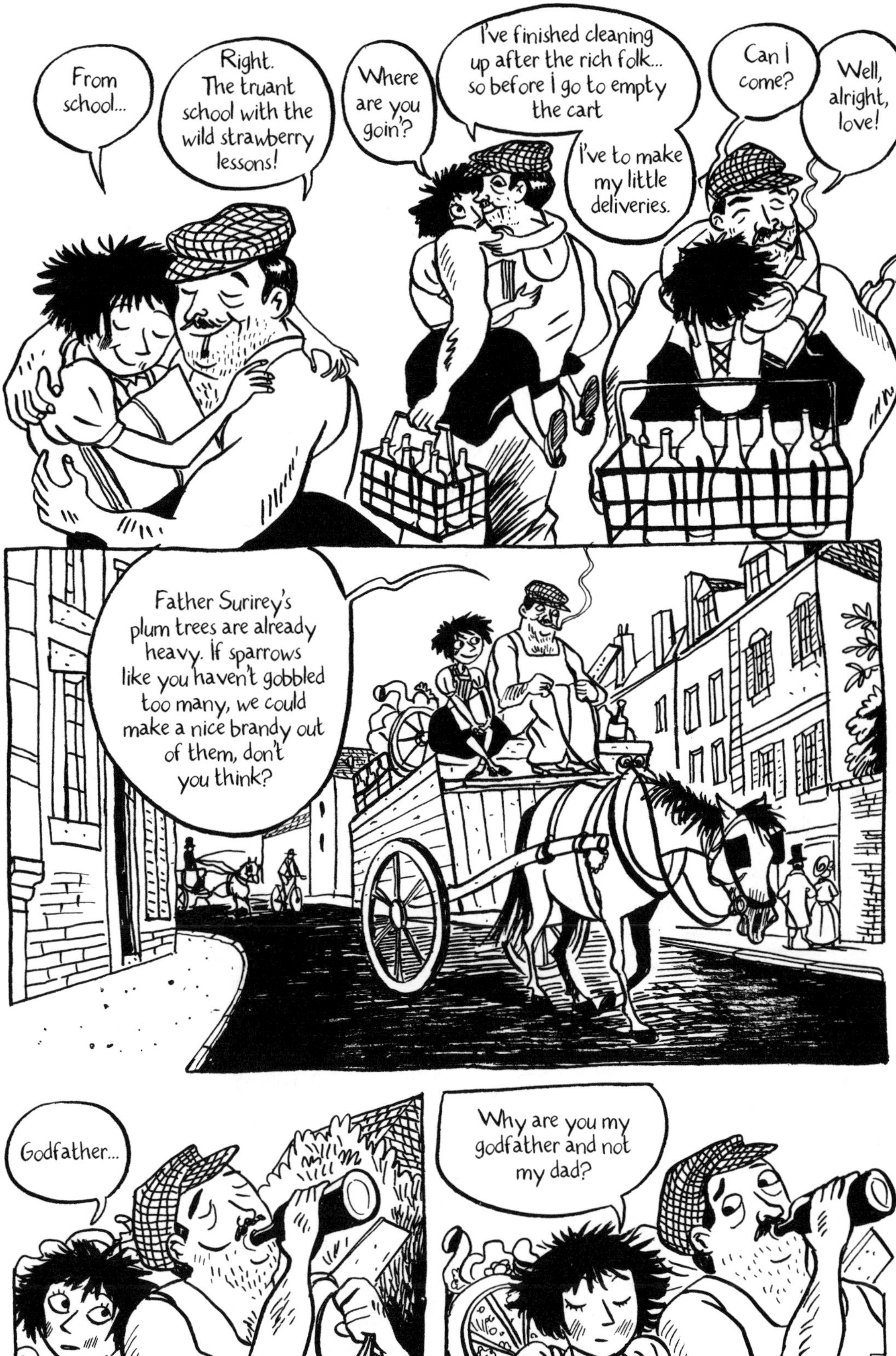
From school...
Right. The truant school with the wild strawberry lessons!
Where are you goin'?
I've finished cleaning up after the rich folk... so before I go to empty the cart
I've to make my little deliveries.
Can I come?
Well, alright, love!
Father Surirey's plum trees are already heavy. If sparrows like you haven't gobbled too many, we could make a nice brandy out of them, don't you think?
Godfather...
Why are you my godfather and not my dad?
15

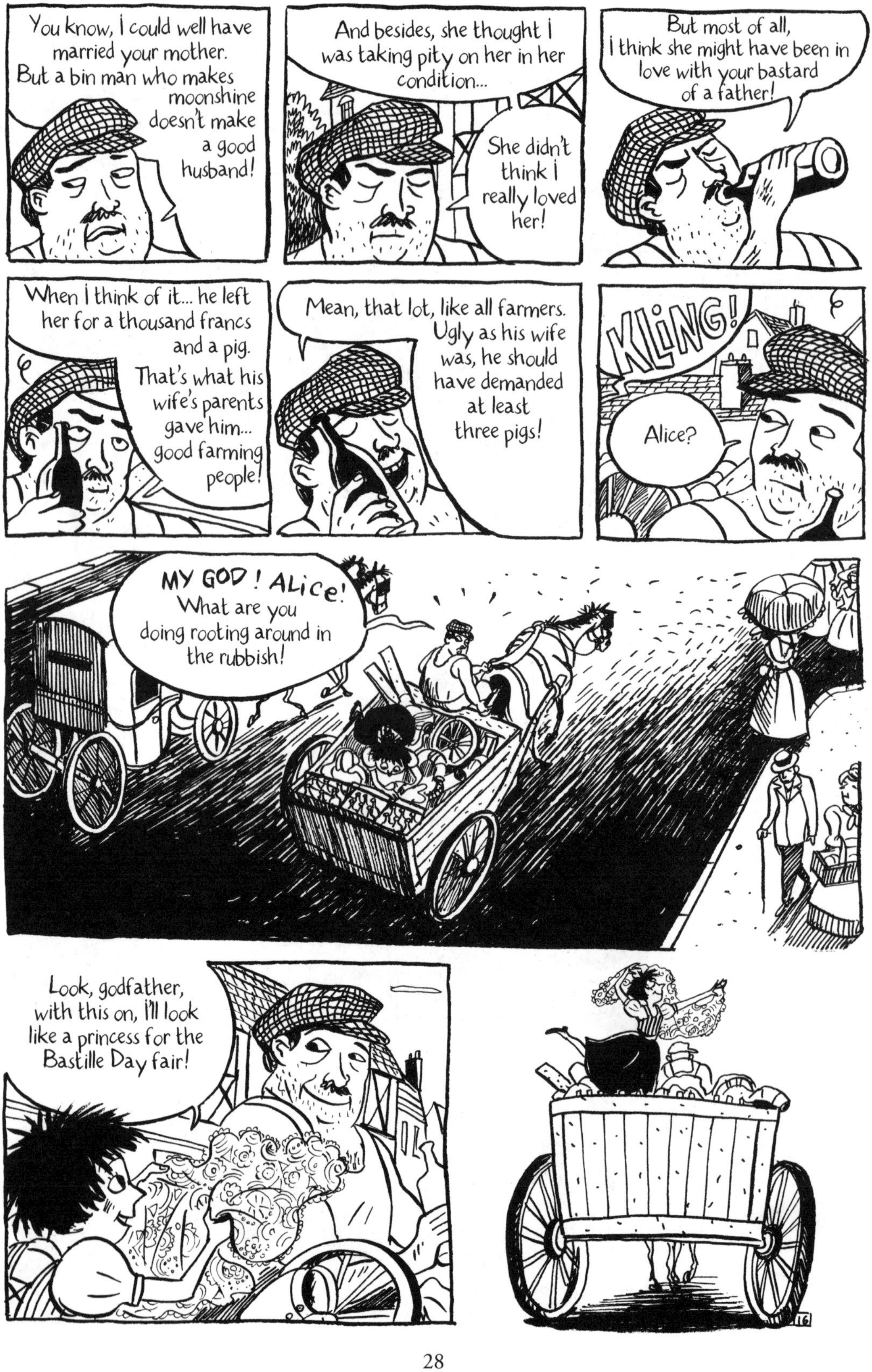
You know, I could well have married your mother. But a bin man who makes moonshine doesn't make a good husband!
And besides, she thought I was taking pity on her in her condition...
She didn't think I really loved her!
But most of all, I think she might have been in love with your bastard of a father!
When I think of it... he left her for a thousand francs and a pig. That's what his wife's parents gave him... good farming people!
Mean, that lot, like all farmers. Ugly as his wife was, he should have demanded at least three pigs!
KLING!
Alice?
MY GOD ! ALICE! What are you doing rooting around in the rubbish!
Look, godfather, with this on, I'll look like a princess for the Bastille Day fair!
16

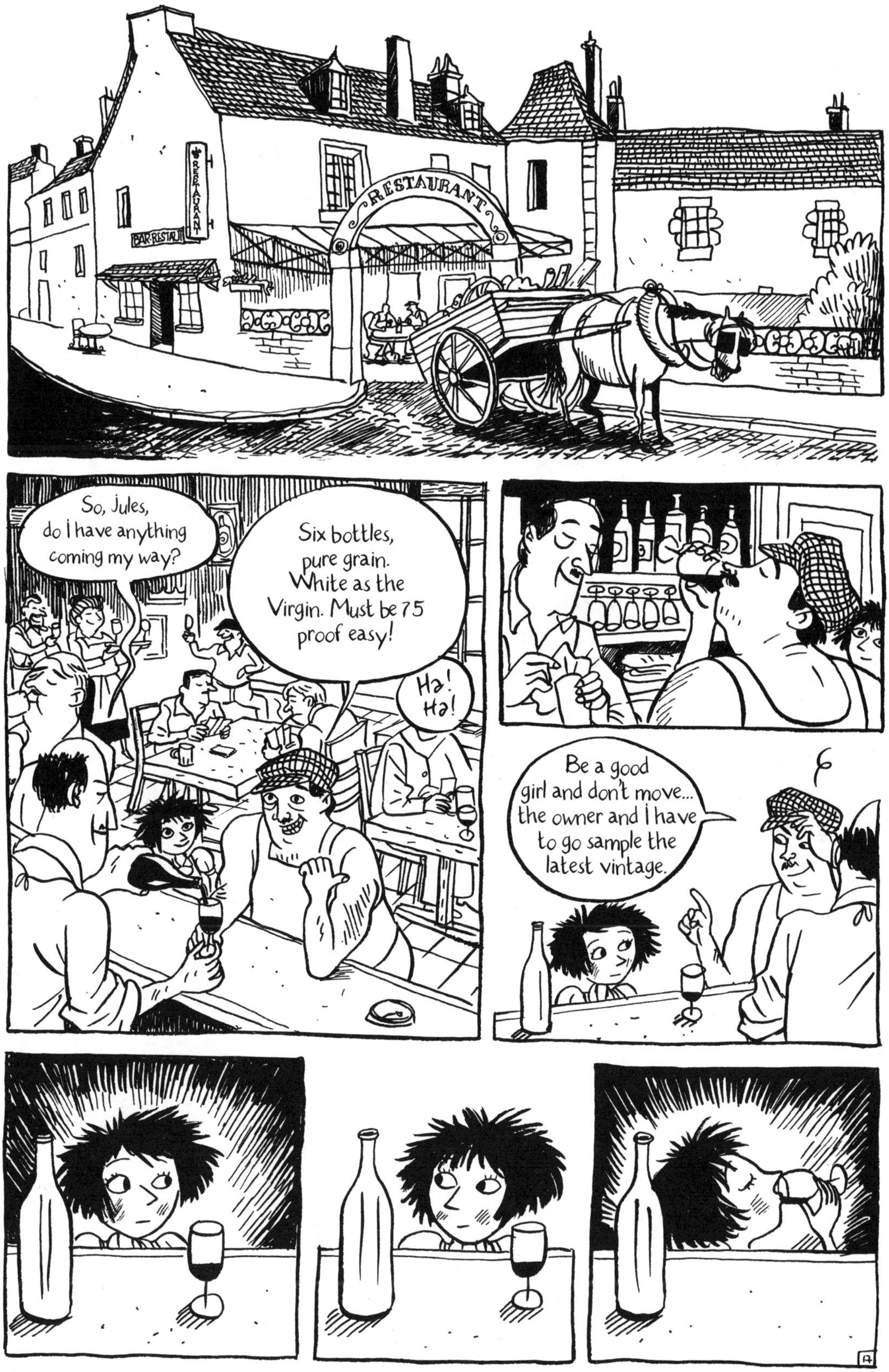
RESTAURANT
RESTAURANT
So, Jules, do I have anything coming my way?
Six bottles, pure grain. White as the Virgin. Must be 75 proof easy!
Ha! Ha!
Be a good girl and don't move... the owner and I have to go sample the latest vintage.
17

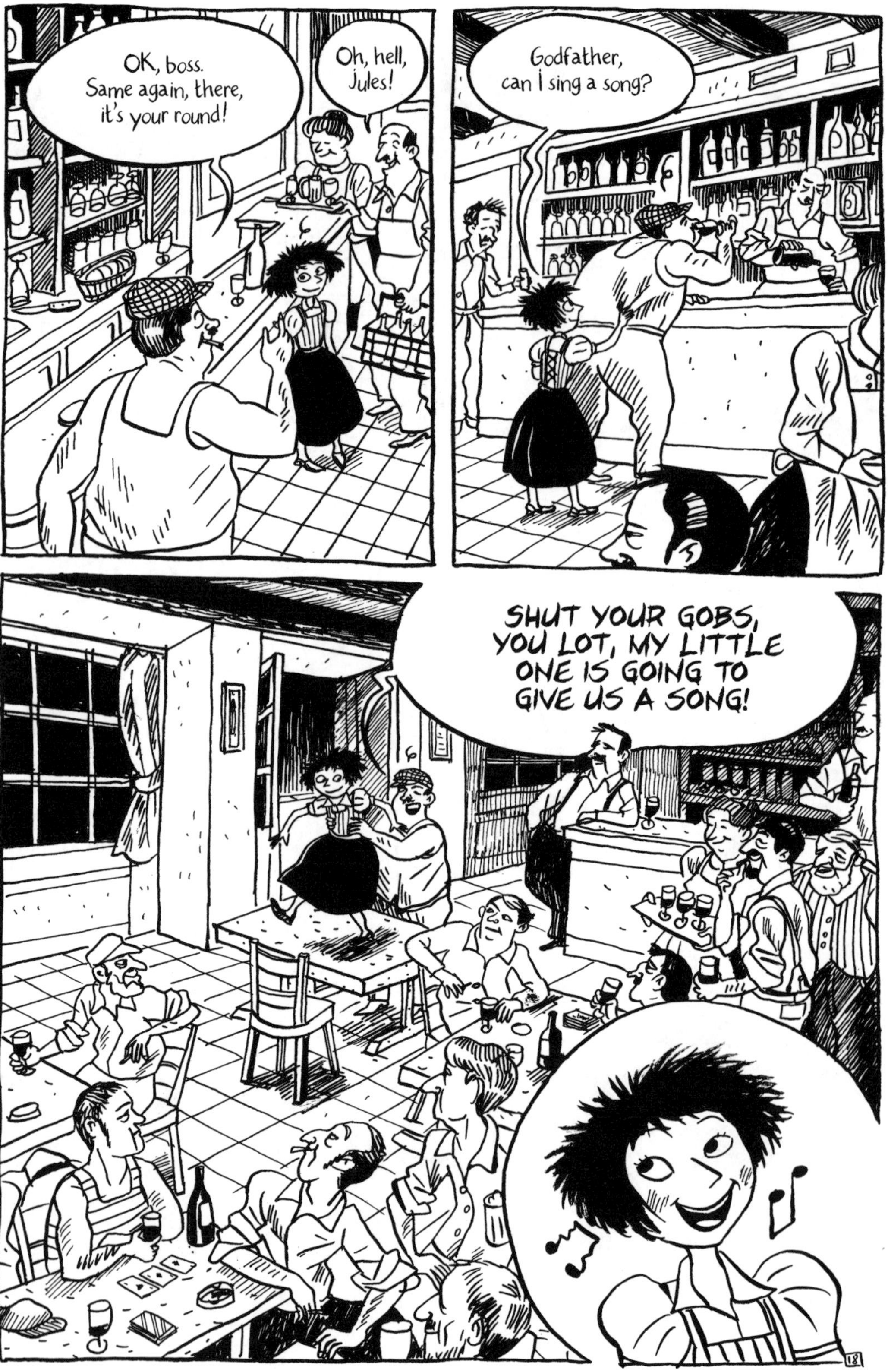
OK, boss.
Same again, there, it's your round!
Oh, hell, Jules!
Godfather, can I sing a song?
SHUT YOUR GOBS, YOU LOT, MY LITTLE ONE IS GOING TO GIVE US A SONG!
18

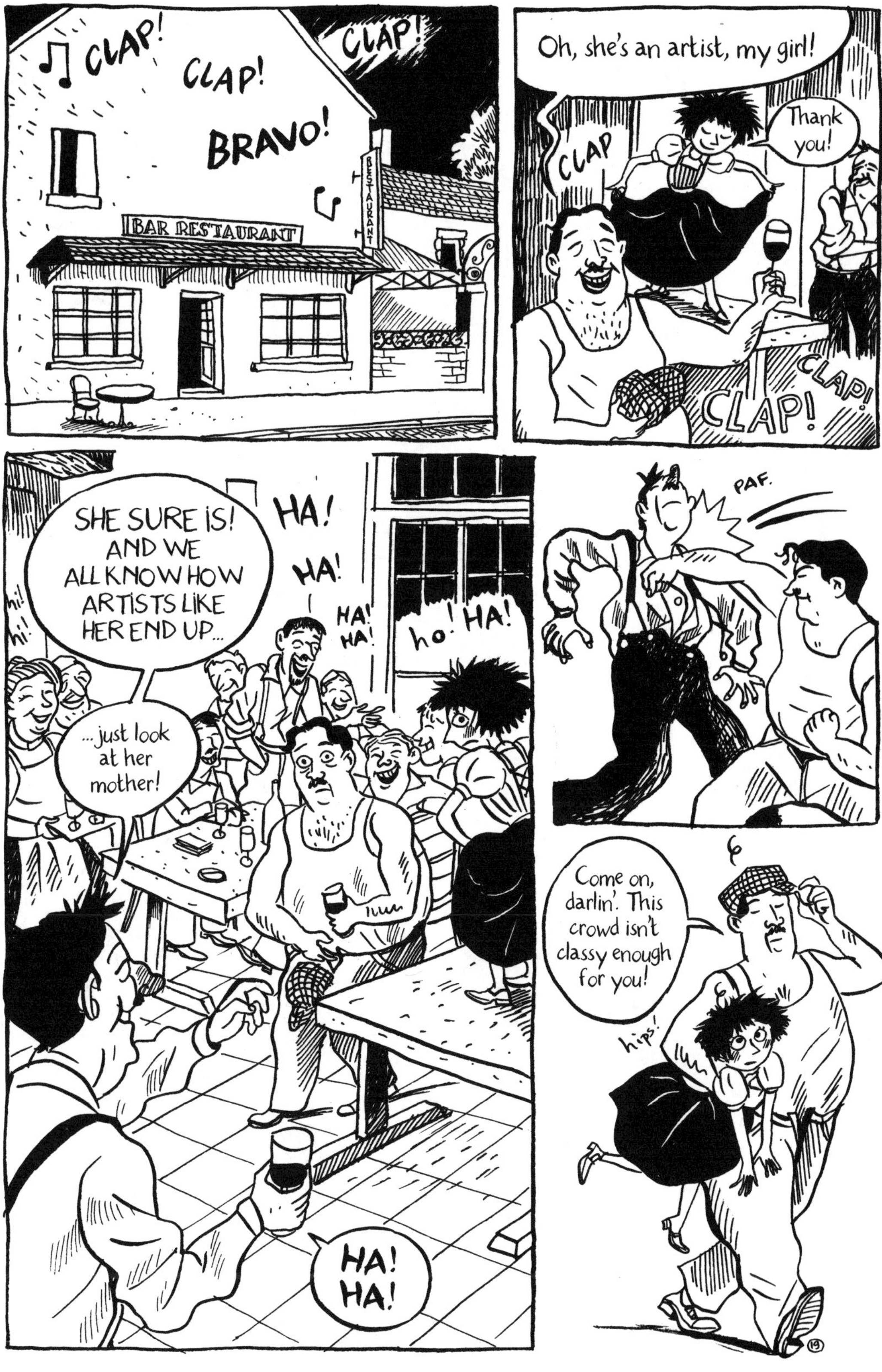

CLAP!
CLAP!
CLAP!
BRAVO!
BAR RESTAURANT
RESTAURANT
Oh, she's an artist, my girl!
CLAP
Thank you!
CLAP!
CLAP!
SHE SURE IS! AND WE ALL KNOW HOW ARTISTS LIKE HER END UP...
HA!
HA!
HA! HA!
ho! HA!
hi! hi!
...just look at her mother!
HA! HA!
PAF.
Come on, darlin'. This crowd isn't classy enough for you!
hips!
19

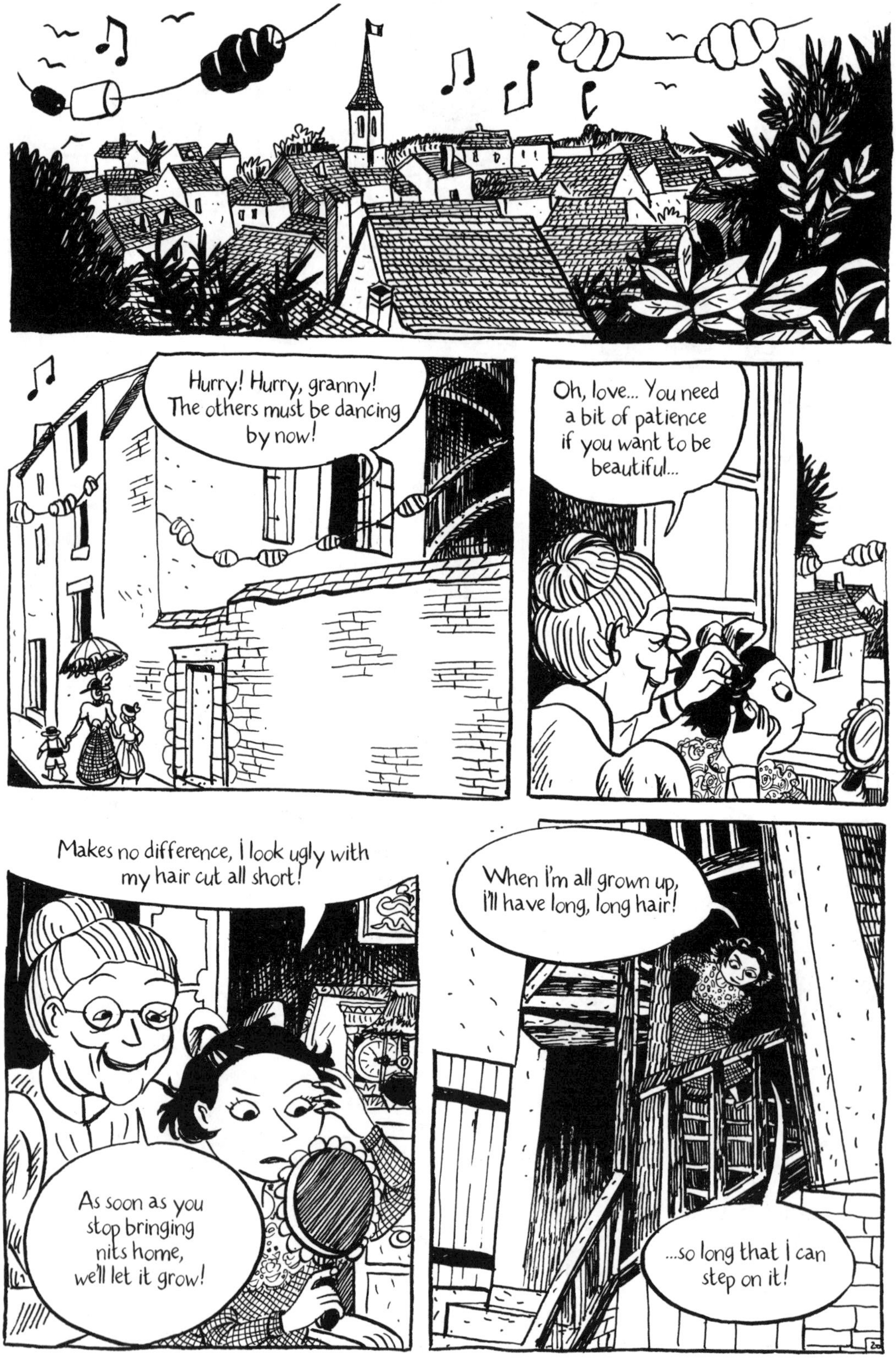
Hurry! Hurry, granny! The others must be dancing by now!
Oh, love... You need a bit of patience if you want to be beautiful...
Makes no difference, I look ugly with my hair cut all short!
As soon as you stop bringing nits home, we'll let it grow!
When I'm all grown up, I'll have long, long hair!
...so long that I can step on it!

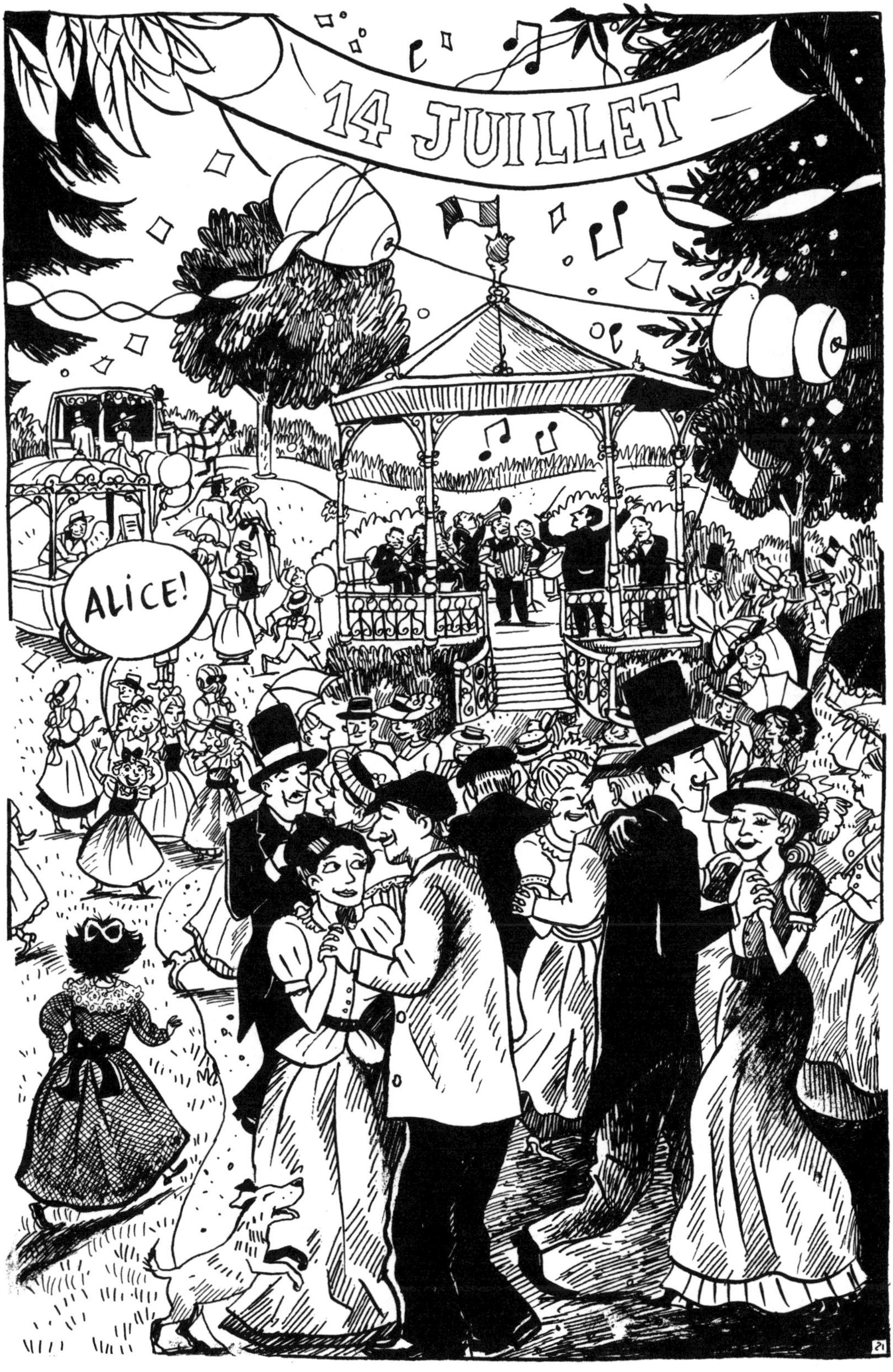
14 JUILLET
ALICE!
21

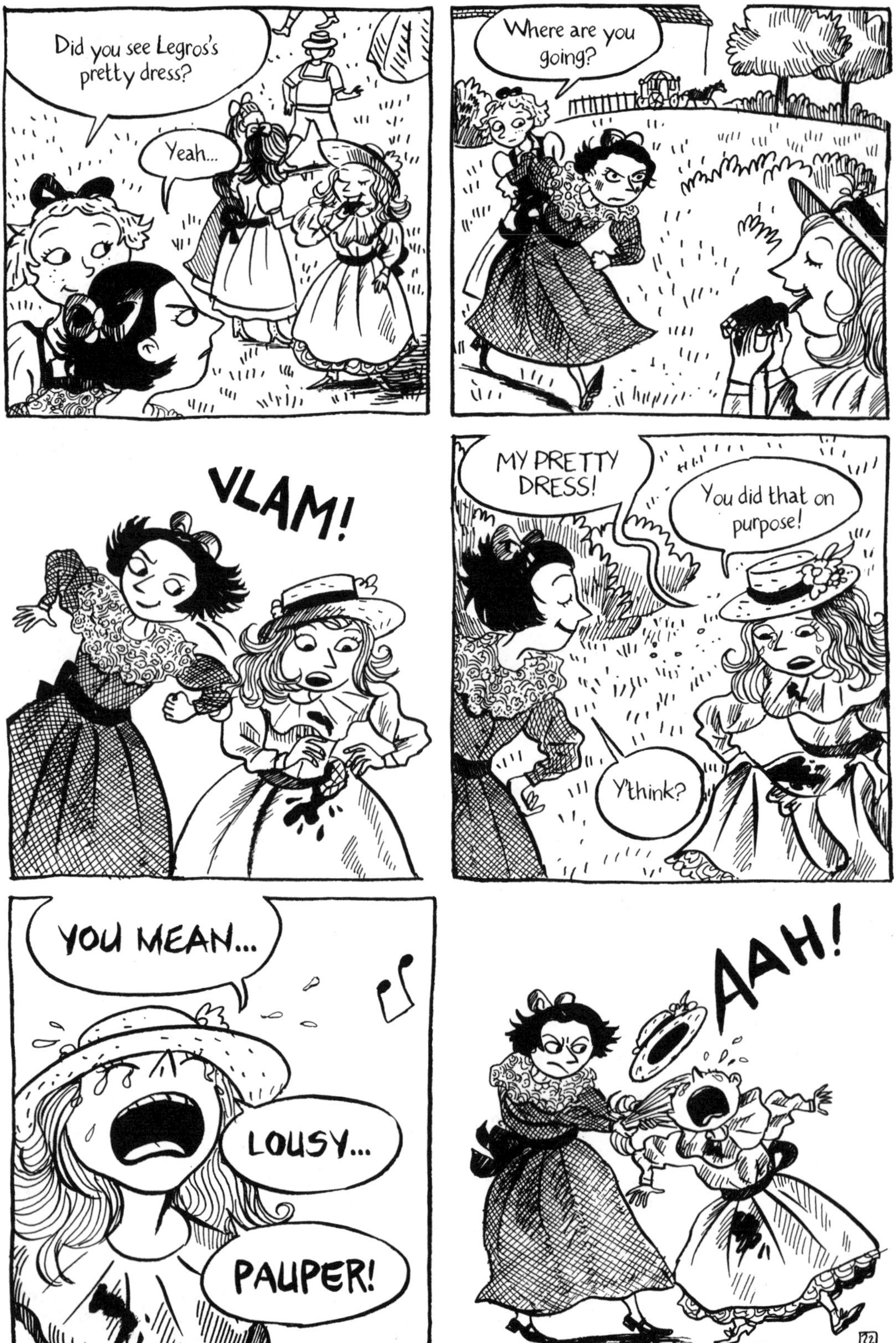
Did you see Legros's pretty dress?
Yeah...
Where are you going?
VLAM!
MY PRETTY DRESS!
You did that on purpose!
Y'think?
YOU MEAN...
LOUSY...
PAUPER!
AAH!
22

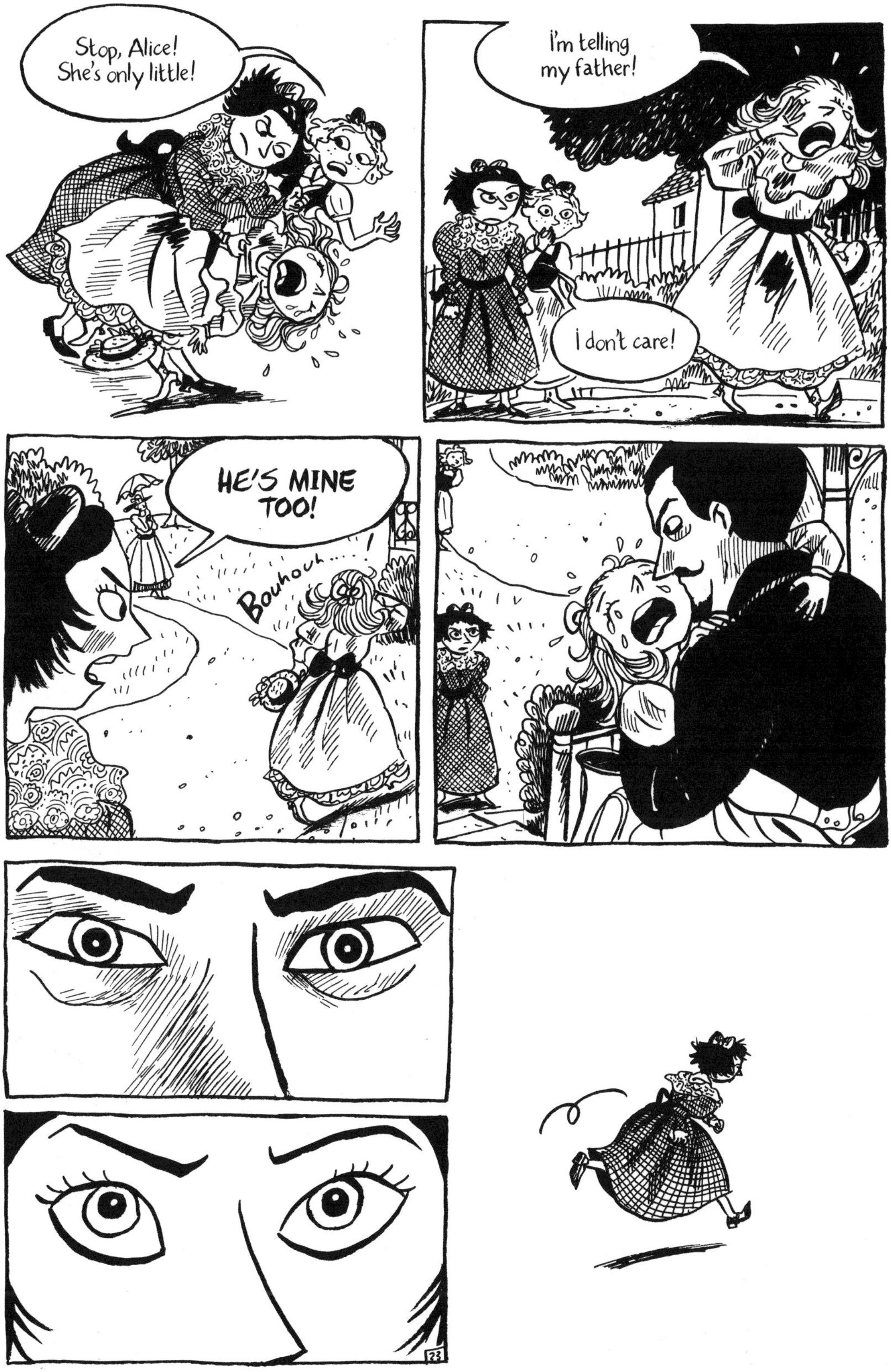

Stop, Alice! She's only little!
I'm telling my father!
I don't care!
HE'S MINE TOO!
Bouhouh....
23

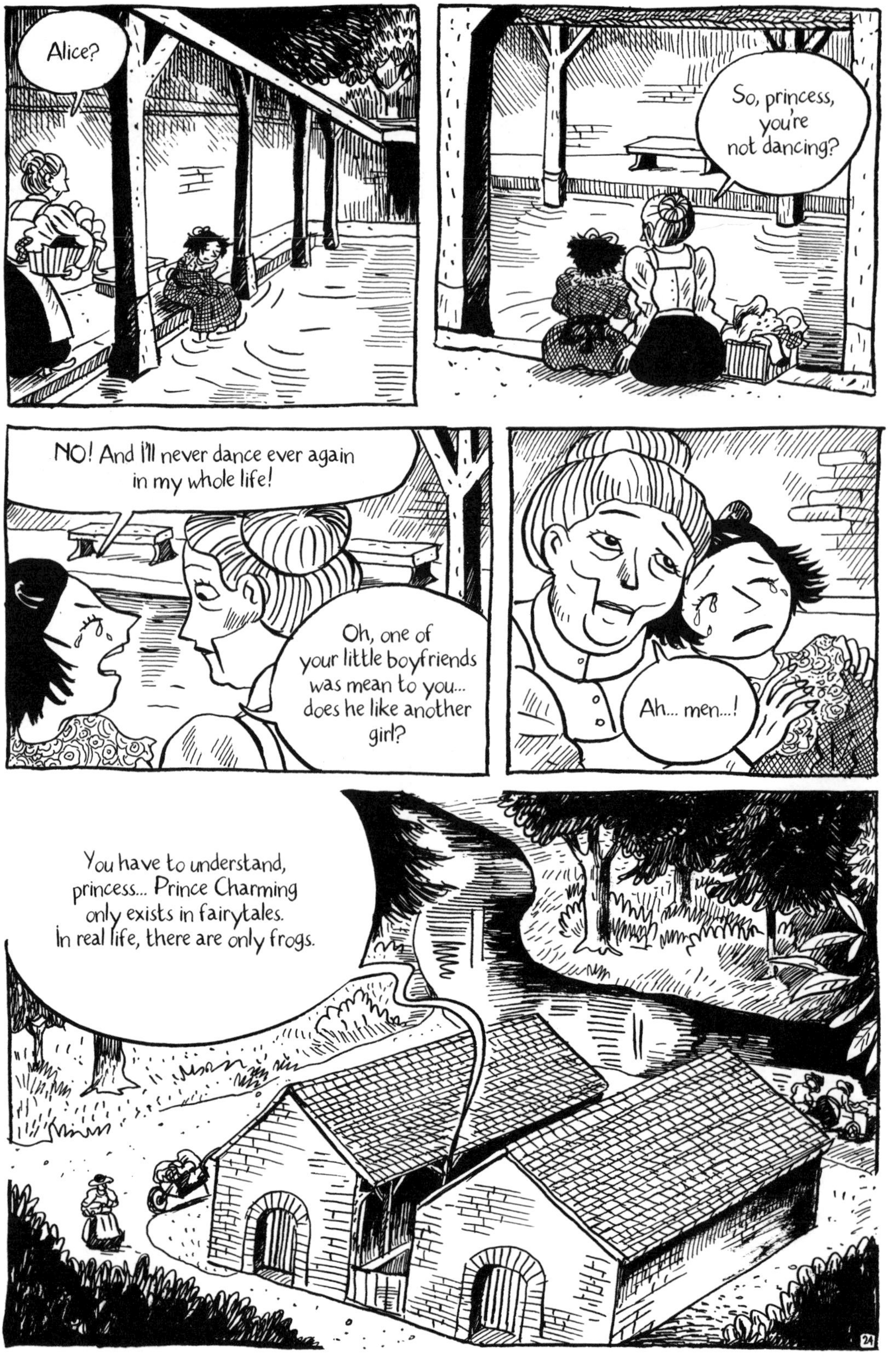
Alice?
So, princess, you're not dancing?
NO! And I'll never dance ever again in my whole life!
Oh, one of your little boyfriends was mean to you... does he like another girl?
Ah... men...!
You have to understand, princess... Prince Charming only exists in fairytales. In real life, there are only frogs.
24

1913 - Gare de l'Est

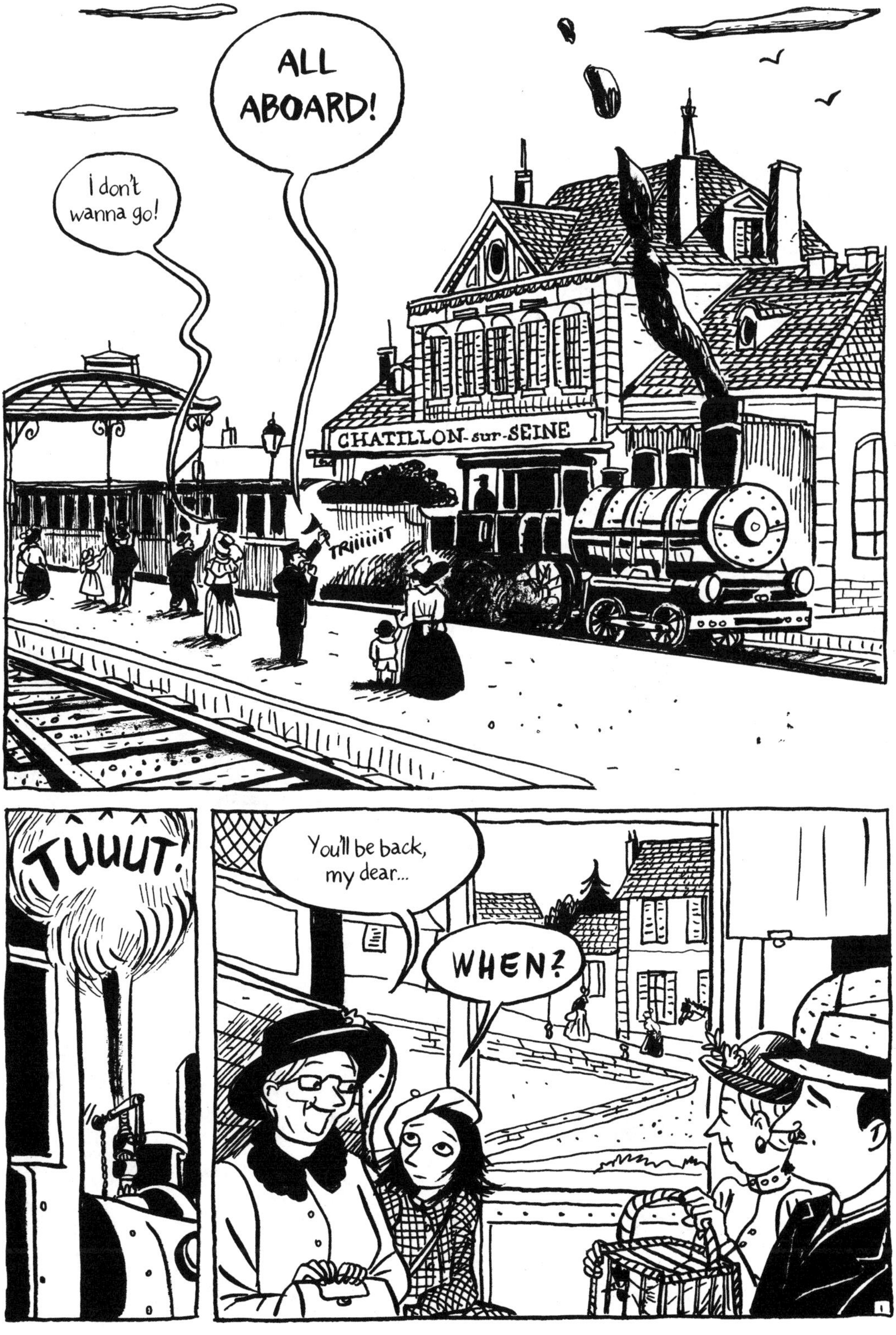
I don't wanna go!
ALL ABOARD!
CHATILLON-sur-SEINE
TRIiiiiiT
TÛÛÛT!
You'll be back, my dear...
WHEN?

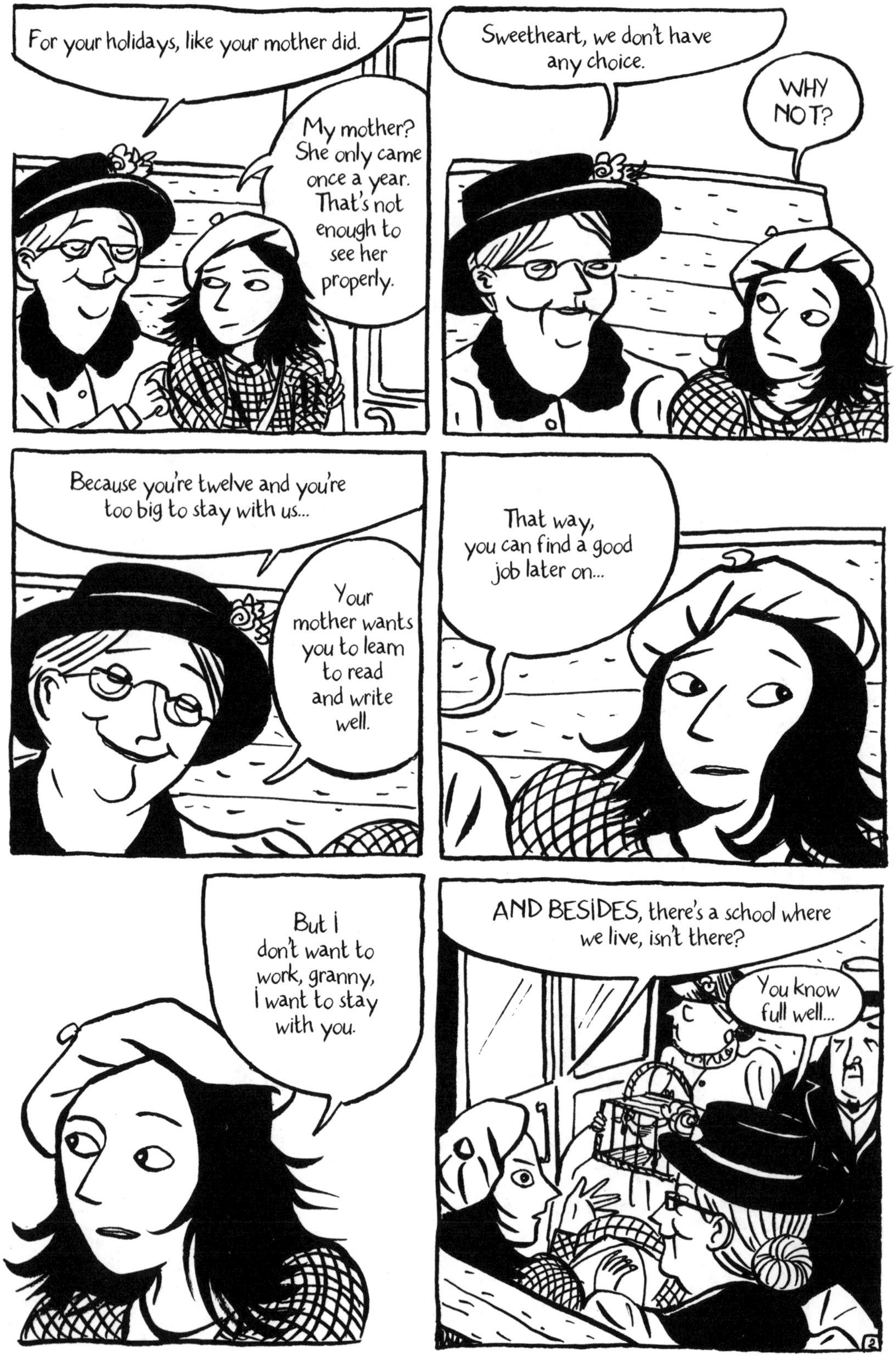
For your holidays, like your mother did.
My mother? She only came once a year. That's not enough to see her properly.
Sweetheart, we don't have any choice.
WHY NOT?
Because you're twelve and you're too big to stay with us...
Your mother wants you to learn to read and write well.
That way, you can find a good job later on...
But I don't want to work, granny, I want to stay with you.
AND BESIDES, there's a school where we live, isn't there?
You know full well...

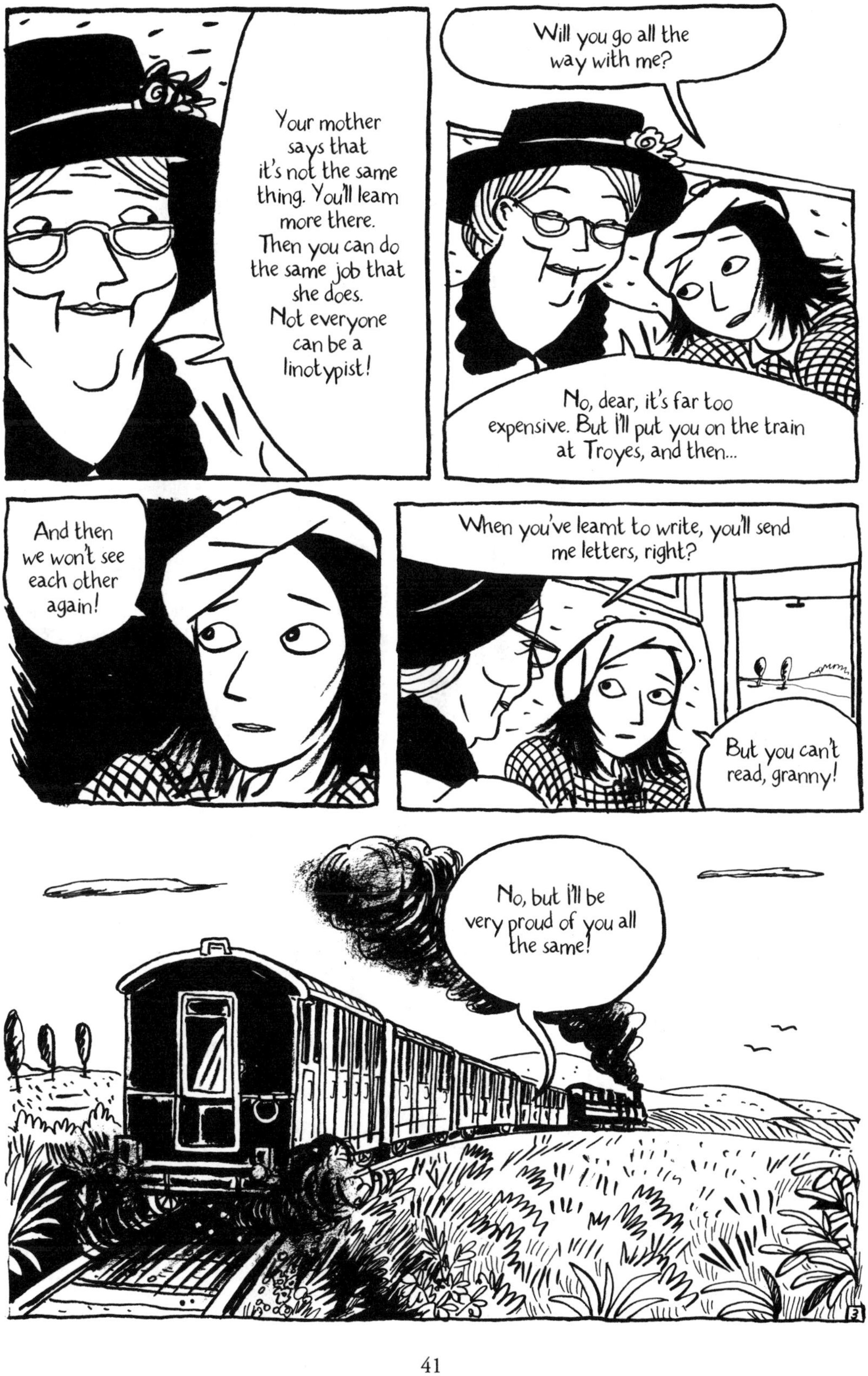
Your mother says that it's not the same thing. You'll learn more there. Then you can do the same job that she does. Not everyone can be a linotypist!
Will you go all the way with me?
No, dear, it's far too expensive. But I'll put you on the train at Troyes, and then...
And then we won't see each other again!
When you've learnt to write, you'll send me letters, right?
But you can't read, granny!
No, but I'll be very proud of you all the same!

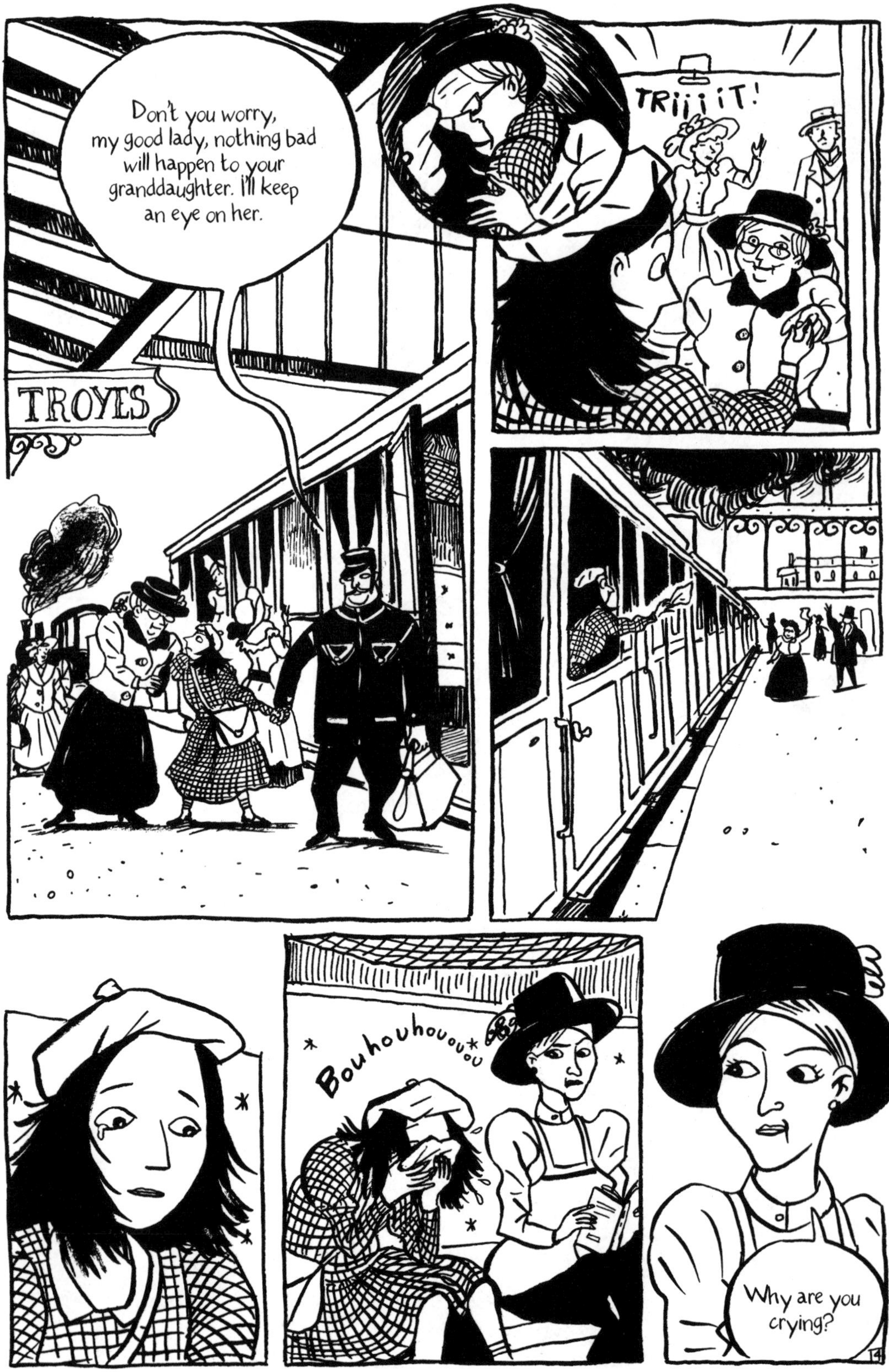

Don't you worry, my good lady, nothing bad will happen to your granddaughter. I'll keep an eye on her.
TROYES
TRIiiiT!
Bouhouhououou
Why are you crying?
14

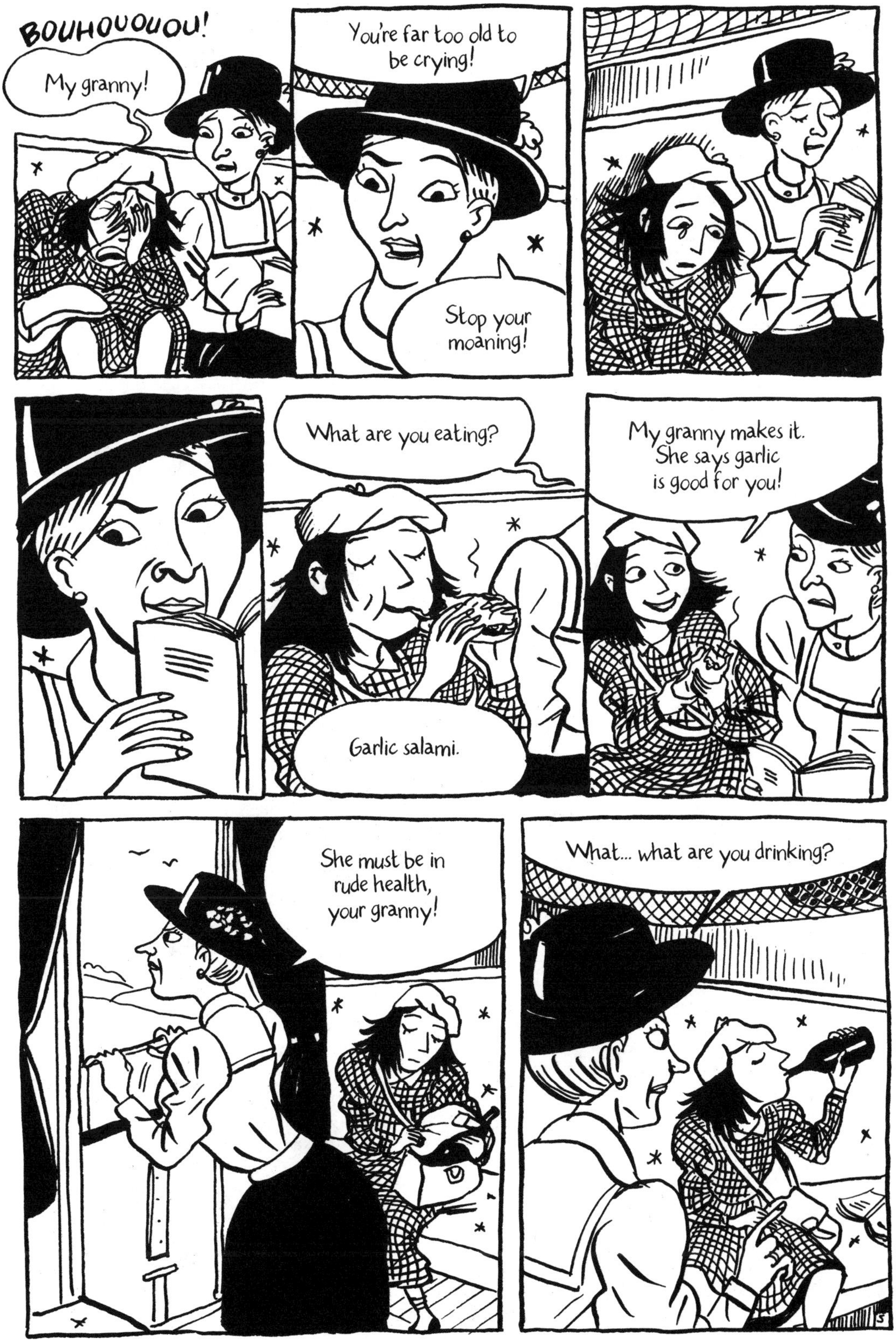
BOUHOUOUOU!
My granny!
You're far too old to be crying!
Stop your moaning!
What are you eating?
Garlic salami.
My granny makes it. She says garlic is good for you!
She must be in rude health, your granny!
What... what are you drinking?

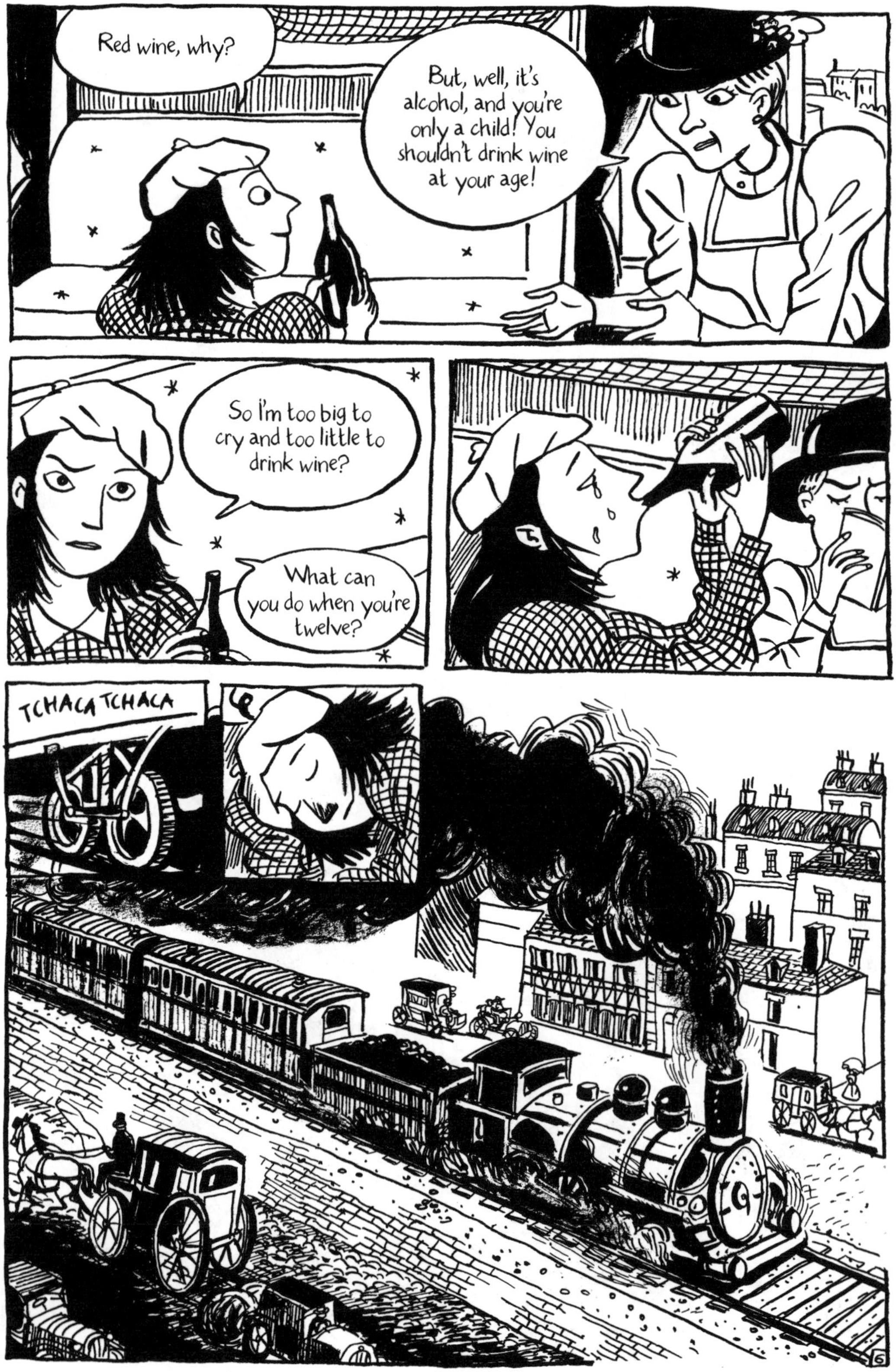
Red wine, why?
But, well, it's alcohol, and you're only a child! You shouldn't drink wine at your age!
So I'm too big to cry and too little to drink wine?
What can you do when you're twelve?
TCHACA TCHACA

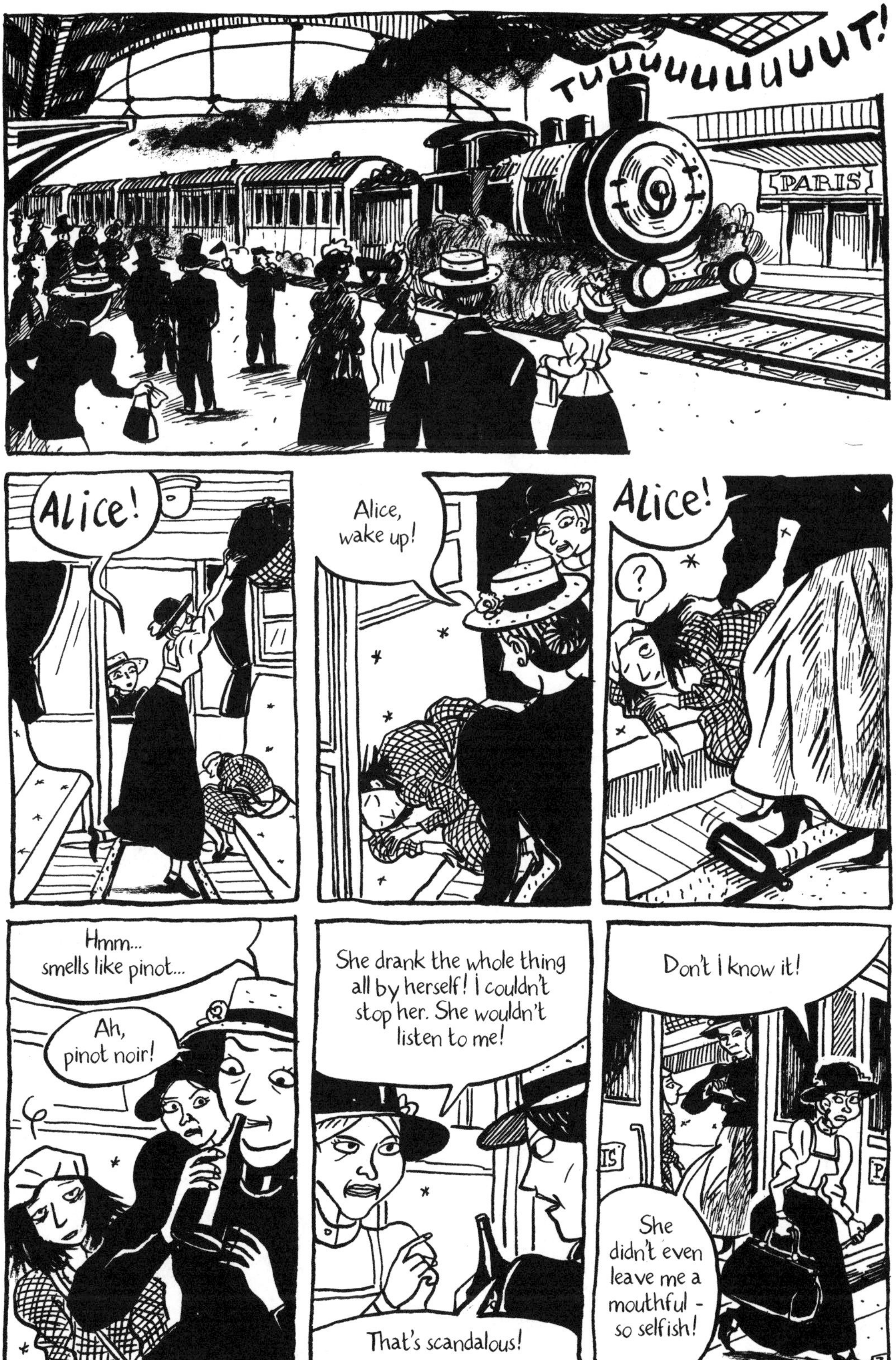
TUUUUUUUUUT!
PARIS
Alice!
Alice, wake up!
Alice!
?
Hmm... smells like pinot...
Ah, pinot noir!
She drank the whole thing all by herself! I couldn't stop her. She wouldn't listen to me!
That's scandalous!
Don't I know it!
She didn't even leave me a mouthful - so selfish!
7

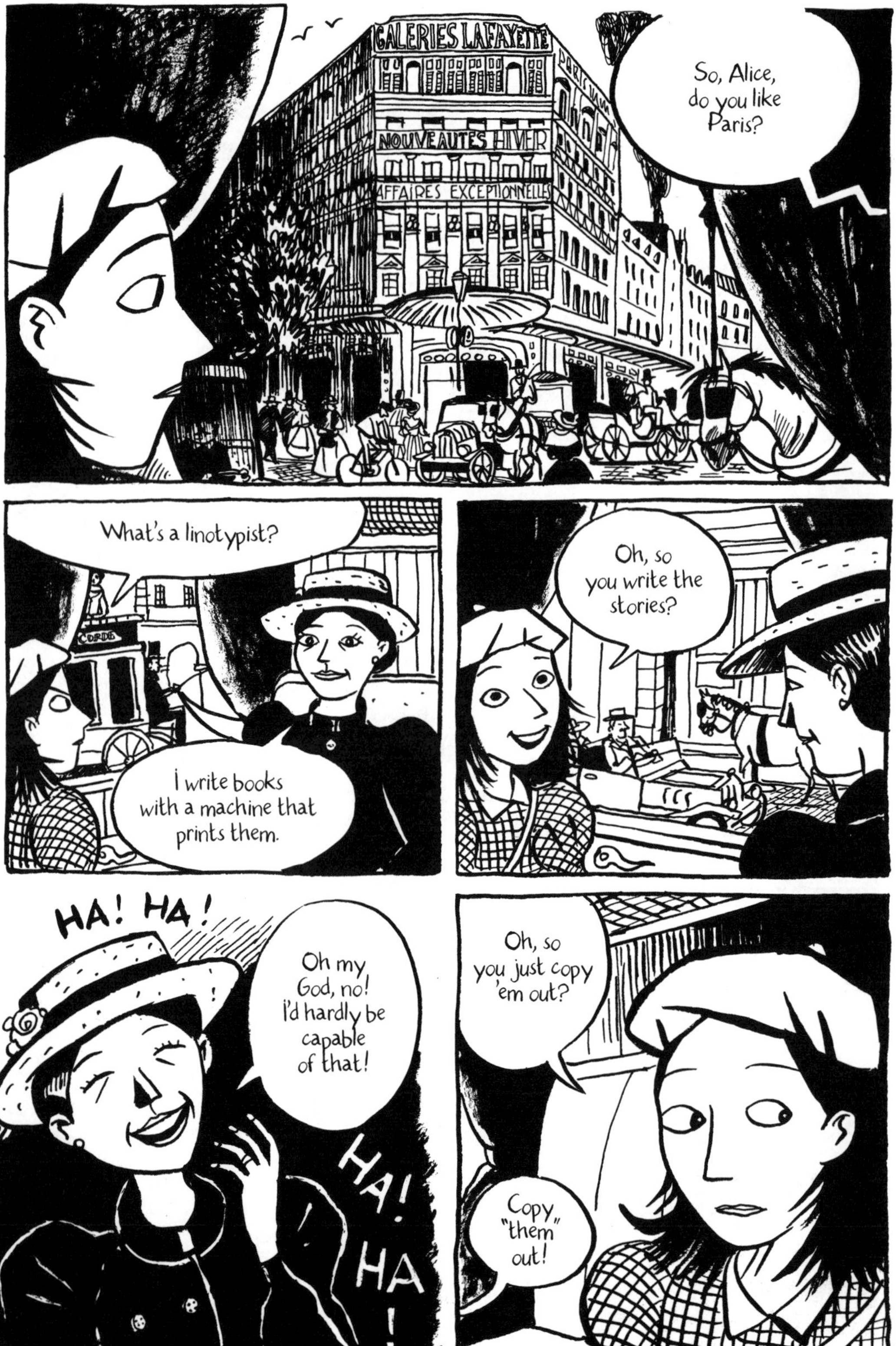
GALERIES LAFAYETTE
NOUVEAUTÉS HIVER
AFFAIRES EXCEPTIONNELLES
So, Alice, do you like Paris?
What's a linotypist?
I write books with a machine that prints them.
Oh, so you write the stories?
HA! HA!
Oh my God, no! I'd hardly be capable of that!
HA! HA!
Oh, so you just copy 'em out?
Copy "them" out!

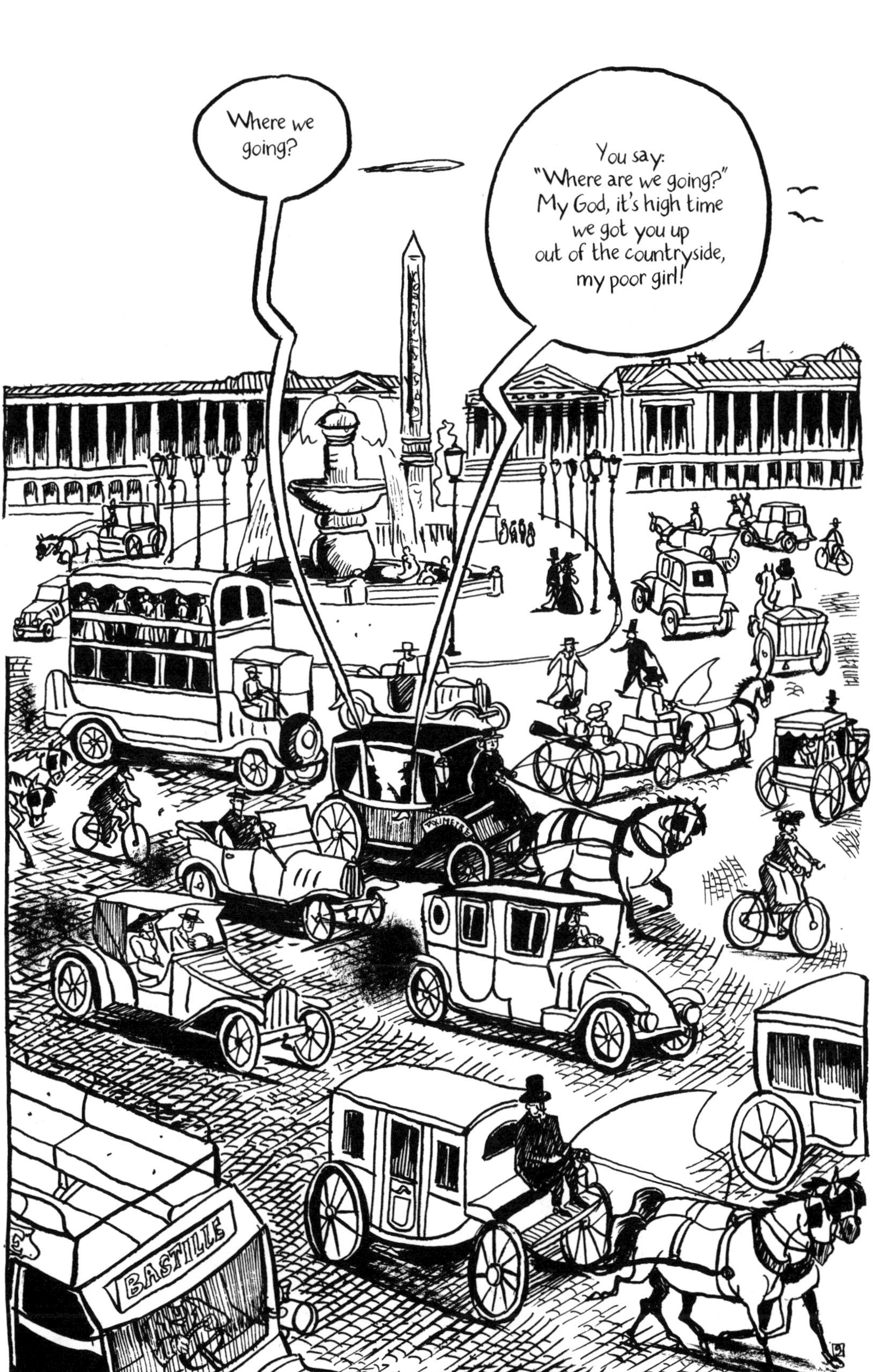
Where we going?
You say: "Where are we going?" My God, it's high time we got you up out of the countryside, my poor girl!
TAXIMETRE
BASTILLE

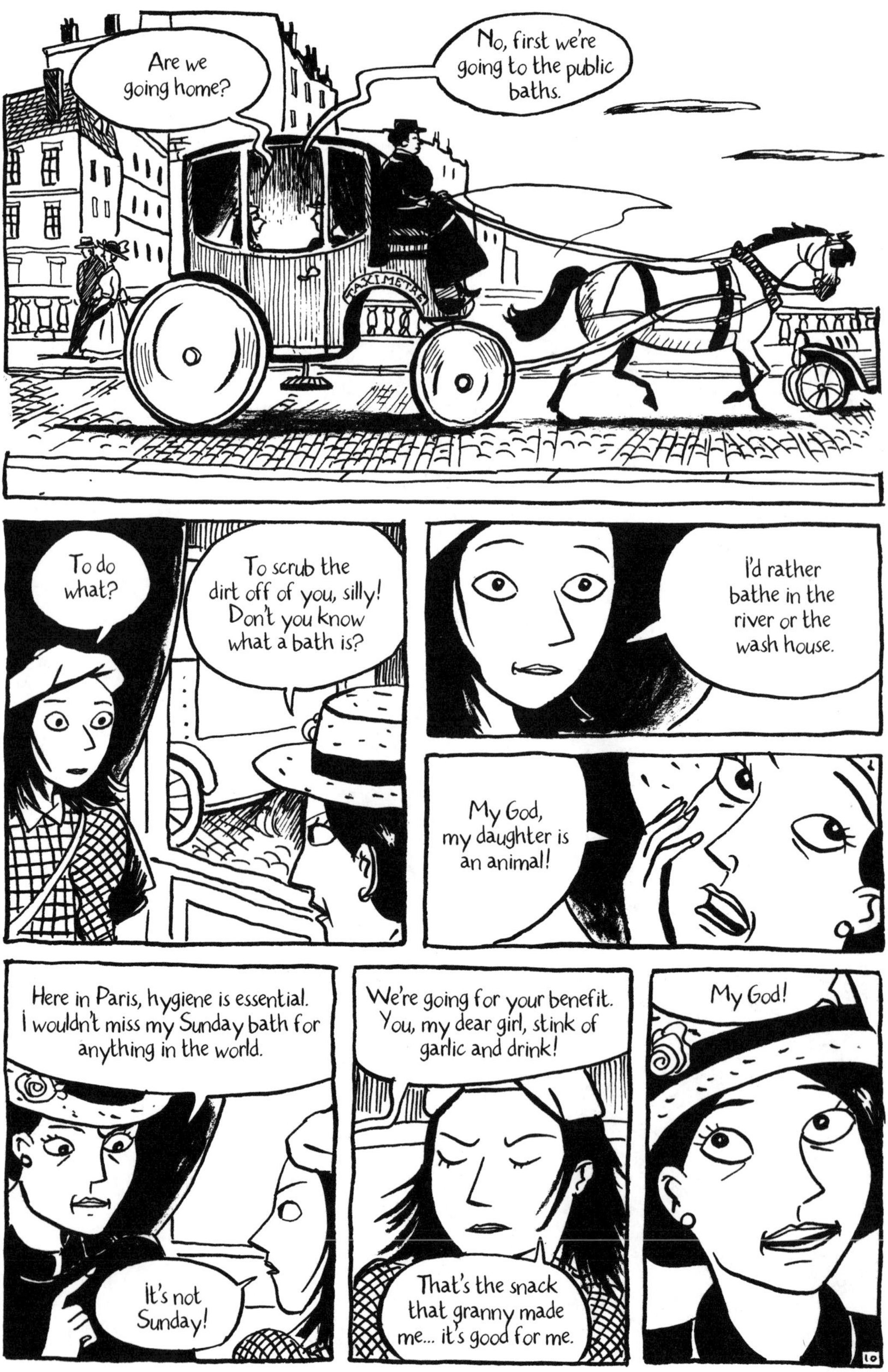

Are we going home?
No, first we're going to the public baths.
TAXIMETRE
To do what?
To scrub the dirt off of you, silly! Don't you know what a bath is?
I'd rather bathe in the river or the wash house.
My God, my daughter is an animal!
Here in Paris, hygiene is essential. I wouldn't miss my Sunday bath for anything in the world.
It's not Sunday!
We're going for your benefit. You, my dear girl, stink of garlic and drink!
That's the snack that granny made me... it's good for me.
My God!
10

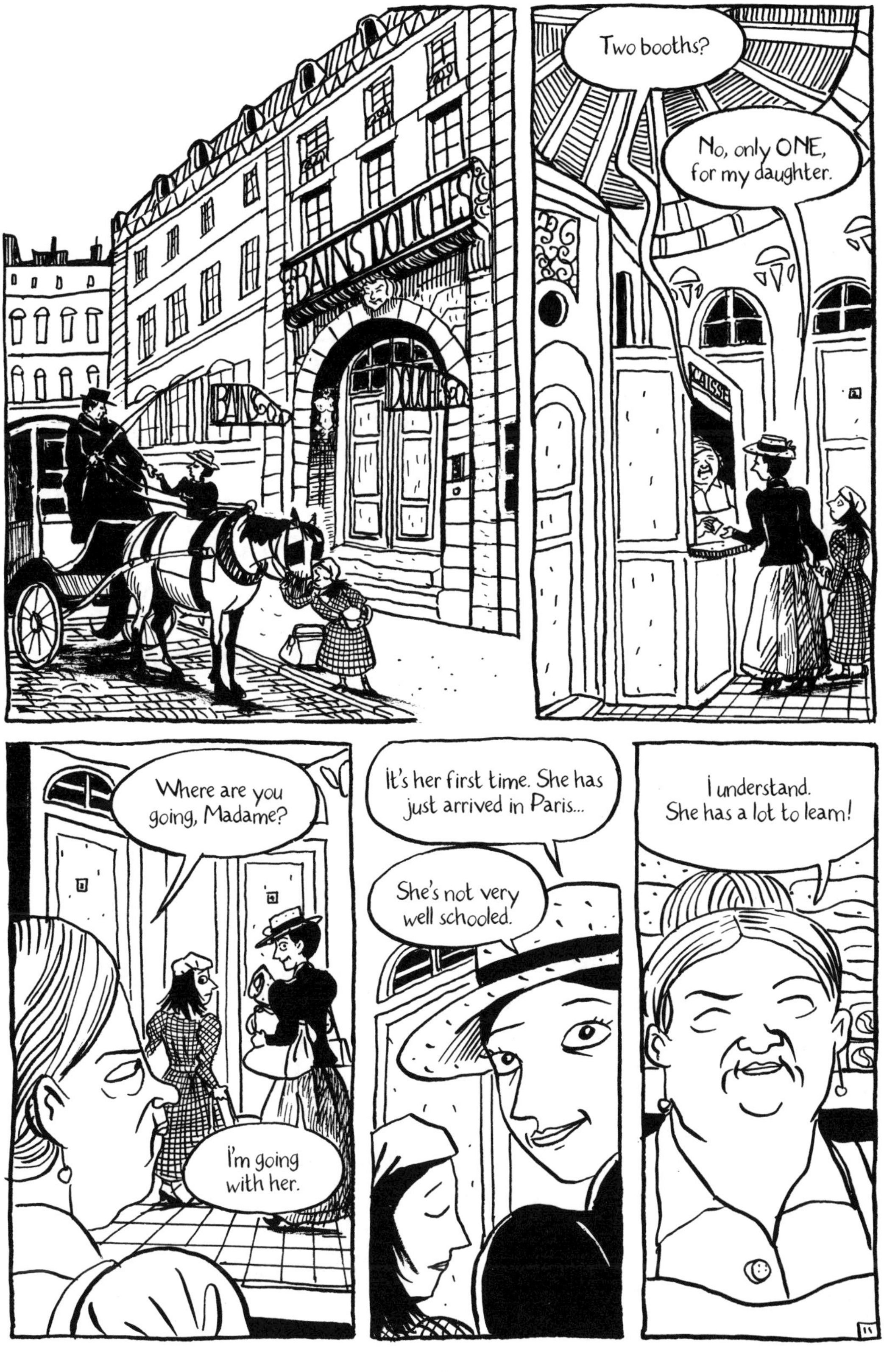
BAINS DOUCHES
Two booths?
No, only ONE, for my daughter.
CAISSE
Where are you going, Madame?
I'm going with her.
It's her first time. She has just arrived in Paris...
She's not very well schooled.
I understand. She has a lot to learn!

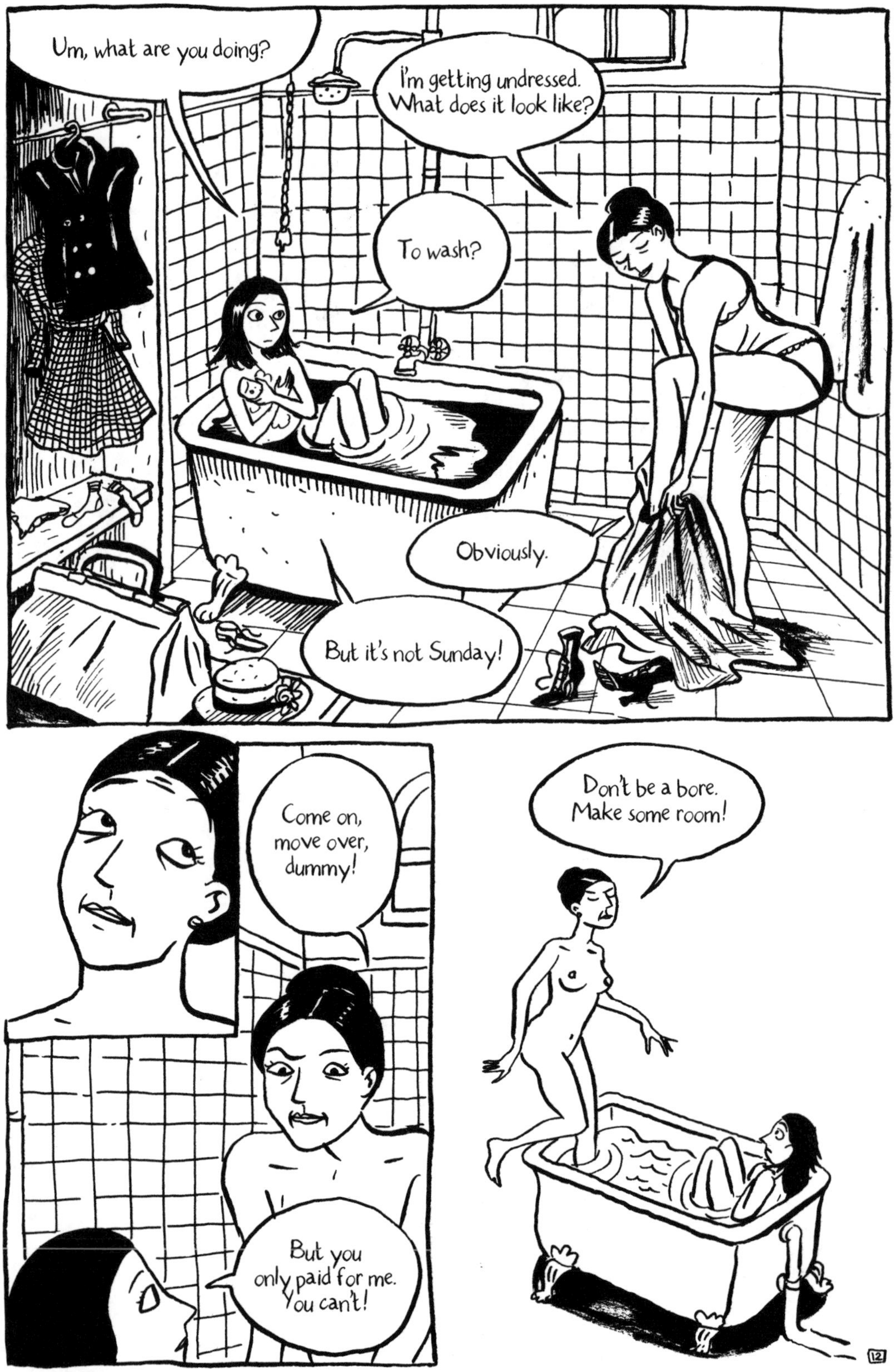

Um, what are you doing?
I'm getting undressed. What does it look like?
To wash?
Obviously.
But it's not Sunday!
Come on, move over, dummy!
But you only paid for me. You can't!
Don't be a bore. Make some room!
12

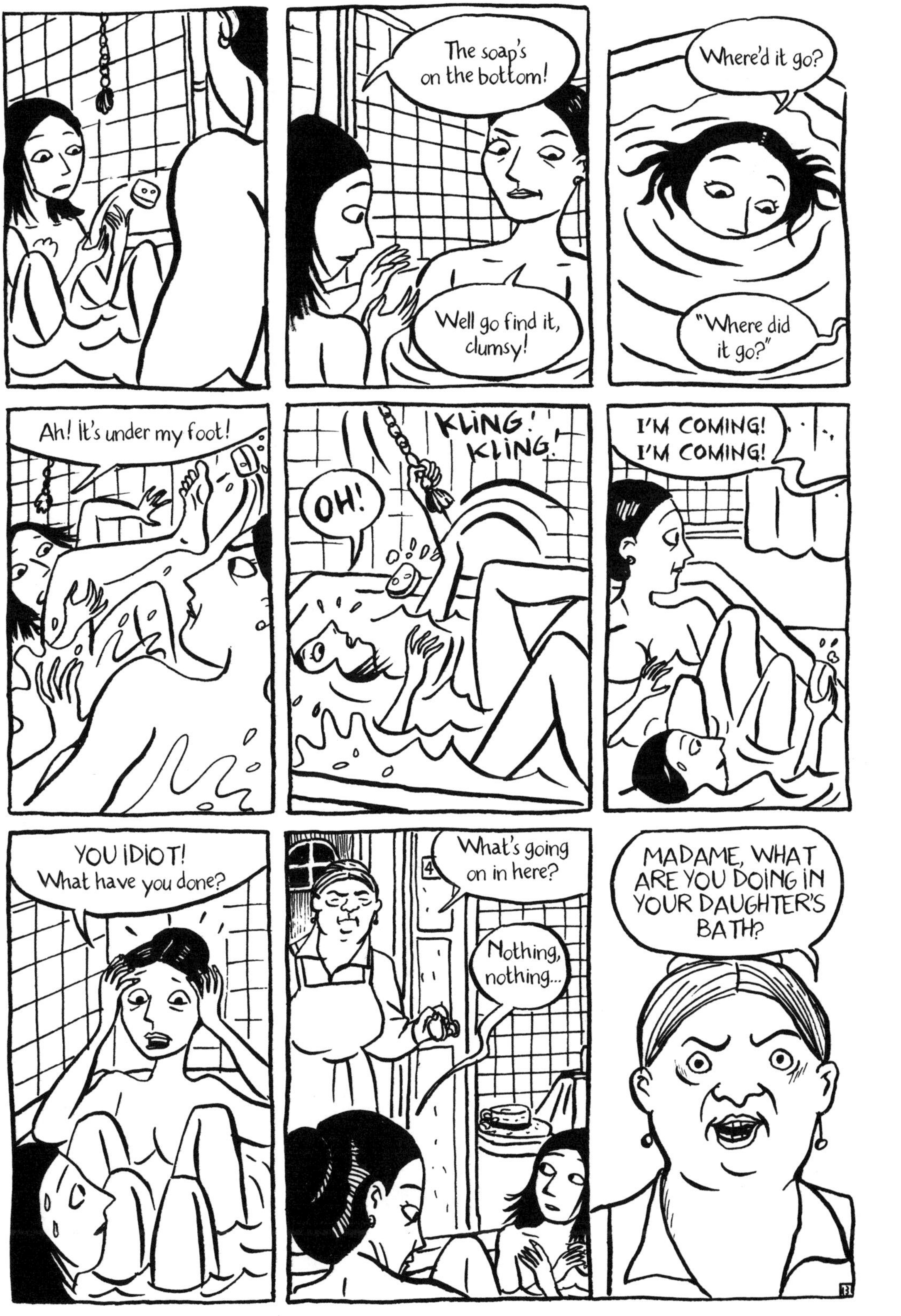
The soap's on the bottom!
Well go find it, clumsy!
Where'd it go?
"Where did it go?"
Ah! It's under my foot!
KLING! KLING!
OH!
I'M COMING! I'M COMING!
YOU IDIOT! What have you done?
What's going on in here?
Nothing, nothing...
MADAME, WHAT ARE YOU DOING IN YOUR DAUGHTER'S BATH?

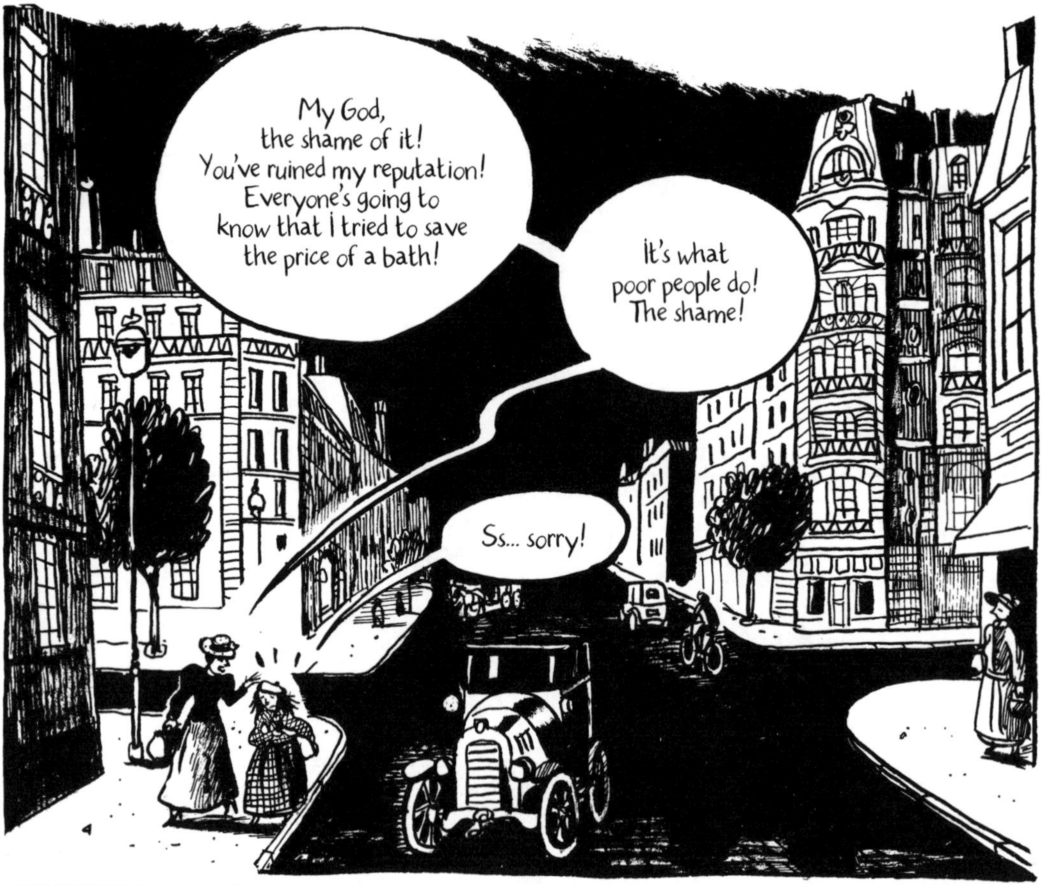
My God, the shame of it! You've ruined my reputation! Everyone's going to know that I tried to save the price of a bath!
It's what poor people do! The shame!
Ss... sorry!

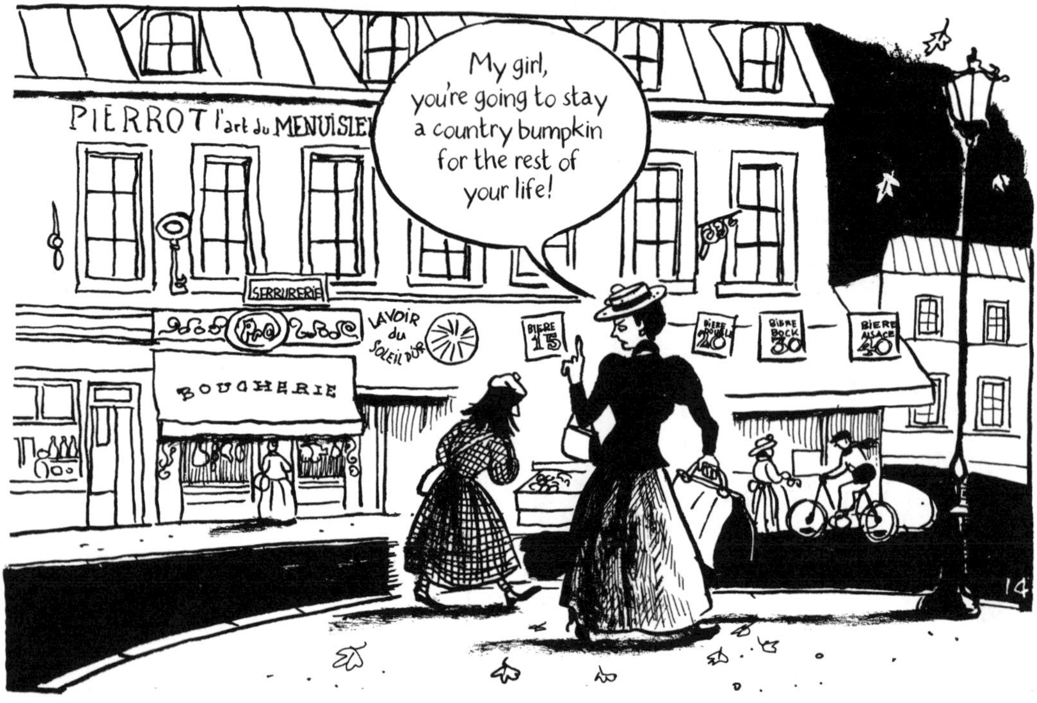
PIERROT l'art du MENUISIE
My girl, you're going to stay a country bumpkin for the rest of your life!
SERRURERIE
BOUCHERIE
LAVOIR du SOLEIL D'OR
BIERE 15
BIERE DOUBLE 20
BIERE BOCK 30
BIERE ALSACE 40
14

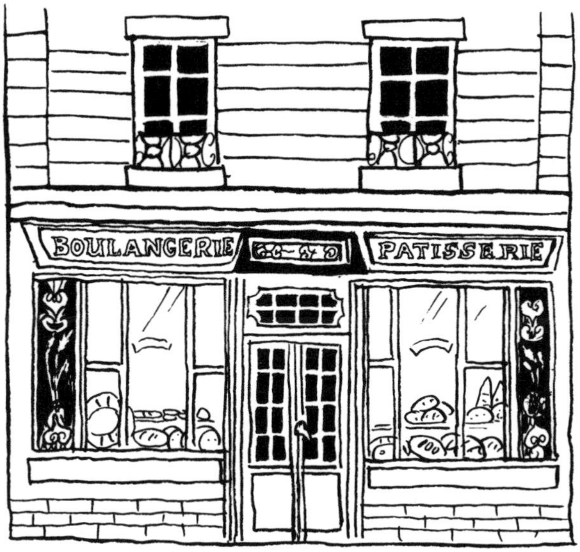
BOULANGERIE
PATISSERIE

1916 - Place Saint-Charles

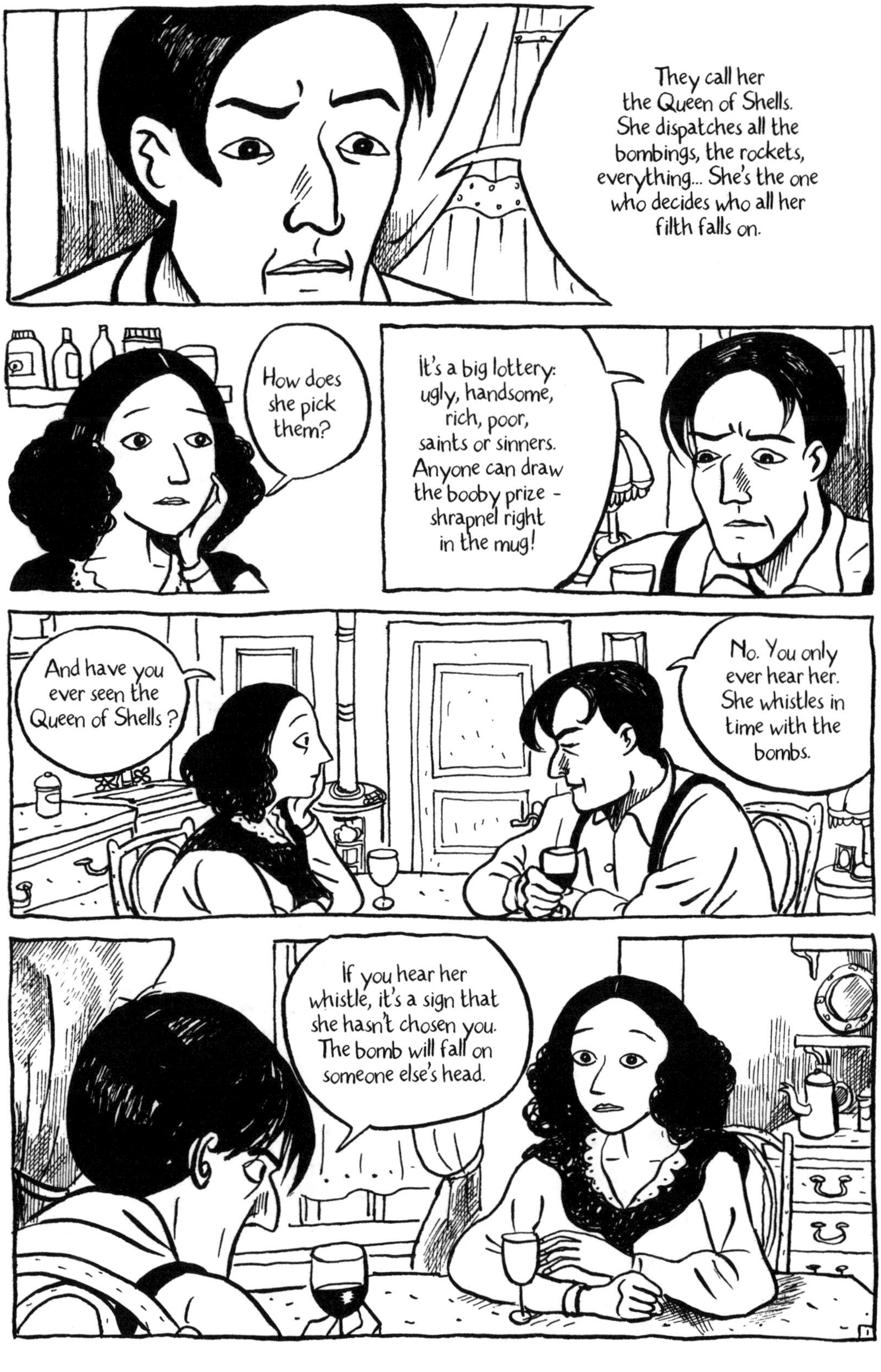
They call her the Queen of Shells. She dispatches all the bombings, the rockets, everything... She's the one who decides who all her filth falls on.
How does she pick them?
It's a big lottery: ugly, handsome, rich, poor, saints or sinners. Anyone can draw the booby prize - shrapnel right in the mug!
And have you ever seen the Queen of Shells?
No. You only ever hear her. She whistles in time with the bombs.
If you hear her whistle, it's a sign that she hasn't chosen you. The bomb will fall on someone else's head.

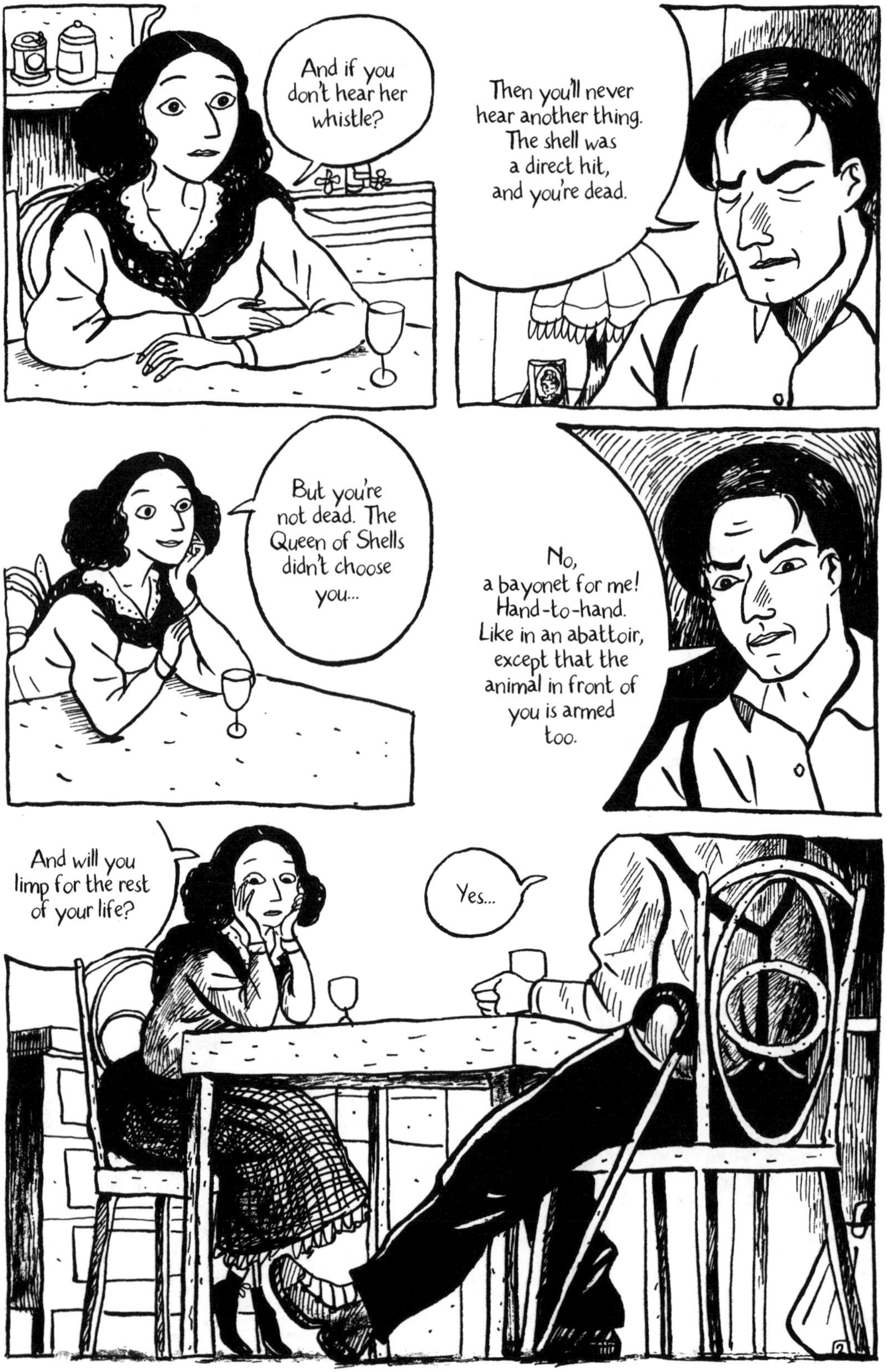
And if you don't hear her whistle?
Then you'll never hear another thing. The shell was a direct hit, and you're dead.
But you're not dead. The Queen of Shells didn't choose you...
No, a bayonet for me! Hand-to-hand. Like in an abattoir, except that the animal in front of you is armed too.
And will you limp for the rest of your life?
Yes...

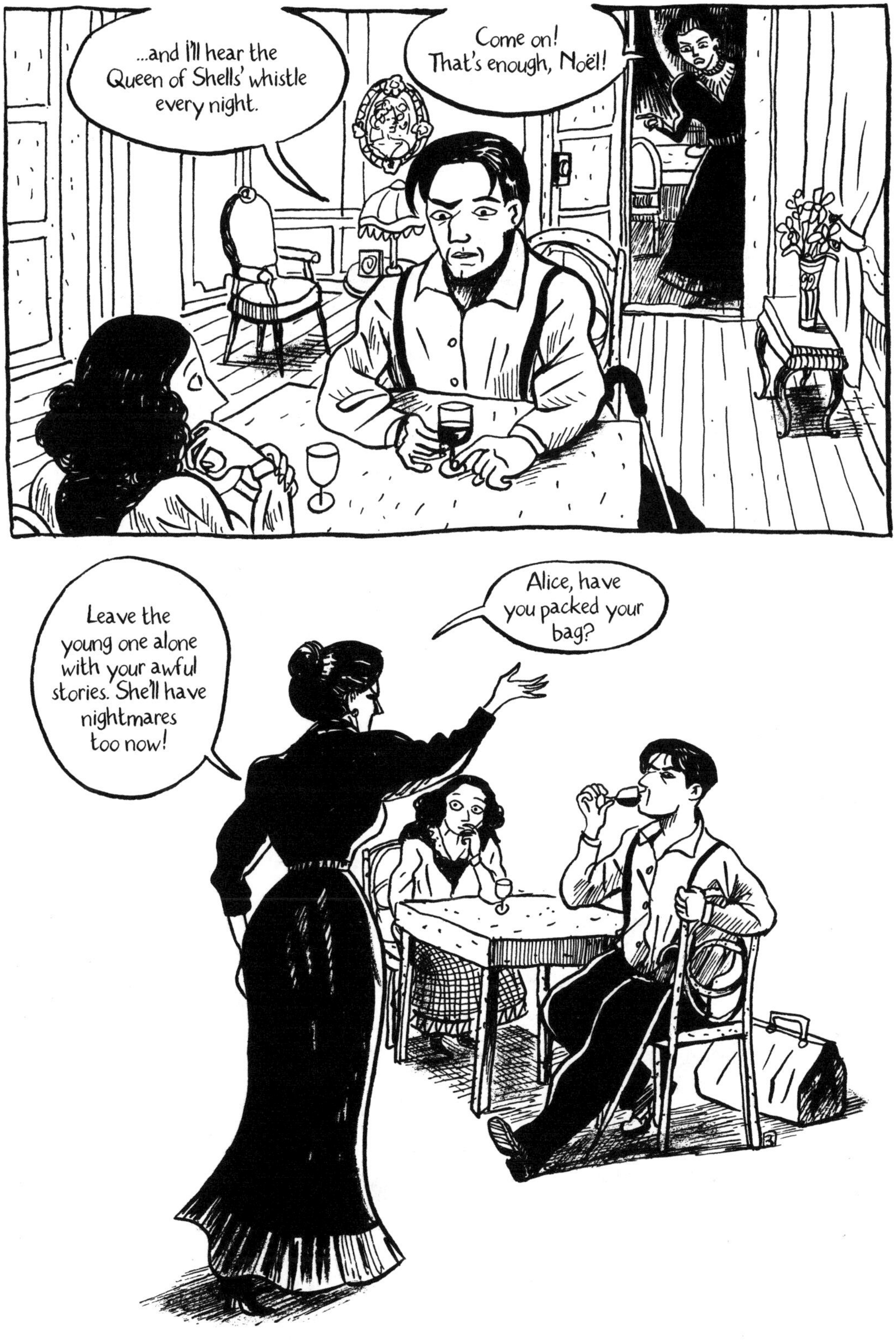
...and I'll hear the Queen of Shells' whistle every night.
Come on! That's enough, Noël!
Leave the young one alone with your awful stories. She'll have nightmares too now!
Alice, have you packed your bag?

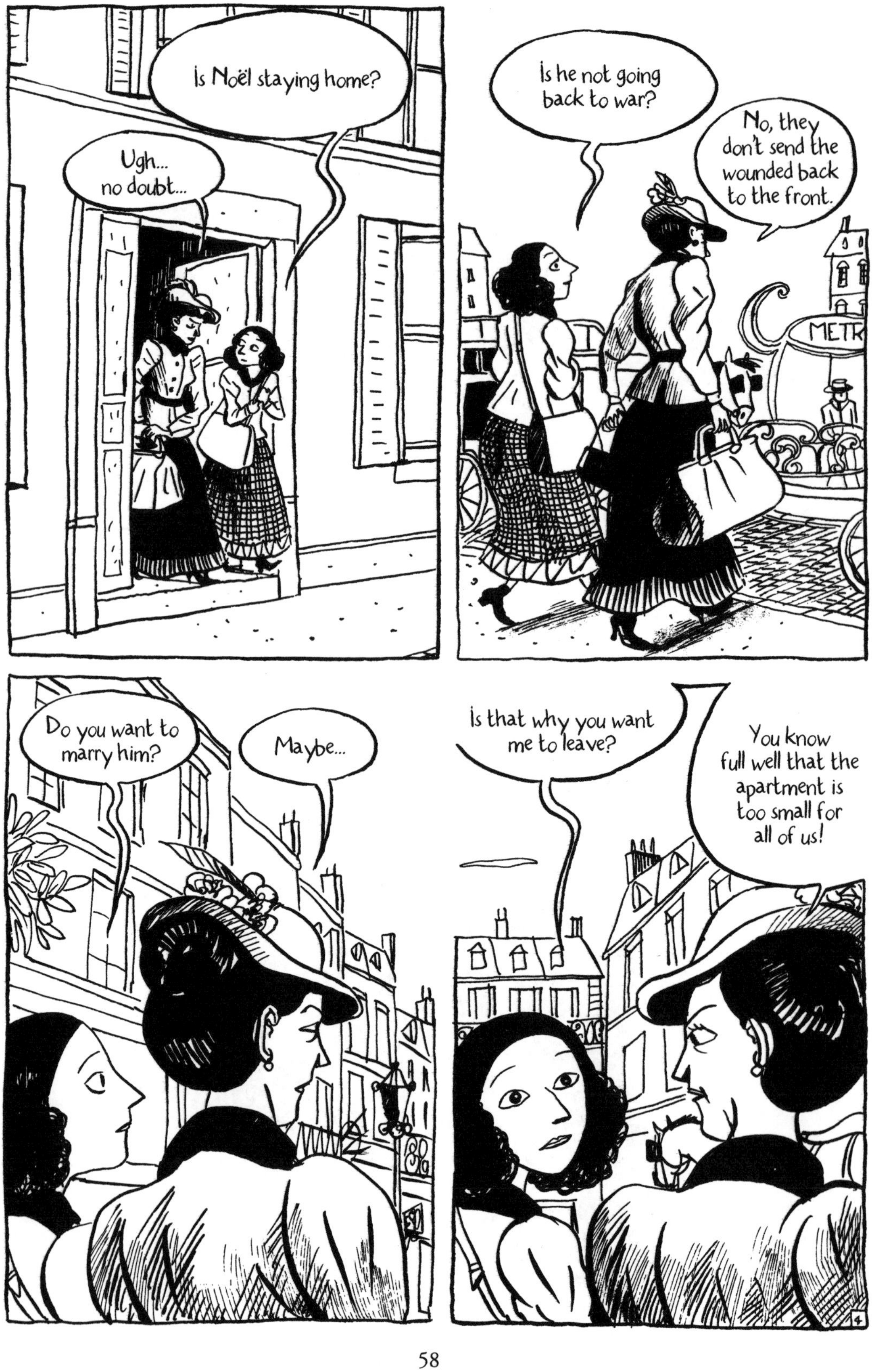
Is Noël staying home?
Ugh... no doubt...
Is he not going back to war?
No, they don't send the wounded back to the front.
METR
Do you want to marry him?
Maybe...
Is that why you want me to leave?
You know full well that the apartment is too small for all of us!

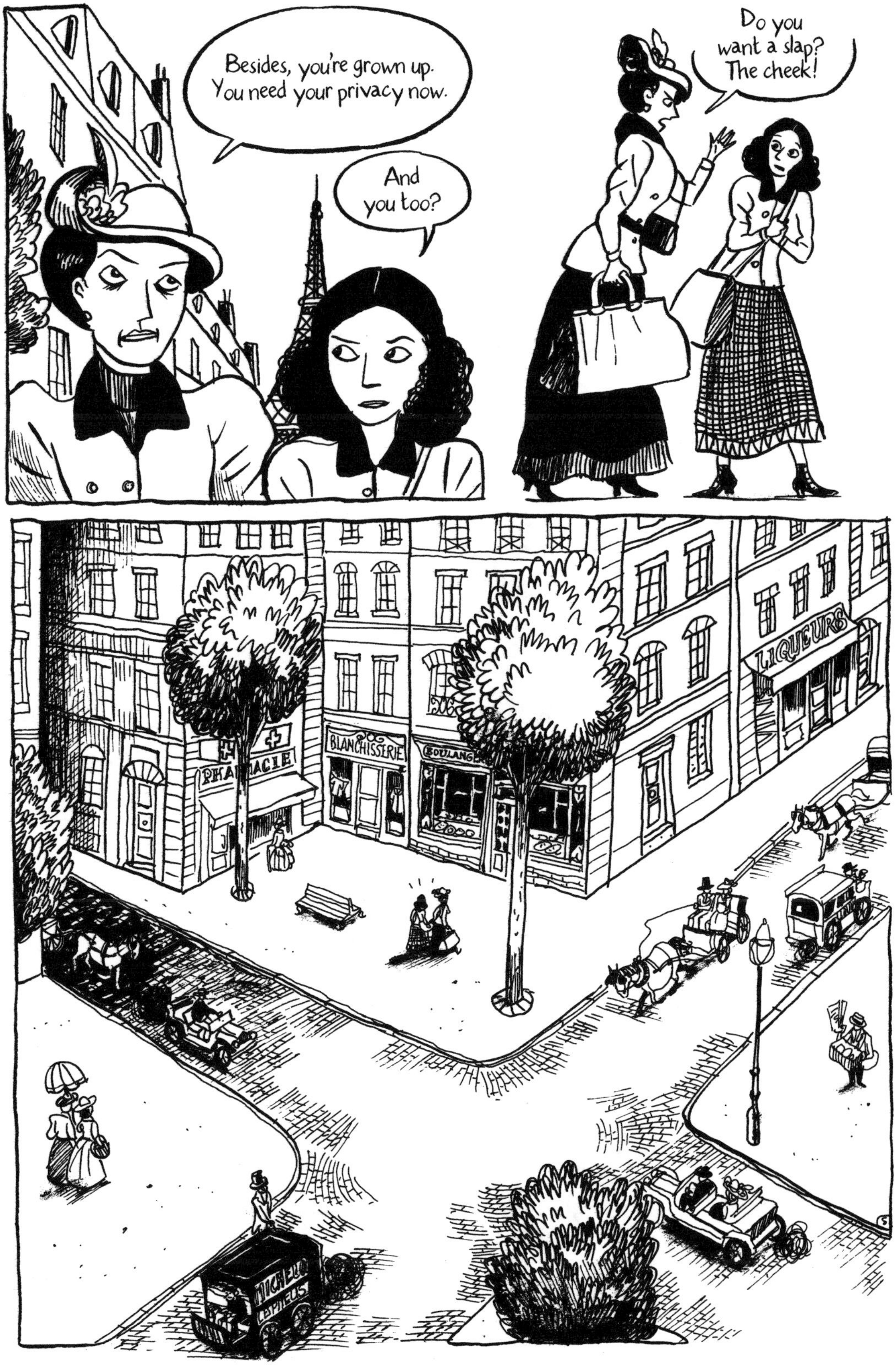
Besides, you're grown up. You need your privacy now.
And you too?
Do you want a slap? The cheek!
BLANCHISSERIE
LIQUEURS

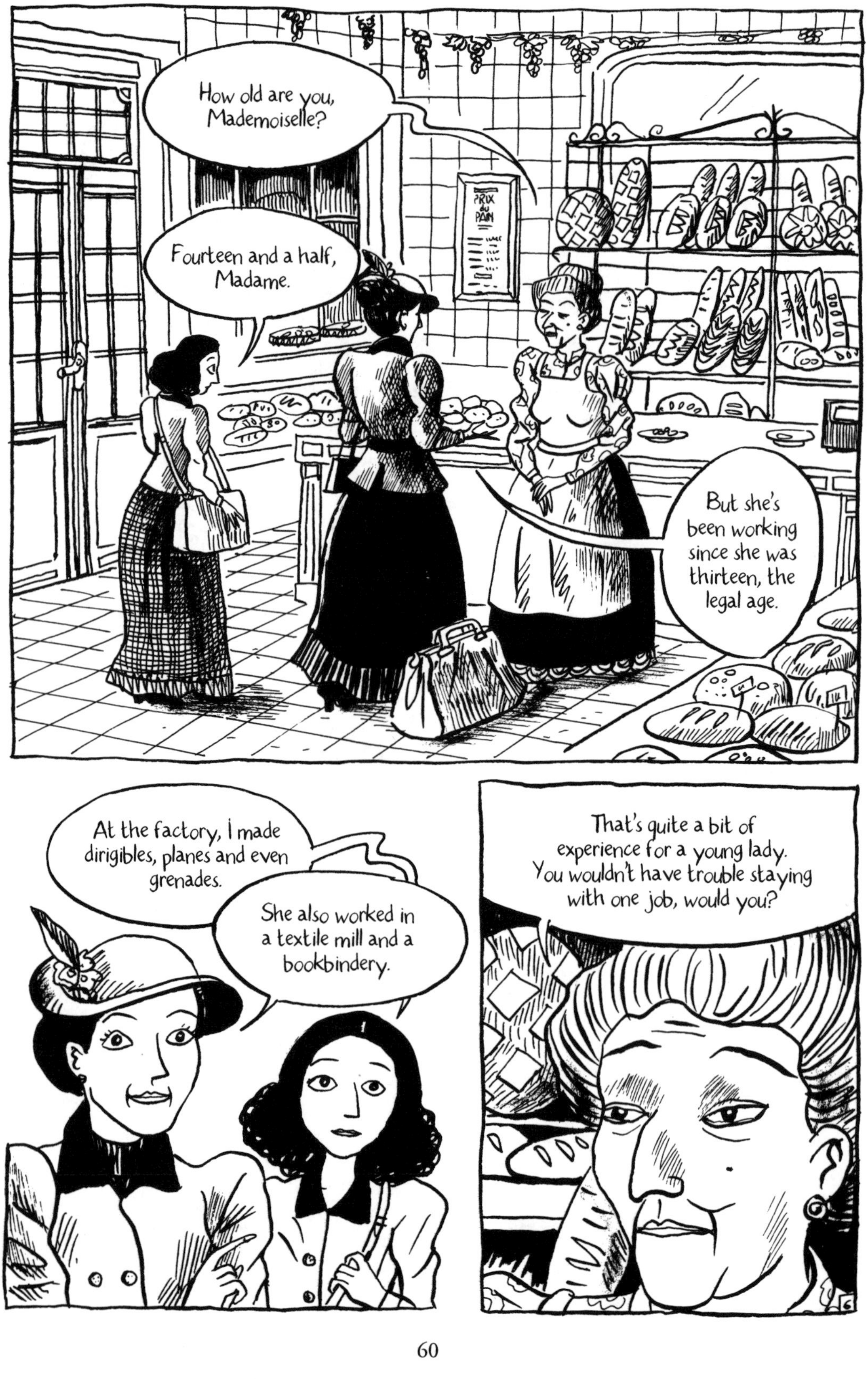
How old are you, Mademoiselle?
Fourteen and a half, Madame.
PRIX du PAIN
But she's been working since she was thirteen, the legal age.
At the factory, I made dirigibles, planes and even grenades.
She also worked in a textile mill and a bookbindery.
That's quite a bit of experience for a young lady. You wouldn't have trouble staying with one job, would you?

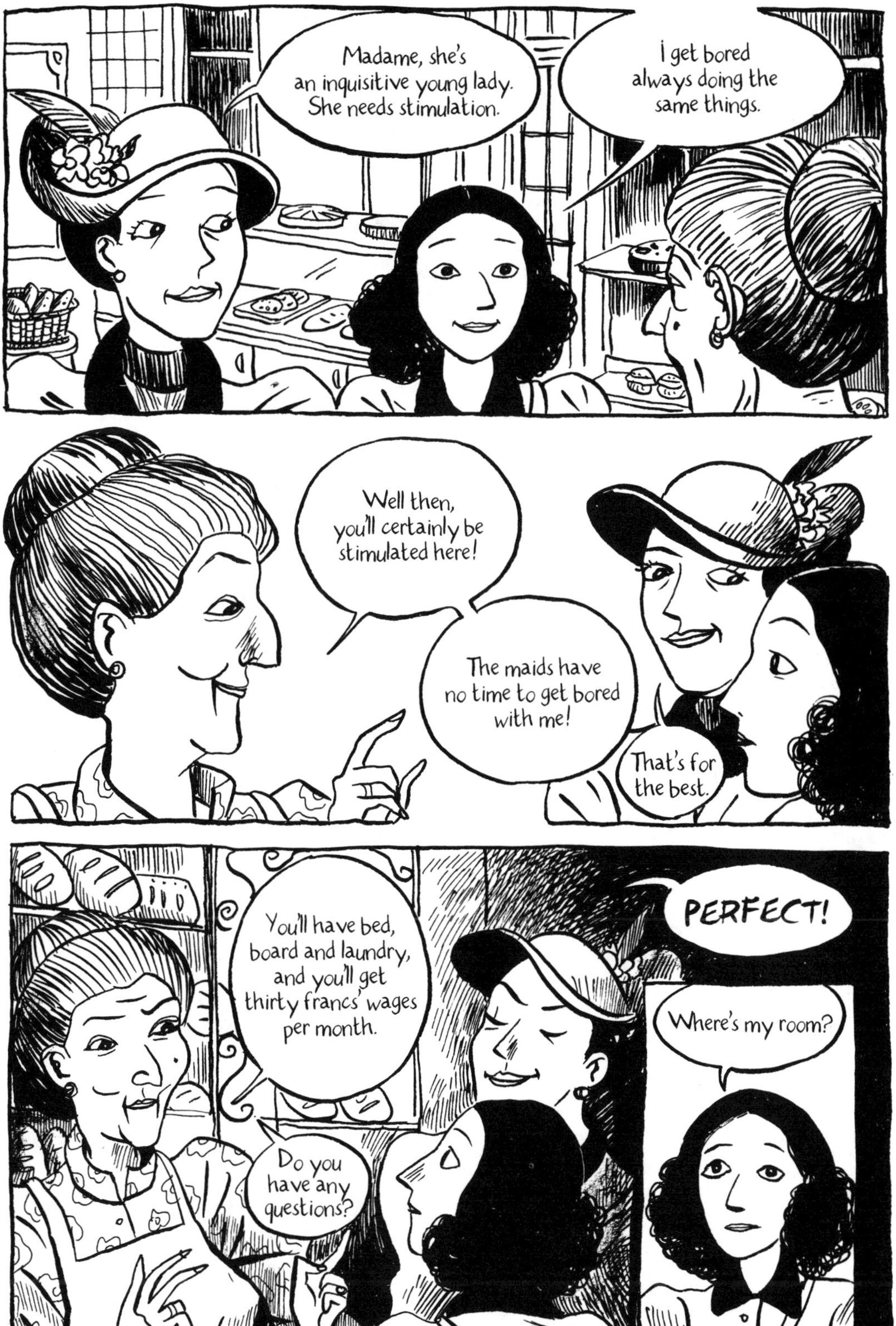
Madame, she's an inquisitive young lady. She needs stimulation.
I get bored always doing the same things.
Well then, you'll certainly be stimulated here!
The maids have no time to get bored with me!
That's for the best.
You'll have bed, board and laundry, and you'll get thirty francs' wages per month.
Do you have any questions?
PERFECT!
Where's my room?
7

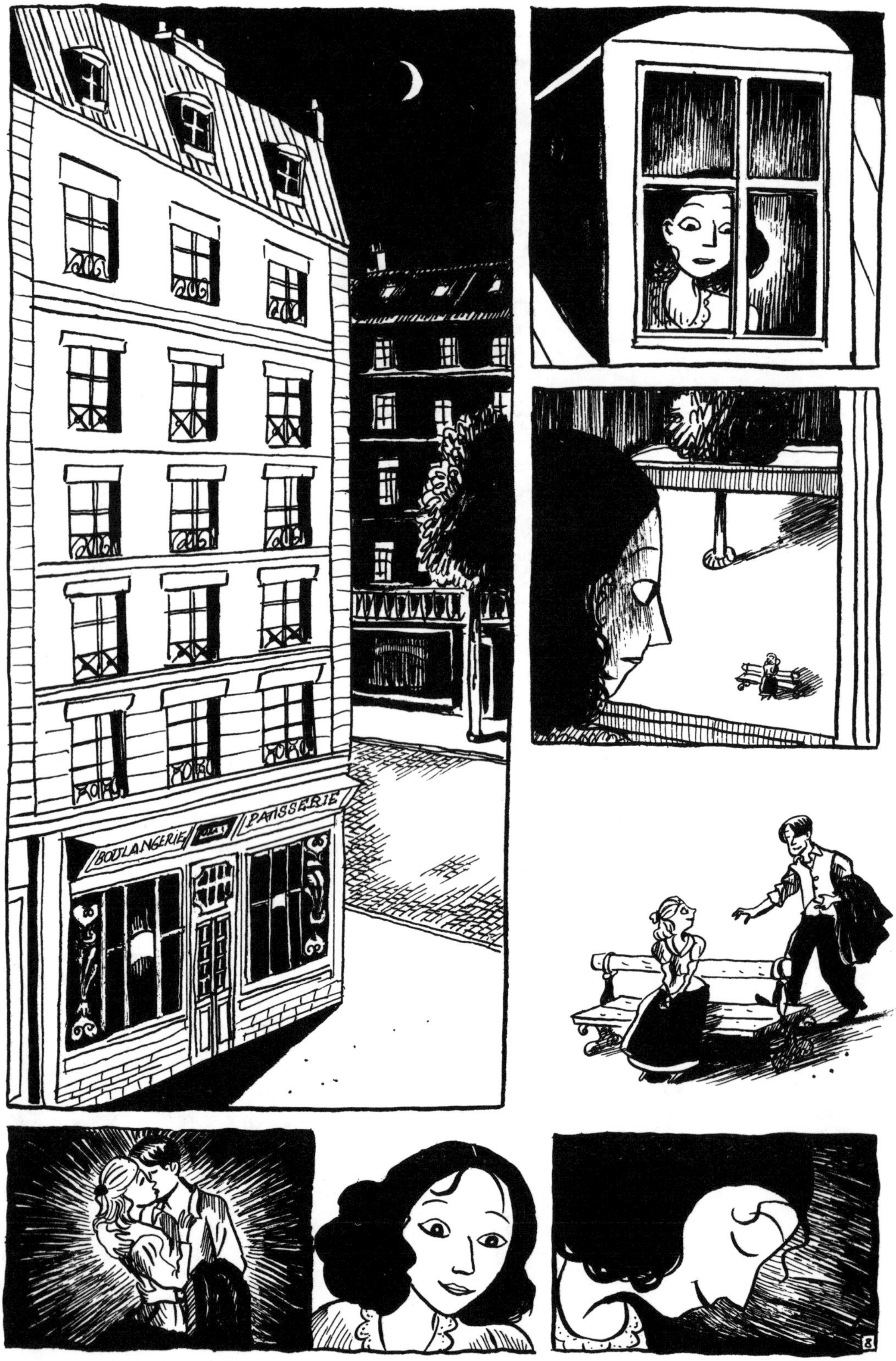
PATISSERIE
BOULANGERIE

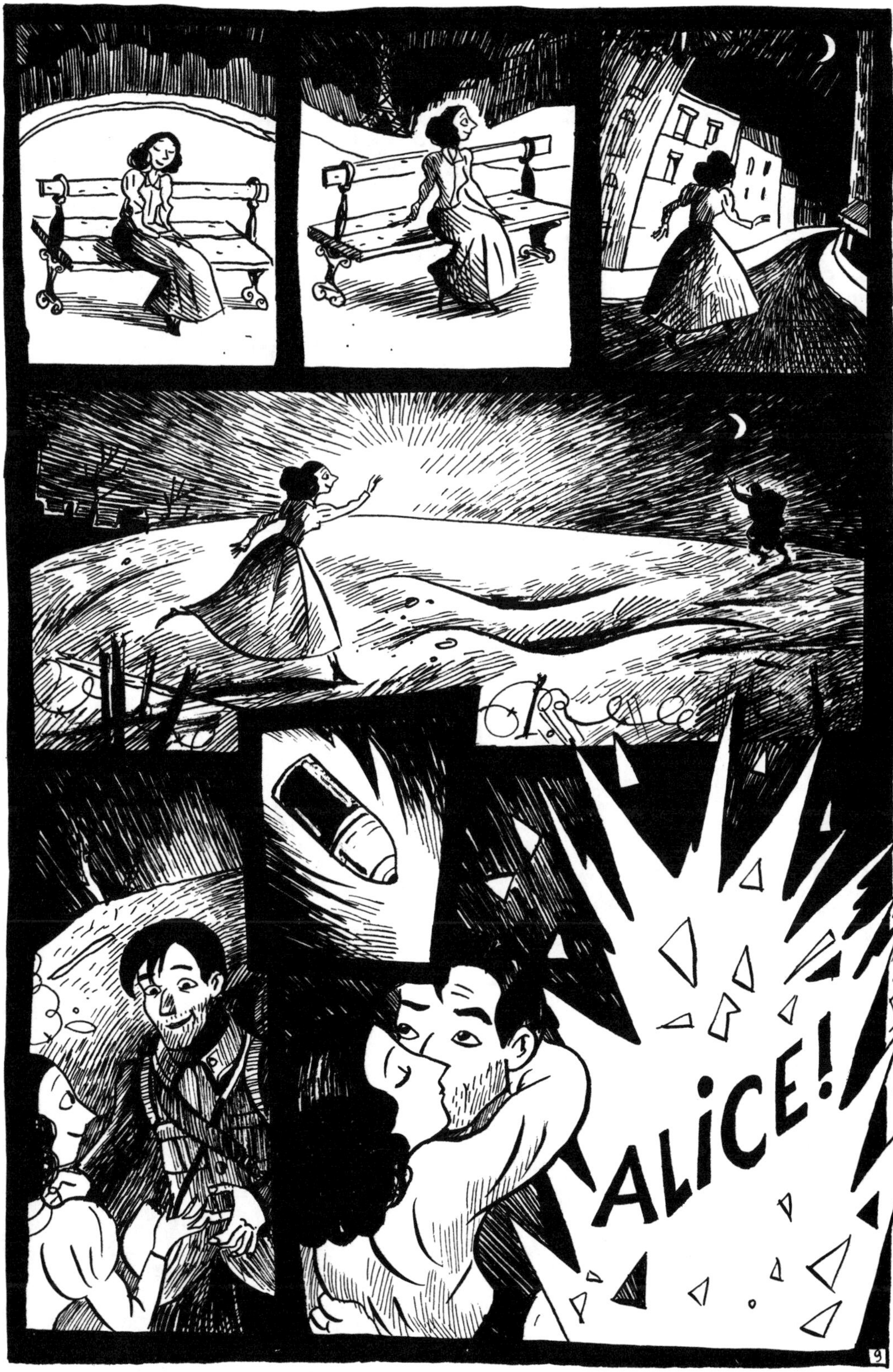
ALICE!
9

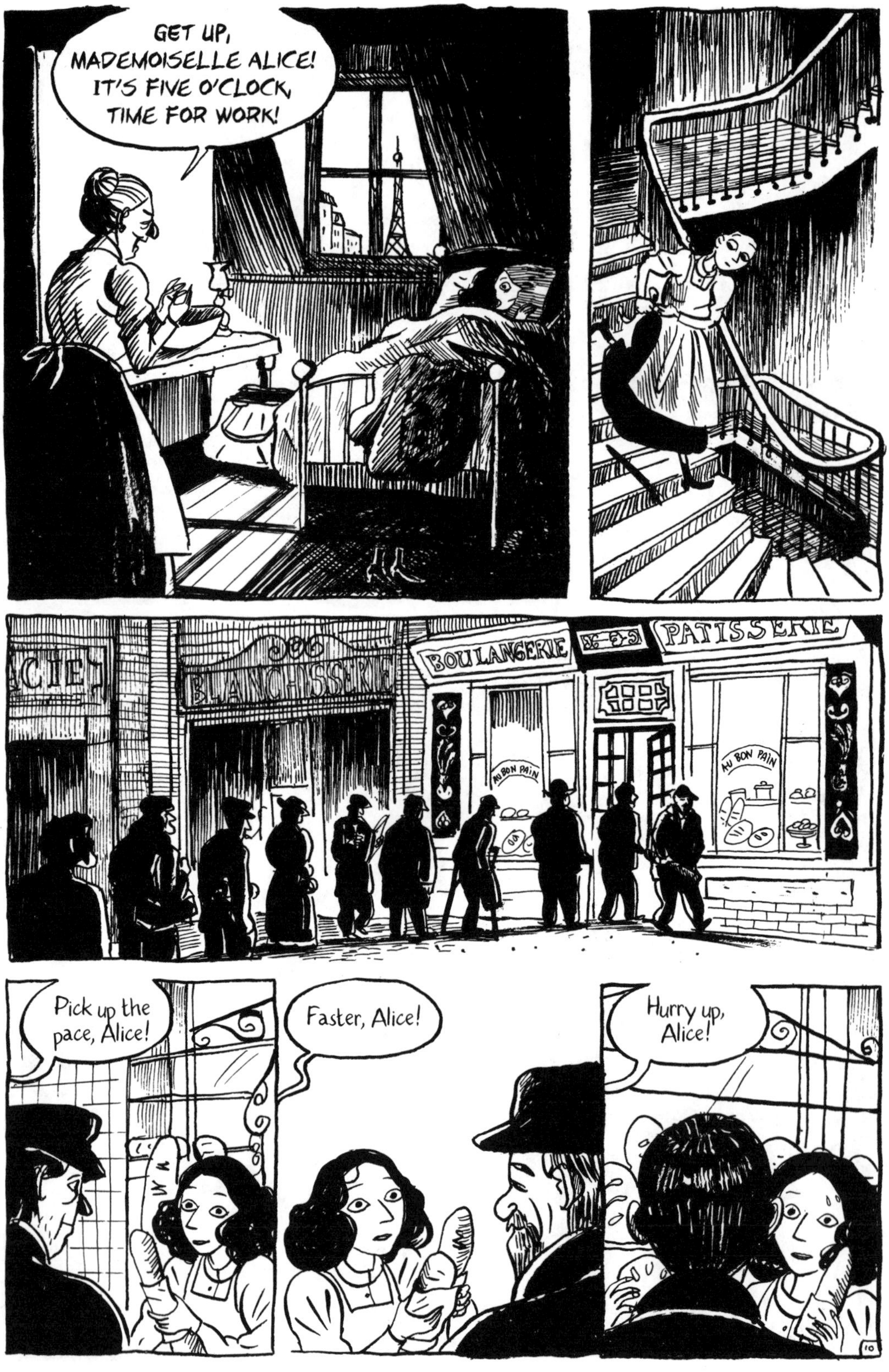
GET UP, MADEMOISELLE ALICE! IT'S FIVE O'CLOCK, TIME FOR WORK!
BLANCHISSERIE
BOULANGERIE
PATISSERIE
AU BON PAIN
AU BON PAIN
Pick up the pace, Alice!
Faster, Alice!
Hurry up, Alice!

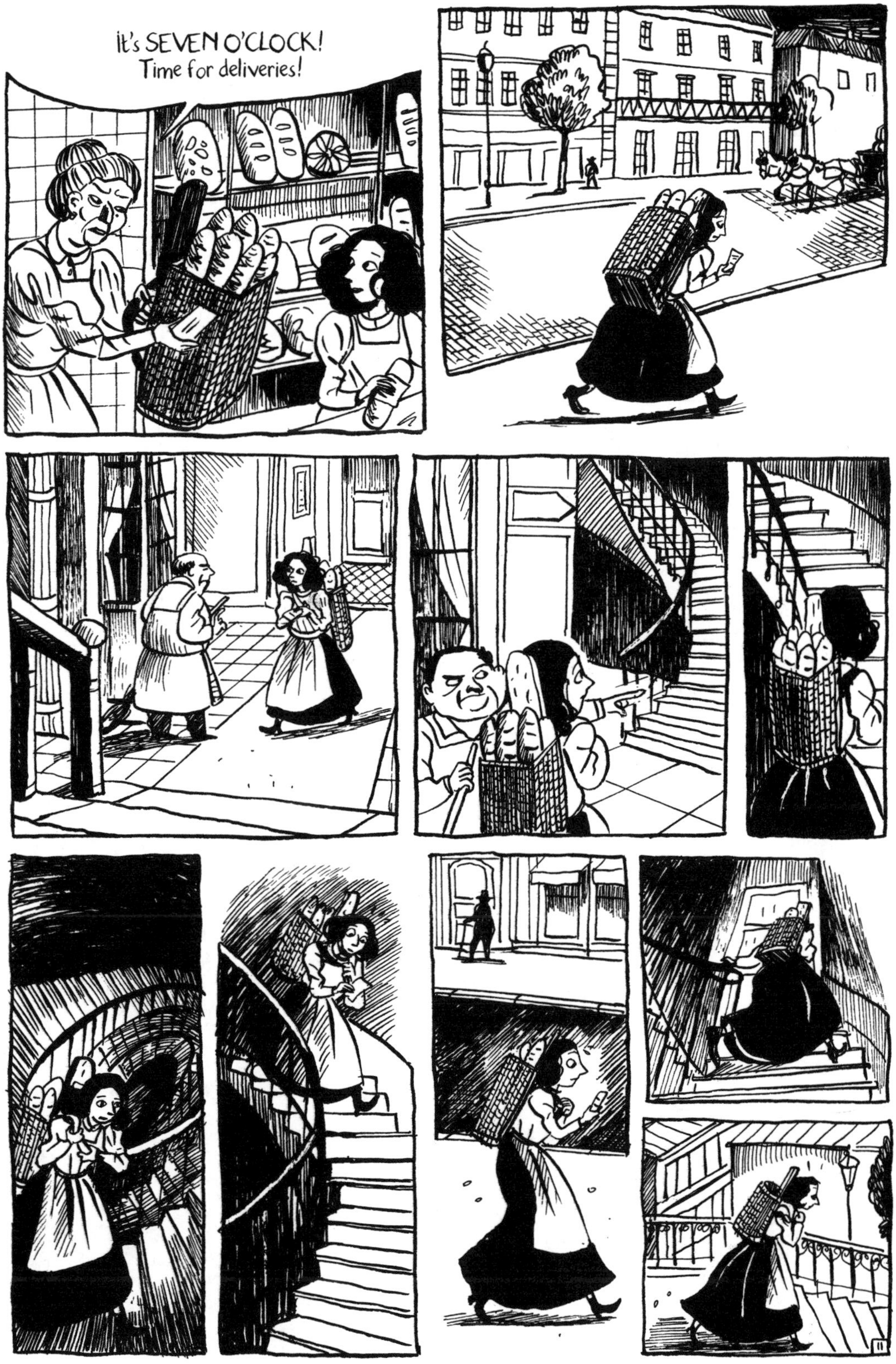
It's SEVEN O'CLOCK!
Time for deliveries!

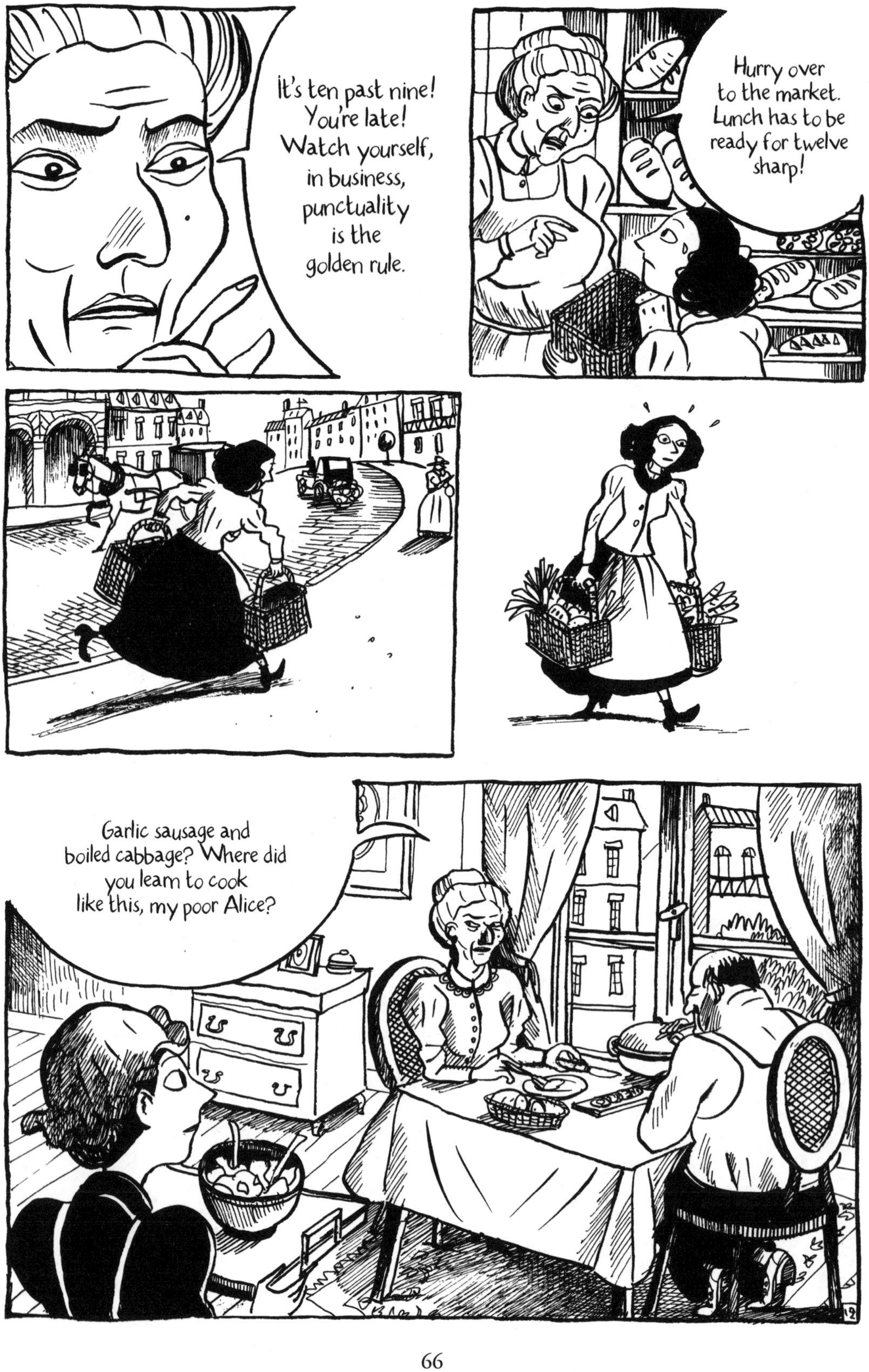

It's ten past nine! You're late! Watch yourself, in business, punctuality is the golden rule.
Hurry over to the market. Lunch has to be ready for twelve sharp!
Garlic sausage and boiled cabbage? Where did you learn to cook like this, my poor Alice?

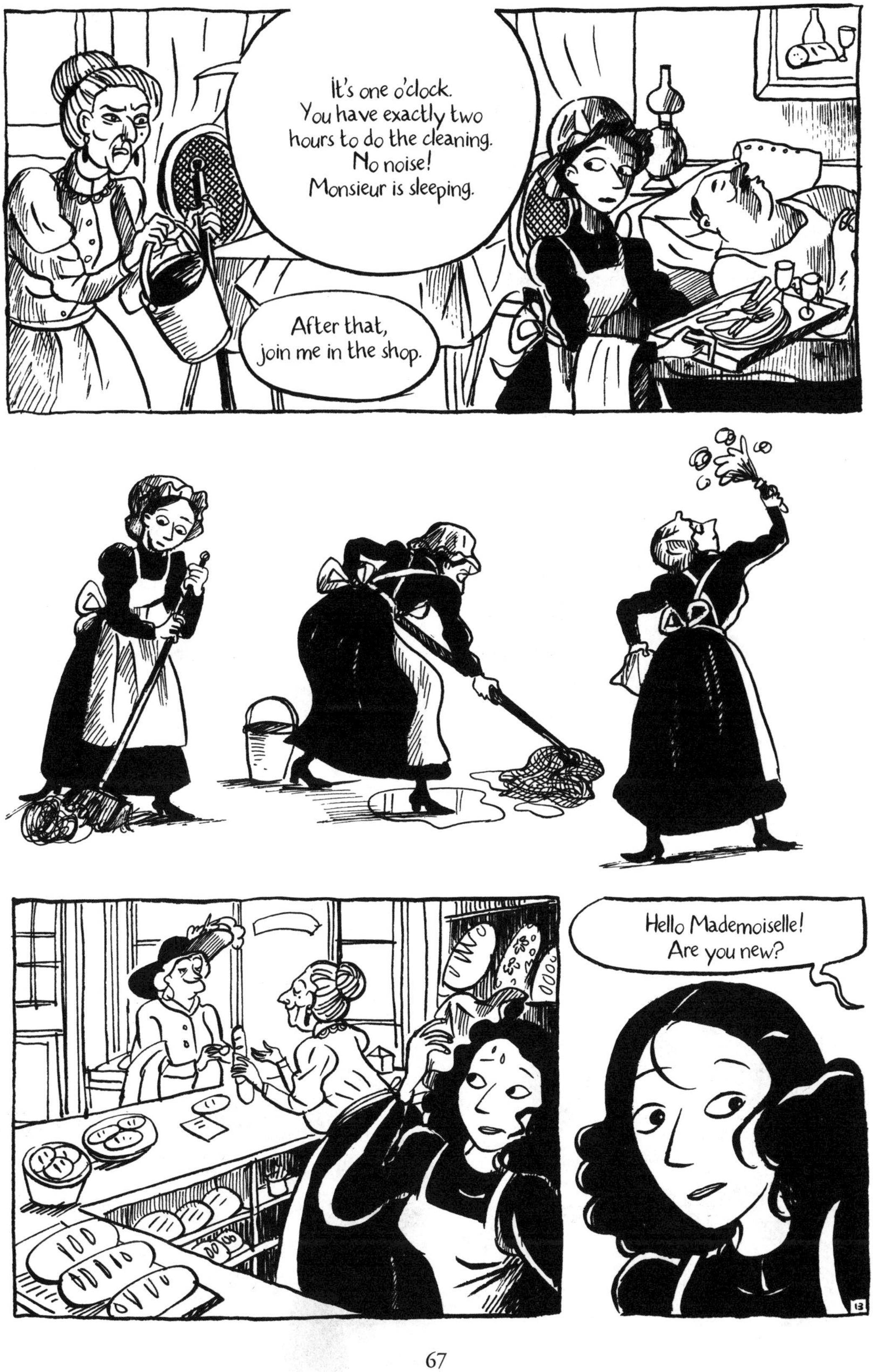
It's one o'clock. You have exactly two hours to do the cleaning. No noise! Monsieur is sleeping.
After that, join me in the shop.
Hello Mademoiselle! Are you new?

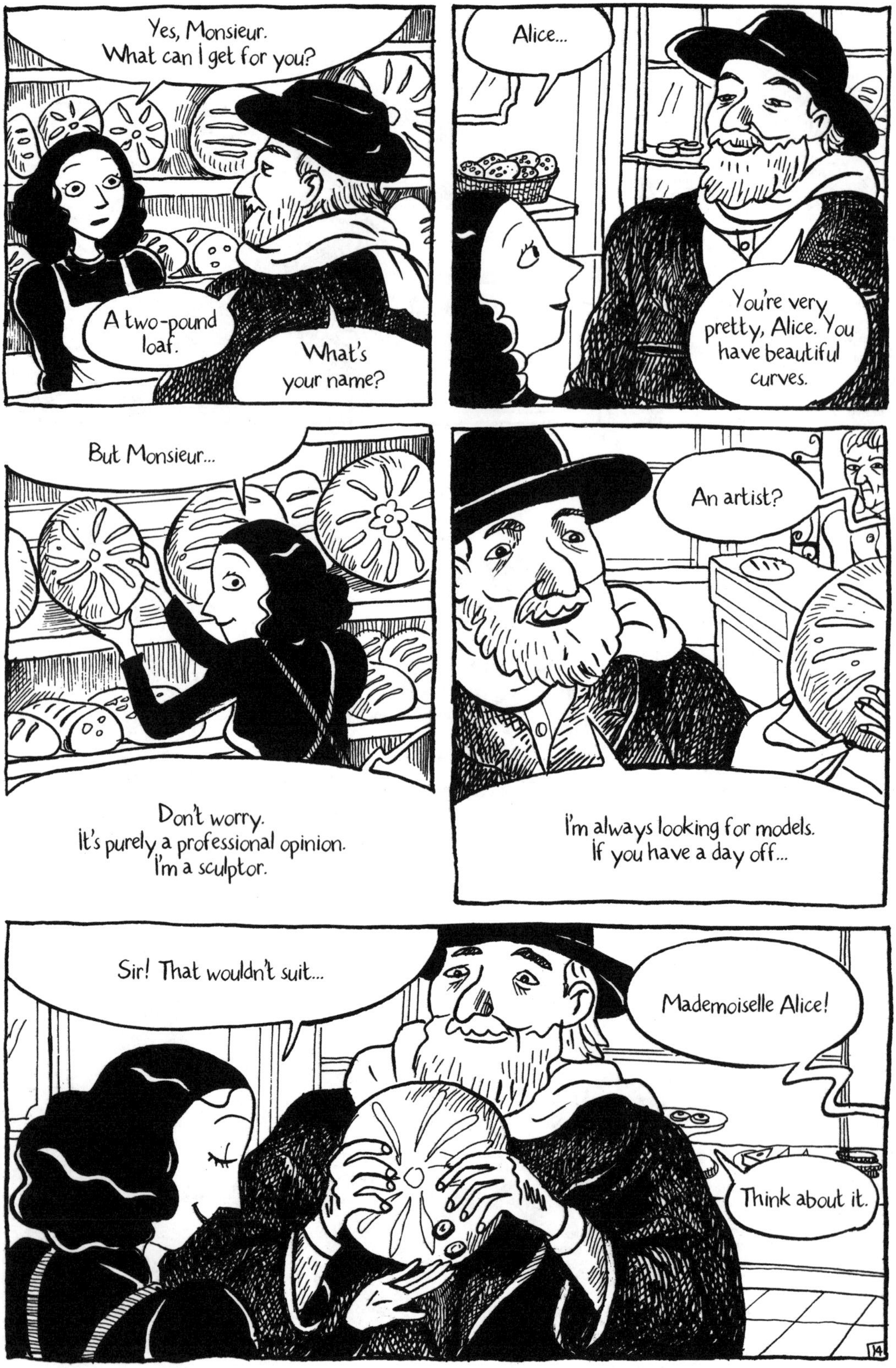
Yes, Monsieur. What can I get for you?
A two-pound loaf.
What's your name?
Alice...
You're very pretty, Alice. You have beautiful curves.
But Monsieur...
Don't worry. It's purely a professional opinion. I'm a sculptor.
An artist?
I'm always looking for models. If you have a day off...
Sir! That wouldn't suit...
Mademoiselle Alice!
Think about it.
14

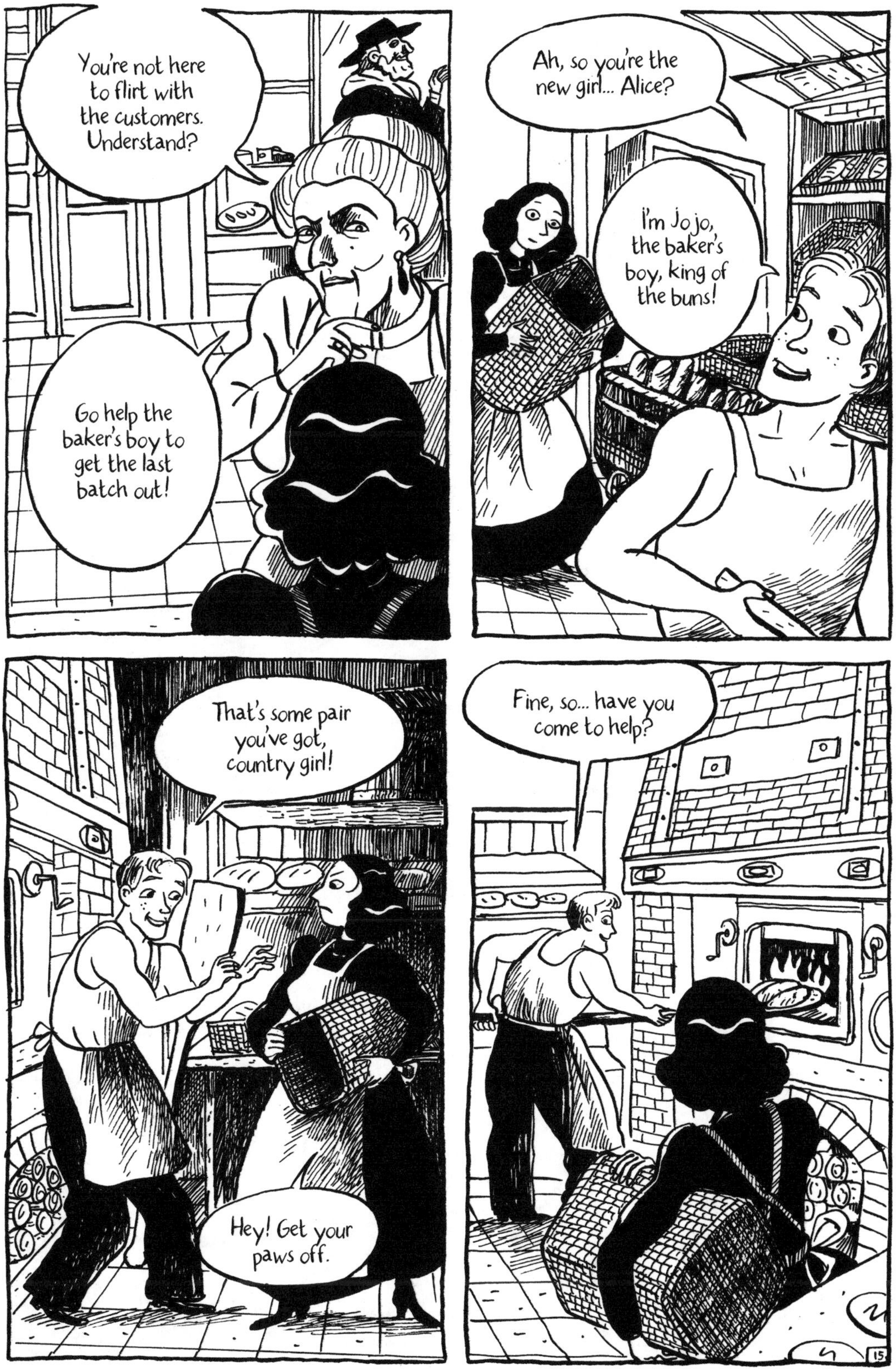
You're not here to flirt with the customers. Understand?
Go help the baker's boy to get the last batch out!
Ah, so you're the new girl... Alice?
I'm Jo jo, the baker's boy, king of the buns!
That's some pair you've got, country girl!
Hey! Get your paws off.
Fine, so... have you come to help?
15

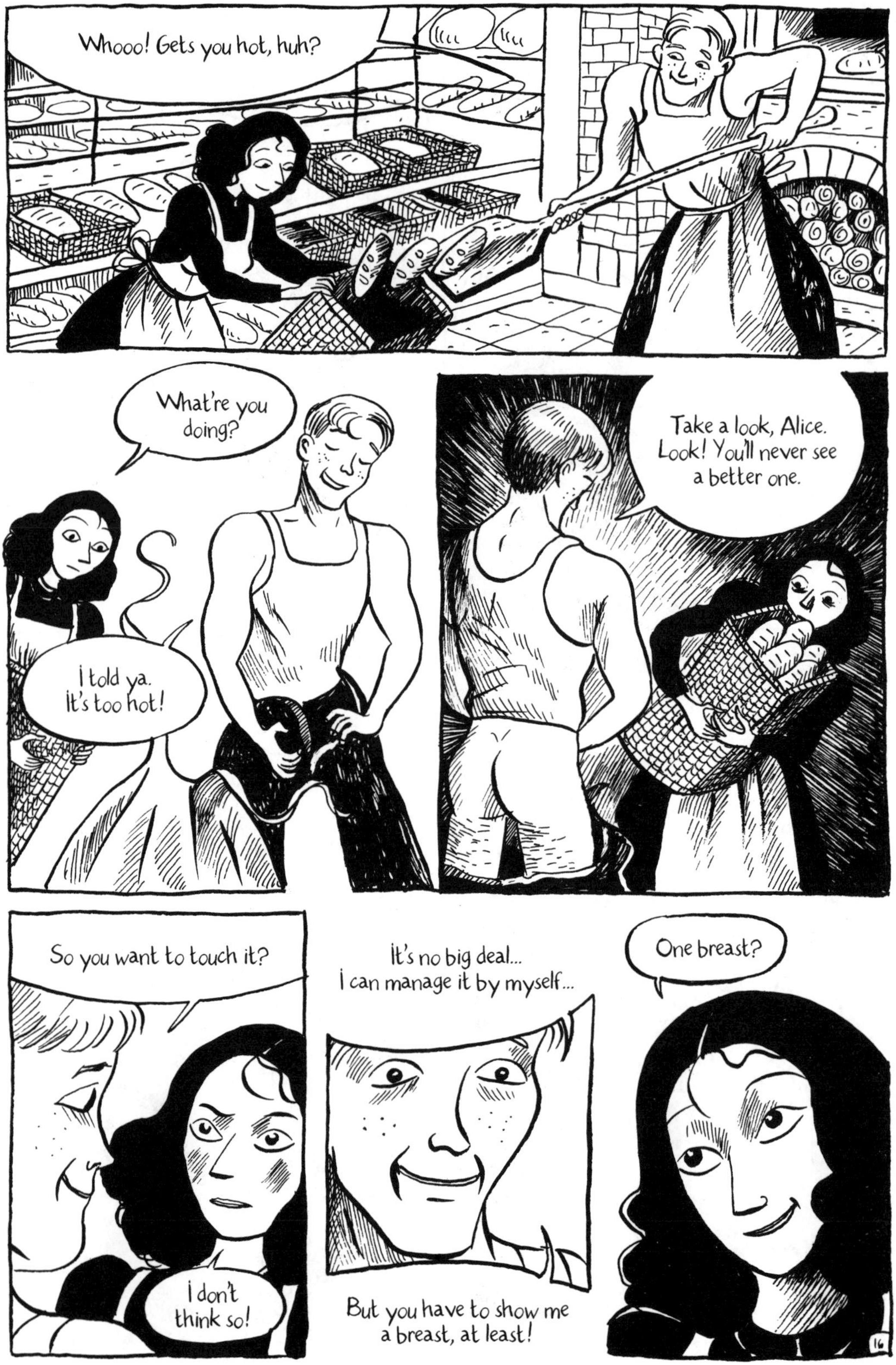
Whooo! Gets you hot, huh?
What're you doing?
I told ya. It's too hot!
Take a look, Alice. Look! You'll never see a better one.
So you want to touch it?
I don't think so!
It's no big deal... I can manage it by myself...
But you have to show me a breast, at least!
One breast?

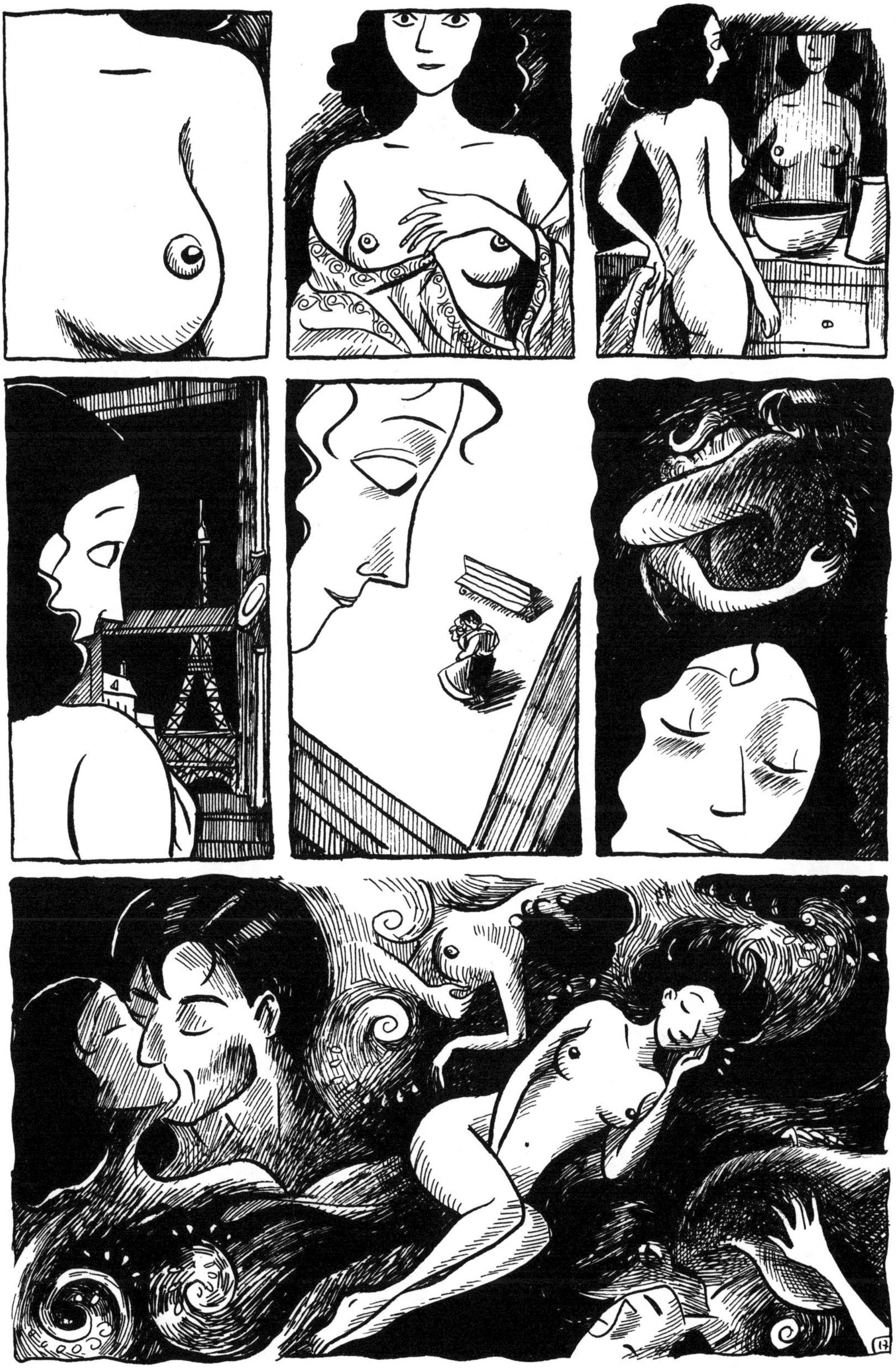
17

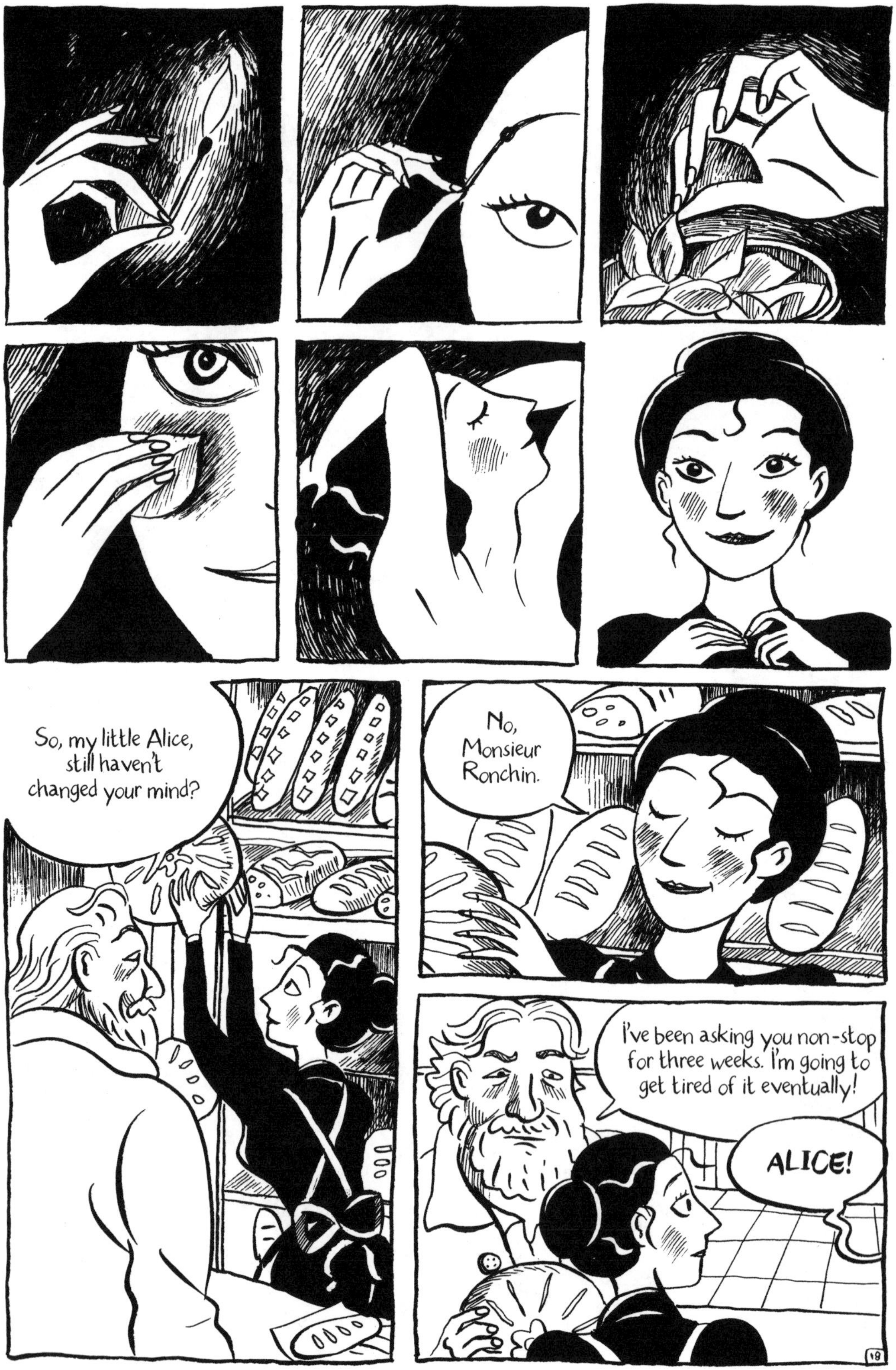
So, my little Alice, still haven't changed your mind?
No, Monsieur Ronchin.
I've been asking you non-stop for three weeks. I'm going to get tired of it eventually!
ALICE!
18

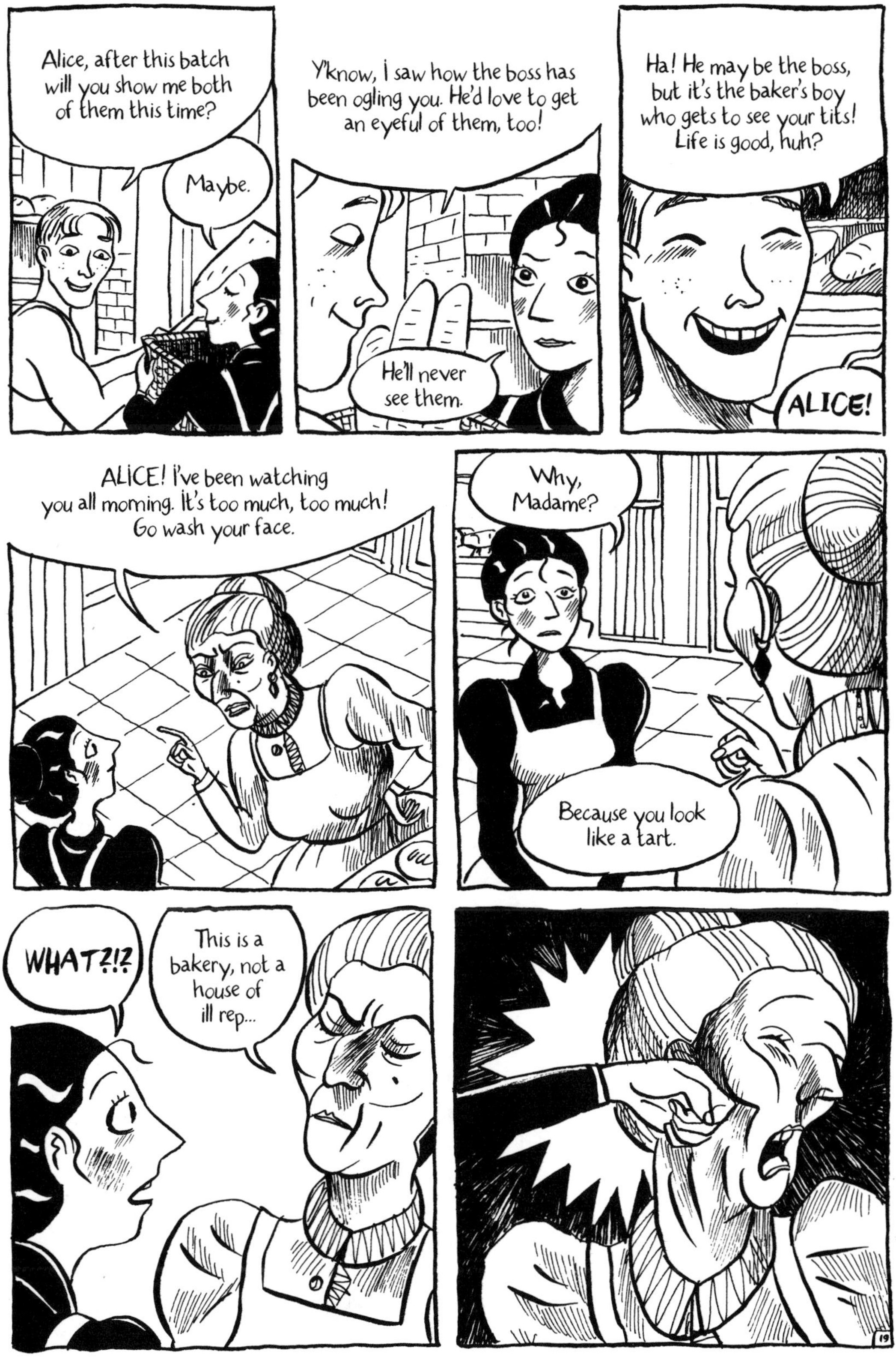
Alice, after this batch will you show me both of them this time?
Maybe.
Y'know, I saw how the boss has been ogling you. He'd love to get an eyeful of them, too!
He'll never see them.
Ha! He may be the boss, but it's the baker's boy who gets to see your tits! Life is good, huh?
ALICE!
ALICE! I've been watching you all morning. It's too much, too much! Go wash your face.
Why, Madame?
Because you look like a tart.
WHAT?!?
This is a bakery, not a house of ill rep...
19

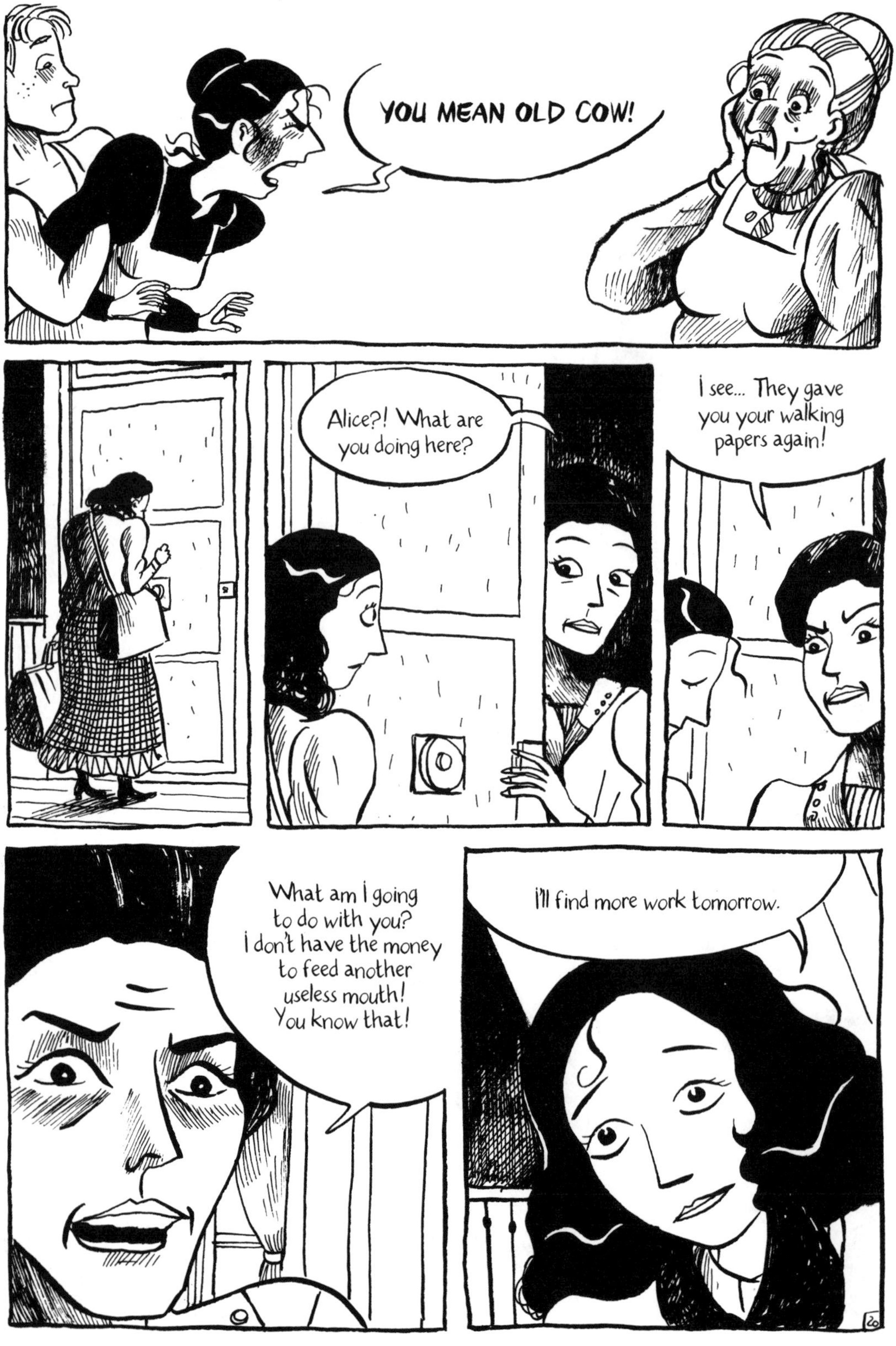
YOU MEAN OLD COW!
Alice?! What are you doing here?
I see... They gave you your walking papers again!
What am I going to do with you? I don't have the money to feed another useless mouth! You know that!
I'll find more work tomorrow.
20

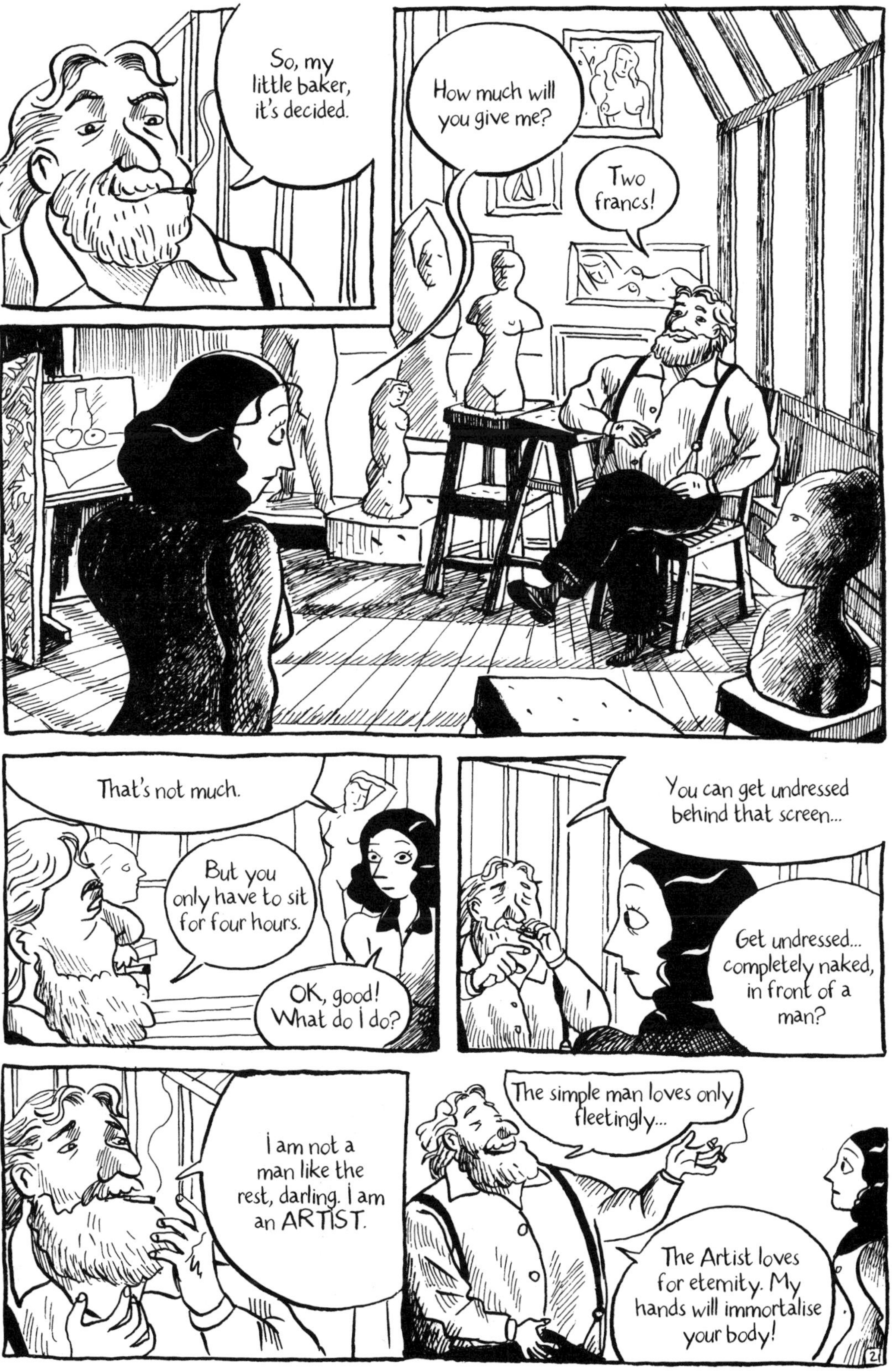
So, my little baker, it's decided.
How much will you give me?
Two francs!
That's not much.
But you only have to sit for four hours.
OK, good! What do I do?
You can get undressed behind that screen...
Get undressed... completely naked, in front of a man?
I am not a man like the rest, darling. I am an ARTIST.
The simple man loves only fleetingly...
The Artist loves for eternity. My hands will immortalise your body!
2

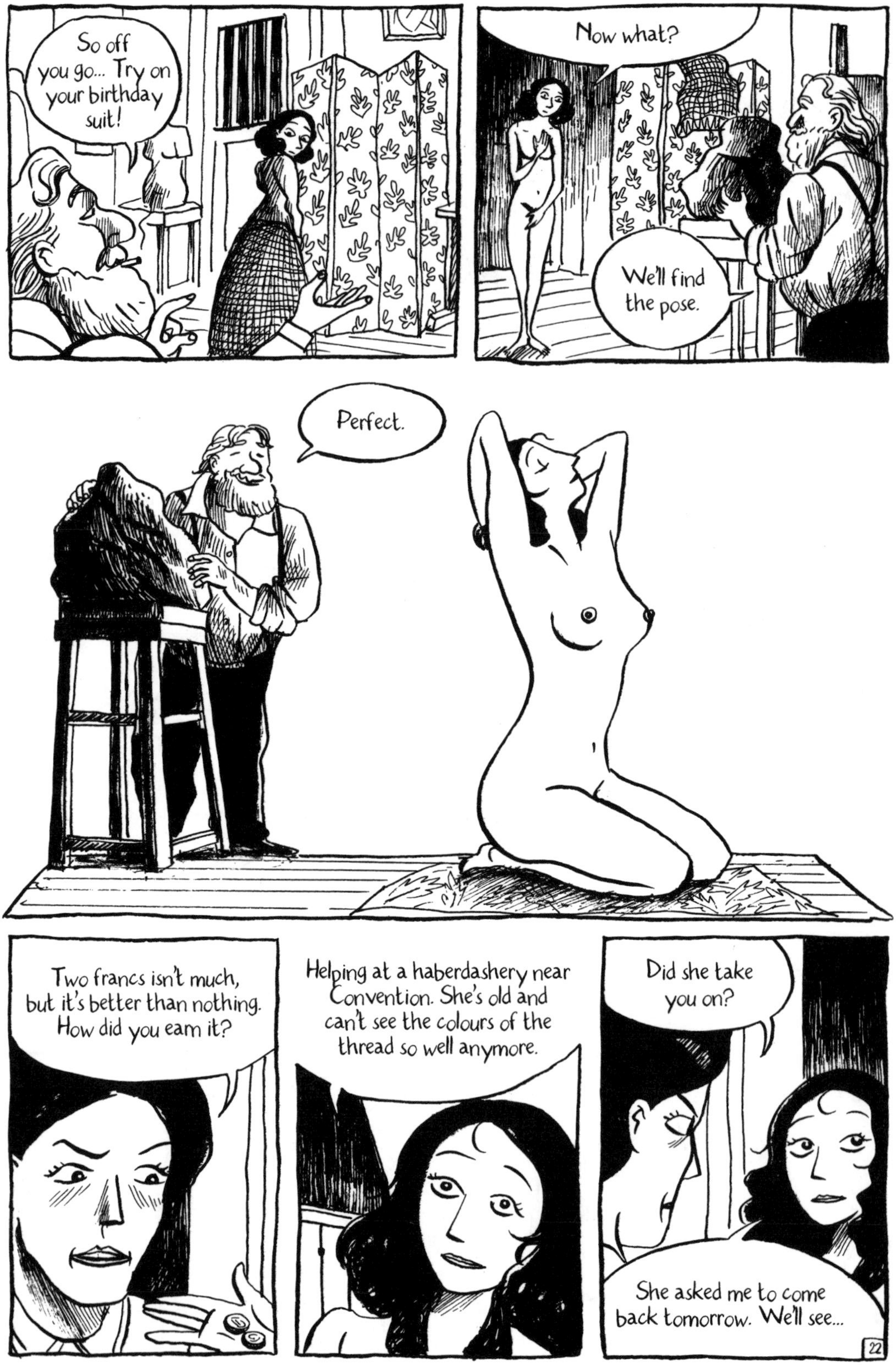
So off you go... Try on your birthday suit!
Now what?
We'll find the pose.
Perfect.
Two francs isn't much, but it's better than nothing. How did you earn it?
Helping at a haberdashery near Convention. She's old and can't see the colours of the thread so well anymore.
Did she take you on?
She asked me to come back tomorrow. We'll see...
22

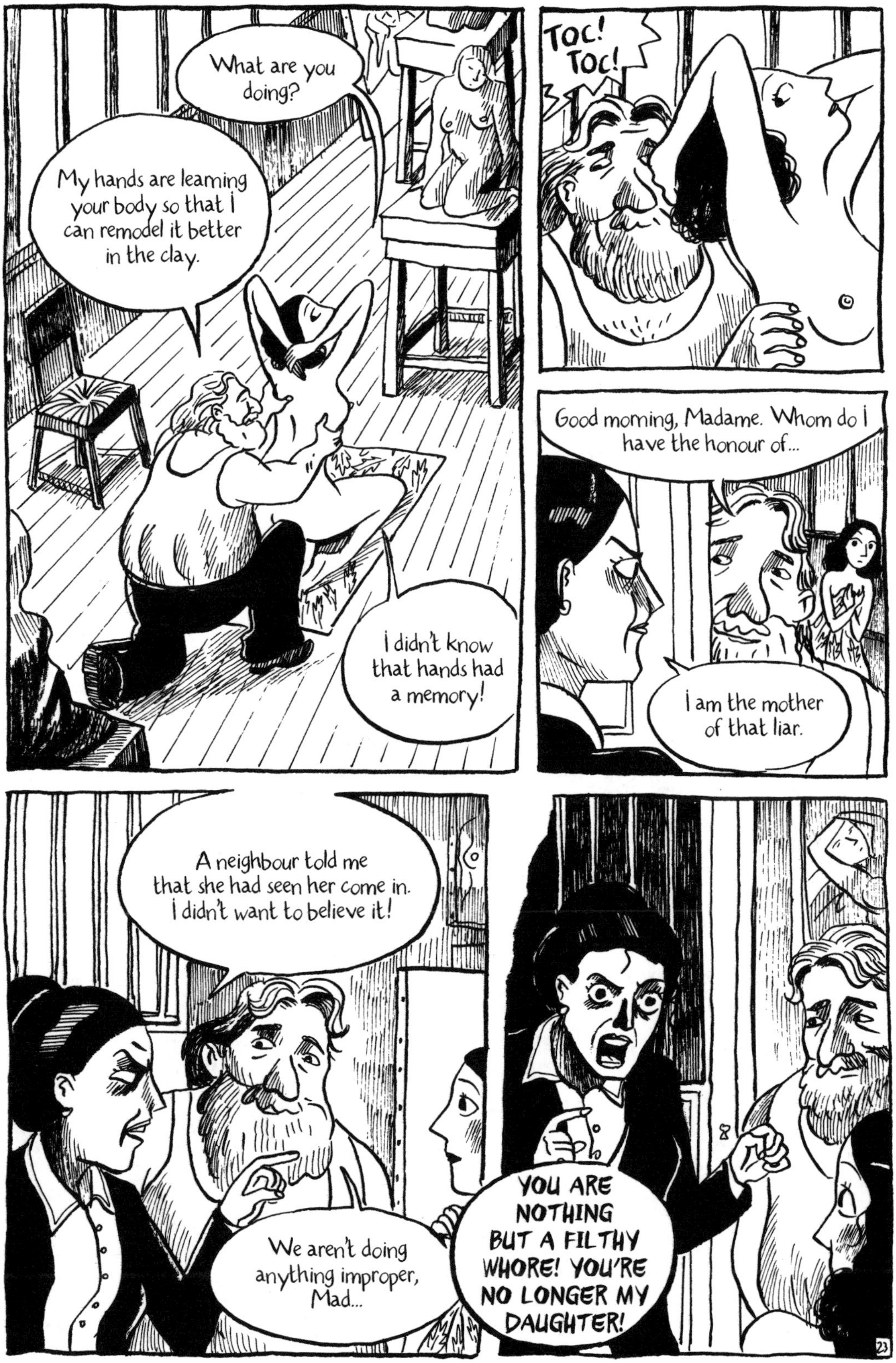
What are you doing?
My hands are learning your body so that I can remodel it better in the clay.
I didn't know that hands had a memory!
TOC! TOC!
Good morning, Madame. Whom do I have the honour of...
I am the mother of that liar.
A neighbour told me that she had seen her come in. I didn't want to believe it!
We aren't doing anything improper, Mad...
YOU ARE NOTHING BUT A FILTHY WHORE! YOU'RE NO LONGER MY DAUGHTER!
23

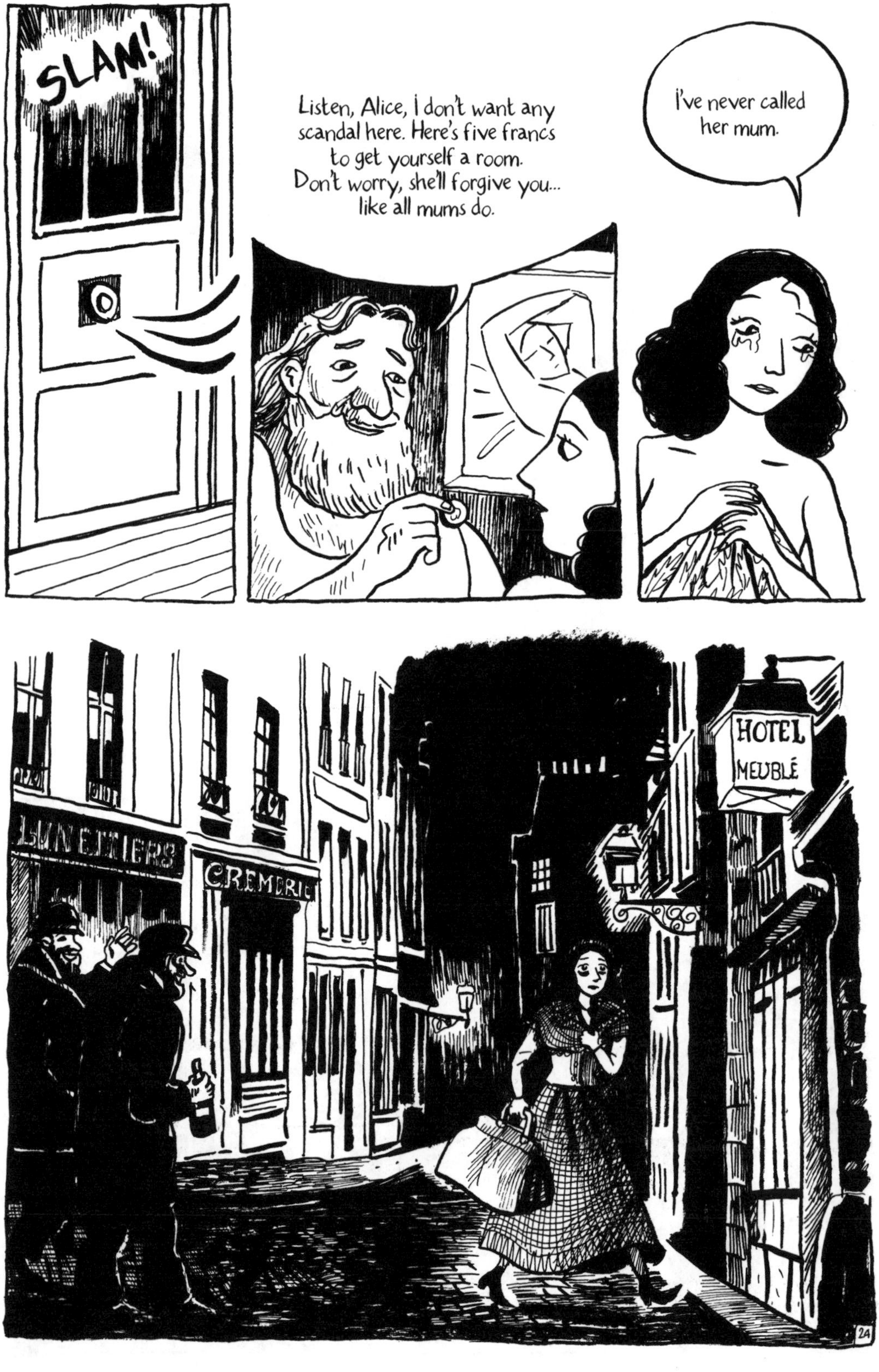
SLAM!
Listen, Alice, I don't want any scandal here. Here's five francs to get yourself a room. Don't worry, she'll forgive you... like all mums do.
I've never called her mum.
HOTEL MEUBLÉ
CREMERIE
24

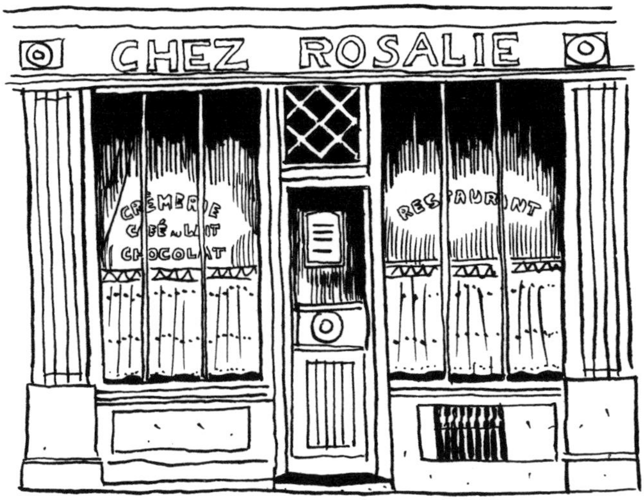
CHEZ ROSALIE
CRÉMERIE
CAFÉ AU LAIT
CHOCOLAT
RESTAURANT

1918 - 3, rue Campagne-Premiére

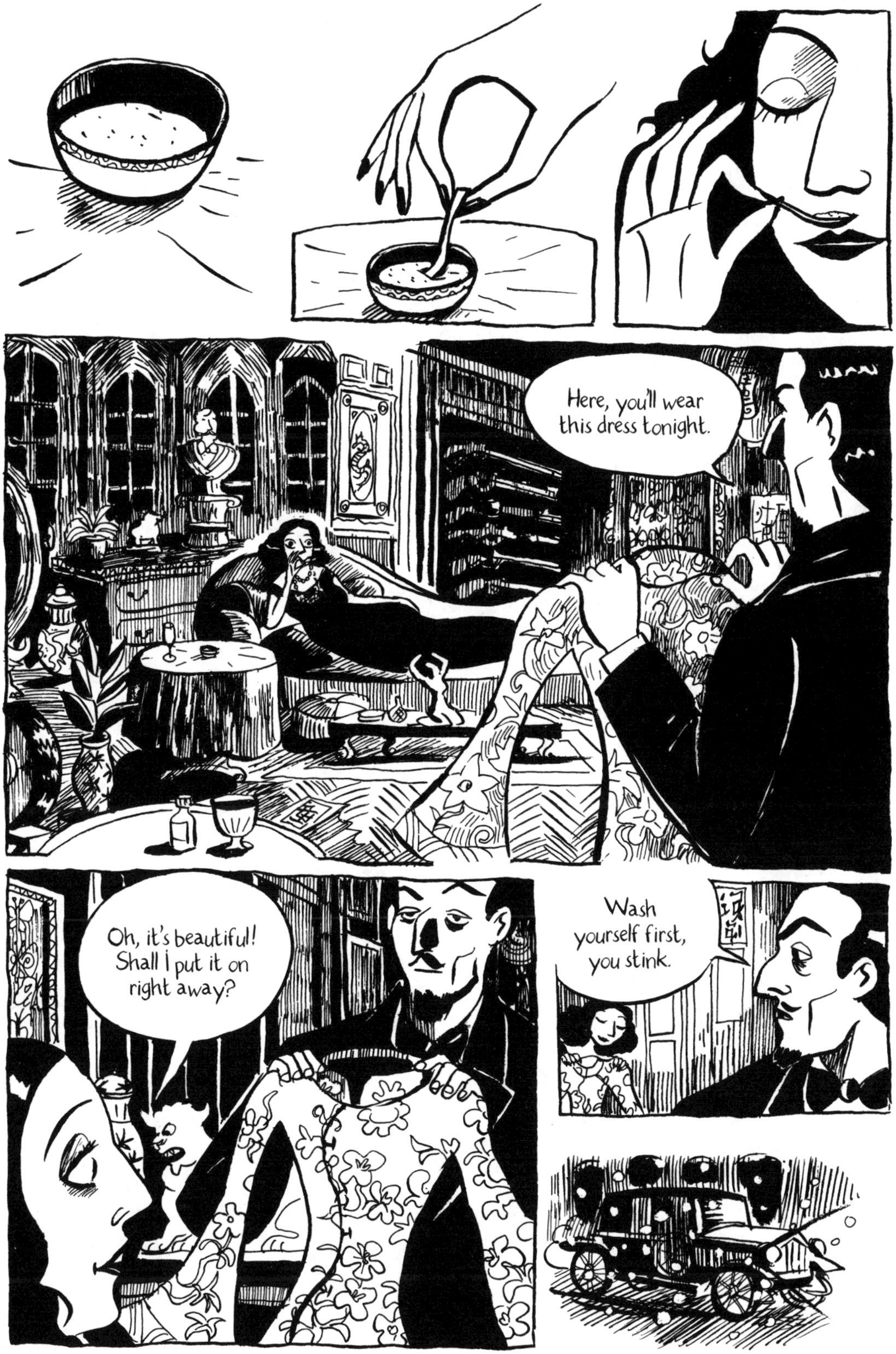
Here, you'll wear this dress tonight.
Oh, it's beautiful! Shall I put it on right away?
Wash yourself first, you stink.

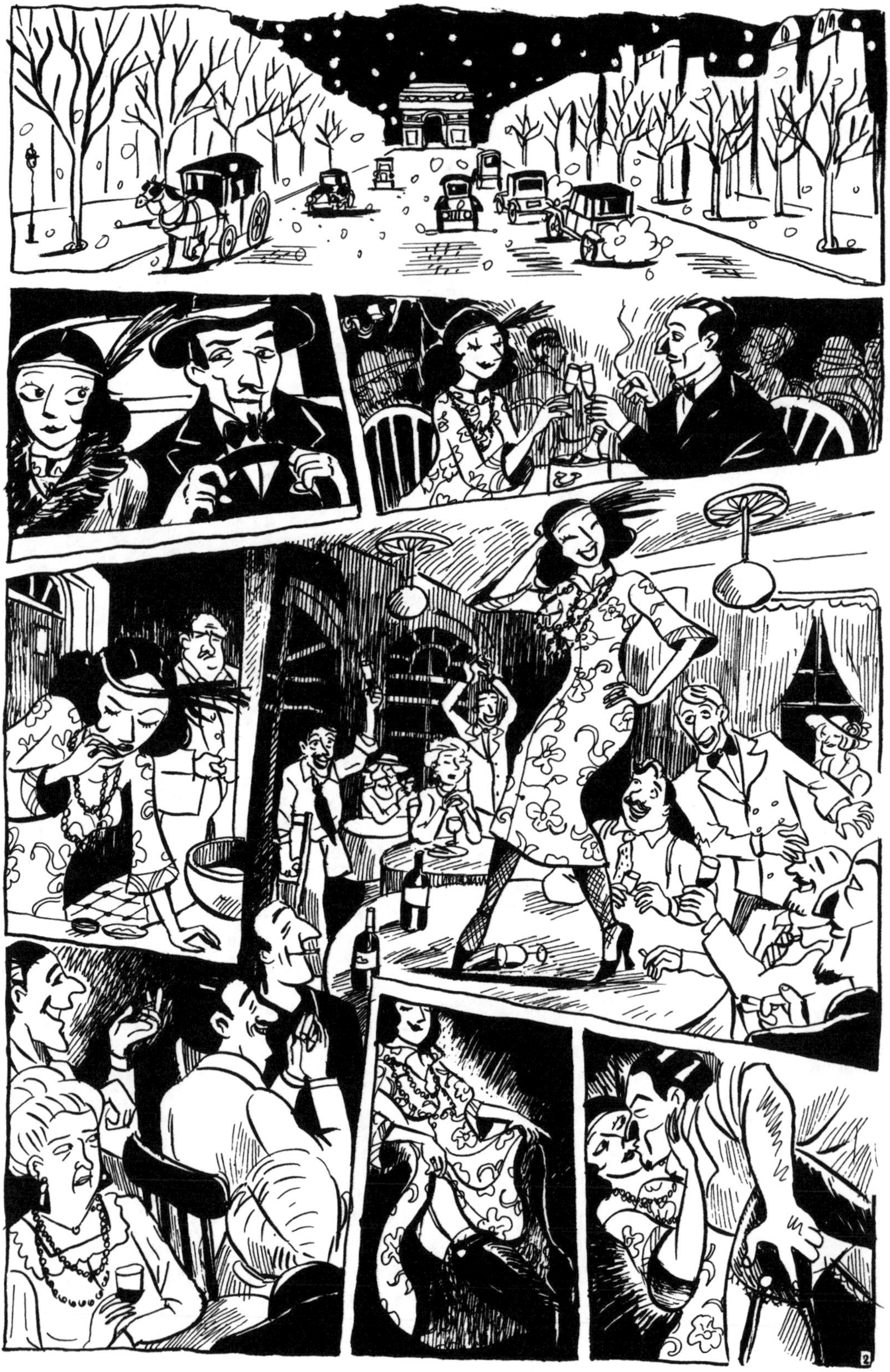

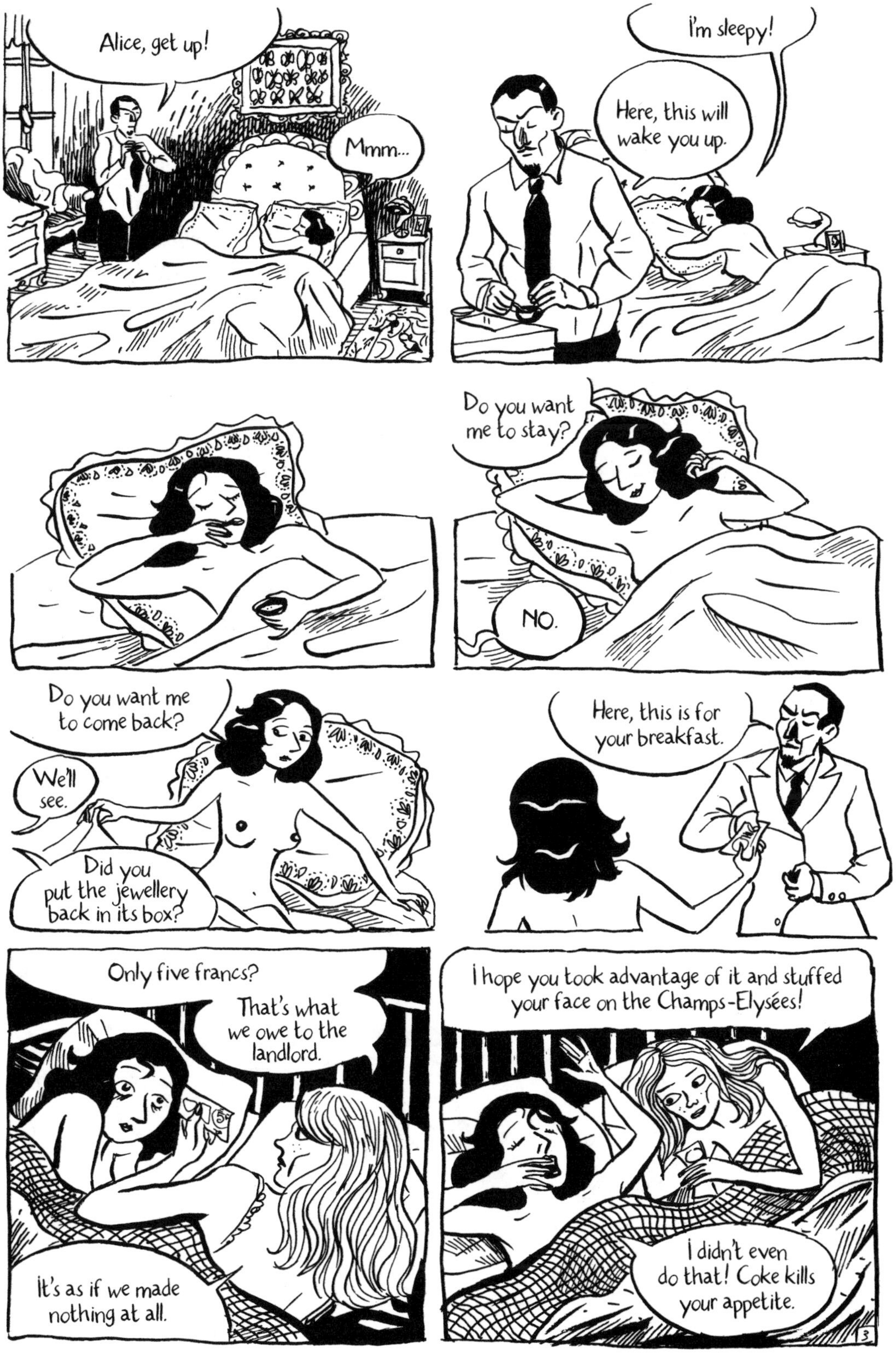

Alice, get up!
Mmm...
I'm sleepy!
Here, this will wake you up.
Do you want me to stay?
NO.
Do you want me to come back?
We'll see.
Did you put the jewellery back in its box?
Here, this is for your breakfast.
Only five francs?
That's what we owe to the landlord.
It's as if we made nothing at all.
I hope you took advantage of it and stuffed your face on the Champs-Elysées!
I didn't even do that! Coke kills your appetite.
3

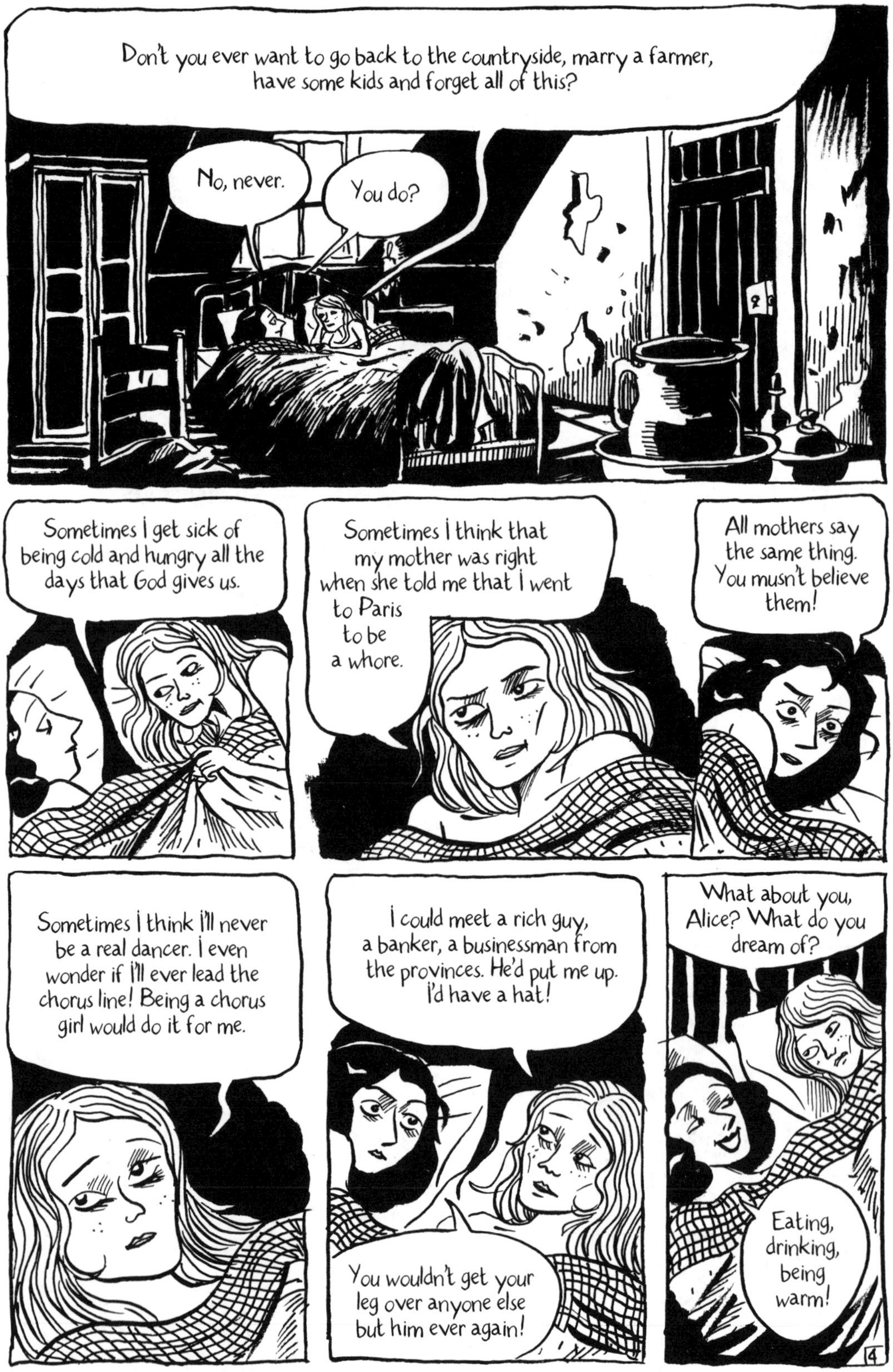
Don't you ever want to go back to the countryside, marry a farmer, have some kids and forget all of this?
No, never.
You do?
Sometimes I get sick of being cold and hungry all the days that God gives us.
Sometimes I think that my mother was right when she told me that I went to Paris to be a whore.
All mothers say the same thing. You musn't believe them!
Sometimes I think I'll never be a real dancer. I even wonder if I'll ever lead the chorus line! Being a chorus girl would do it for me.
I could meet a rich guy, a banker, a businessman from the provinces. He'd put me up. I'd have a hat!
You wouldn't get your leg over anyone else but him ever again!
What about you, Alice? What do you dream of?
Eating, drinking, being warm!
4

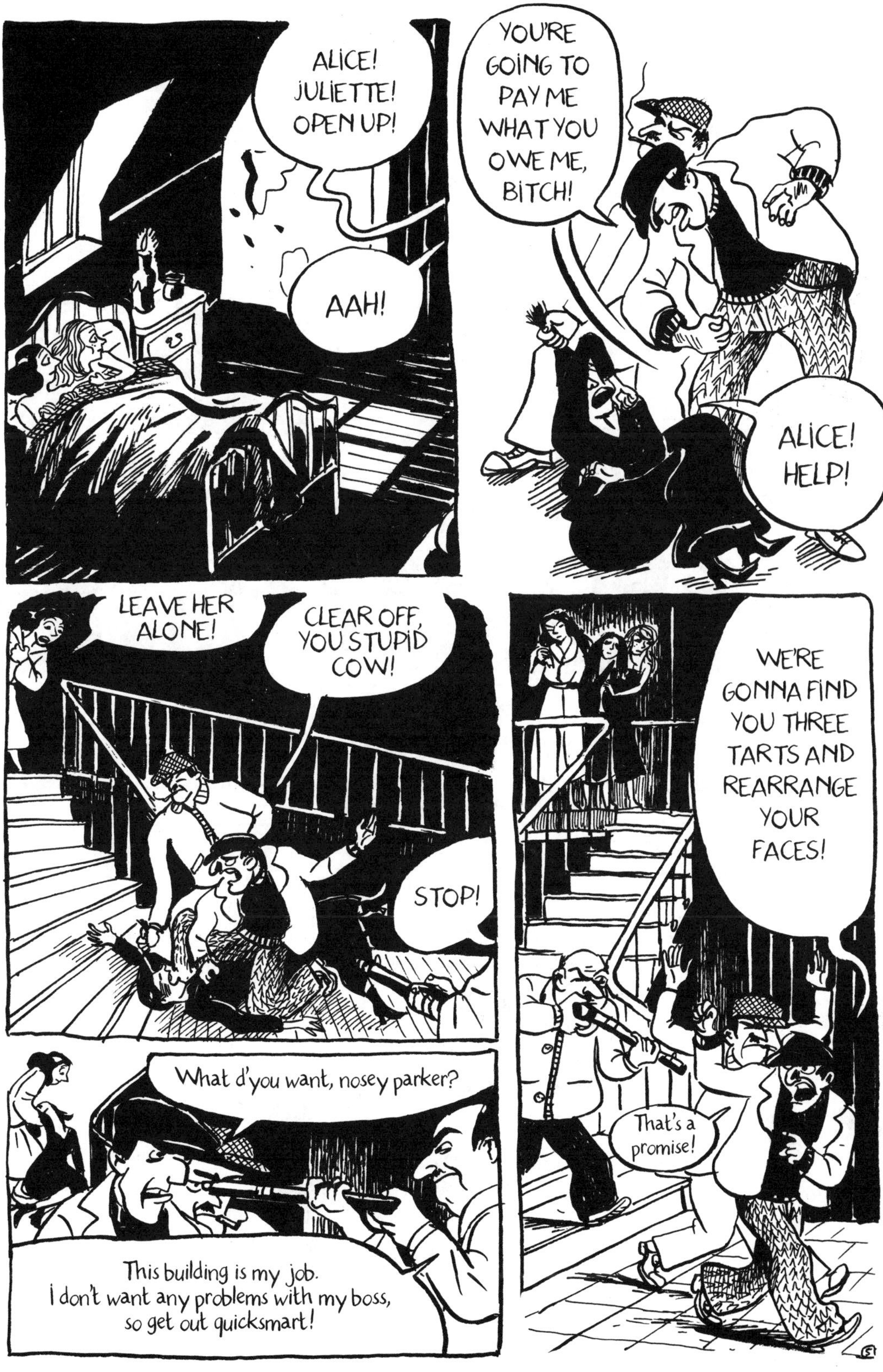
ALICE! JULIETTE! OPEN UP!
AAH!
YOU'RE GOING TO PAY ME WHAT YOU OWE ME, BITCH!
ALICE! HELP!
LEAVE HER ALONE!
CLEAR OFF, YOU STUPID COW!
STOP!
What d'you want, nosey parker?
This building is my job. I don't want any problems with my boss, so get out quicksmart!
WE'RE GONNA FIND YOU THREE TARTS AND REARRANGE YOUR FACES!
That's a promise!

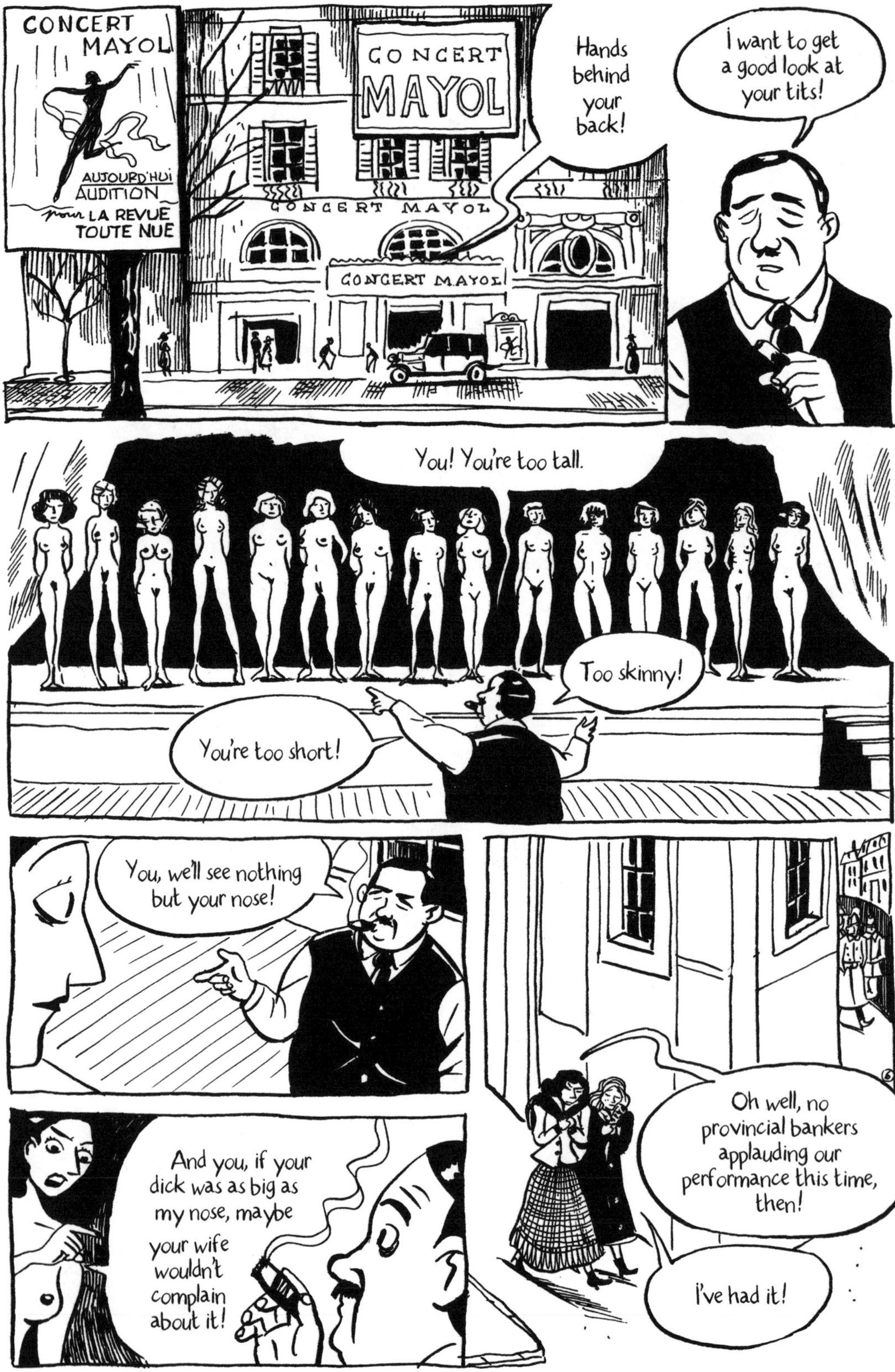
CONCERT MAYOL
AUJOURD'HUI AUDITION pour LA REVUE TOUTE NUE
CONCERT MAYOL
CONCERT MAYOL
CONCERT MAYOL
Hands behind your back!
I want to get a good look at your tits!
You! You're too tall.
Too skinny!
You're too short!
You, we'll see nothing but your nose!
And you, if your dick was as big as my nose, maybe your wife wouldn't complain about it!
Oh well, no provincial bankers applauding our performance this time, then!
I've had it!

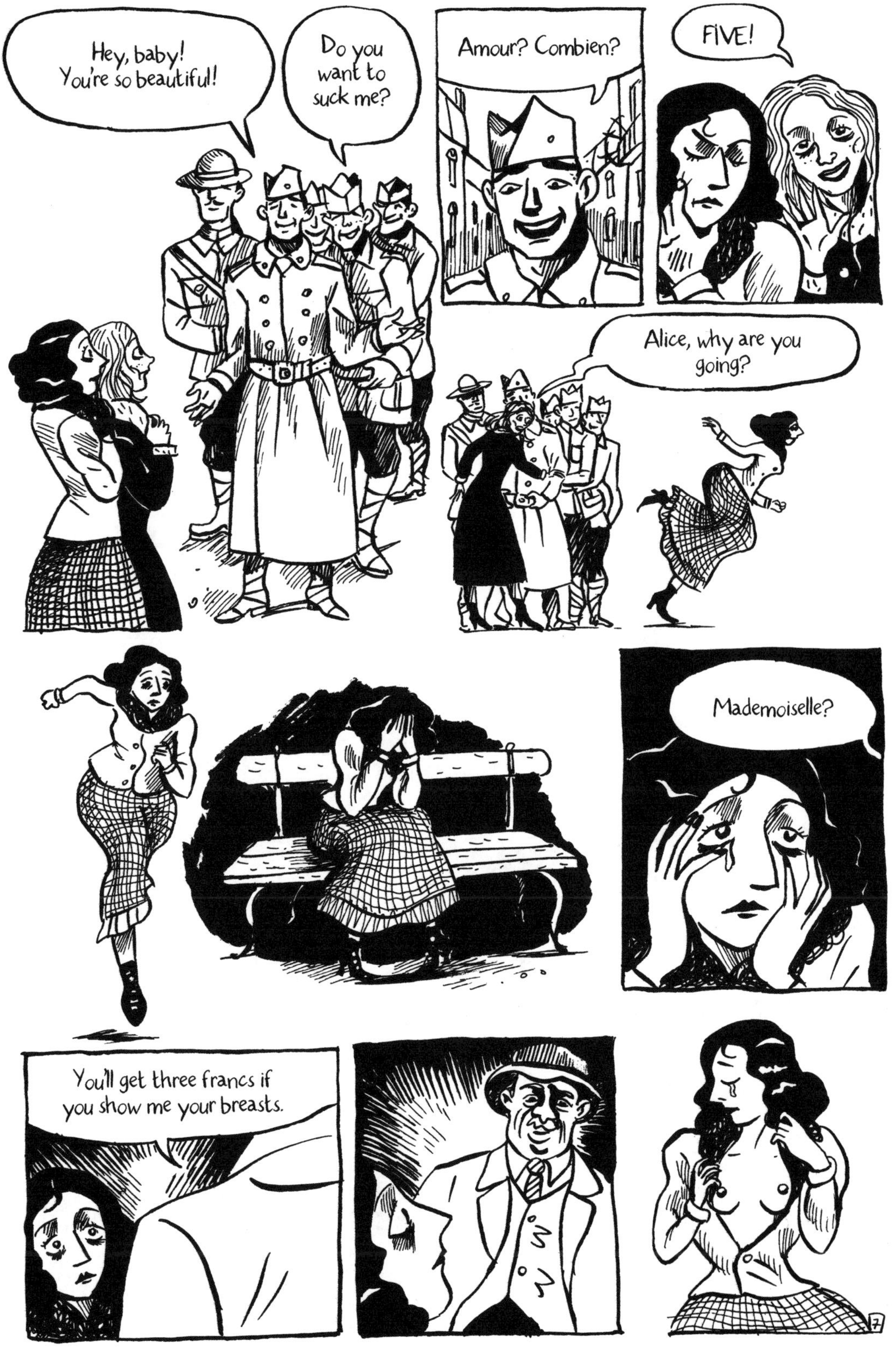
Hey, baby! You're so beautiful!
Do you want to suck me?
Amour? Combien?
FIVE!
Alice, why are you going?
Mademoiselle?
You'll get three francs if you show me your breasts.
7

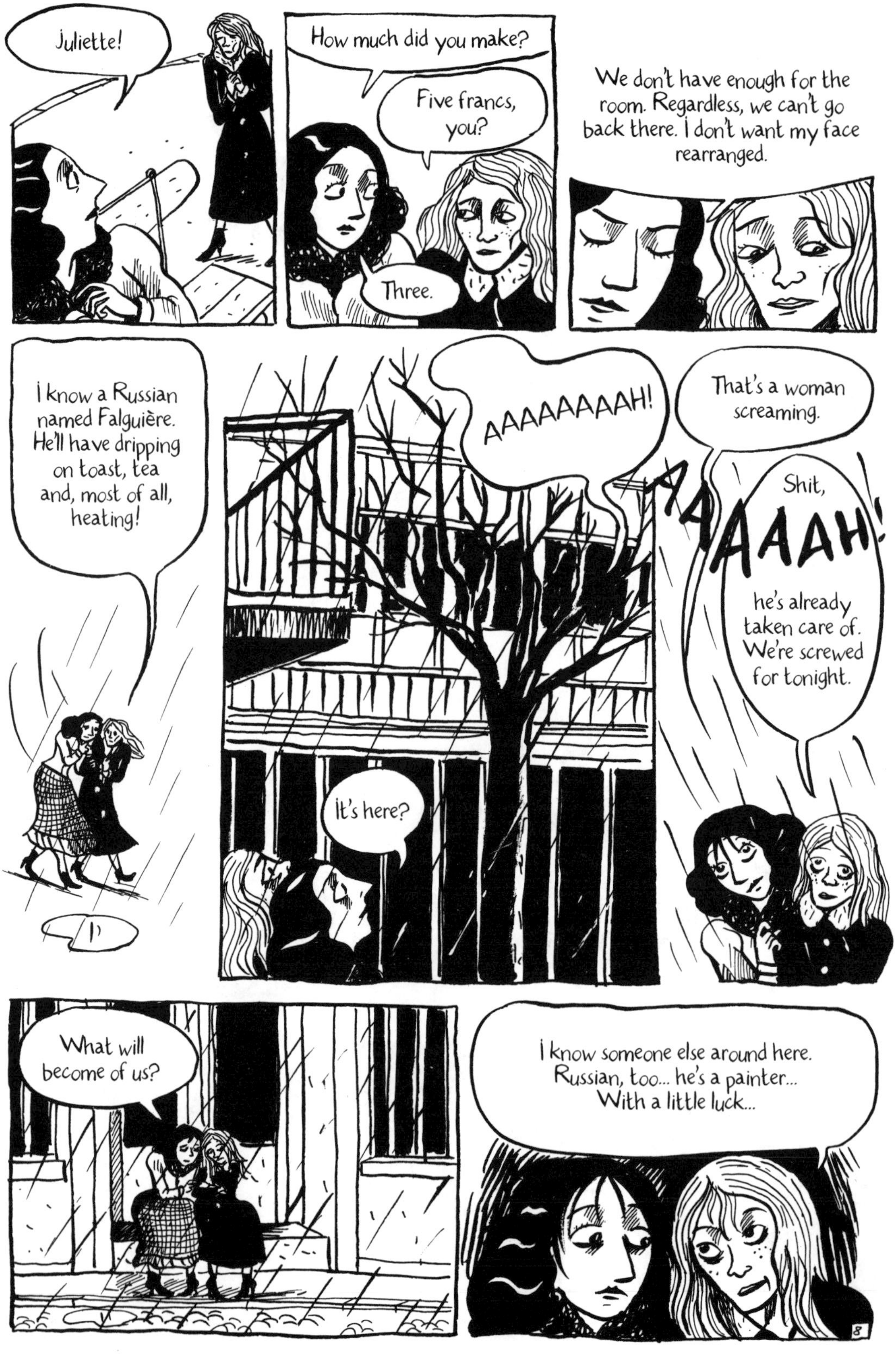
Juliette!
How much did you make?
Five francs, you?
Three.
We don't have enough for the room. Regardless, we can't go back there. I don't want my face rearranged.
I know a Russian named Falguière. He'll have dripping on toast, tea and, most of all, heating!
AAAAAAAAH!
That's a woman screaming.
AAAAAH!
It's here?
Shit, he's already taken care of. We're screwed for tonight.
What will become of us?
I know someone else around here. Russian, too... he's a painter... With a little luck...

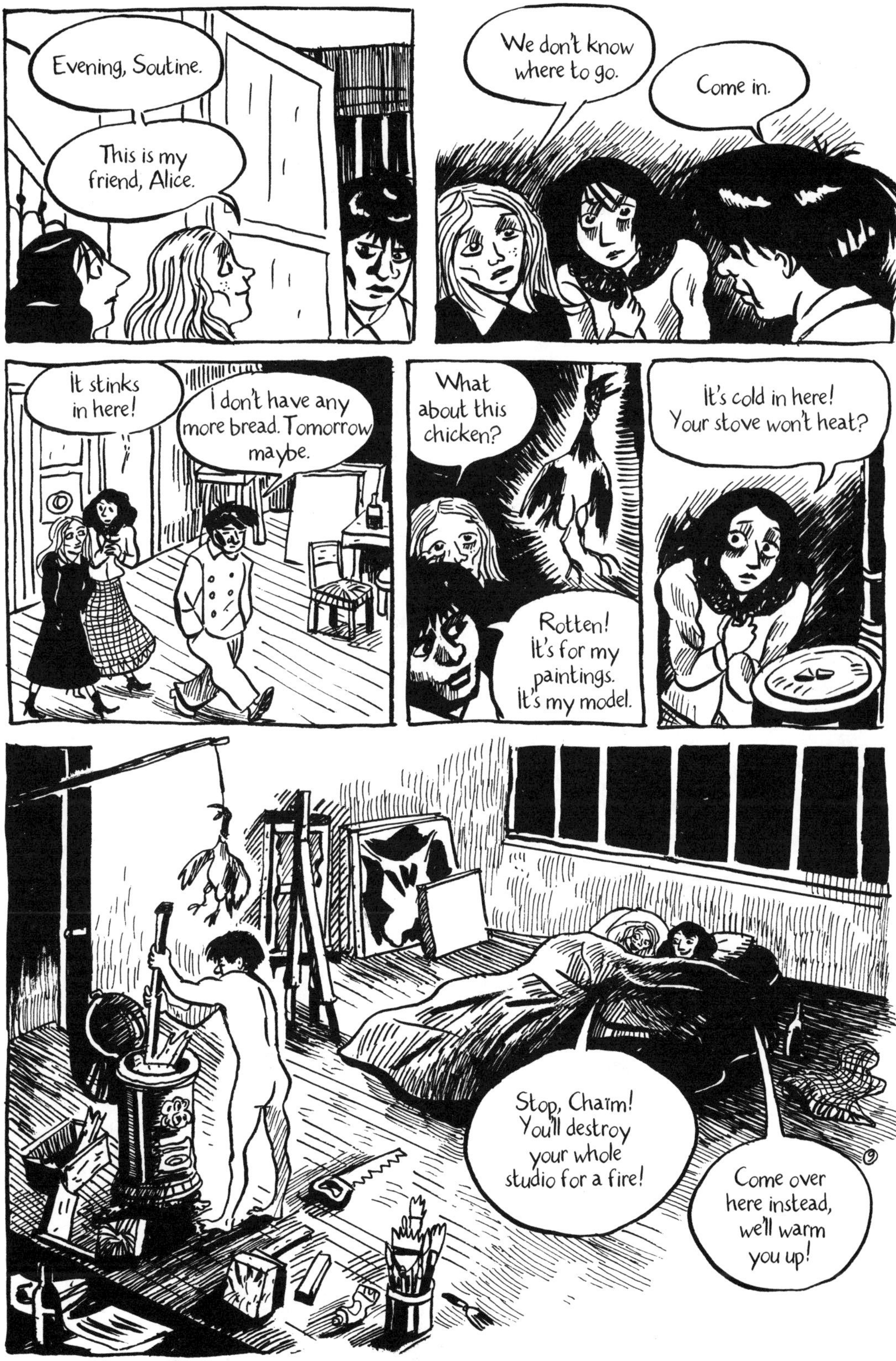
Evening, Soutine.
This is my friend, Alice.
We don't know where to go.
Come in.
It stinks in here!
I don't have any more bread. Tomorrow maybe.
What about this chicken?
Rotten! It's for my paintings. It's my model.
It's cold in here! Your stove won't heat?
Stop, Chaïm! You'll destroy your whole studio for a fire!
Come over here instead, we'll warm you up!

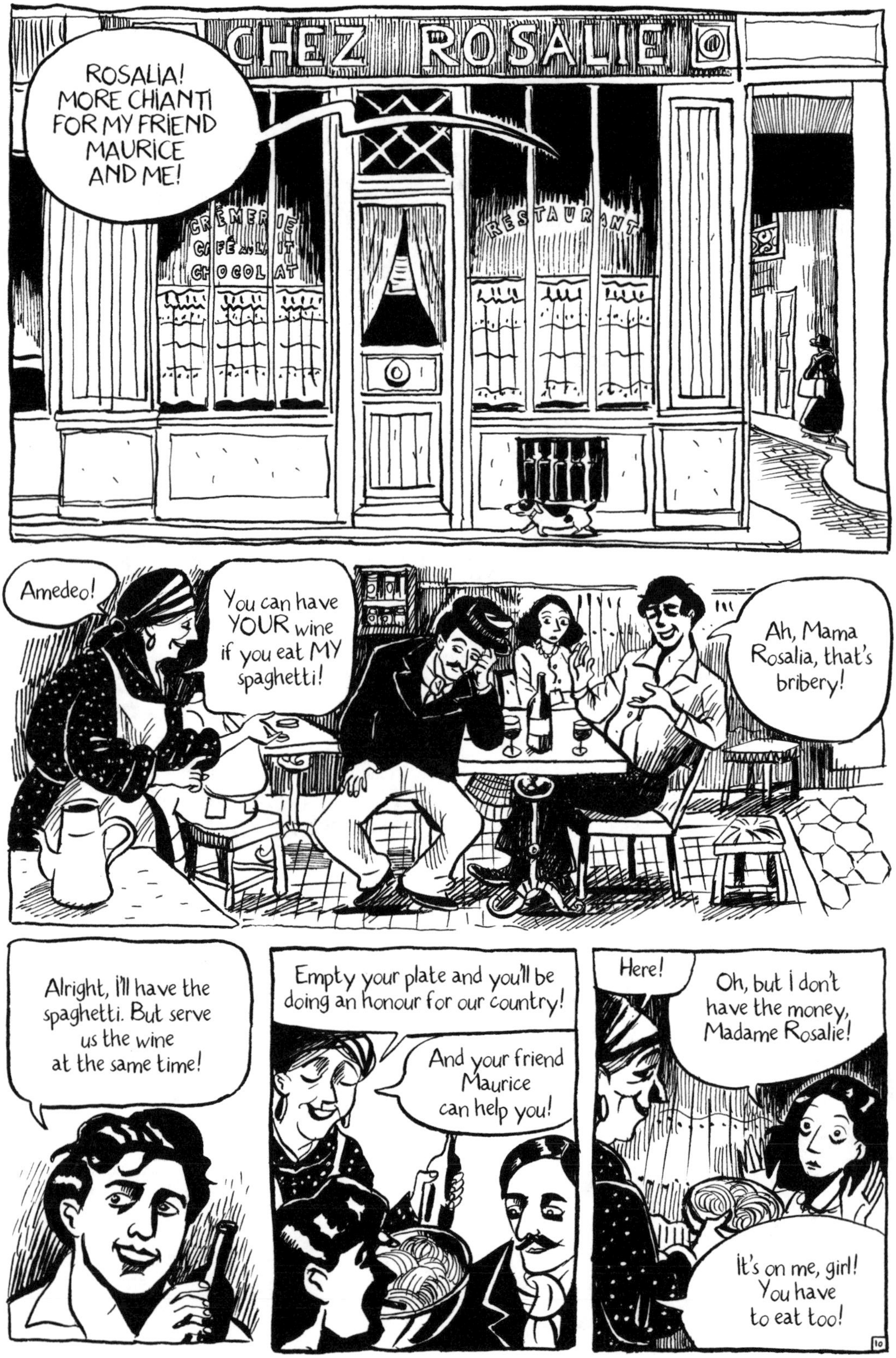
CHEZ ROSALIE
ROSALIA! MORE CHIANTI FOR MY FRIEND MAURICE AND ME!
CRÉMERIE CAFÉ AU LAIT CHOCOLAT
RESTAURANT
Amedeo!
You can have YOUR wine if you eat MY spaghetti!
Ah, Mama Rosalia, that's bribery!
Alright, I'll have the spaghetti. But serve us the wine at the same time!
Empty your plate and you'll be doing an honour for our country!
And your friend Maurice can help you!
Here!
Oh, but I don't have the money, Madame Rosalie!
It's on me, girl! You have to eat too!
10

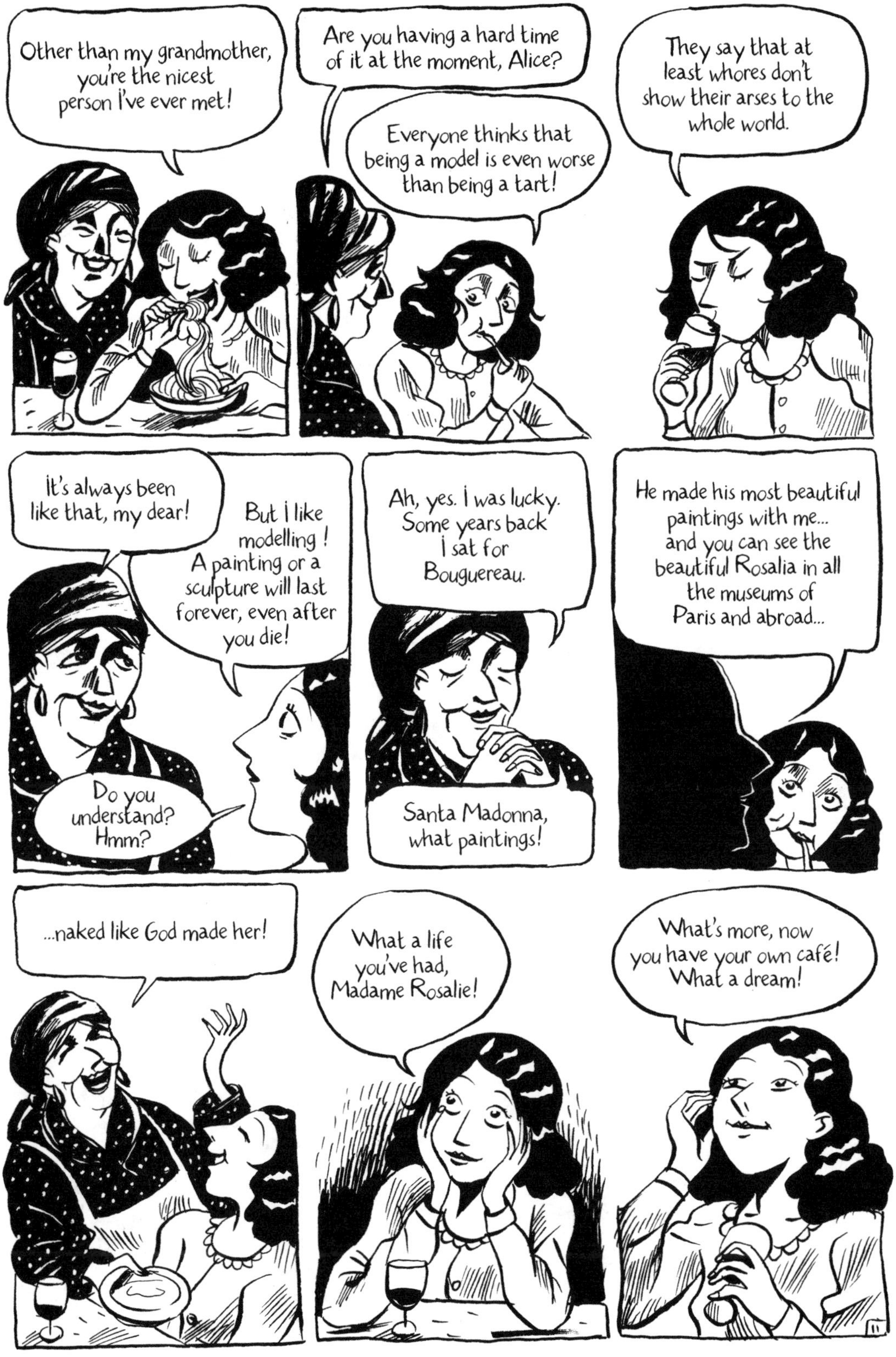
Other than my grandmother, you're the nicest person I've ever met!
Are you having a hard time of it at the moment, Alice?
Everyone thinks that being a model is even worse than being a tart!
They say that at least whores don't show their arses to the whole world.
It's always been like that, my dear!
But I like modelling! A painting or a sculpture will last forever, even after you die!
Do you understand? Hmm?
Ah, yes. I was lucky. Some years back I sat for Bouguereau.
Santa Madonna, what paintings!
He made his most beautiful paintings with me... and you can see the beautiful Rosalia in all the museums of Paris and abroad...
...naked like God made her!
What a life you've had, Madame Rosalie!
What's more, now you have your own café! What a dream!

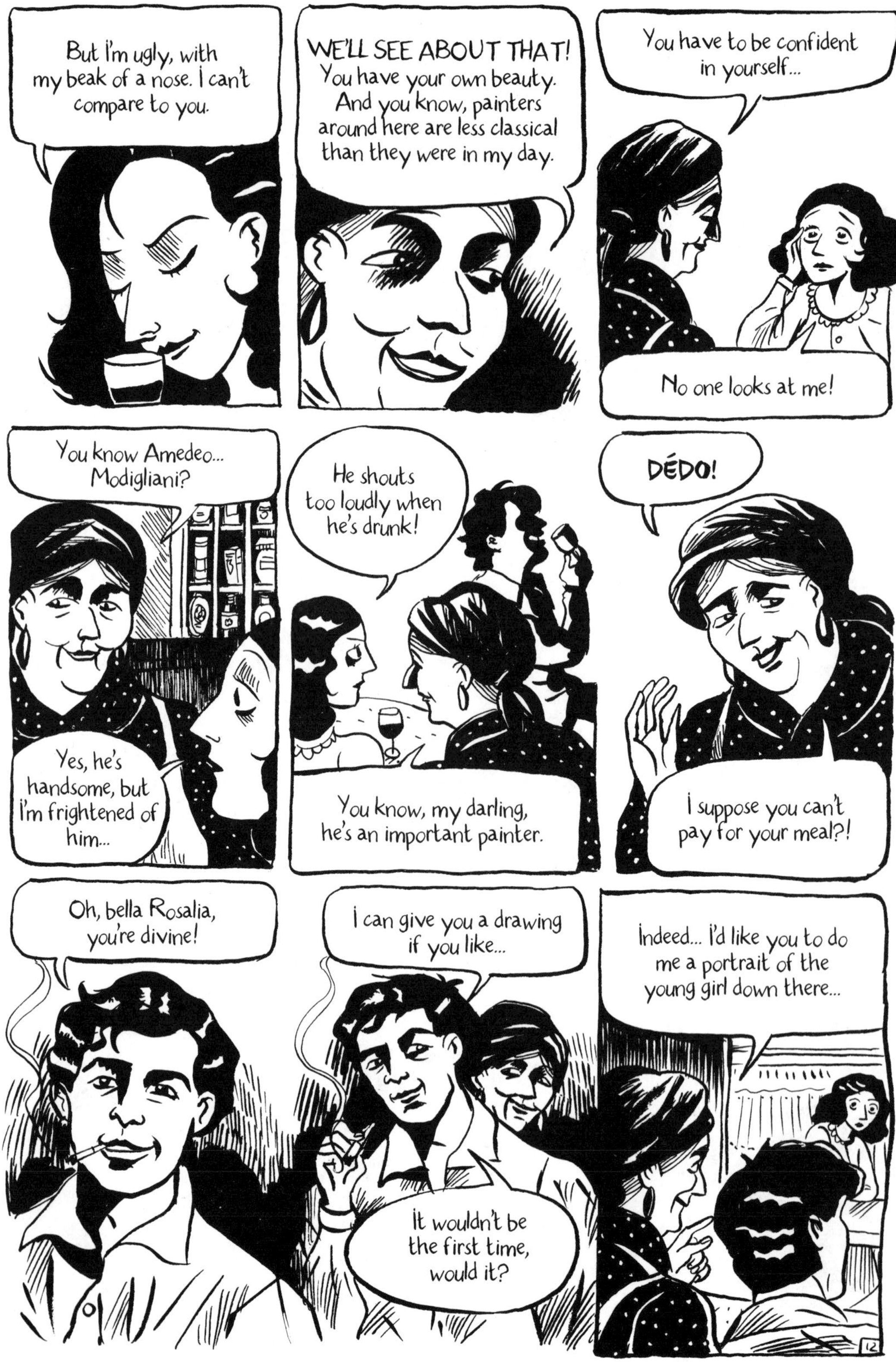
But I'm ugly, with my beak of a nose. I can't compare to you.
WE'LL SEE ABOUT THAT! You have your own beauty. And you know, painters around here are less classical than they were in my day.
You have to be confident in yourself...
No one looks at me!
You know Amedeo... Modigliani?
Yes, he's handsome, but I'm frightened of him...
He shouts too loudly when he's drunk!
You know, my darling, he's an important painter.
DÉDO!
I suppose you can't pay for your meal?!
Oh, bella Rosalia, you're divine!
I can give you a drawing if you like...
It wouldn't be the first time, would it?
Indeed... I'd like you to do me a portrait of the young girl down there...
12

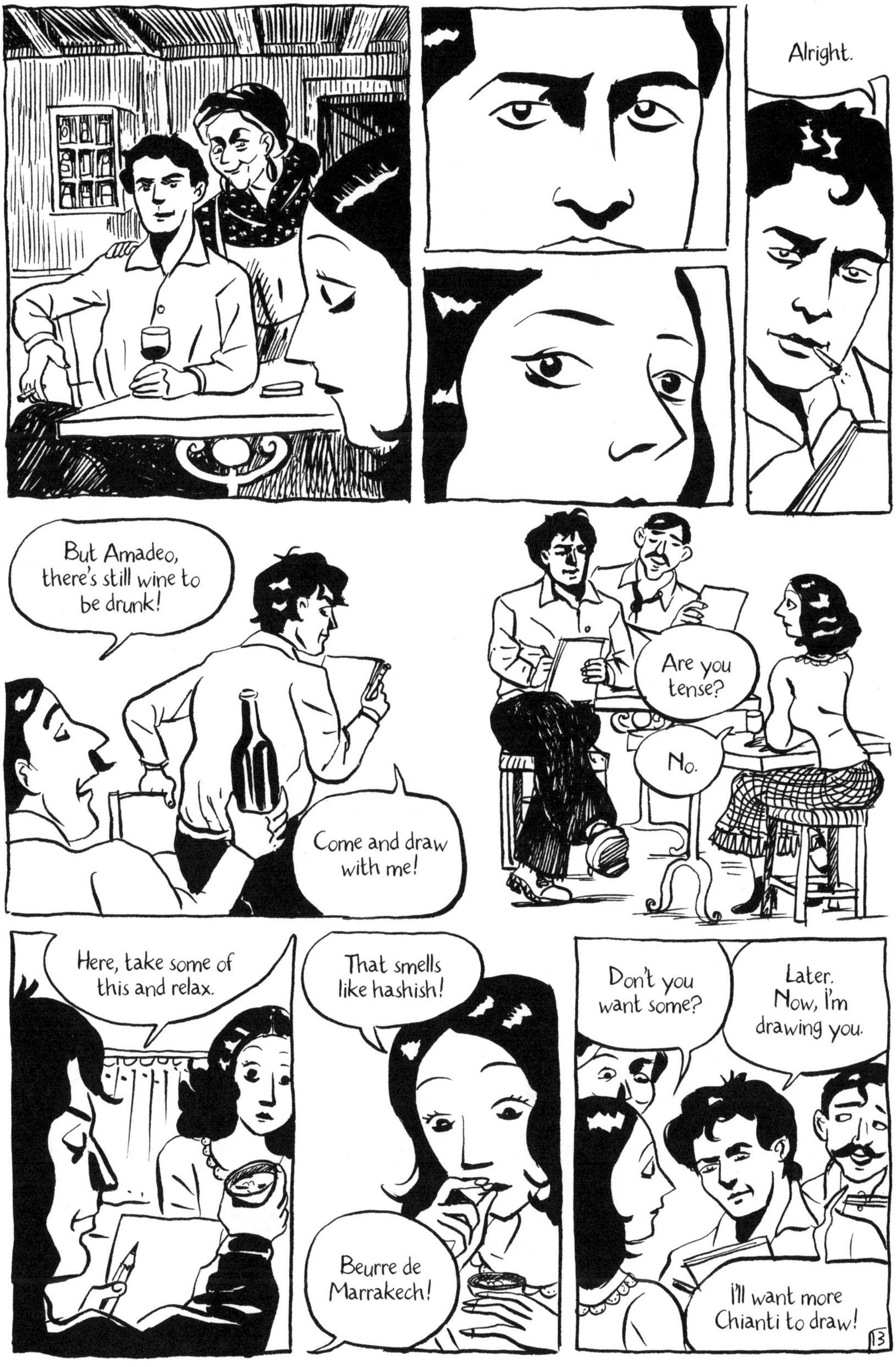
Alright.
But Amadeo, there's still wine to be drunk!
Come and draw with me!
Are you tense?
No.
Here, take some of this and relax.
That smells like hashish!
Beurre de Marrakech!
Don't you want some?
Later. Now, I'm drawing you.
I'll want more Chianti to draw!
13

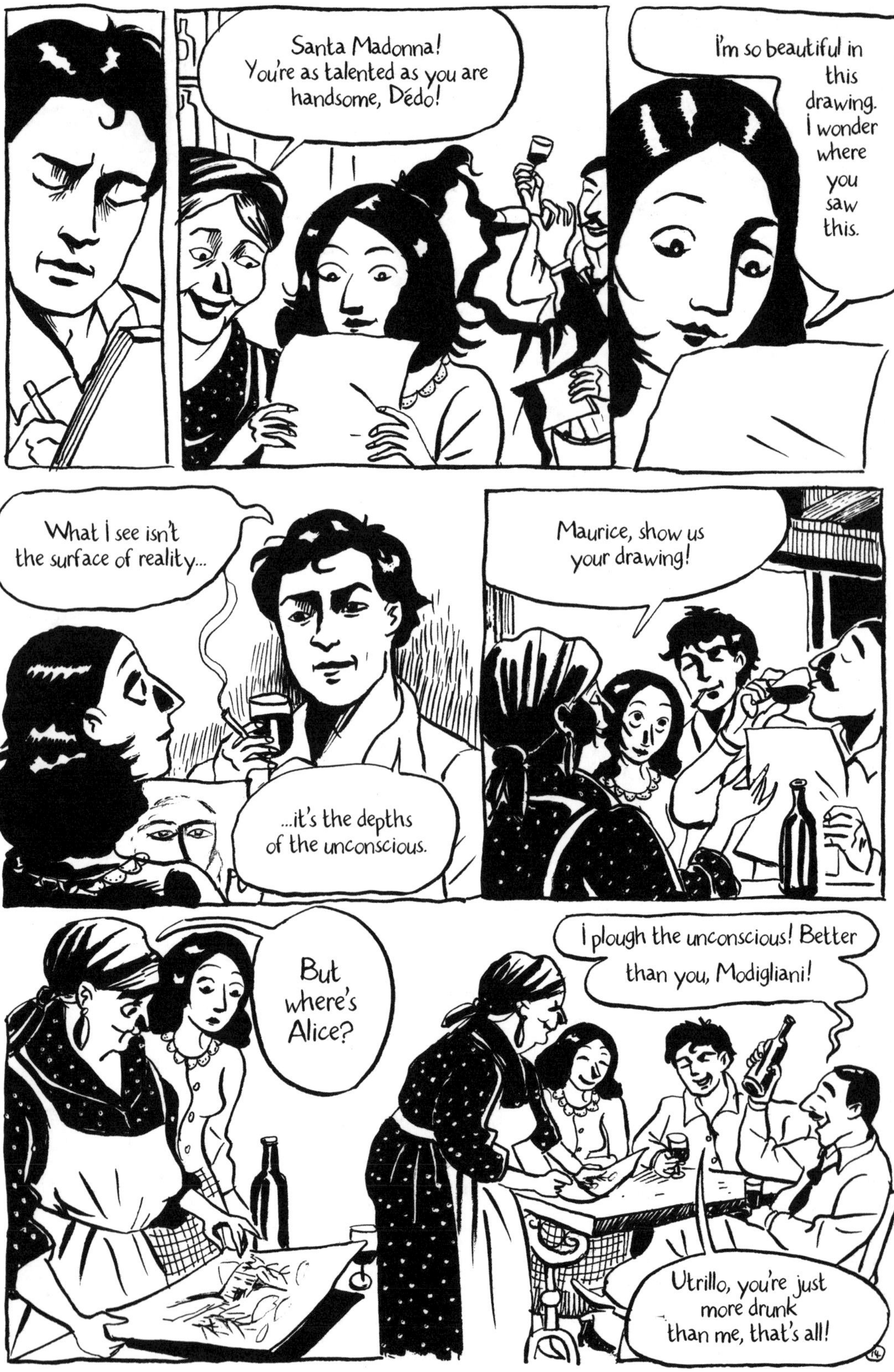
Santa Madonna! You're as talented as you are handsome, Dédo!
I'm so beautiful in this drawing. I wonder where you saw this.
What I see isn't the surface of reality...
...it's the depths of the unconscious.
Maurice, show us your drawing!
But where's Alice?
I plough the unconscious! Better than you, Modigliani!
Utrillo, you're just more drunk than me, that's all!

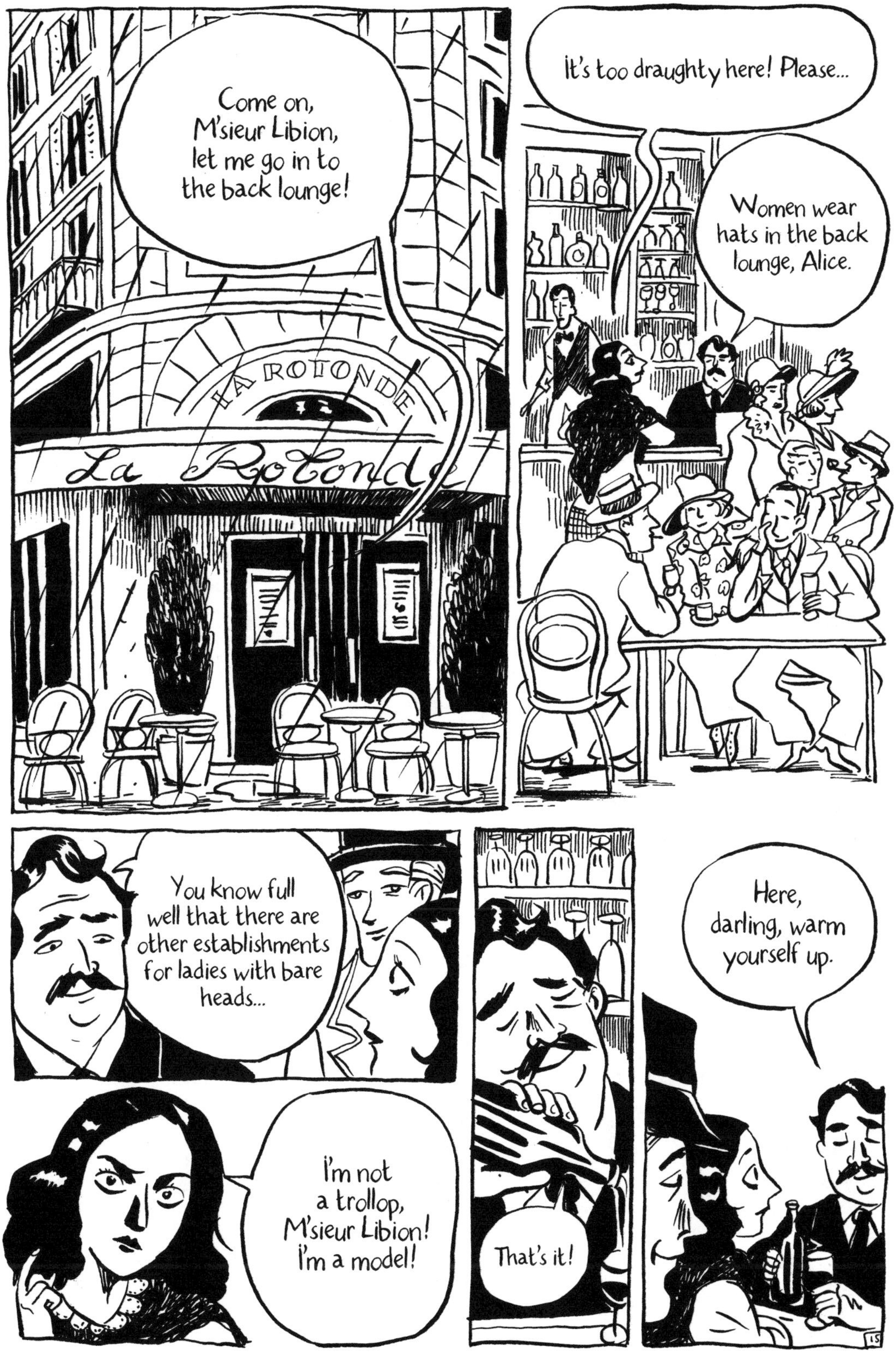
Come on, M'sieur Libion, let me go in to the back lounge!
LA ROTONDE
La Rotonde
It's too draughty here! Please...
Women wear hats in the back lounge, Alice.
You know full well that there are other establishments for ladies with bare heads...
I'm not a trollop, M'sieur Libion! I'm a model!
That's it!
Here, darling, warm yourself up.

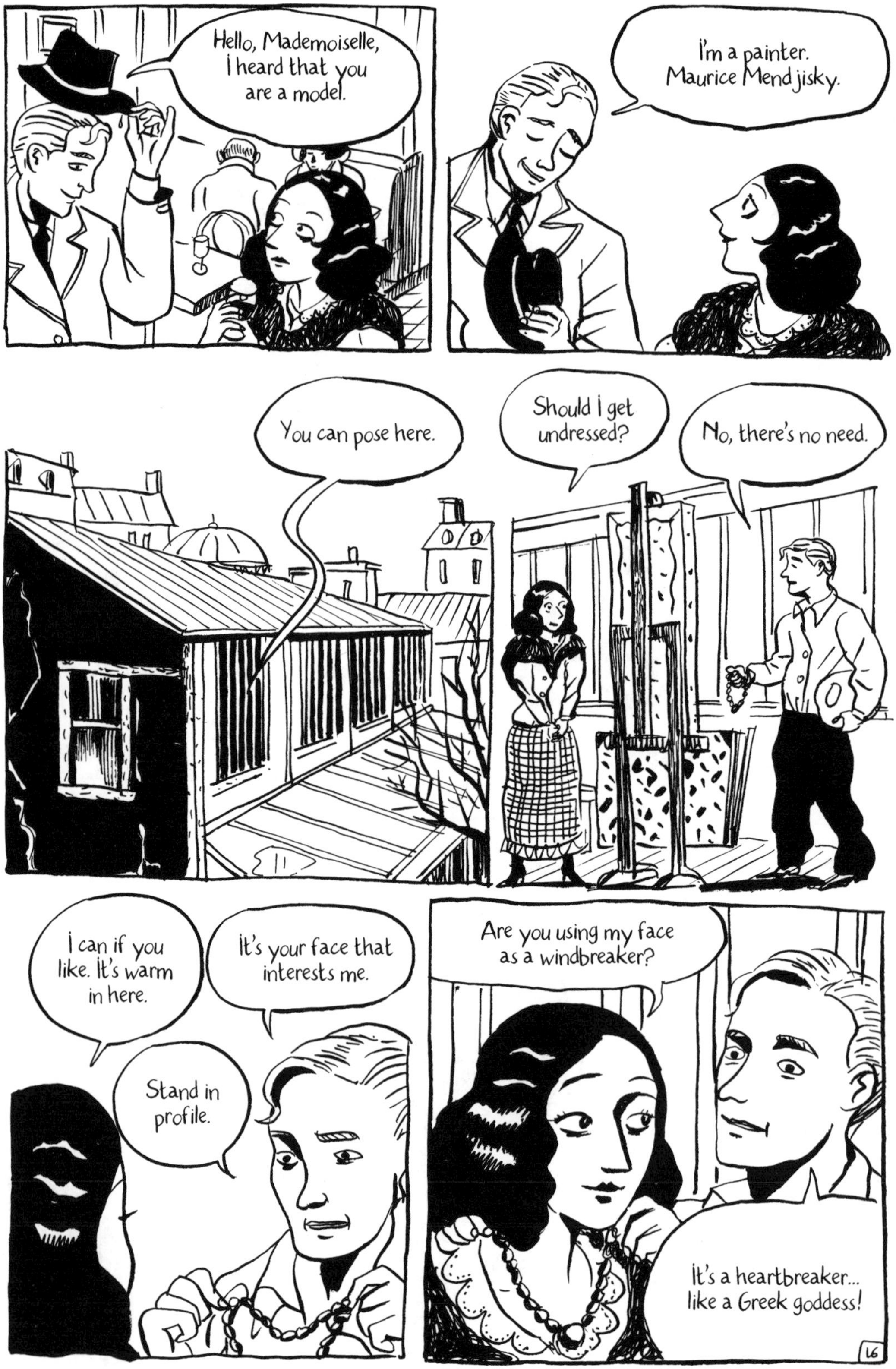
Hello, Mademoiselle, I heard that you are a model.
I'm a painter. Maurice Mendjisky.
You can pose here.
Should I get undressed?
No, there's no need.
I can if you like. It's warm in here.
It's your face that interests me.
Stand in profile.
Are you using my face as a windbreaker?
It's a heartbreaker... like a Greek goddess!
16

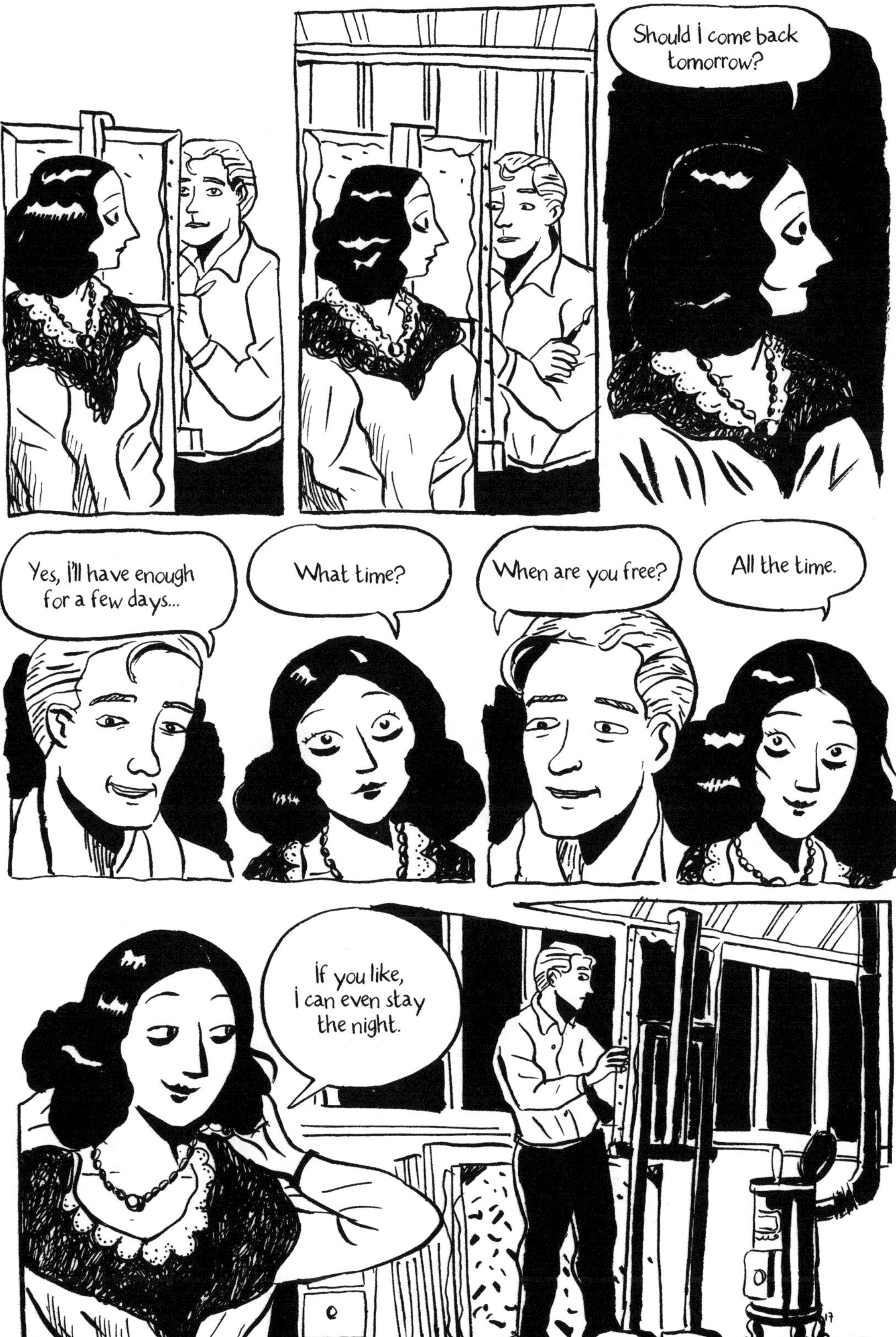
Should I come back tomorrow?
Yes, I'll have enough for a few days...
What time?
When are you free?
All the time.
If you like, I can even stay the night.

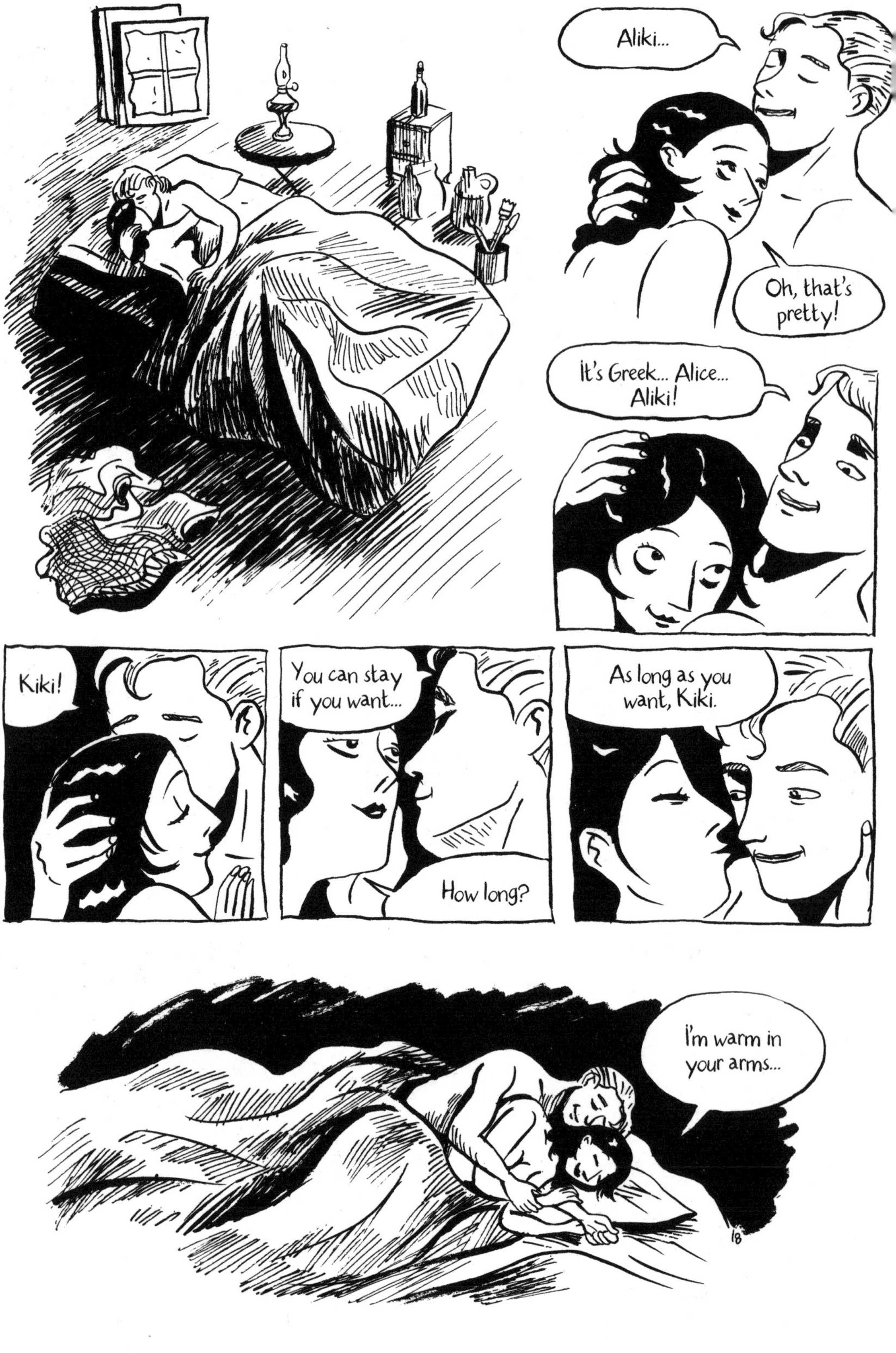
Aliki...
Oh, that's pretty!
It's Greek... Alice... Aliki!
Kiki!
You can stay if you want...
How long?
As long as you want, Kiki.
I'm warm in your arms...
18

1920 - 3, rue Bara

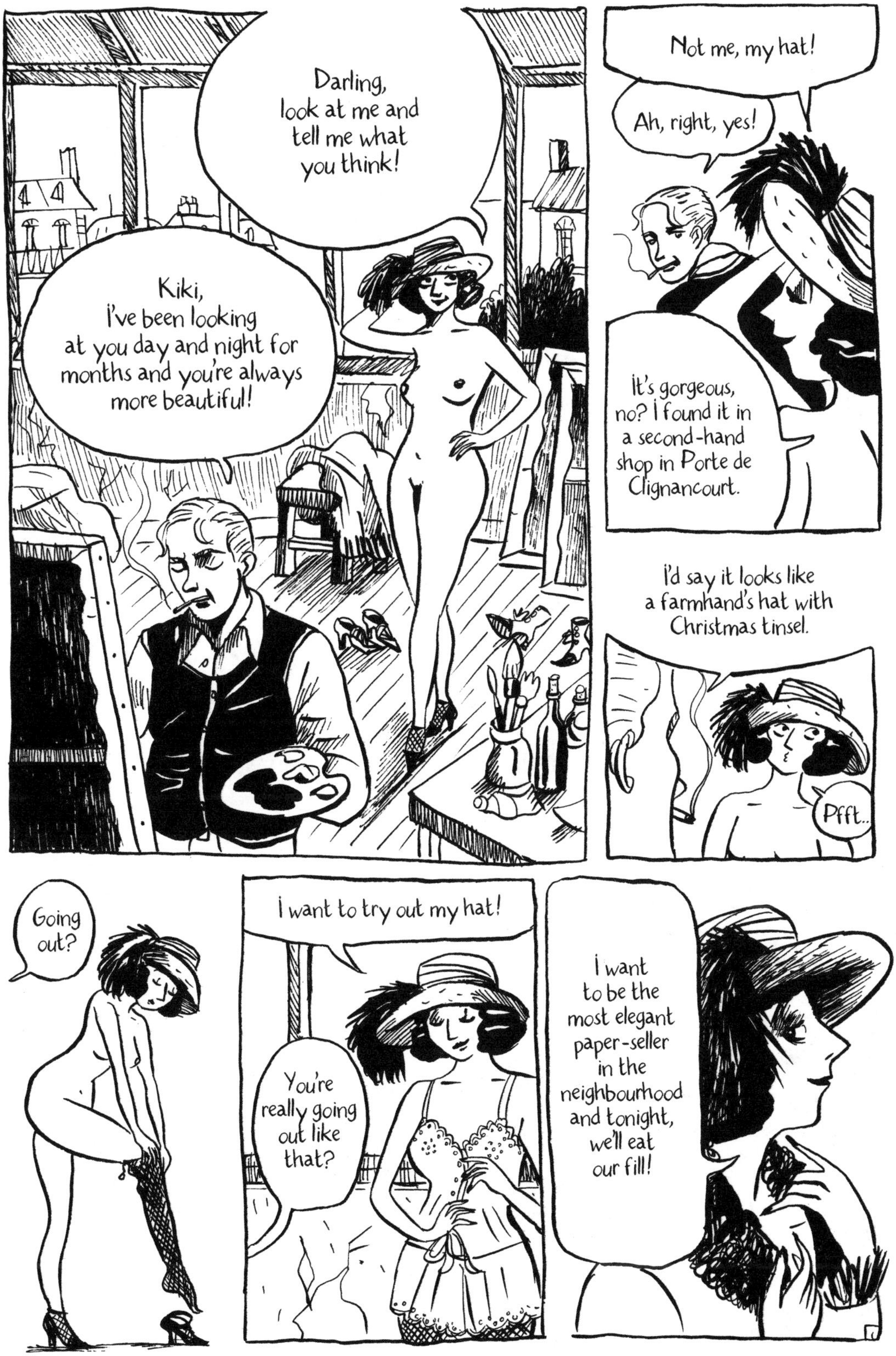
Darling, look at me and tell me what you think!
Kiki, I've been looking at you day and night for months and you're always more beautiful!
Not me, my hat!
Ah, right, yes!
It's gorgeous, no? I found it in a second-hand shop in Porte de Clignancourt.
I'd say it looks like a farmhand's hat with Christmas tinsel.
Pfft...
Going out?
I want to try out my hat!
You're really going out like that?
I want to be the most elegant paper-seller in the neighbourhood and tonight, we'll eat our fill!

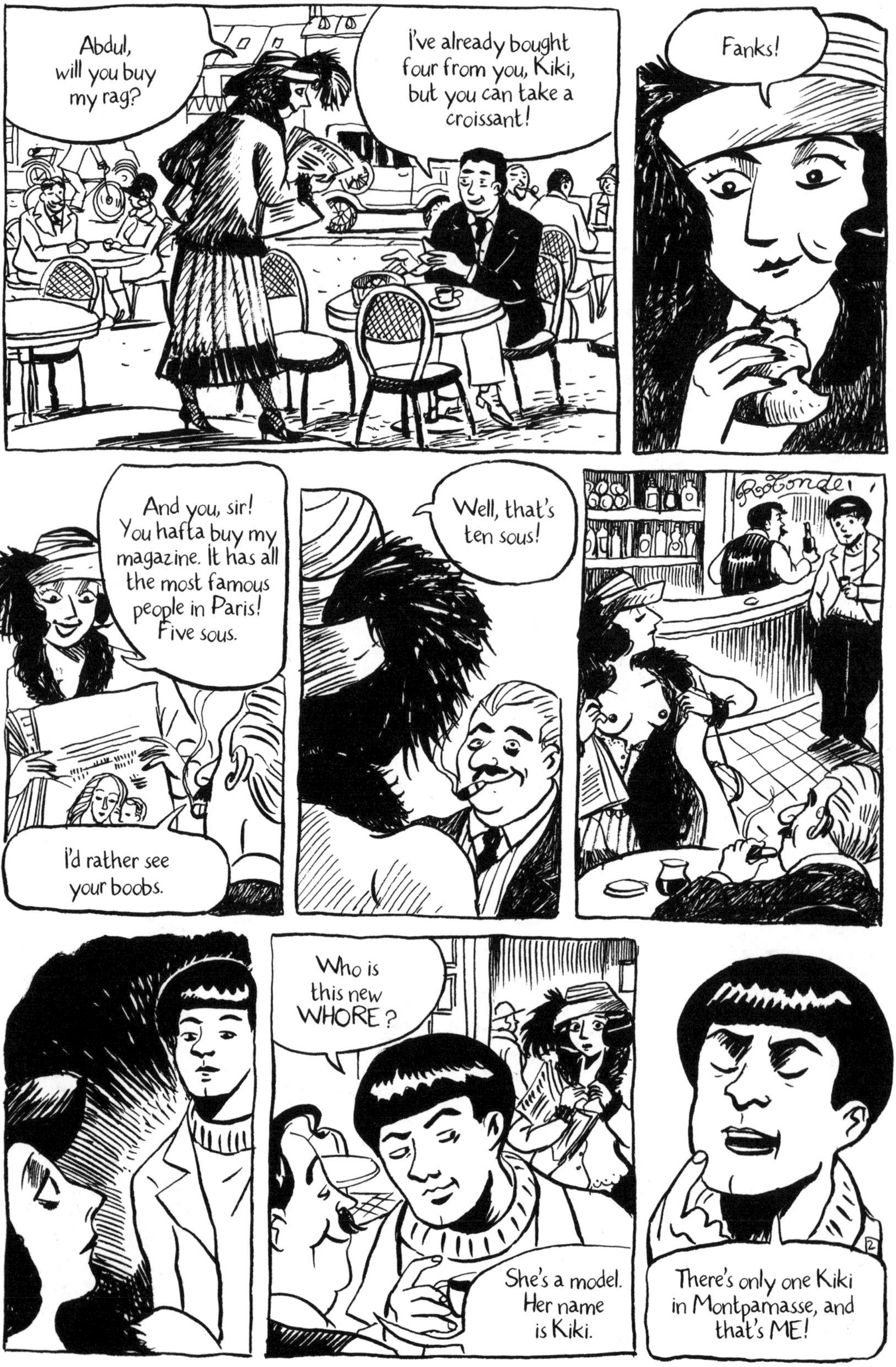
Abdul, will you buy my rag?
I've already bought four from you, Kiki, but you can take a croissant!
Fanks!
And you, sir! You hafta buy my magazine. It has all the most famous people in Paris! Five sous.
I'd rather see your boobs.
Well, that's ten sous!
Rotonde
Who is this new WHORE?
She's a model. Her name is Kiki.
There's only one Kiki in Montparnasse, and that's ME!

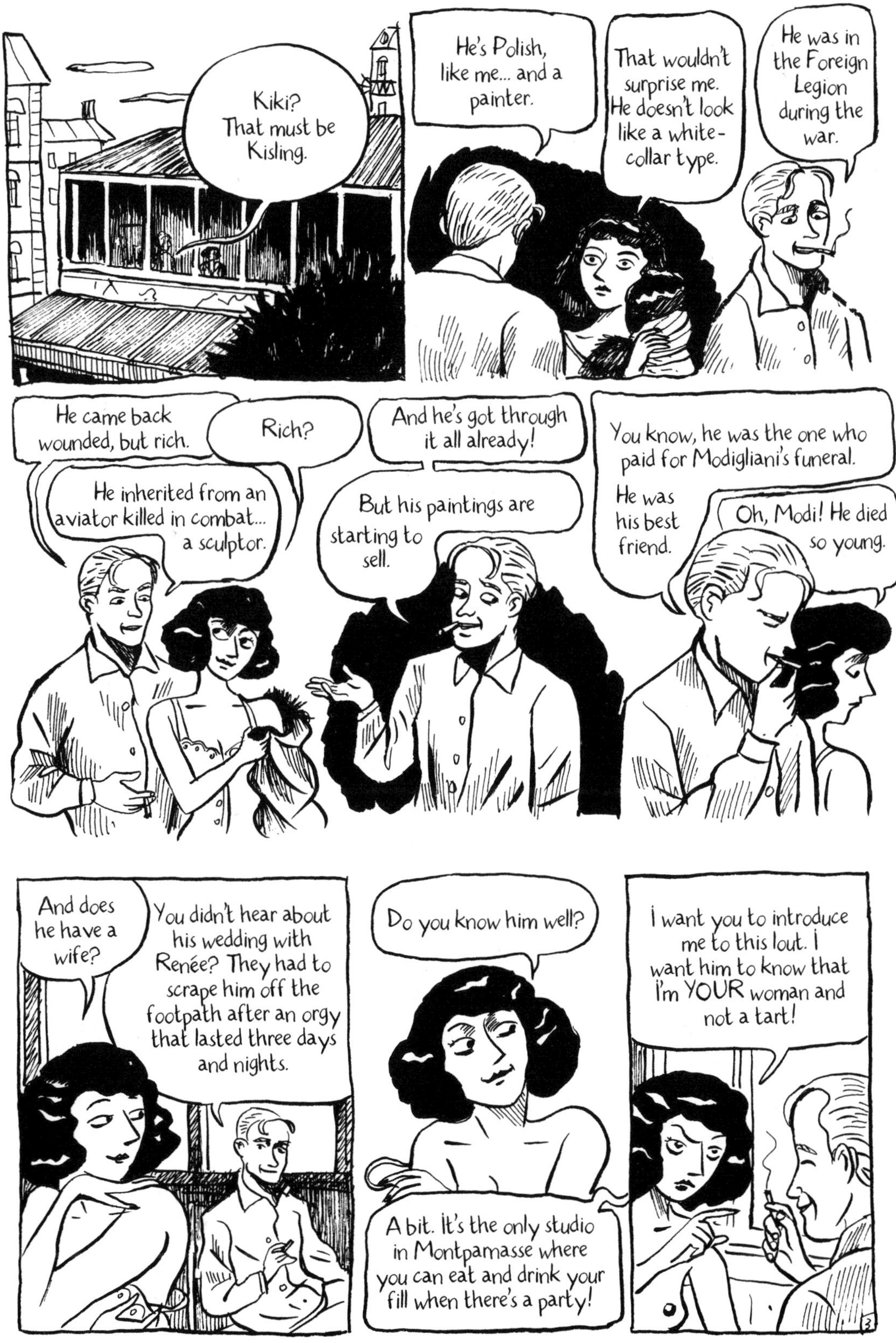
Kiki? That must be Kisling.
He's Polish, like me... and a painter.
That wouldn't surprise me. He doesn't look like a white-collar type.
He was in the Foreign Legion during the war.
He came back wounded, but rich.
Rich?
He inherited from an aviator killed in combat... a sculptor.
And he's got through it all already!
But his paintings are starting to sell.
You know, he was the one who paid for Modigliani's funeral.
He was his best friend.
Oh, Modi! He died so young.
And does he have a wife?
You didn't hear about his wedding with Renée? They had to scrape him off the footpath after an orgy that lasted three days and nights.
Do you know him well?
A bit. It's the only studio in Montparnasse where you can eat and drink your fill when there's a party!
I want you to introduce me to this lout. I want him to know that I'm YOUR woman and not a tart!
3

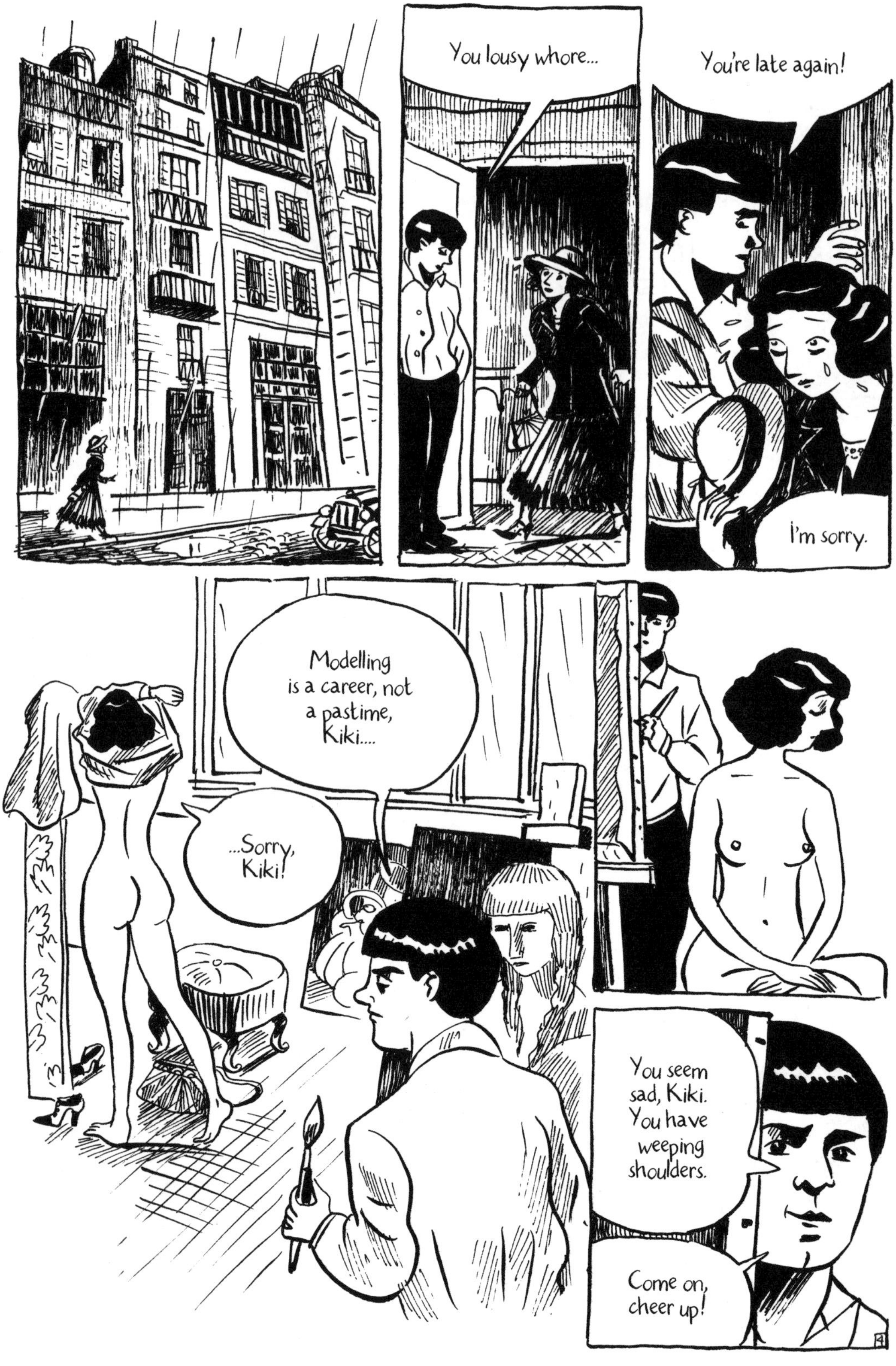
You lousy whore...
You're late again!
I'm sorry.
Modelling is a career, not a pastime, Kiki....
...Sorry, Kiki!
You seem sad, Kiki. You have weeping shoulders.
Come on, cheer up!
4

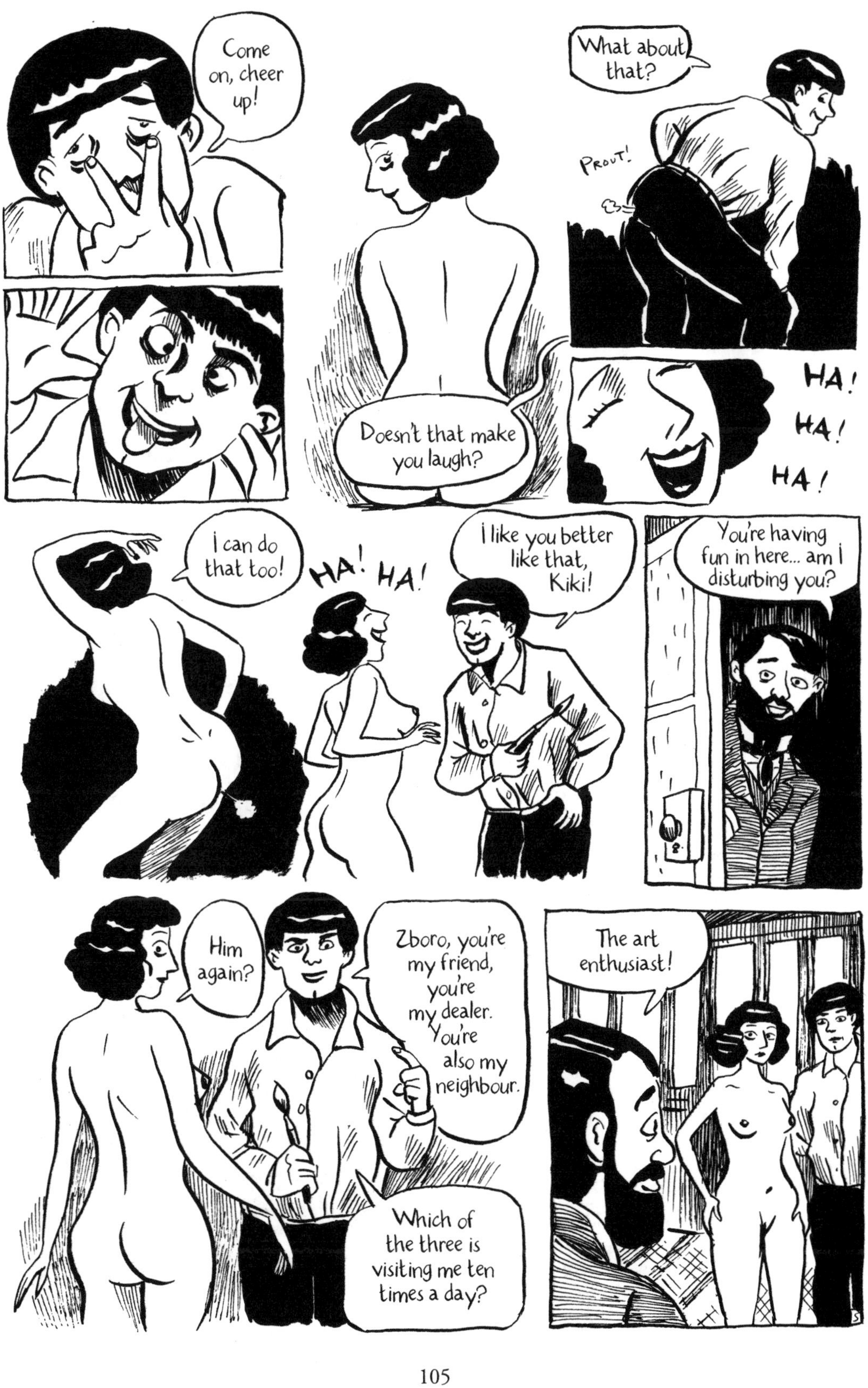
Come on, cheer up!
What about that?
PROUT!
Doesn't that make you laugh?
HA! HA! HA!
I can do that too!
HA! HA!
I like you better like that, Kiki!
You're having fun in here... am I disturbing you?
Him again?
Zboro, you're my friend, you're my dealer. You're also my neighbour.
Which of the three is visiting me ten times a day?
The art enthusiast!

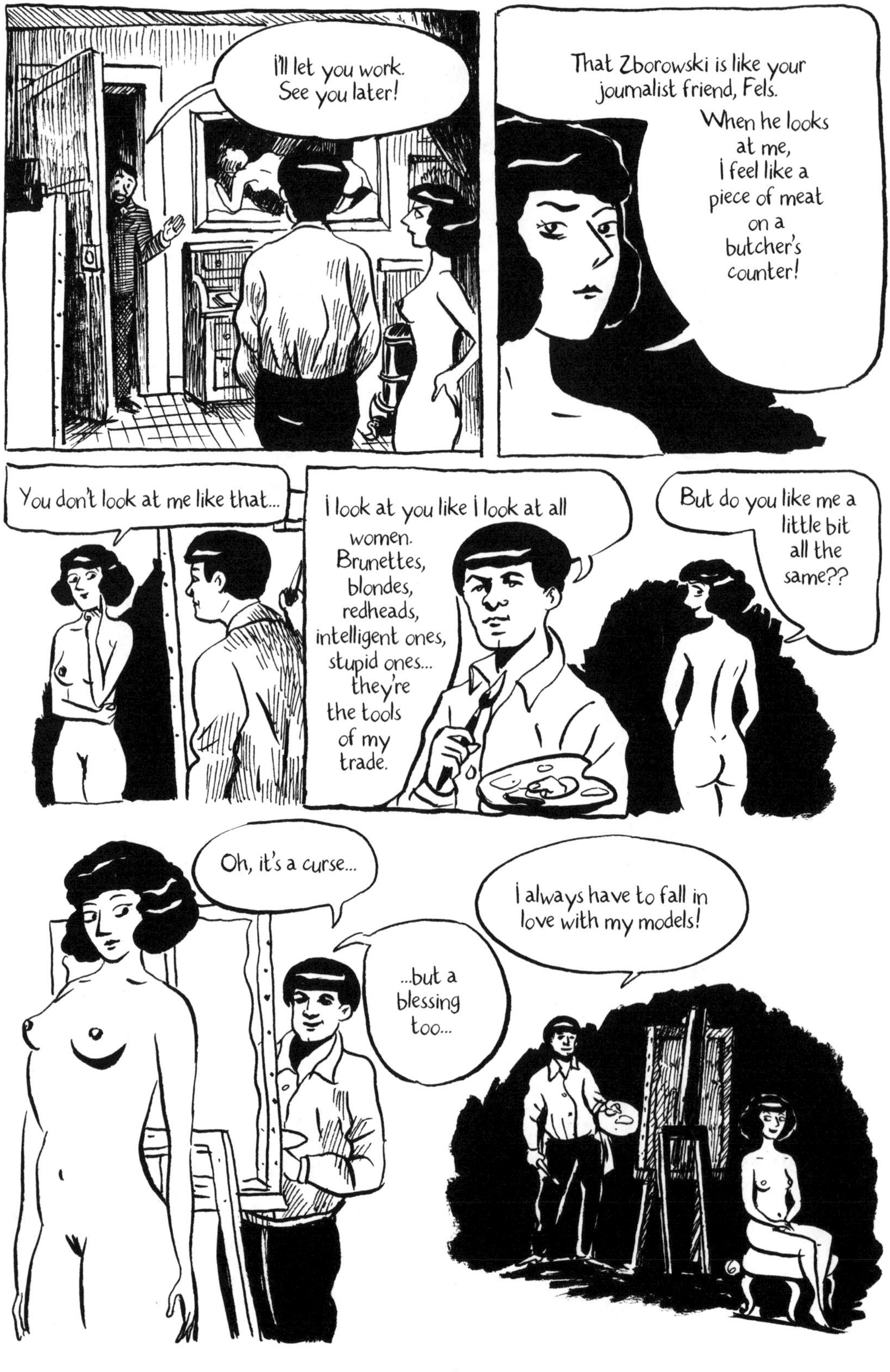
I'll let you work. See you later!
That Zborowski is like your journalist friend, Fels.
When he looks at me, I feel like a piece of meat on a butcher's counter!
You don't look at me like that...
I look at you like I look at all women. Brunettes, blondes, redheads, intelligent ones, stupid ones... they're the tools of my trade.
But do you like me a little bit all the same??
Oh, it's a curse...
...but a blessing too...
I always have to fall in love with my models!

1921 – 5, rue Delambre

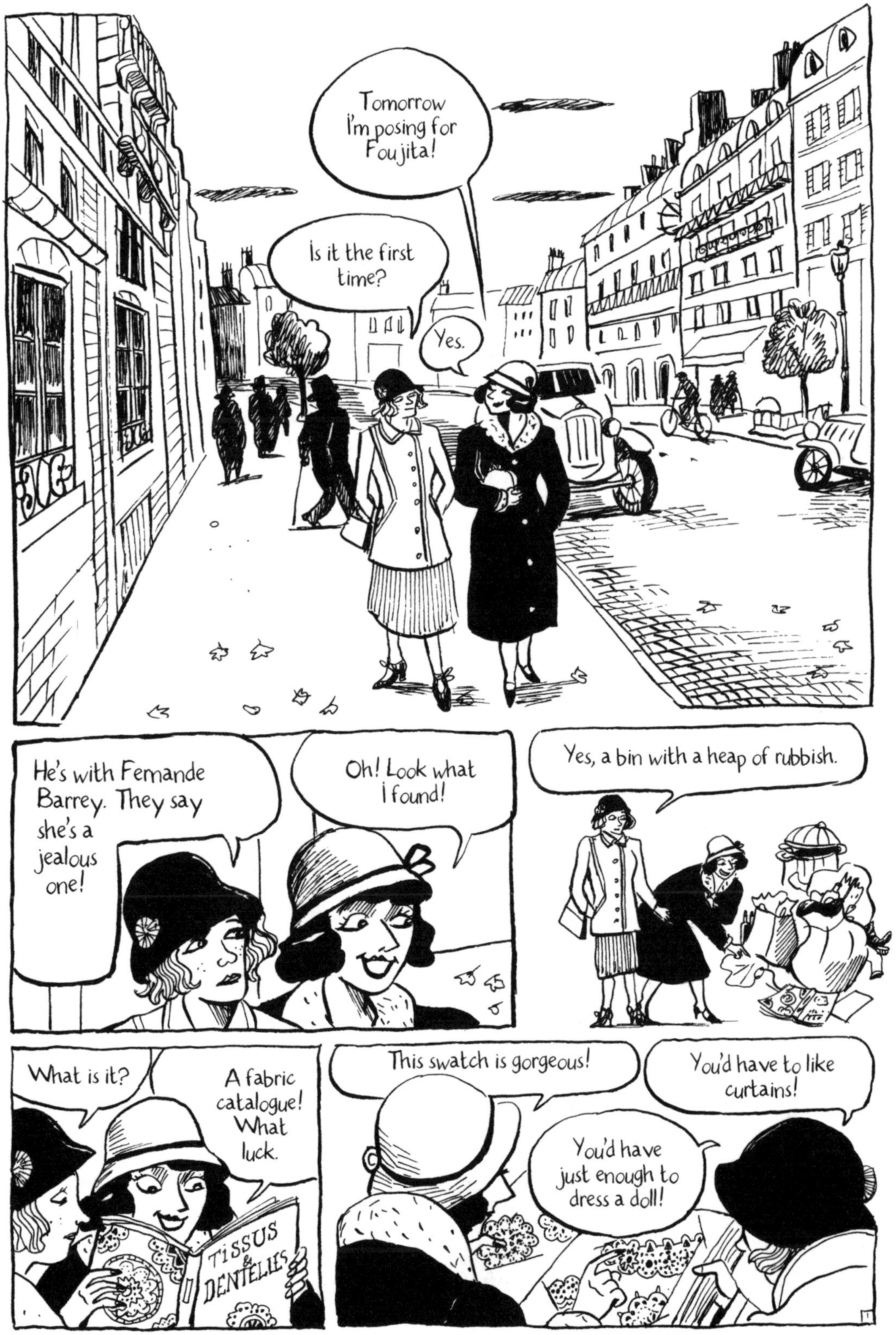
Tomorrow I'm posing for Foujita!
Is it the first time?
Yes.
He's with Fernande Barrey. They say she's a jealous one!
Oh! Look what I found!
Yes, a bin with a heap of rubbish.
What is it?
A fabric catalogue! What luck.
TISSUS & DENTELLES
This swatch is gorgeous!
You'd have to like curtains!
You'd have just enough to dress a doll!

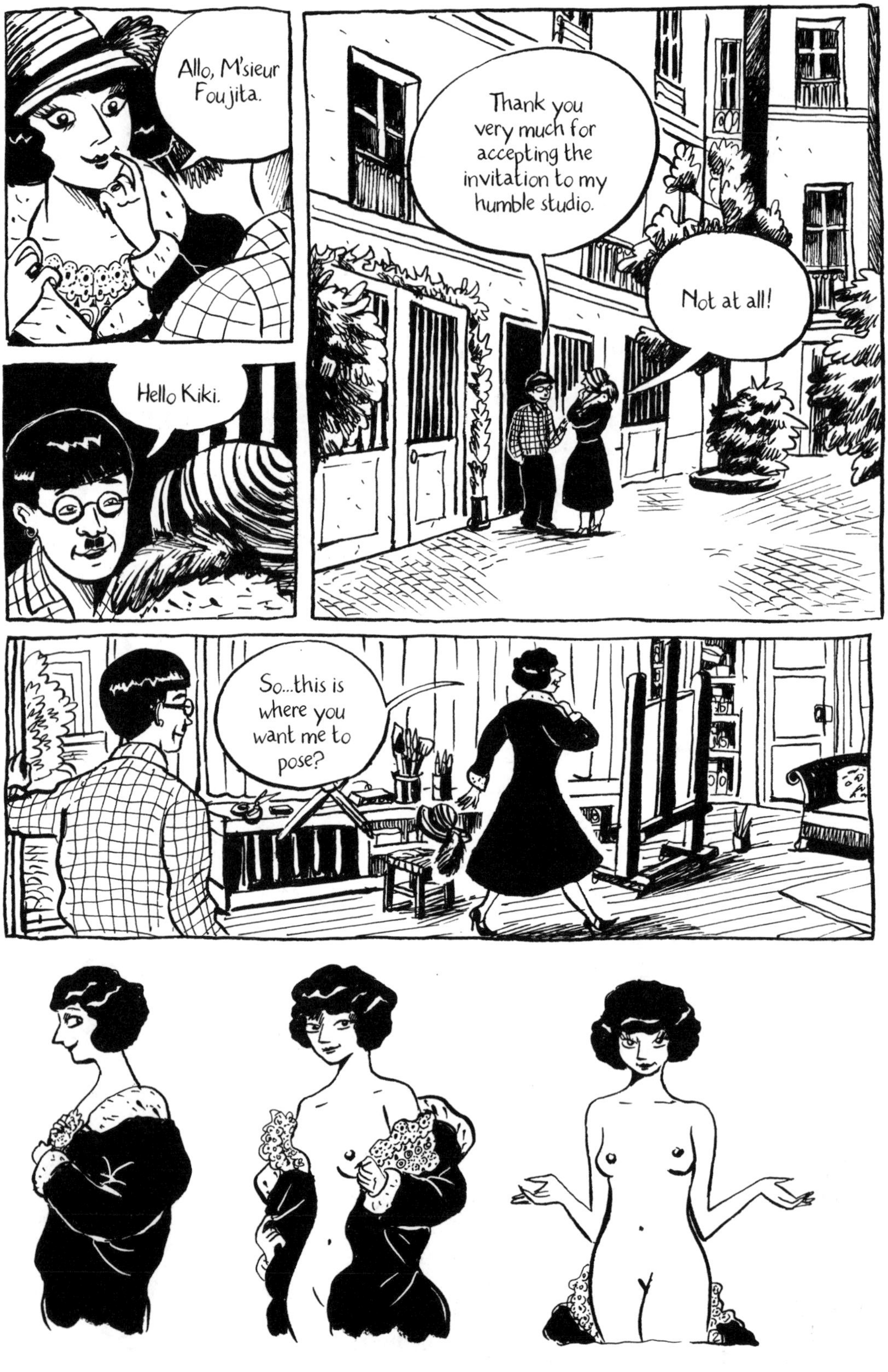
Allo, M'sieur Foujita.
Hello Kiki.
Thank you very much for accepting the invitation to my humble studio.
Not at all!
So...this is where you want me to pose?

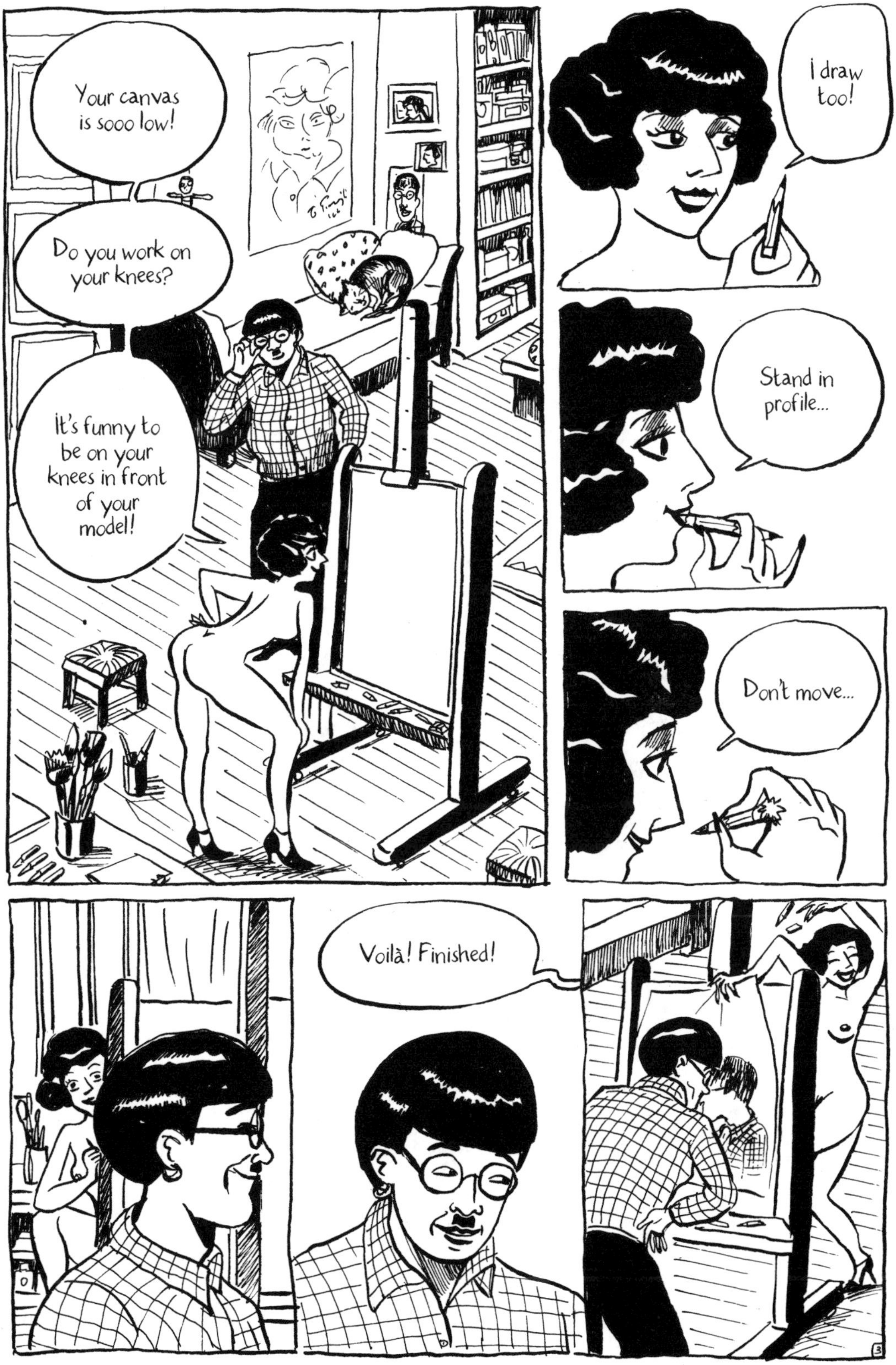
Your canvas is sooo low!
Do you work on your knees?
It's funny to be on your knees in front of your model!
I draw too!
Stand in profile...
Don't move...
Voilà! Finished!
3

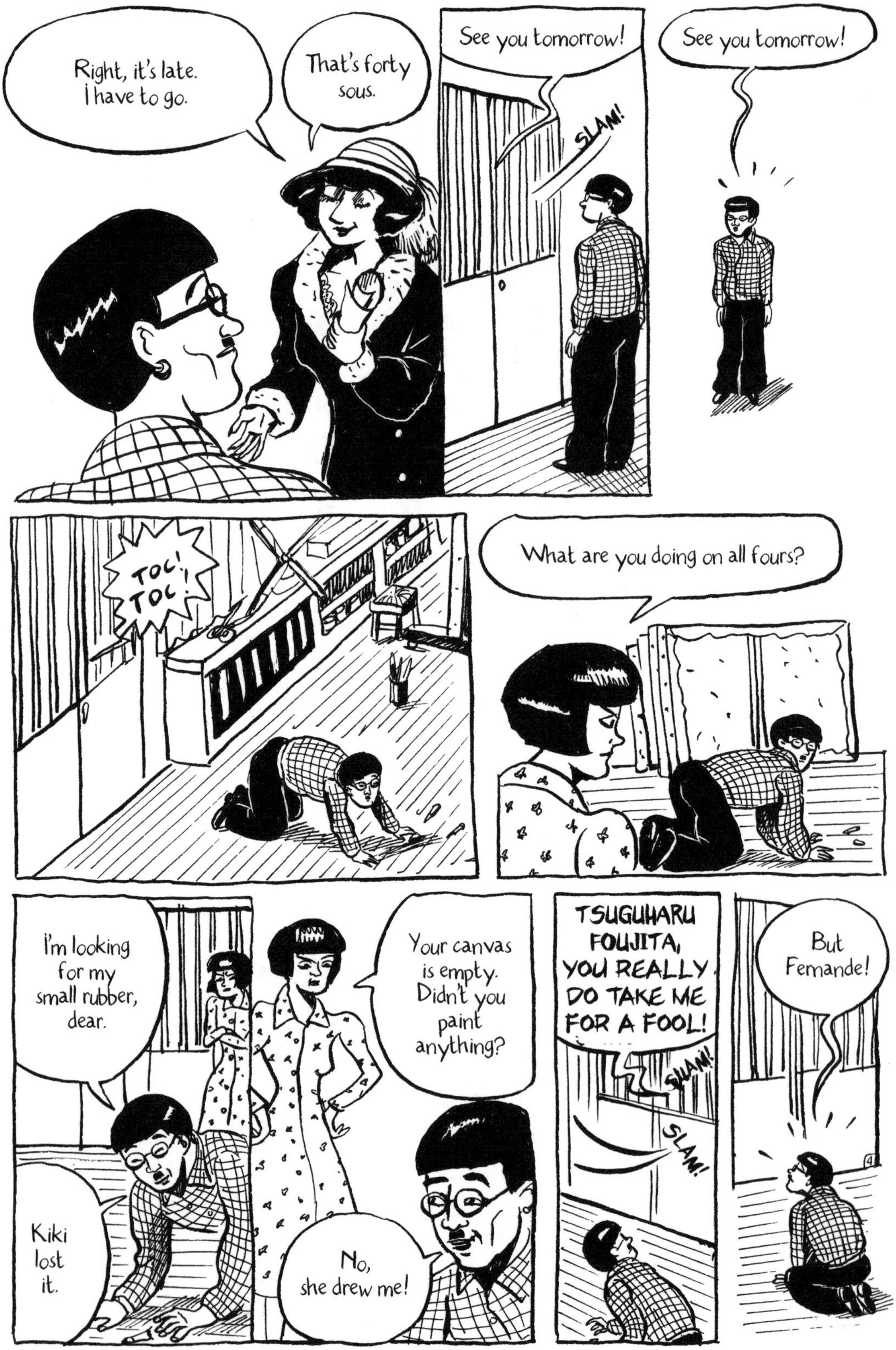
Right, it's late.
I have to go.
That's forty sous.
See you tomorrow!
SLAM!
See you tomorrow!
TOC! TOC!
What are you doing on all fours?
I'm looking for my small rubber, dear.
Kiki lost it.
Your canvas is empty. Didn't you paint anything?
No, she drew me!
TSUGUHARU FOUJITA, YOU REALLY DO TAKE ME FOR A FOOL!
SLAM!
SLAM!
But Fernande!

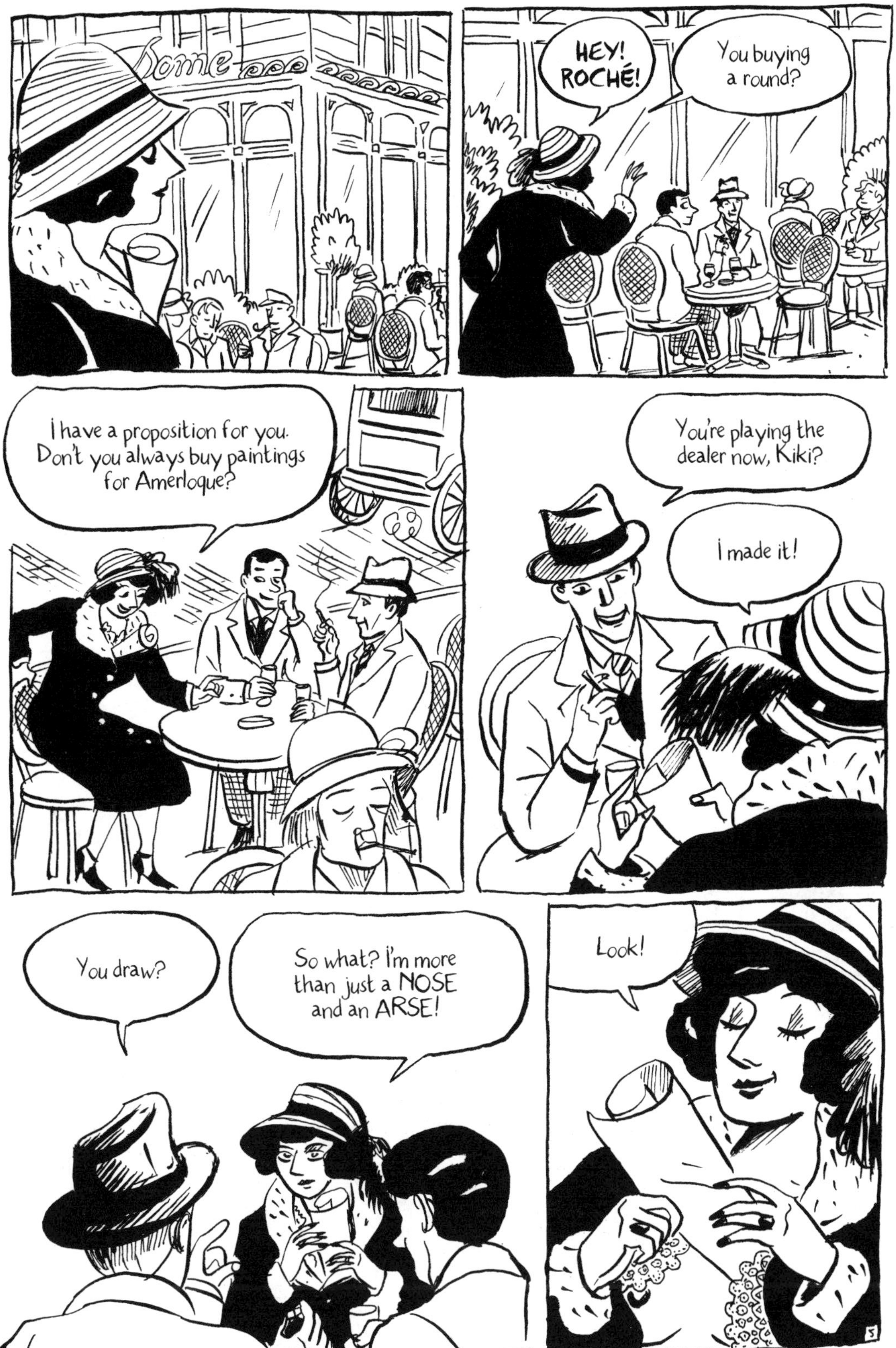

Dome
HEY! ROCHÉ!
You buying a round?
I have a proposition for you. Don't you always buy paintings for Amerloque?
You're playing the dealer now, Kiki?
I made it!
You draw?
So what? I'm more than just a NOSE and an ARSE!
Look!

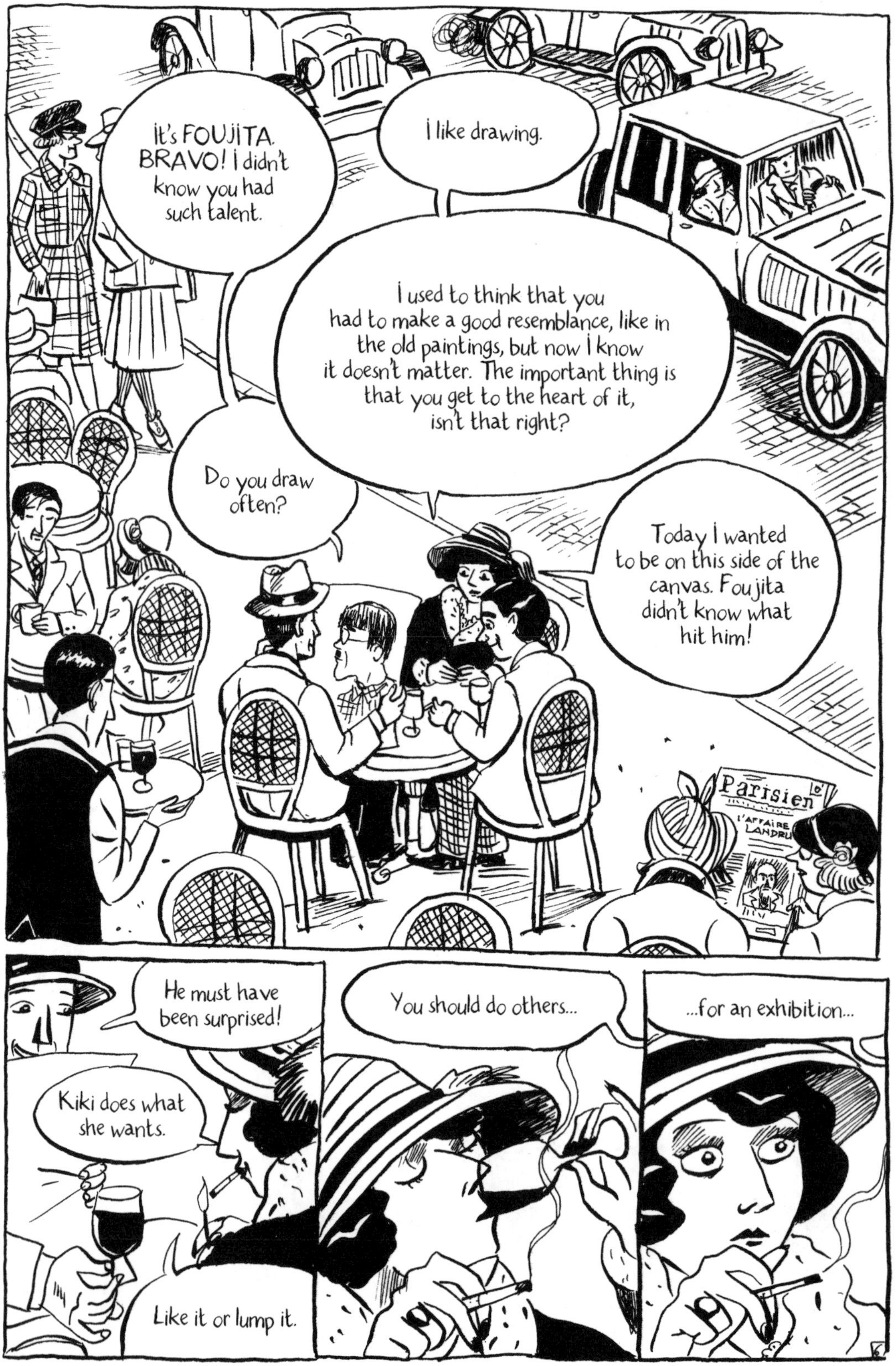
It's FOUJITA. BRAVO! I didn't know you had such talent.
I like drawing.
I used to think that you had to make a good resemblance, like in the old paintings, but now I know it doesn't matter. The important thing is that you get to the heart of it, isn't that right?
Do you draw often?
Today I wanted to be on this side of the canvas. Foujita didn't know what hit him!
Parisien
L'AFFAIRE LANDRU
He must have been surprised!
Kiki does what she wants.
Like it or lump it.
You should do others...
...for an exhibition...

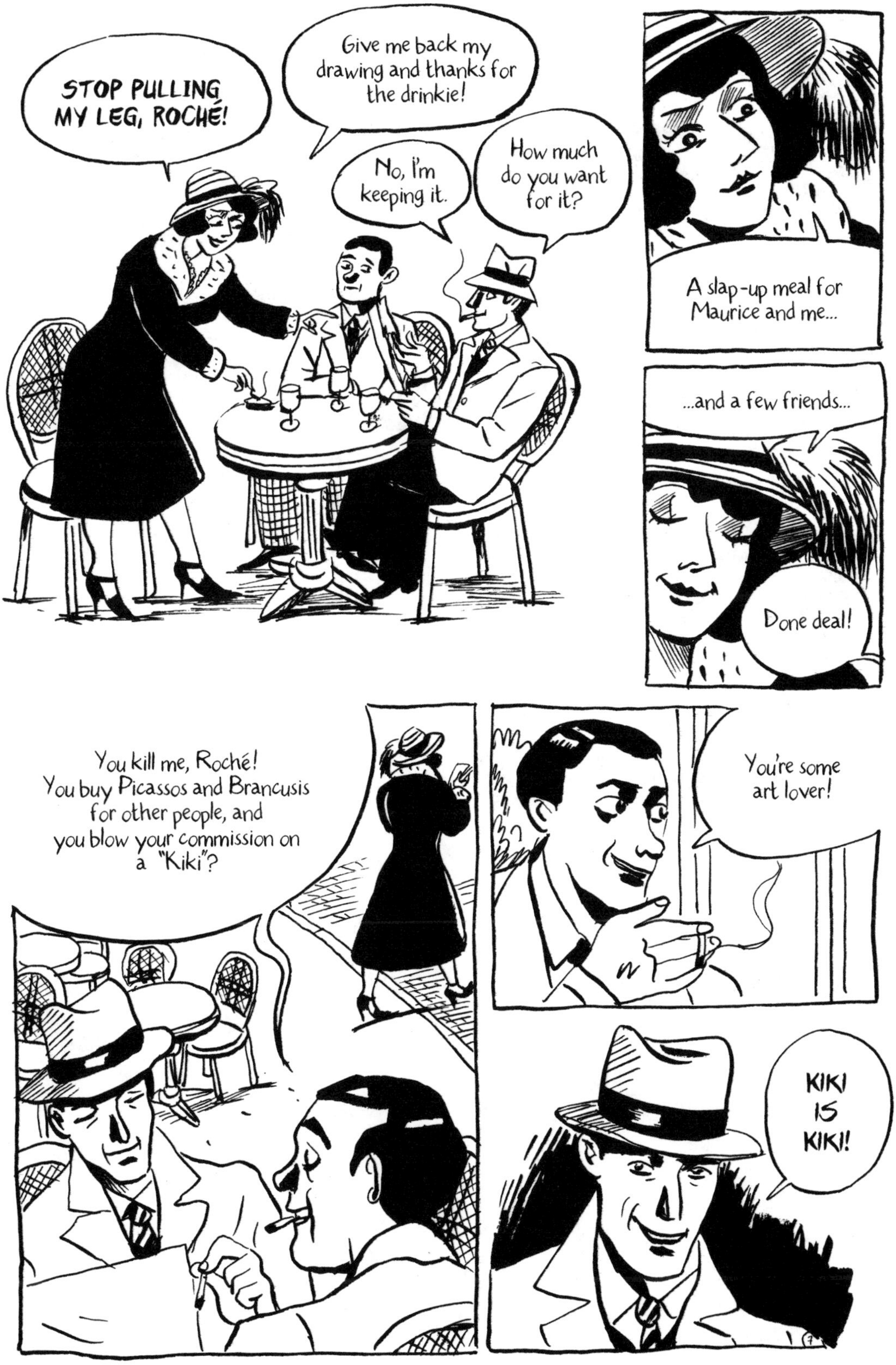
STOP PULLING MY LEG, ROCHÉ!
Give me back my drawing and thanks for the drinkie!
No, I'm keeping it.
How much do you want for it?
A slap-up meal for Maurice and me...
...and a few friends...
Done deal!
You kill me, Roché! You buy Picassos and Brancusis for other people, and you blow your commission on a "Kiki"?
You're some art lover!
KIKI IS KIKI!

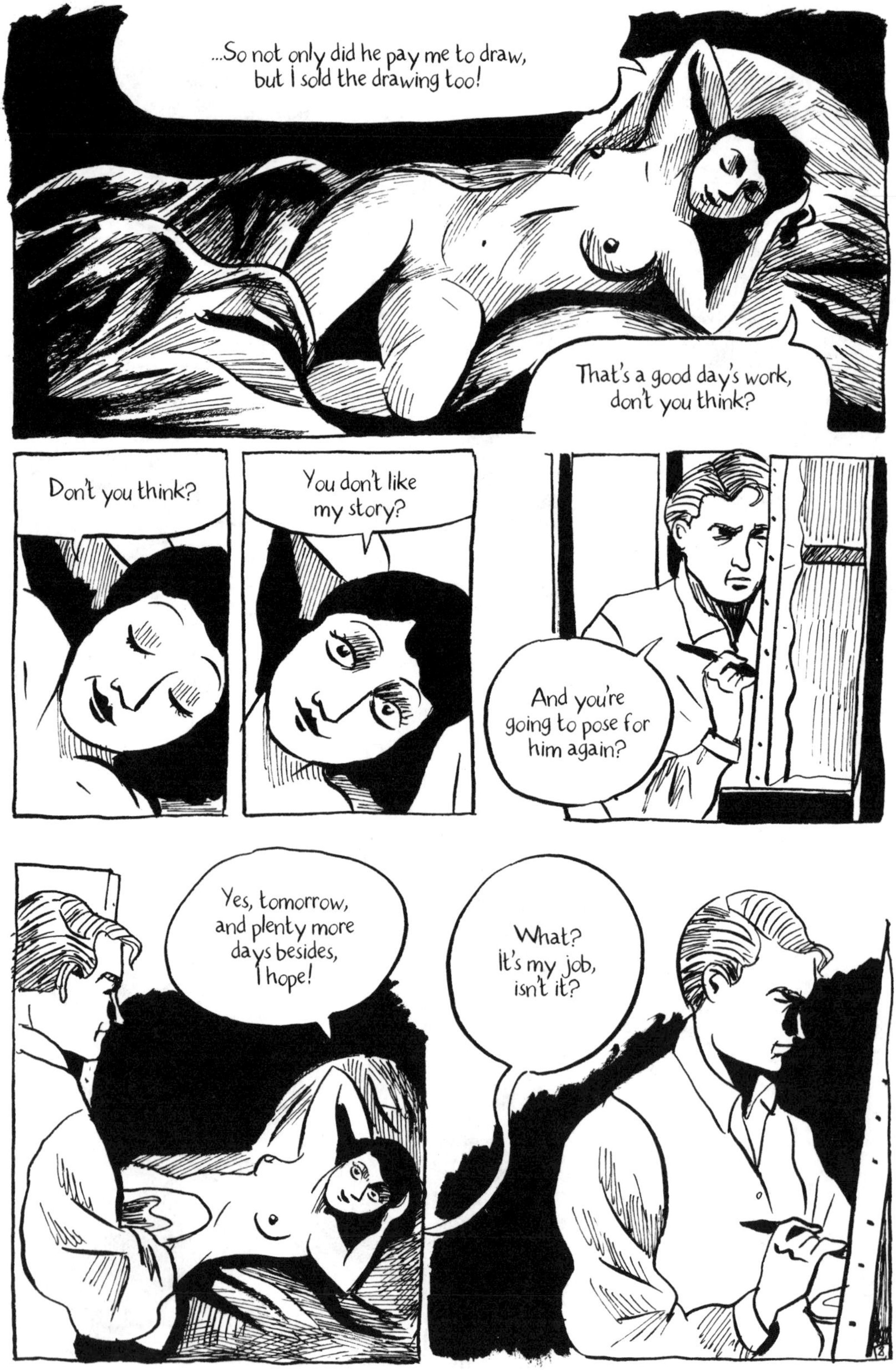
...So not only did he pay me to draw, but I sold the drawing too!
That's a good day's work, don't you think?
Don't you think?
You don't like my story?
And you're going to pose for him again?
Yes, tomorrow, and plenty more days besides, I hope!
What? It's my job, isn't it?

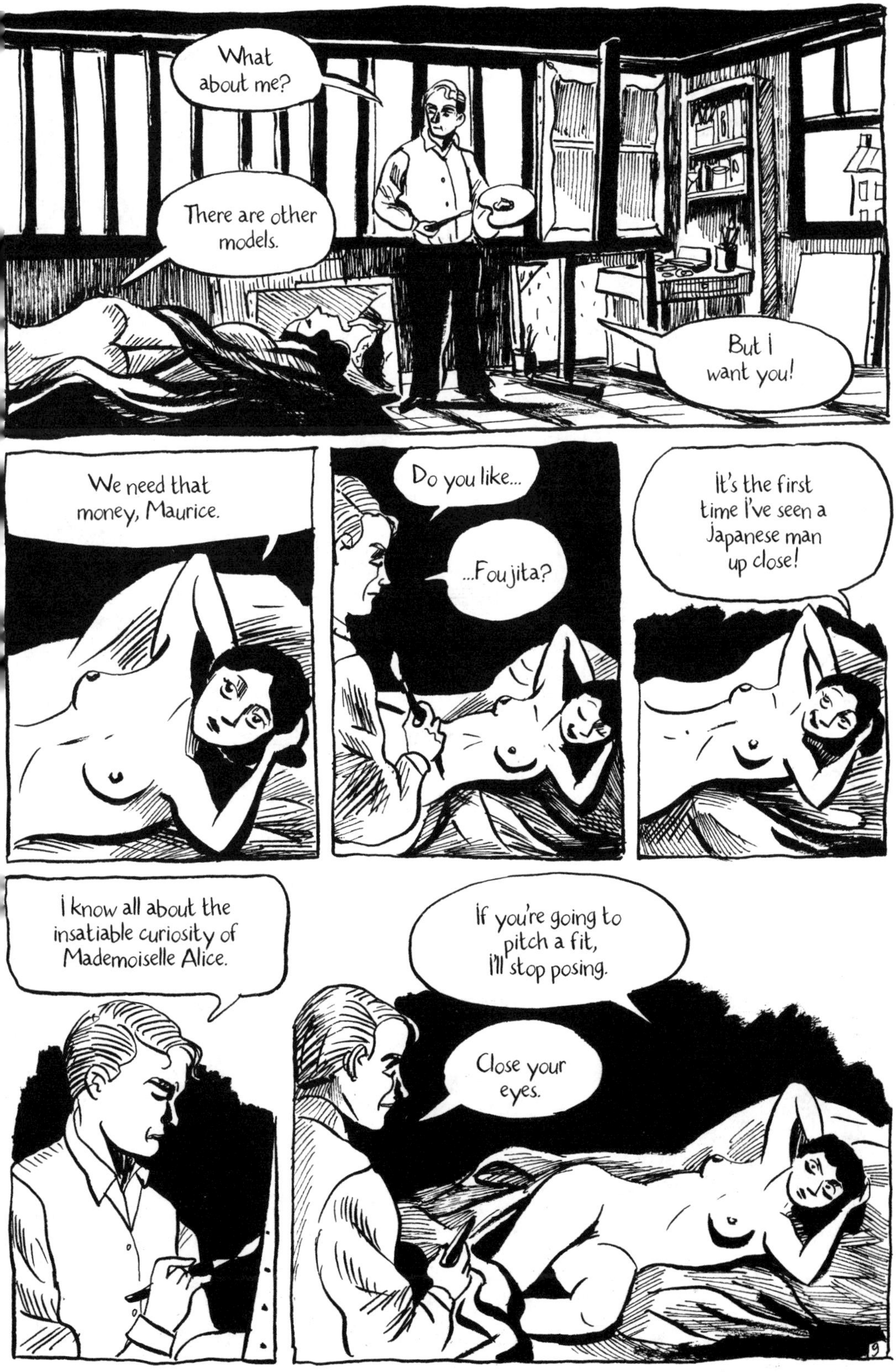
What about me?
There are other models.
But I want you!
We need that money, Maurice.
Do you like...
...Foujita?
It's the first time I've seen a Japanese man up close!
I know all about the insatiable curiosity of Mademoiselle Alice.
If you're going to pitch a fit, I'll stop posing.
Close your eyes.
9

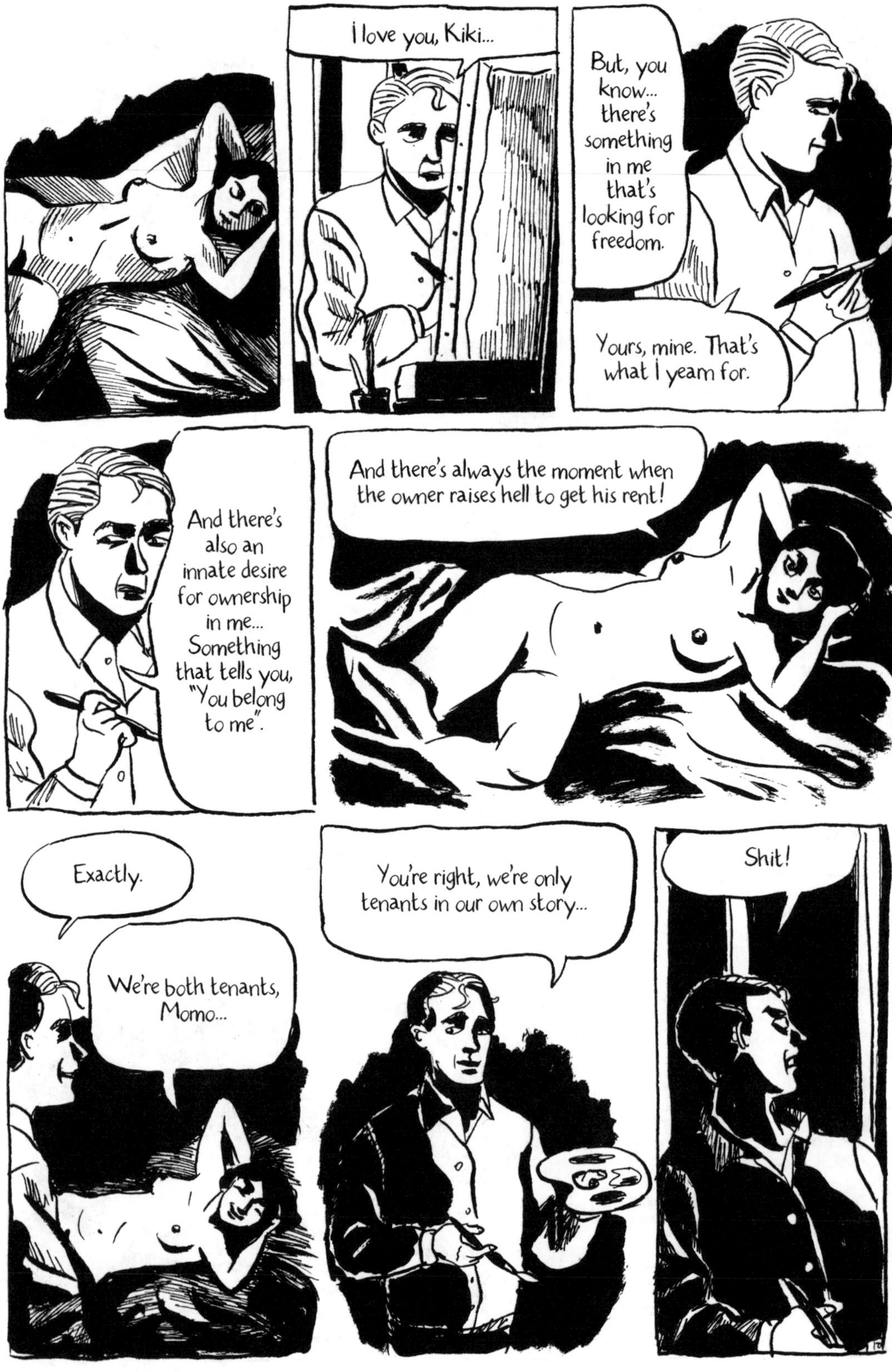
I love you, Kiki...
But, you know... there's something in me that's looking for freedom.
Yours, mine. That's what I yeam for.
And there's also an innate desire for ownership in me... Something that tells you, "You belong to me".
And there's always the moment when the owner raises hell to get his rent!
Exactly.
We're both tenants, Momo...
You're right, we're only tenants in our own story...
Shit!

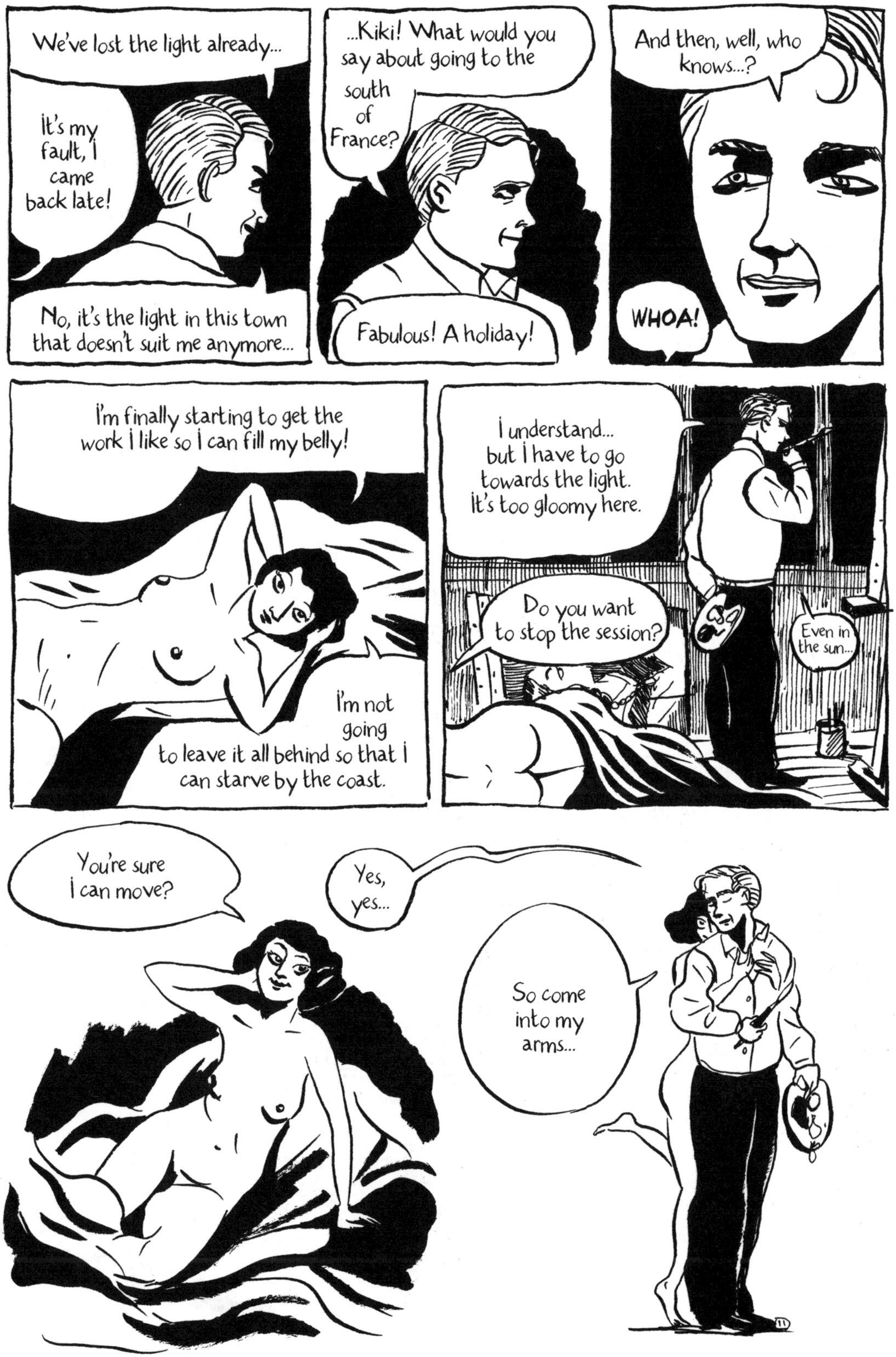
We've lost the light already...
It's my fault, I came back late!
No, it's the light in this town that doesn't suit me anymore...
...Kiki! What would you say about going to the south of France?
Fabulous! A holiday!
And then, well, who knows...?
WHOA!
I'm finally starting to get the work I like so I can fill my belly!
I'm not going to leave it all behind so that I can starve by the coast.
I understand... but I have to go towards the light. It's too gloomy here.
Do you want to stop the session?
Even in the sun...
You're sure I can move?
Yes, yes...
So come into my arms...

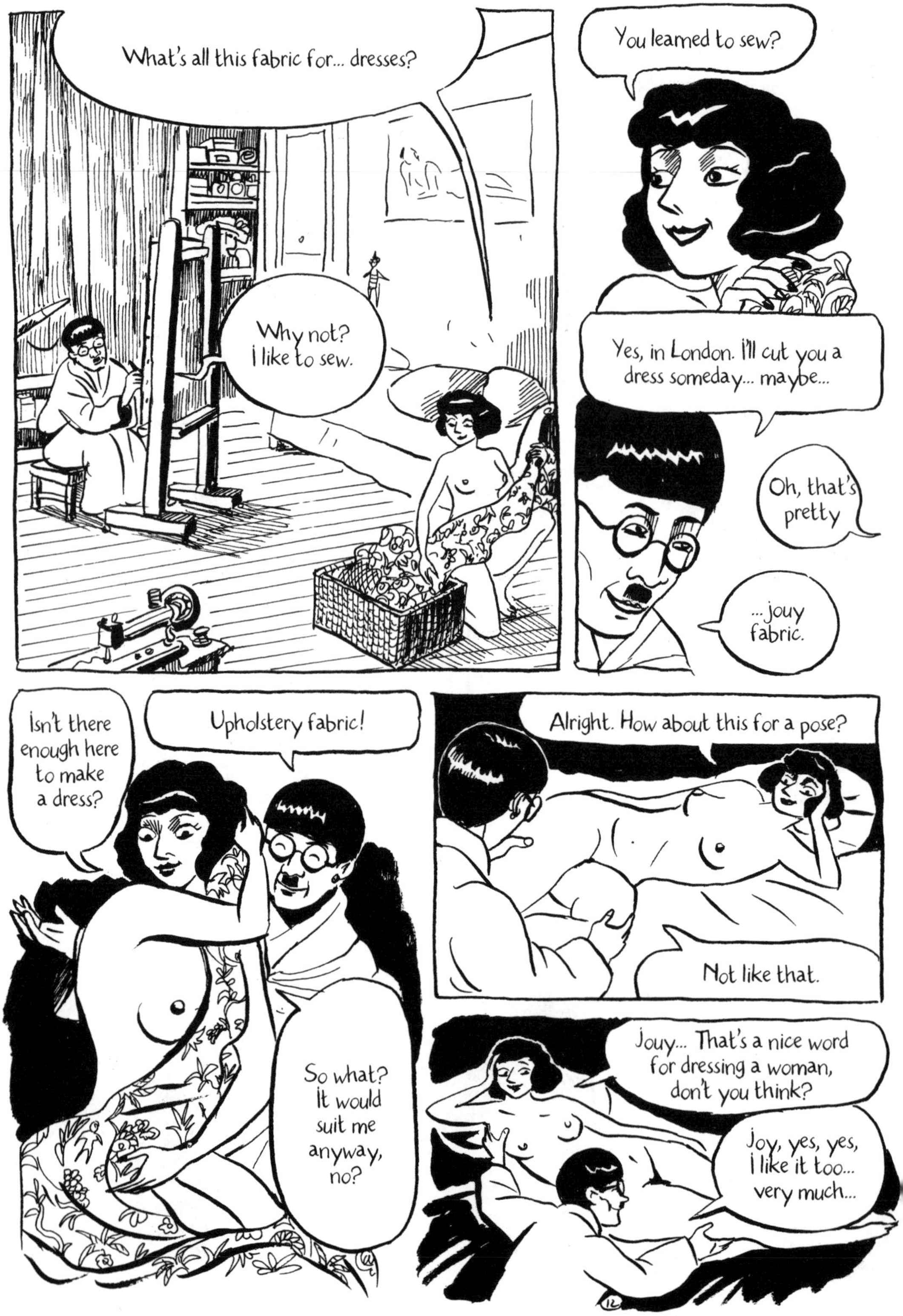
What's all this fabric for... dresses?
Why not? I like to sew.
You learned to sew?
Yes, in London. I'll cut you a dress someday... maybe...
Oh, that's pretty
...jouy fabric.
Isn't there enough here to make a dress?
Upholstery fabric!
So what? It would suit me anyway, no?
Alright. How about this for a pose?
Not like that.
Jouy... That's a nice word for dressing a woman, don't you think?
Joy, yes, yes, I like it too... very much...

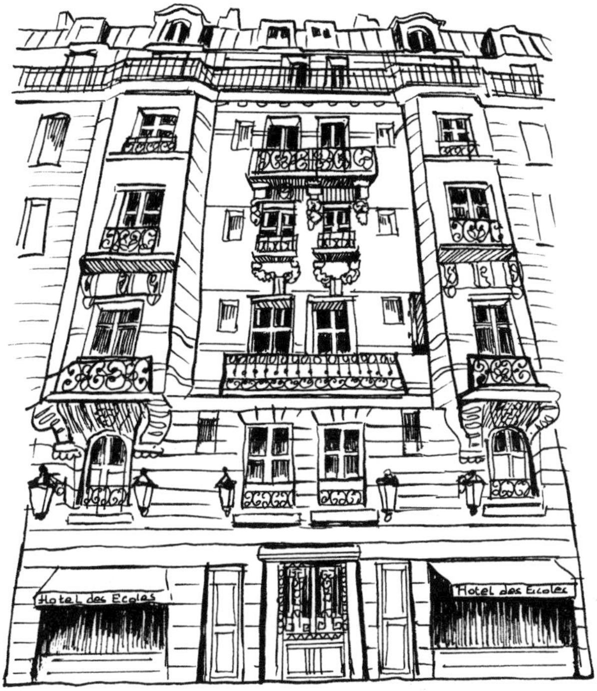
Hotel des Ecoles
Hotel des Ecoles

1922 - Grand Hôtel des Écoles, 15, rue Delambre

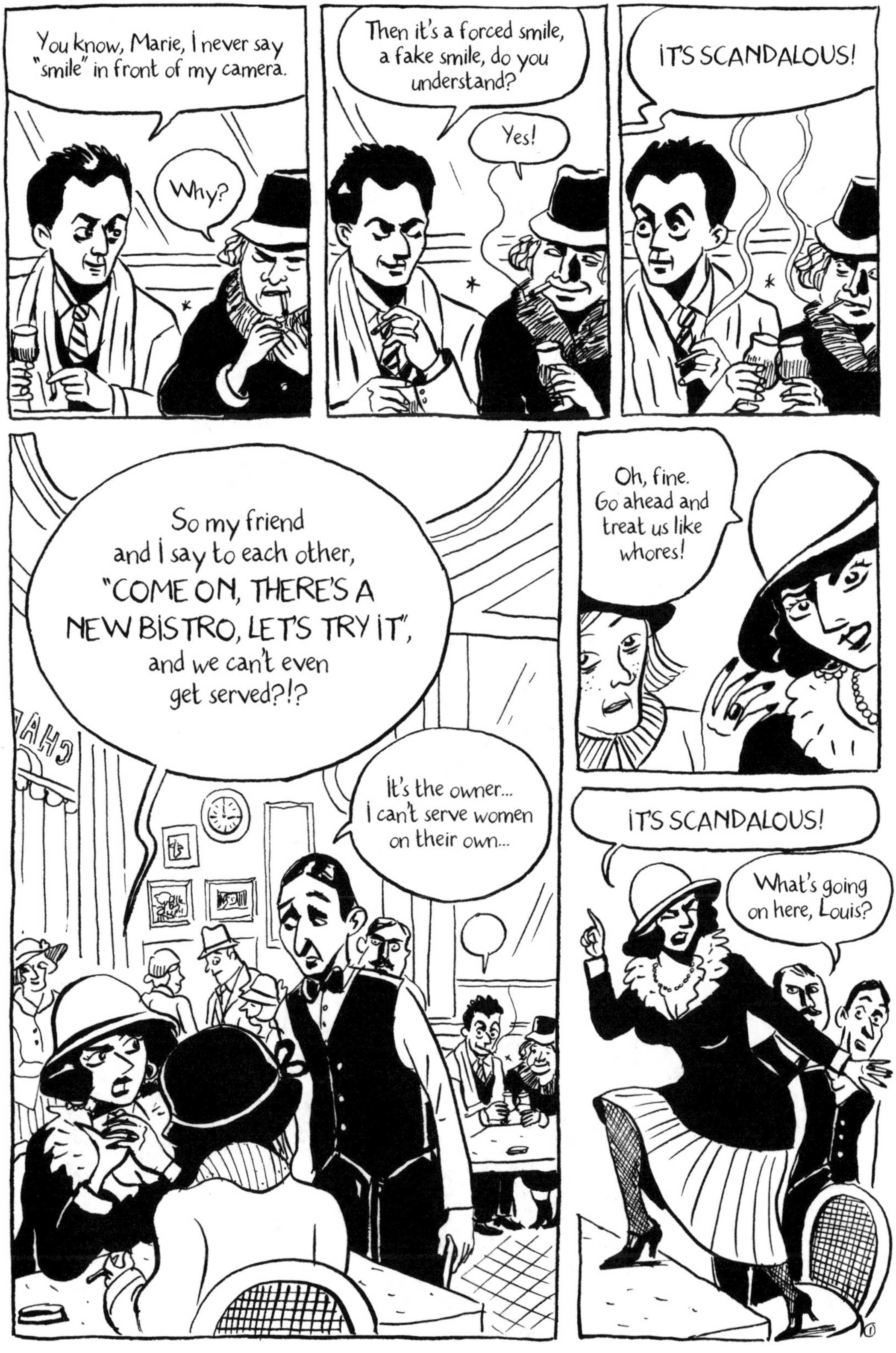
You know, Marie, I never say "smile" in front of my camera.
Why?
Then it's a forced smile, a fake smile, do you understand?
Yes!
IT'S SCANDALOUS!
So my friend and I say to each other, "COME ON, THERE'S A NEW BISTRO, LET'S TRY IT", and we can't even get served?!?
It's the owner... I can't serve women on their own...
Oh, fine. Go ahead and treat us like whores!
IT'S SCANDALOUS!
What's going on here, Louis?

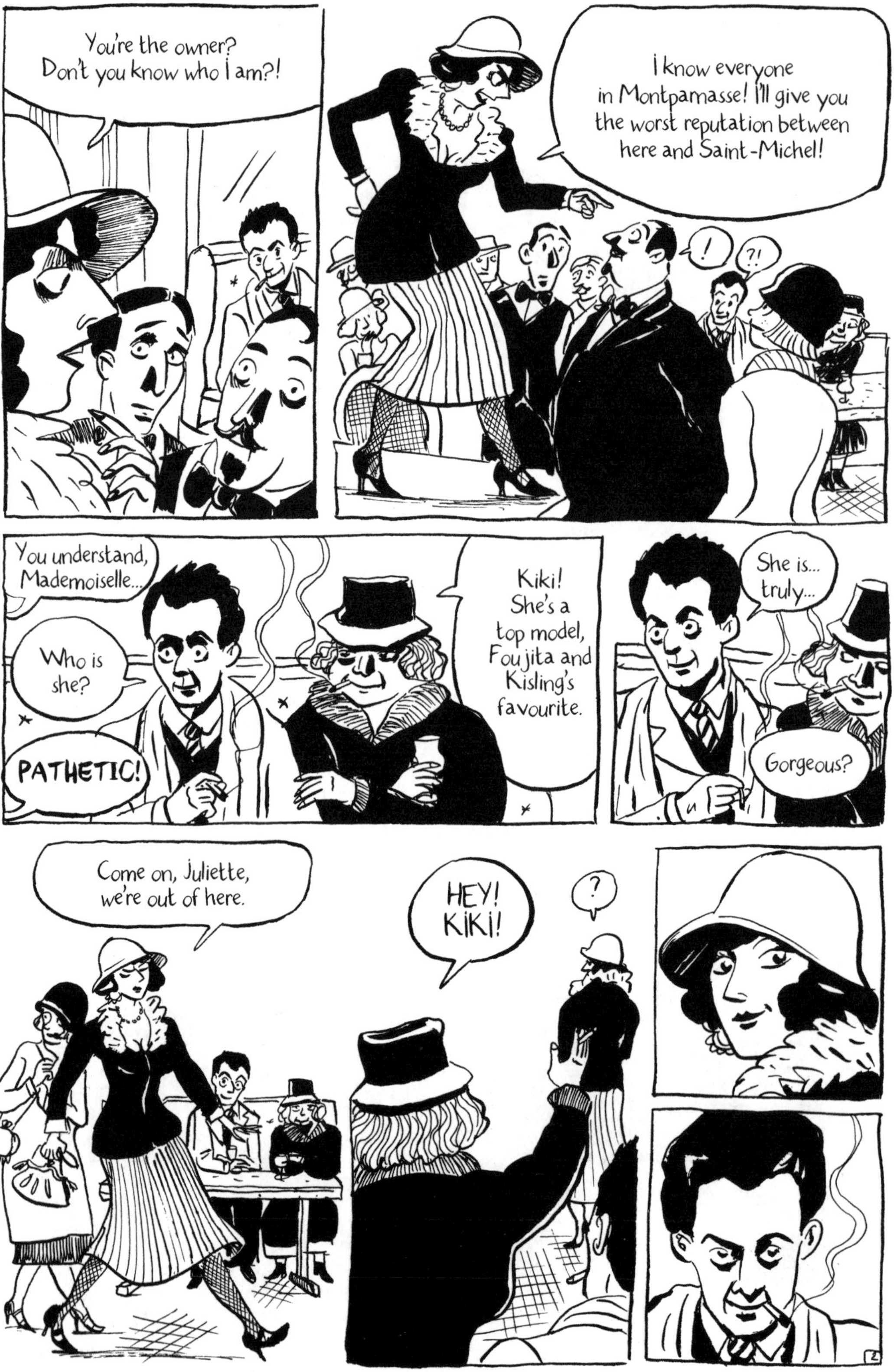
You're the owner? Don't you know who I am?!
I know everyone in Montpamasse! I'll give you the worst reputation between here and Saint-Michel!
!
?!
You understand, Mademoiselle...
Who is she?
PATHETIC!
Kiki! She's a top model, Foujita and Kisling's favourite.
She is... truly...
Gorgeous?
Come on, Juliette, we're out of here.
HEY! KIKI!
?

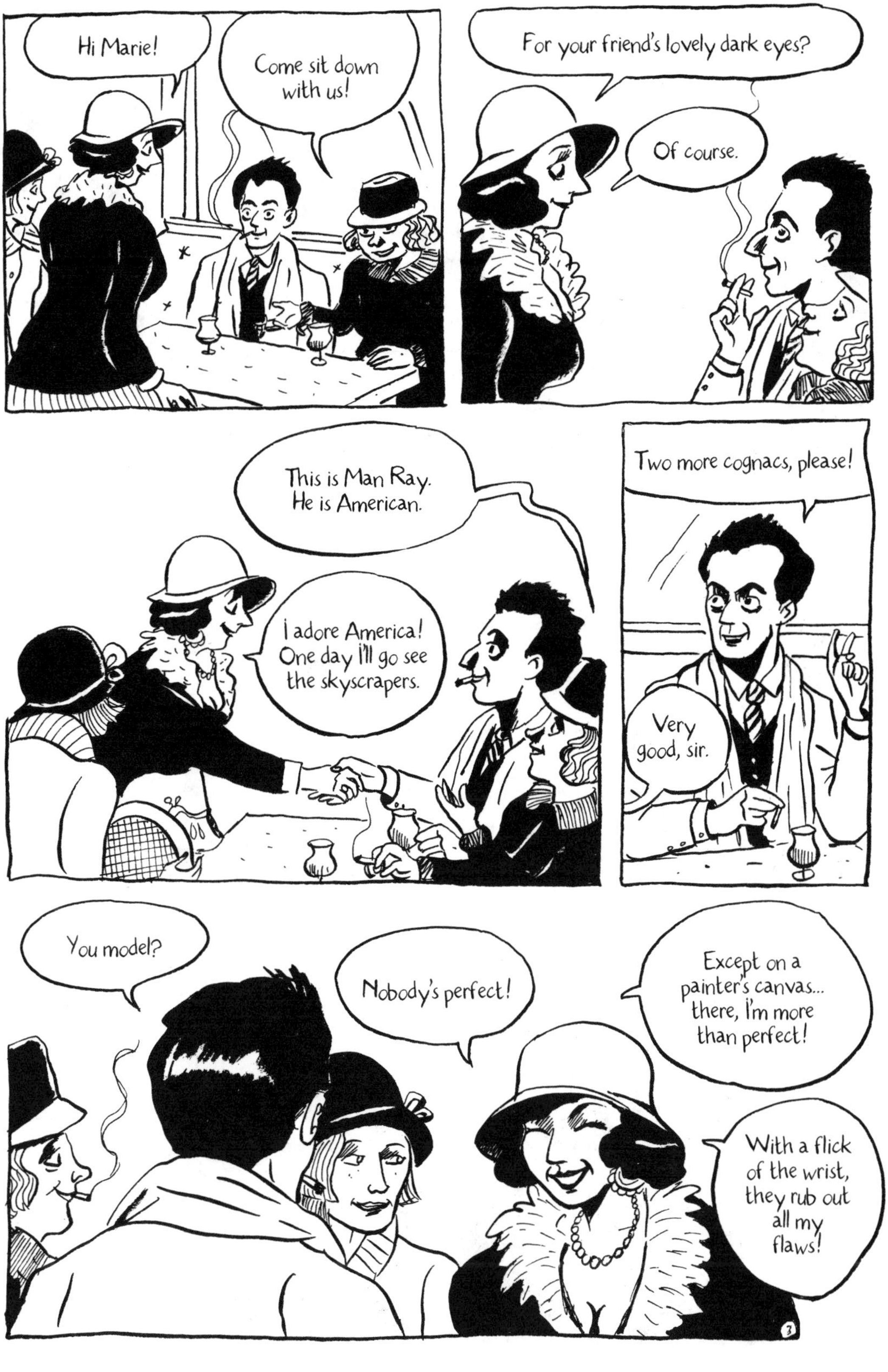
Hi Marie!
Come sit down with us!
For your friend's lovely dark eyes?
Of course.
This is Man Ray. He is American.
I adore America! One day I'll go see the skyscrapers.
Two more cognacs, please!
Very good, sir.
You model?
Nobody's perfect!
Except on a painter's canvas... there, I'm more than perfect!
With a flick of the wrist, they rub out all my flaws!

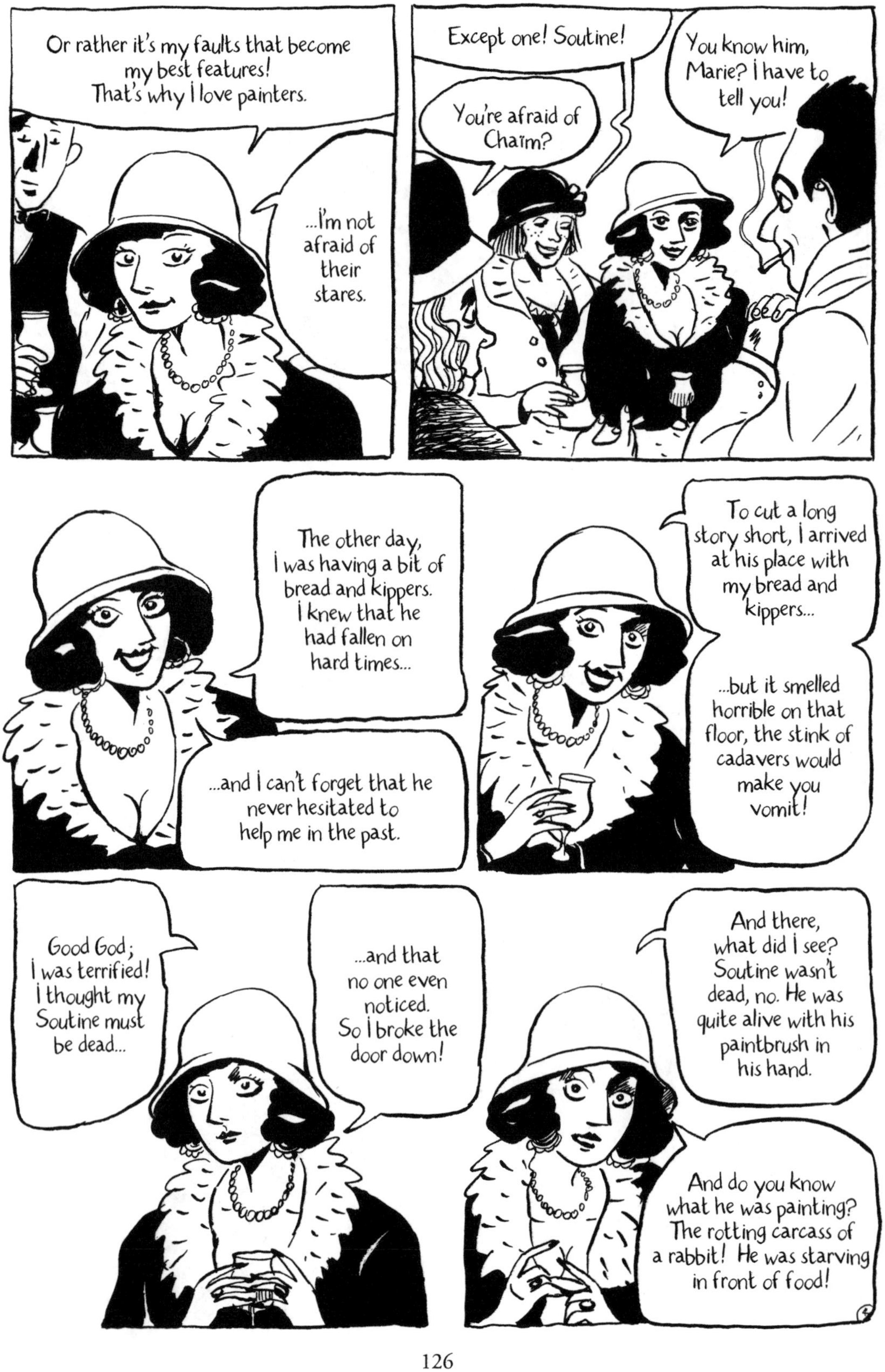
Or rather it's my faults that become my best features! That's why I love painters.
...I'm not afraid of their stares.
Except one! Soutine!
You're afraid of Chaïm?
You know him, Marie? I have to tell you!
The other day, I was having a bit of bread and kippers. I knew that he had fallen on hard times...
...and I can't forget that he never hesitated to help me in the past.
To cut a long story short, I arrived at his place with my bread and kippers...
...but it smelled horrible on that floor, the stink of cadavers would make you vomit!
Good God; I was terrified! I thought my Soutine must be dead...
...and that no one even noticed. So I broke the door down!
And there, what did I see? Soutine wasn't dead, no. He was quite alive with his paintbrush in his hand.
And do you know what he was painting? The rotting carcass of a rabbit! He was starving in front of food!

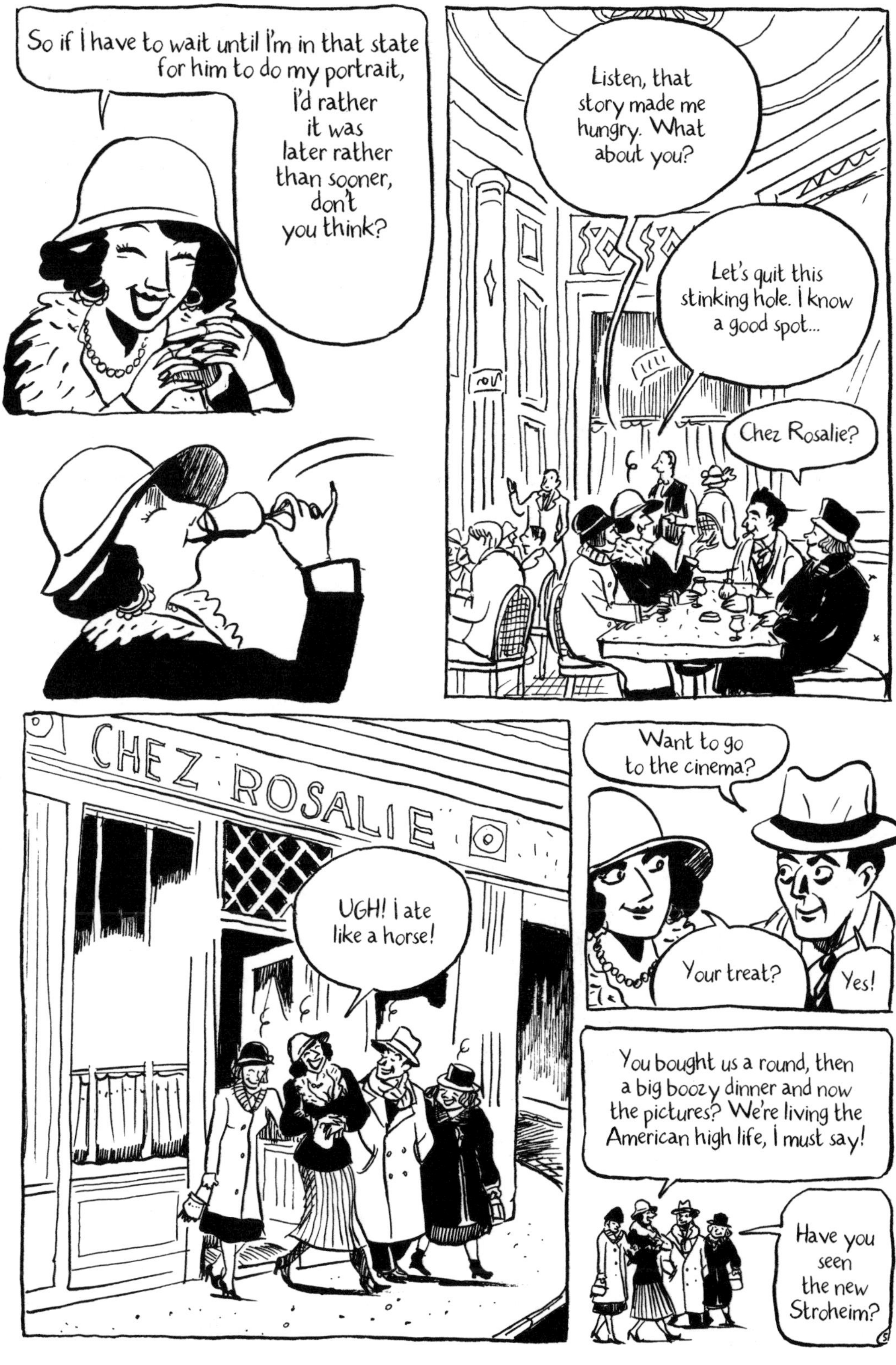
So if I have to wait until I'm in that state for him to do my portrait, I'd rather it was later rather than sooner, don't you think?
Listen, that story made me hungry. What about you?
Let's quit this stinking hole. I know a good spot...
Chez Rosalie?
CHEZ ROSALIE
UGH! I ate like a horse!
Want to go to the cinema?
Your treat?
Yes!
You bought us a round, then a big boozy dinner and now the pictures? We're living the American high life, I must say!
Have you seen the new Stroheim?

CARL LAEMMLE
présente

FOOLISH WIVES

de
Erich von Stroheim

MONTE CARLO, LAPPED BY THE WAVES OF THE MEDITERRANEAN AND ENVELOPED BY THE SMELLS OF PROVENCE. ROULETTE, POKER, BLACK JACK, KINGS, HUSTLERS... SYCOPHANTS AND SUICIDES, AND THE WAVES... ALWAYS THE WAVES...

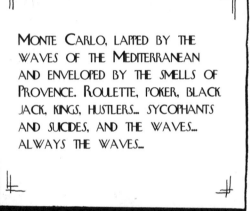

FOR THE AVERAGE AMERICAN, THE CODE OF HONOUR, WHETHER WRITTEN OR SPOKEN, DOESN'T EXIST, AND MEN PREFER THE CHASE TO DOLLARS. IN THIS BUSINESS BATTLE, SOMETIMES THEY FORGET THEIR BASIC VALUES...

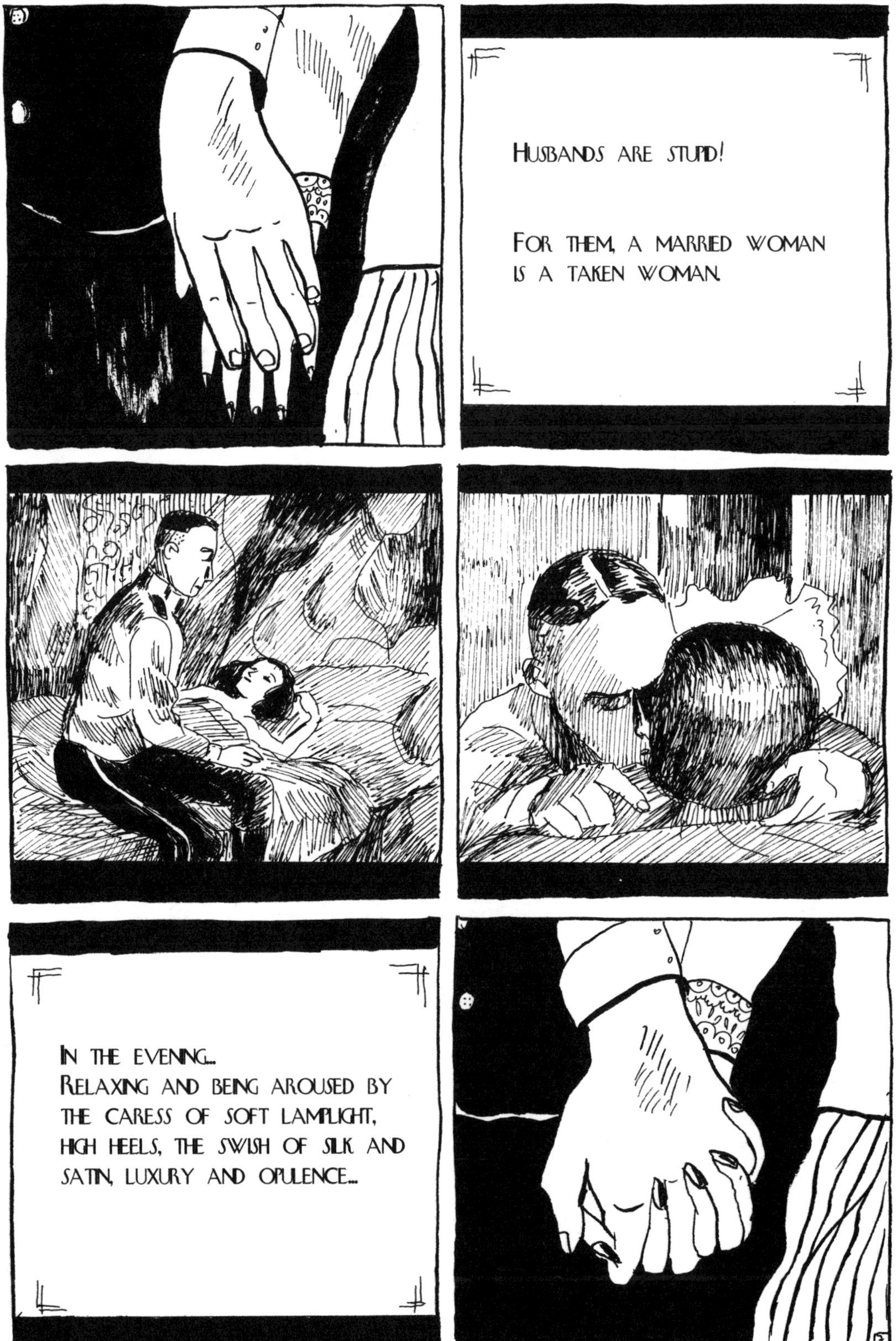
HUSBANDS ARE STUPID!
FOR THEM, A MARRIED WOMAN IS A TAKEN WOMAN.
IN THE EVENING...
RELAXING AND BEING AROUSED BY THE CARESS OF SOFT LAMPLIGHT, HIGH HEELS, THE SWISH OF SILK AND SATIN, LUXURY AND OPULENCE...

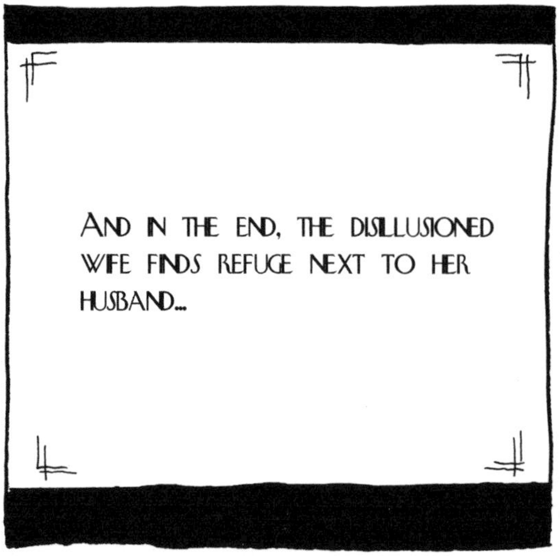
AND IN THE END, THE DISILLUSIONED WIFE FINDS REFUGE NEXT TO HER HUSBAND...

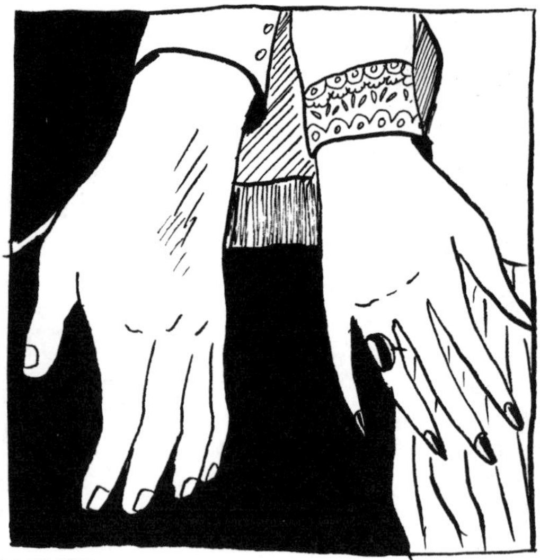

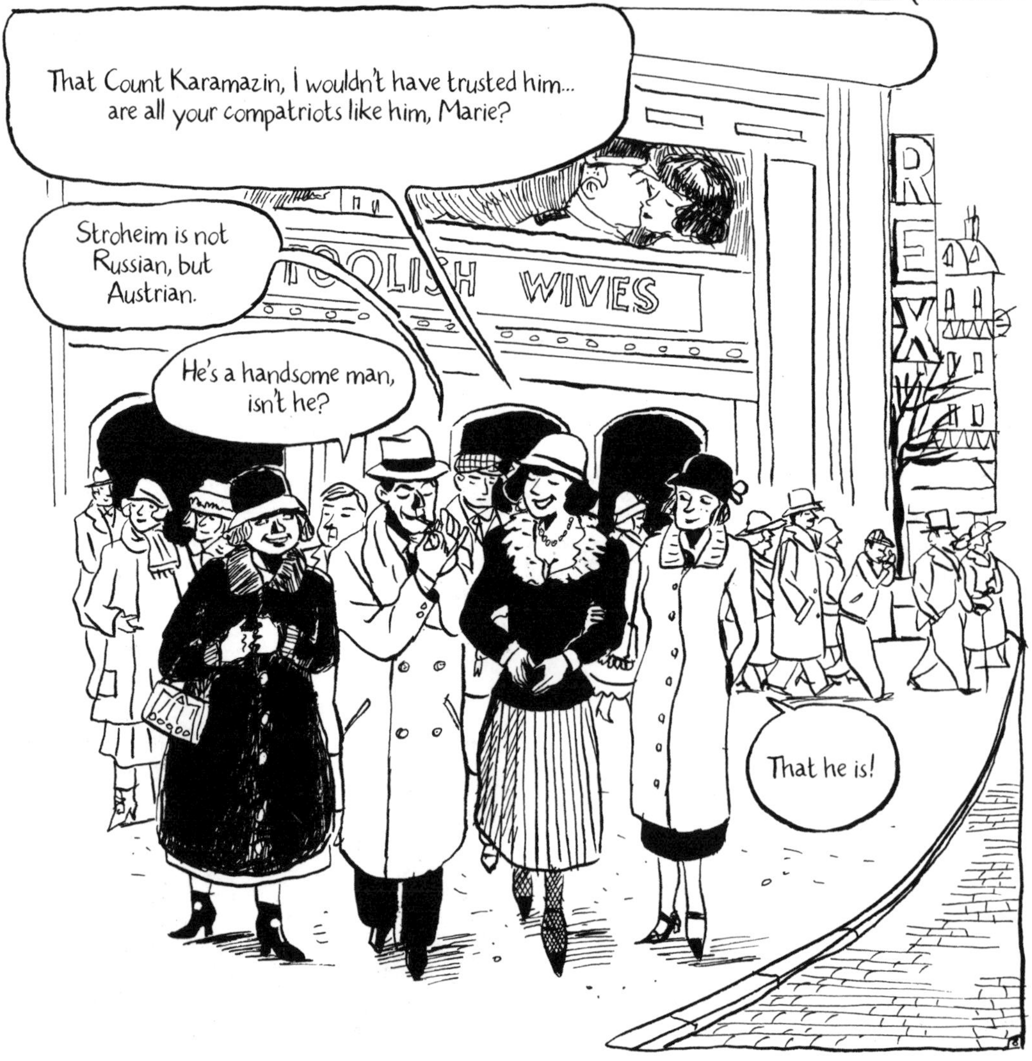
That Count Karamazin, I wouldn't have trusted him... are all your compatriots like him, Marie?
Stroheim is not Russian, but Austrian.
FOOLISH WIVES
REX
He's a handsome man, isn't he?
That he is!

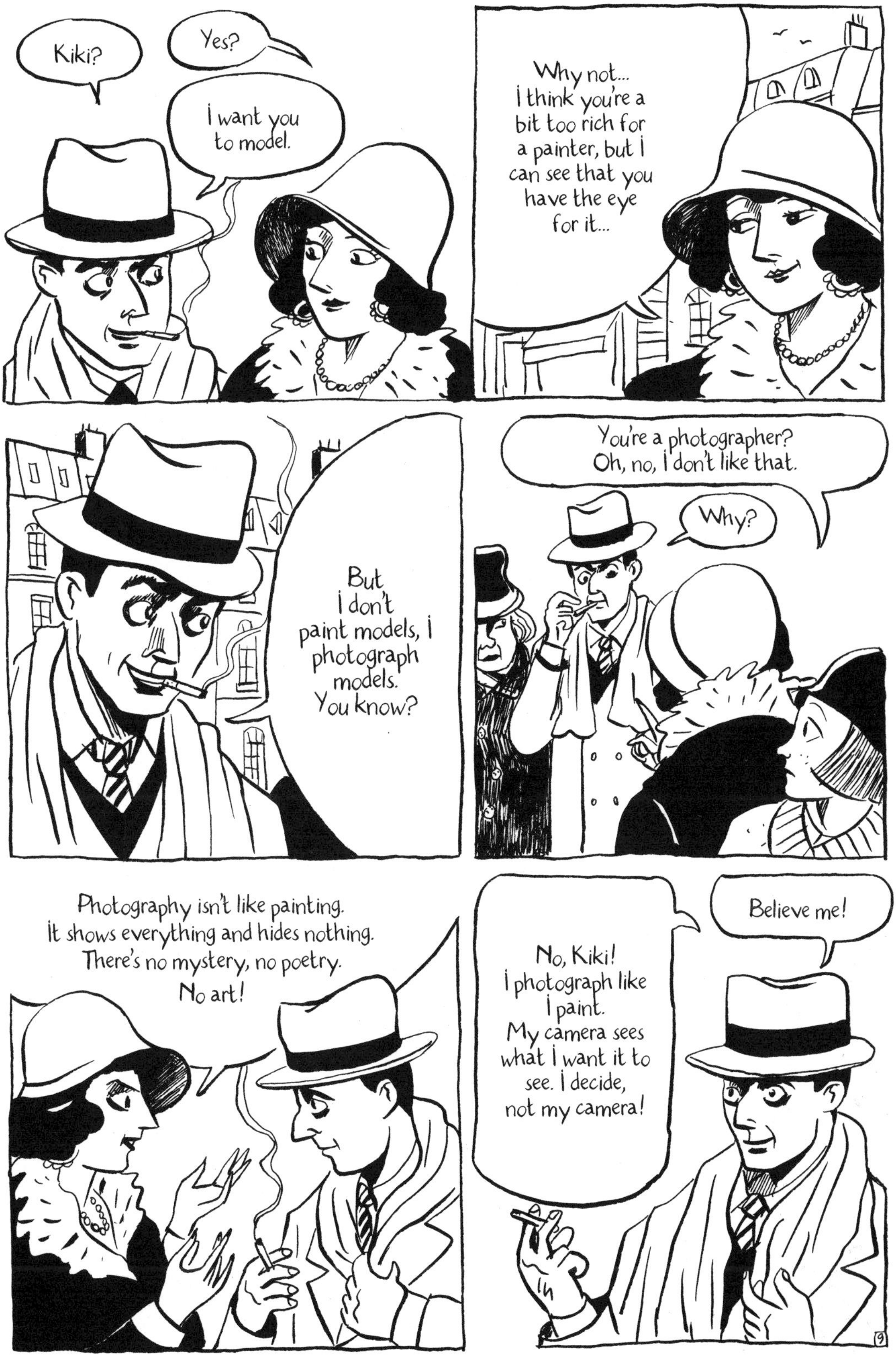
Kiki?
Yes?
I want you to model.
Why not... I think you're a bit too rich for a painter, but I can see that you have the eye for it...
But I don't paint models, I photograph models. You know?
You're a photographer? Oh, no, I don't like that.
Why?
Photography isn't like painting. It shows everything and hides nothing. There's no mystery, no poetry. No art!
No, Kiki! I photograph like I paint. My camera sees what I want it to see. I decide, not my camera!
Believe me!
9

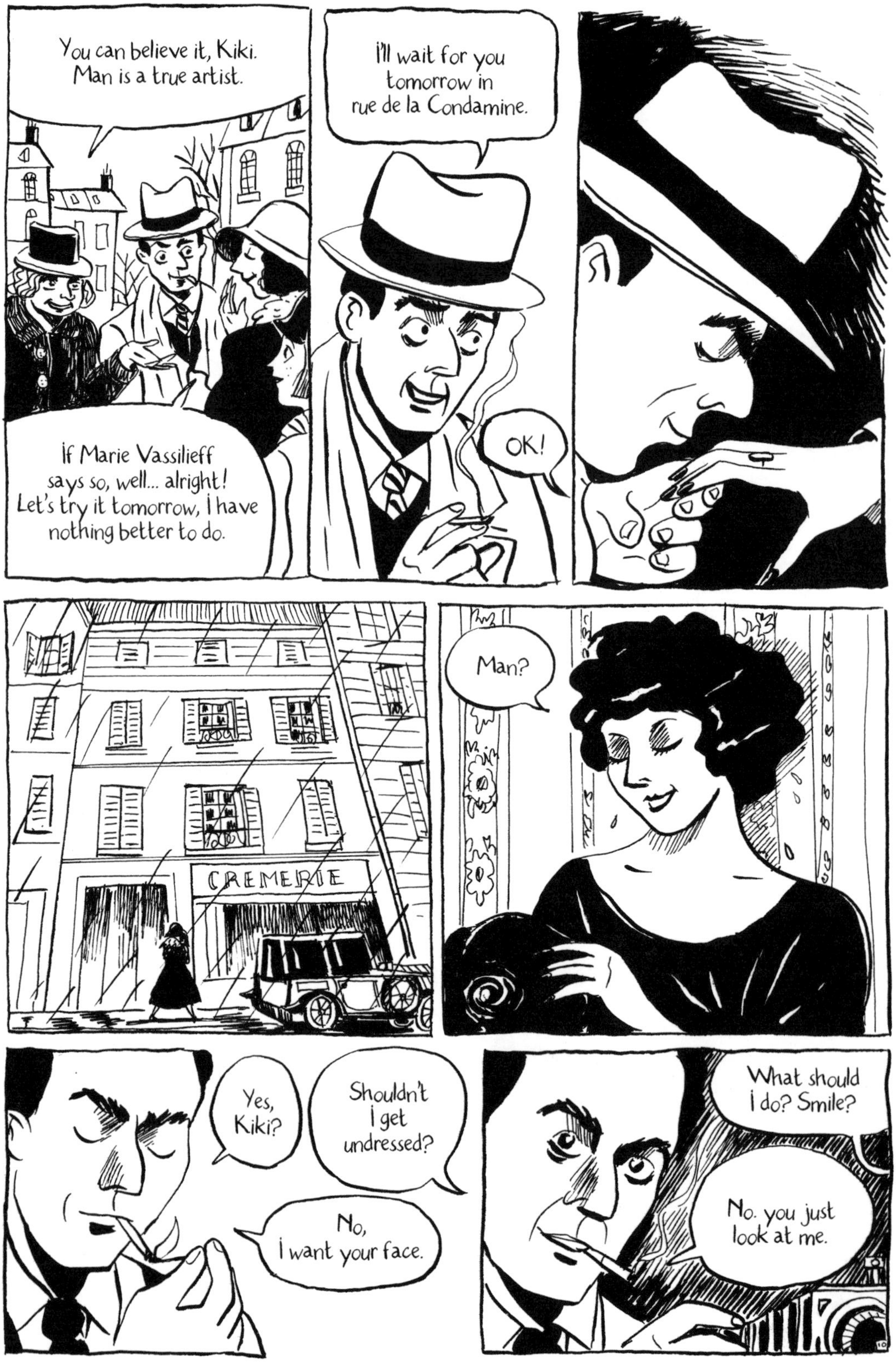
You can believe it, Kiki. Man is a true artist.
If Marie Vassilieff says so, well... alright! Let's try it tomorrow, I have nothing better to do.
I'll wait for you tomorrow in rue de la Condamine.
OK!
CREMERIE
Man?
Yes, Kiki?
Shouldn't I get undressed?
No, I want your face.
What should I do? Smile?
No. you just look at me.

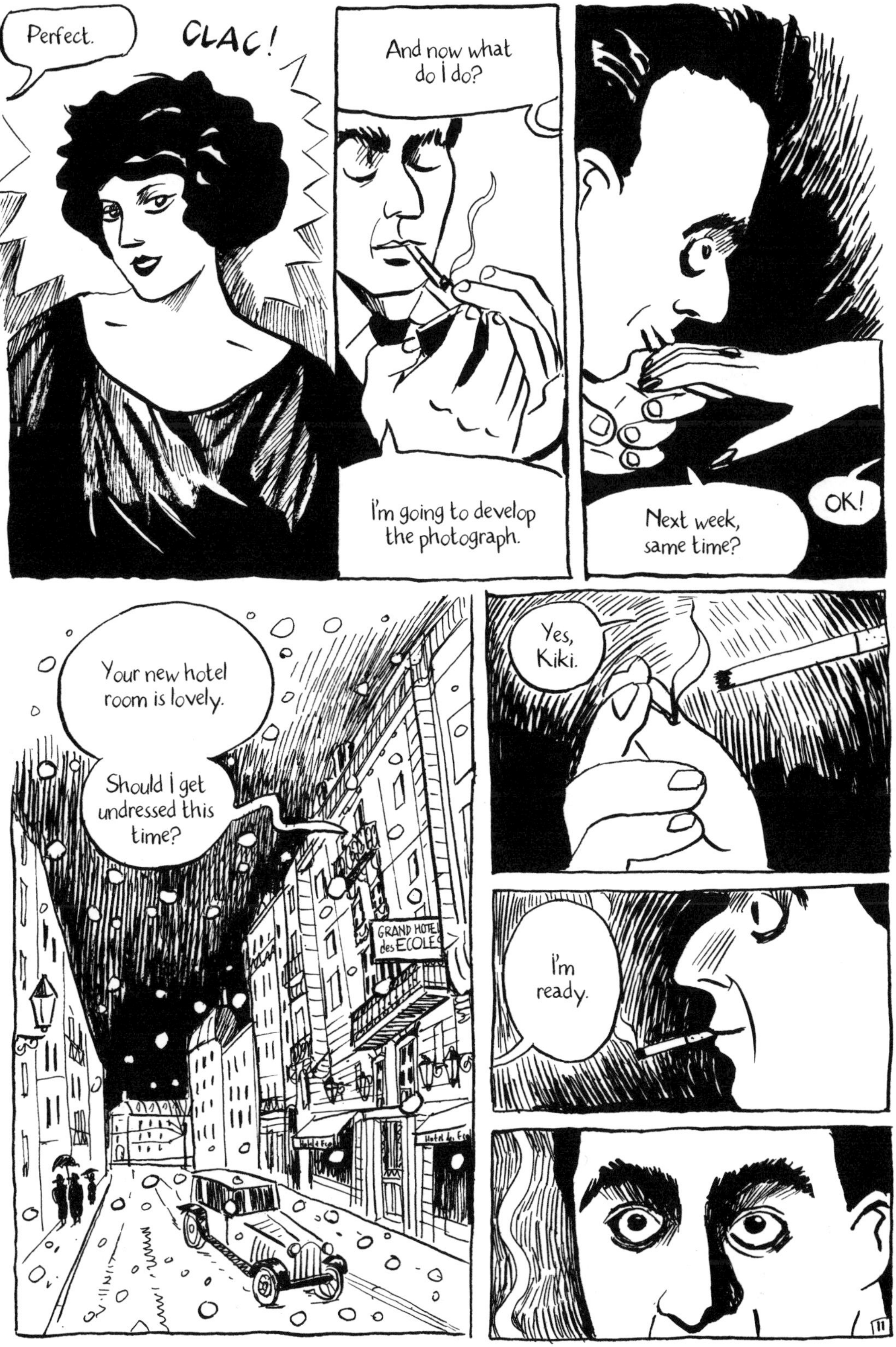

Perfect.
CLAC!
And now what do I do?
I'm going to develop the photograph.
Next week, same time?
OK!
Your new hotel room is lovely.
Should I get undressed this time?
GRAND HOTEL des ECOLES
Yes, Kiki.
I'm ready.

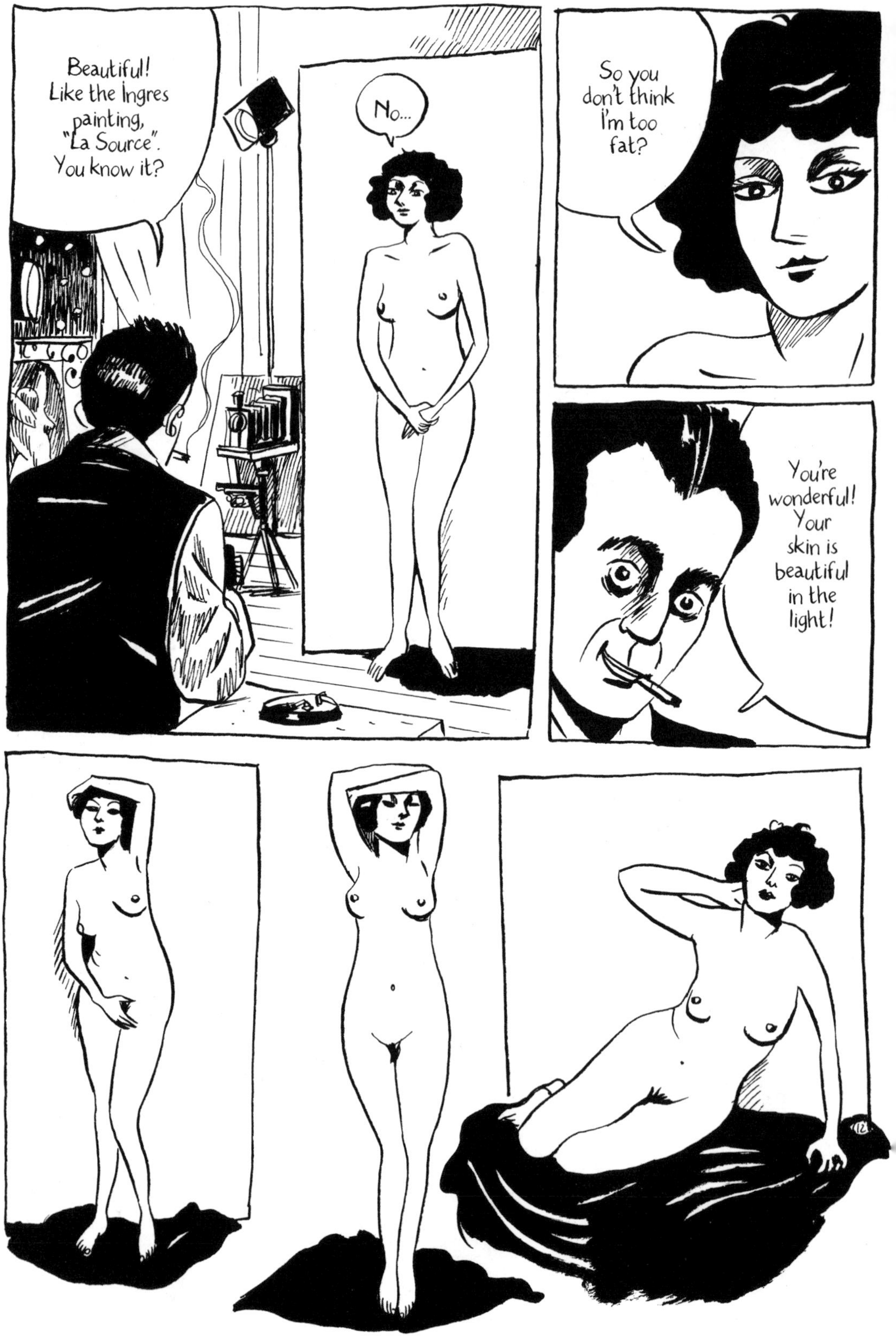
Beautiful! Like the Ingres painting, "La Source". You know it?
No...
So you don't think I'm too fat?
You're wonderful! Your skin is beautiful in the light!

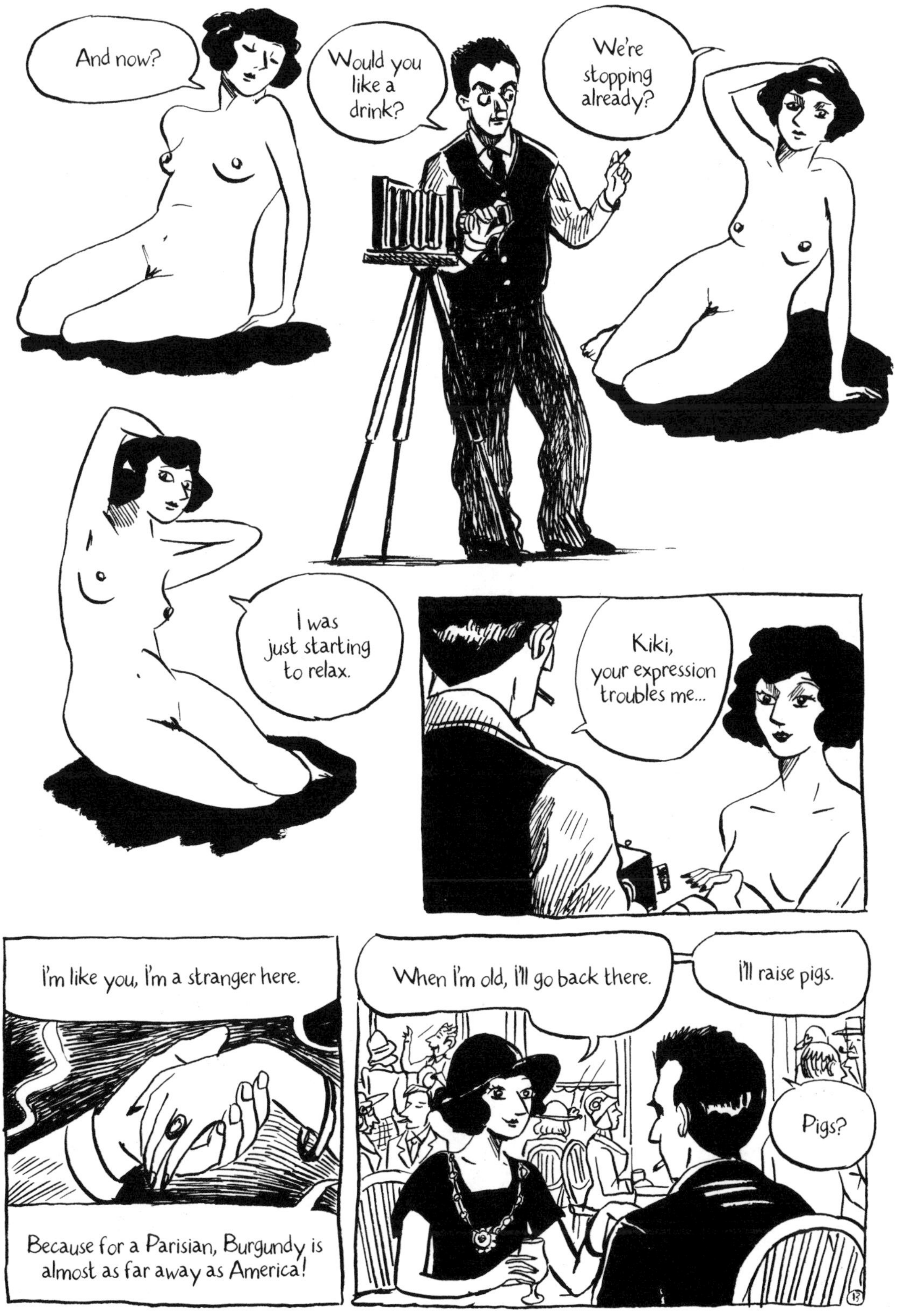
And now?
Would you like a drink?
We're stopping already?
I was just starting to relax.
Kiki, your expression troubles me...
I'm like you, I'm a stranger here.
Because for a Parisian, Burgundy is almost as far away as America!
When I'm old, I'll go back there.
I'll raise pigs.
Pigs?

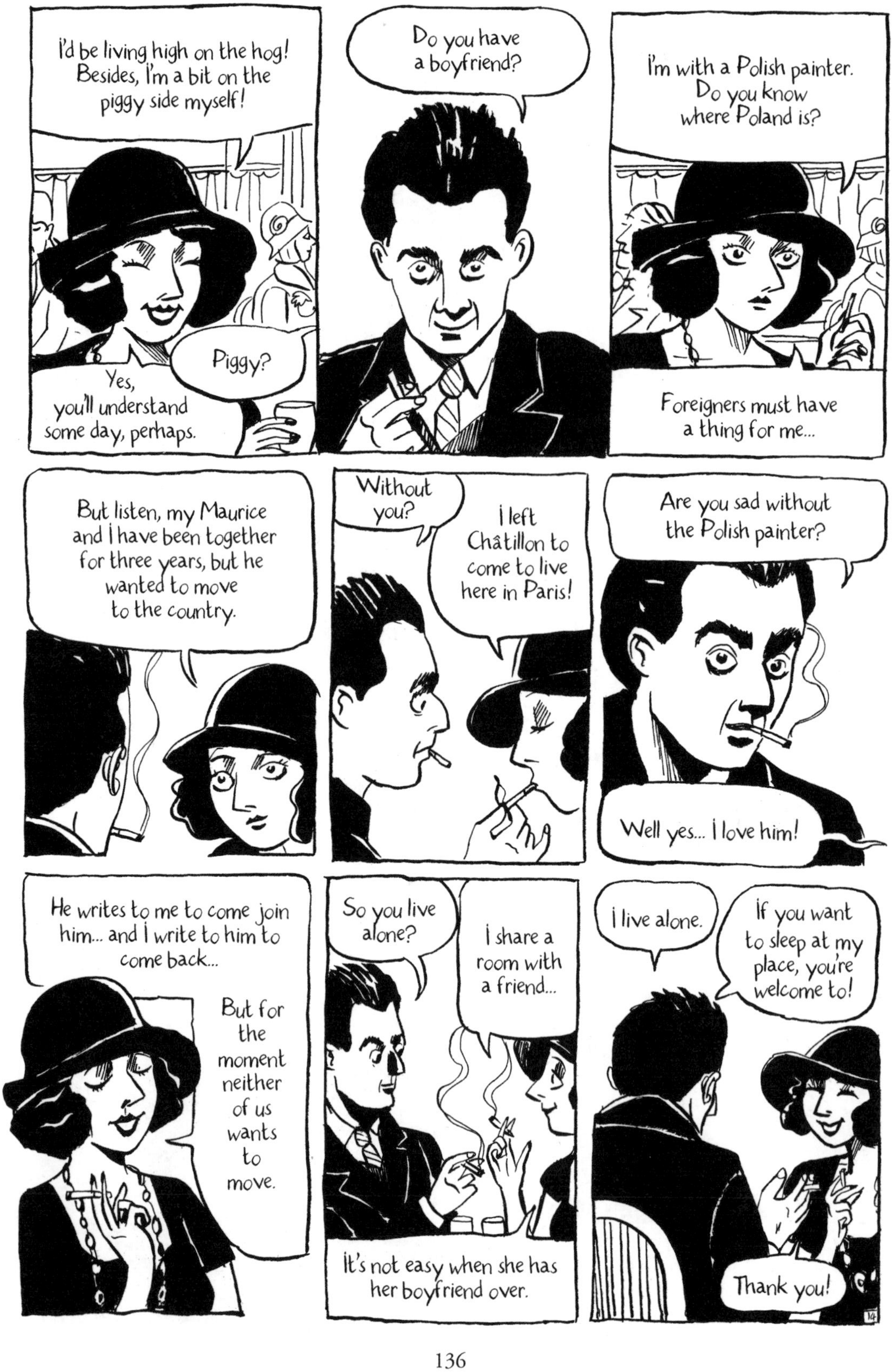
I'd be living high on the hog! Besides, I'm a bit on the piggy side myself!
Piggy?
Yes, you'll understand some day, perhaps.
Do you have a boyfriend?
I'm with a Polish painter. Do you know where Poland is?
Foreigners must have a thing for me...
But listen, my Maurice and I have been together for three years, but he wanted to move to the country.
Without you?
I left Châtillon to come to live here in Paris!
Are you sad without the Polish painter?
Well yes... I love him!
He writes to me to come join him... and I write to him to come back...
But for the moment neither of us wants to move.
So you live alone?
I share a room with a friend...
It's not easy when she has her boyfriend over.
I live alone.
If you want to sleep at my place, you're welcome to!
Thank you!
14

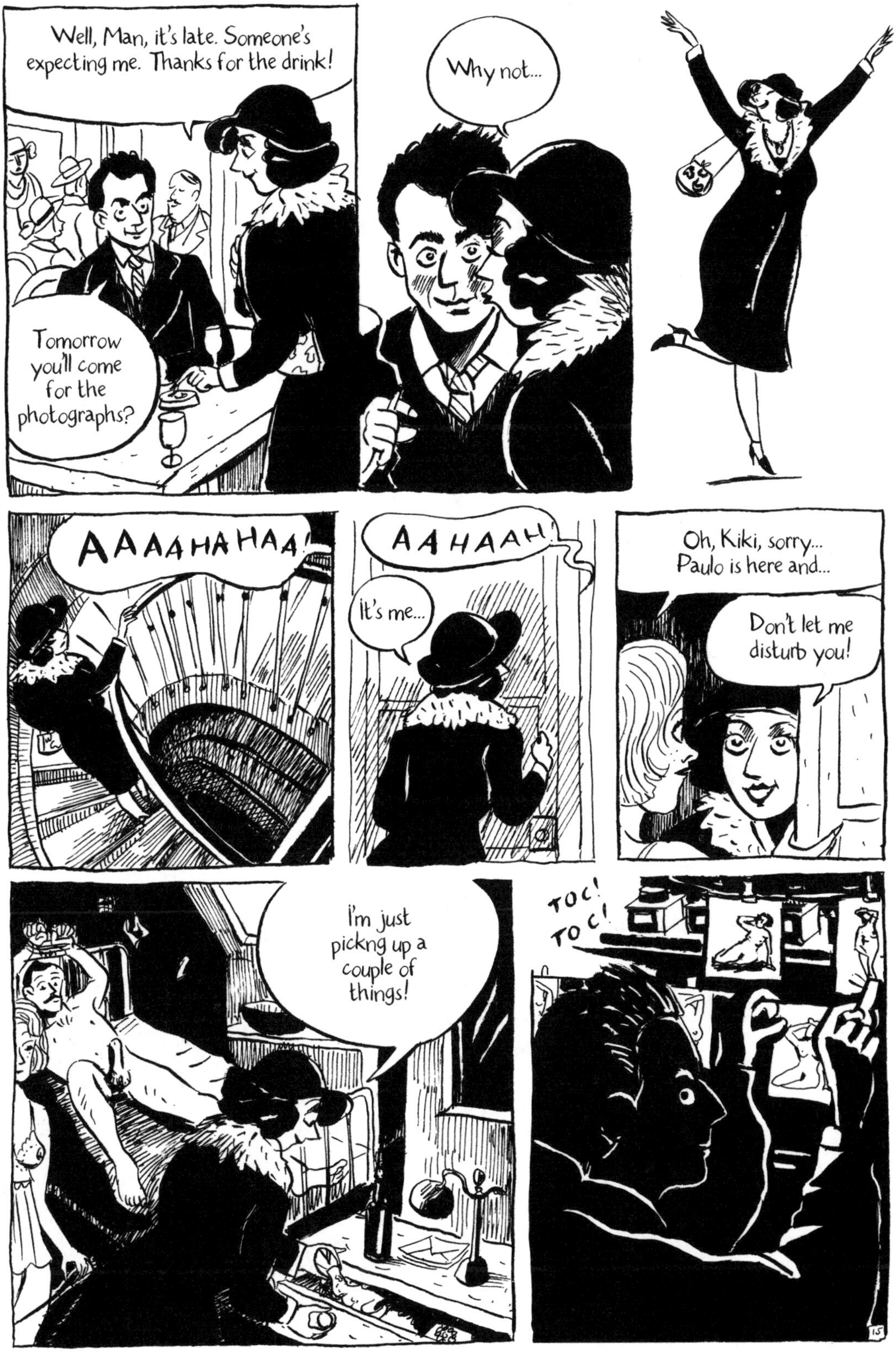

Well, Man, it's late. Someone's expecting me. Thanks for the drink!
Tomorrow you'll come for the photographs?
Why not...
AAAAHAHAA!
AAHAAH!
It's me...
Oh, Kiki, sorry... Paulo is here and...
Don't let me disturb you!
I'm just pickng up a couple of things!
TOC! TOC!
15

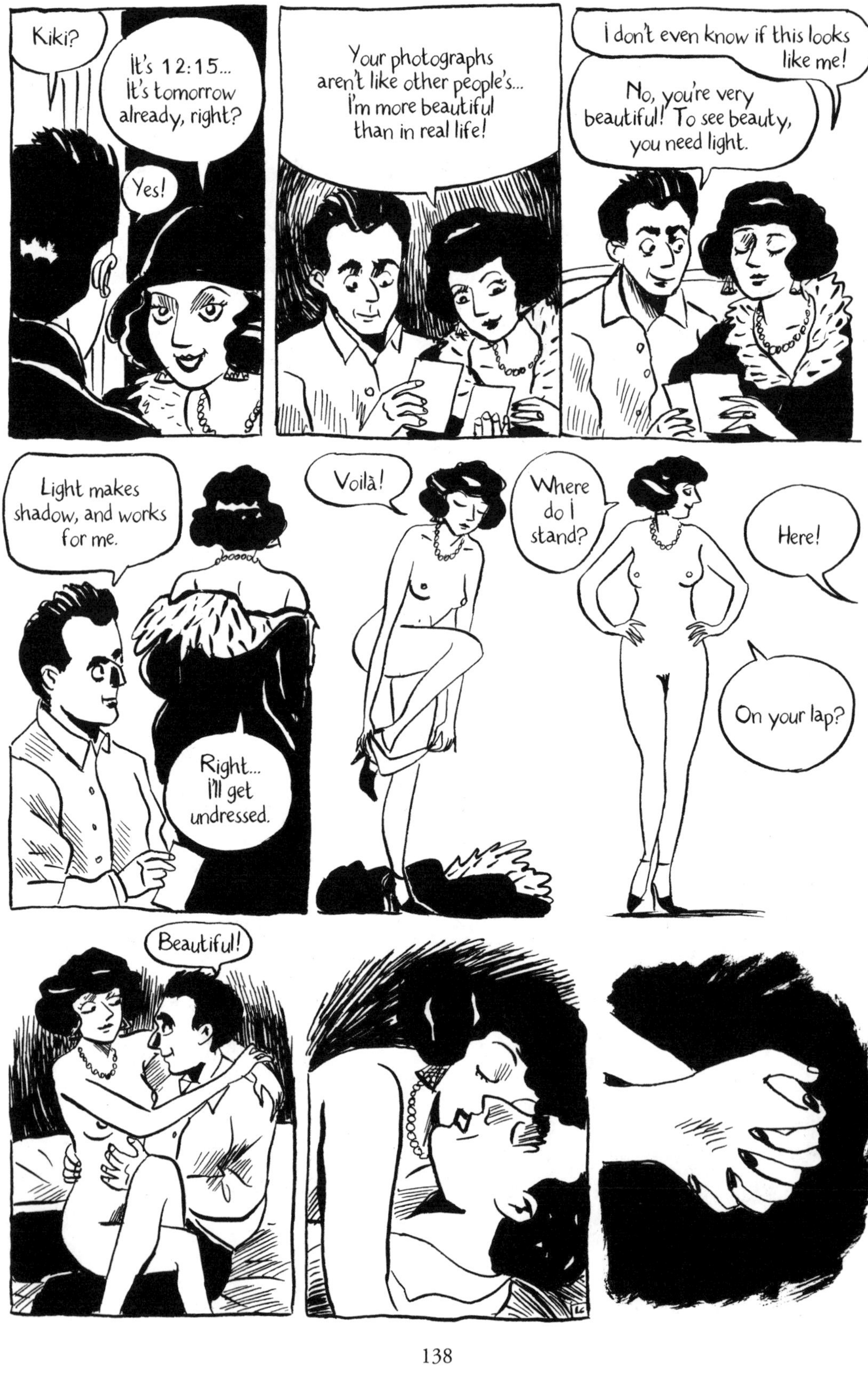
Kiki?
It's 12:15... It's tomorrow already, right?
Yes!
Your photographs aren't like other people's... I'm more beautiful than in real life!
I don't even know if this looks like me!
No, you're very beautiful! To see beauty, you need light.
Light makes shadow, and works for me.
Right... I'll get undressed.
Voilà!
Where do I stand?
Here!
On your lap?
Beautiful!

1922 - 23, rue La Boétie

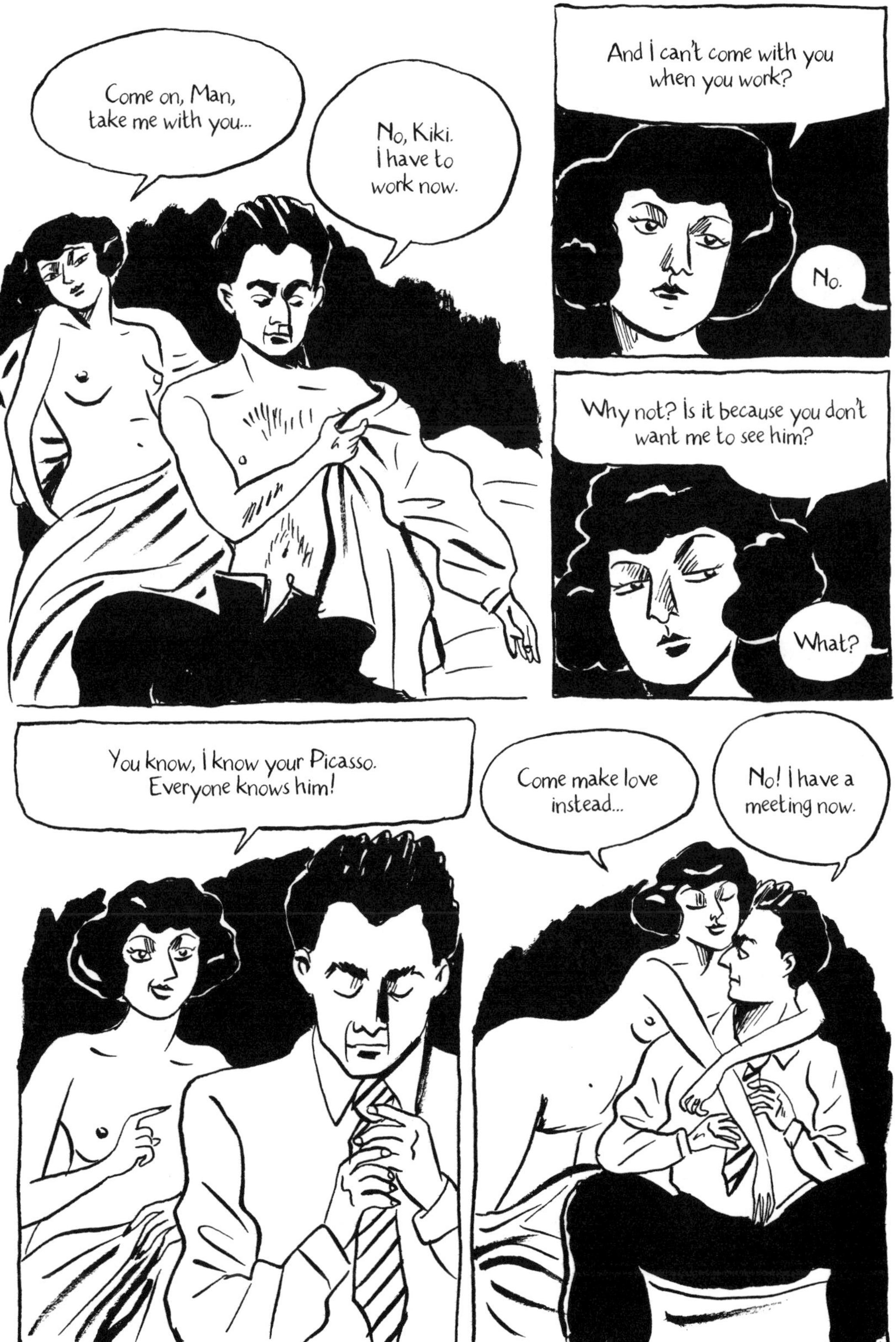
Come on, Man, take me with you...
No, Kiki. I have to work now.
And I can't come with you when you work?
No.
Why not? Is it because you don't want me to see him?
What?
You know, I know your Picasso. Everyone knows him!
Come make love instead...
No! I have a meeting now.

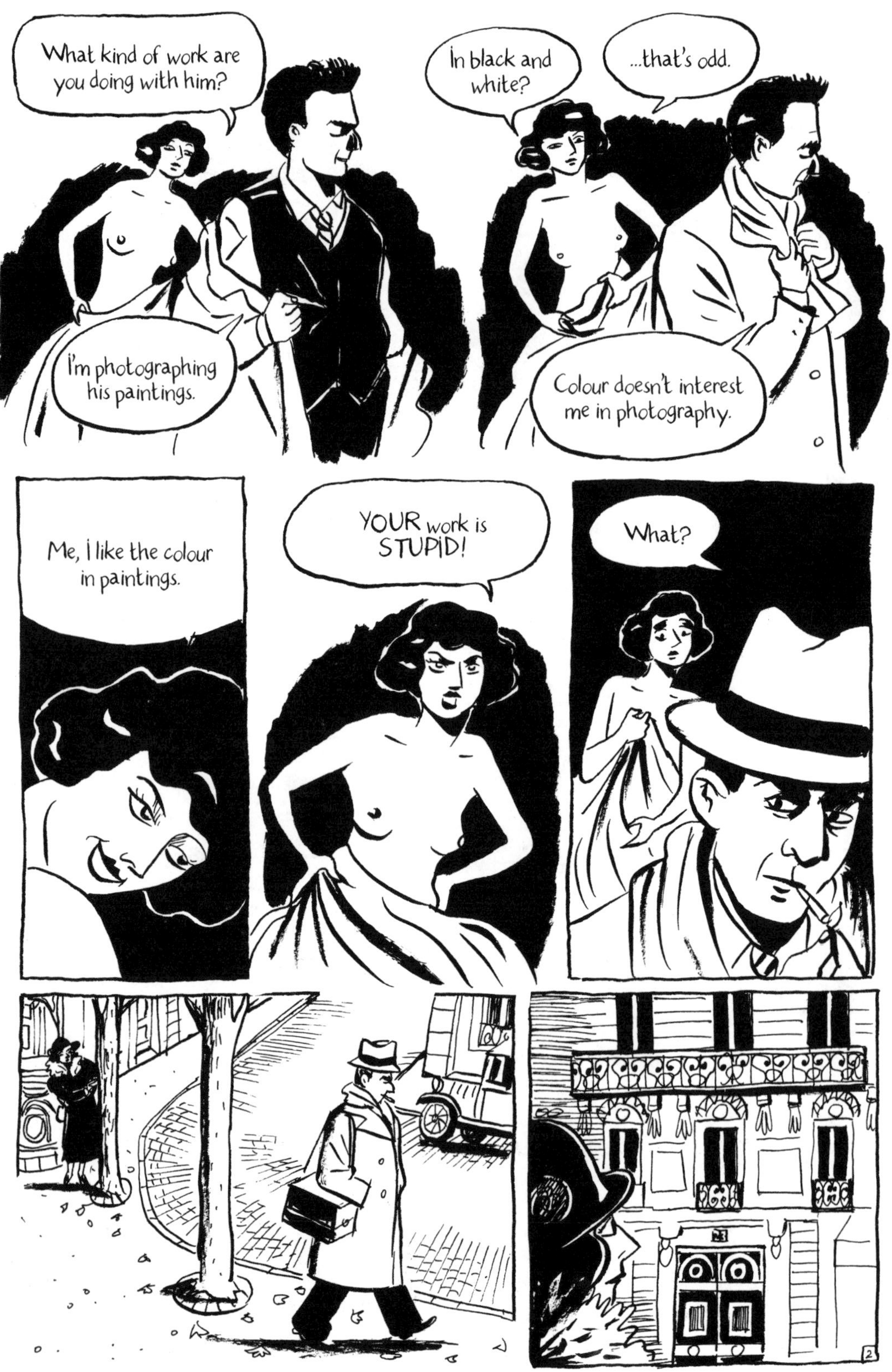
What kind of work are you doing with him?
I'm photographing his paintings.
In black and white?
...that's odd.
Colour doesn't interest me in photography.
Me, I like the colour in paintings.
YOUR work is STUPID!
What?
2

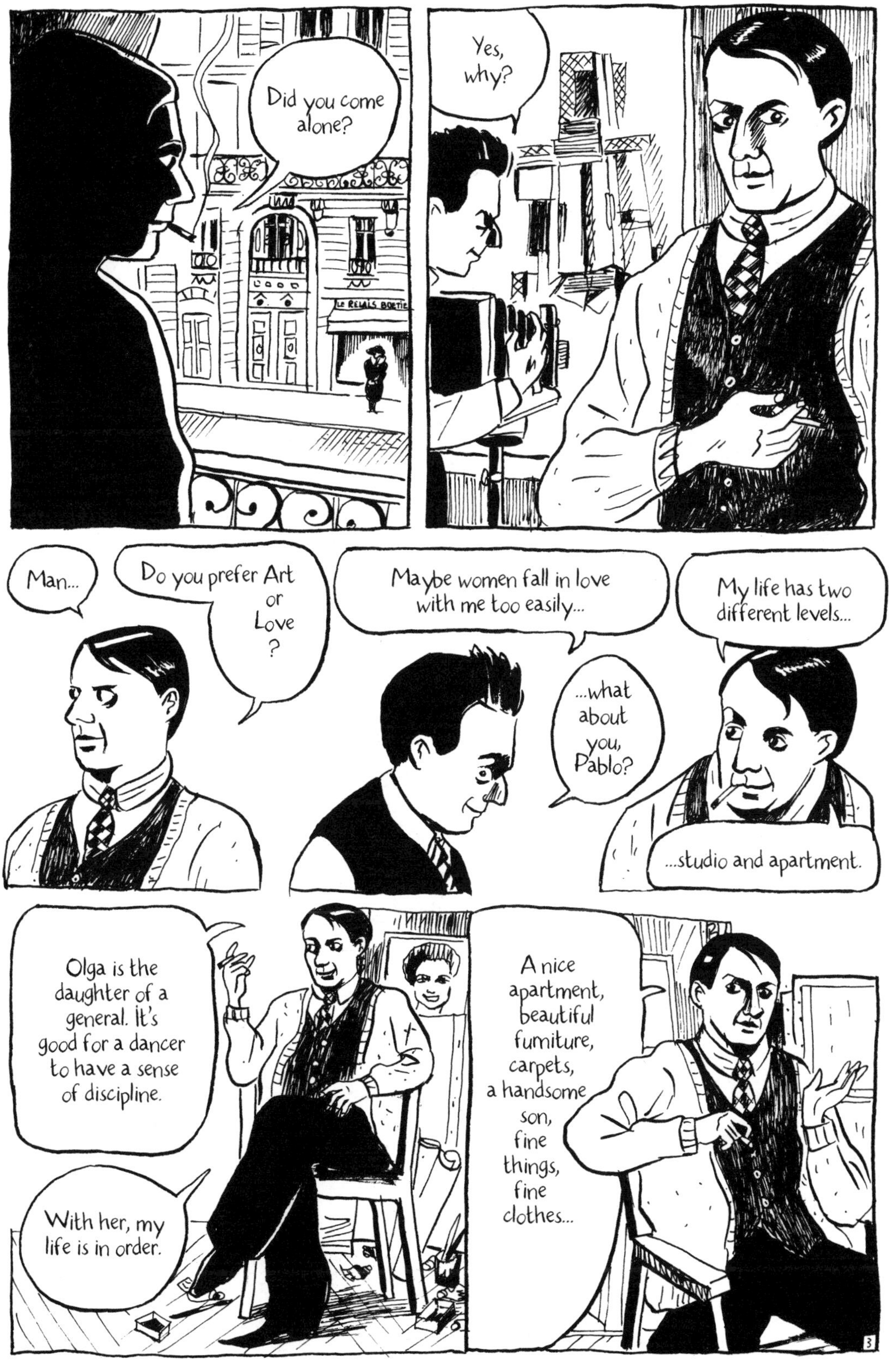
Did you come alone?
Yes, why?
Man...
Do you prefer Art or Love ?
Maybe women fall in love with me too easily...
...what about you, Pablo?
My life has two different levels...
...studio and apartment.
Olga is the daughter of a general. It's good for a dancer to have a sense of discipline.
With her, my life is in order.
A nice apartment, beautiful furniture, carpets, a handsome son, fine things, fine clothes...

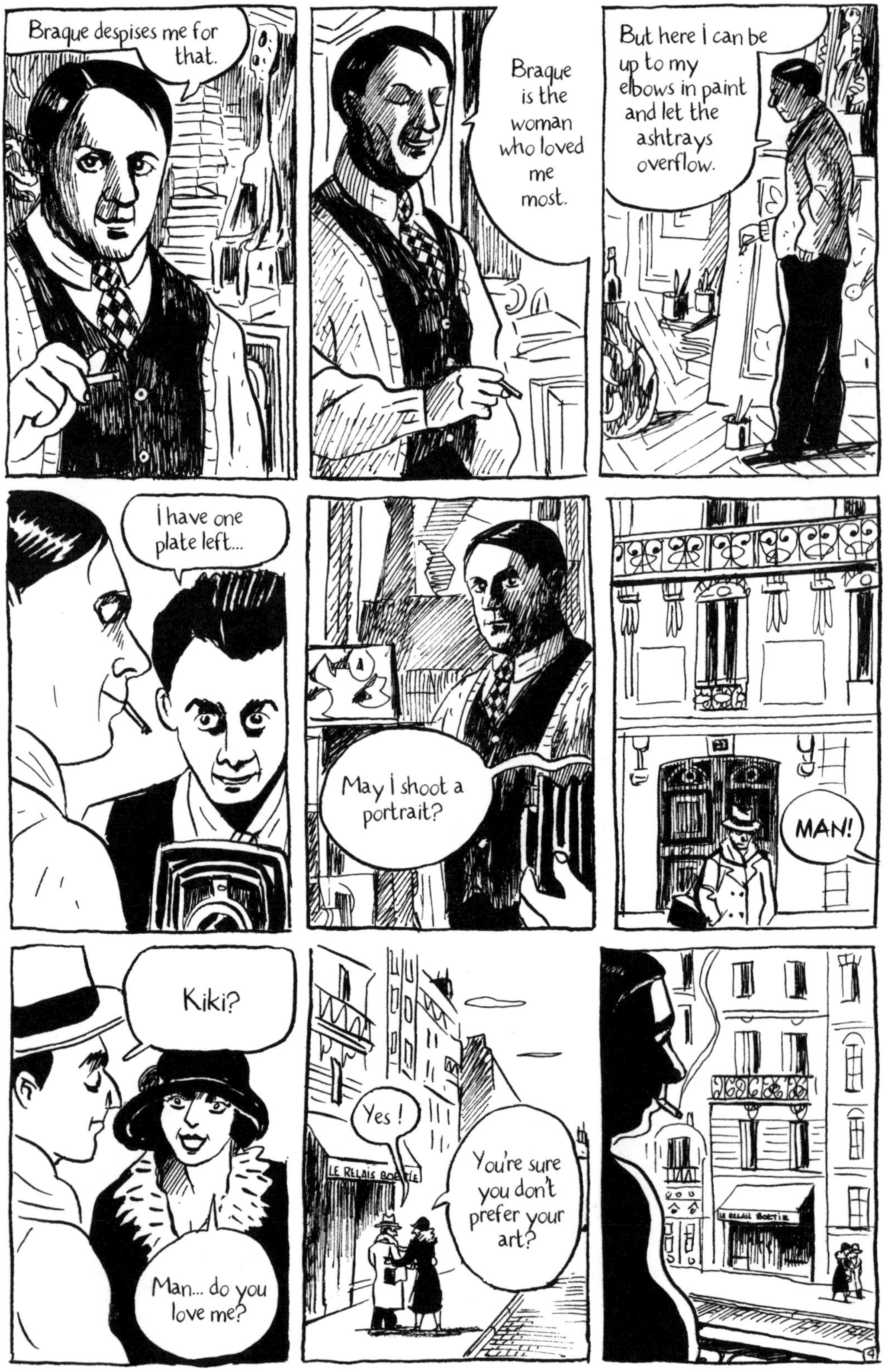
Braque despises me for that.
Braque is the woman who loved me most.
But here I can be up to my elbows in paint and let the ashtrays overflow.
I have one plate left...
May I shoot a portrait?
MAN!
Kiki?
Man... do you love me?
Yes!
You're sure you don't prefer your art?
LE RELAIS BOETIE
4

1922 - Grand Palais

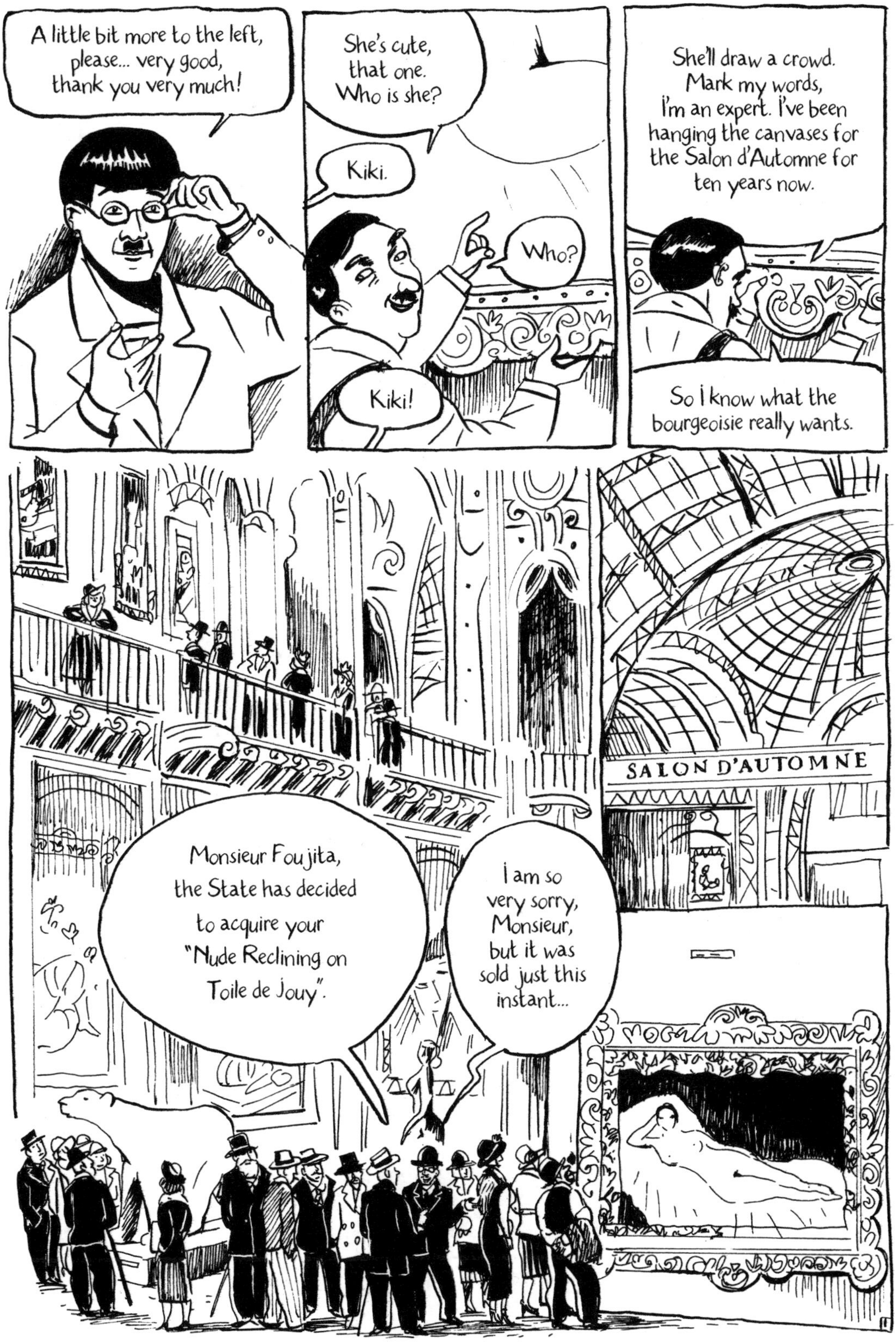
A little bit more to the left, please... very good, thank you very much!
She's cute, that one. Who is she?
Kiki.
Who?
Kiki!
She'll draw a crowd. Mark my words, I'm an expert. I've been hanging the canvases for the Salon d'Automne for ten years now.
So I know what the bourgeoisie really wants.
SALON D'AUTOMNE
Monsieur Foujita, the State has decided to acquire your "Nude Reclining on Toile de Jouy".
I am so very sorry, Monsieur, but it was sold just this instant...

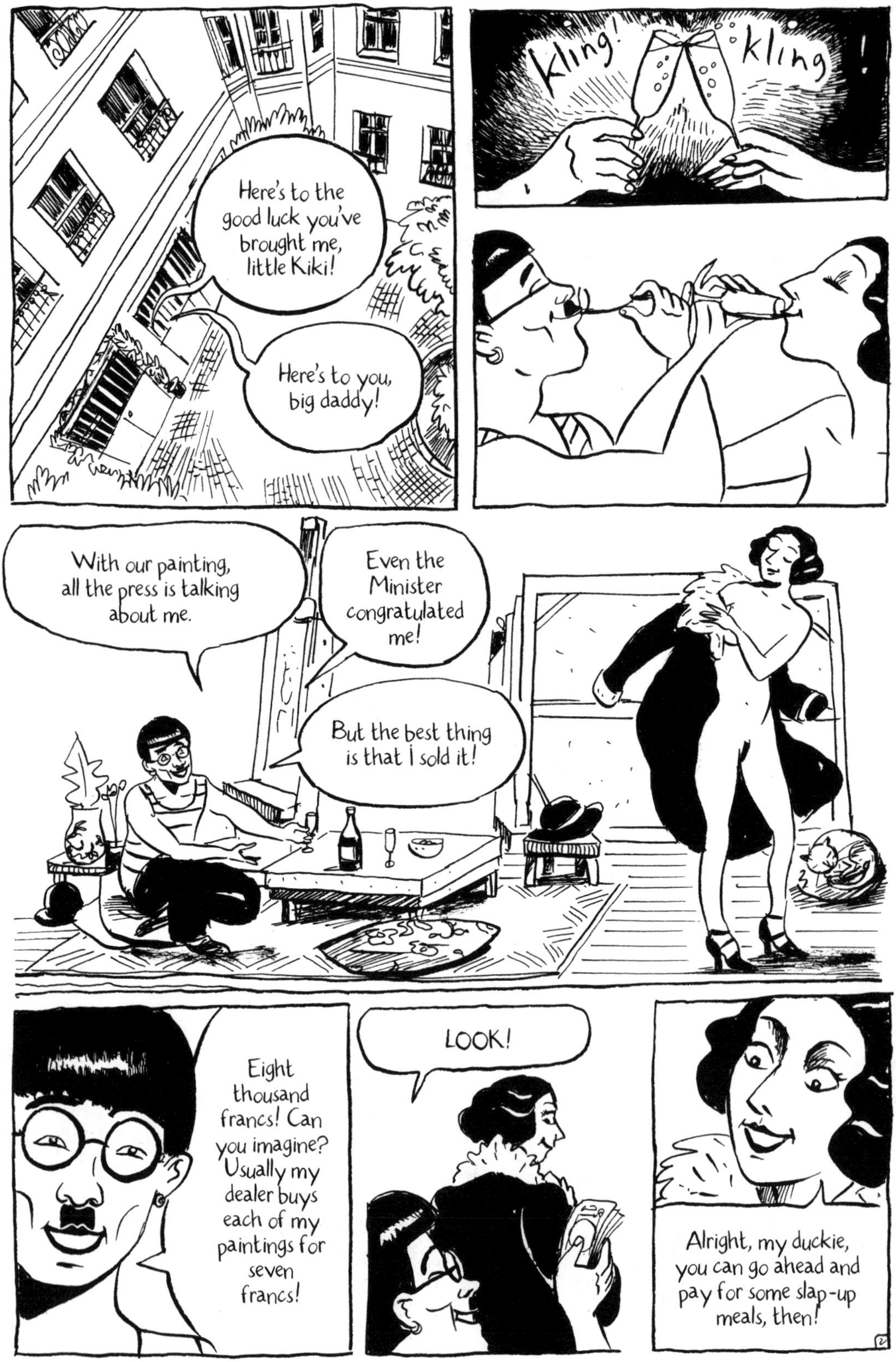
Here's to the good luck you've brought me, little Kiki!
Here's to you, big daddy!
kling! kling
With our painting, all the press is talking about me.
Even the Minister congratulated me!
But the best thing is that I sold it!
Eight thousand francs! Can you imagine? Usually my dealer buys each of my paintings for seven francs!
LOOK!
Alright, my duckie, you can go ahead and pay for some slap-up meals, then!

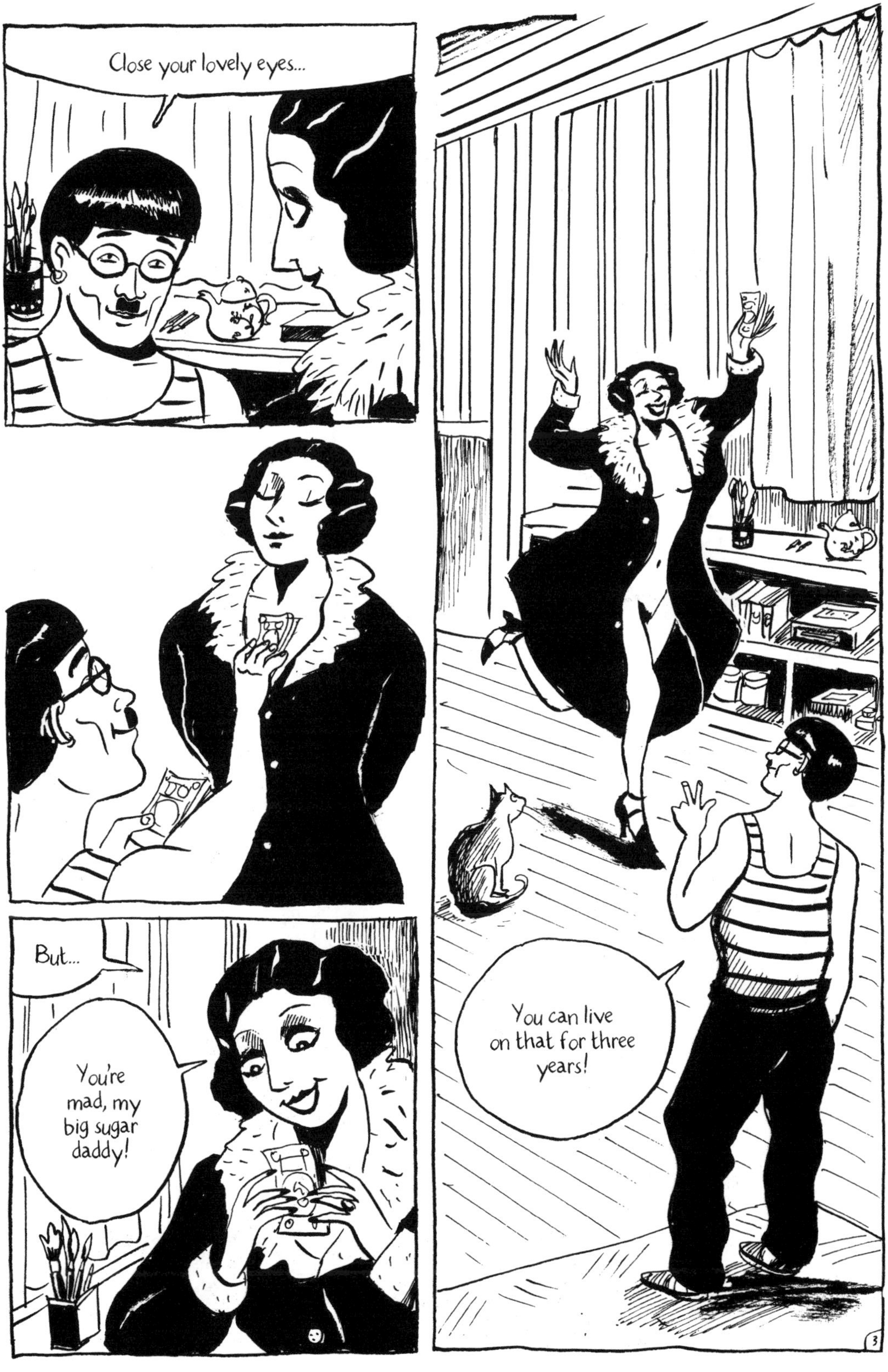
Close your lovely eyes...
But...
You're mad, my big sugar daddy!
You can live on that for three years!
3

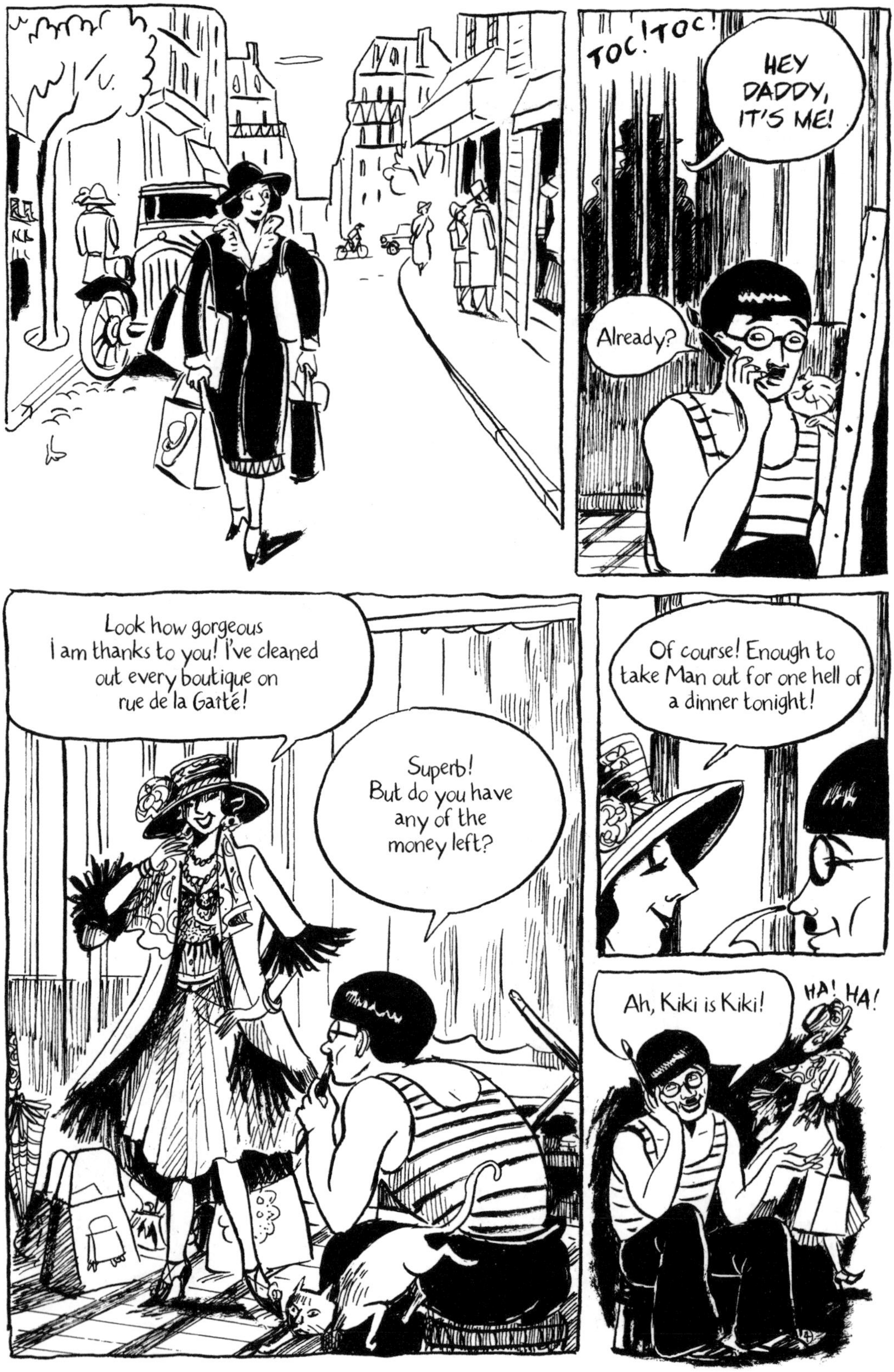

TOC! TOC!
HEY DADDY, IT'S ME!
Already?
Look how gorgeous I am thanks to you! I've cleaned out every boutique on rue de la Gaîté!
Superb! But do you have any of the money left?
Of course! Enough to take Man out for one hell of a dinner tonight!
Ah, Kiki is Kiki!
HA! HA!

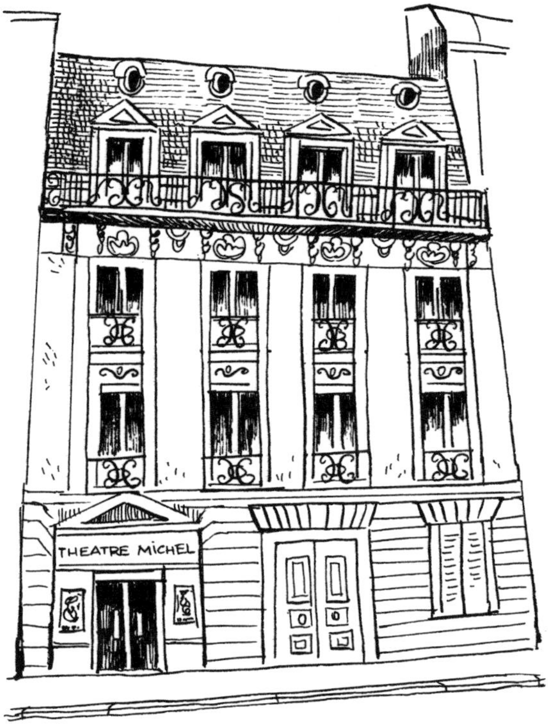
THEATRE MICHEL

1923 - 36, rue des Mathurins

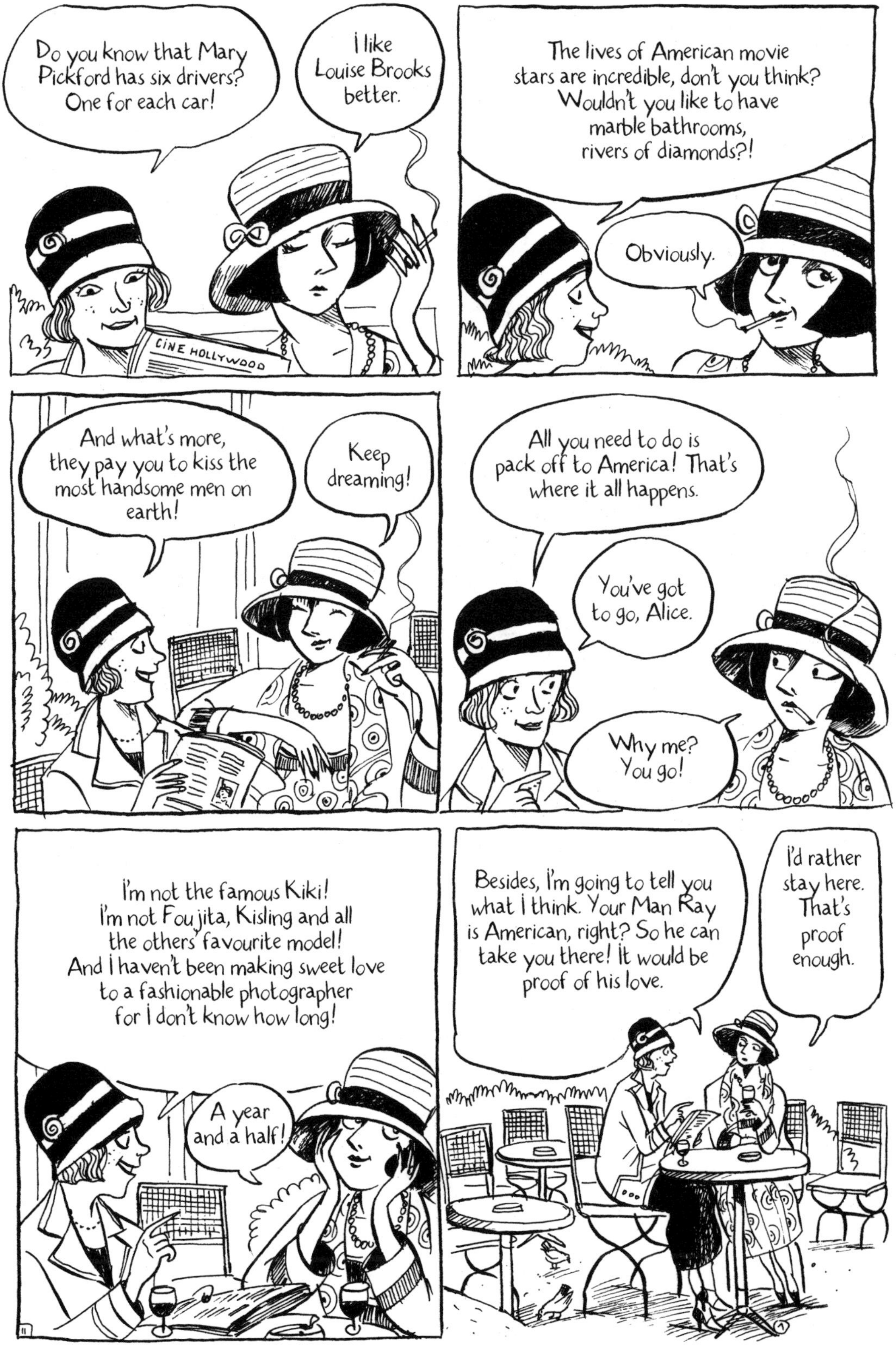

Do you know that Mary Pickford has six drivers? One for each car!
I like Louise Brooks better.
CINE HOLLYWOOD
The lives of American movie stars are incredible, don't you think? Wouldn't you like to have marble bathrooms, rivers of diamonds?!
Obviously.
And what's more, they pay you to kiss the most handsome men on earth!
Keep dreaming!
All you need to do is pack off to America! That's where it all happens.
You've got to go, Alice.
Why me? You go!
I'm not the famous Kiki! I'm not Foujita, Kisling and all the others' favourite model! And I haven't been making sweet love to a fashionable photographer for I don't know how long!
A year and a half!
Besides, I'm going to tell you what I think. Your Man Ray is American, right? So he can take you there! It would be proof of his love.
I'd rather stay here. That's proof enough.

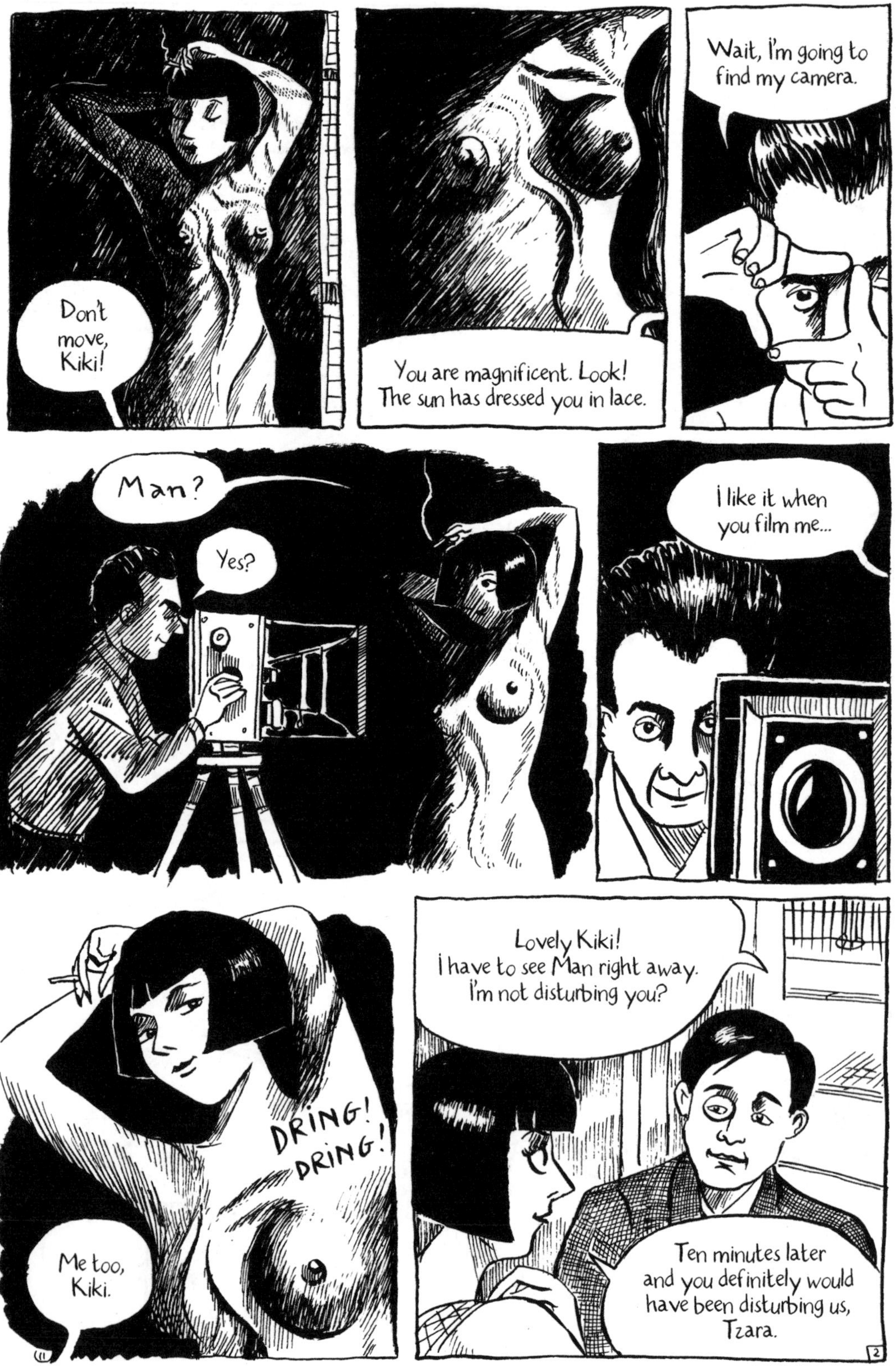
Don't move, Kiki!
You are magnificent. Look! The sun has dressed you in lace.
Wait, I'm going to find my camera.
Man?
Yes?
I like it when you film me...
DRING! DRING!
Me too, Kiki.
Lovely Kiki! I have to see Man right away. I'm not disturbing you?
Ten minutes later and you definitely would have been disturbing us, Tzara.

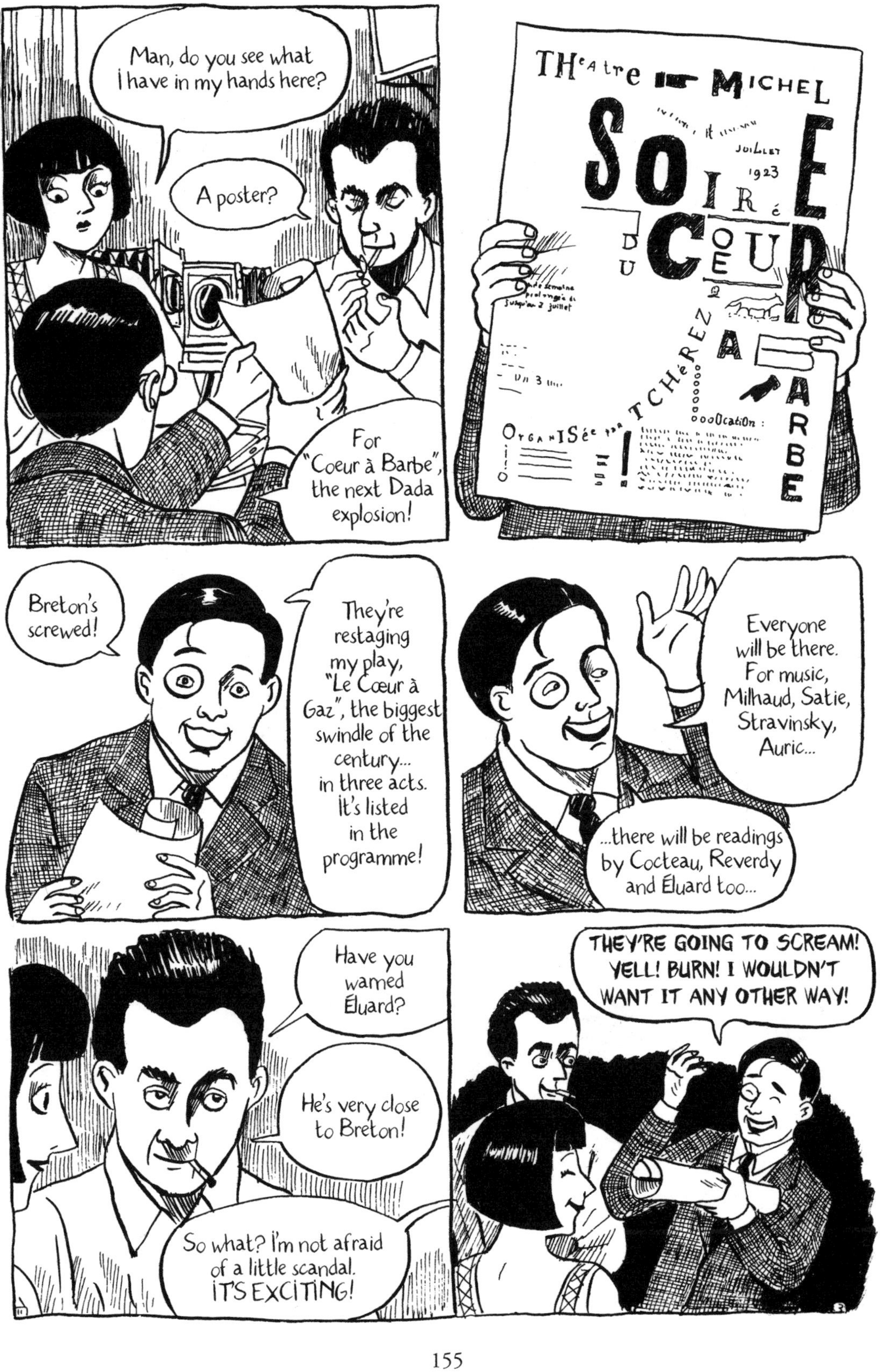

Man, do you see what I have in my hands here?
A poster?
THeatre MICHEL
SOIRÉE DU CŒUR À BARBE
JUILLET 1923
TCHÉREZ
ORGANISée par
For "Coeur à Barbe", the next Dada explosion!
Breton's screwed!
They're restaging my play, "Le Cœur à Gaz", the biggest swindle of the century... in three acts. It's listed in the programme!
Everyone will be there. For music, Milhaud, Satie, Stravinsky, Auric...
...there will be readings by Cocteau, Reverdy and Éluard too...
Have you warned Éluard?
He's very close to Breton!
So what? I'm not afraid of a little scandal. IT'S EXCITING!
THEY'RE GOING TO SCREAM! YELL! BURN! I WOULDN'T WANT IT ANY OTHER WAY!

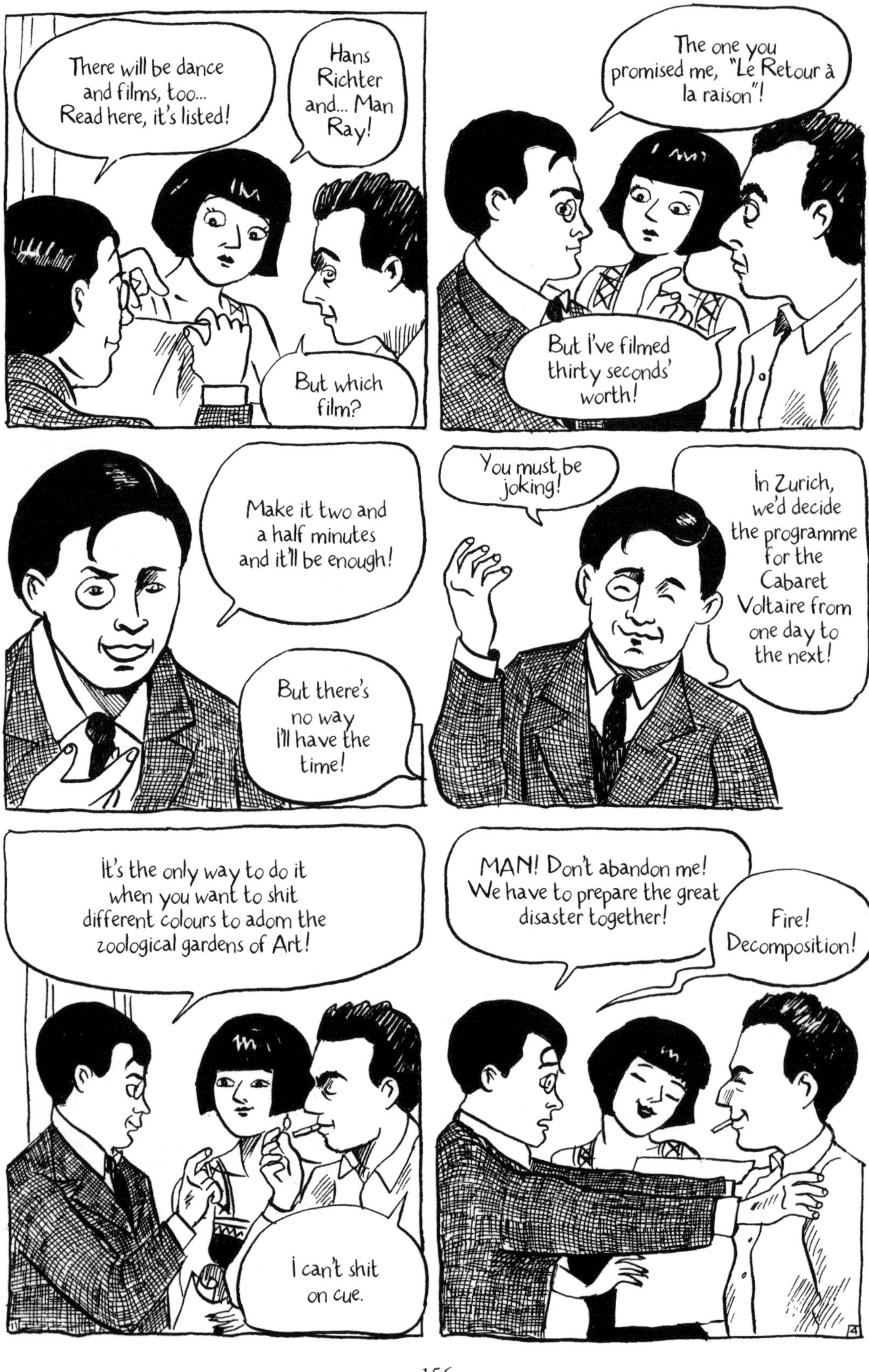
There will be dance and films, too... Read here, it's listed!
Hans Richter and... Man Ray!
But which film?
The one you promised me, "Le Retour à la raison"!
But I've filmed thirty seconds' worth!
Make it two and a half minutes and it'll be enough!
But there's no way I'll have the time!
You must be joking!
In Zurich, we'd decide the programme for the Cabaret Voltaire from one day to the next!
It's the only way to do it when you want to shit different colours to adorn the zoological gardens of Art!
I can't shit on cue.
MAN! Don't abandon me! We have to prepare the great disaster together!
Fire! Decomposition!

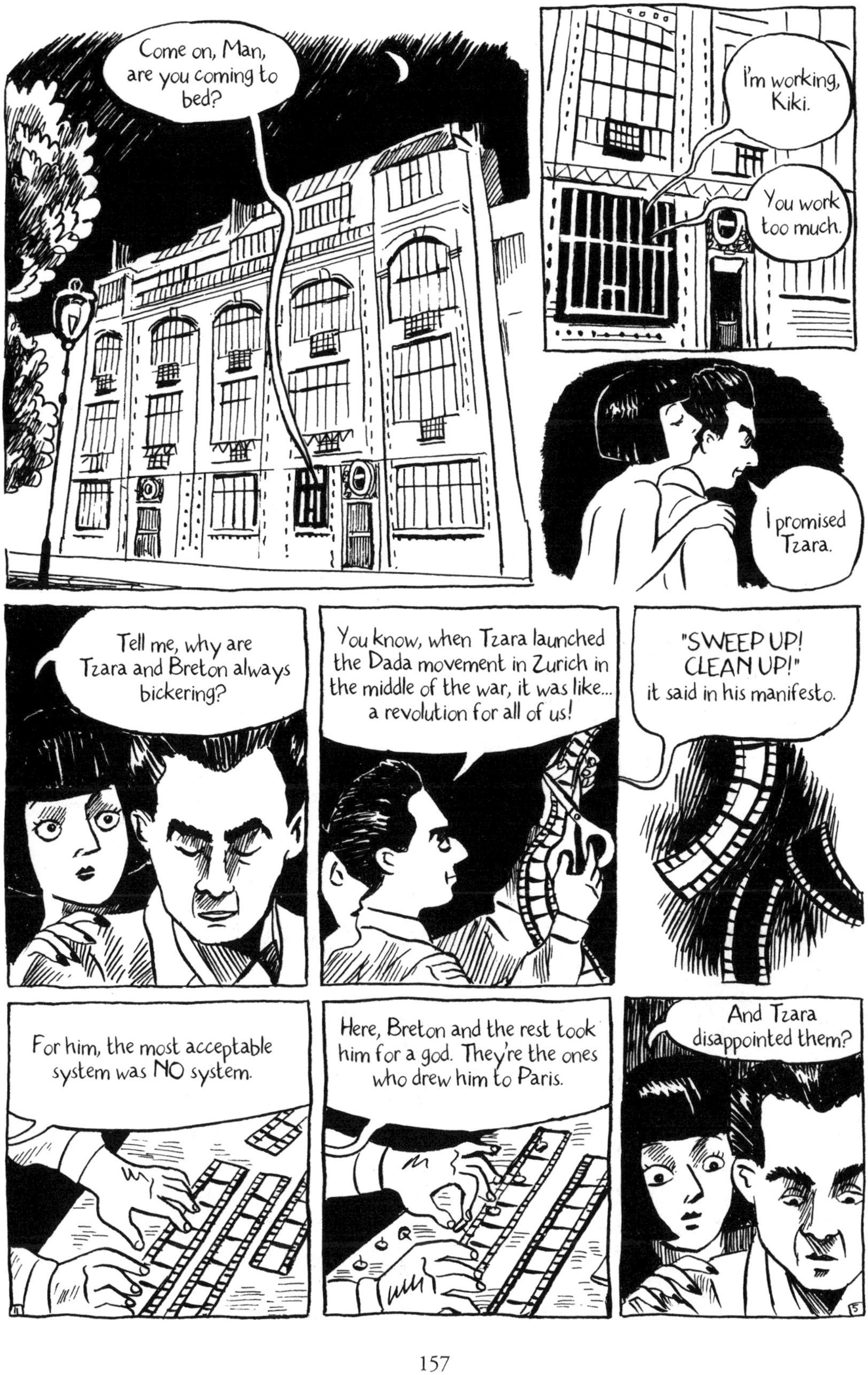
Come on, Man, are you coming to bed?
I'm working, Kiki.
You work too much.
I promised Tzara.
Tell me, why are Tzara and Breton always bickering?
You know, when Tzara launched the Dada movement in Zurich in the middle of the war, it was like... a revolution for all of us!
"SWEEP UP! CLEAN UP!" it said in his manifesto.
For him, the most acceptable system was NO system.
Here, Breton and the rest took him for a god. They're the ones who drew him to Paris.
And Tzara disappointed them?

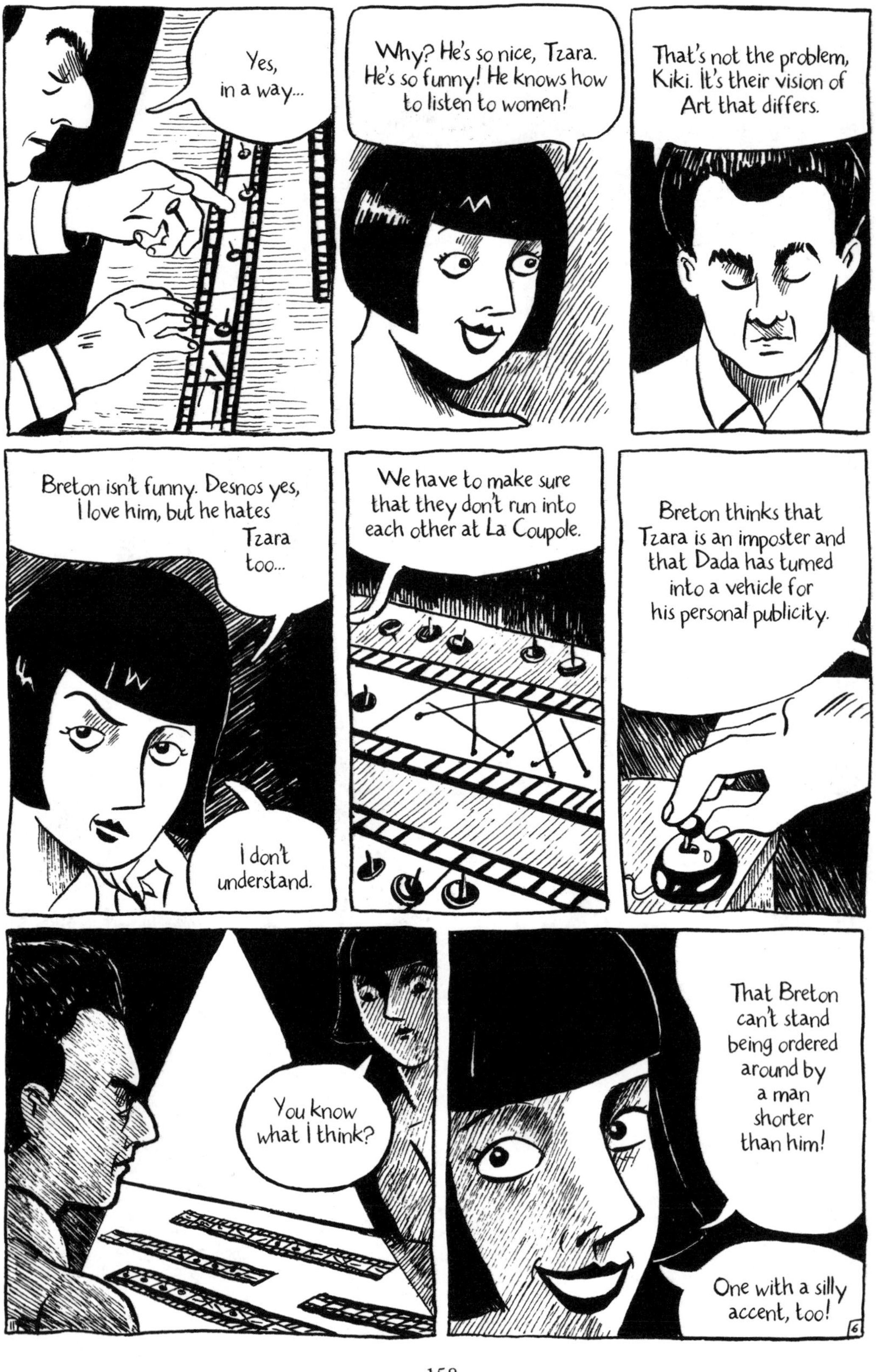
Yes, in a way...
Why? He's so nice, Tzara. He's so funny! He knows how to listen to women!
That's not the problem, Kiki. It's their vision of Art that differs.
Breton isn't funny. Desnos yes, I love him, but he hates Tzara too...
I don't understand.
We have to make sure that they don't run into each other at La Coupole.
Breton thinks that Tzara is an imposter and that Dada has turned into a vehicle for his personal publicity.
You know what I think?
That Breton can't stand being ordered around by a man shorter than him!
One with a silly accent, too!

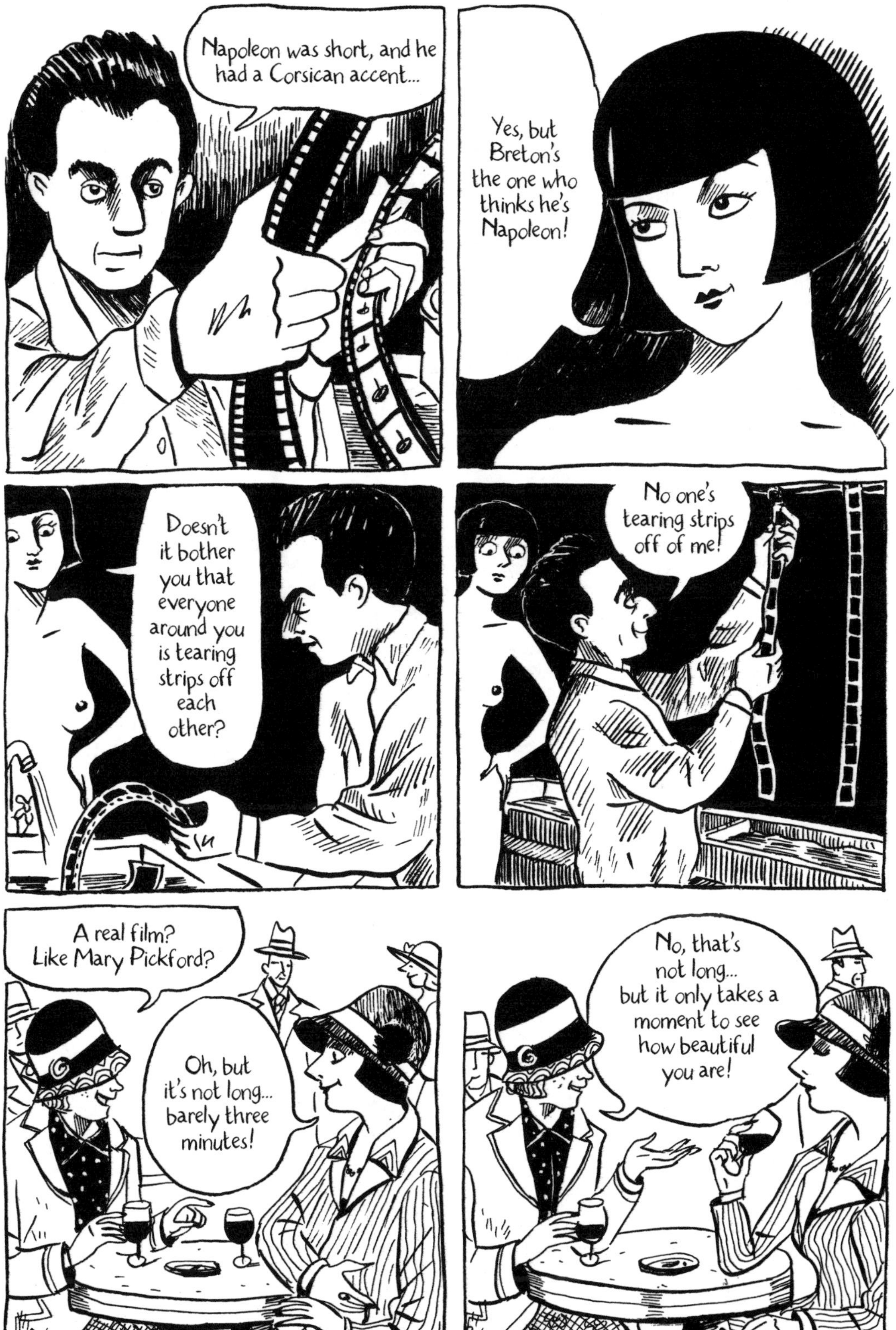
Napoleon was short, and he had a Corsican accent...
Yes, but Breton's the one who thinks he's Napoleon!
Doesn't it bother you that everyone around you is tearing strips off each other?
No one's tearing strips off of me!
A real film? Like Mary Pickford?
Oh, but it's not long... barely three minutes!
No, that's not long... but it only takes a moment to see how beautiful you are!
7

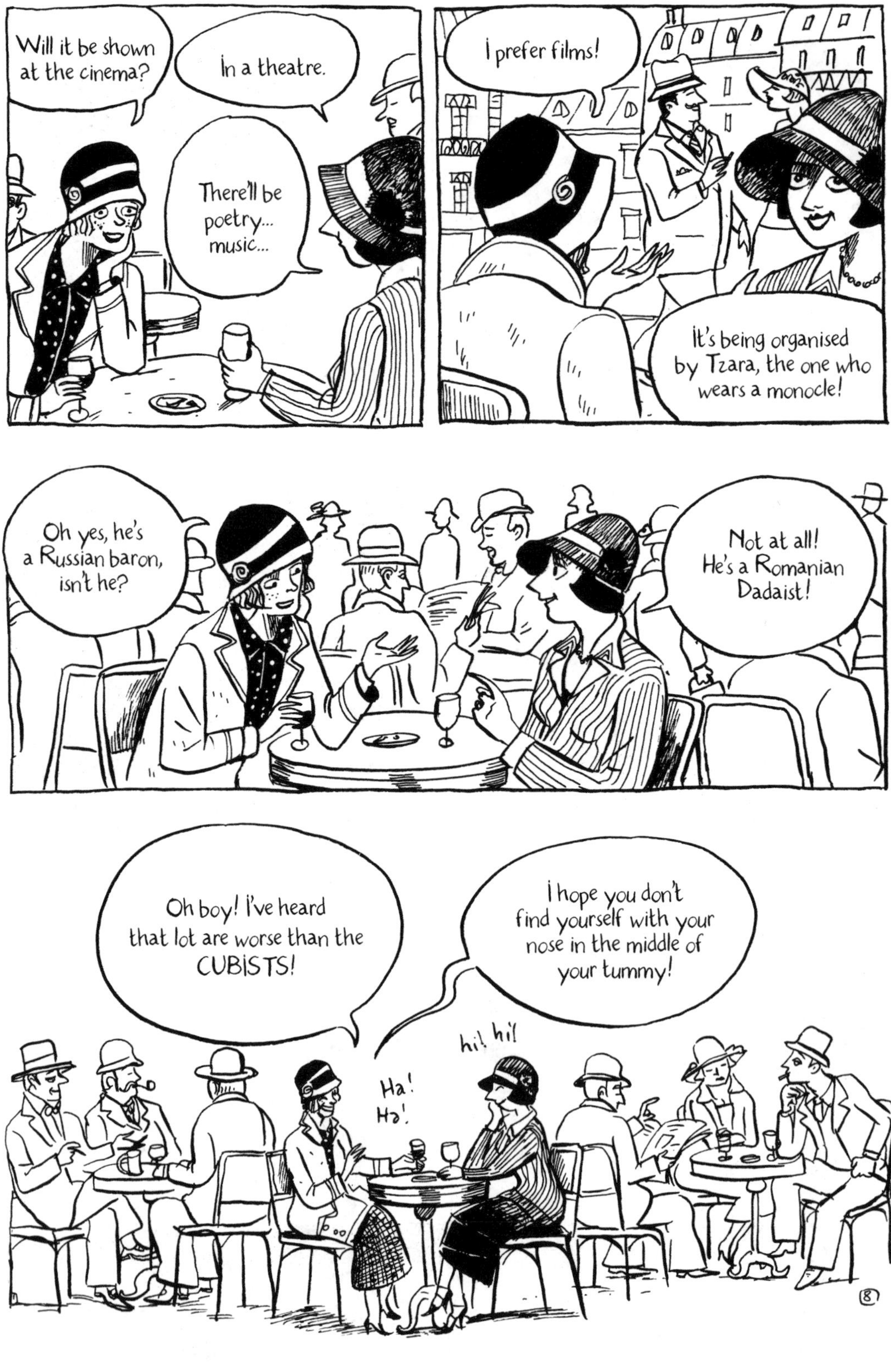
Will it be shown at the cinema?
In a theatre.
There'll be poetry... music...
I prefer films!
It's being organised by Tzara, the one who wears a monocle!
Oh yes, he's a Russian baron, isn't he?
Not at all! He's a Romanian Dadaist!
Oh boy! I've heard that lot are worse than the CUBISTS!
I hope you don't find yourself with your nose in the middle of your tummy!
Ha! Ha!
hi! hi!
8

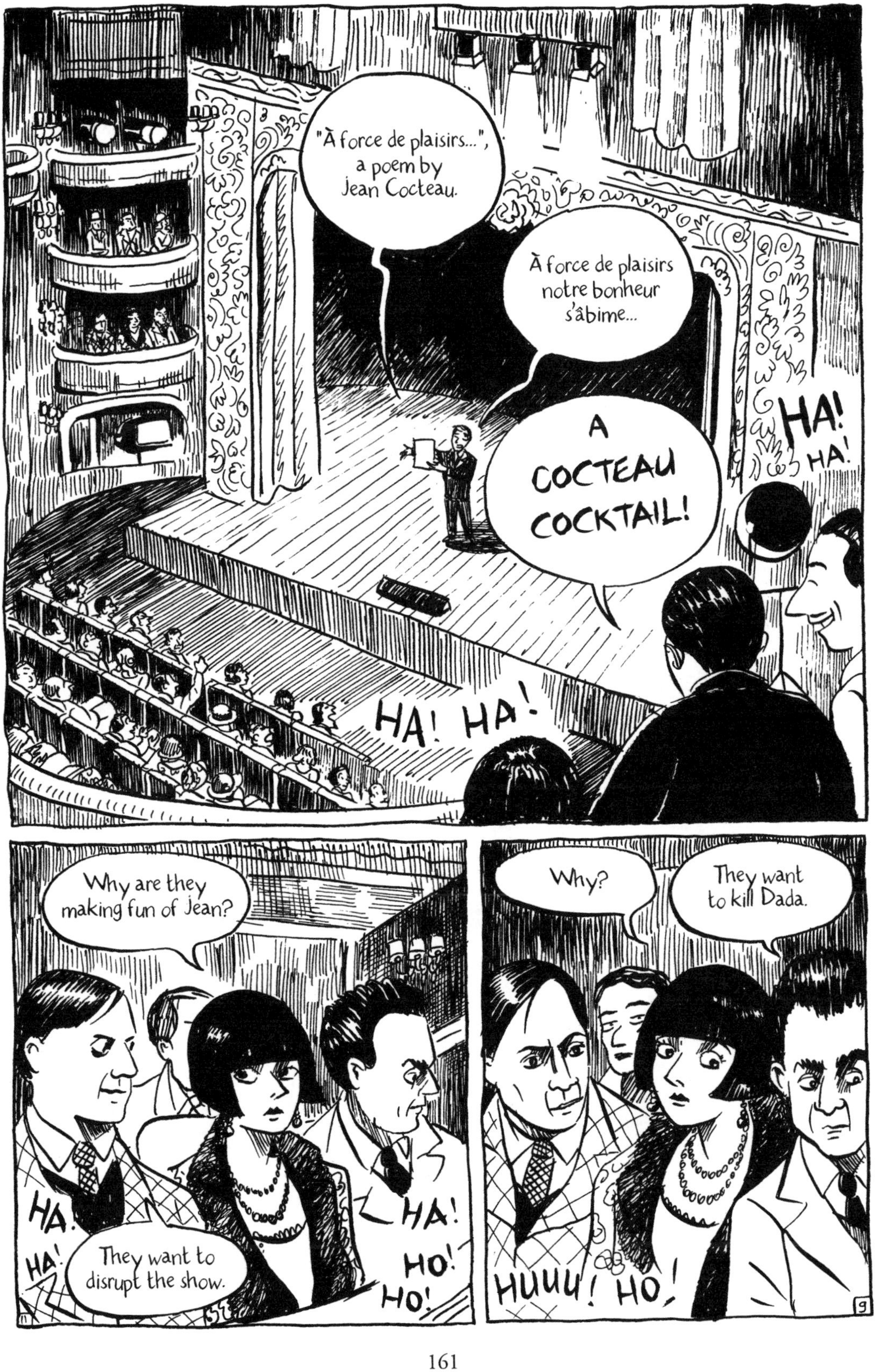
"À force de plaisirs...", a poem by Jean Cocteau.
À force de plaisirs notre bonheur s'âbime...
A COCTEAU COCKTAIL!
HA! HA!
HA! HA!
Why are they making fun of Jean?
HA. HA!
HA! HO! HO!
They want to disrupt the show.
Why?
They want to kill Dada.
HUUU! HO!

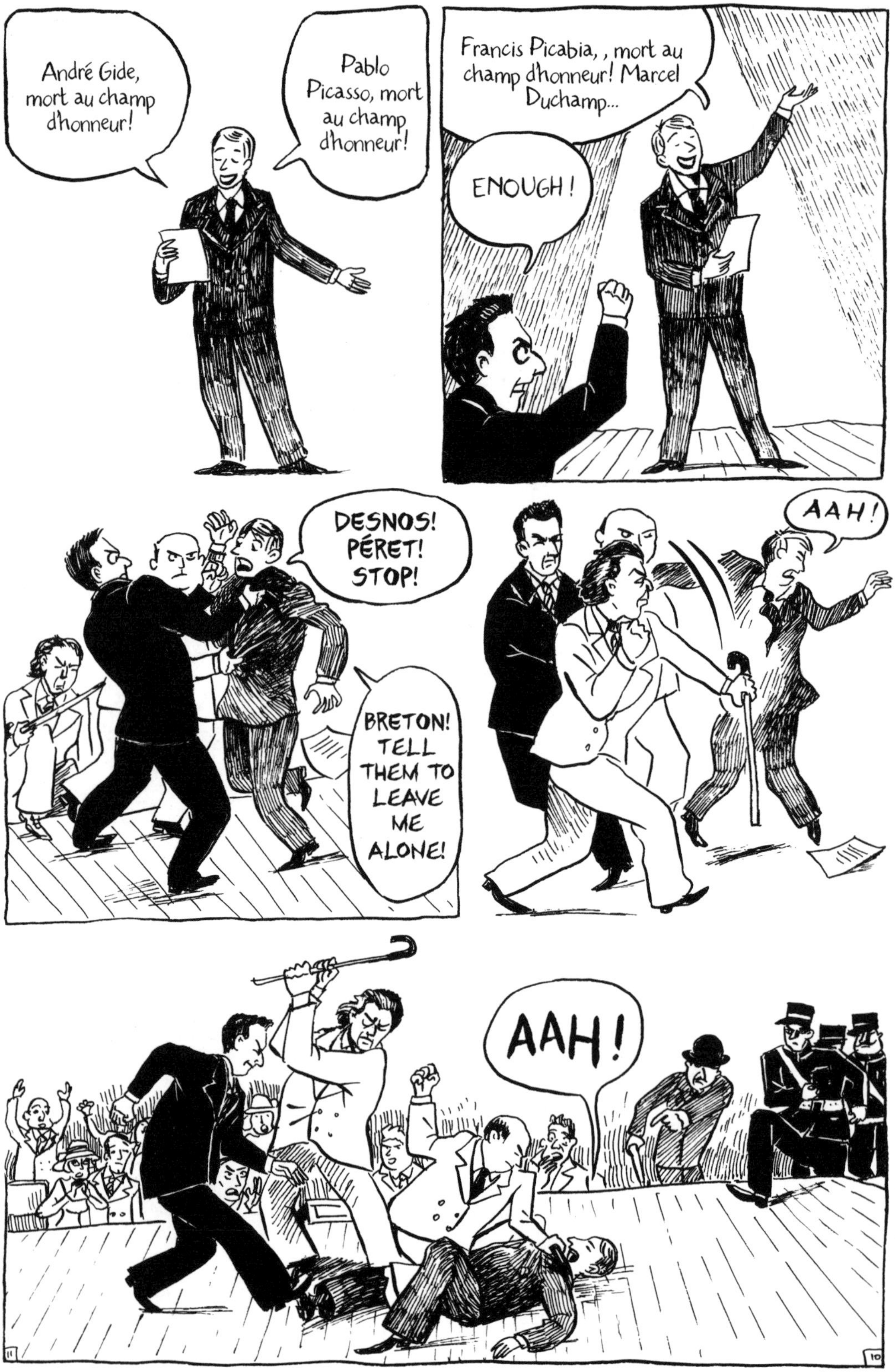
André Gide, mort au champ d'honneur!
Pablo Picasso, mort au champ d'honneur!
Francis Picabia, , mort au champ d'honneur! Marcel Duchamp...
ENOUGH!
DESNOS! PÉRET! STOP!
BRETON! TELL THEM TO LEAVE ME ALONE!
AAH!
AAH!
11
10

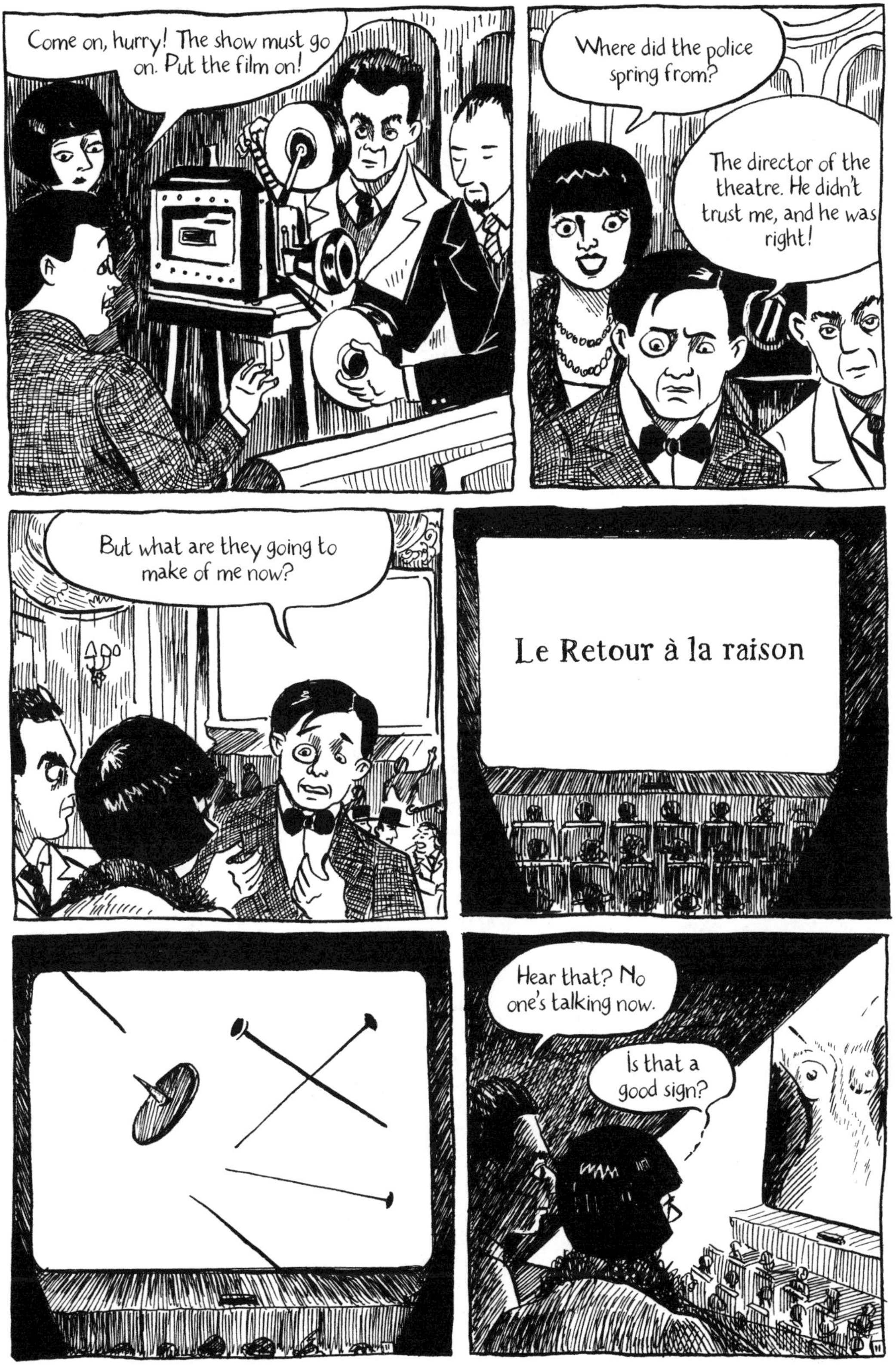
Come on, hurry! The show must go on. Put the film on!
Where did the police spring from?
The director of the theatre. He didn't trust me, and he was right!
But what are they going to make of me now?
Le Retour à la raison
Hear that? No one's talking now.
Is that a good sign?

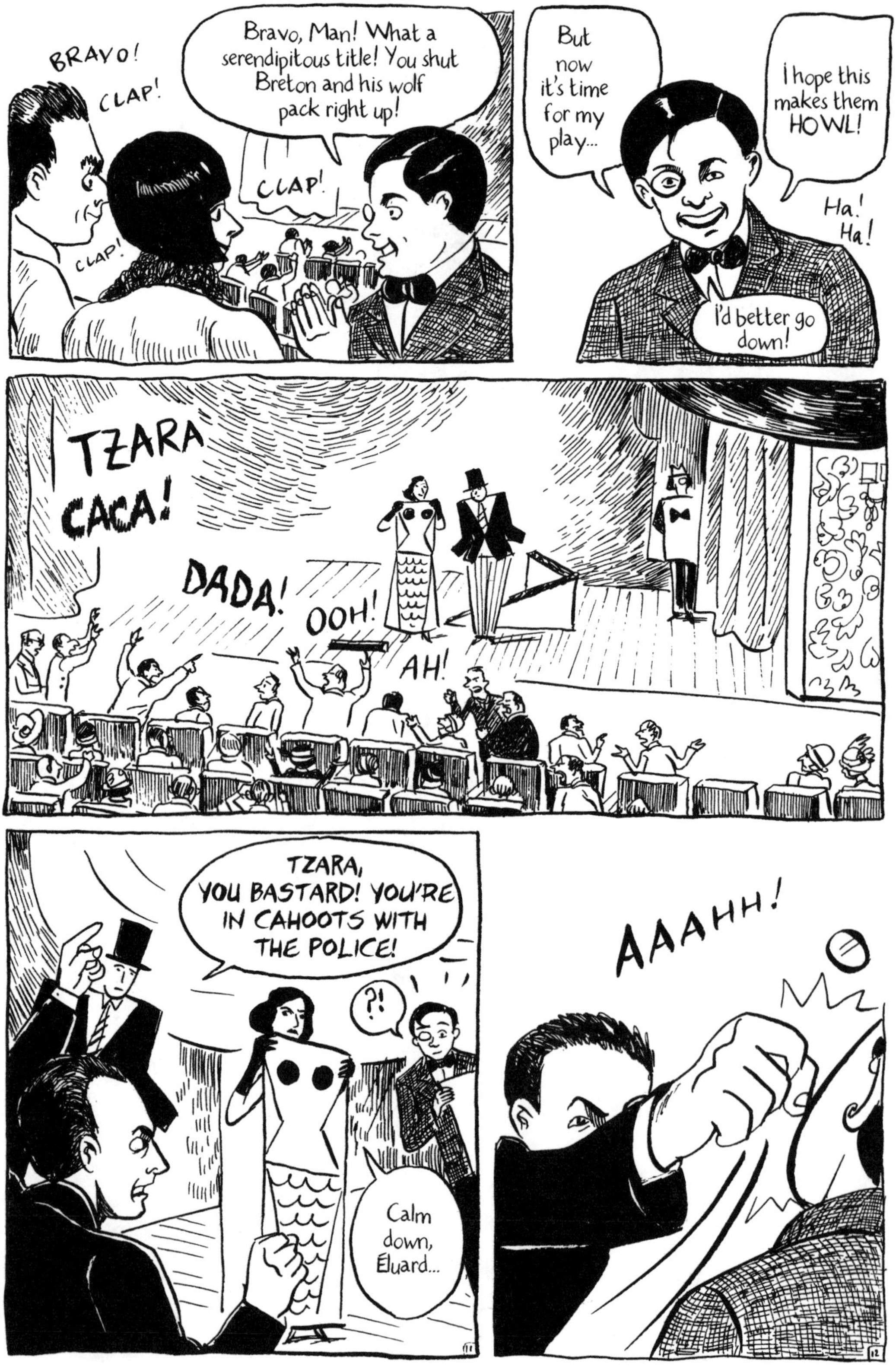
BRAVO!
CLAP!
Bravo, Man! What a serendipitous title! You shut Breton and his wolf pack right up!
CLAP!
CLAP!
But now it's time for my play...
I hope this makes them HOWL!
Ha! Ha!
I'd better go down!
TZARA CACA!
DADA!
OOH!
AH!
TZARA, YOU BASTARD! YOU'RE IN CAHOOTS WITH THE POLICE!
?!
Calm down, Éluard...
AAAHH!

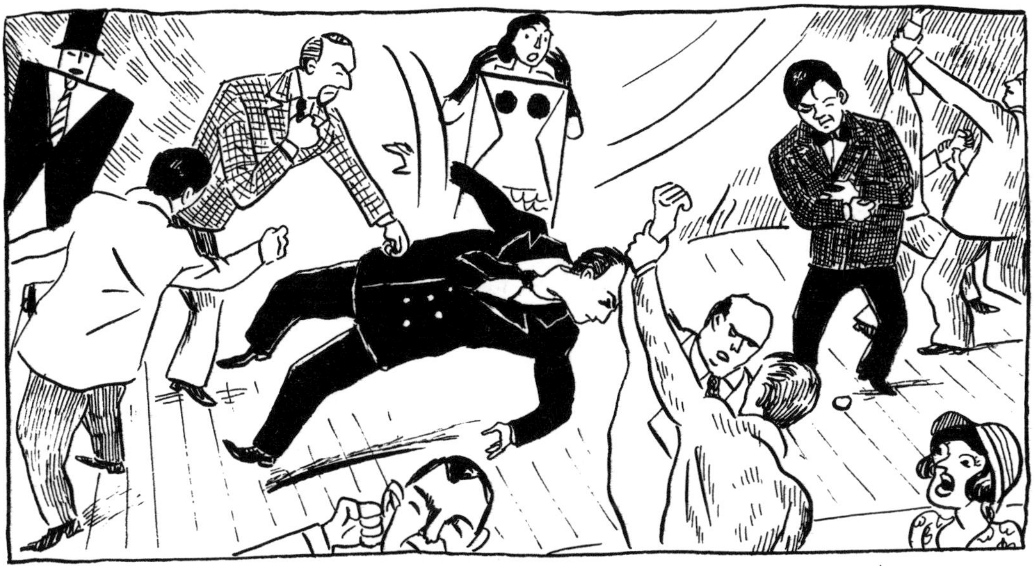

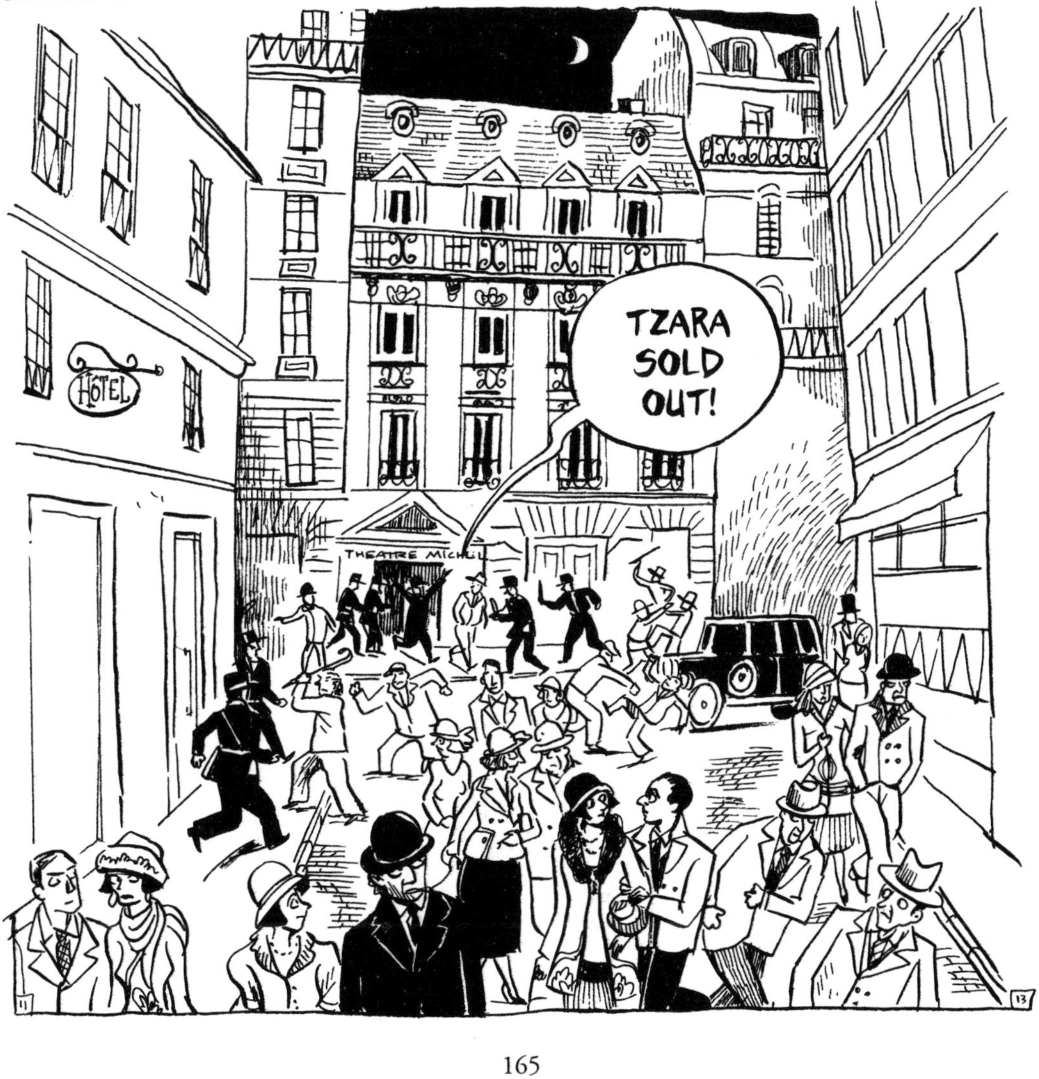
TZARA SOLD OUT!
THEATRE MICHEL
HÔTEL

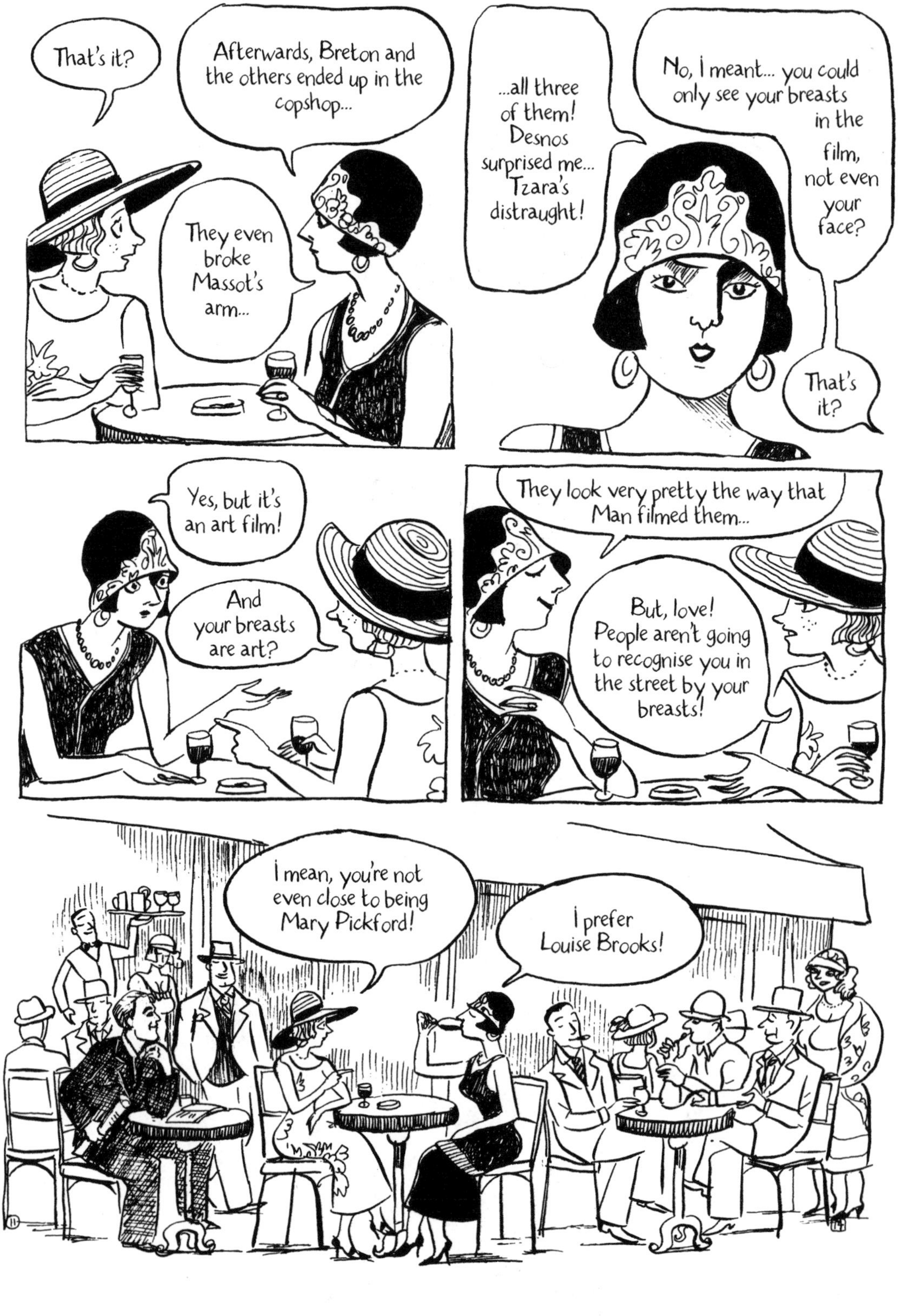
That's it?
Afterwards, Breton and the others ended up in the copshop...
They even broke Massot's arm...
...all three of them! Desnos surprised me... Tzara's distraught!
No, I meant... you could only see your breasts in the film, not even your face?
That's it?
Yes, but it's an art film!
And your breasts are art?
They look very pretty the way that Man filmed them...
But, love! People aren't going to recognise you in the street by your breasts!
I mean, you're not even close to being Mary Pickford!
I prefer Louise Brooks!

1923 - 31 bis, rue Campagne-Premiére

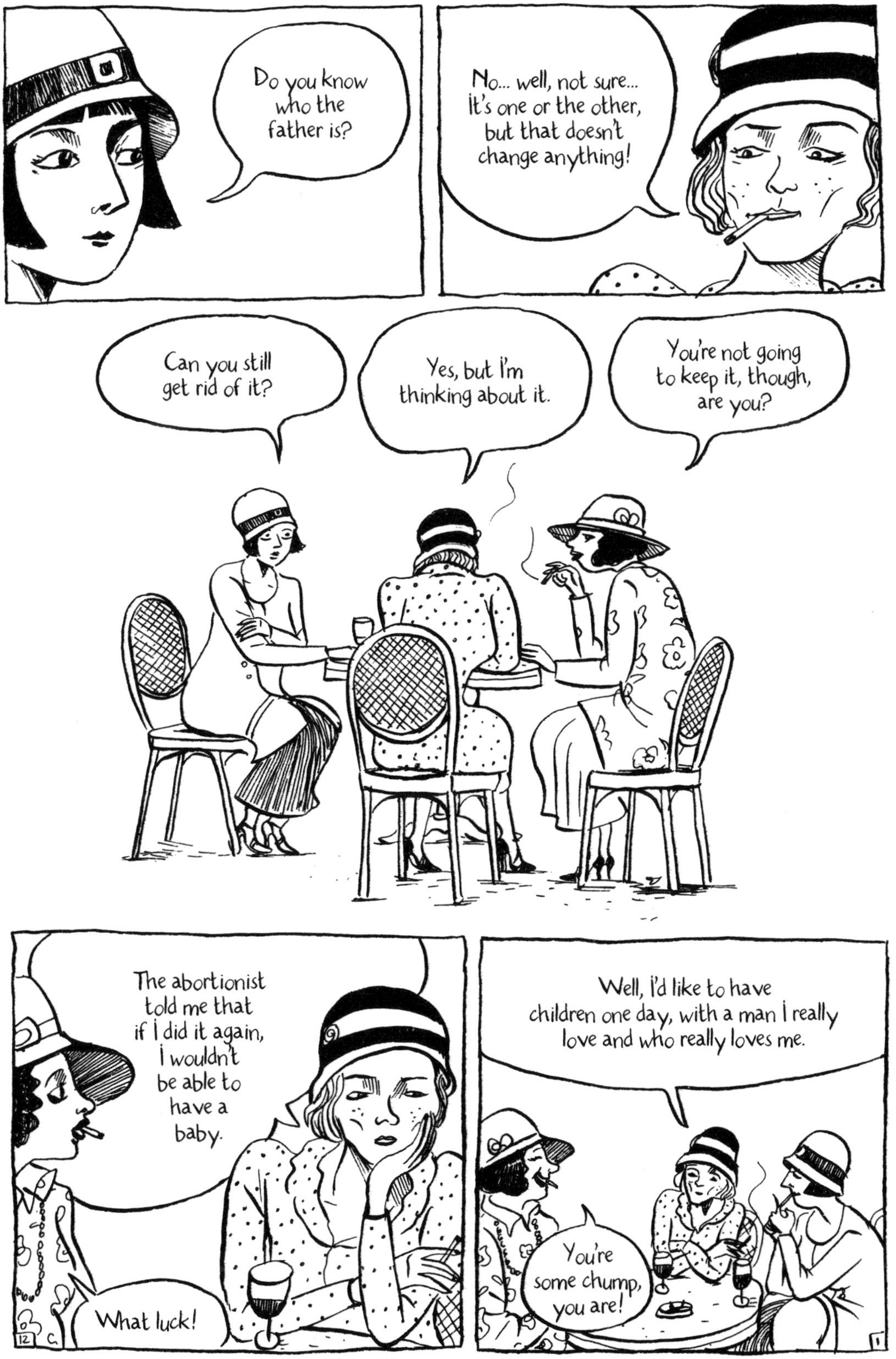
Do you know who the father is?
No... well, not sure... It's one or the other, but that doesn't change anything!
Can you still get rid of it?
Yes, but I'm thinking about it.
You're not going to keep it, though, are you?
The abortionist told me that if I did it again, I wouldn't be able to have a baby.
What luck!
Well, I'd like to have children one day, with a man I really love and who really loves me.
You're some chump, you are!

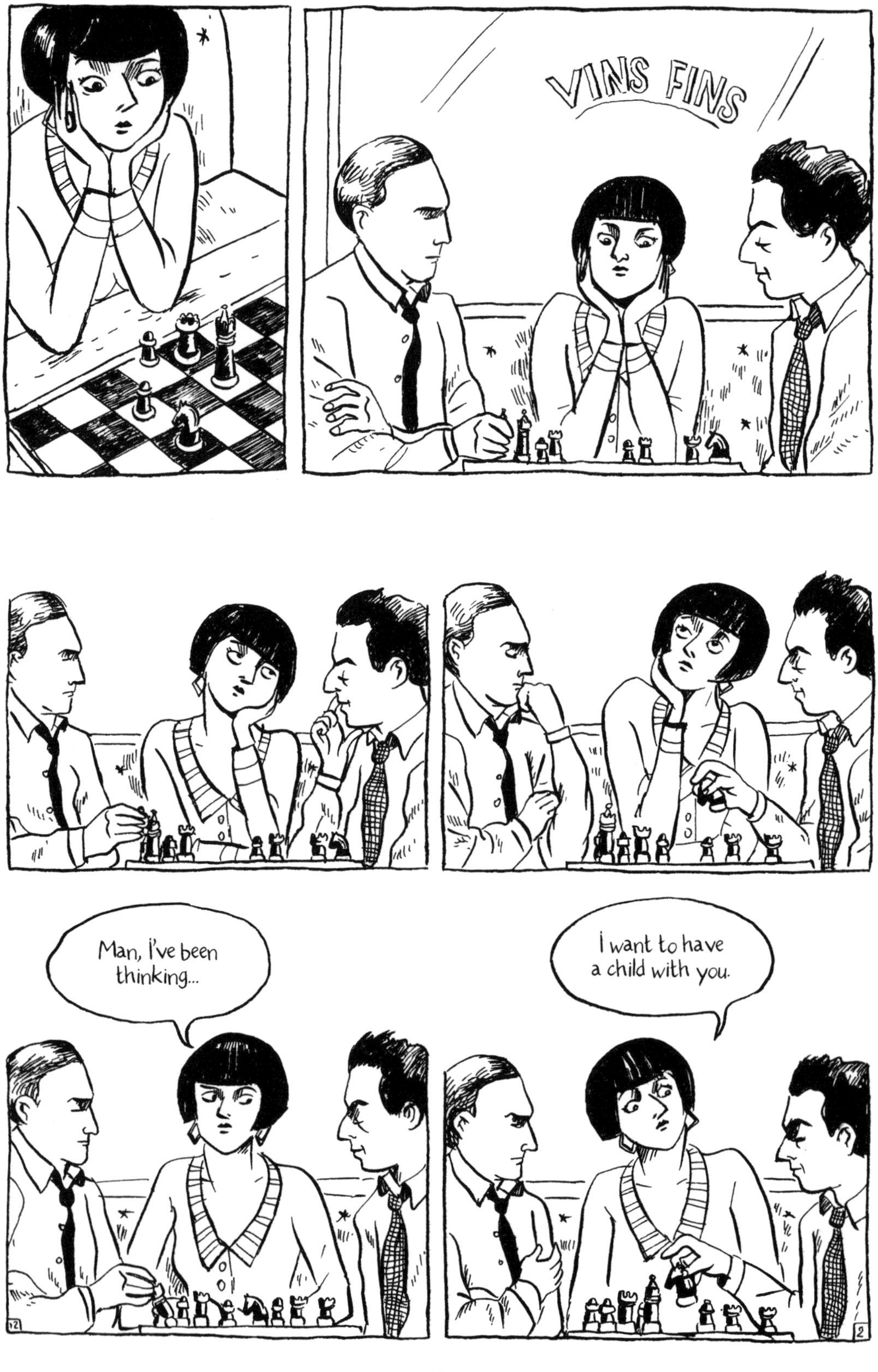

VINS FINS
Man, I've been thinking...
I want to have a child with you.

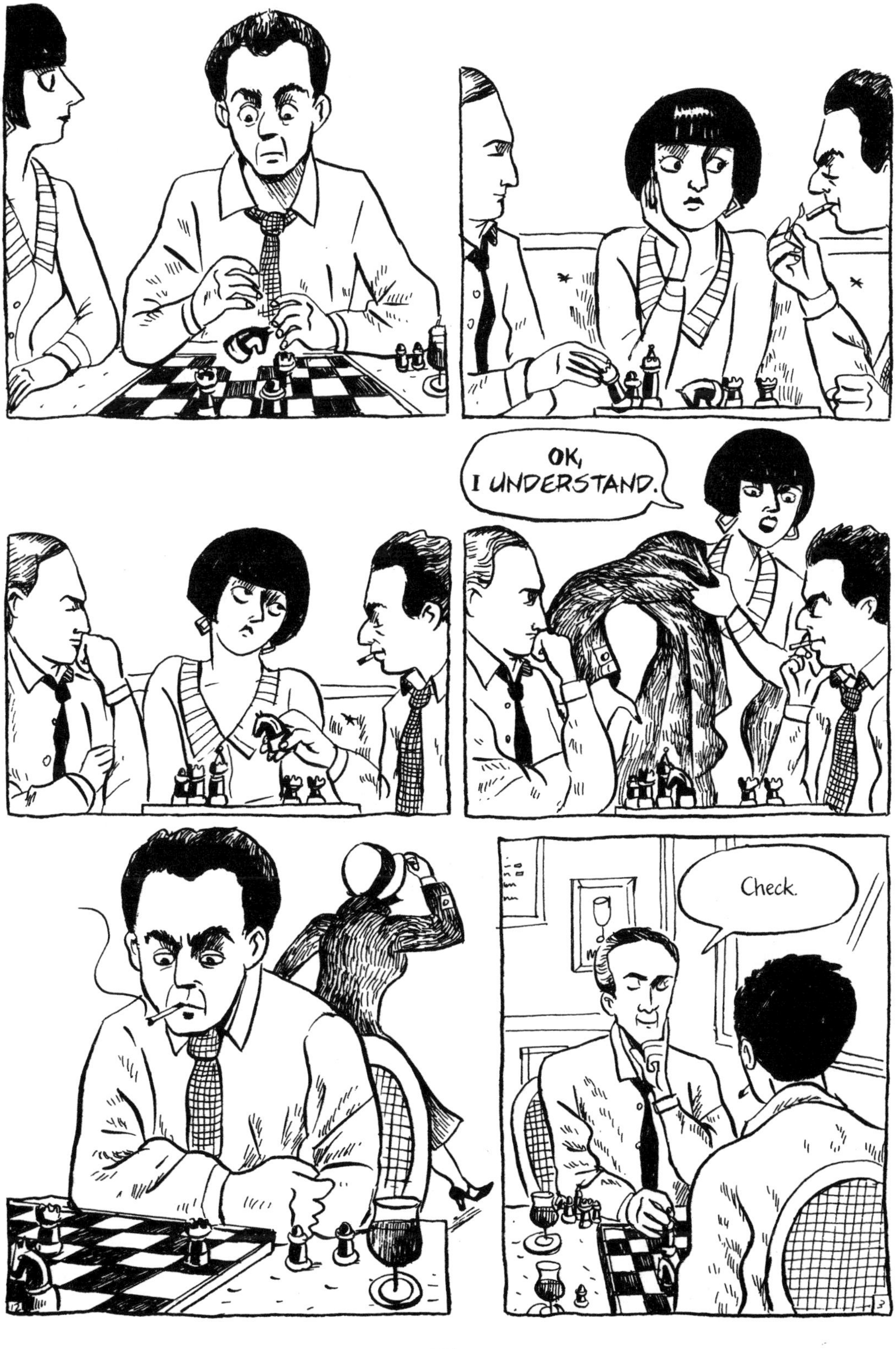
OK, I UNDERSTAND.
Check.

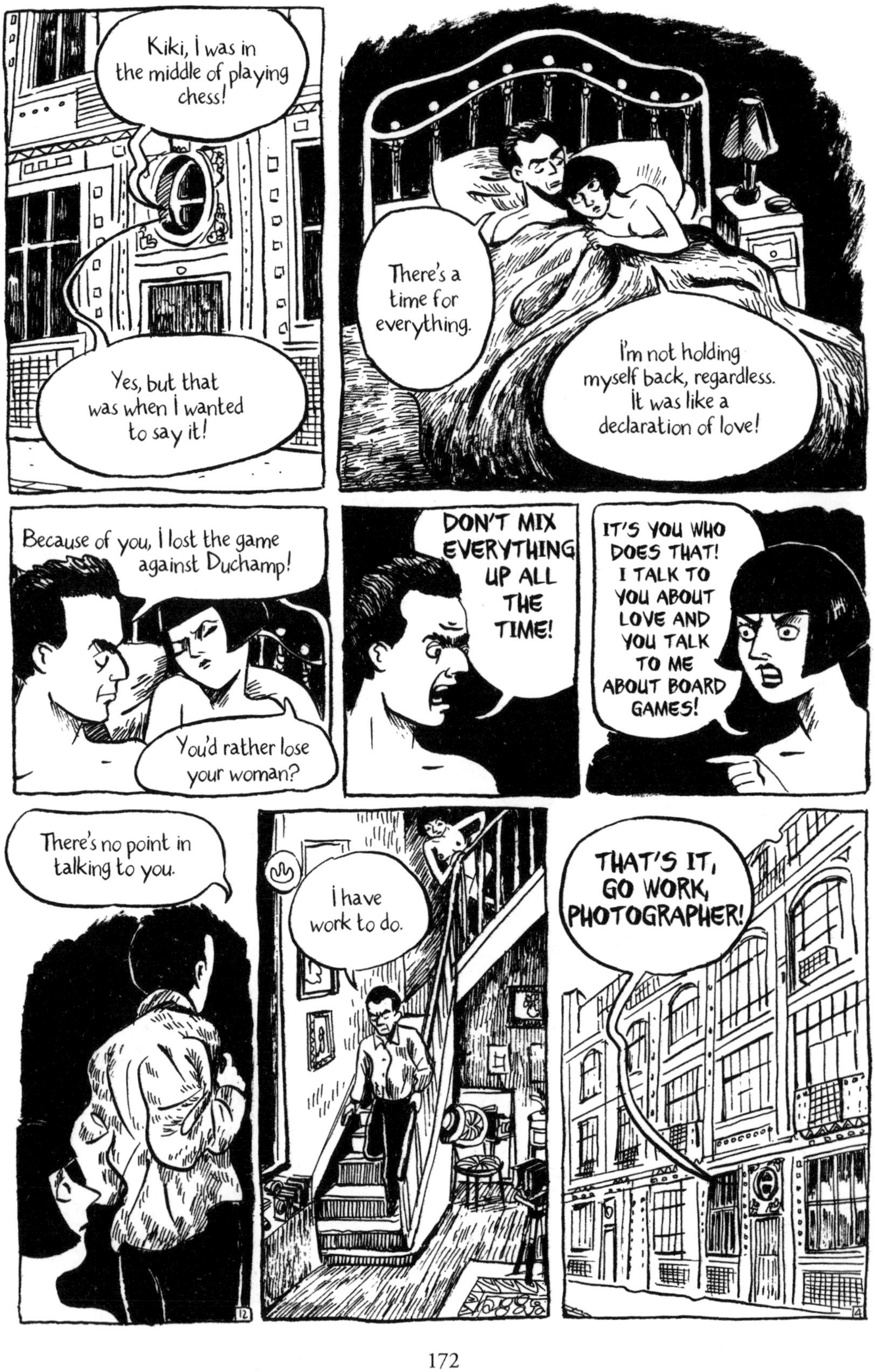
Kiki, I was in the middle of playing chess!
Yes, but that was when I wanted to say it!
There's a time for everything.
I'm not holding myself back, regardless. It was like a declaration of love!
Because of you, I lost the game against Duchamp!
You'd rather lose your woman?
DON'T MIX EVERYTHING UP ALL THE TIME!
IT'S YOU WHO DOES THAT! I TALK TO YOU ABOUT LOVE AND YOU TALK TO ME ABOUT BOARD GAMES!
There's no point in talking to you.
I have work to do.
THAT'S IT, GO WORK, PHOTOGRAPHER!

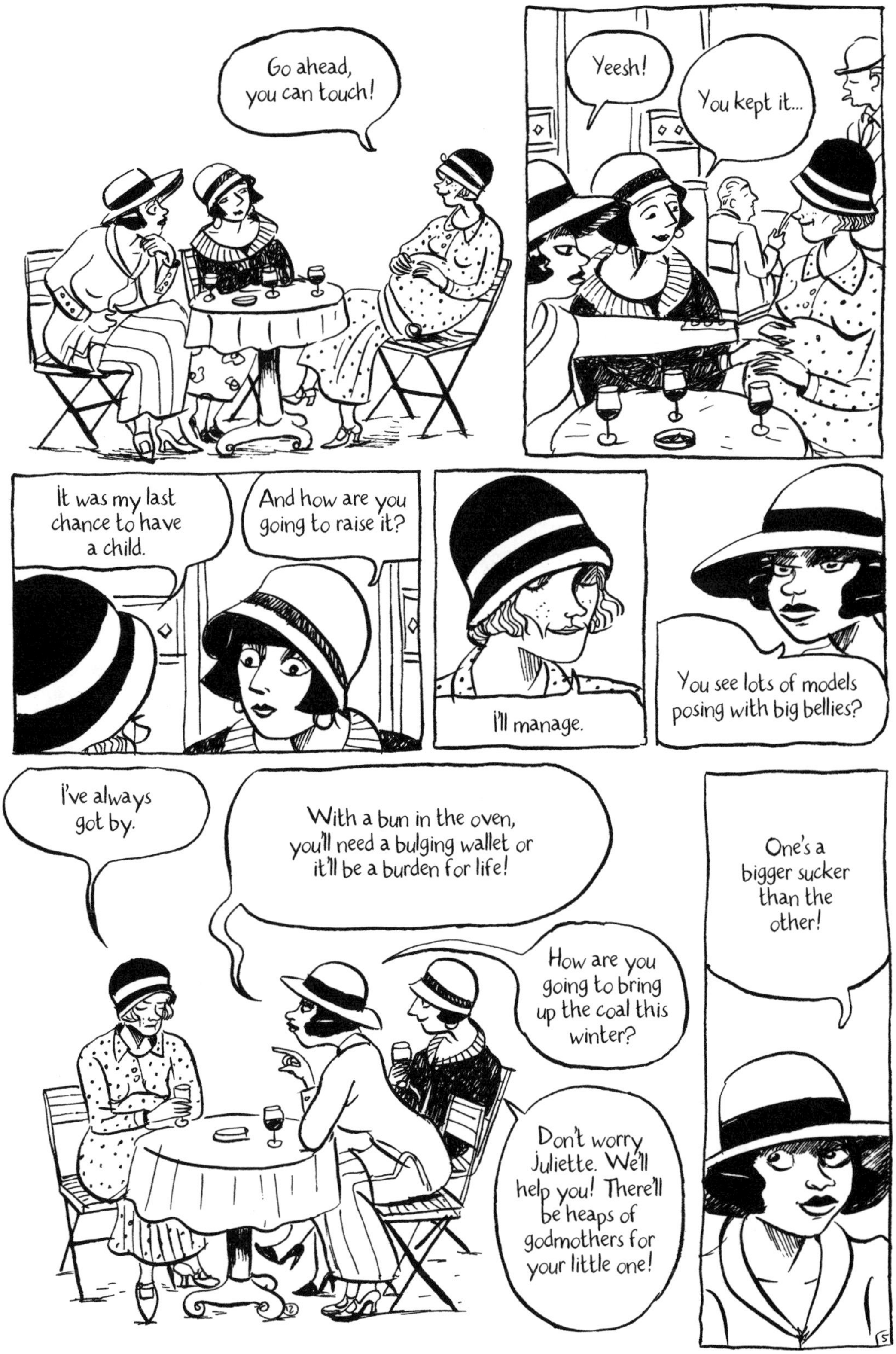
Go ahead, you can touch!
Yeesh!
You kept it...
It was my last chance to have a child.
And how are you going to raise it?
I'll manage.
You see lots of models posing with big bellies?
I've always got by.
With a bun in the oven, you'll need a bulging wallet or it'll be a burden for life!
How are you going to bring up the coal this winter?
Don't worry Juliette. We'll help you! There'll be heaps of godmothers for your little one!
One's a bigger sucker than the other!

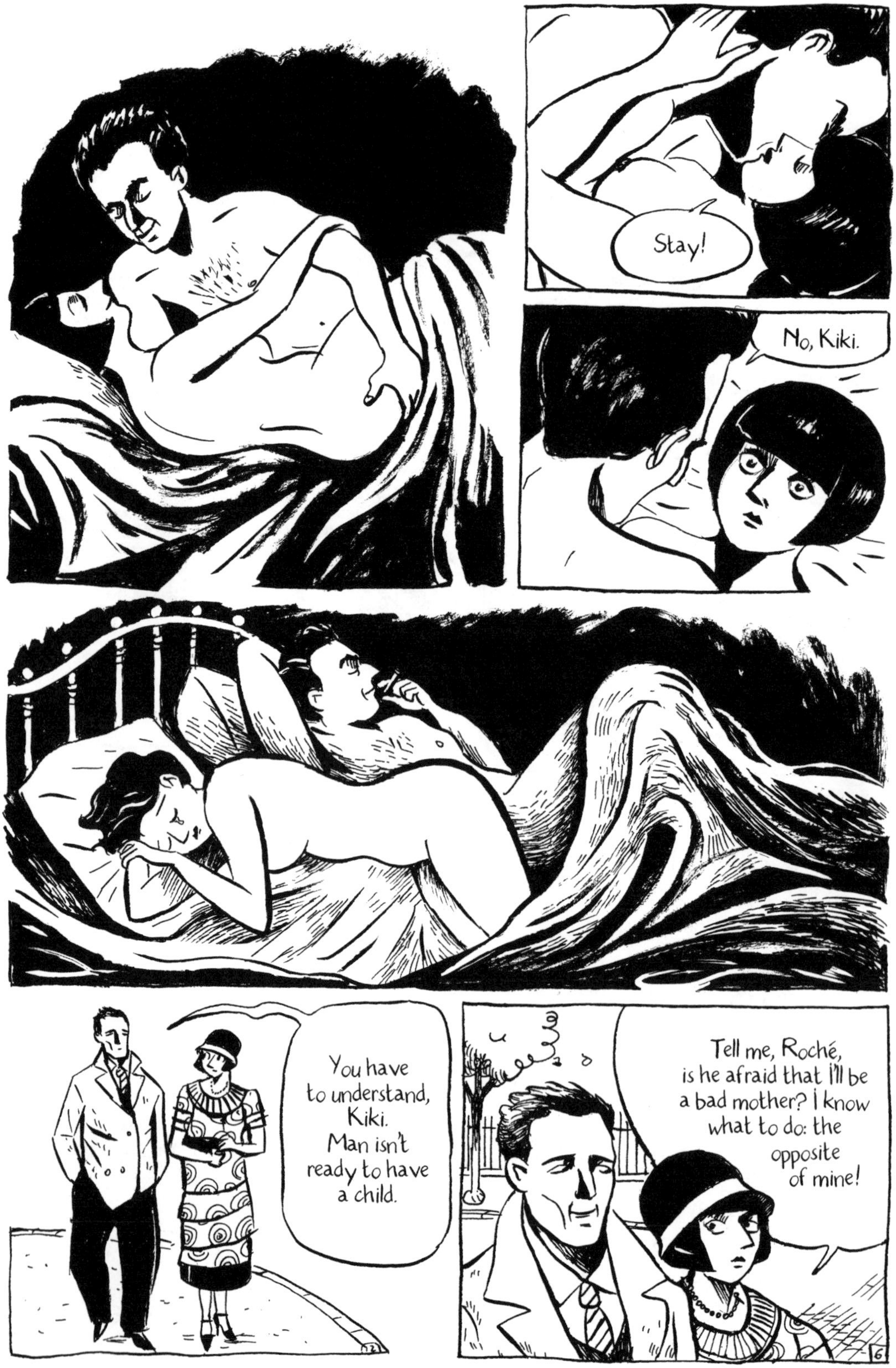
Stay!
No, Kiki.
You have to understand, Kiki. Man isn't ready to have a child.
Tell me, Roché, is he afraid that I'll be a bad mother? I know what to do: the opposite of mine!

That's not why, Kiki. For the moment, Man is totally giving himself to creating.

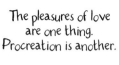

He must think of other things...

...I know it!

The pleasures of love are one thing. Procreation is another.

Procreation/creation. An artist has to choose.

He's afraid that a child will make him sterile? That's egotism!

Creation comes at a price, Kiki.

WHAT BULLSHIT!

It's like this: an artist can't be encumbered by a child.

What about ME?

But you are an artist, Kiki.

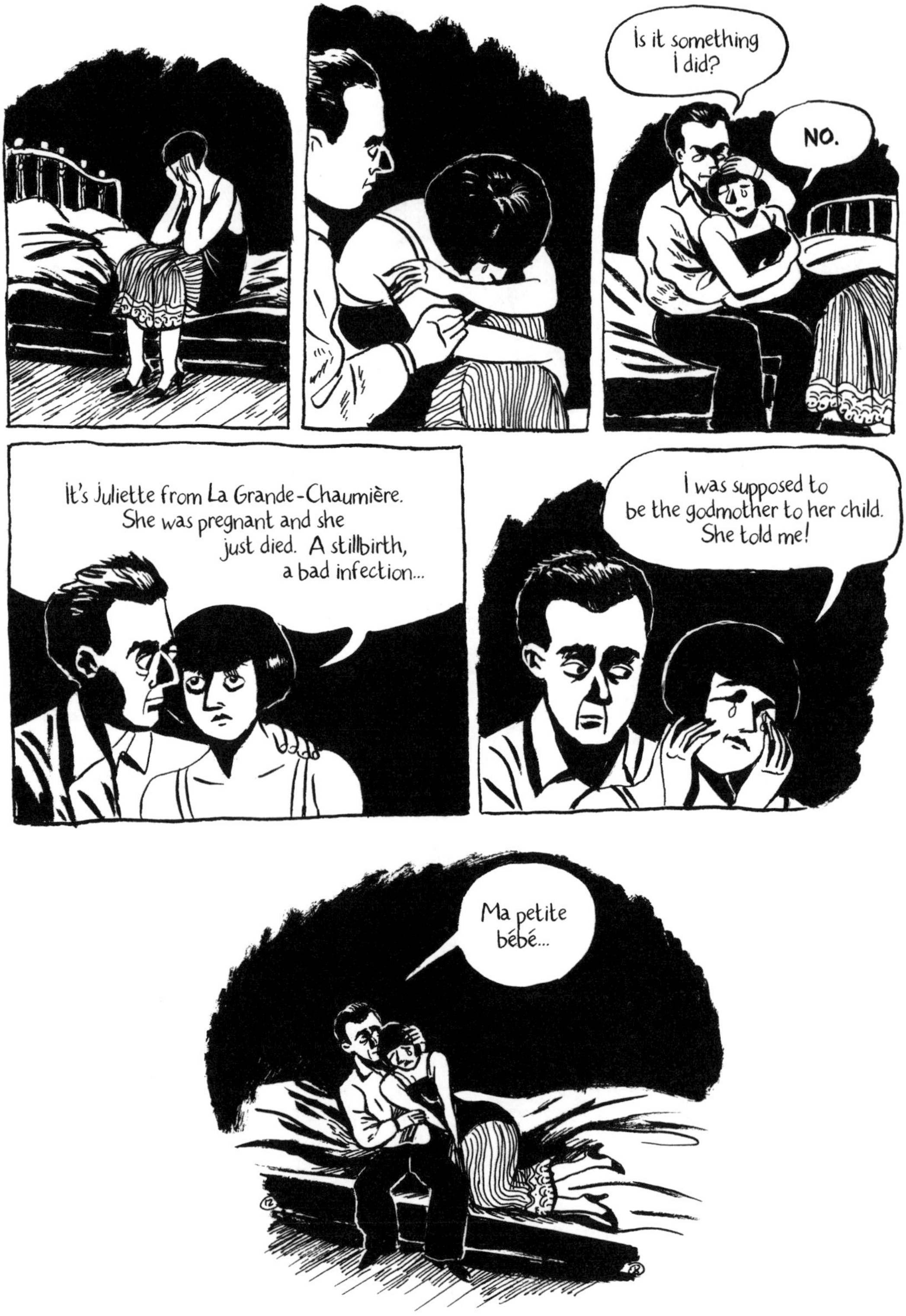
Is it something I did?
NO.
It's Juliette from La Grande-Chaumière. She was pregnant and she just died. A stillbirth, a bad infection...
I was supposed to be the godmother to her child. She told me!
Ma petite bébé...

1923 - New York

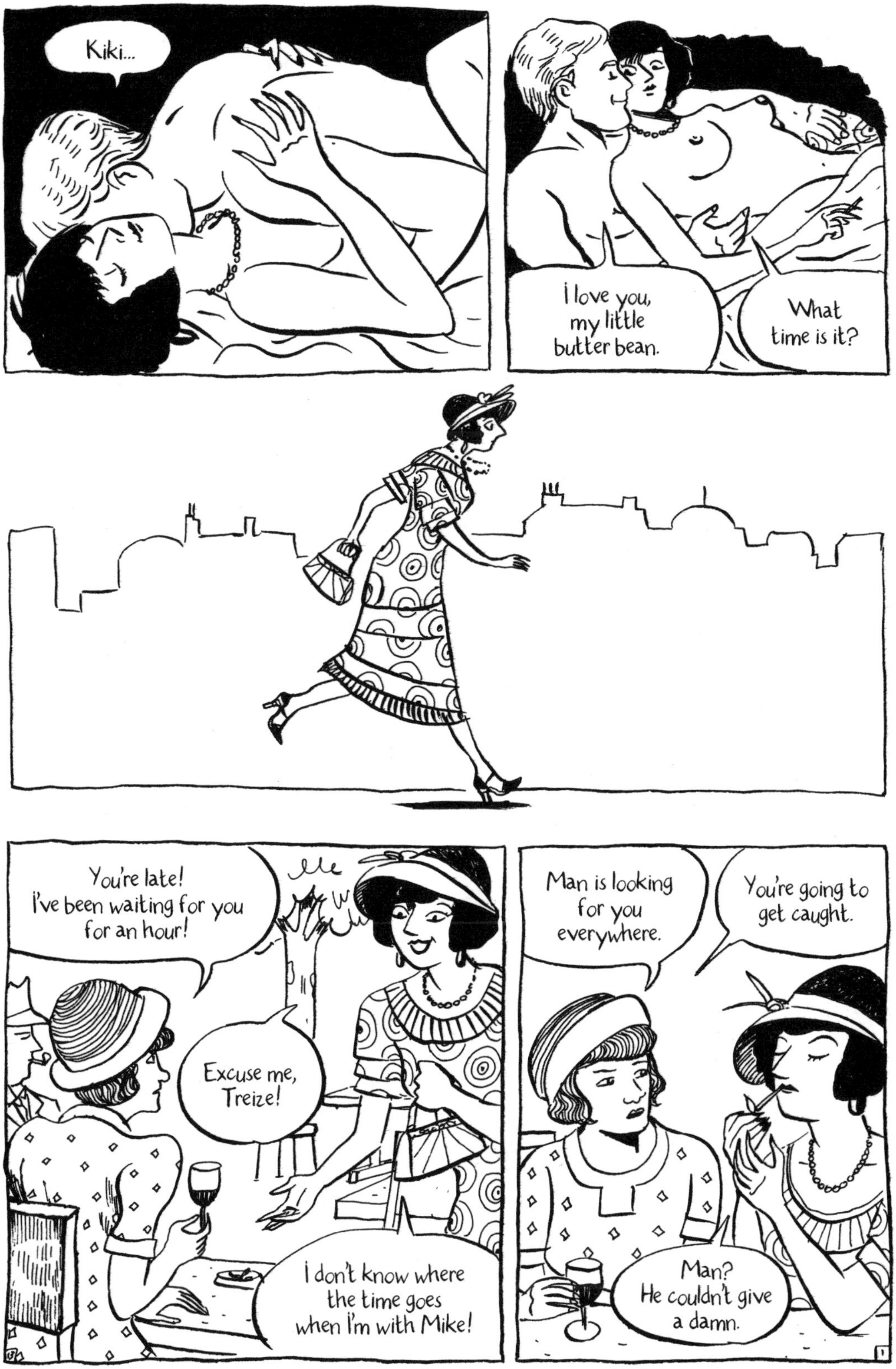
Kiki...
I love you, my little butter bean.
What time is it?
You're late! I've been waiting for you for an hour!
Excuse me, Treize!
I don't know where the time goes when I'm with Mike!
Man is looking for you everywhere.
You're going to get caught.
Man? He couldn't give a damn.

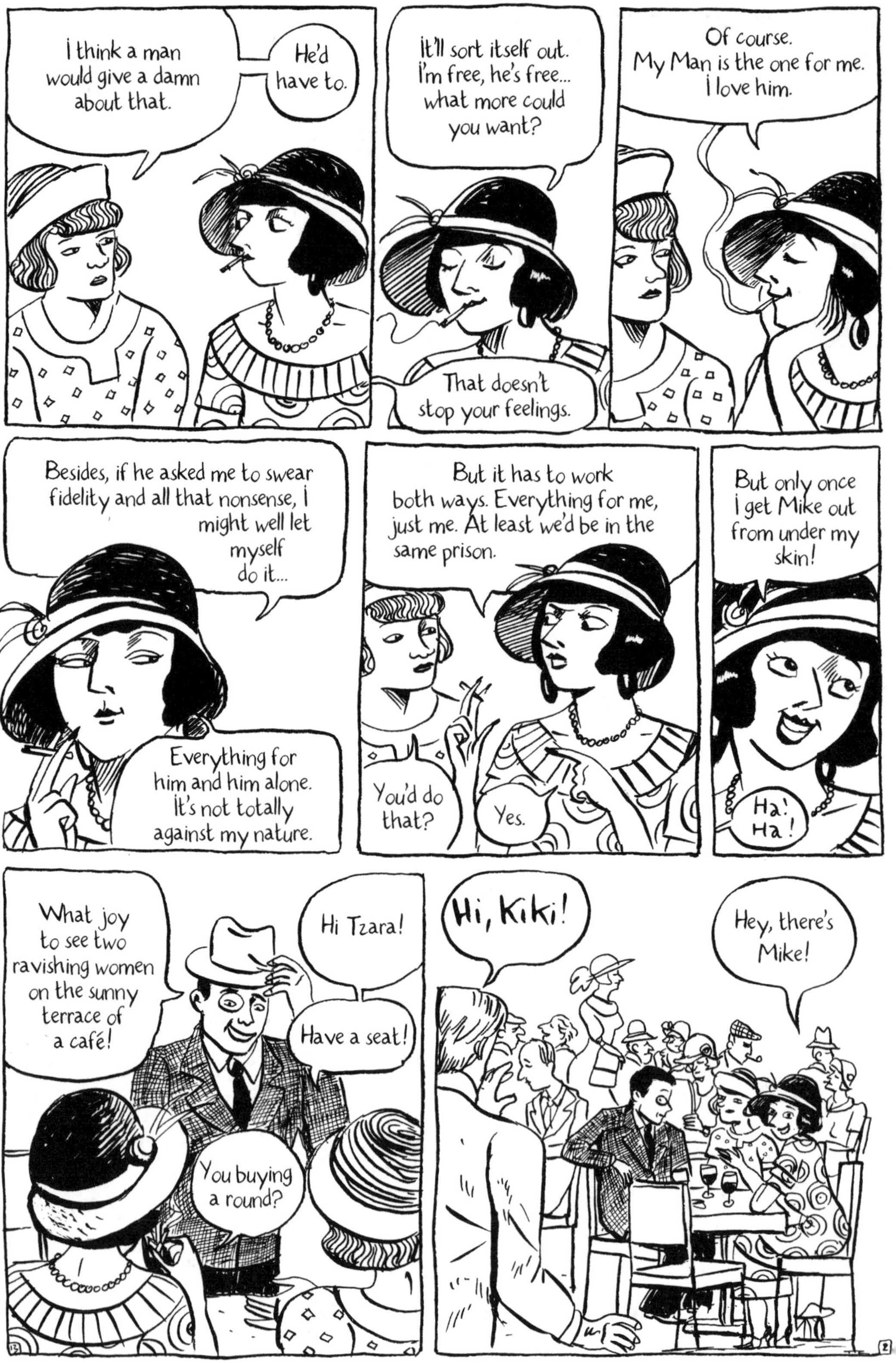
I think a man would give a damn about that.
He'd have to.
It'll sort itself out. I'm free, he's free... what more could you want?
That doesn't stop your feelings.
Of course. My Man is the one for me. I love him.
Besides, if he asked me to swear fidelity and all that nonsense, I might well let myself do it...
Everything for him and him alone. It's not totally against my nature.
But it has to work both ways. Everything for me, just me. At least we'd be in the same prison.
You'd do that?
Yes.
But only once I get Mike out from under my skin!
Ha! Ha!
What joy to see two ravishing women on the sunny terrace of a café!
Hi Tzara!
Have a seat!
You buying a round?
Hi, Kiki!
Hey, there's Mike!

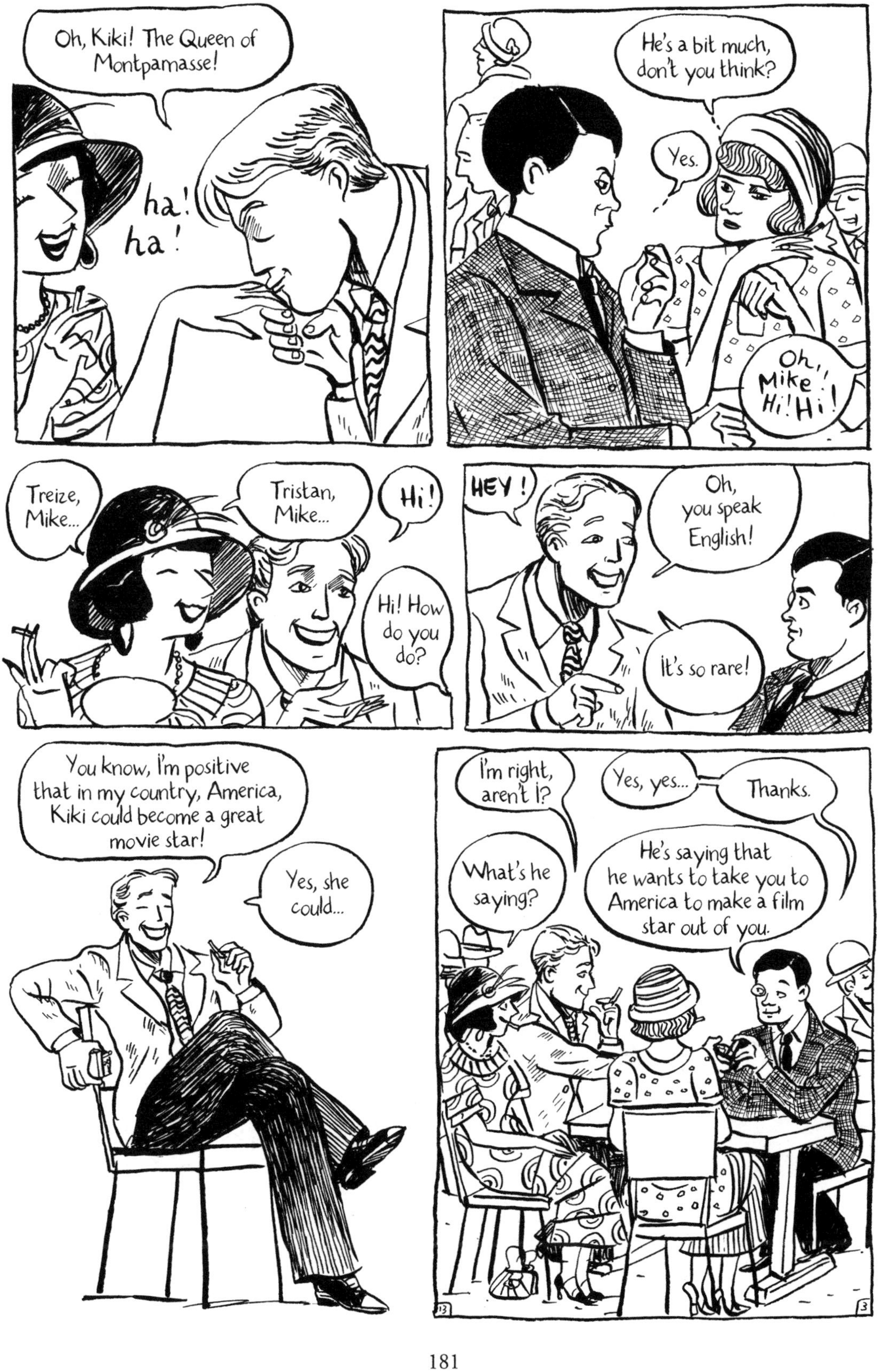
Oh, Kiki! The Queen of Montparnasse!
ha! ha!
He's a bit much, don't you think?
Yes.
Oh, Mike! Hi! Hi!
Treize, Mike...
Tristan, Mike...
Hi!
Hi! How do you do?
HEY!
Oh, you speak English!
It's so rare!
You know, I'm positive that in my country, America, Kiki could become a great movie star!
Yes, she could...
I'm right, aren't I?
Yes, yes...
Thanks.
What's he saying?
He's saying that he wants to take you to America to make a film star out of you.

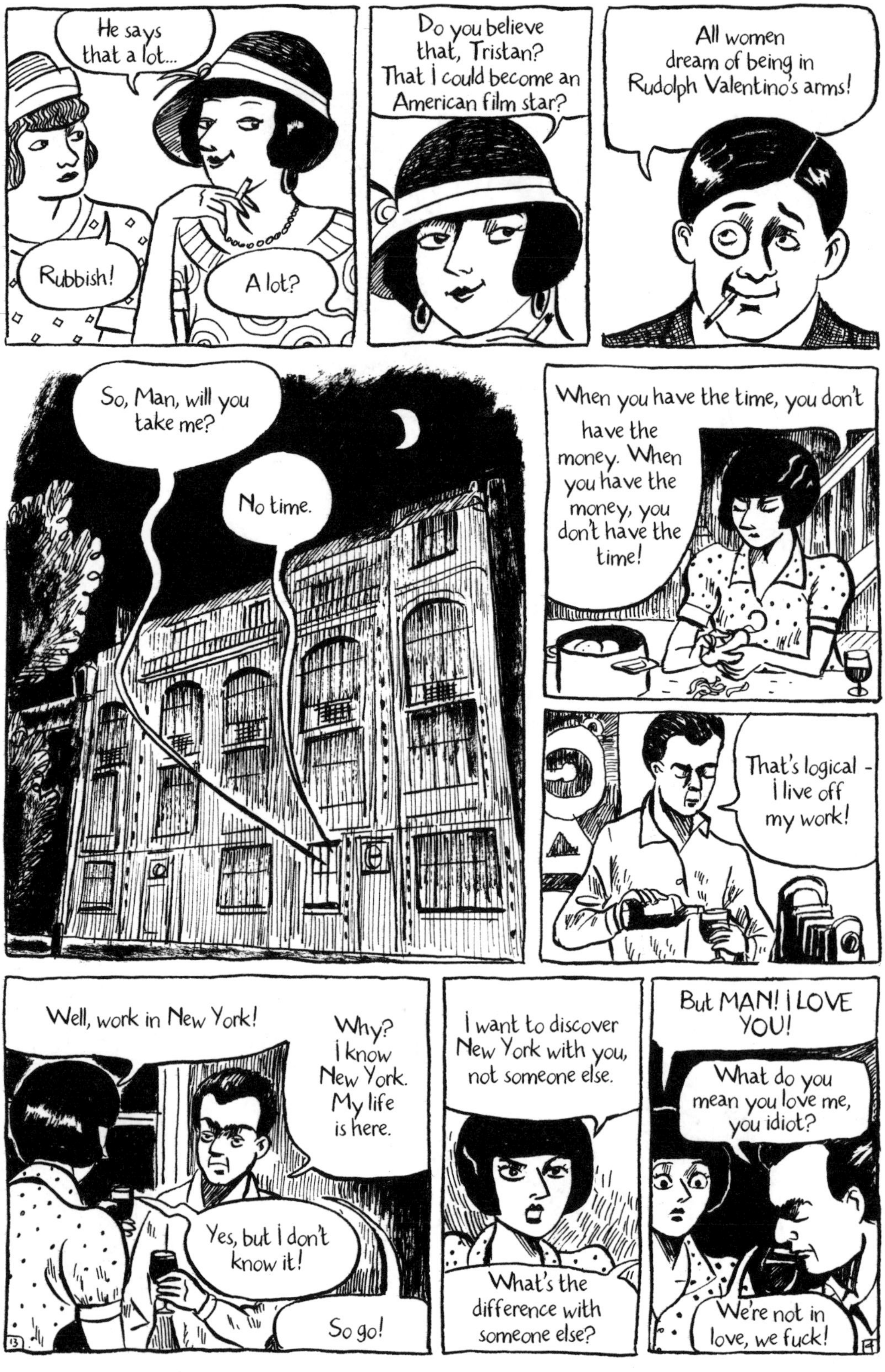
He says that a lot...
Rubbish!
A lot?
Do you believe that, Tristan? That I could become an American film star?
All women dream of being in Rudolph Valentino's arms!
So, Man, will you take me?
No time.
When you have the time, you don't have the money. When you have the money, you don't have the time!
That's logical - I live off my work!
Well, work in New York!
Why? I know New York. My life is here.
Yes, but I don't know it!
So go!
13
I want to discover New York with you, not someone else.
What's the difference with someone else?
But MAN! I LOVE YOU!
What do you mean you love me, you idiot?
We're not in love, we fuck!
14

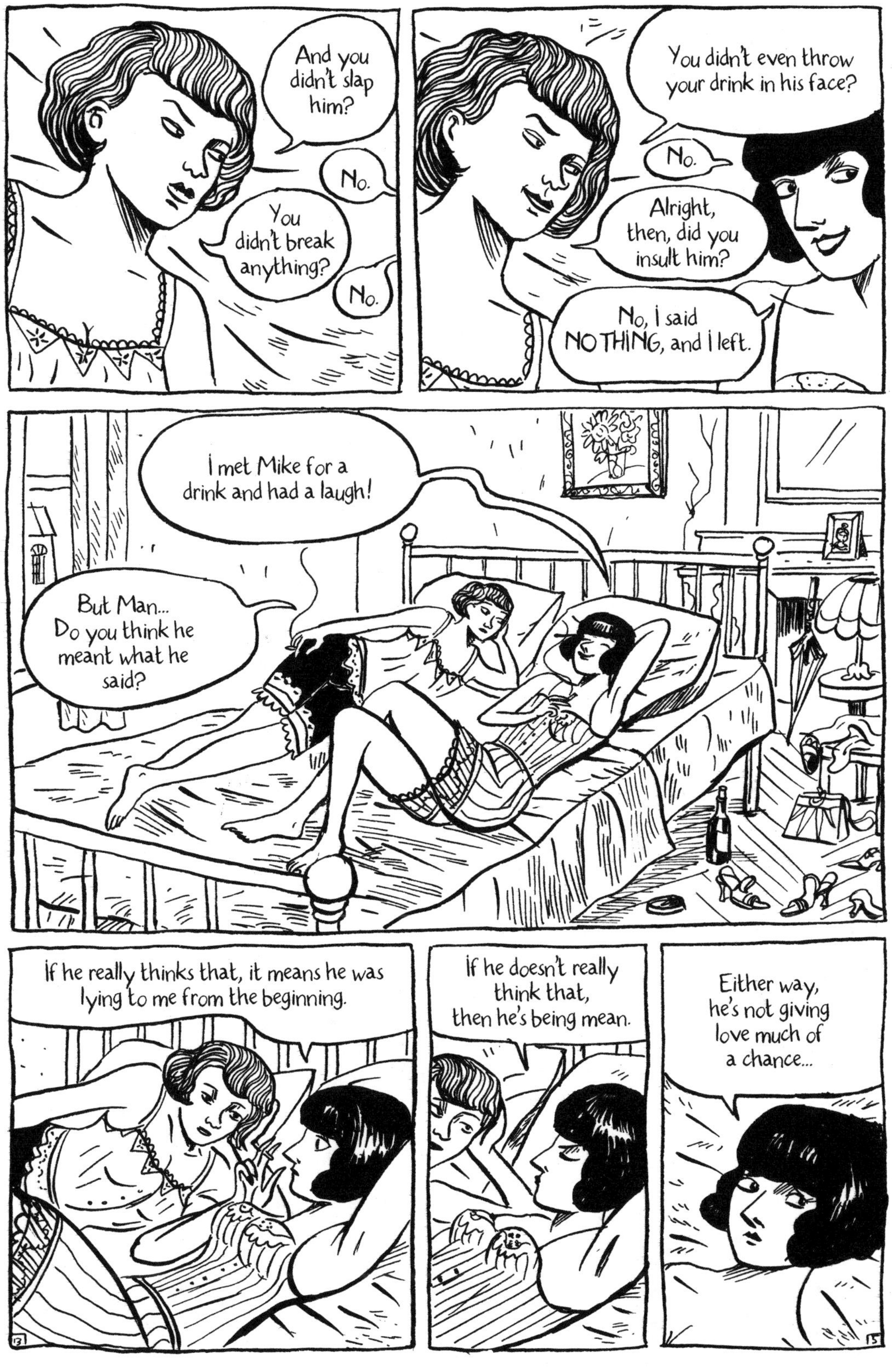
And you didn't slap him?
No.
You didn't break anything?
No.
You didn't even throw your drink in his face?
No.
Alright, then, did you insult him?
No, I said NOTHING, and I left.
I met Mike for a drink and had a laugh!
But Man... Do you think he meant what he said?
If he really thinks that, it means he was lying to me from the beginning.
If he doesn't really think that, then he's being mean.
Either way, he's not giving love much of a chance...

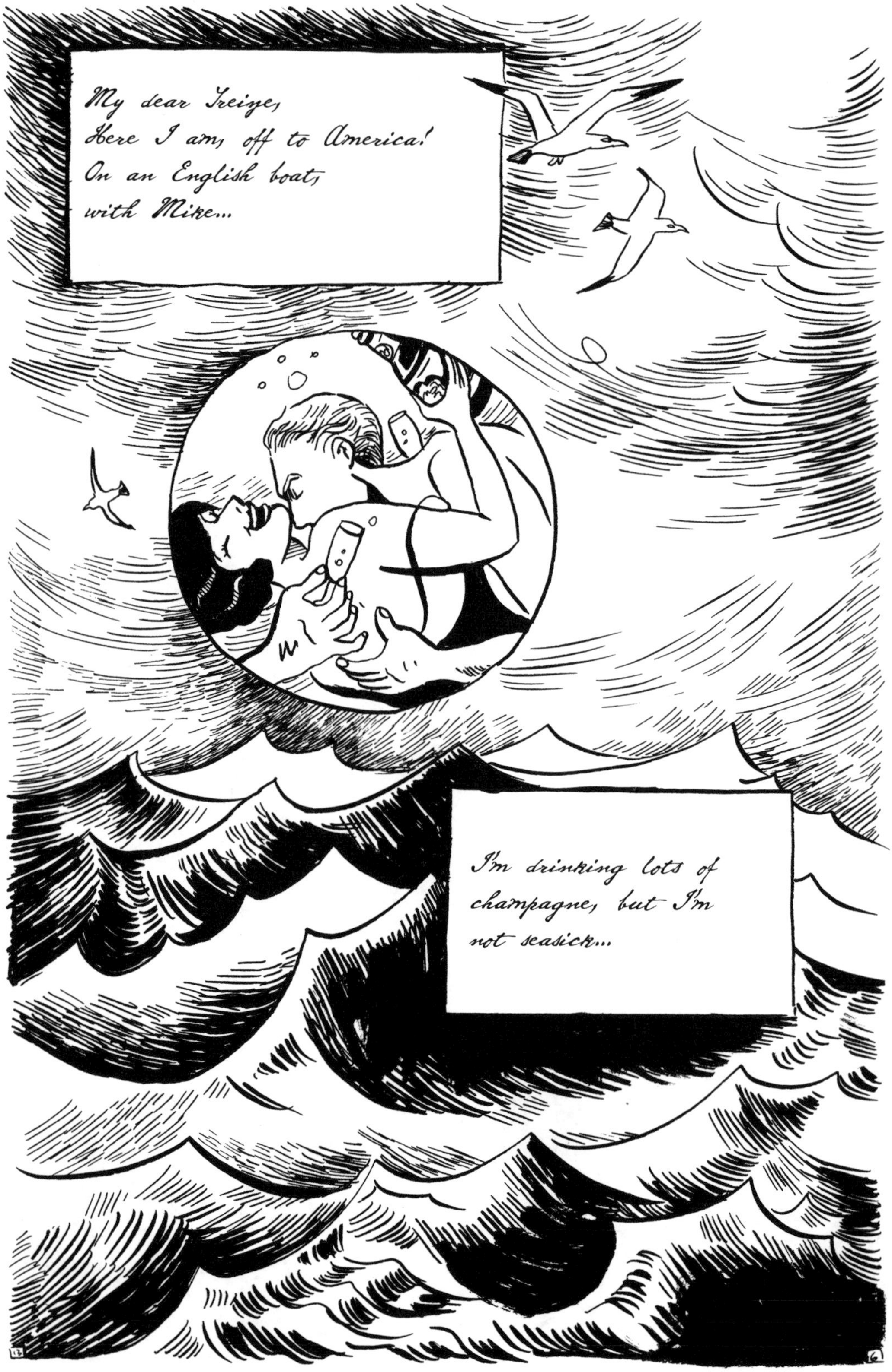
My dear Ireize,
Here I am, off to America!
On an English boat,
with Mike...
I'm drinking lots of champagne, but I'm not seasick...

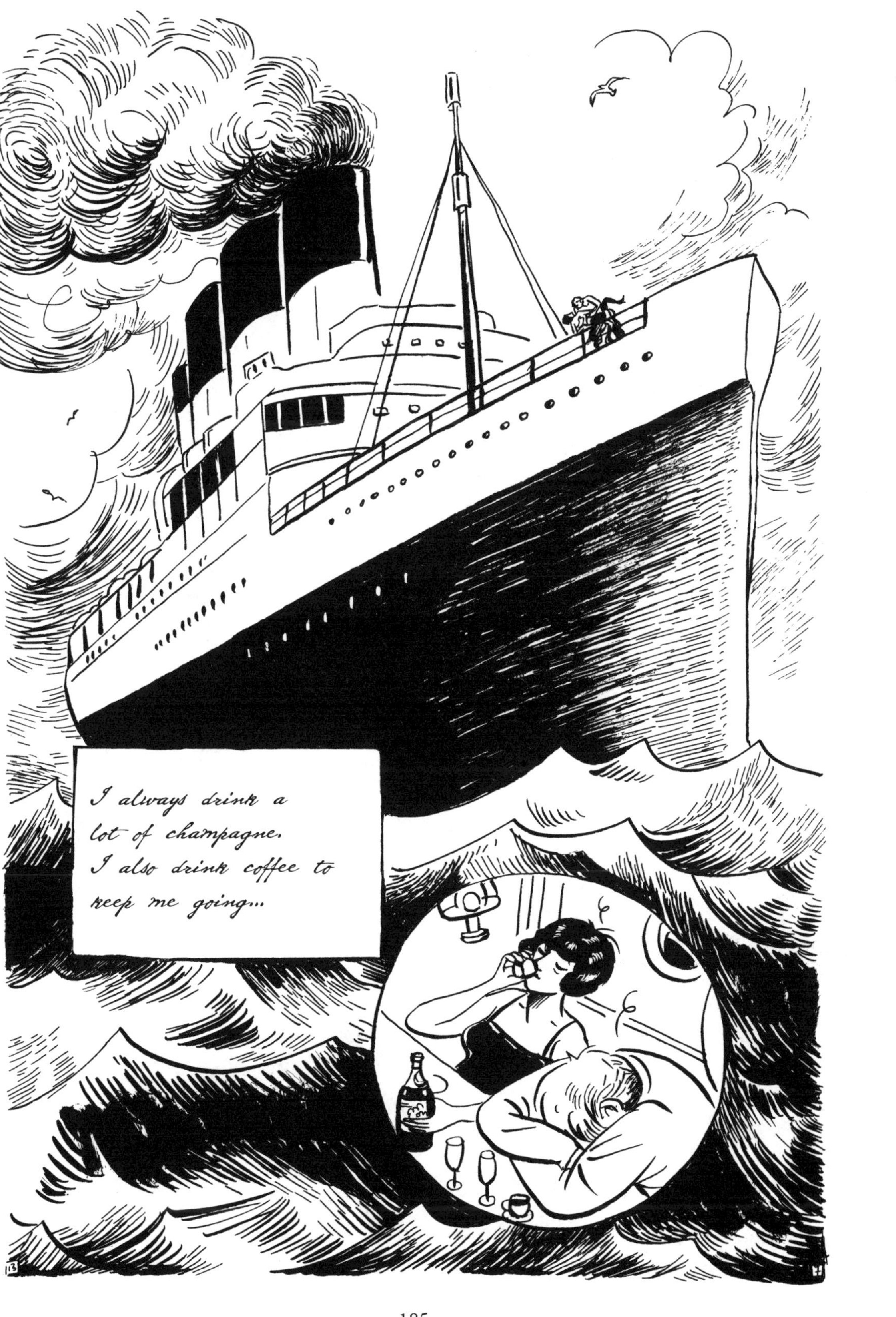
I always drink a
lot of champagne.
I also drink coffee to
keep me going...

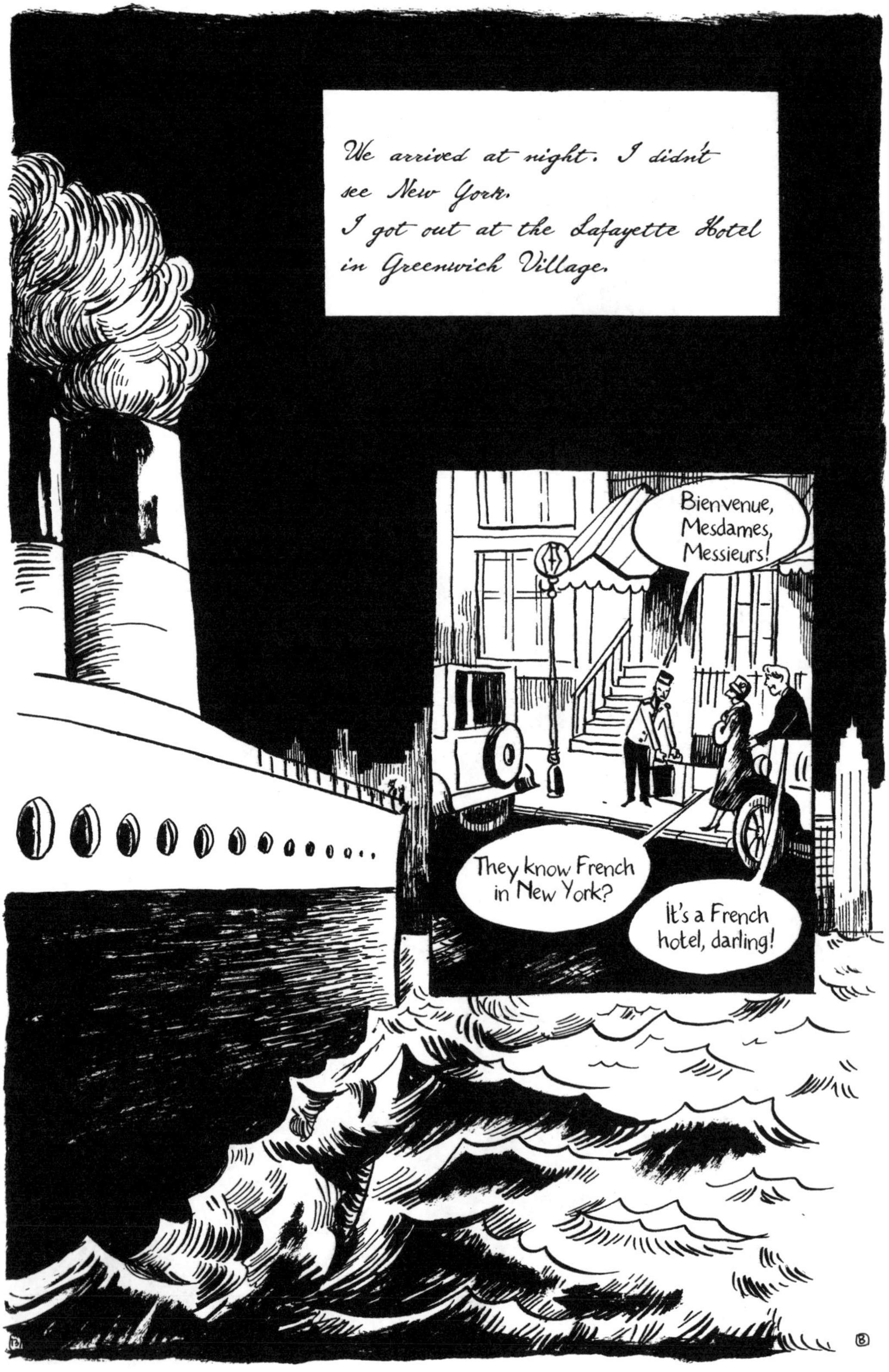
We arrived at night. I didn't see New York.
I got out at the Lafayette Hotel in Greenwich Village.
Bienvenue, Mesdames, Messieurs!
They know French in New York?
It's a French hotel, darling!

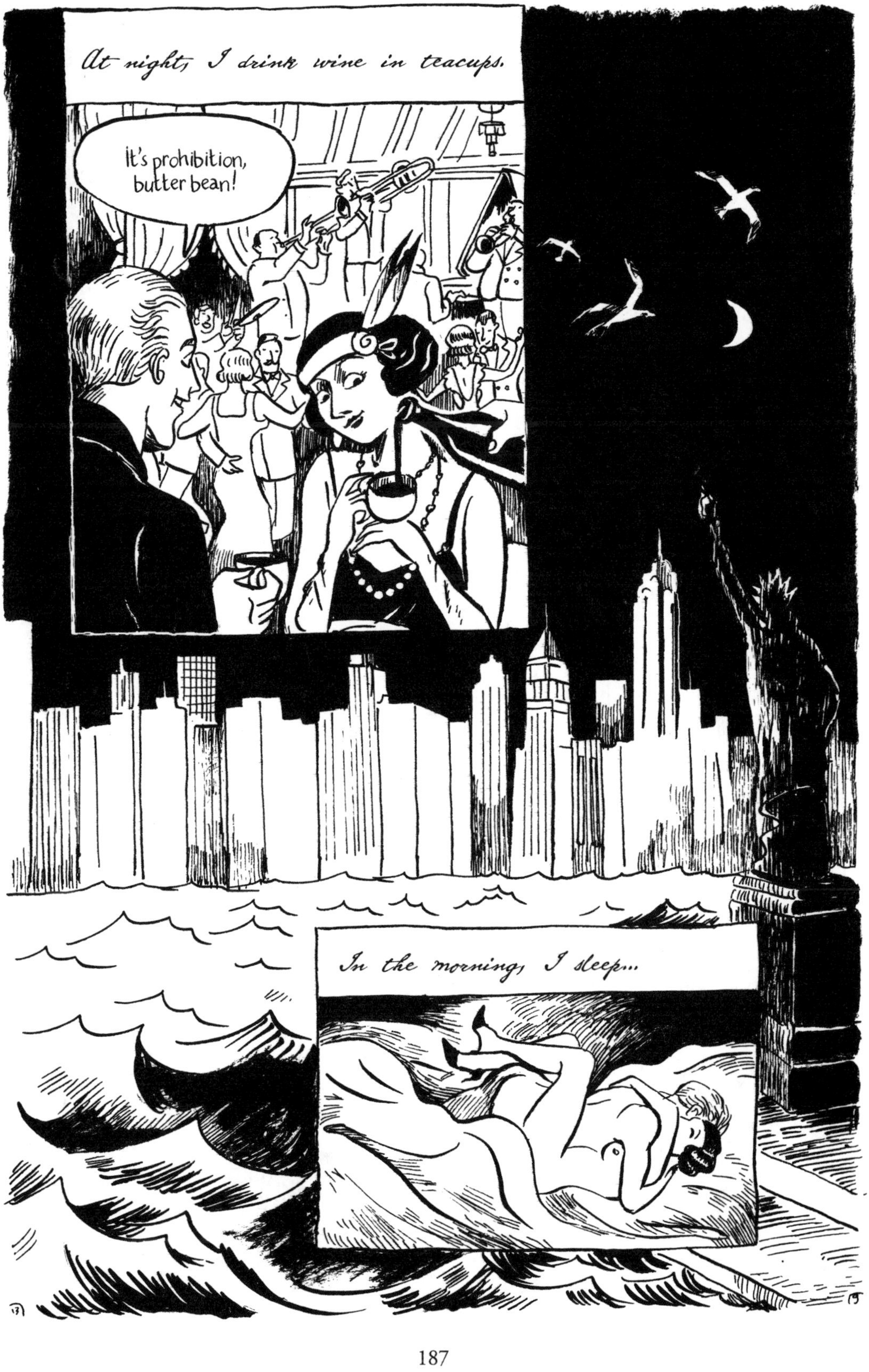
At night, I drink wine in teacups.
It's prohibition, butter bean!
In the morning, I sleep...

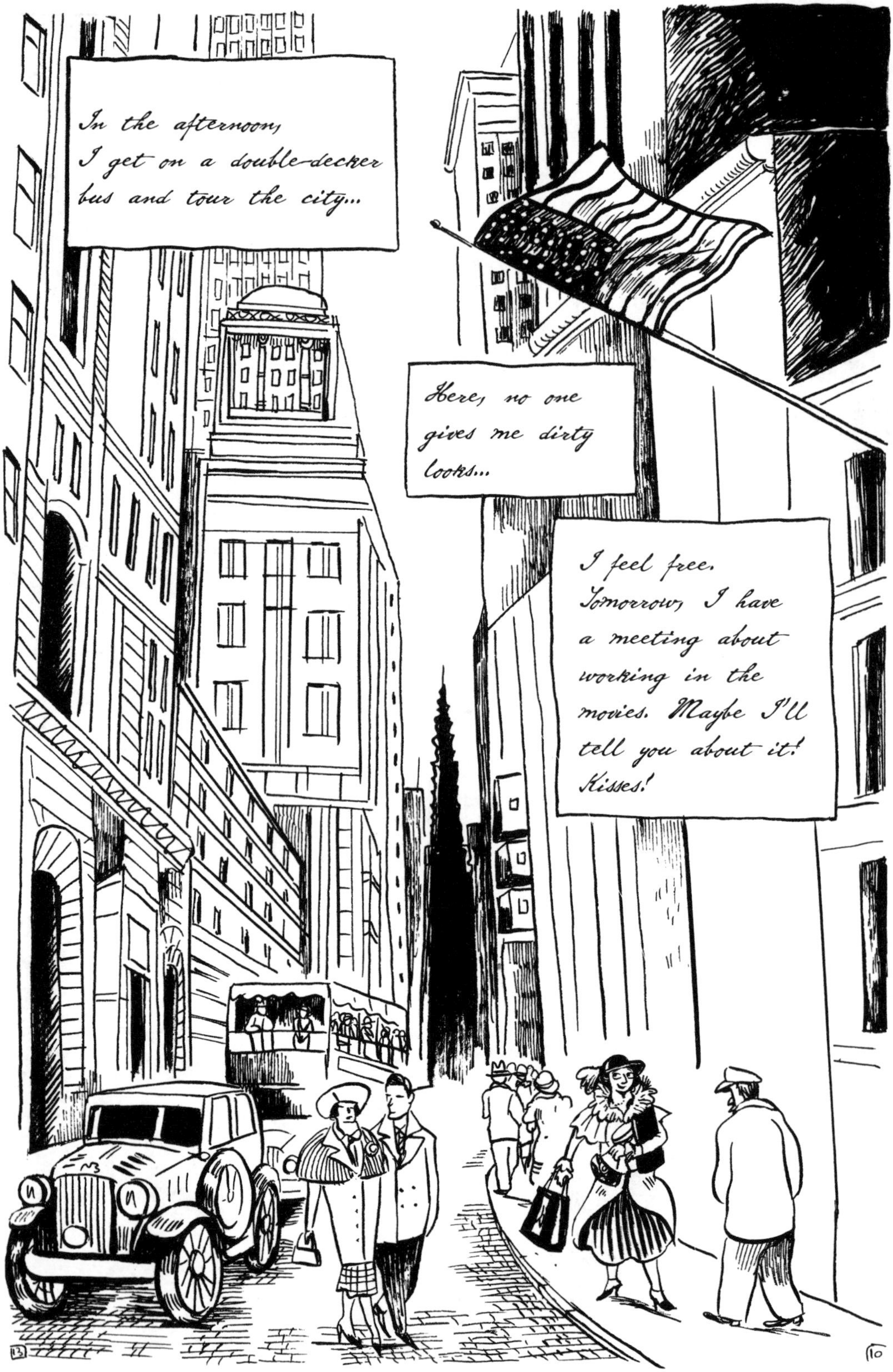
In the afternoon, I get on a double-decker bus and tour the city...
Here, no one gives me dirty looks...
I feel free. Tomorrow, I have a meeting about working in the movies. Maybe I'll tell you about it! Kisses!

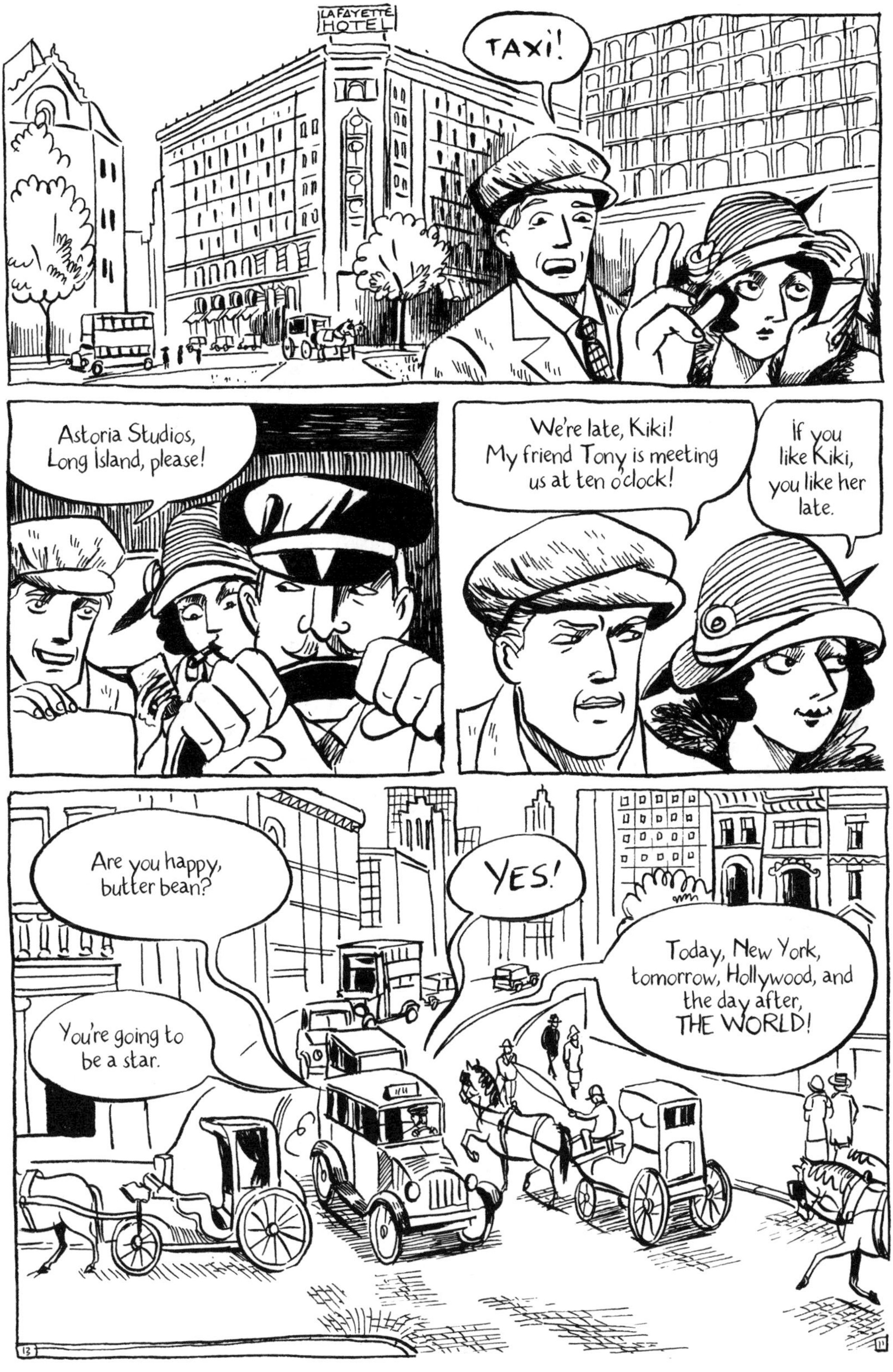
LAFAYETTE HOTEL
TAXI!
Astoria Studios, Long Island, please!
We're late, Kiki! My friend Tony is meeting us at ten o'clock!
If you like Kiki, you like her late.
Are you happy, butter bean?
YES!
You're going to be a star.
Today, New York, tomorrow, Hollywood, and the day after, THE WORLD!

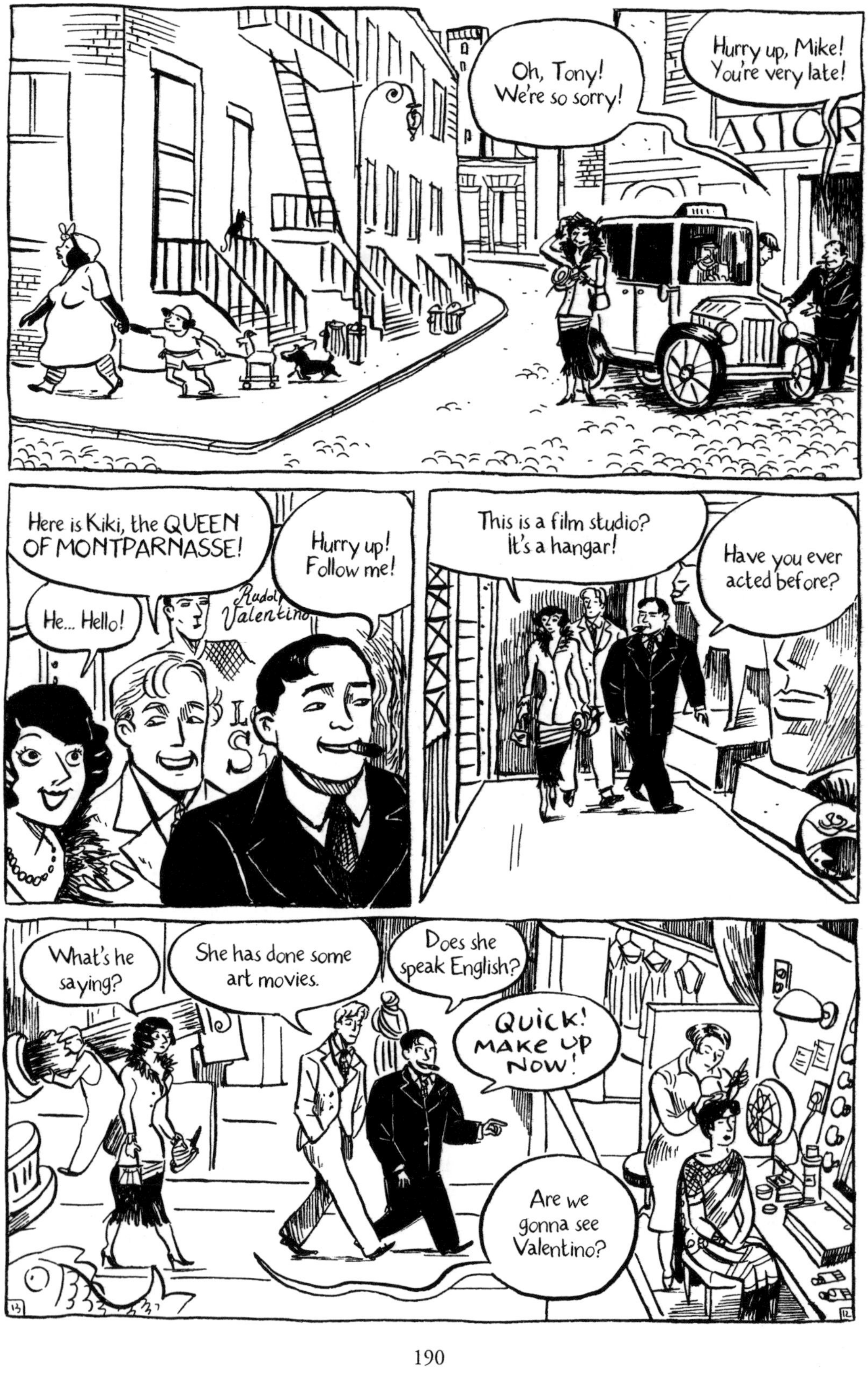
Oh, Tony! We're so sorry!
Hurry up, Mike! You're very late!
ASTOR
Here is Kiki, the QUEEN OF MONTPARNASSE!
He... Hello!
Hurry up! Follow me!
Rudol
Valentino
This is a film studio? It's a hangar!
Have you ever acted before?
What's he saying?
She has done some art movies.
Does she speak English?
QUICK! MAKE UP NOW!
Are we gonna see Valentino?

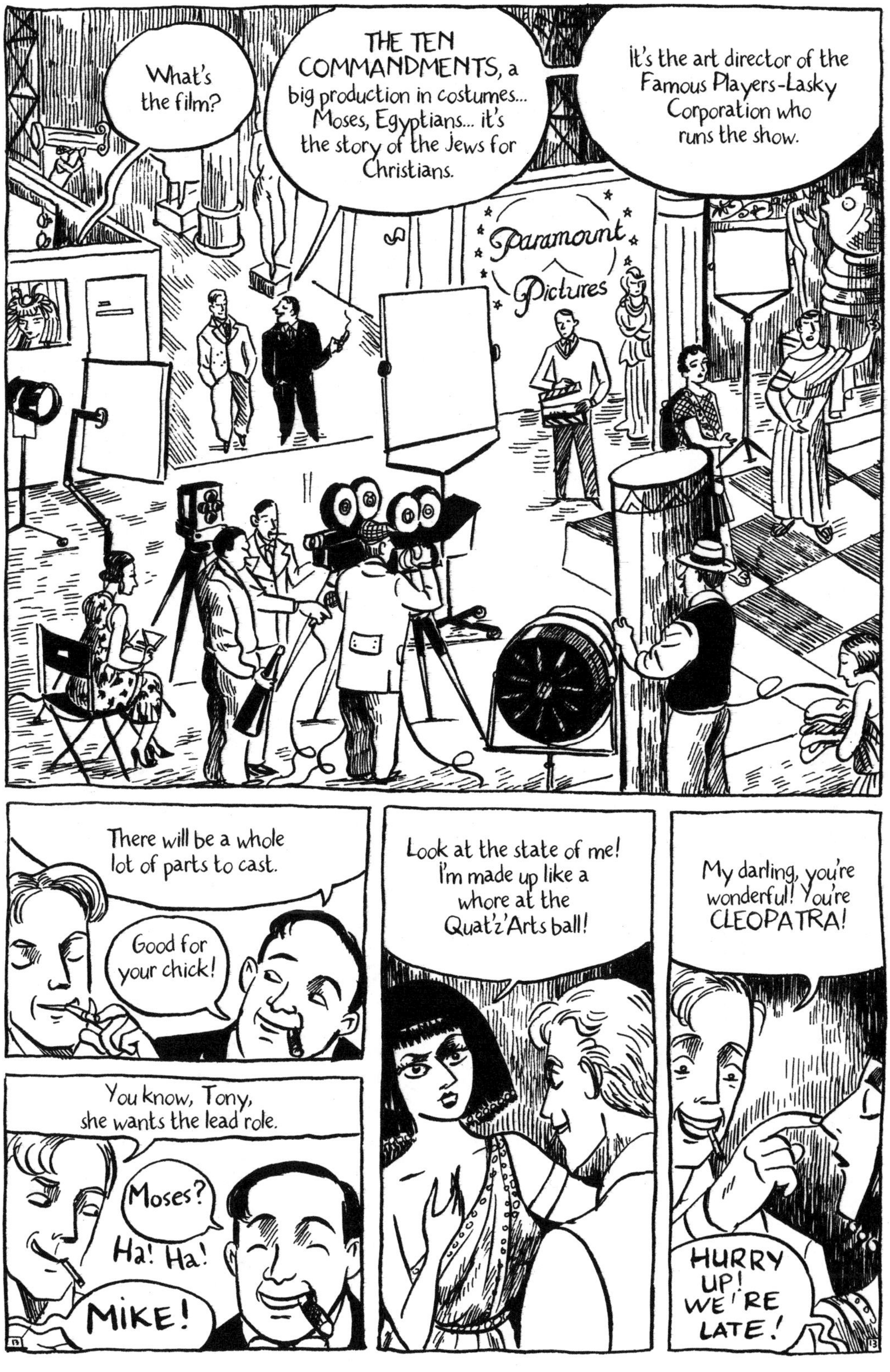
What's the film?
THE TEN COMMANDMENTS, a big production in costumes... Moses, Egyptians... it's the story of the Jews for Christians.
It's the art director of the Famous Players-Lasky Corporation who runs the show.
Paramount Pictures
There will be a whole lot of parts to cast.
Good for your chick!
You know, Tony, she wants the lead role.
Moses?
Ha! Ha!
MIKE!
Look at the state of me! I'm made up like a whore at the Quat'z'Arts ball!
My darling, you're wonderful! You're CLEOPATRA!
HURRY UP! WE'RE LATE!

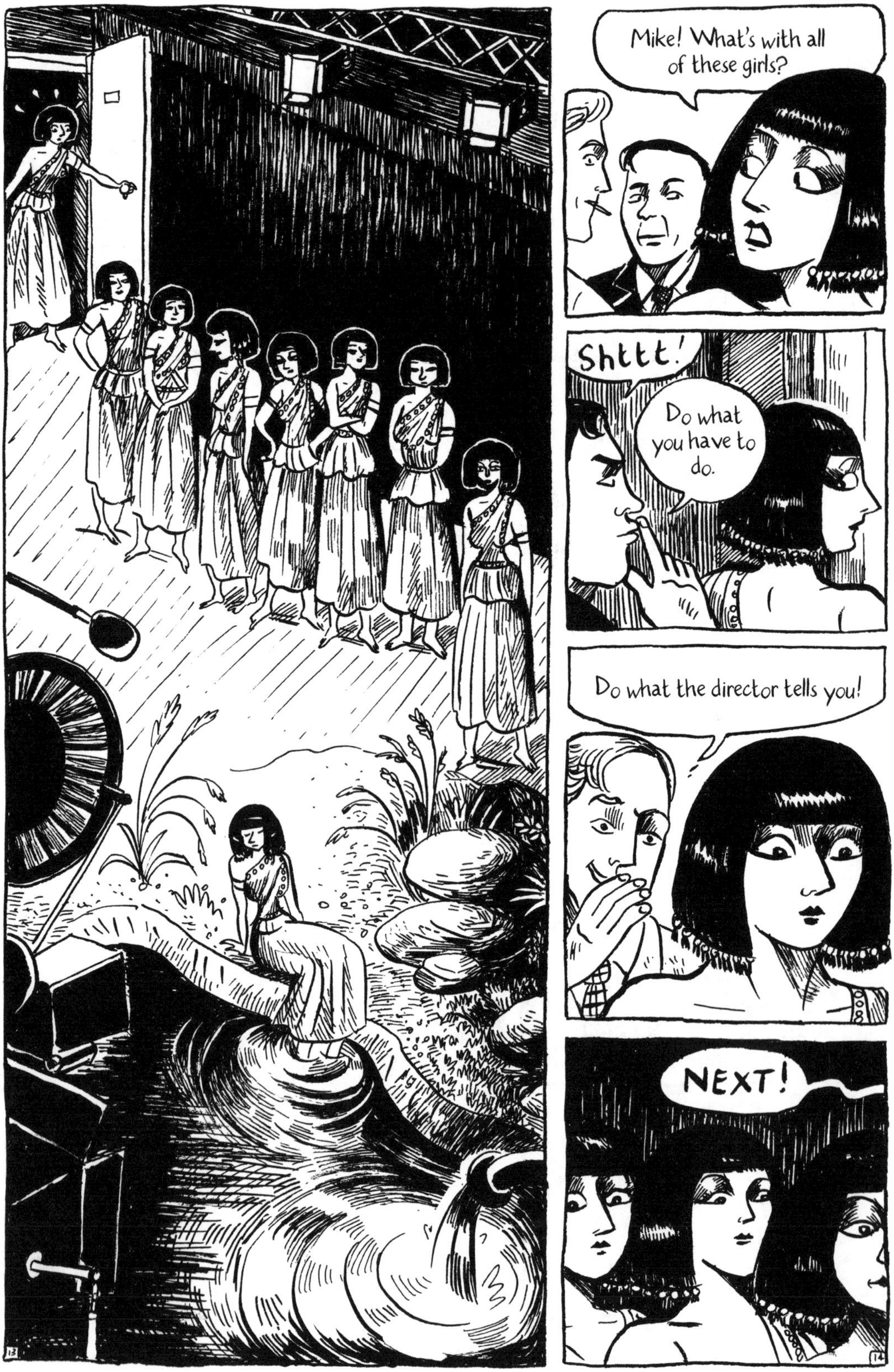
Mike! What's with all of these girls?
Shttt!
Do what you have to do.
Do what the director tells you!
NEXT!

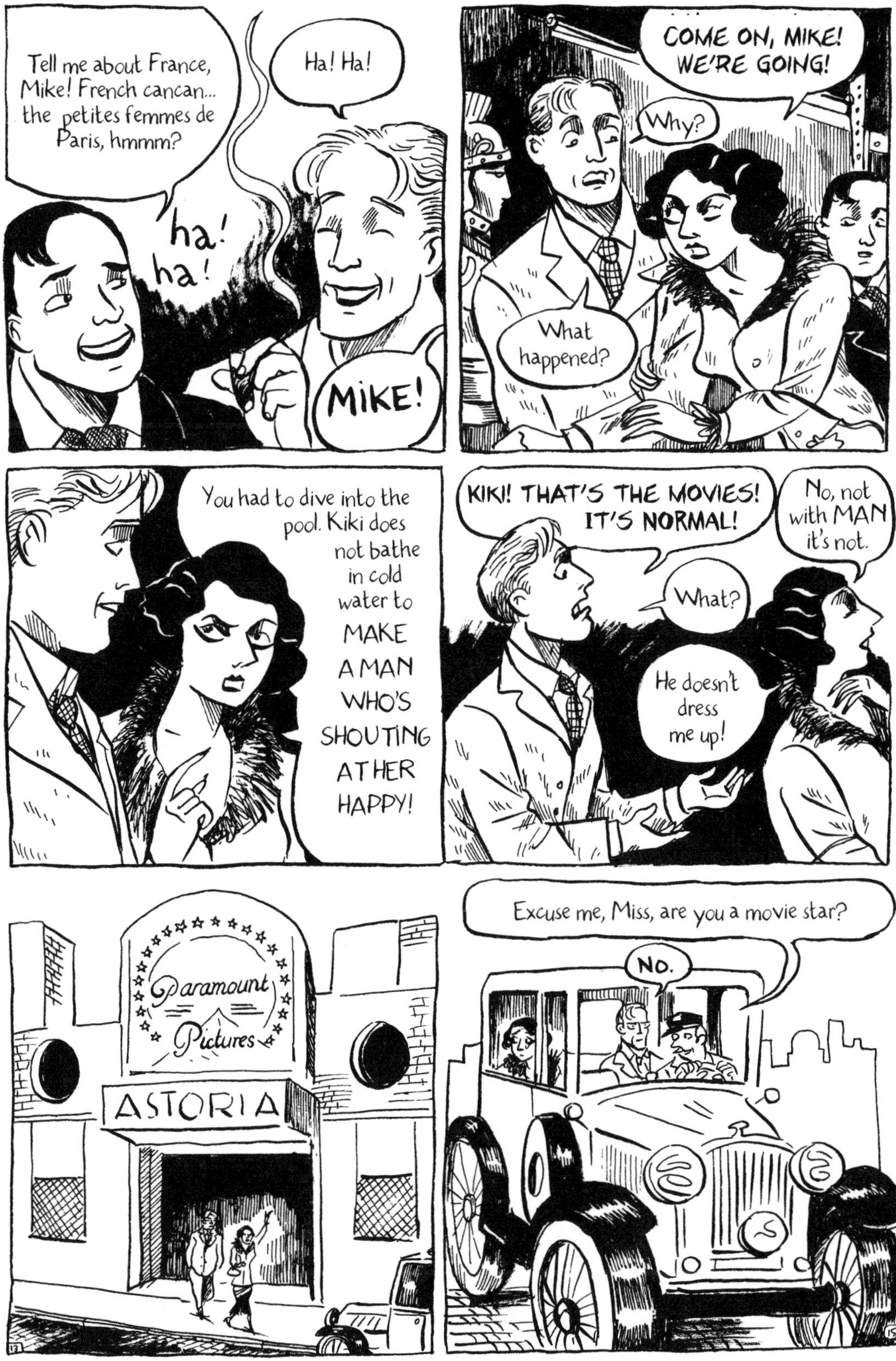
Tell me about France, Mike! French cancan... the petites femmes de Paris, hmmm?
Ha! Ha!
ha! ha!
MIKE!
COME ON, MIKE! WE'RE GOING!
Why?
What happened?
You had to dive into the pool. Kiki does not bathe in cold water to MAKE A MAN WHO'S SHOUTING AT HER HAPPY!
KIKI! THAT'S THE MOVIES! IT'S NORMAL!
No, not with MAN it's not.
What?
He doesn't dress me up!
Paramount Pictures
ASTORIA
Excuse me, Miss, are you a movie star?
NO.

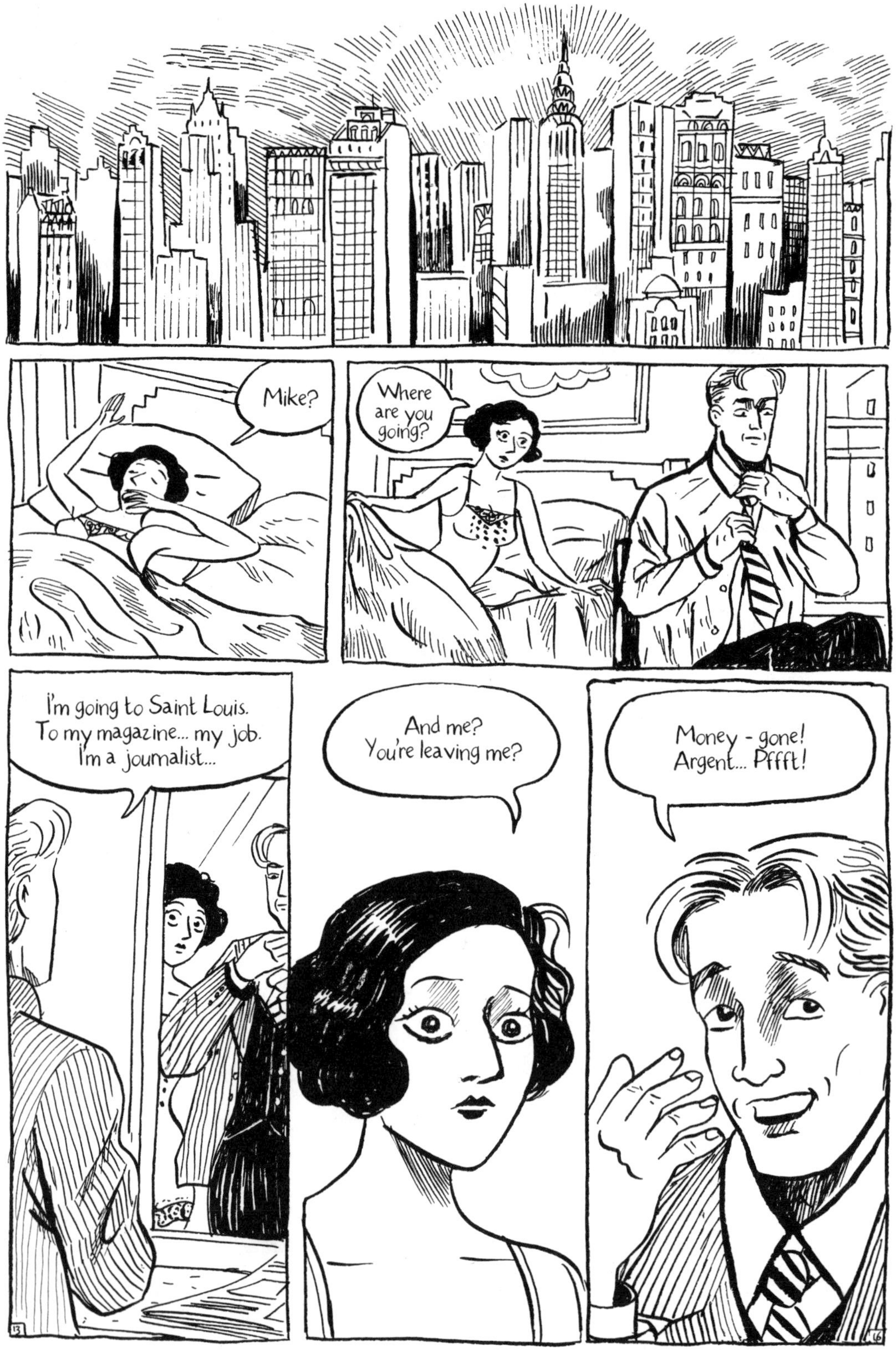
Mike?
Where are you going?
I'm going to Saint Louis. To my magazine... my job. I'm a journalist...
And me? You're leaving me?
Money - gone! Argent... Pffft!

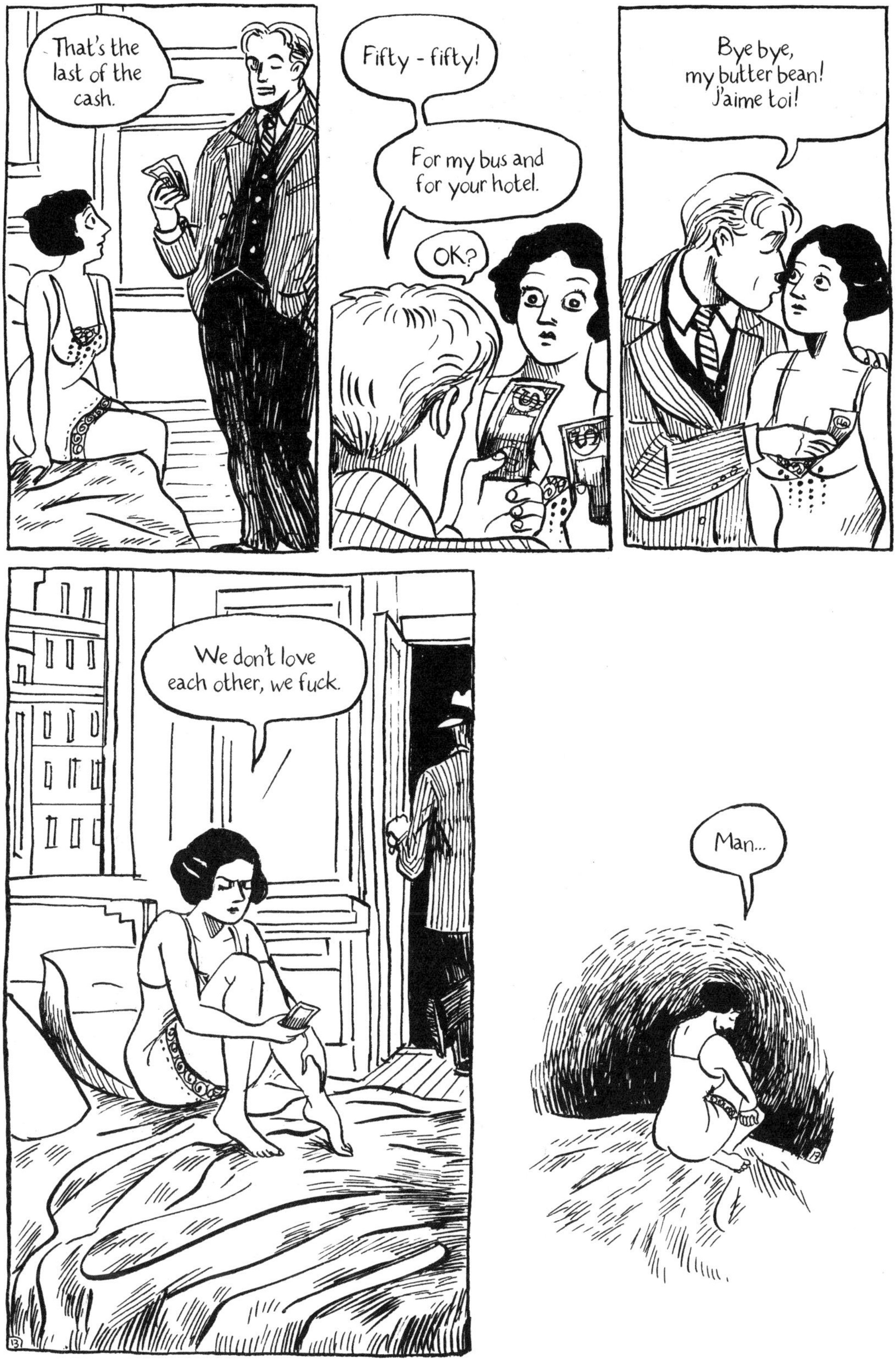
That's the last of the cash.
Fifty - fifty!
For my bus and for your hotel.
OK?
Bye bye, my butter bean! j'aime toi!
We don't love each other, we fuck.
Man...

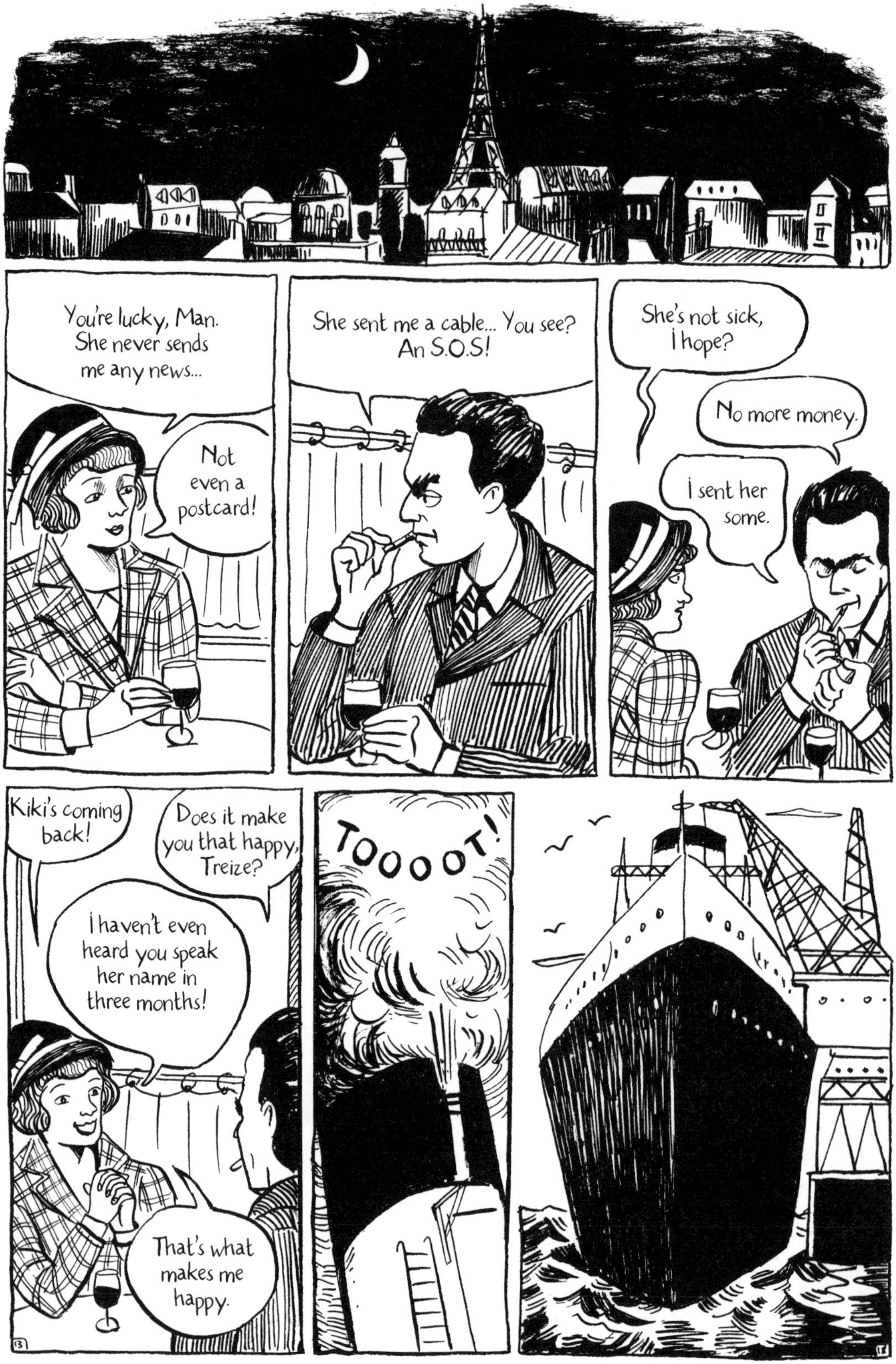

You're lucky, Man. She never sends me any news...
Not even a postcard!
She sent me a cable... You see? An S.O.S!
She's not sick, I hope?
No more money.
I sent her some.
Kiki's coming back!
Does it make you that happy, Treize?
I haven't even heard you speak her name in three months!
That's what makes me happy.
TOOOOT!

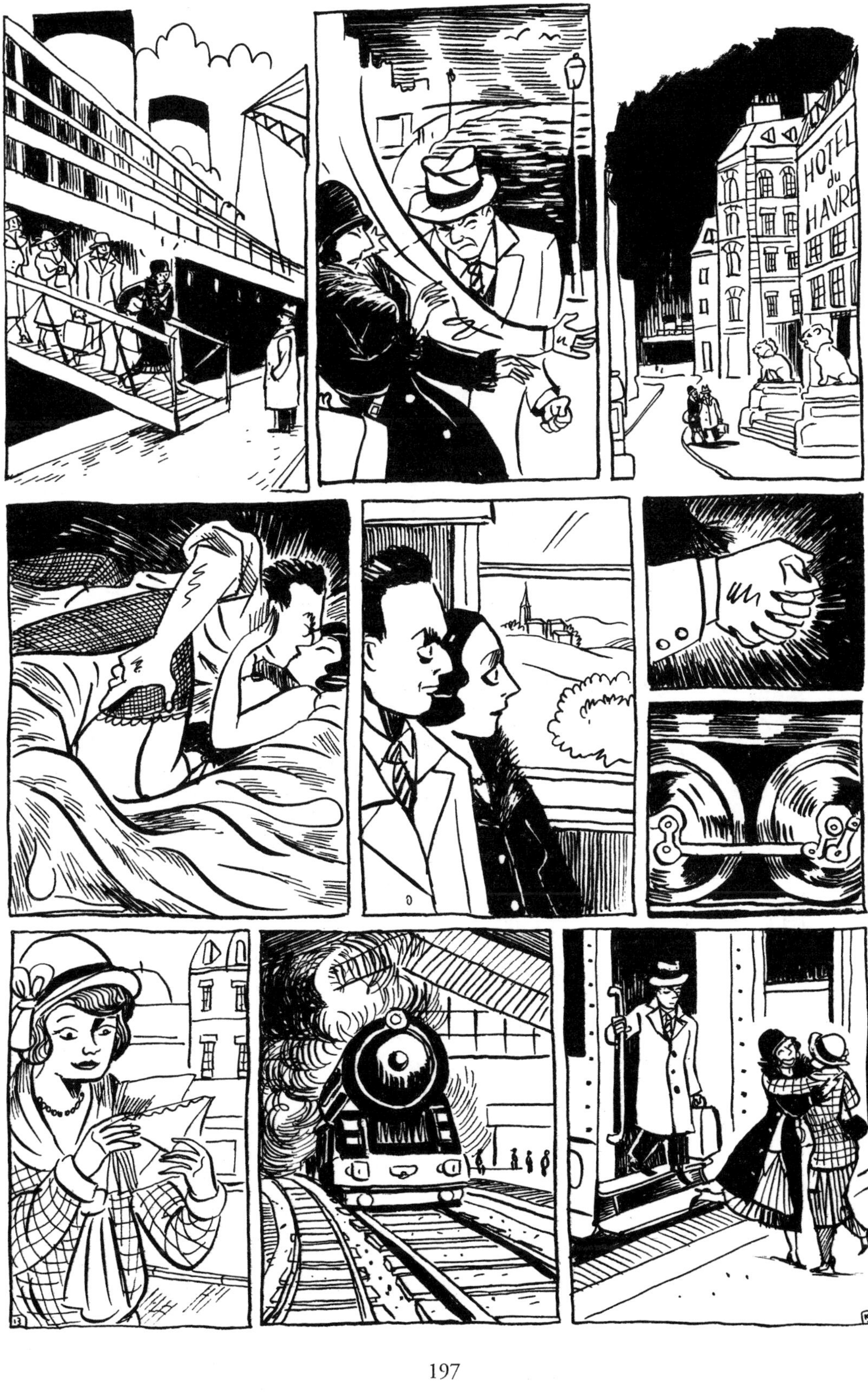
HOTEL du HAVRE

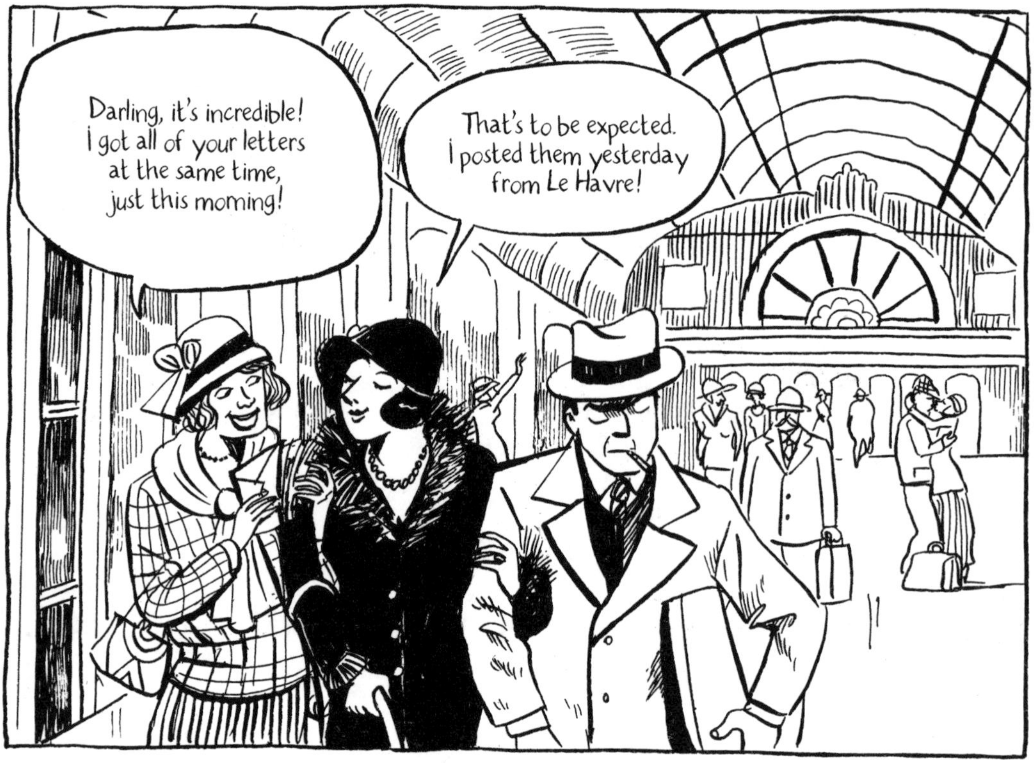
Darling, it's incredible! I got all of your letters at the same time, just this morning!
That's to be expected. I posted them yesterday from Le Havre!

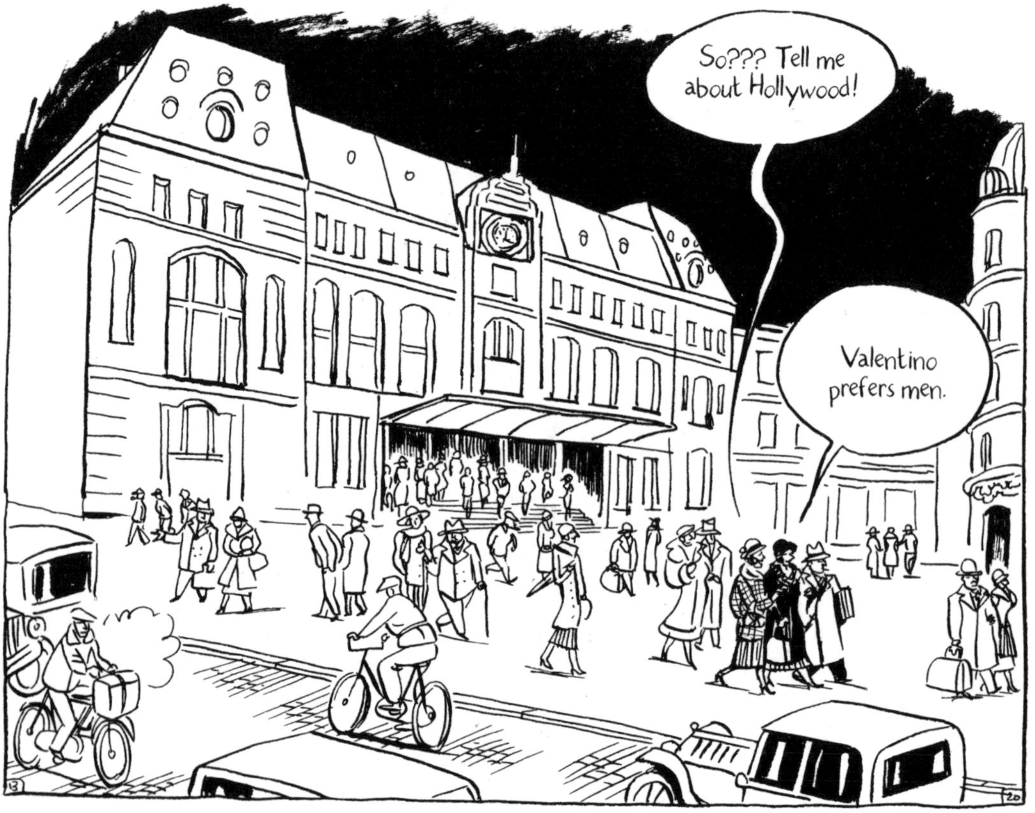
So??? Tell me about Hollywood!
Valentino prefers men.

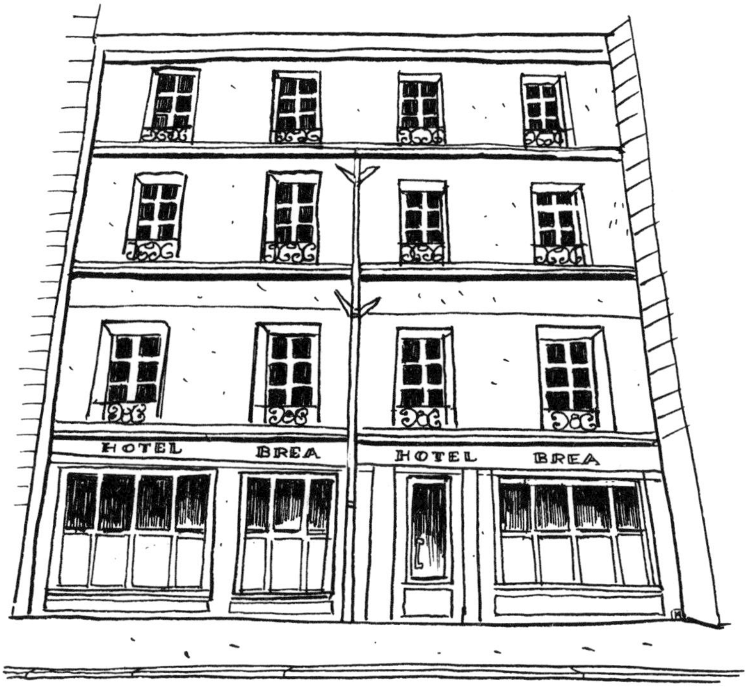
HOTEL BREA
HOTEL BREA

1923 - Hôtel Bréa 14, rue Bréa

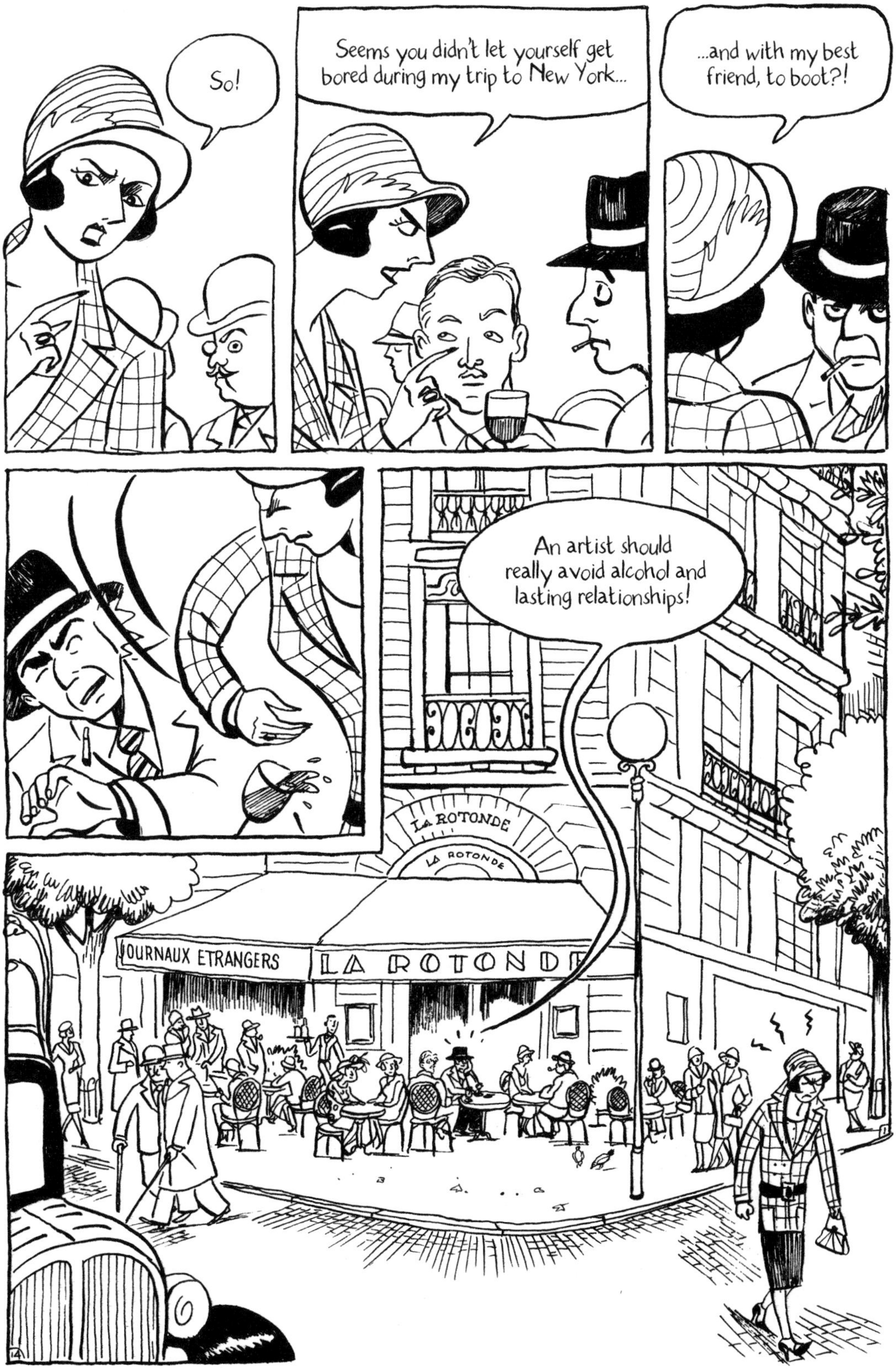
So!
Seems you didn't let yourself get bored during my trip to New York...
...and with my best friend, to boot?!
An artist should really avoid alcohol and lasting relationships!
LA ROTONDE
LA ROTONDE
JOURNAUX ETRANGERS
LA ROTONDE

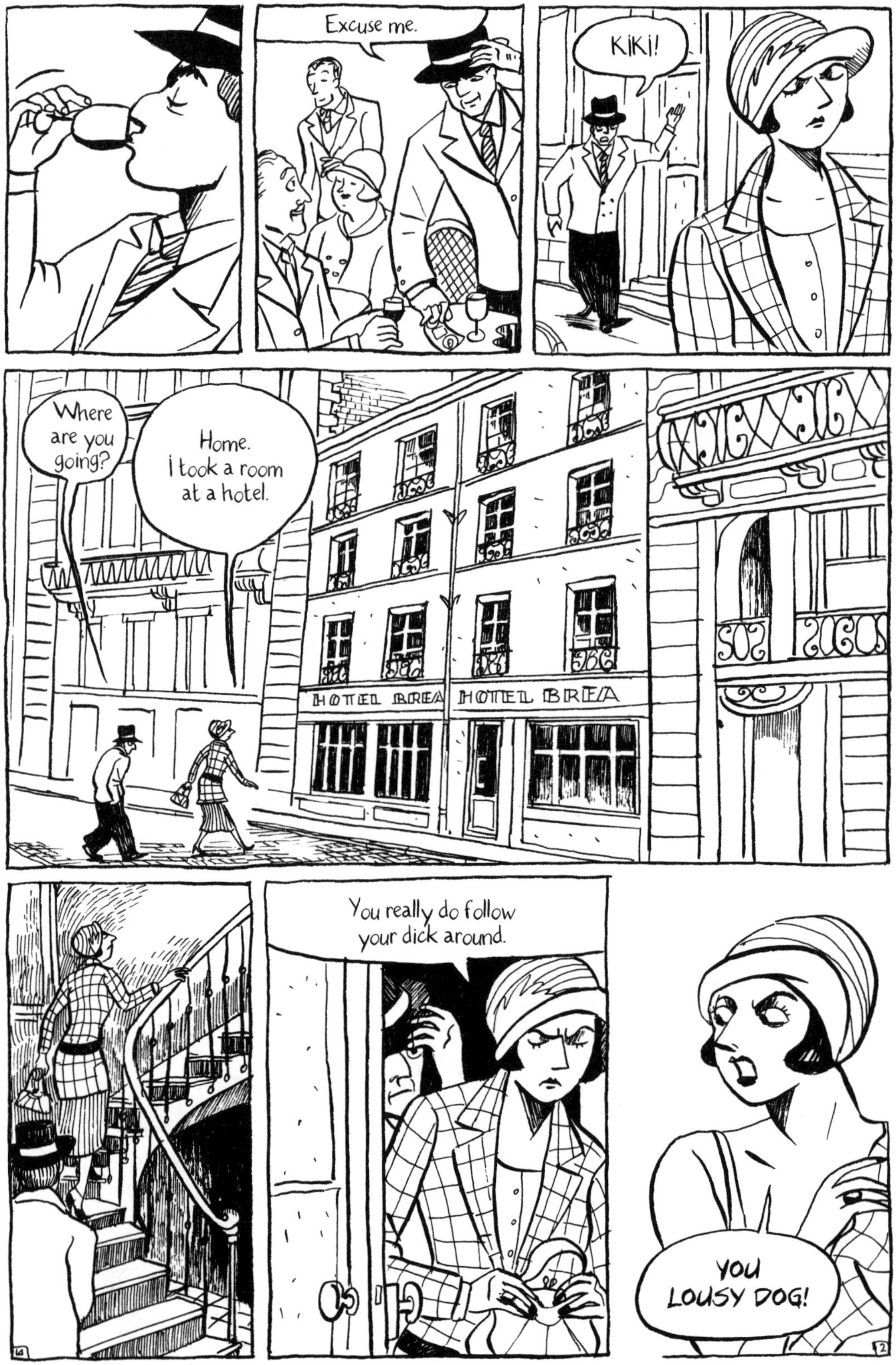
Excuse me.
KiKi!
Where are you going?
Home. I took a room at a hotel.
HOTEL BREA HOTEL BREA
You really do follow your dick around.
YOU LOUSY DOG!

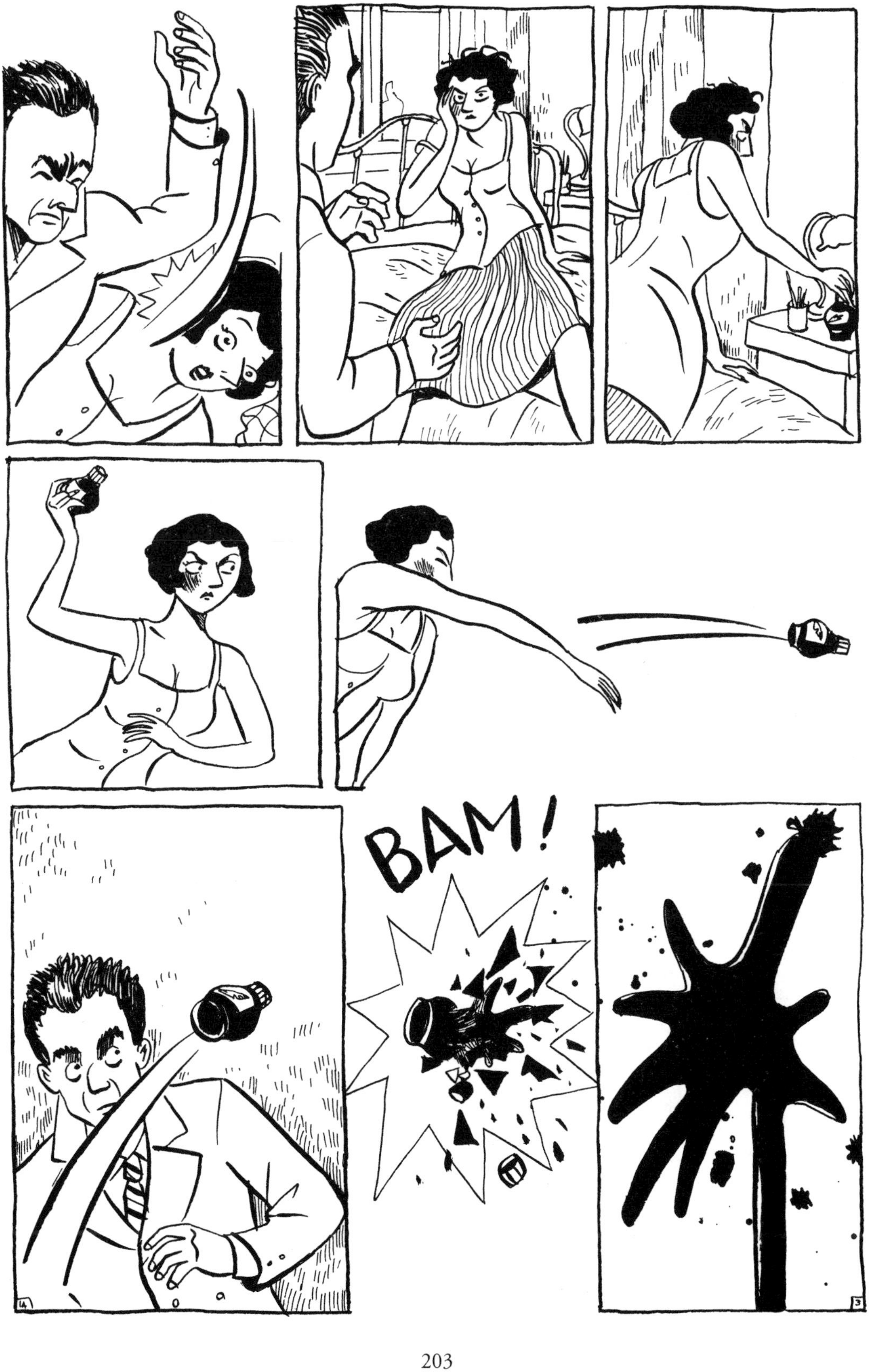
BAM!

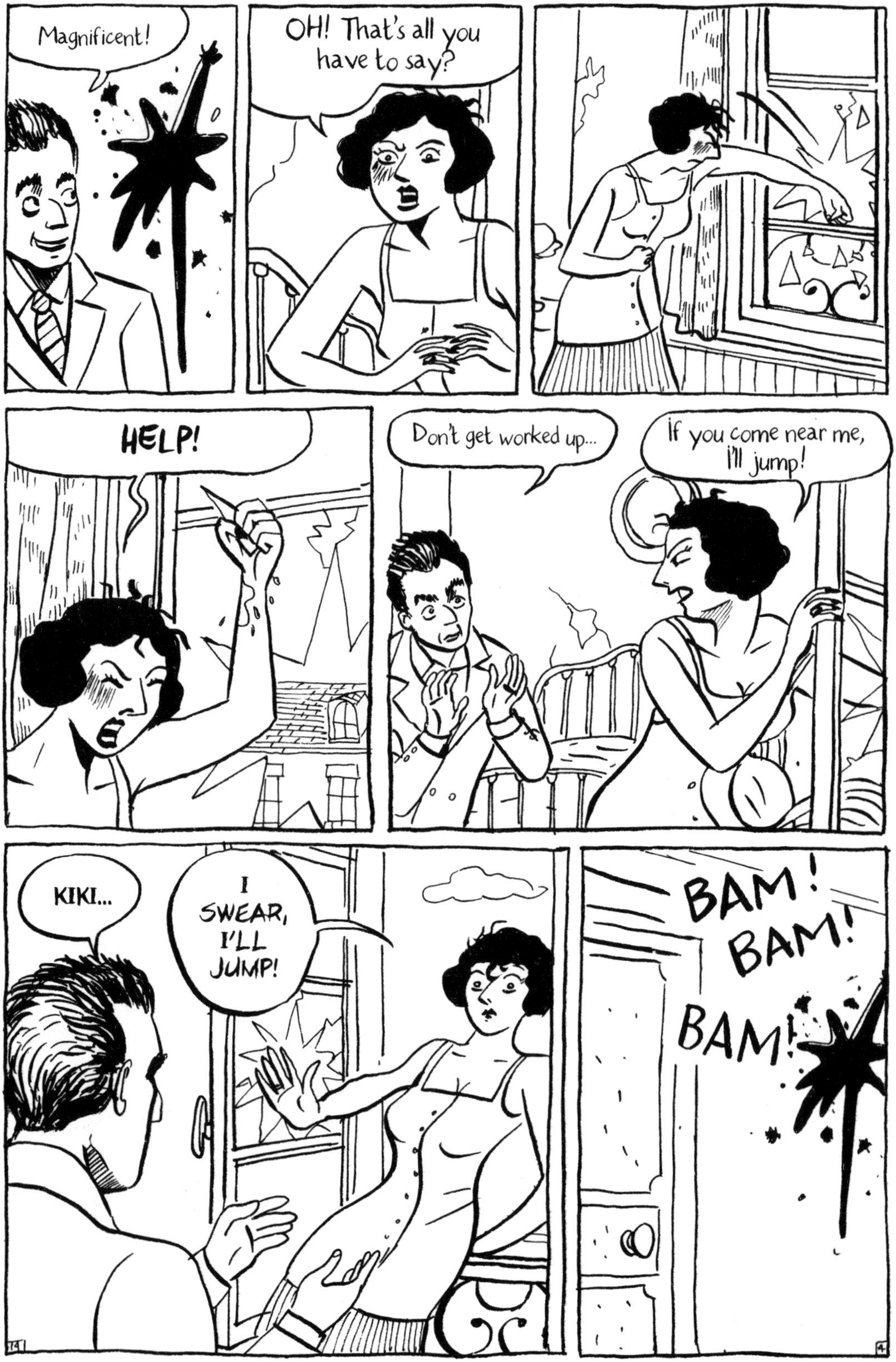
Magnificent!
OH! That's all you have to say?
HELP!
Don't get worked up...
If you come near me, I'll jump!
KIKI...
I SWEAR, I'LL JUMP!
BAM! BAM! BAM!

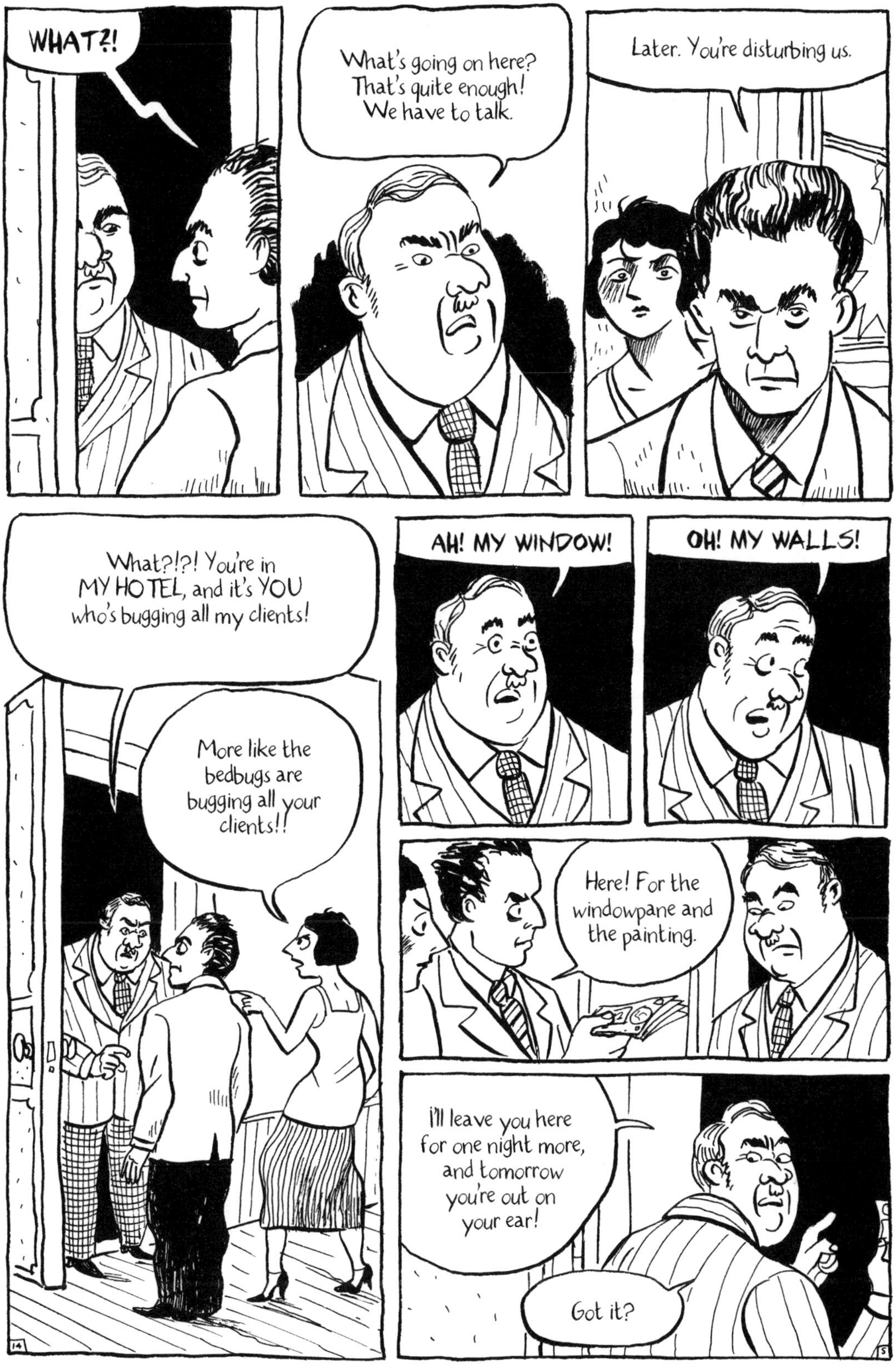
WHAT?!
What's going on here? That's quite enough! We have to talk.
Later. You're disturbing us.
What?!?! You're in MY HOTEL, and it's YOU who's bugging all my clients!
More like the bedbugs are bugging all your clients!!
AH! MY WINDOW!
OH! MY WALLS!
Here! For the windowpane and the painting.
I'll leave you here for one night more, and tomorrow you're out on your ear!
Got it?

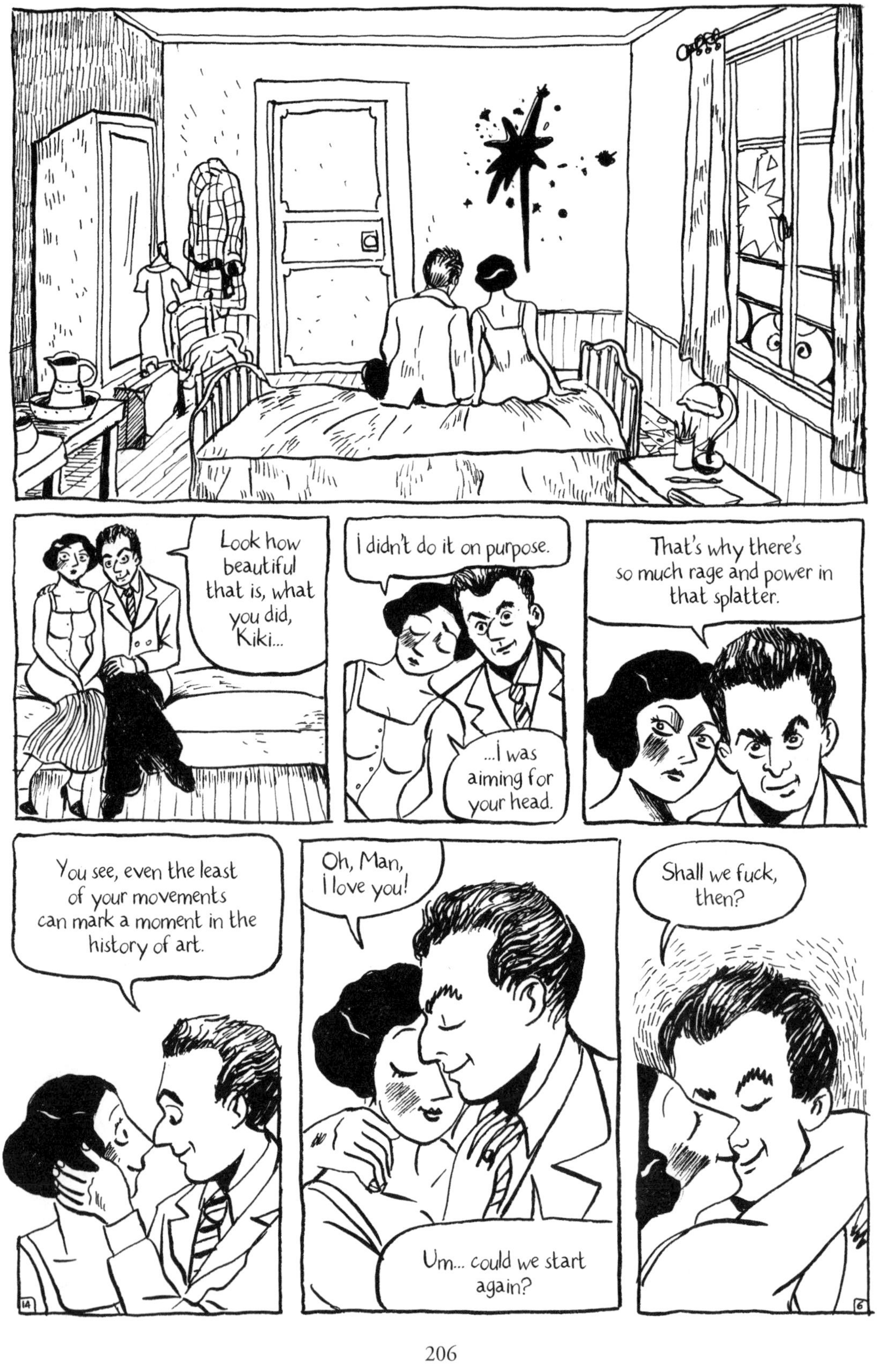
Look how beautiful that is, what you did, Kiki...
I didn't do it on purpose.
...I was aiming for your head.
That's why there's so much rage and power in that splatter.
You see, even the least of your movements can mark a moment in the history of art.
Oh, Man, I love you!
Um... could we start again?
Shall we fuck, then?

1924 - Côte bretonne

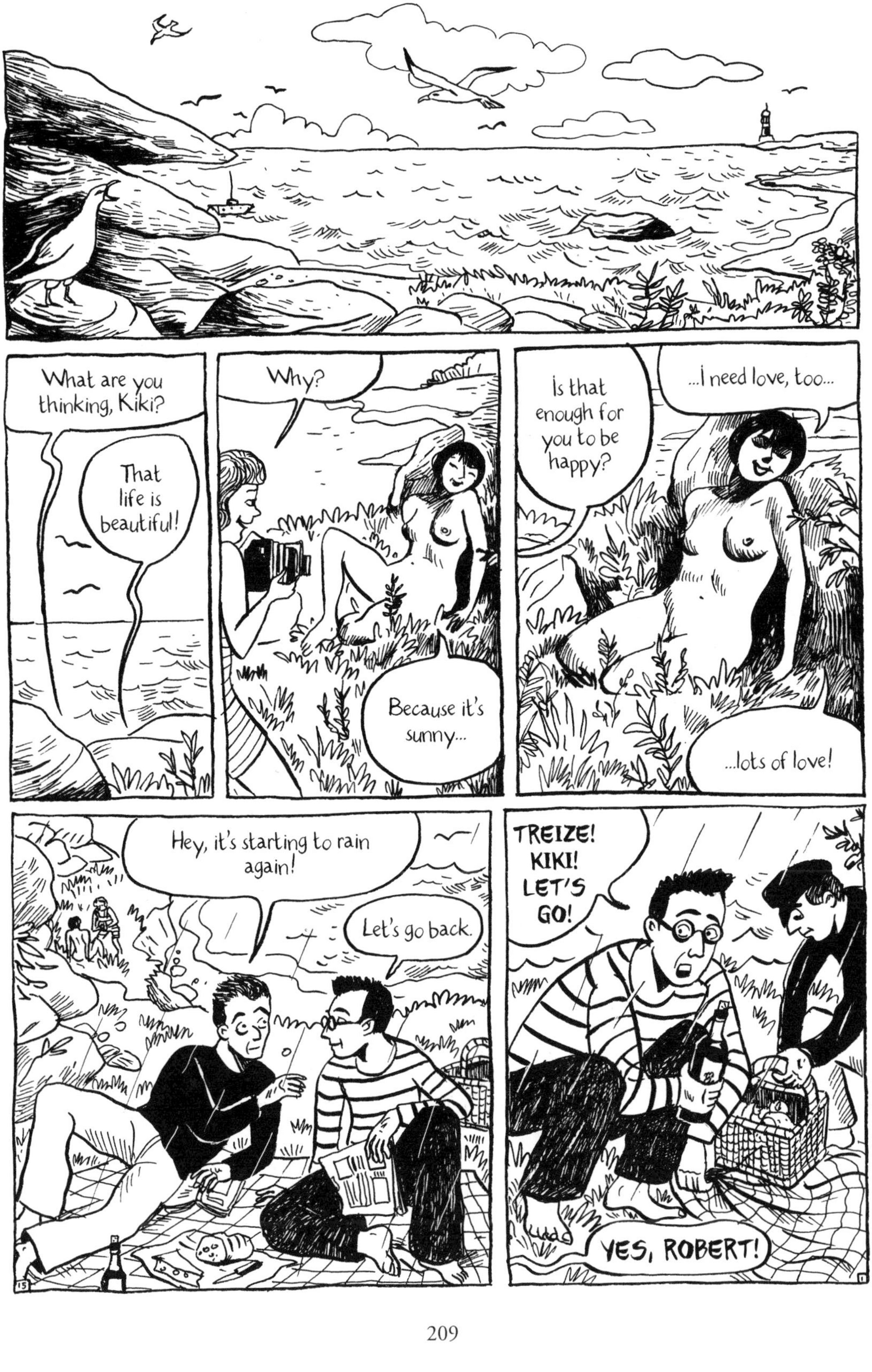
What are you thinking, Kiki?
That life is beautiful!
Why?
Because it's sunny...
Is that enough for you to be happy?
...I need love, too...
...lots of love!
Hey, it's starting to rain again!
Let's go back.
TREIZE! KIKI! LET'S GO!
YES, ROBERT!

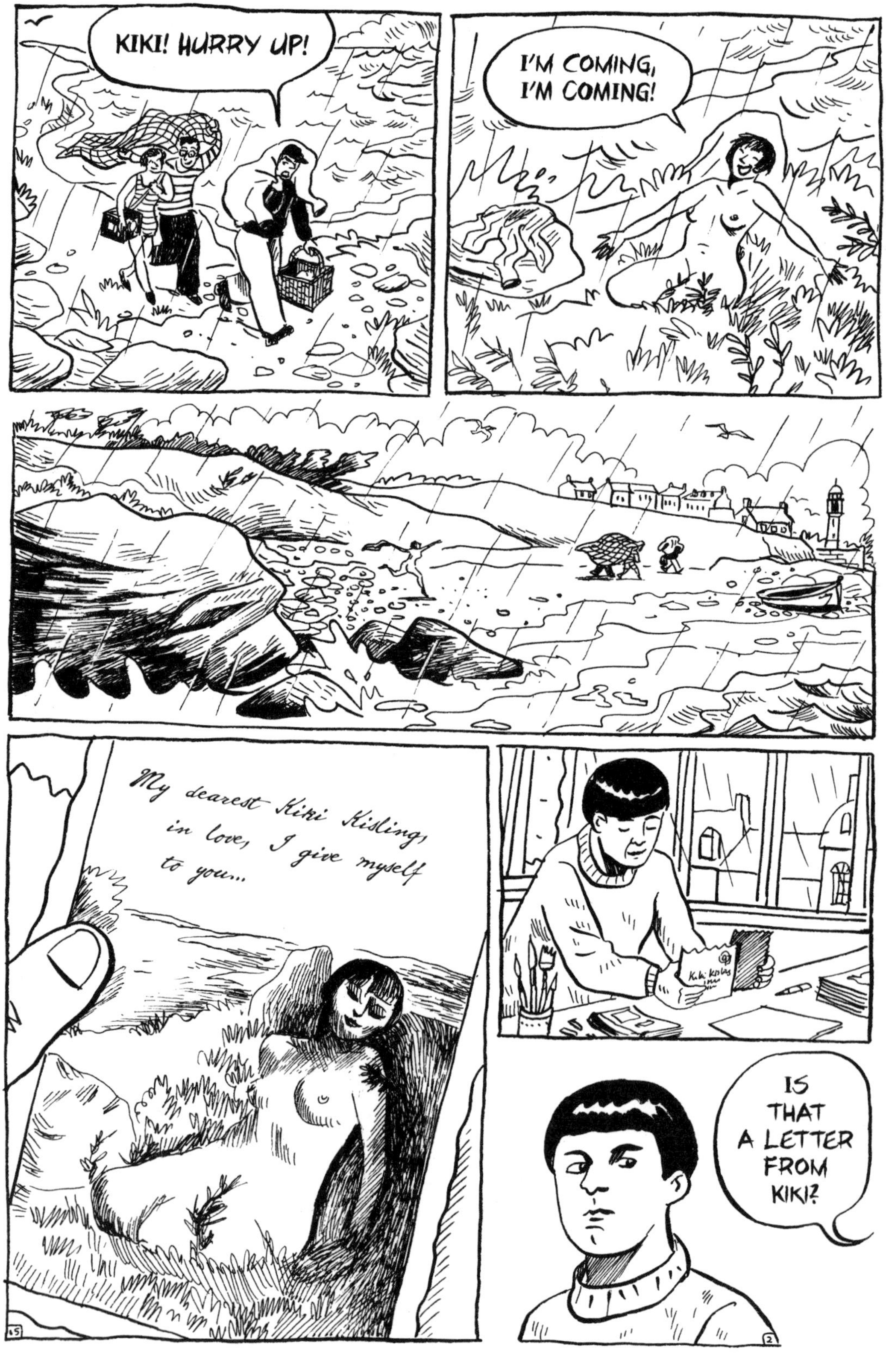
KIKI! HURRY UP!
I'M COMING, I'M COMING!
My dearest Kiki Kisling, in love, I give myself to you...
IS THAT A LETTER FROM KIKI?

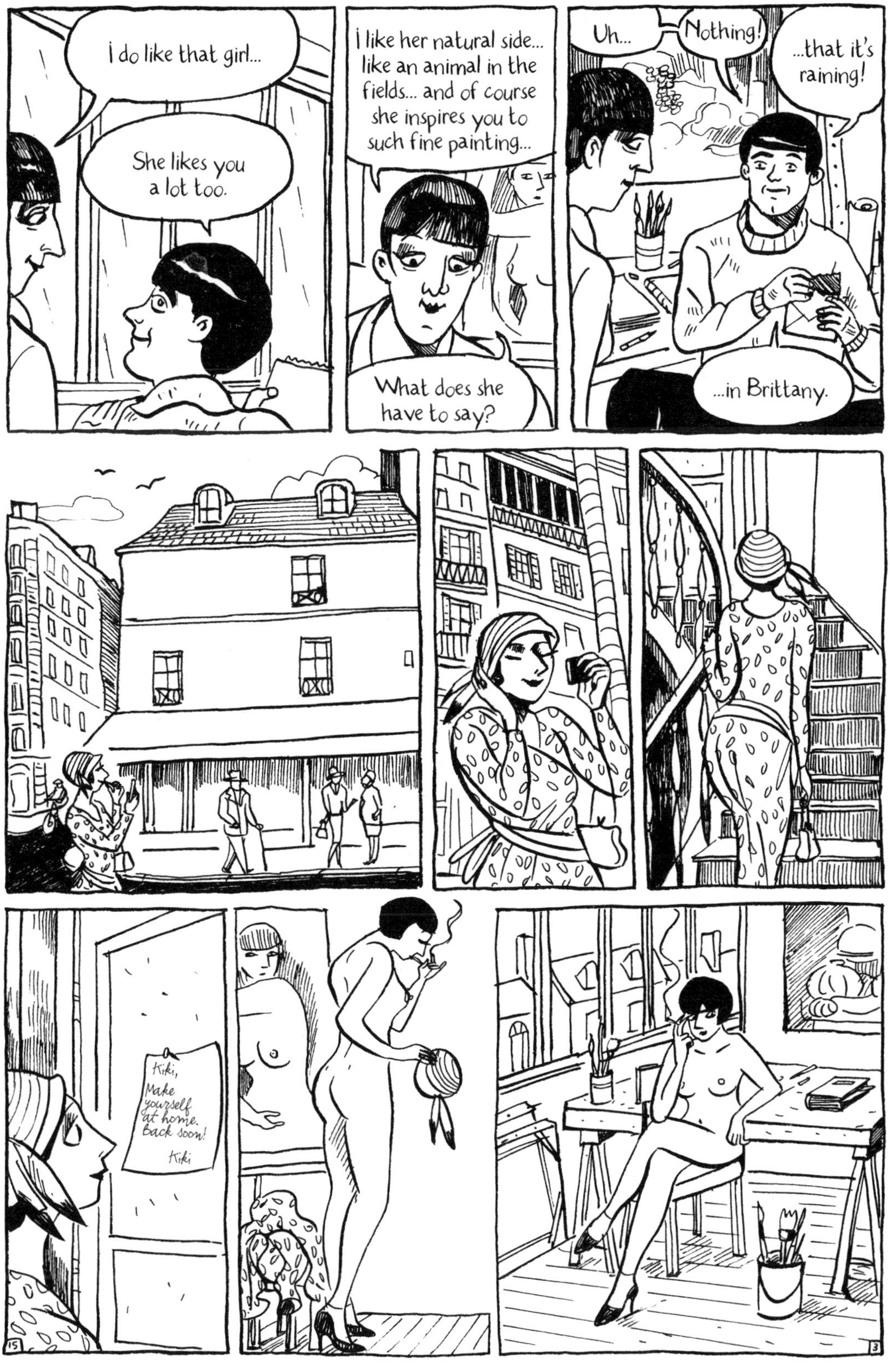
I do like that girl...
She likes you a lot too.
I like her natural side... like an animal in the fields... and of course she inspires you to such fine painting...
What does she have to say?
Uh...
Nothing!
...that it's raining!
...in Brittany.
Kiki, Make yourself at home. Back soon! Kiki

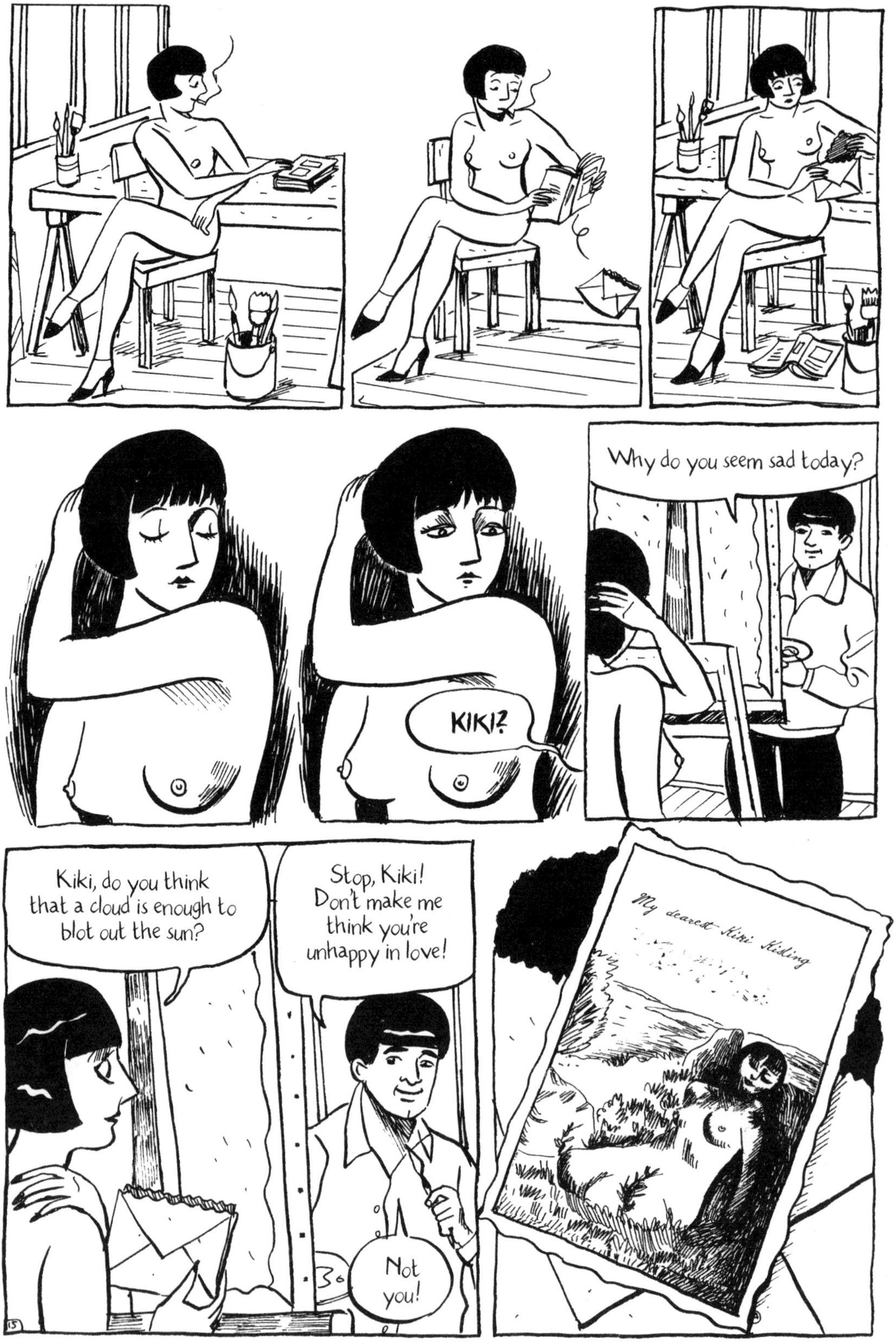
KIKI?
Why do you seem sad today?
Kiki, do you think that a cloud is enough to blot out the sun?
Stop, Kiki! Don't make me think you're unhappy in love!
Not you!
My dearest Kiki Kisling

1924 - Châtillon-sur-Seine

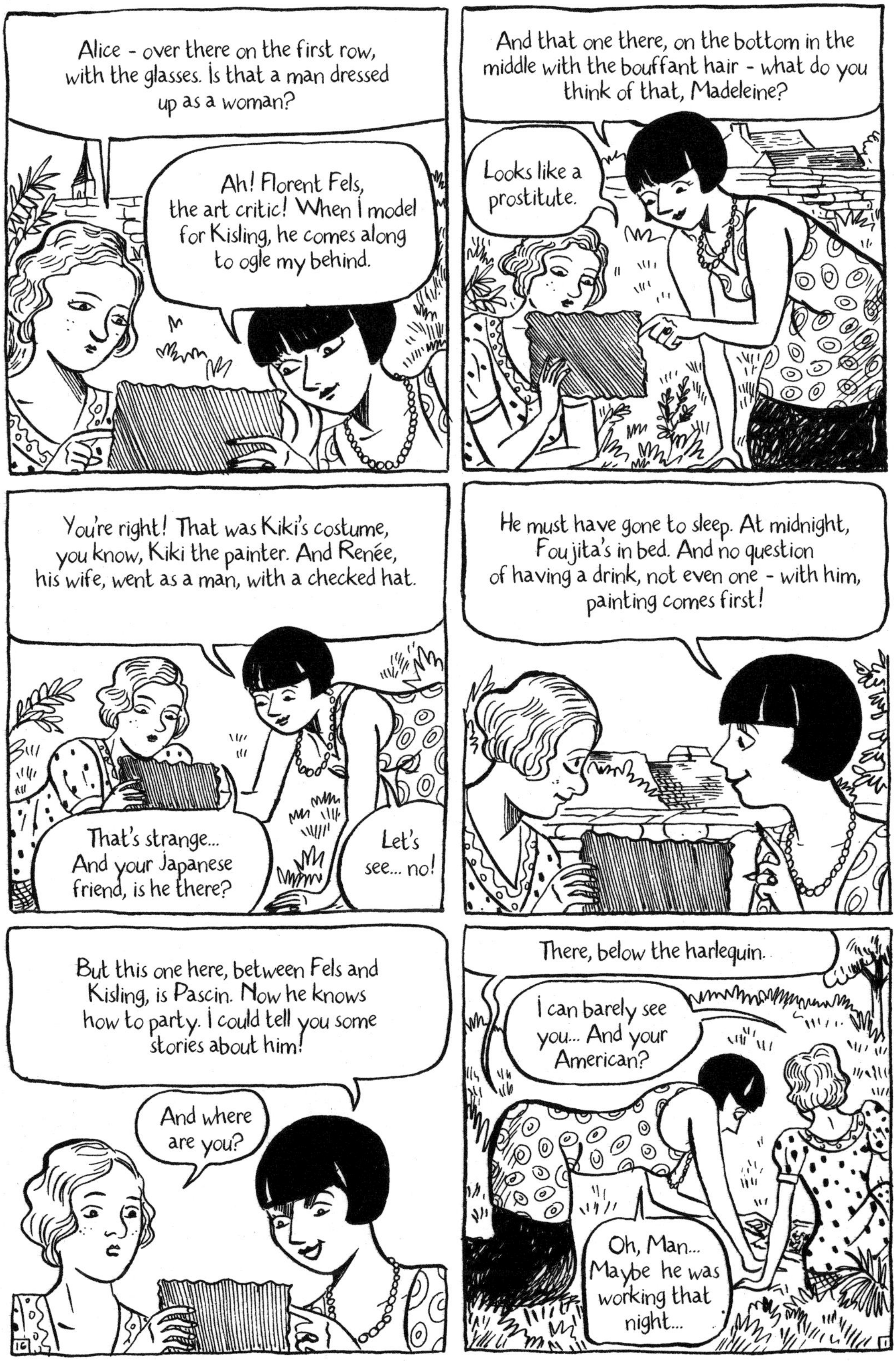
Alice - over there on the first row, with the glasses. Is that a man dressed up as a woman?
Ah! Florent Fels, the art critic! When I model for Kisling, he comes along to ogle my behind.
And that one there, on the bottom in the middle with the bouffant hair - what do you think of that, Madeleine?
Looks like a prostitute.
You're right! That was Kiki's costume, you know, Kiki the painter. And Renée, his wife, went as a man, with a checked hat.
That's strange... And your Japanese friend, is he there?
Let's see... no!
He must have gone to sleep. At midnight, Foujita's in bed. And no question of having a drink, not even one - with him, painting comes first!
But this one here, between Fels and Kisling, is Pascin. Now he knows how to party. I could tell you some stories about him!
And where are you?
There, below the harlequin.
I can barely see you... And your American?
Oh, Man... Maybe he was working that night...

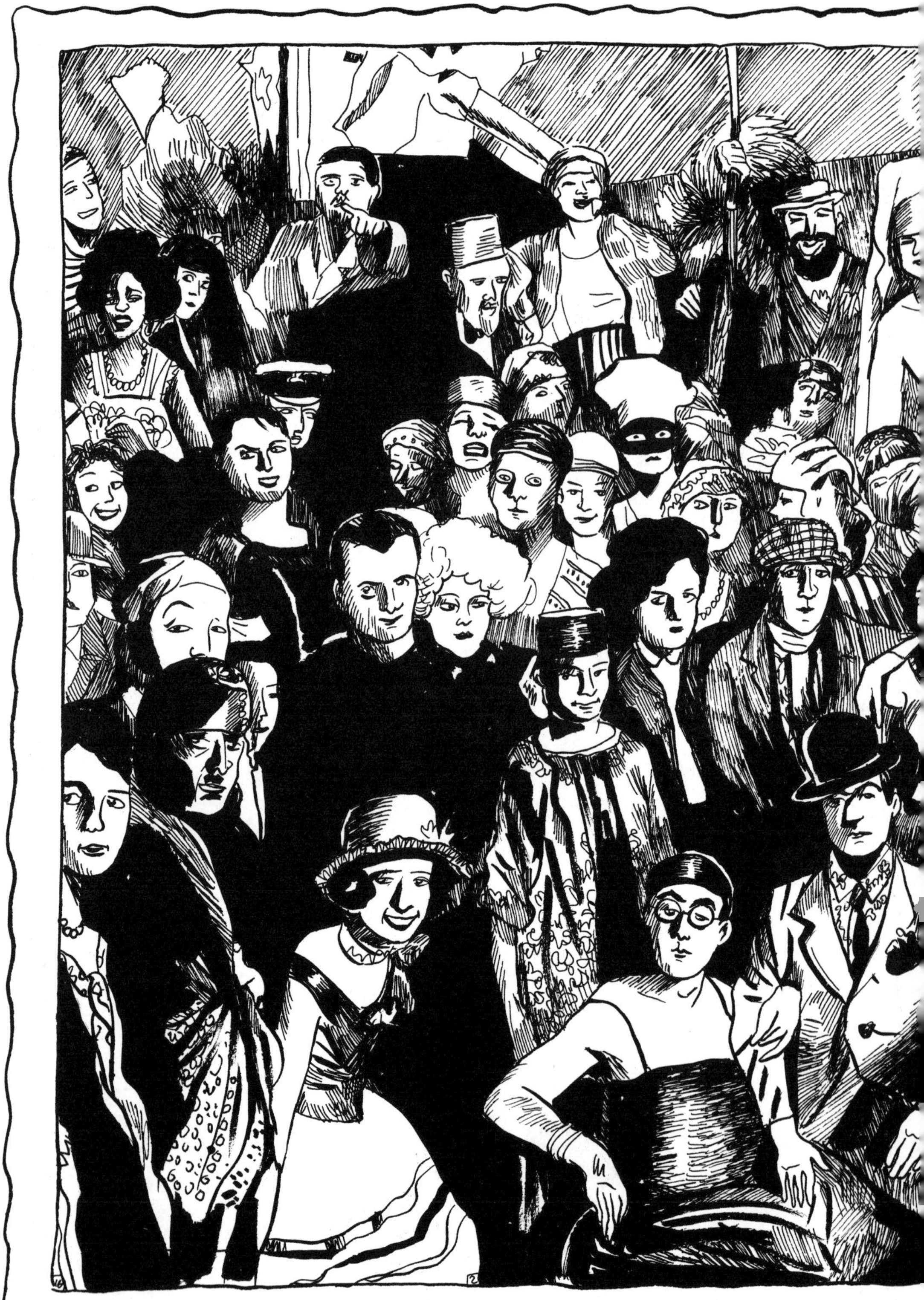

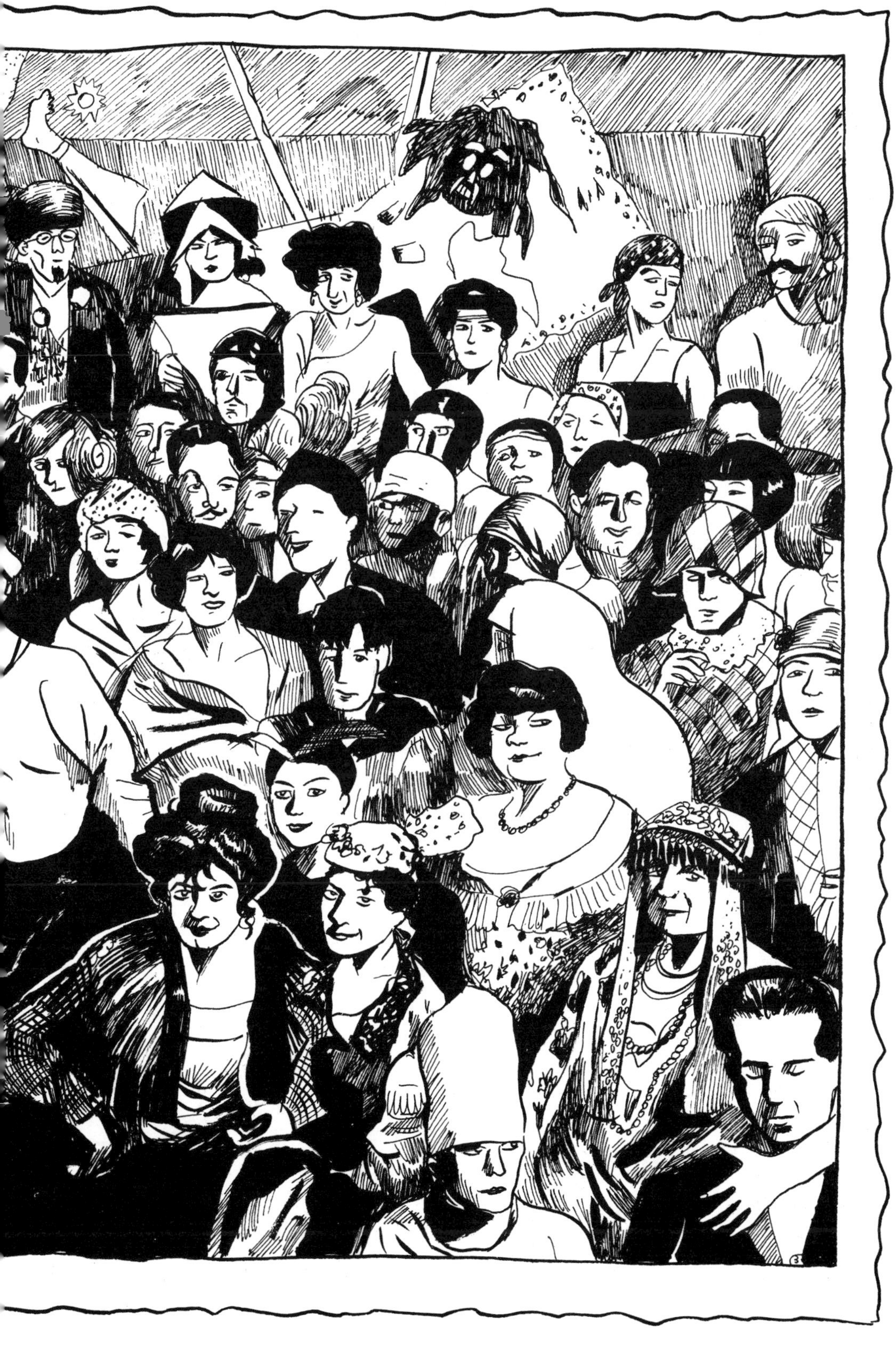

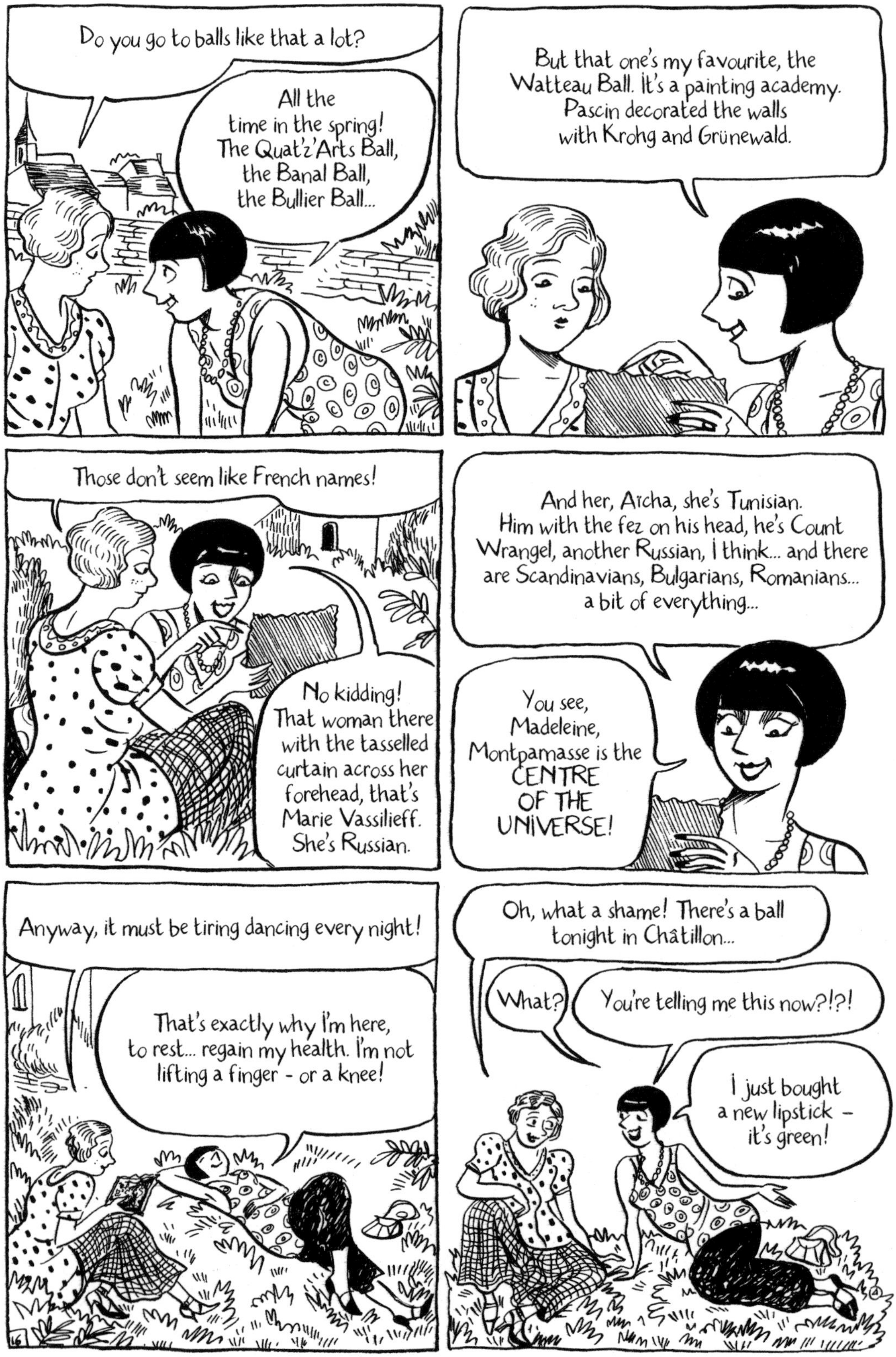
Do you go to balls like that a lot?
All the time in the spring! The Quat'z'Arts Ball, the Banal Ball, the Bullier Ball...
But that one's my favourite, the Watteau Ball. It's a painting academy. Pascin decorated the walls with Krohg and Grünewald.
Those don't seem like French names!
No kidding! That woman there with the tasselled curtain across her forehead, that's Marie Vassilieff. She's Russian.
And her, Aïcha, she's Tunisian. Him with the fez on his head, he's Count Wrangel, another Russian, I think... and there are Scandinavians, Bulgarians, Romanians... a bit of everything...
You see, Madeleine, Montparnasse is the CENTRE OF THE UNIVERSE!
Anyway, it must be tiring dancing every night!
That's exactly why I'm here, to rest... regain my health. I'm not lifting a finger - or a knee!
Oh, what a shame! There's a ball tonight in Châtillon...
What?
You're telling me this now?!?!
I just bought a new lipstick - it's green!

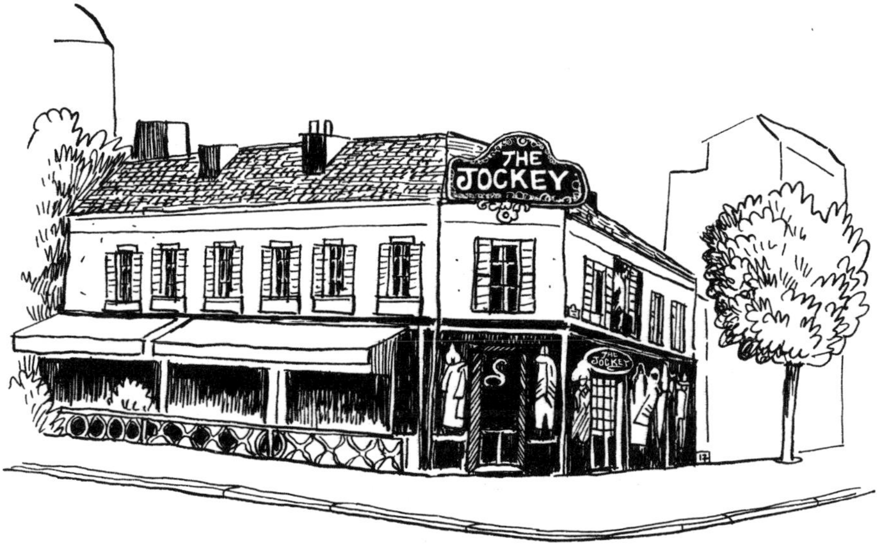
THE
JOCKEY

1924 - 146, boulevard du Montparnasse

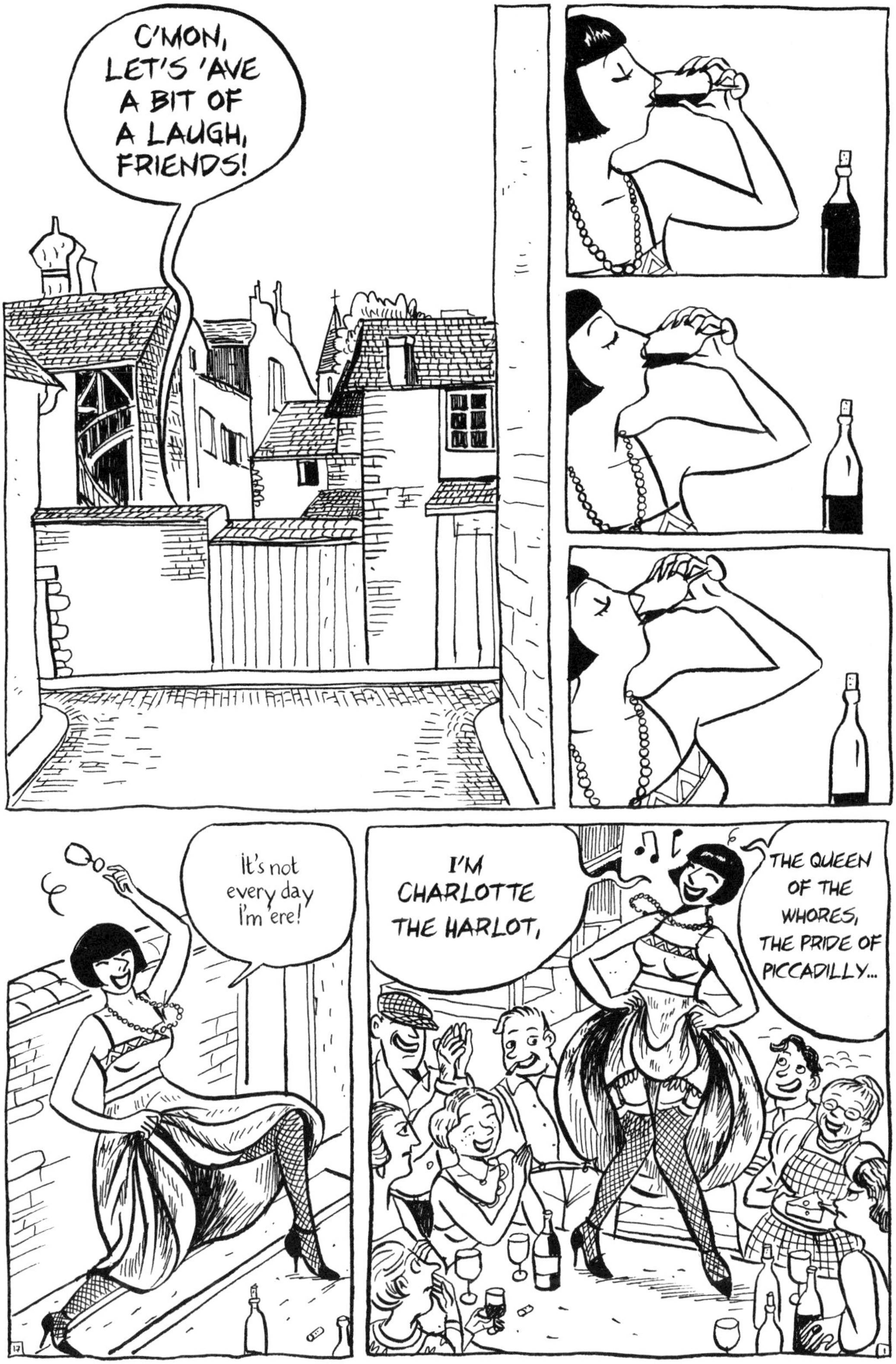
C'MON, LET'S 'AVE A BIT OF A LAUGH, FRIENDS!
It's not every day I'm 'ere!
I'M CHARLOTTE THE HARLOT,
THE QUEEN OF THE WHORES, THE PRIDE OF PICCADILLY...

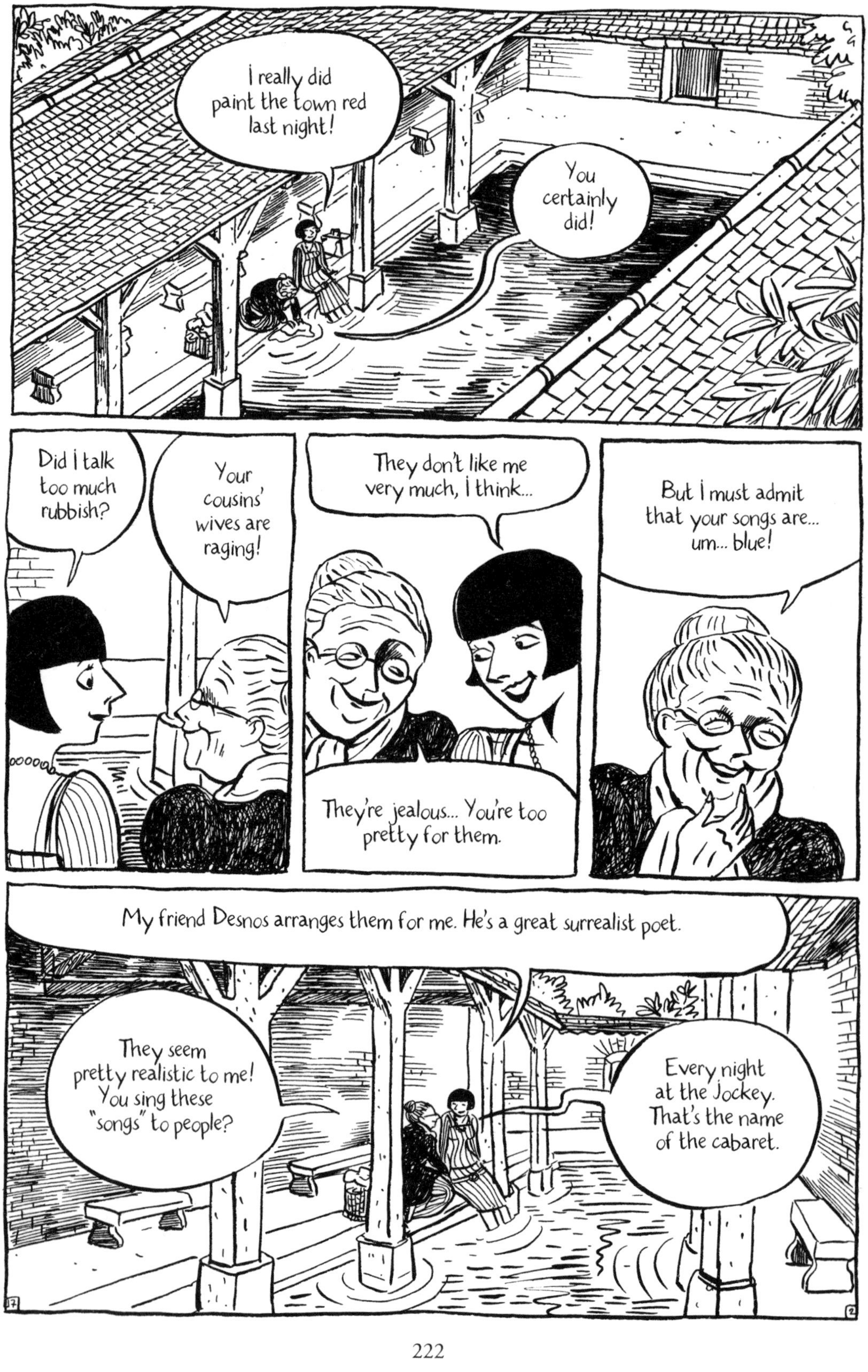
I really did paint the town red last night!
You certainly did!
Did I talk too much rubbish?
Your cousins' wives are raging!
They don't like me very much, I think...
They're jealous... You're too pretty for them.
But I must admit that your songs are... um... blue!
My friend Desnos arranges them for me. He's a great surrealist poet.
They seem pretty realistic to me! You sing these "songs" to people?
Every night at the Jockey. That's the name of the cabaret.

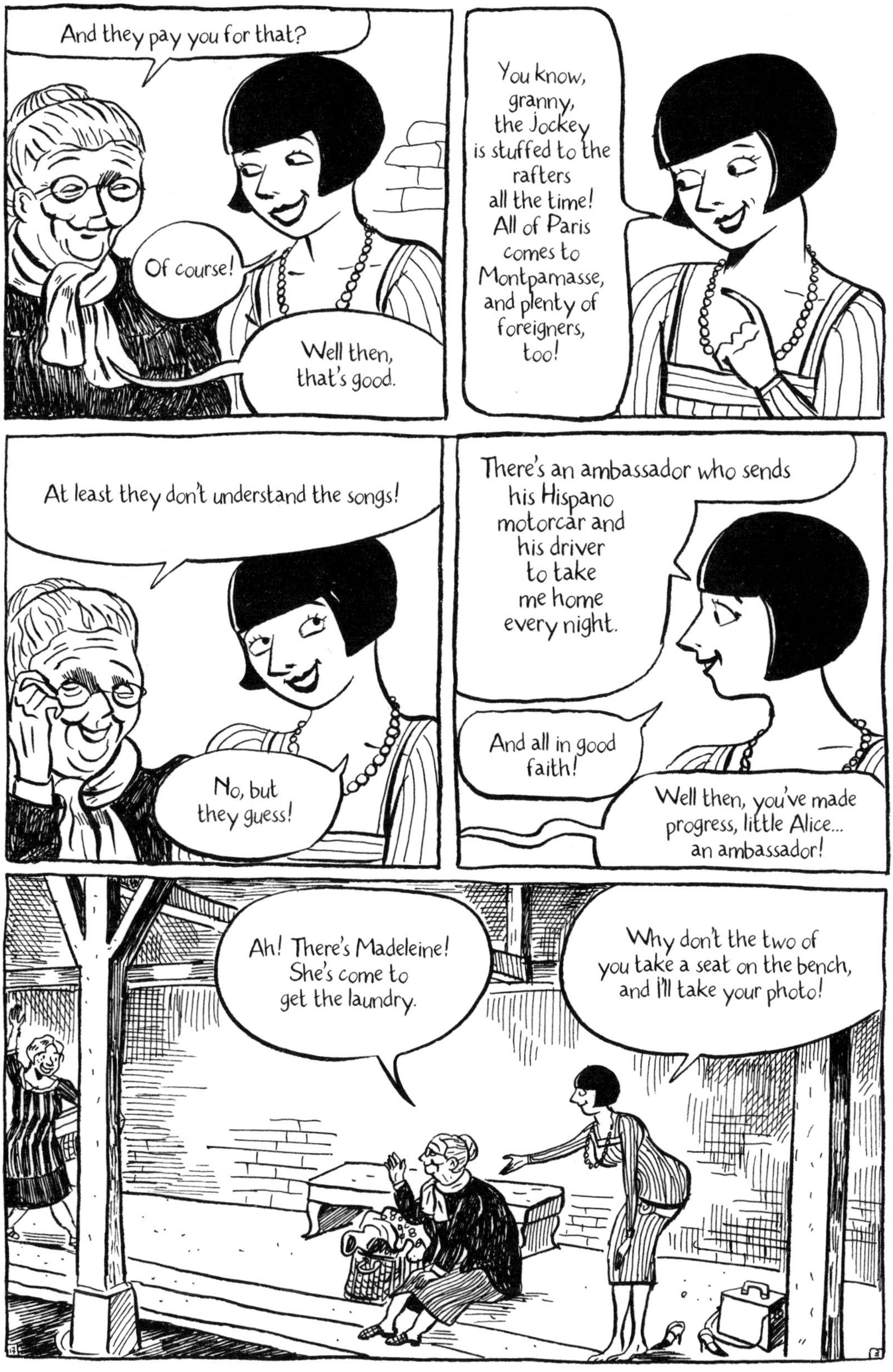
And they pay you for that?
Of course!
Well then, that's good.
You know, granny, the Jockey is stuffed to the rafters all the time! All of Paris comes to Montparnasse, and plenty of foreigners, too!
At least they don't understand the songs!
No, but they guess!
There's an ambassador who sends his Hispano motorcar and his driver to take me home every night.
And all in good faith!
Well then, you've made progress, little Alice... an ambassador!
Ah! There's Madeleine! She's come to get the laundry.
Why don't the two of you take a seat on the bench, and I'll take your photo!

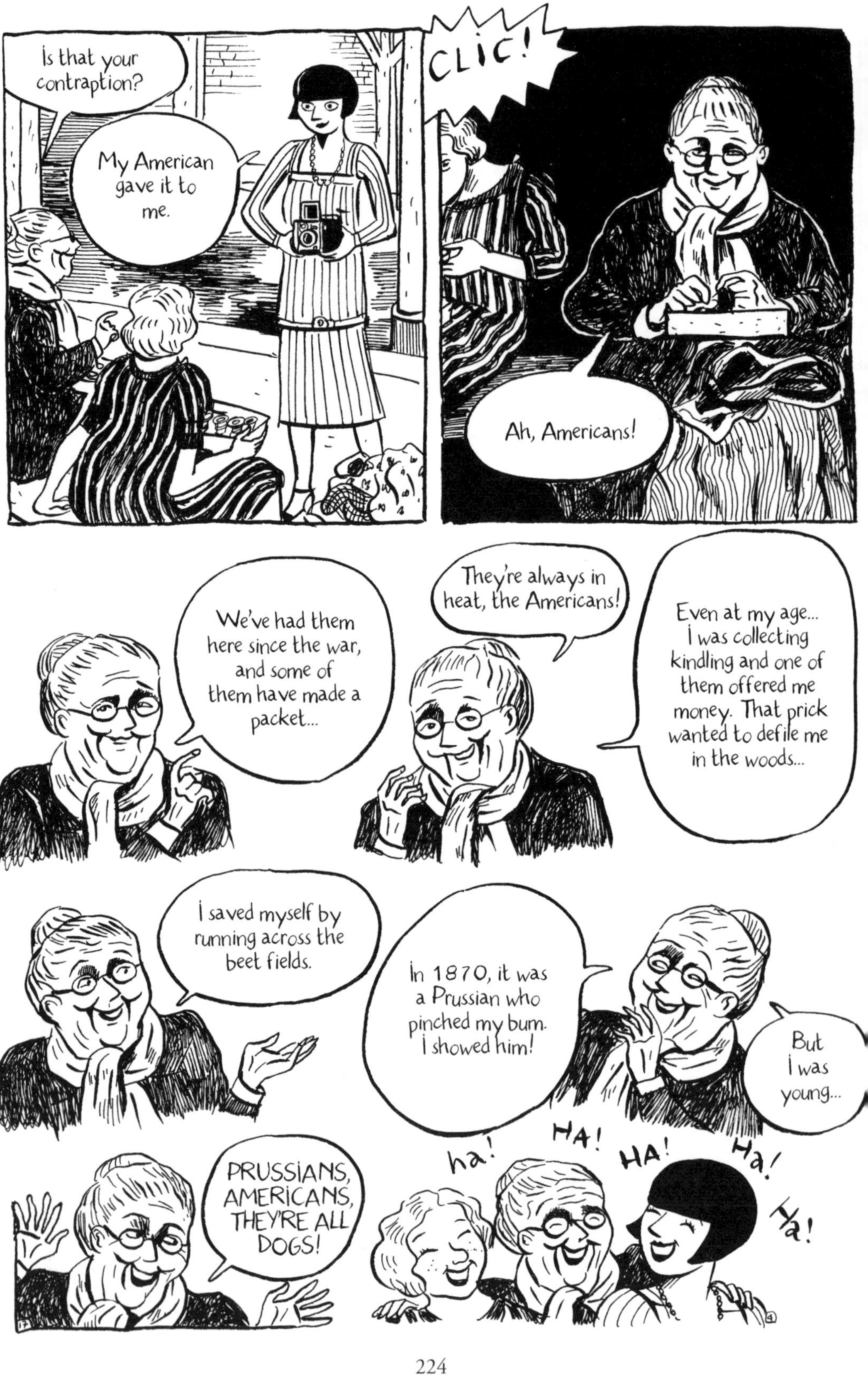

Is that your contraption?
My American gave it to me.
CLIC!
Ah, Americans!
We've had them here since the war, and some of them have made a packet...
They're always in heat, the Americans!
Even at my age... I was collecting kindling and one of them offered me money. That prick wanted to defile me in the woods...
I saved myself by running across the beet fields.
In 1870, it was a Prussian who pinched my bum. I showed him!
But I was young...
PRUSSIANS, AMERICANS, THEY'RE ALL DOGS!
ha!
HA!
HA!
Ha!
Ha!

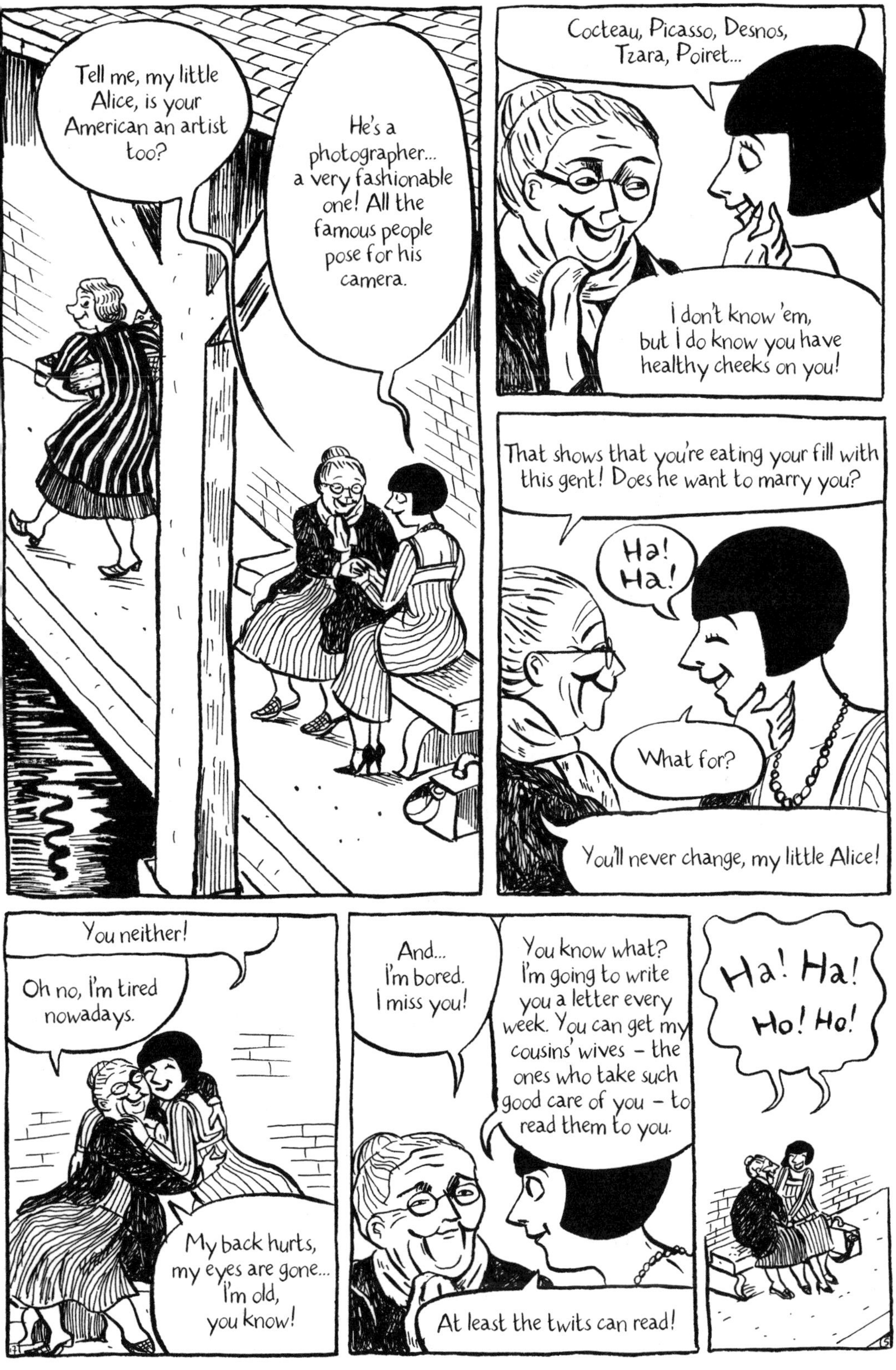
Tell me, my little Alice, is your American an artist too?
He's a photographer... a very fashionable one! All the famous people pose for his camera.
Cocteau, Picasso, Desnos, Tzara, Poiret...
I don't know 'em, but I do know you have healthy cheeks on you!
That shows that you're eating your fill with this gent! Does he want to marry you?
Ha! Ha!
What for?
You'll never change, my little Alice!
You neither!
Oh no, I'm tired nowadays.
My back hurts, my eyes are gone... I'm old, you know!
And... I'm bored. I miss you!
You know what? I'm going to write you a letter every week. You can get my cousins' wives – the ones who take such good care of you – to read them to you.
At least the twits can read!
Ha! Ha! Ho! Ho!

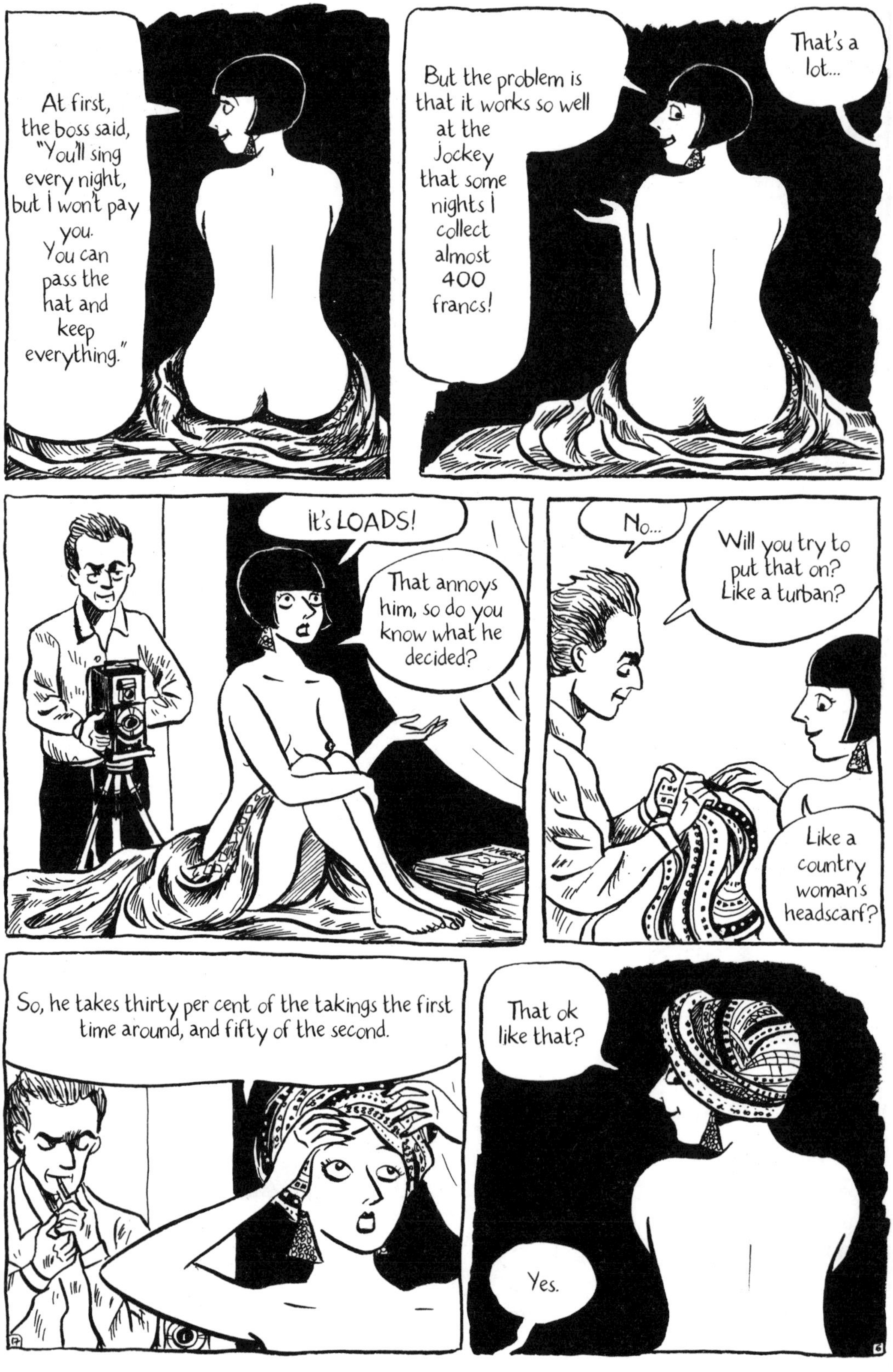

At first, the boss said, "You'll sing every night, but I won't pay you. You can pass the hat and keep everything."
But the problem is that it works so well at the Jockey that some nights I collect almost 400 francs!
That's a lot...
It's LOADS!
That annoys him, so do you know what he decided?
No...
Will you try to put that on? Like a turban?
Like a country woman's headscarf?
So, he takes thirty per cent of the takings the first time around, and fifty of the second.
That ok like that?
Yes.

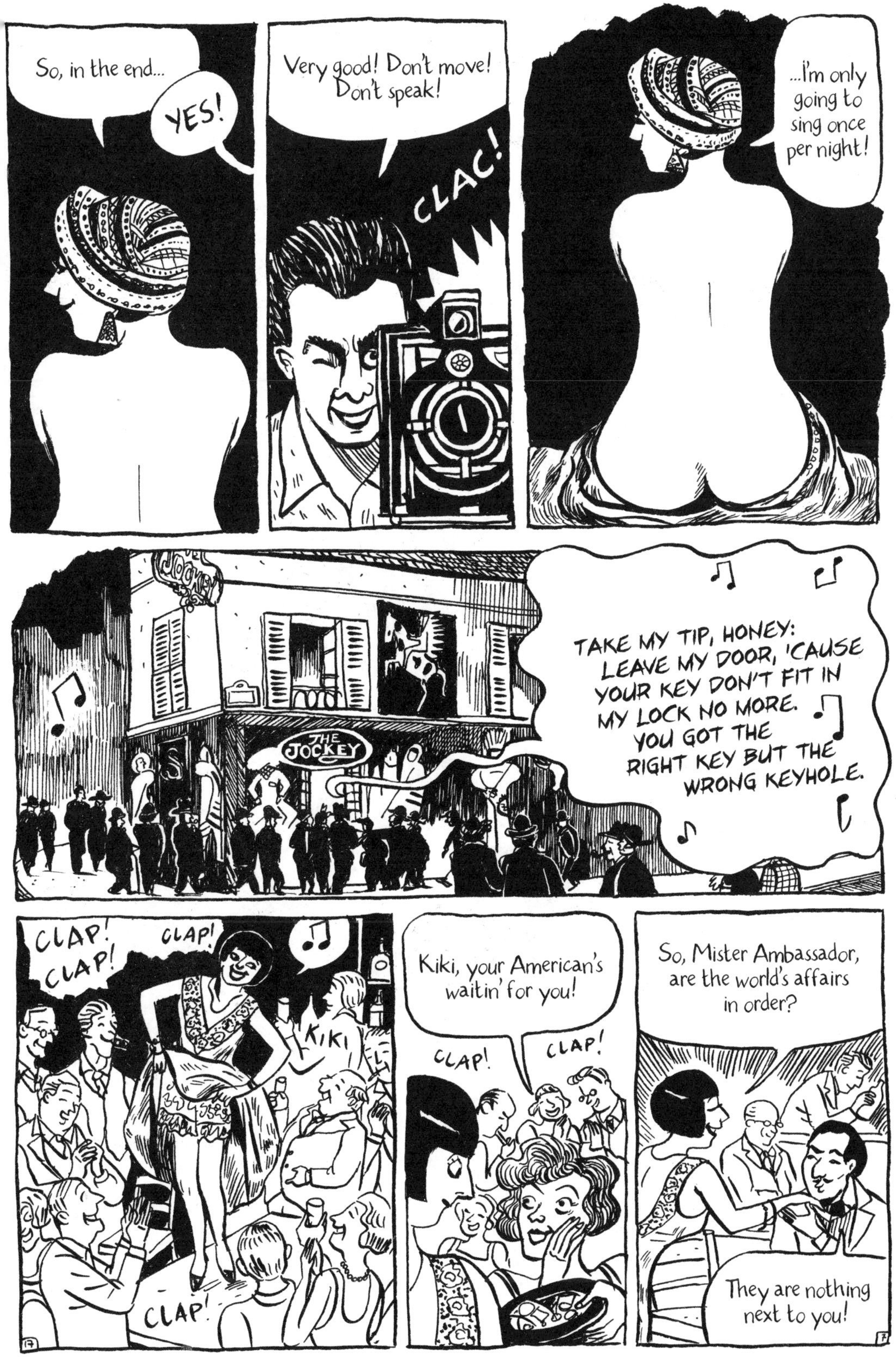
So, in the end...
YES!
Very good! Don't move! Don't speak!
CLAC!
...I'm only going to sing once per night!
JOCKEY
THE JOCKEY
TAKE MY TIP, HONEY: LEAVE MY DOOR, 'CAUSE YOUR KEY DON'T FIT IN MY LOCK NO MORE. YOU GOT THE RIGHT KEY BUT THE WRONG KEYHOLE.
CLAP! CLAP!
CLAP!
KIKI
CLAP!
Kiki, your American's waitin' for you!
CLAP!
CLAP!
So, Mister Ambassador, are the world's affairs in order?
They are nothing next to you!

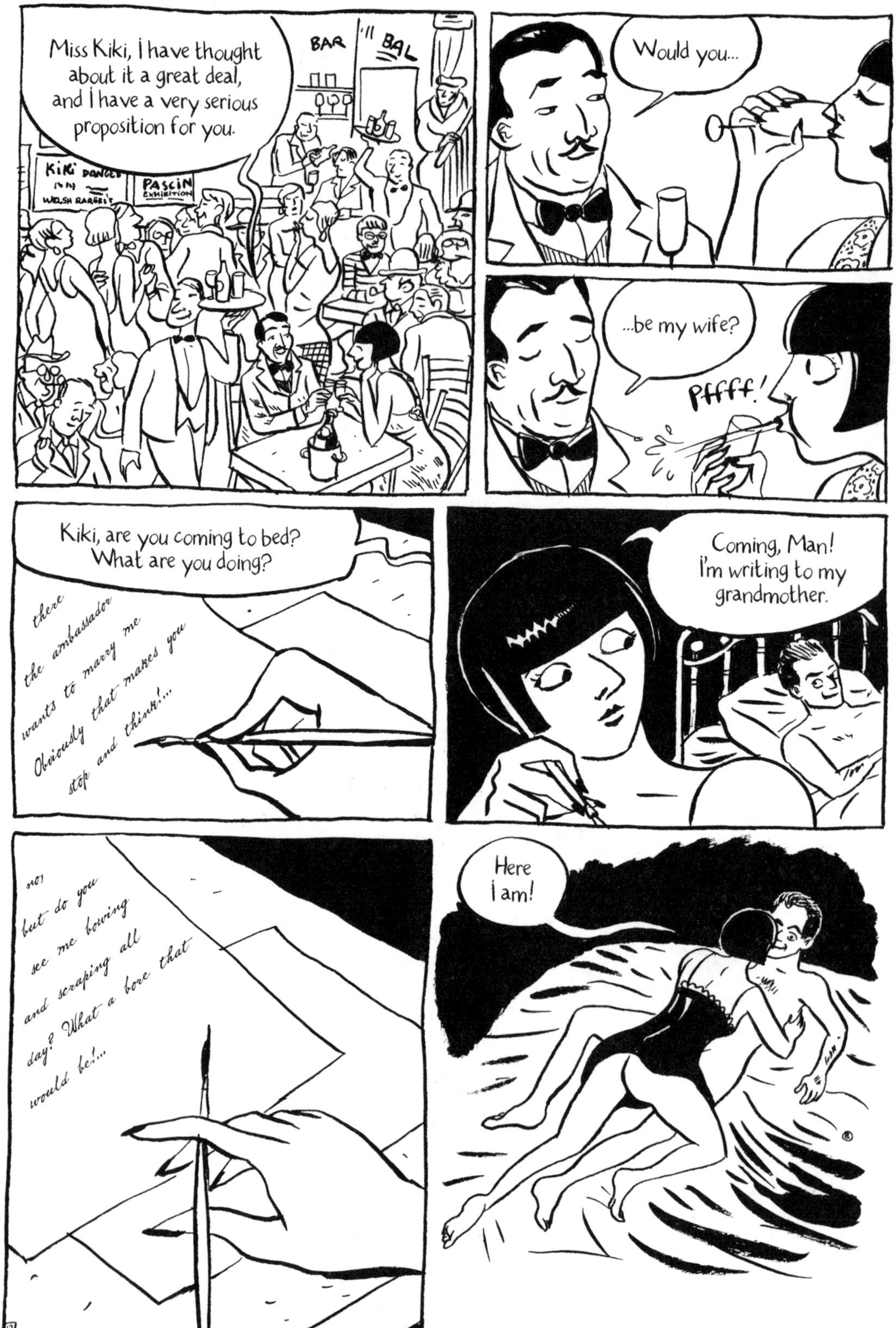
Miss Kiki, I have thought about it a great deal, and I have a very serious proposition for you.
BAR
BAL
KIKI DANCES
WELSH RAREBITS
PASCIN EXHIBITION
Would you...
...be my wife?
Pffff!
Kiki, are you coming to bed? What are you doing?
there
the ambassador
wants to marry me
Obviously that makes you
stop and think!...
Coming, Man! I'm writing to my grandmother.
no,
but do you
see me bowing
and scraping all
day? What a bore that
would be!...
Here I am!

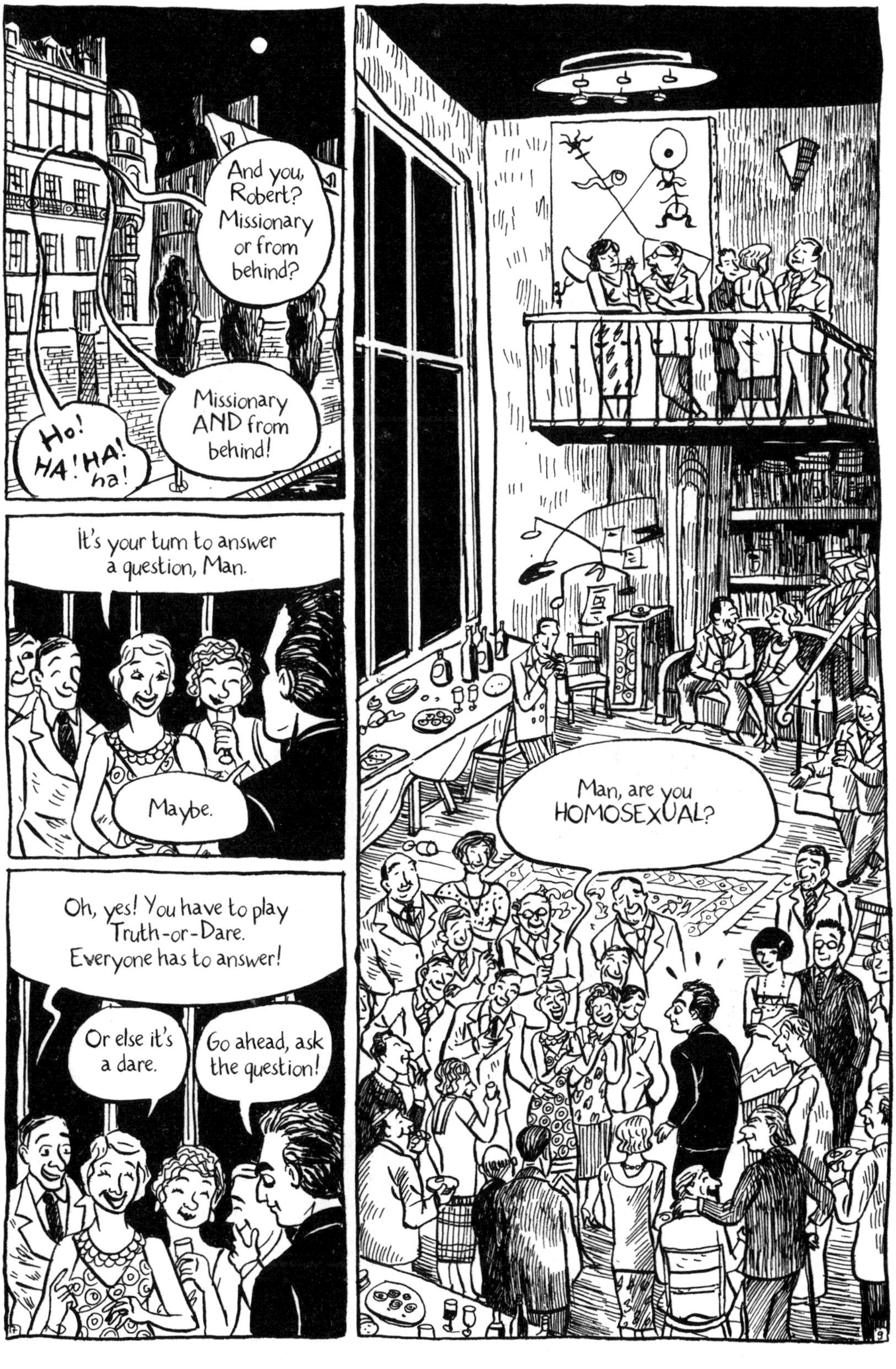
And you, Robert? Missionary or from behind?
Missionary AND from behind!
Ho! HA! HA! ha!
It's your turn to answer a question, Man.
Maybe.
Oh, yes! You have to play Truth-or-Dare. Everyone has to answer!
Or else it's a dare.
Go ahead, ask the question!
Man, are you HOMOSEXUAL?

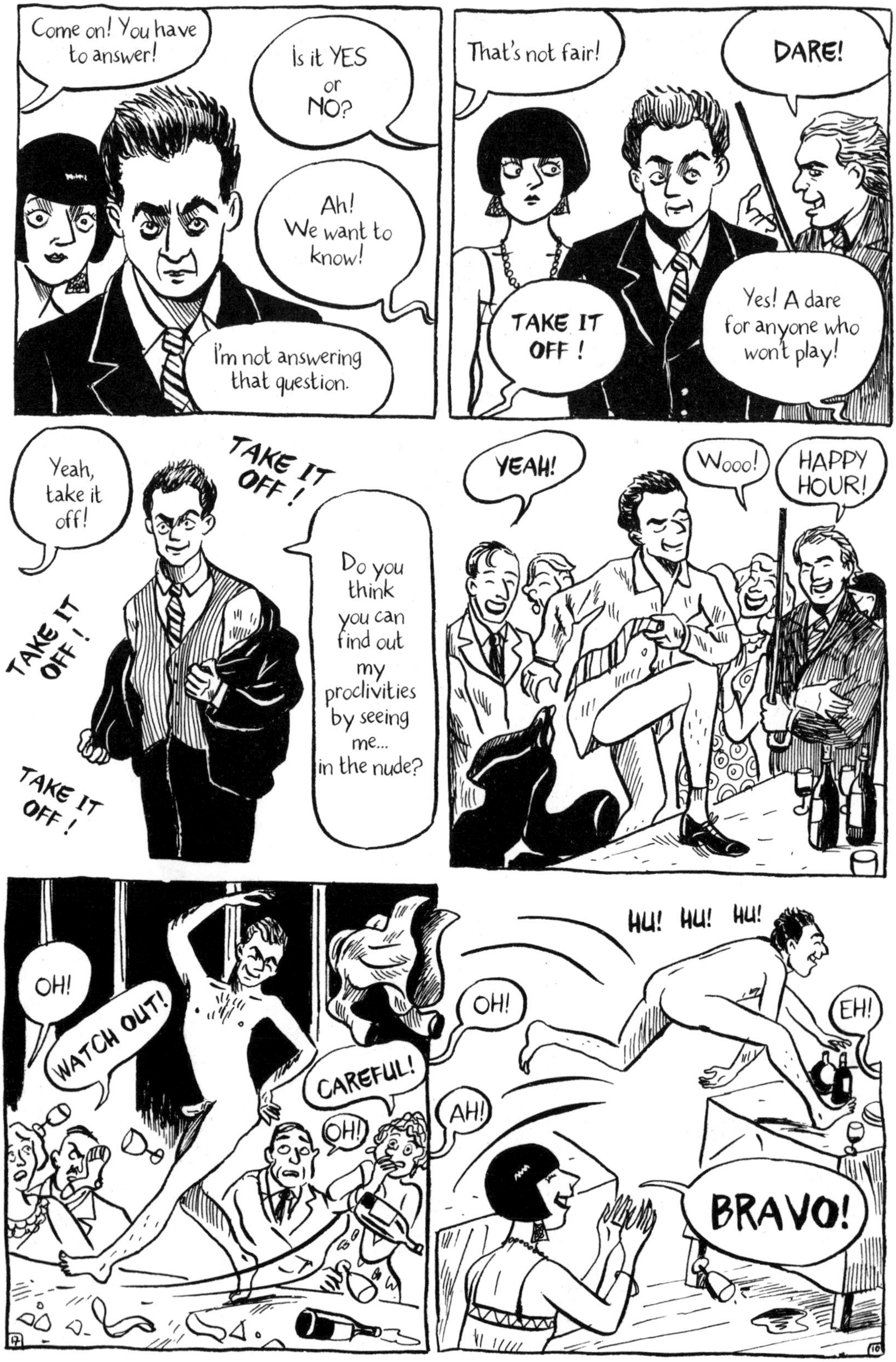
Come on! You have to answer!
Is it YES or NO?
Ah! We want to know!
I'm not answering that question.
That's not fair!
DARE!
TAKE IT OFF!
Yes! A dare for anyone who won't play!
Yeah, take it off!
TAKE IT OFF!
TAKE IT OFF!
TAKE IT OFF!
Do you think you can find out my proclivities by seeing me... in the nude?
YEAH!
Wooo!
HAPPY HOUR!
OH!
WATCH OUT!
CAREFUL!
OH!
OH!
AH!
HU! HU! HU!
EH!
BRAVO!

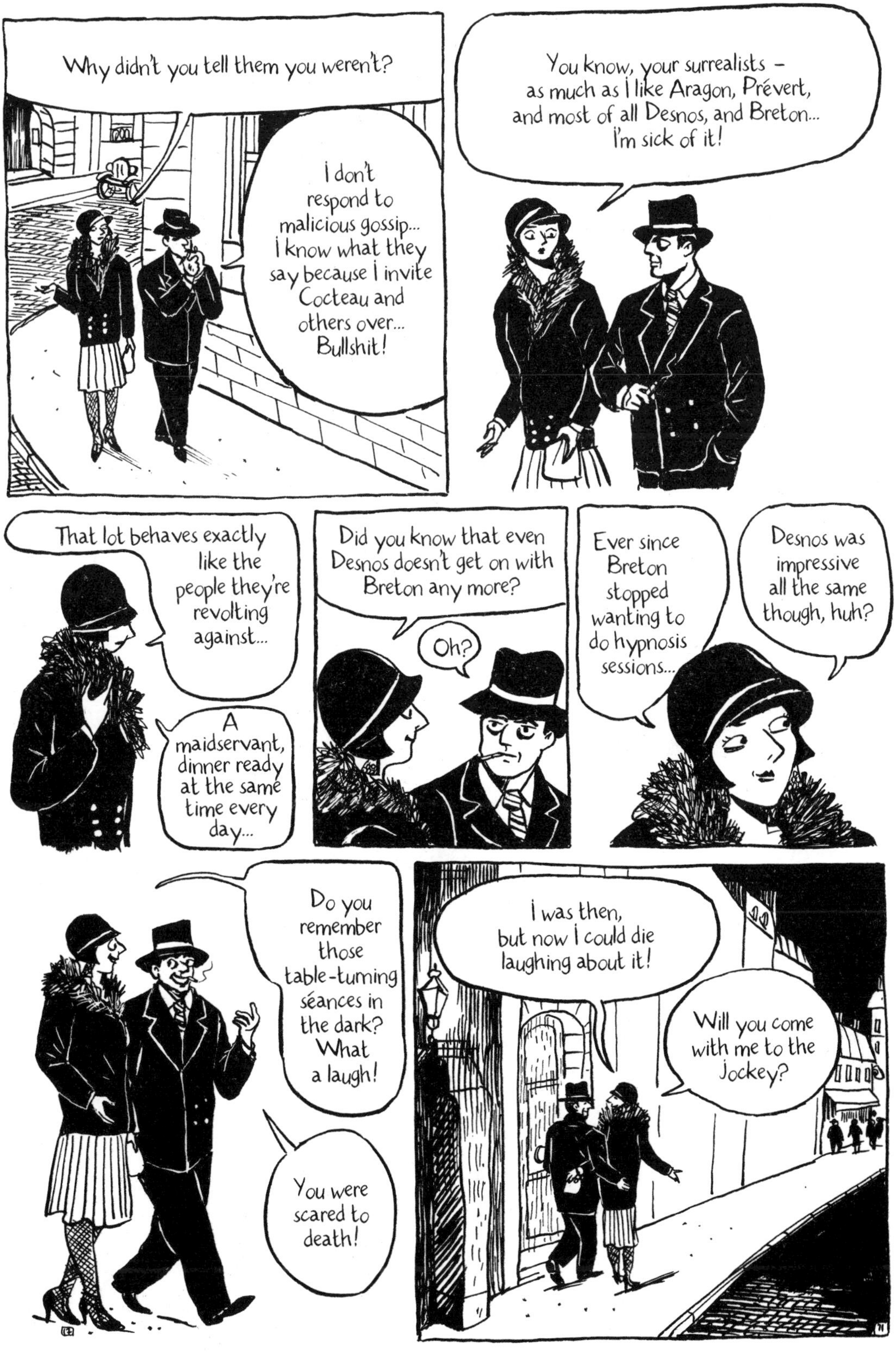
Why didn't you tell them you weren't?
I don't respond to malicious gossip... I know what they say because I invite Cocteau and others over... Bullshit!
You know, your surrealists – as much as I like Aragon, Prévert, and most of all Desnos, and Breton... I'm sick of it!
That lot behaves exactly like the people they're revolting against...
A maidservant, dinner ready at the same time every day...
Did you know that even Desnos doesn't get on with Breton any more?
Oh?
Ever since Breton stopped wanting to do hypnosis sessions...
Desnos was impressive all the same though, huh?
Do you remember those table-turning séances in the dark? What a laugh!
You were scared to death!
I was then, but now I could die laughing about it!
Will you come with me to the Jockey?

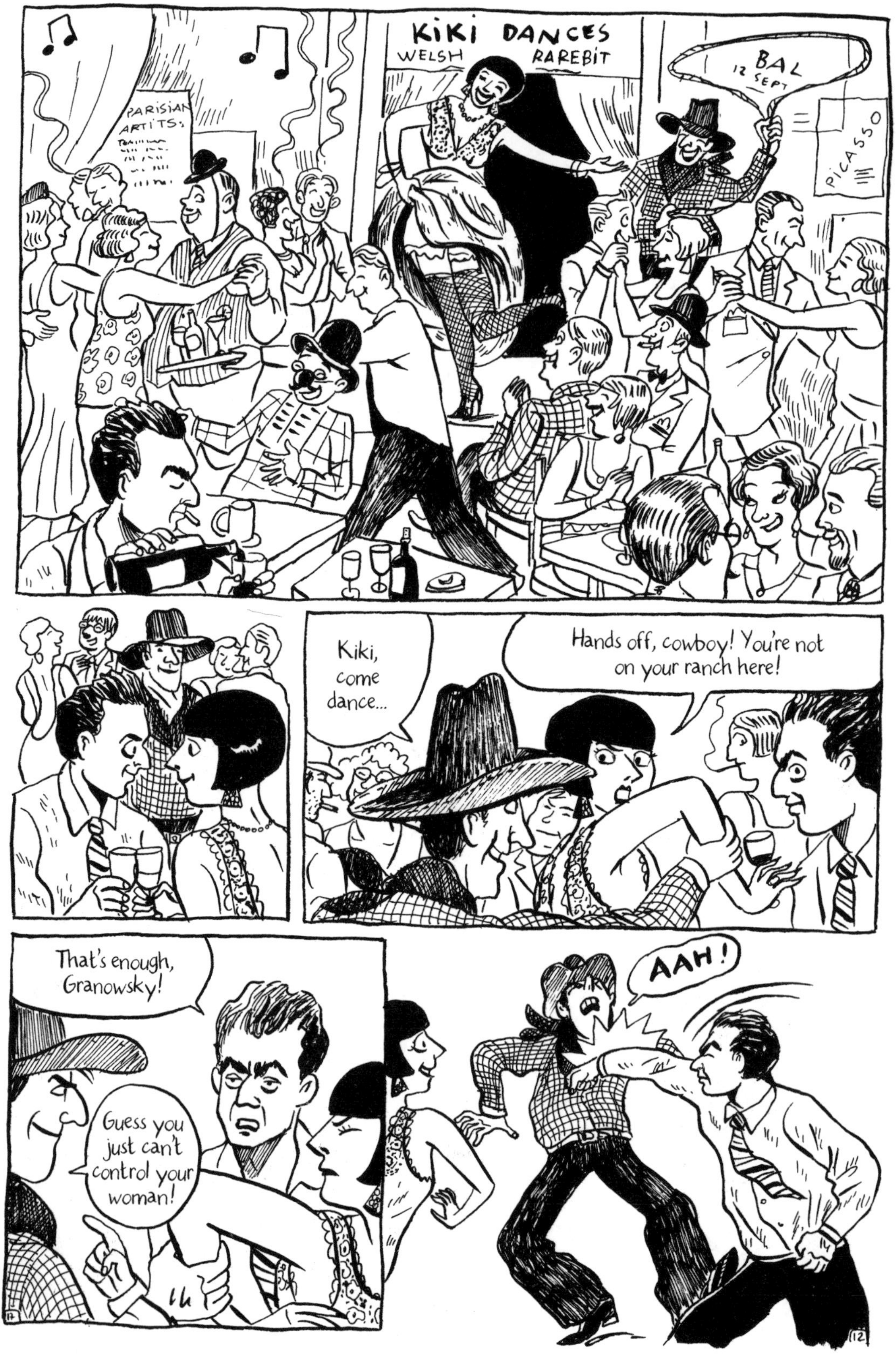
KIKI DANCES
WELSH RAREBIT
PARISIAN ARTISTS:
BAL
12 SEPT
PICASSO
Kiki, come dance...
Hands off, cowboy! You're not on your ranch here!
That's enough, Granowsky!
Guess you just can't control your woman!
AAH!

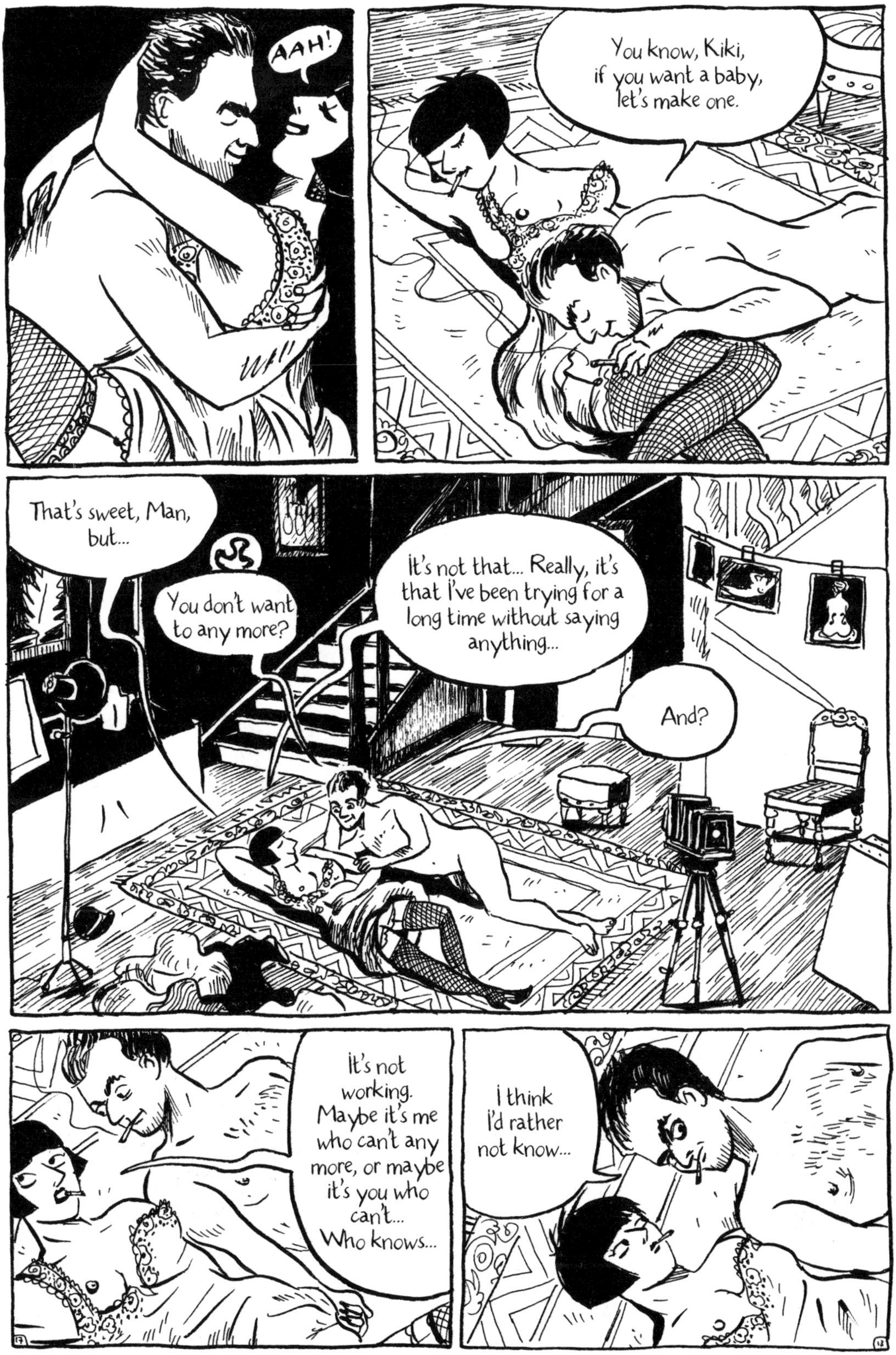
AAH!
You know, Kiki, if you want a baby, let's make one.
That's sweet, Man, but...
You don't want to any more?
It's not that... Really, it's that I've been trying for a long time without saying anything...
And?
It's not working. Maybe it's me who can't any more, or maybe it's you who can't... Who knows...
I think I'd rather not know...

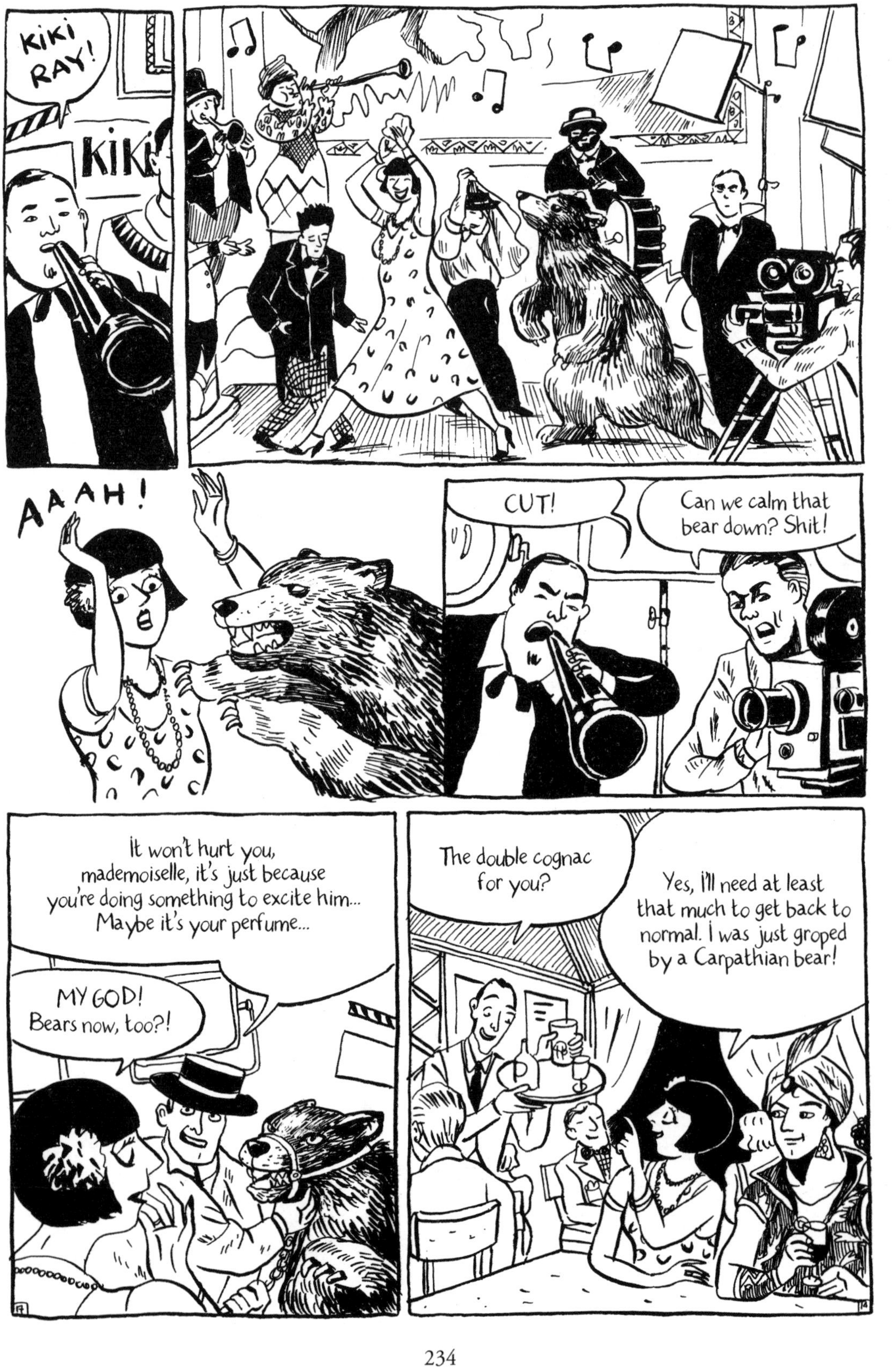
KIKI RAY!
KIKI
AAAH!
CUT!
Can we calm that bear down? Shit!
It won't hurt you, mademoiselle, it's just because you're doing something to excite him... Maybe it's your perfume...
MY GOD! Bears now, too?!
The double cognac for you?
Yes, I'll need at least that much to get back to normal. I was just groped by a Carpathian bear!

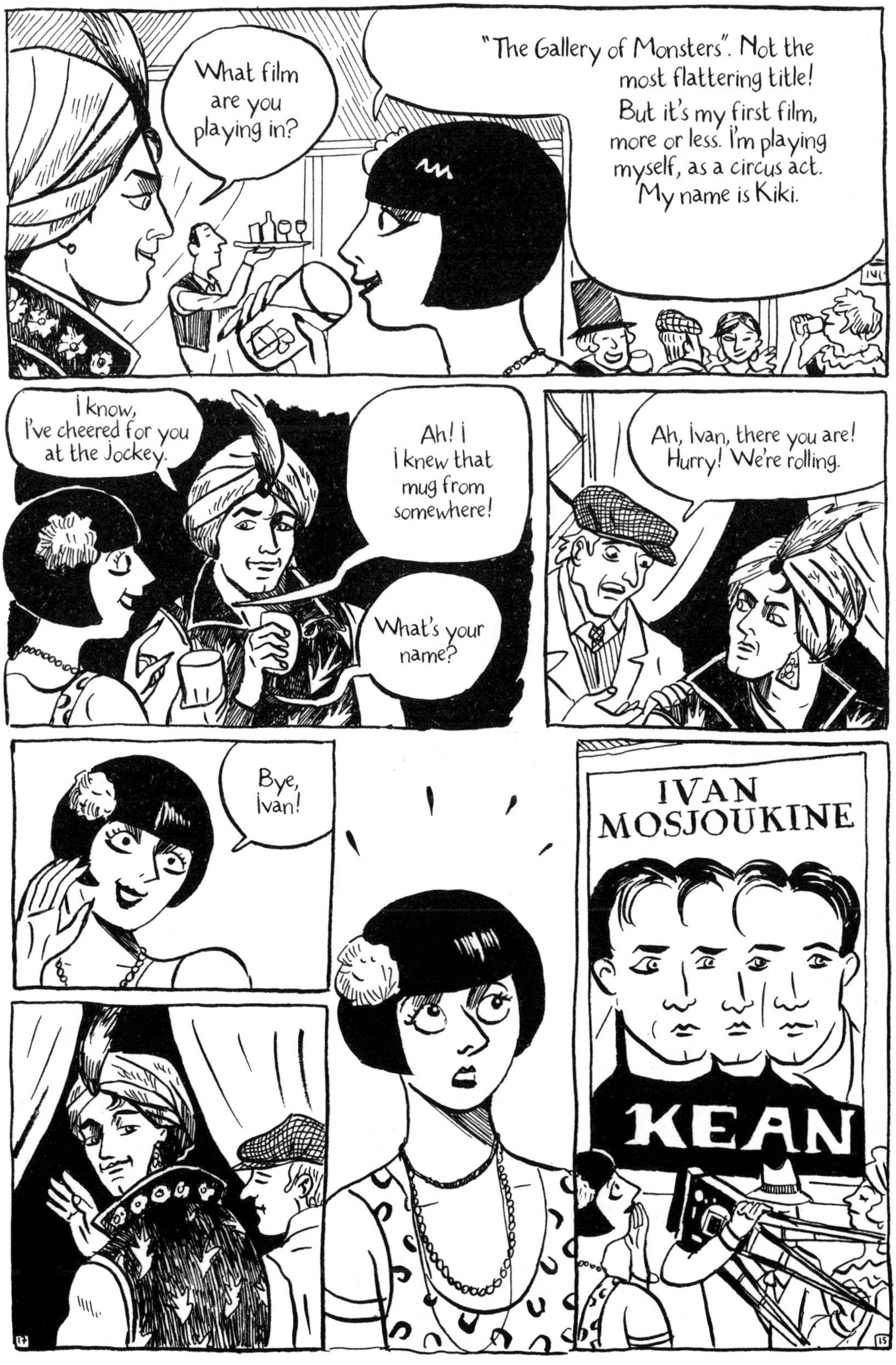
What film are you playing in?
"The Gallery of Monsters". Not the most flattering title! But it's my first film, more or less. I'm playing myself, as a circus act. My name is Kiki.
I know, I've cheered for you at the Jockey.
Ah! I I knew that mug from somewhere!
What's your name?
Ah, Ivan, there you are! Hurry! We're rolling.
Bye, Ivan!
IVAN MOSJOUKINE
KEAN

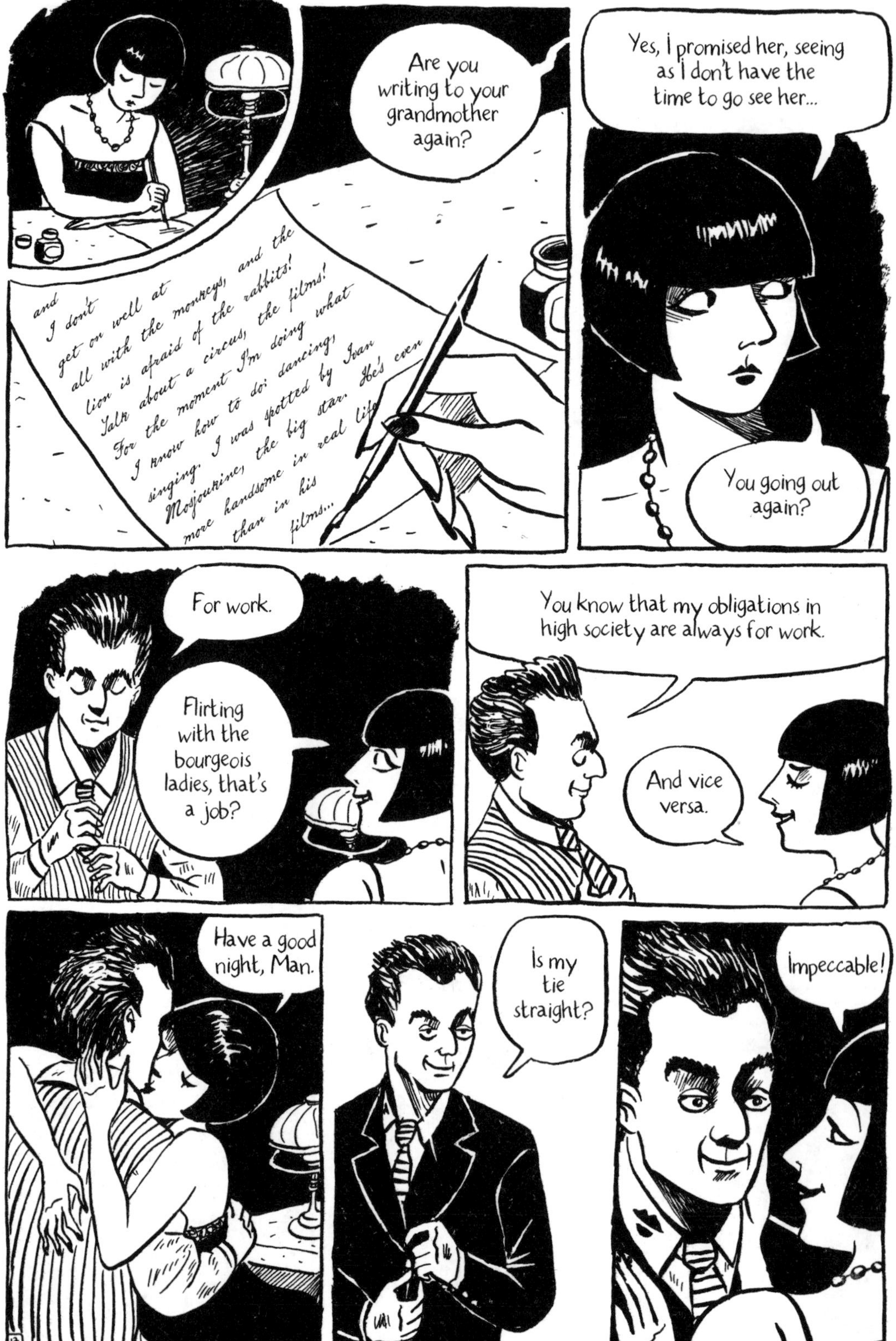

Are you writing to your grandmother again?
and I don't get on well at
all with the monkeys, and the
lion is afraid of the rabbits!
Talk about a circus, the films!
For the moment I'm doing what
I know how to do: dancing,
singing. I was spotted by Ivan
Mosjoukine, the big star. He's even
more handsome in real life
than in his
films...
Yes, I promised her, seeing as I don't have the time to go see her...
You going out again?
For work.
Flirting with the bourgeois ladies, that's a job?
You know that my obligations in high society are always for work.
And vice versa.
Have a good night, Man.
Is my tie straight?
Impeccable!

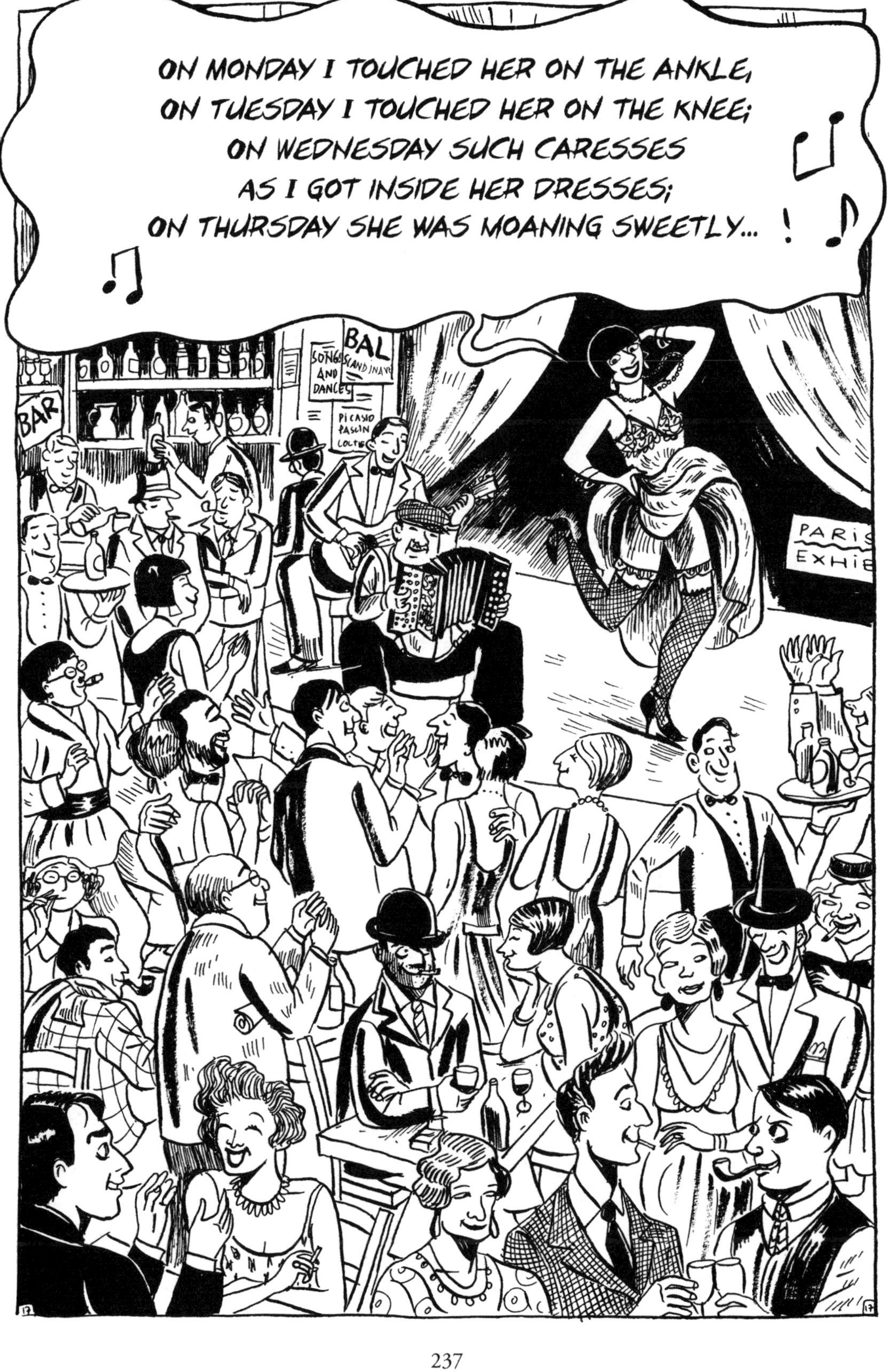
ON MONDAY I TOUCHED HER ON THE ANKLE,
ON TUESDAY I TOUCHED HER ON THE KNEE;
ON WEDNESDAY SUCH CARESSES
AS I GOT INSIDE HER DRESSES;
ON THURSDAY SHE WAS MOANING SWEETLY...
BAR
BAL
SONGS AND DANCES

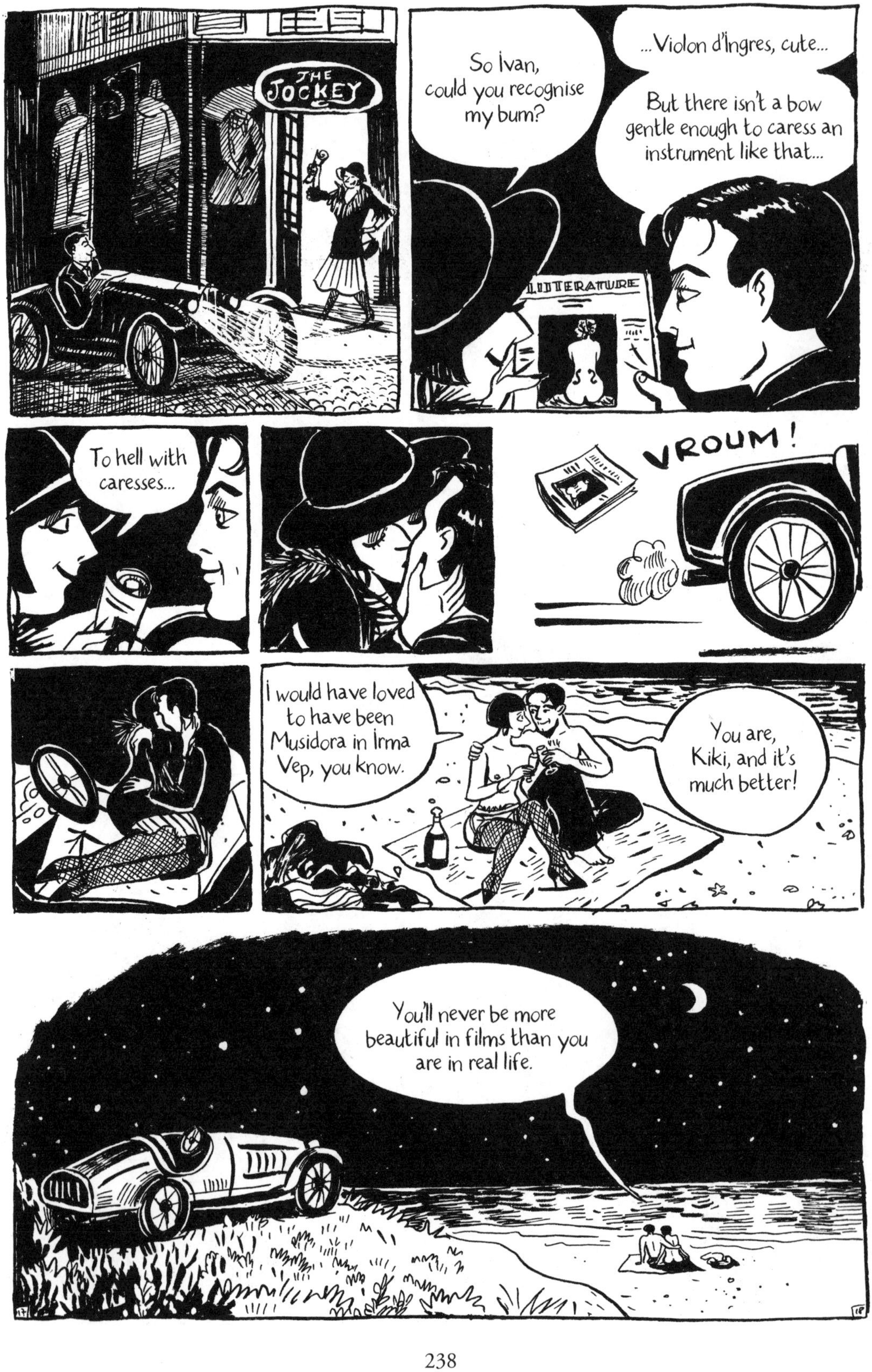
THE JOCKEY
So Ivan, could you recognise my bum?
...Violon d'Ingres, cute...
But there isn't a bow gentle enough to caress an instrument like that...
LITTERATURE
To hell with caresses...
VROUM!
I would have loved to have been Musidora in Irma Vep, you know.
You are, Kiki, and it's much better!
You'll never be more beautiful in films than you are in real life.

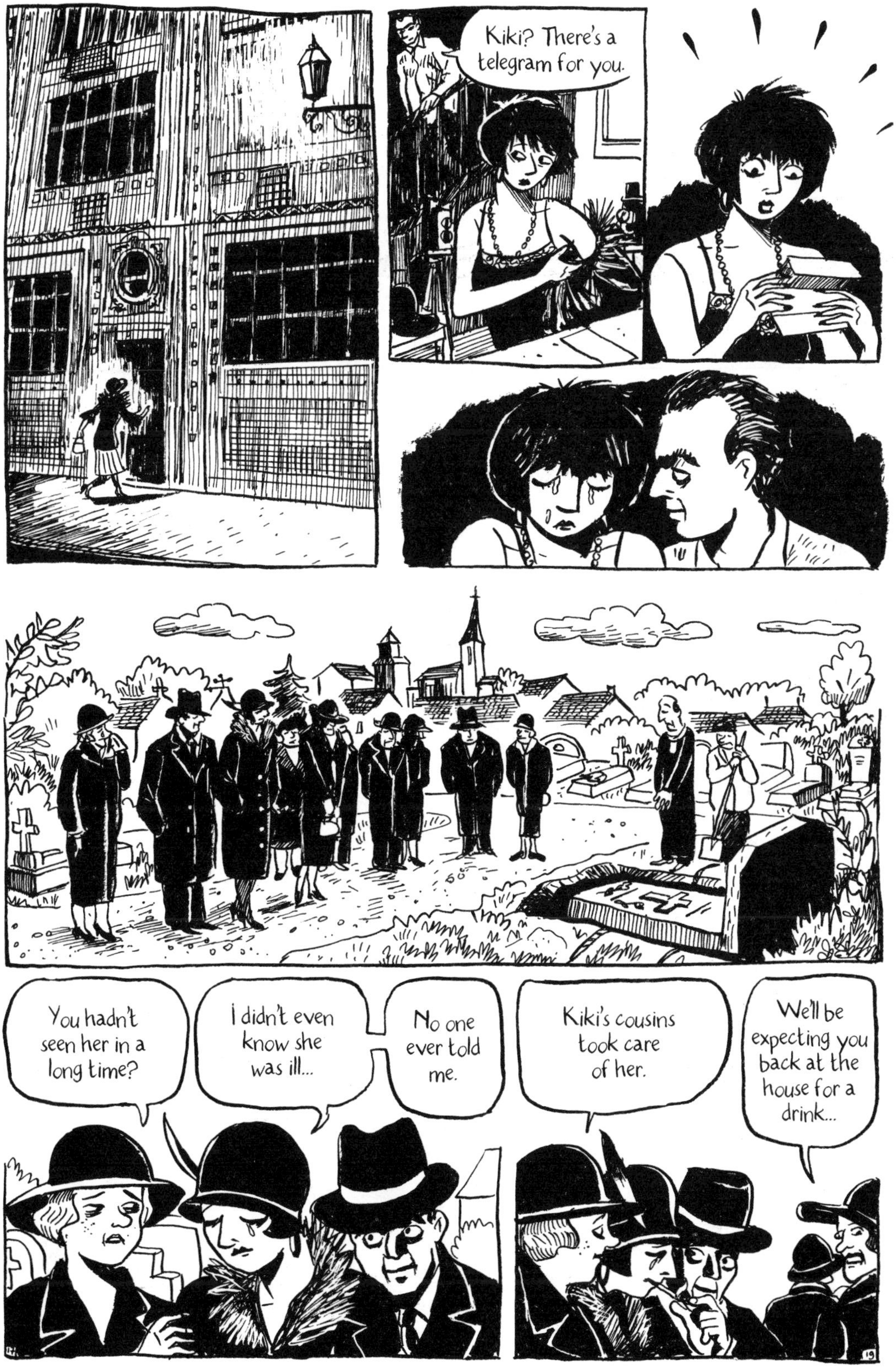
Kiki? There's a telegram for you.
You hadn't seen her in a long time?
I didn't even know she was ill...
No one ever told me.
Kiki's cousins took care of her.
We'll be expecting you back at the house for a drink...

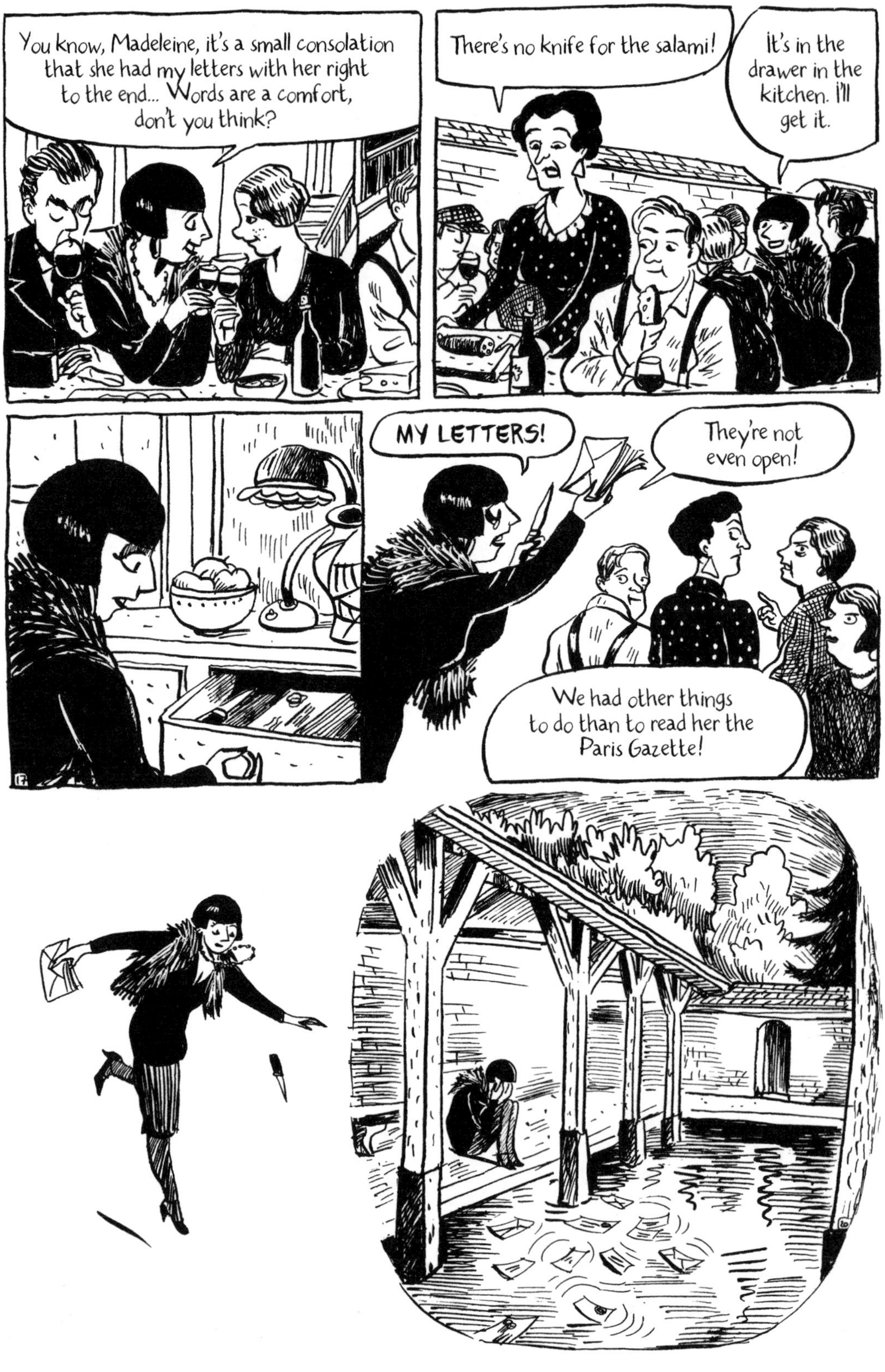
You know, Madeleine, it's a small consolation that she had my letters with her right to the end... Words are a comfort, don't you think?
There's no knife for the salami!
It's in the drawer in the kitchen. I'll get it.
MY LETTERS!
They're not even open!
We had other things to do than to read her the Paris Gazette!

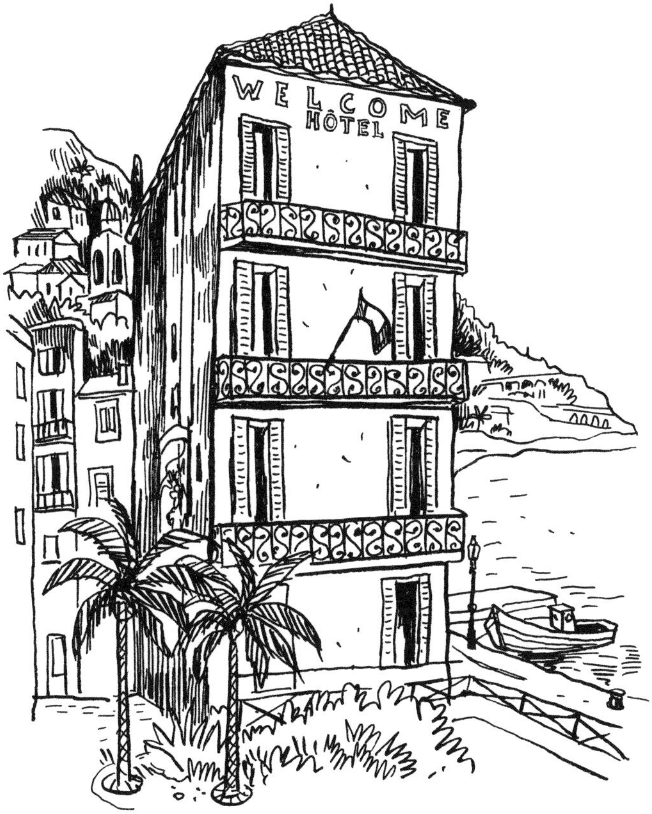
WELCOME
HÔTEL

1925 - Villefranche-sur-Mer

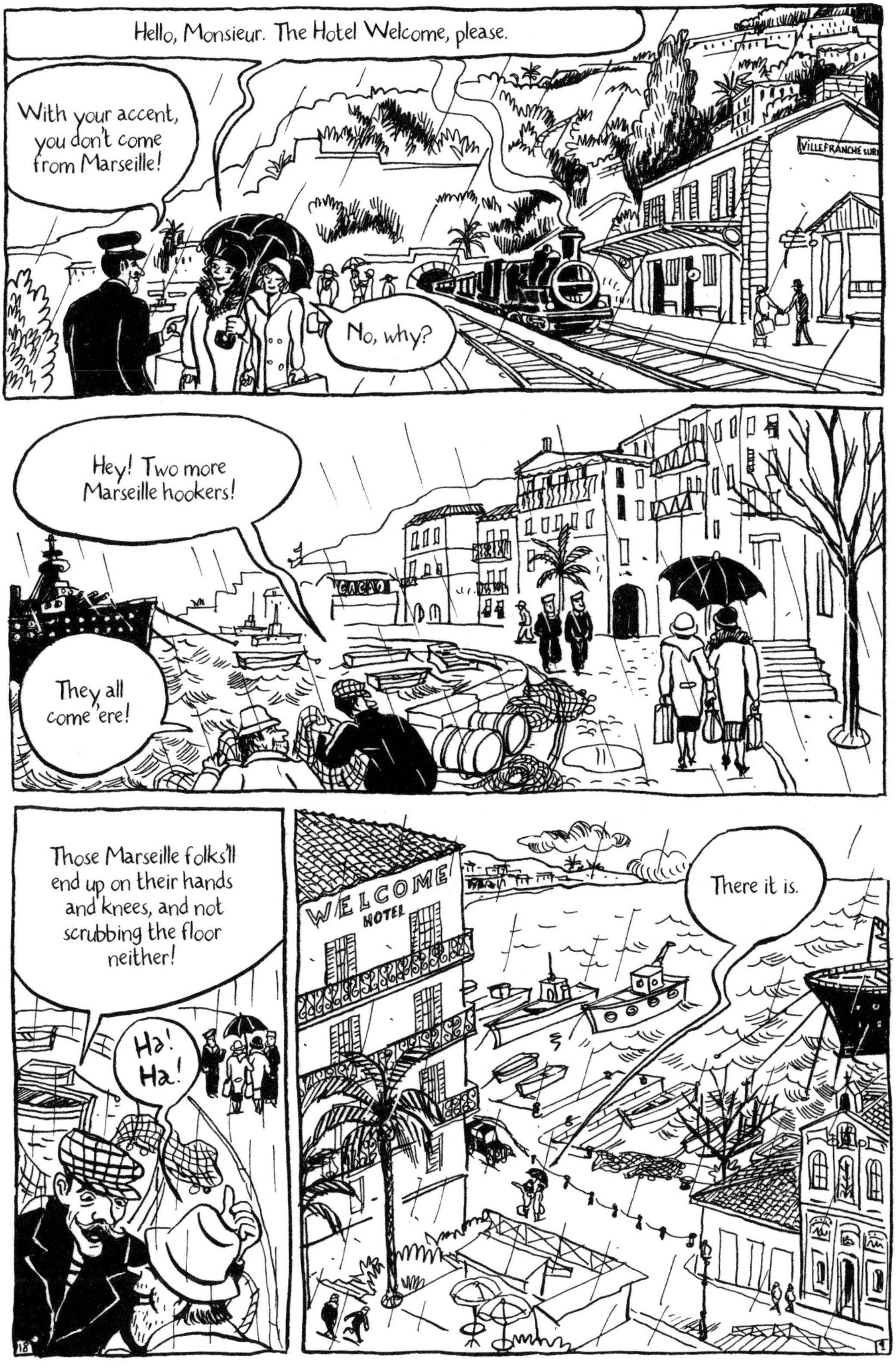
Hello, Monsieur. The Hotel Welcome, please.
With your accent, you don't come from Marseille!
No, why?
VILLEFRANCHE SUR
Hey! Two more Marseille hookers!
They all come 'ere!
CACAO
Those Marseille folks'll end up on their hands and knees, and not scrubbing the floor neither!
Ha! Ha!
WELCOME
HOTEL
There it is.

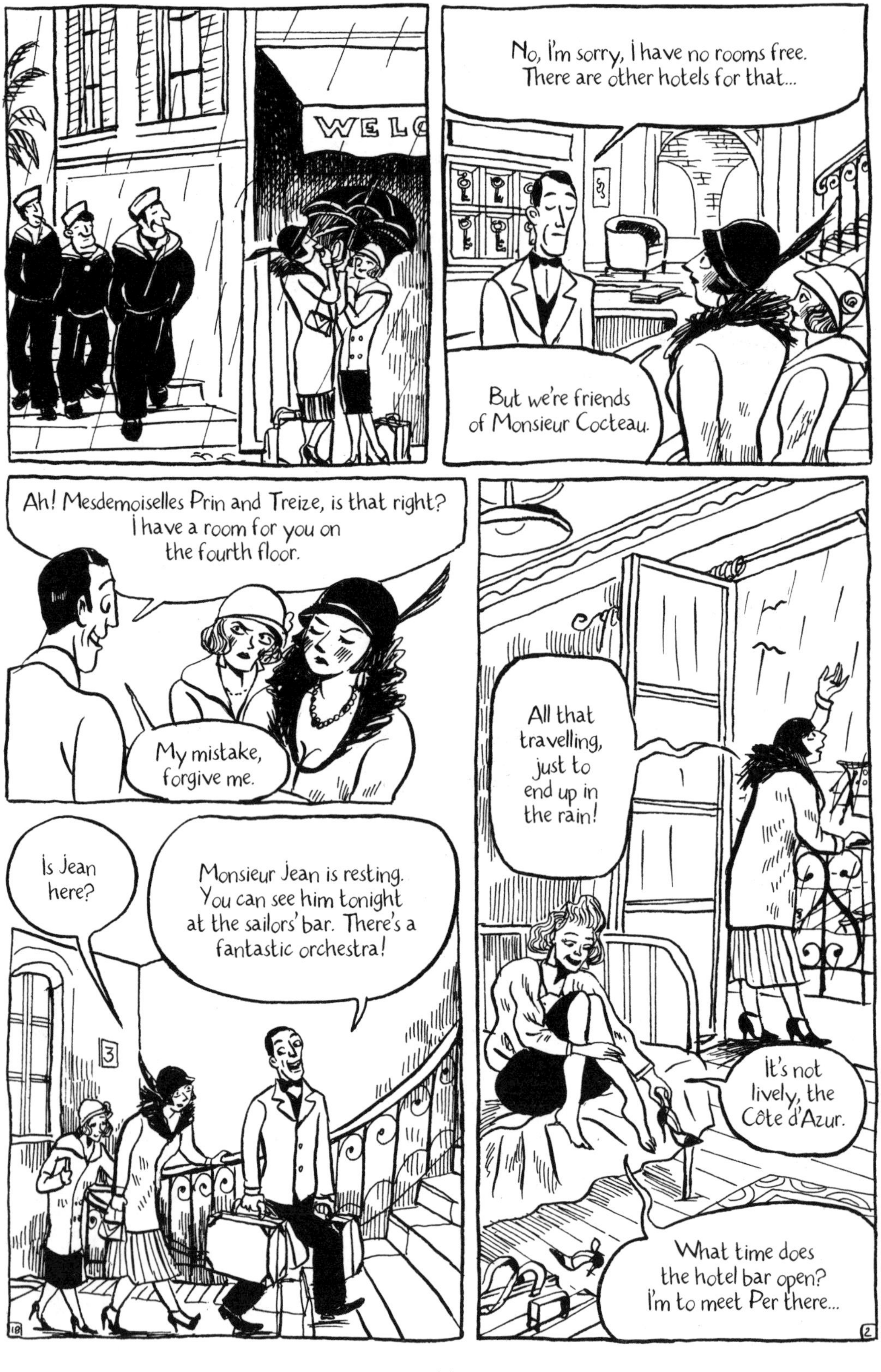

WELC
No, I'm sorry, I have no rooms free. There are other hotels for that...
But we're friends of Monsieur Cocteau.
Ah! Mesdemoiselles Prin and Treize, is that right? I have a room for you on the fourth floor.
My mistake, forgive me.
Is Jean here?
Monsieur Jean is resting. You can see him tonight at the sailors' bar. There's a fantastic orchestra!
3
All that travelling, just to end up in the rain!
It's not lively, the Côte d'Azur.
What time does the hotel bar open? I'm to meet Per there...

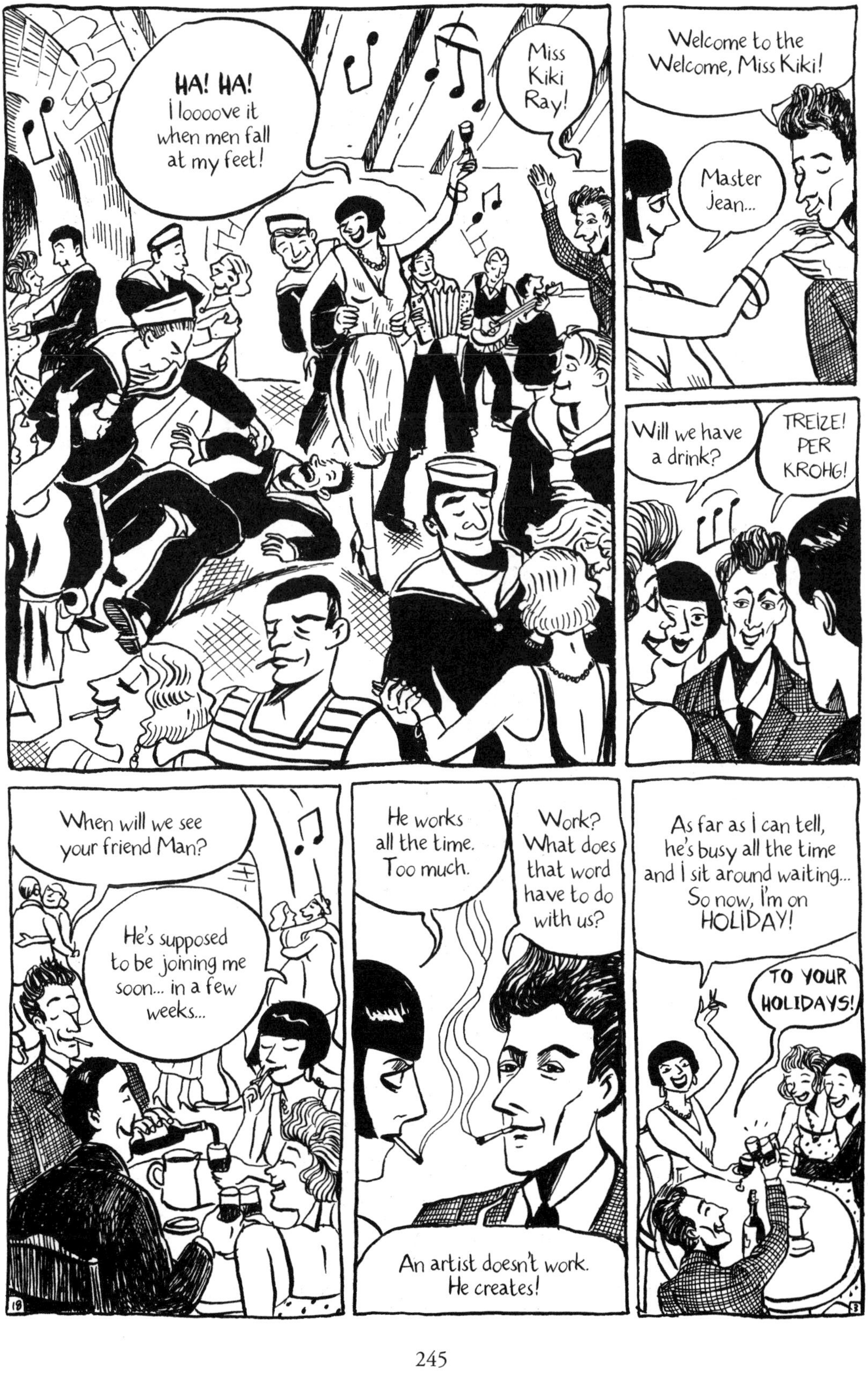
HA! HA! I loooove it when men fall at my feet!
Miss Kiki Ray!
Welcome to the Welcome, Miss Kiki!
Master Jean...
Will we have a drink?
TREIZE! PER KROHG!
When will we see your friend Man?
He's supposed to be joining me soon... in a few weeks...
He works all the time. Too much.
Work? What does that word have to do with us?
An artist doesn't work. He creates!
As far as I can tell, he's busy all the time and I sit around waiting... So now, I'm on HOLIDAY!
TO YOUR HOLIDAYS!

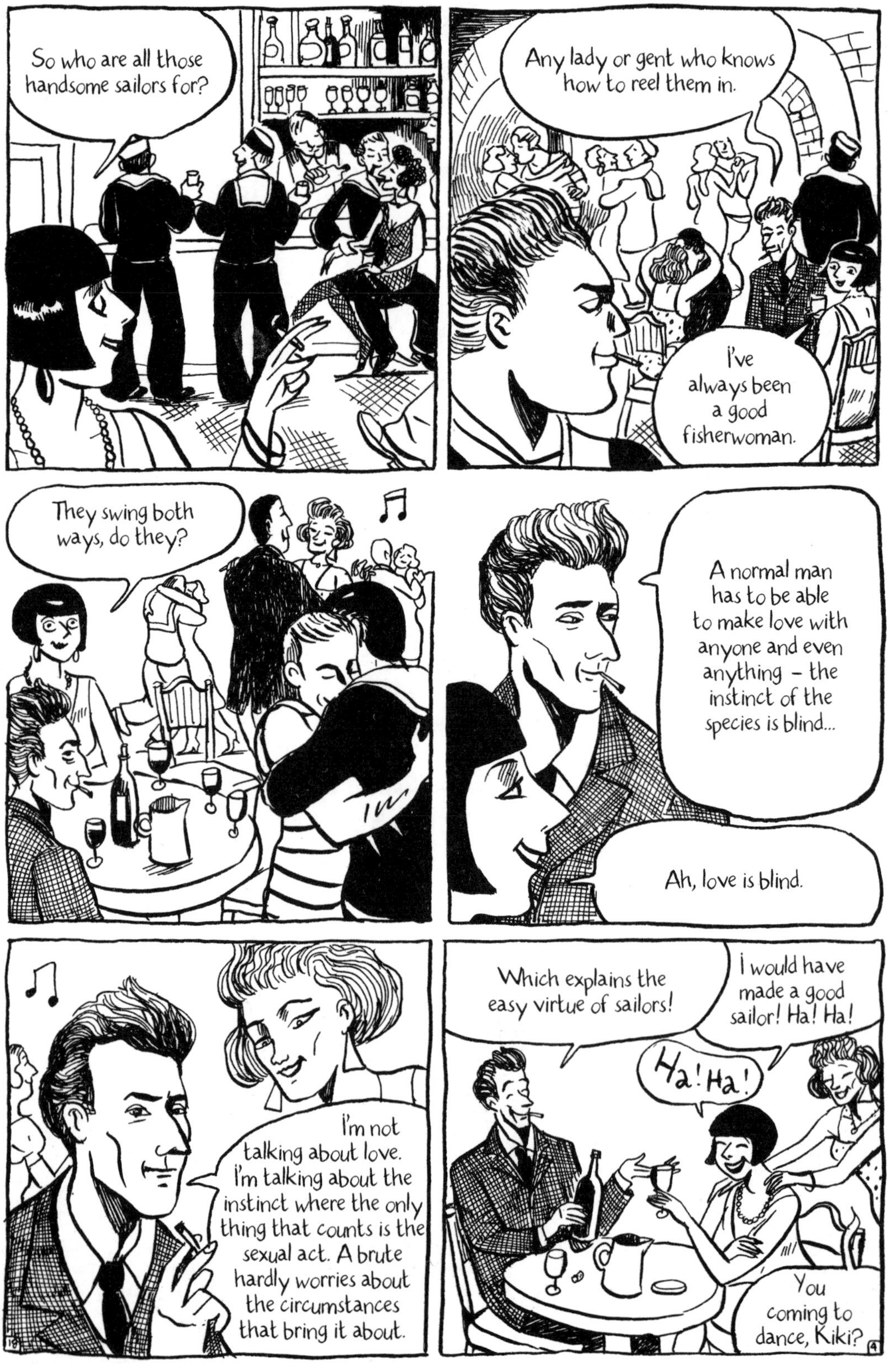
So who are all those handsome sailors for?
Any lady or gent who knows how to reel them in.
I've always been a good fisherwoman.
They swing both ways, do they?
A normal man has to be able to make love with anyone and even anything – the instinct of the species is blind...
Ah, love is blind.
I'm not talking about love. I'm talking about the instinct where the only thing that counts is the sexual act. A brute hardly worries about the circumstances that bring it about.
Which explains the easy virtue of sailors!
I would have made a good sailor! Ha! Ha!
Ha! Ha!
You coming to dance, Kiki?

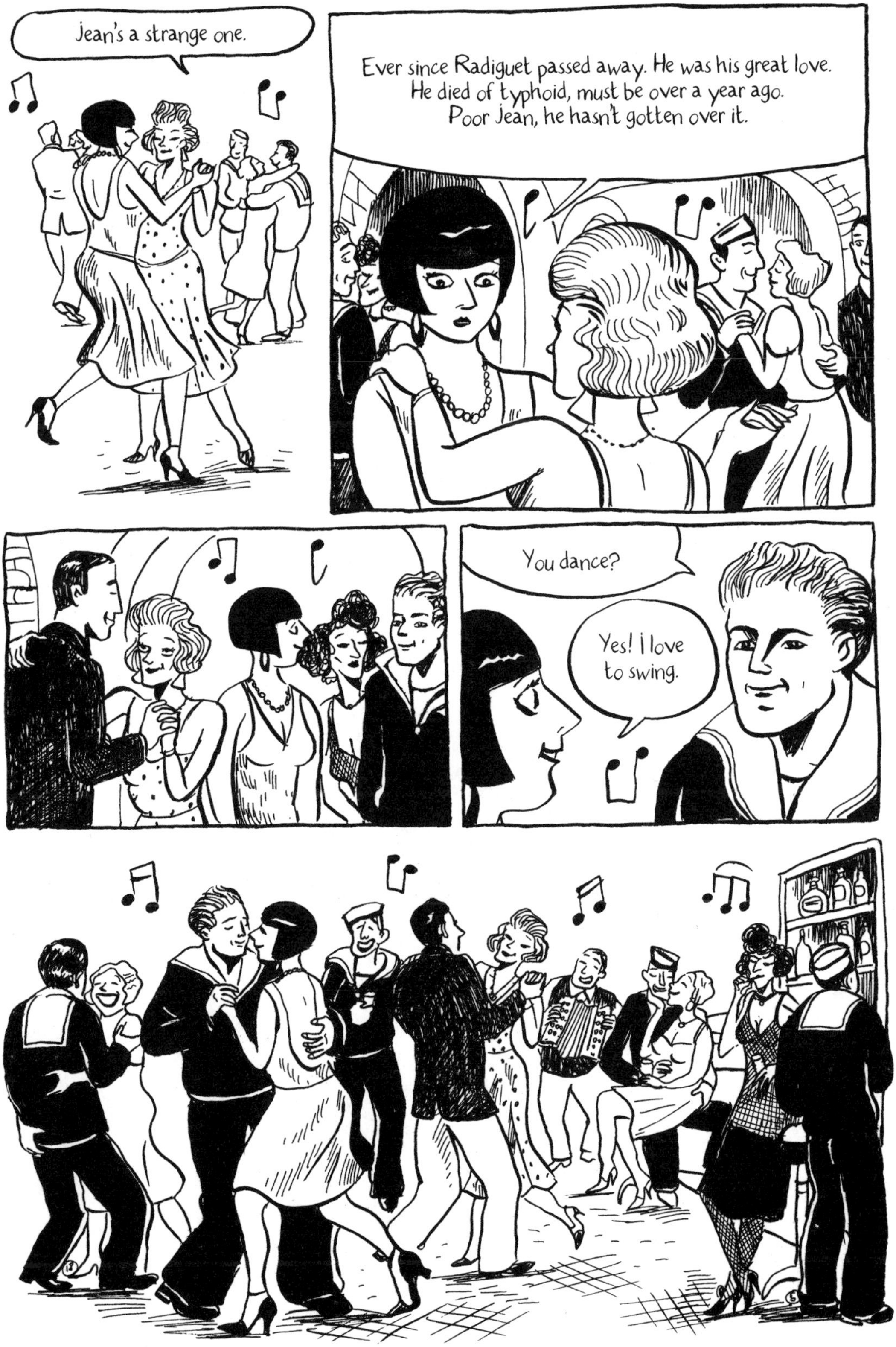
Jean's a strange one.
Ever since Radiguet passed away. He was his great love. He died of typhoid, must be over a year ago. Poor Jean, he hasn't gotten over it.
You dance?
Yes! I love to swing.

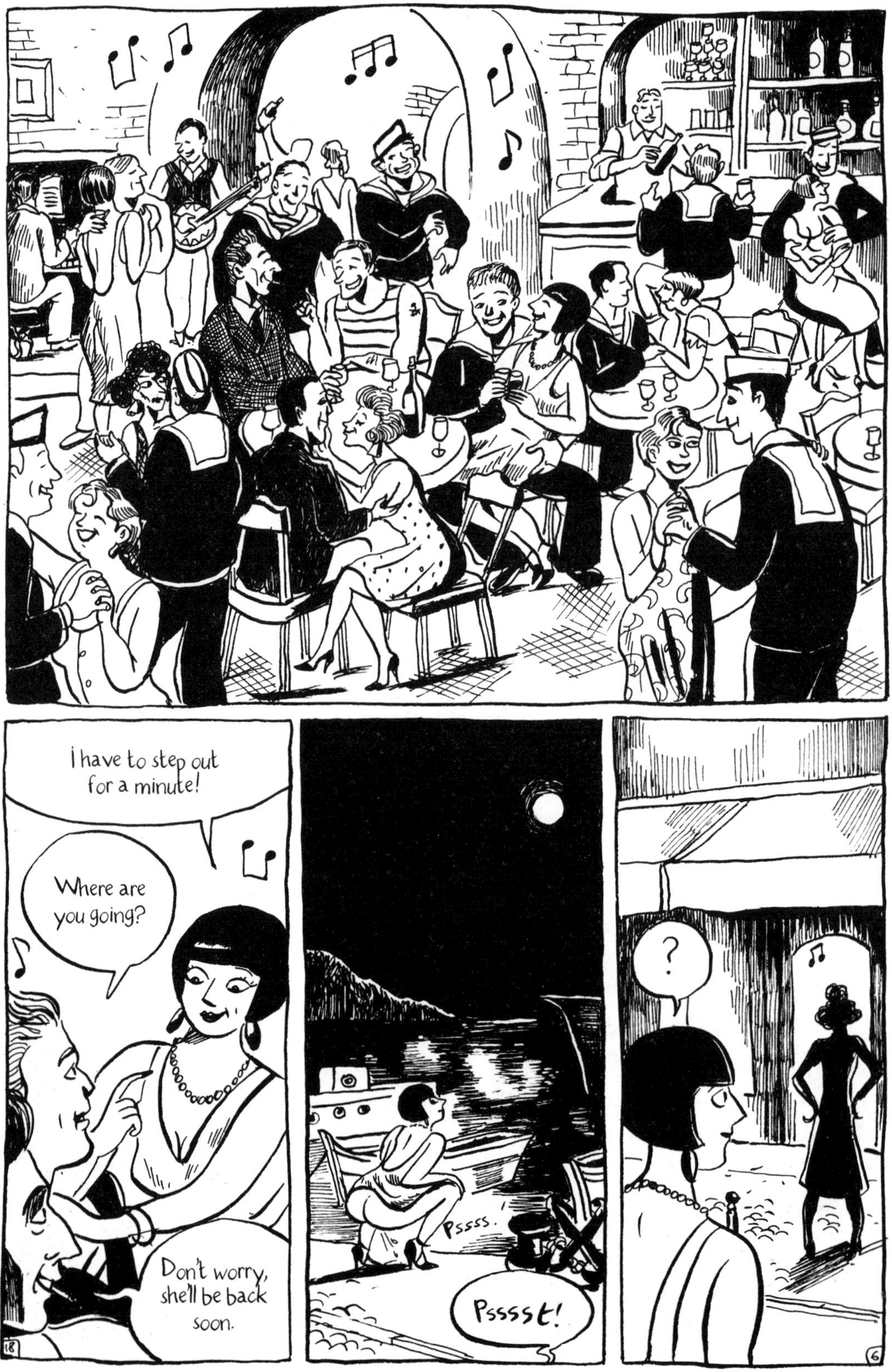
I have to step out for a minute!
Where are you going?
Don't worry, she'll be back soon.
Pssss.
Psssst!
?

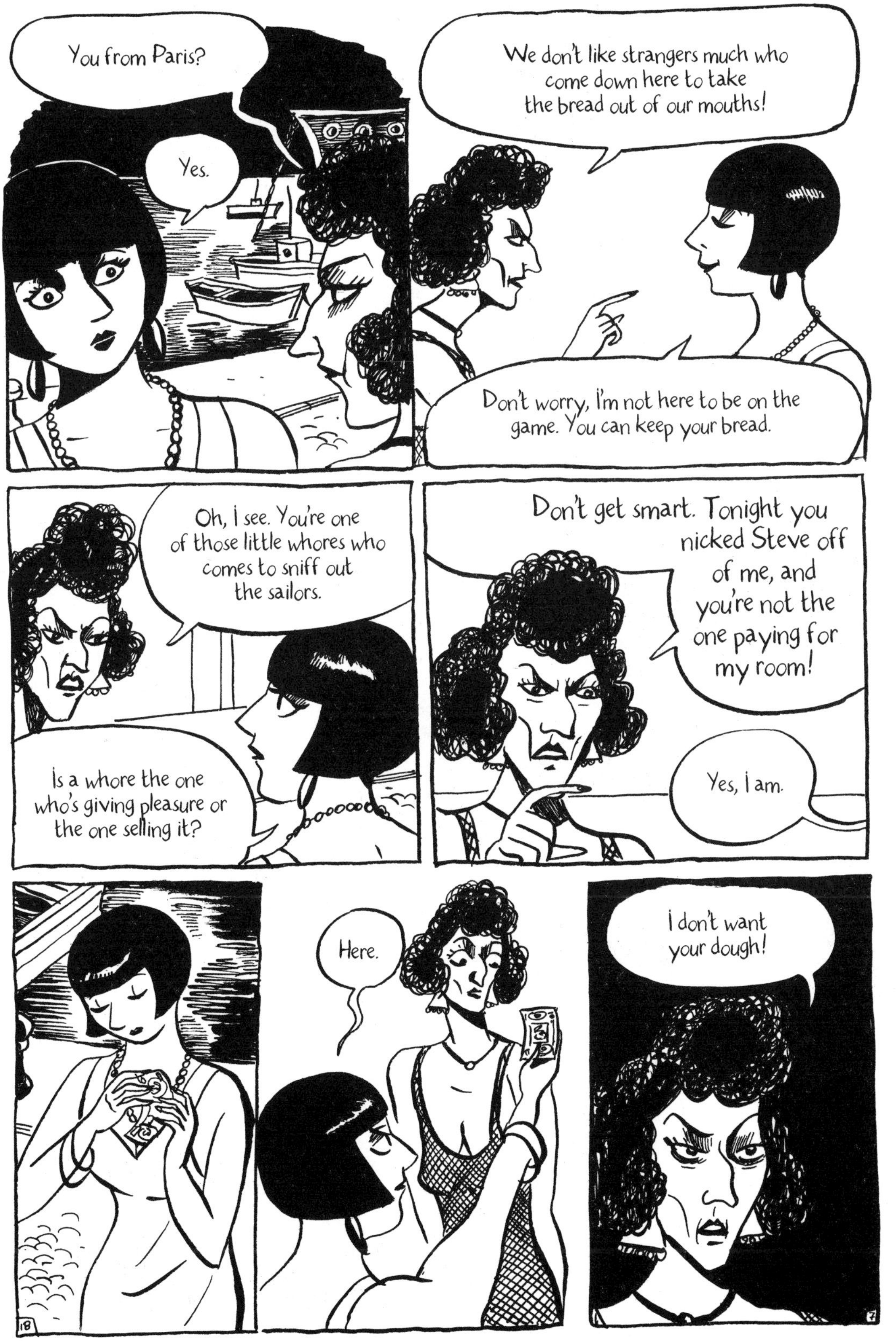
You from Paris?
Yes.
We don't like strangers much who come down here to take the bread out of our mouths!
Don't worry, I'm not here to be on the game. You can keep your bread.
Oh, I see. You're one of those little whores who comes to sniff out the sailors.
Is a whore the one who's giving pleasure or the one selling it?
Don't get smart. Tonight you nicked Steve off of me, and you're not the one paying for my room!
Yes, I am.
Here.
I don't want your dough!

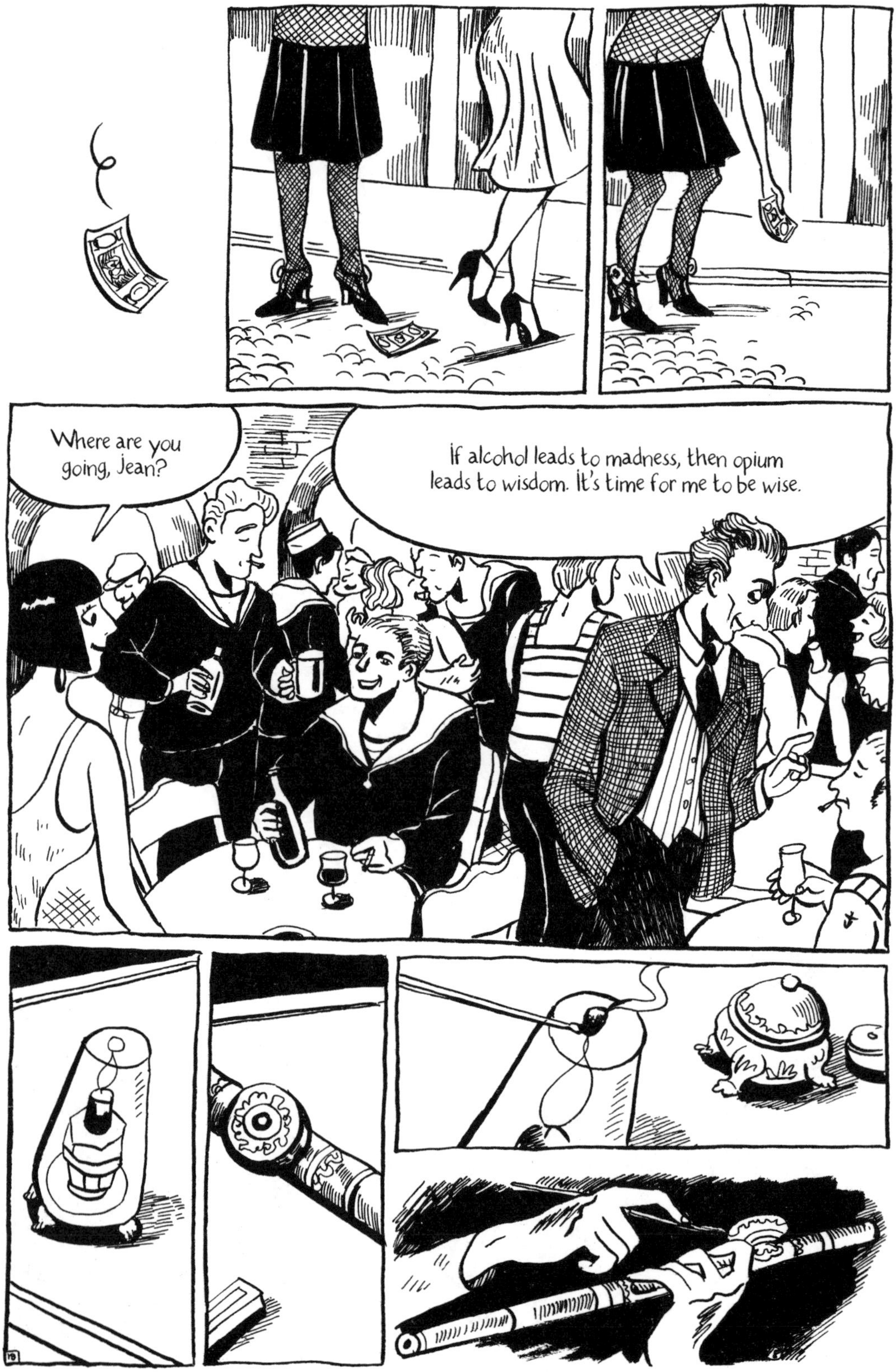
Where are you going, Jean?
If alcohol leads to madness, then opium leads to wisdom. It's time for me to be wise.

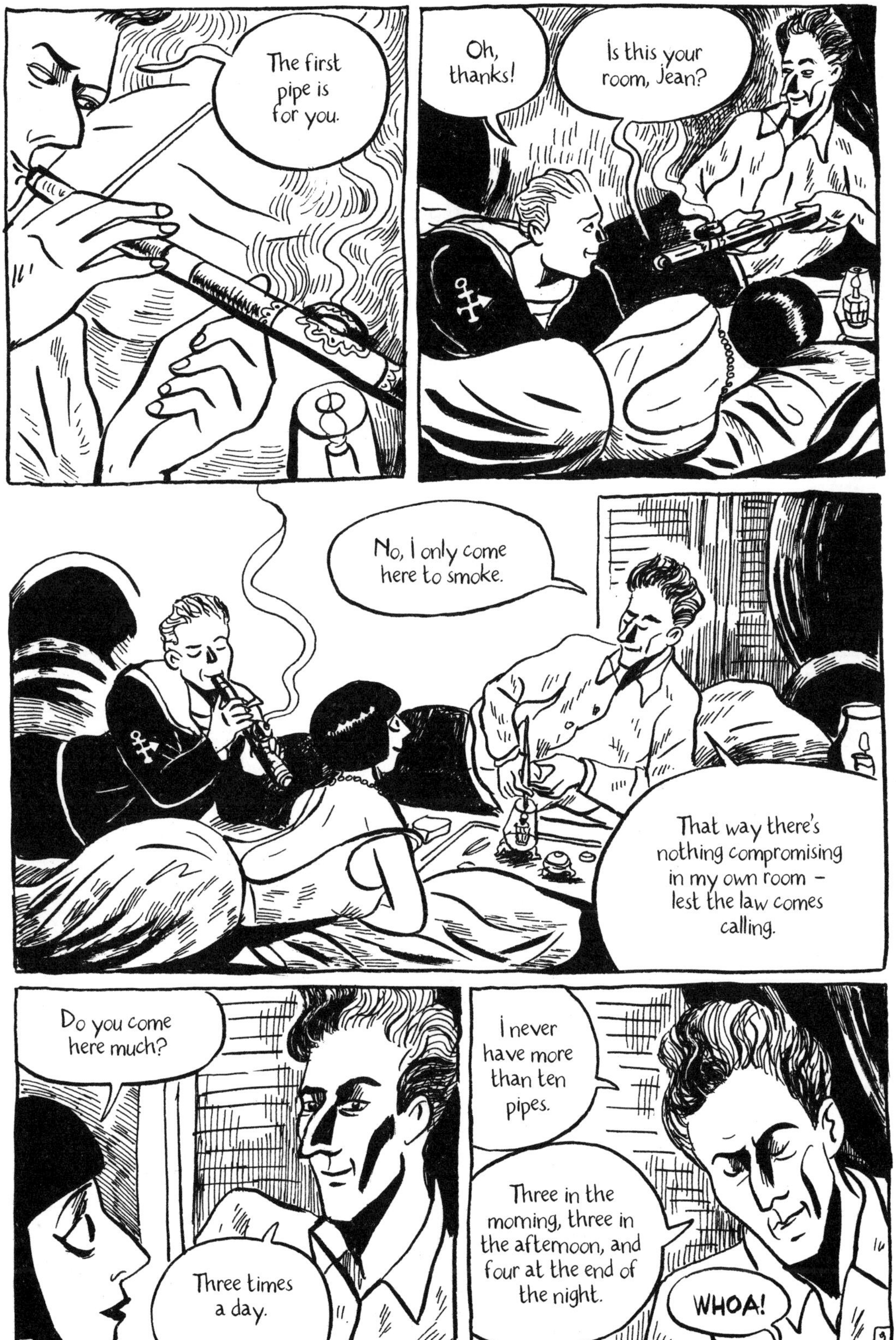
The first pipe is for you.
Oh, thanks!
Is this your room, Jean?
No, I only come here to smoke.
That way there's nothing compromising in my own room – lest the law comes calling.
Do you come here much?
Three times a day.
I never have more than ten pipes.
Three in the morning, three in the afternoon, and four at the end of the night.
WHOA!

Don't you think you're hitting the bamboo a bit hard, Jean?

Ha! Ha! Darling Kiki, convincing an opium addict to change is like telling Tristan, "Kill Isolde, you'll feel better afterwards!"

You like opium that much?

Everything we do in life, even love, we do on the express train to death.

For me, smoking opium is getting off when you're halfway there...

...but you still have to be careful not to fall on your head!

This one's for you...

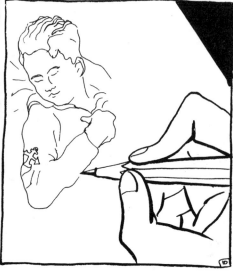

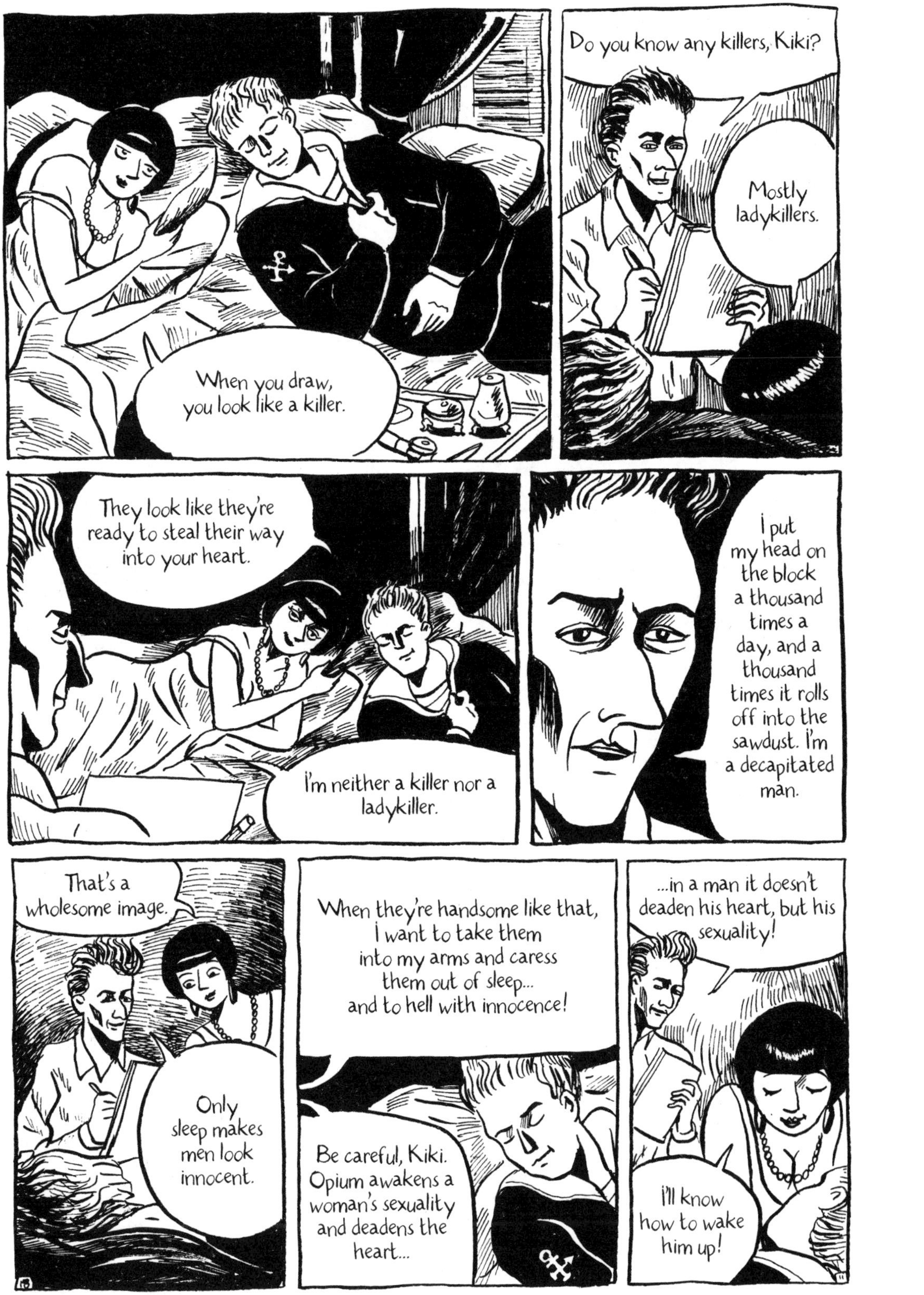
When you draw, you look like a killer.
Do you know any killers, Kiki?
Mostly ladykillers.
They look like they're ready to steal their way into your heart.
I'm neither a killer nor a ladykiller.
I put my head on the block a thousand times a day, and a thousand times it rolls off into the sawdust. I'm a decapitated man.
That's a wholesome image.
Only sleep makes men look innocent.
When they're handsome like that, I want to take them into my arms and caress them out of sleep... and to hell with innocence!
Be careful, Kiki. Opium awakens a woman's sexuality and deadens the heart...
...in a man it doesn't deaden his heart, but his sexuality!
I'll know how to wake him up!

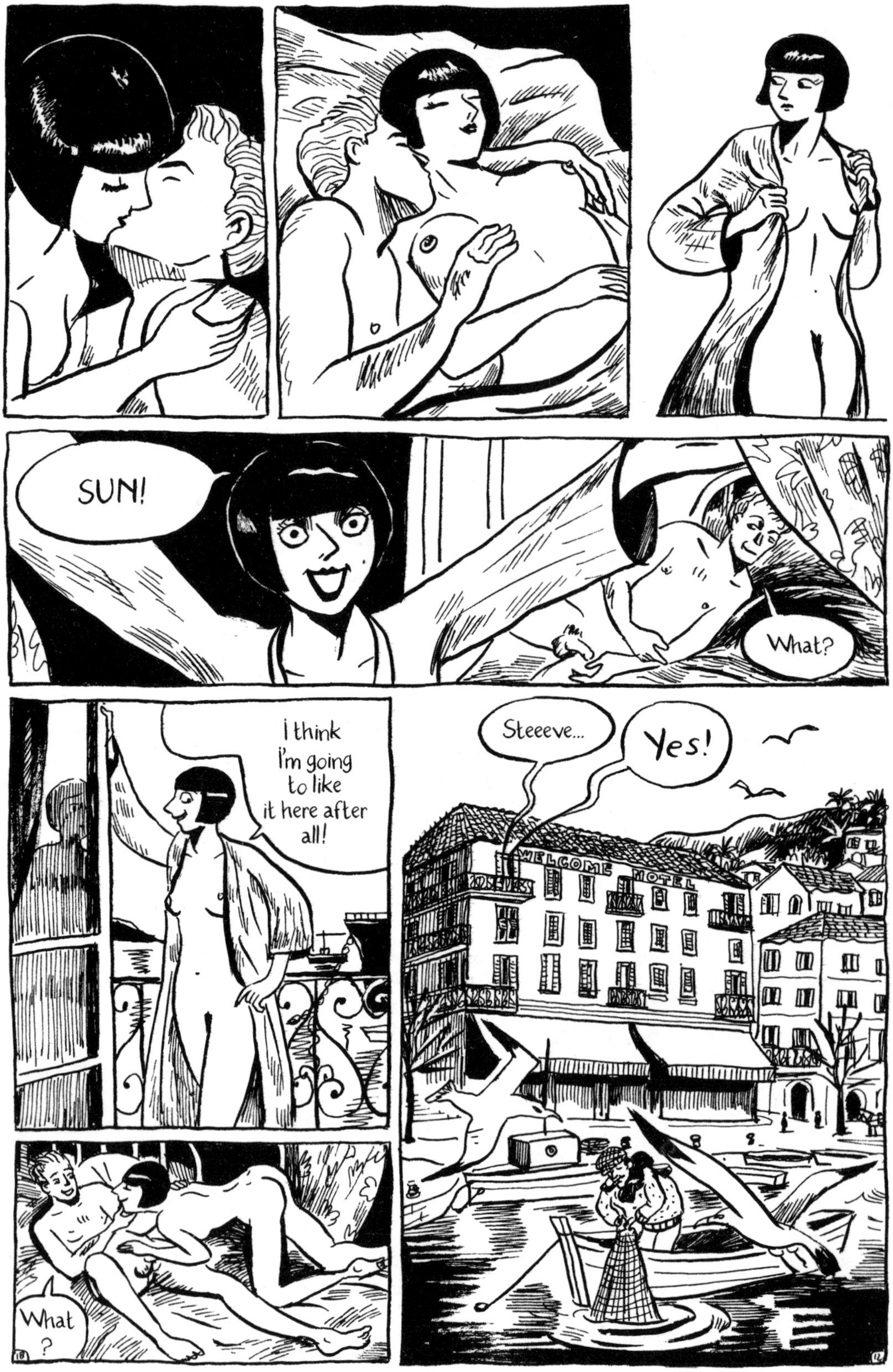
SUN!
What?
I think I'm going to like it here after all!
What ?
Steeeve...
Yes!
WELCOME HOTEL

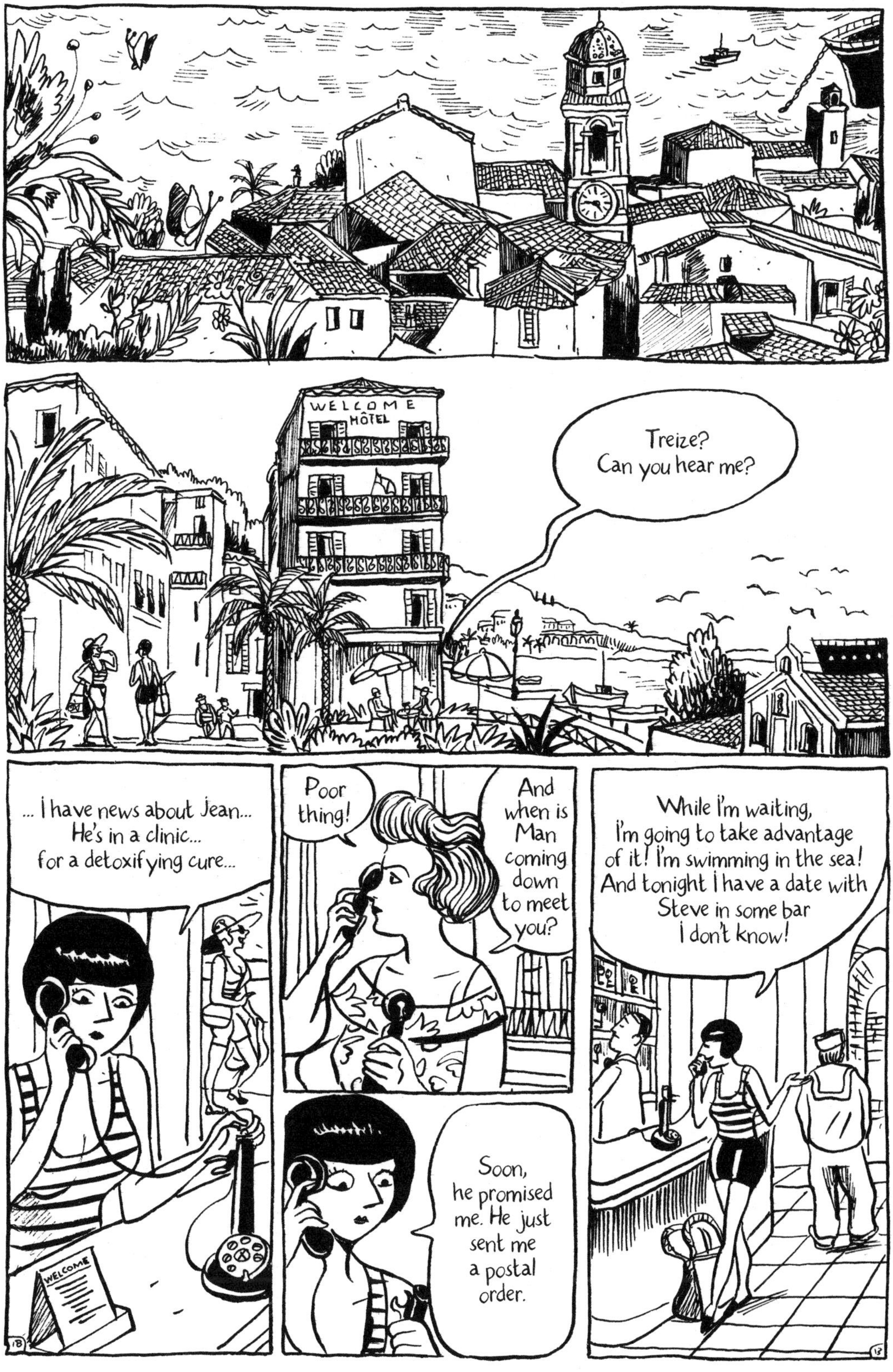
WELCOME HÔTEL
Treize? Can you hear me?
... I have news about Jean... He's in a clinic... for a detoxifying cure...
Poor thing!
And when is Man coming down to meet you?
Soon, he promised me. He just sent me a postal order.
While I'm waiting, I'm going to take advantage of it! I'm swimming in the sea! And tonight I have a date with Steve in some bar I don't know!
WELCOME

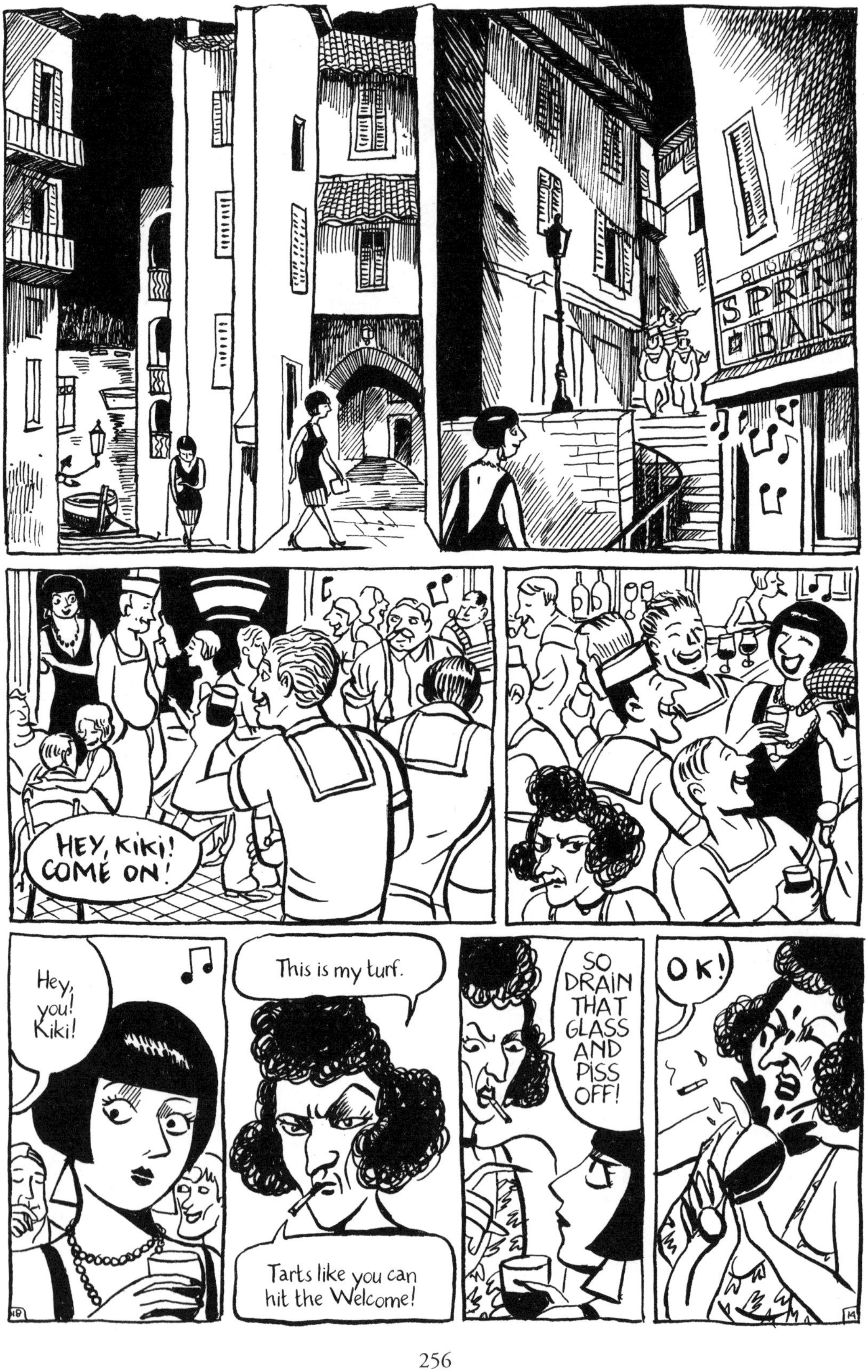
SPRIN
BAR
HEY, KiKi! COME ON!
Hey, you! Kiki!
This is my turf.
Tarts like you can hit the Welcome!
SO DRAIN THAT GLASS AND PiSS OFF!
OK!

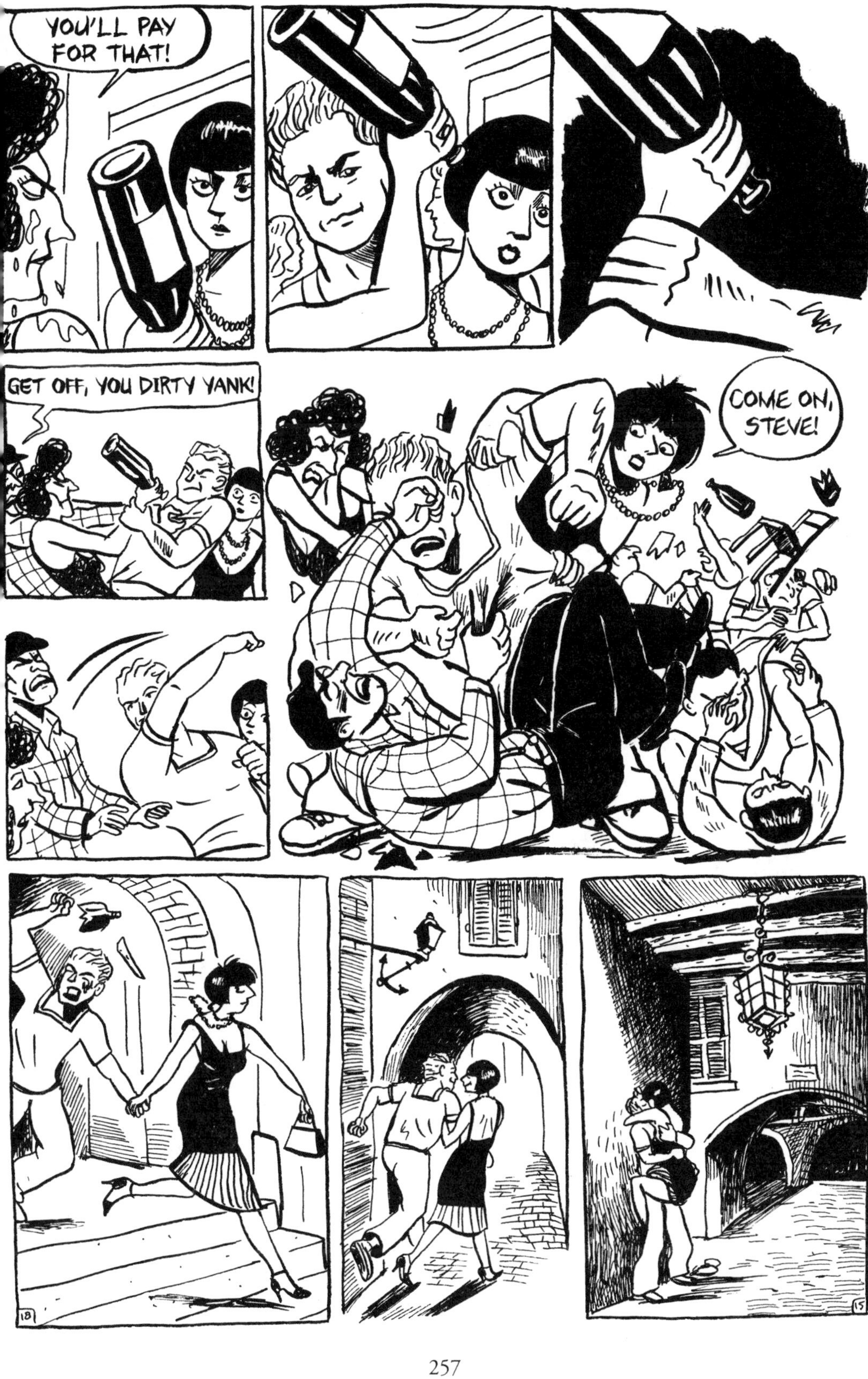
YOU'LL PAY FOR THAT!
GET OFF, YOU DIRTY YANK!
COME ON, STEVE!
18
15

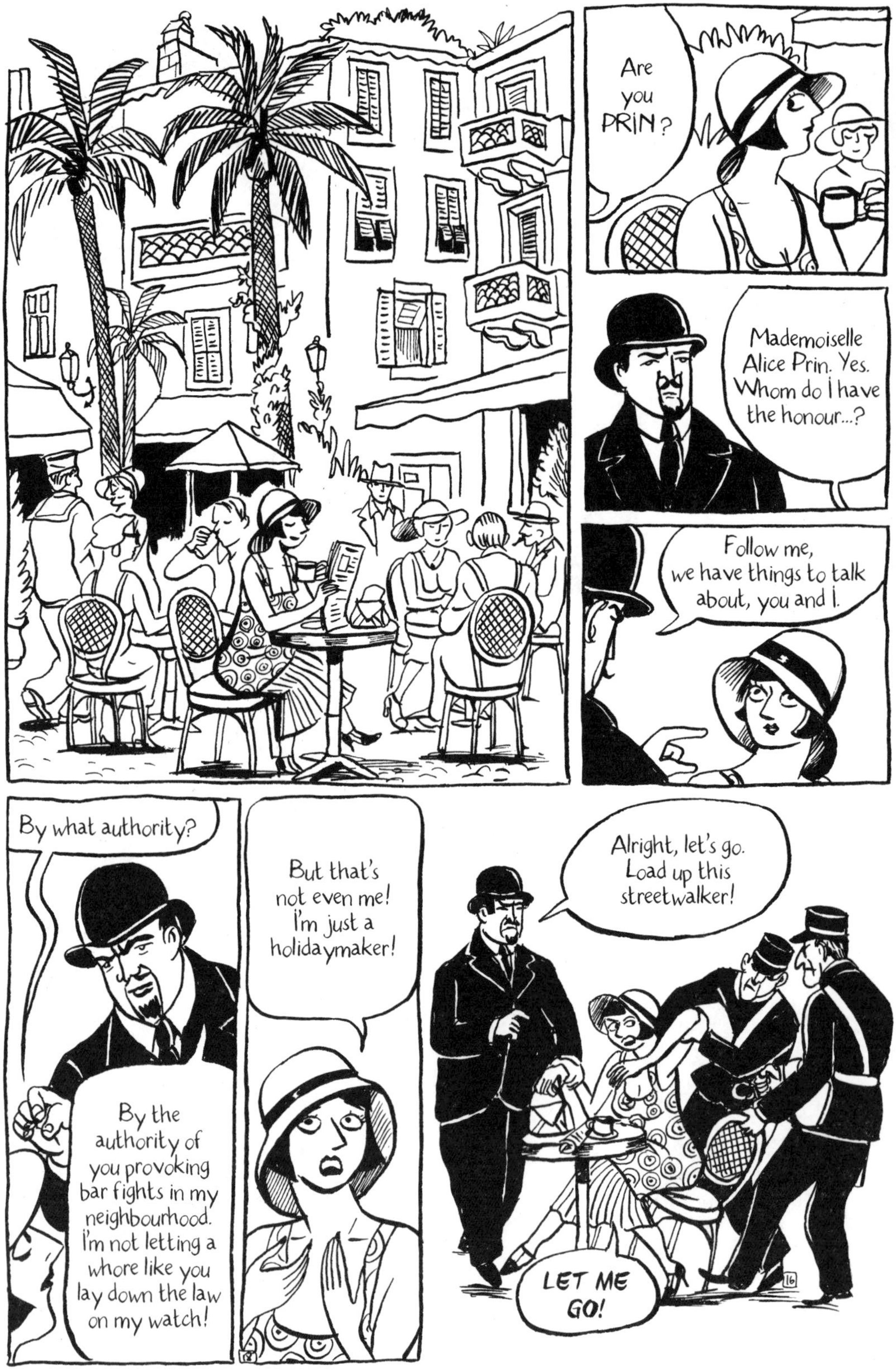
Are you PRIN?
Mademoiselle Alice Prin. Yes. Whom do I have the honour...?
Follow me, we have things to talk about, you and I.
By what authority?
By the authority of you provoking bar fights in my neighbourhood. I'm not letting a whore like you lay down the law on my watch!
But that's not even me! I'm just a holidaymaker!
Alright, let's go. Load up this streetwalker!
LET ME GO!

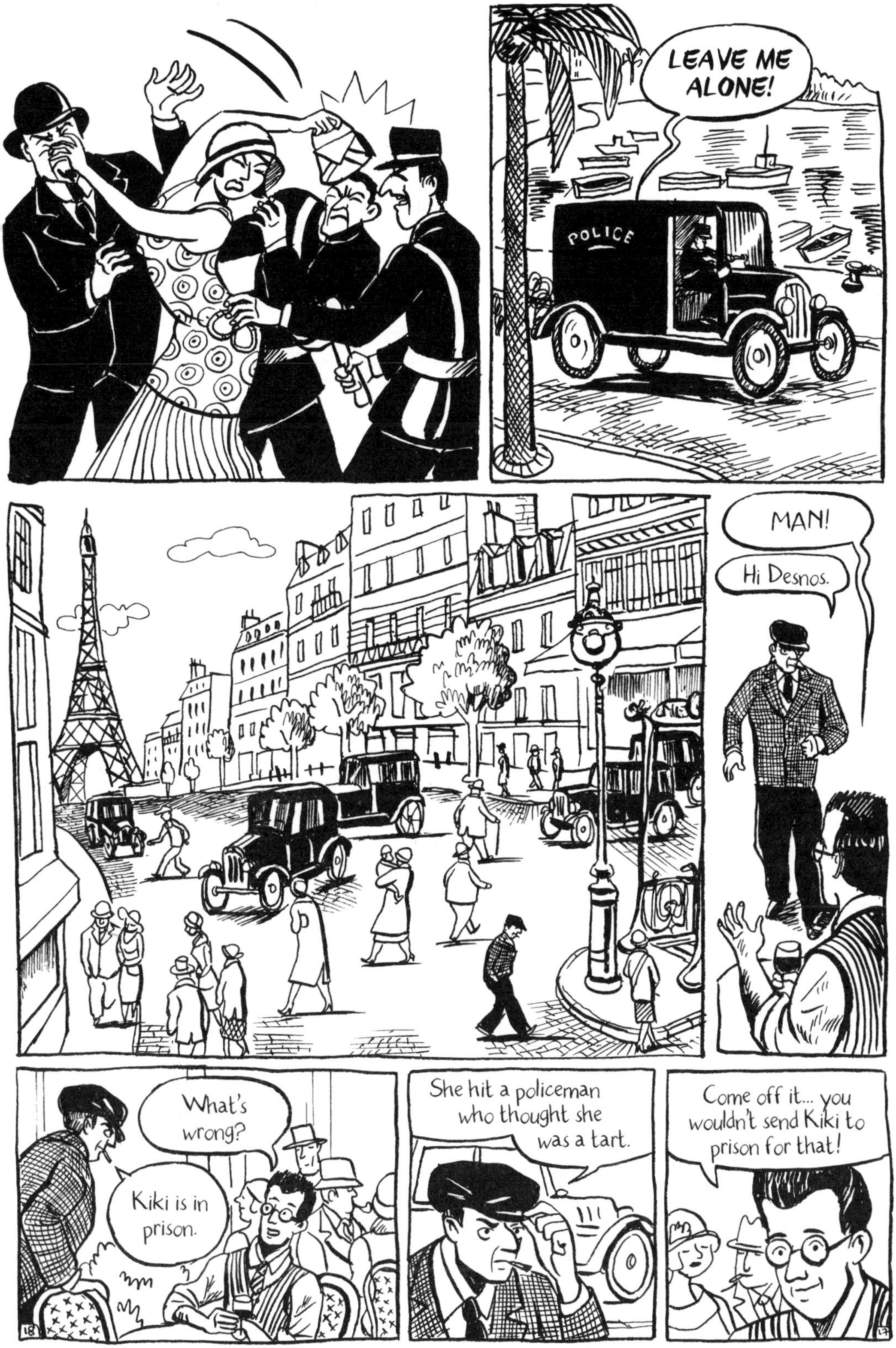
LEAVE ME ALONE!
MAN!
Hi Desnos.
What's wrong?
Kiki is in prison.
She hit a policeman who thought she was a tart.
Come off it... you wouldn't send Kiki to prison for that!

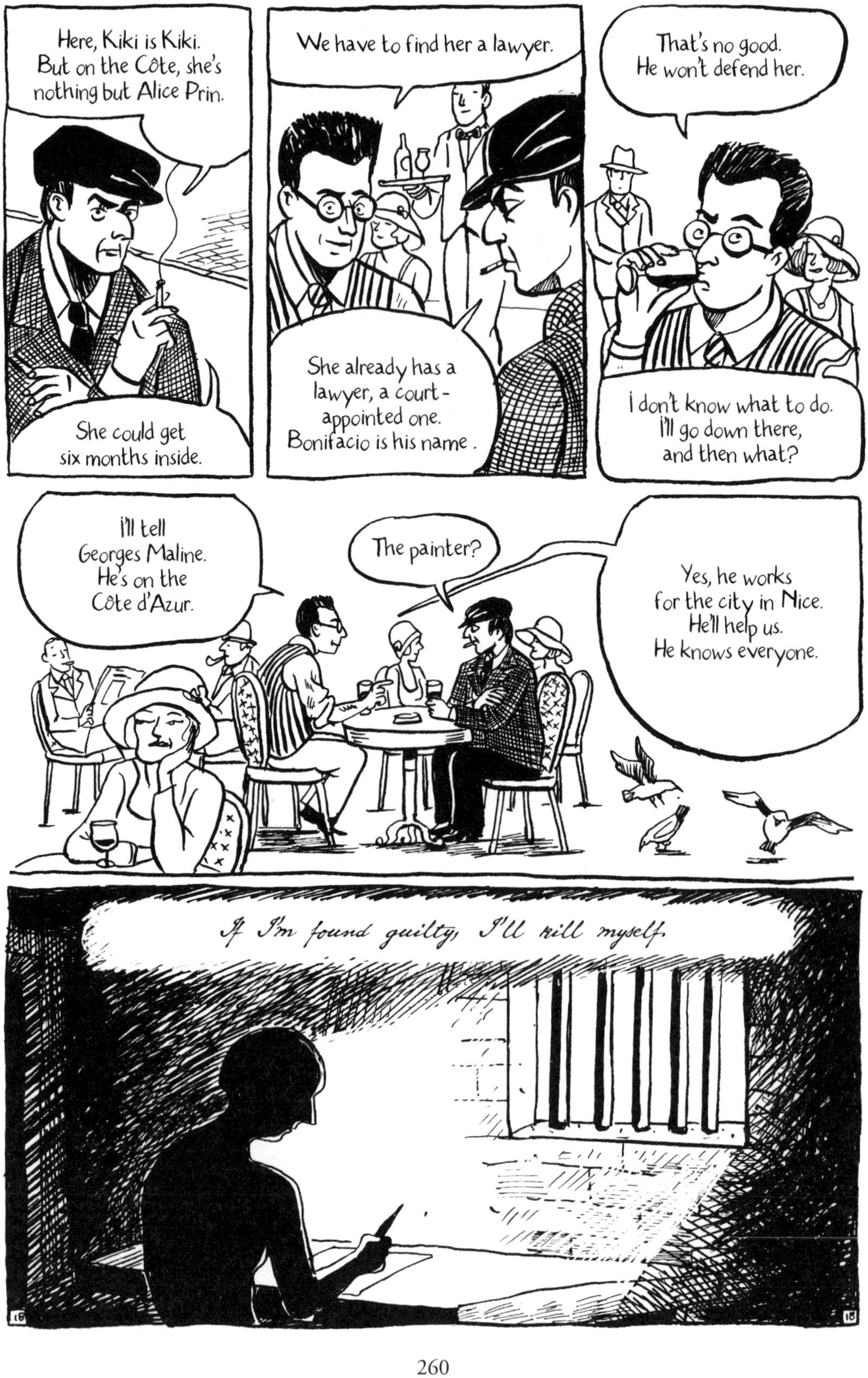
Here, Kiki is Kiki. But on the Côte, she's nothing but Alice Prin.
She could get six months inside.
We have to find her a lawyer.
She already has a lawyer, a court-appointed one. Bonifacio is his name.
That's no good. He won't defend her.
I don't know what to do. I'll go down there, and then what?
I'll tell Georges Maline. He's on the Côte d'Azur.
The painter?
Yes, he works for the city in Nice. He'll help us. He knows everyone.
If I'm found guilty, I'll kill myself.

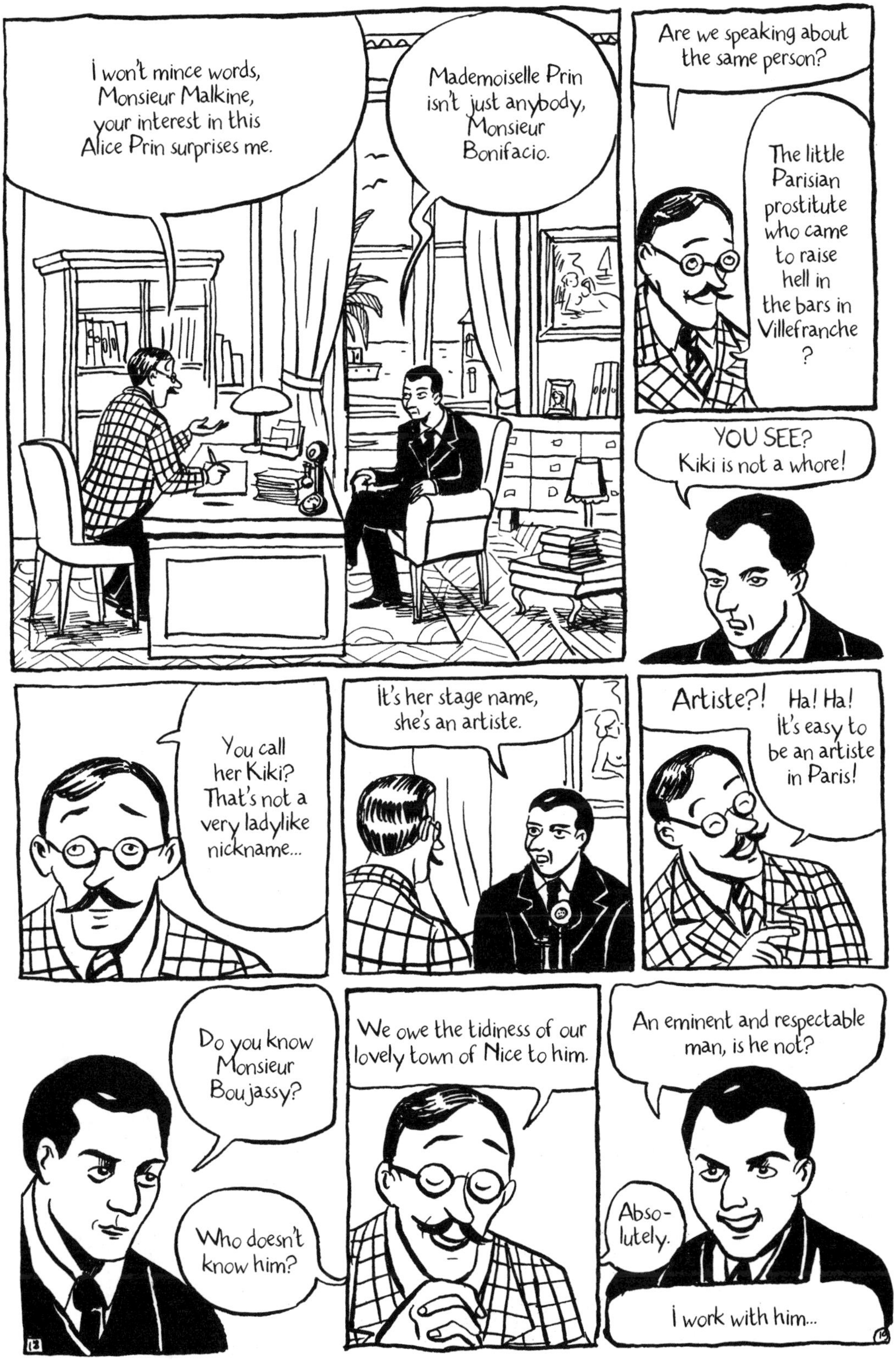
I won't mince words, Monsieur Malkine, your interest in this Alice Prin surprises me.
Mademoiselle Prin isn't just anybody, Monsieur Bonifacio.
Are we speaking about the same person?
The little Parisian prostitute who came to raise hell in the bars in Villefranche ?
YOU SEE? Kiki is not a whore!
You call her Kiki? That's not a very ladylike nickname...
It's her stage name, she's an artiste.
Artiste?!
Ha! Ha! It's easy to be an artiste in Paris!
Do you know Monsieur Boujassy?
Who doesn't know him?
We owe the tidiness of our lovely town of Nice to him.
An eminent and respectable man, is he not?
Abso-lutely.
I work with him...

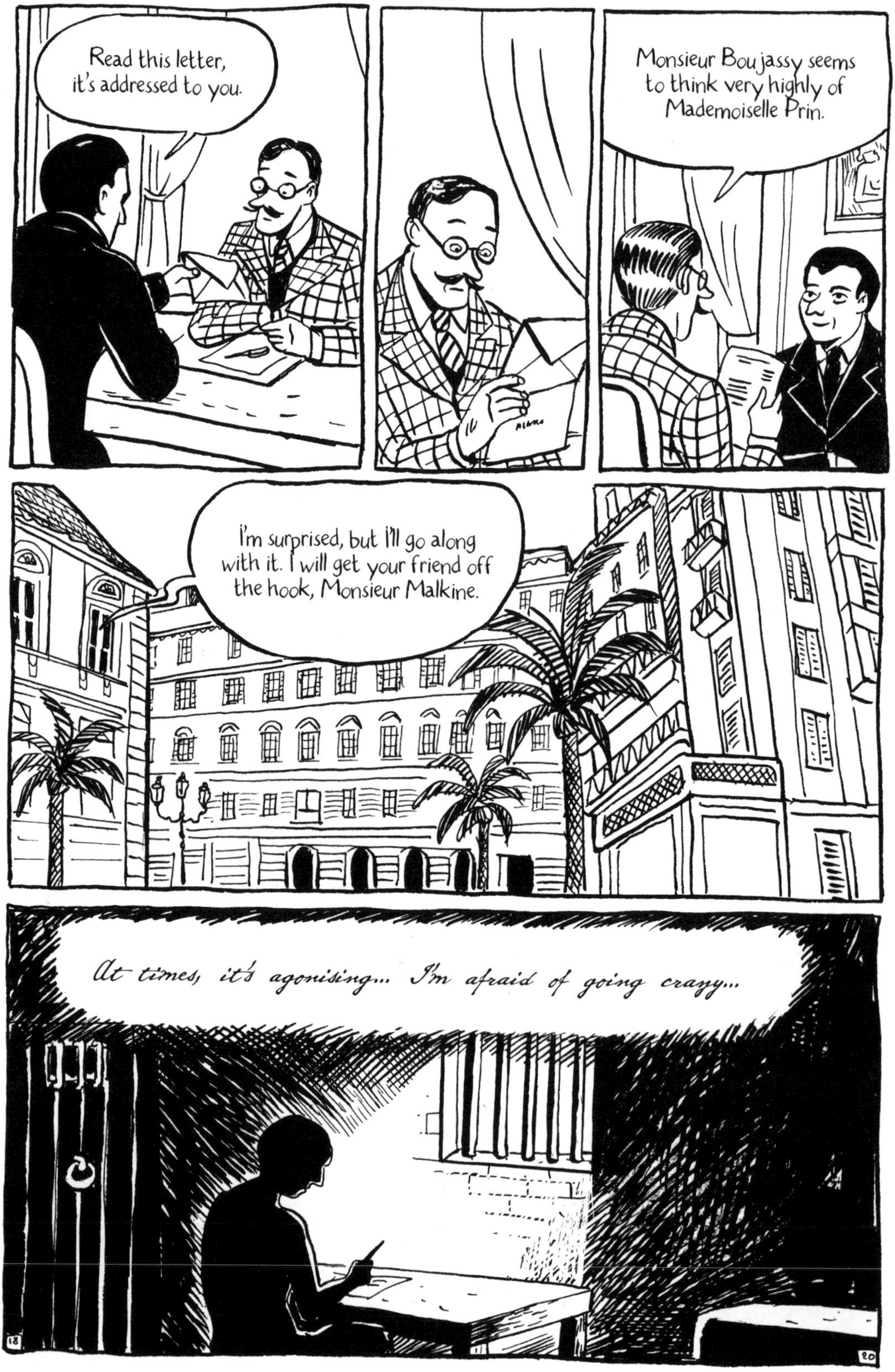
Read this letter, it's addressed to you.
Monsieur Boujassy seems to think very highly of Mademoiselle Prin.
I'm surprised, but I'll go along with it. I will get your friend off the hook, Monsieur Malkine.
At times, it's agonising... I'm afraid of going crazy...

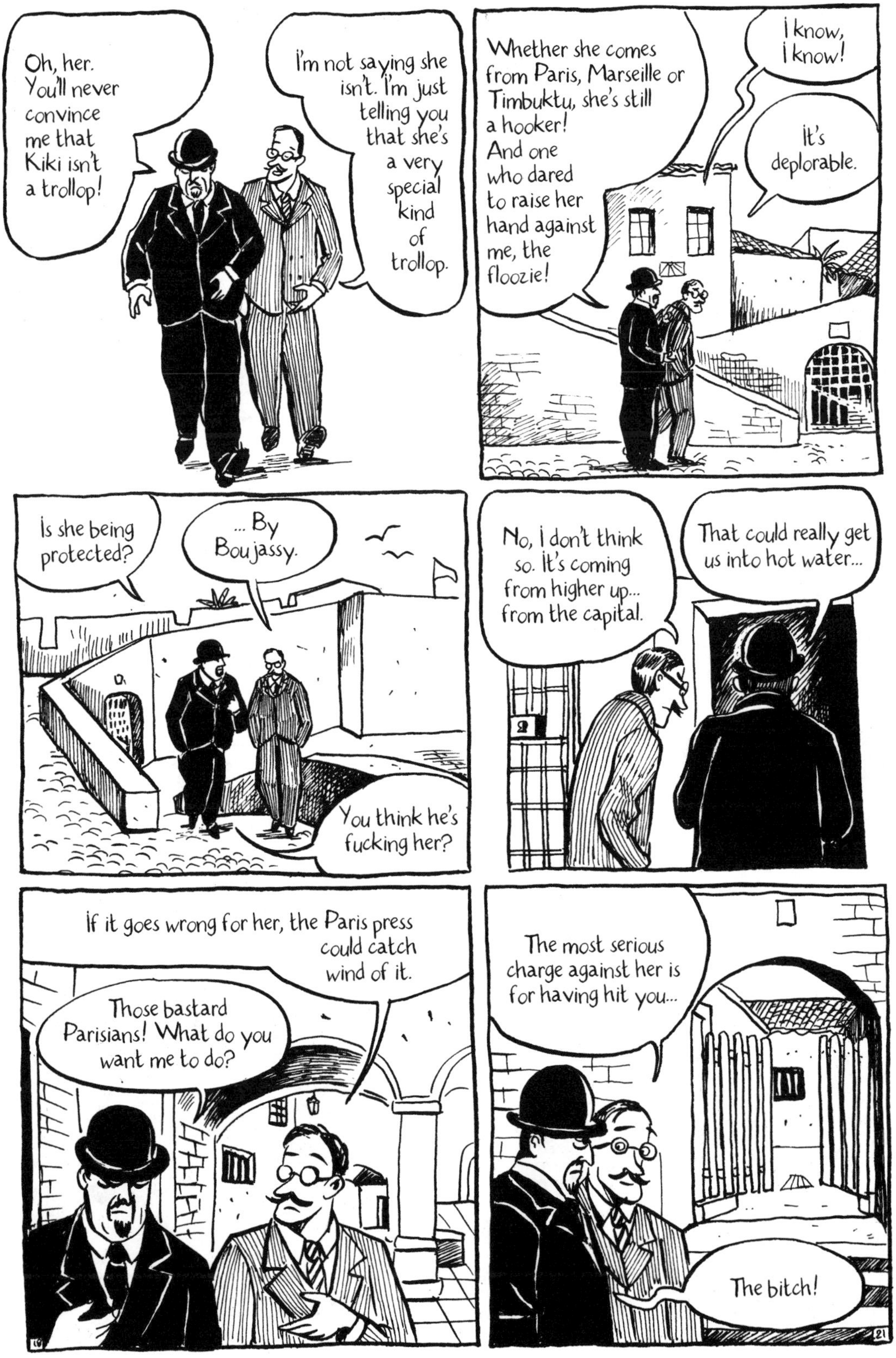

Oh, her. You'll never convince me that Kiki isn't a trollop!
I'm not saying she isn't. I'm just telling you that she's a very special kind of trollop.
Whether she comes from Paris, Marseille or Timbuktu, she's still a hooker! And one who dared to raise her hand against me, the floozie!
I know, I know!
It's deplorable.
Is she being protected?
... By Boujassy.
You think he's fucking her?
No, I don't think so. It's coming from higher up... from the capital.
That could really get us into hot water...
If it goes wrong for her, the Paris press could catch wind of it.
Those bastard Parisians! What do you want me to do?
The most serious charge against her is for having hit you...
The bitch!

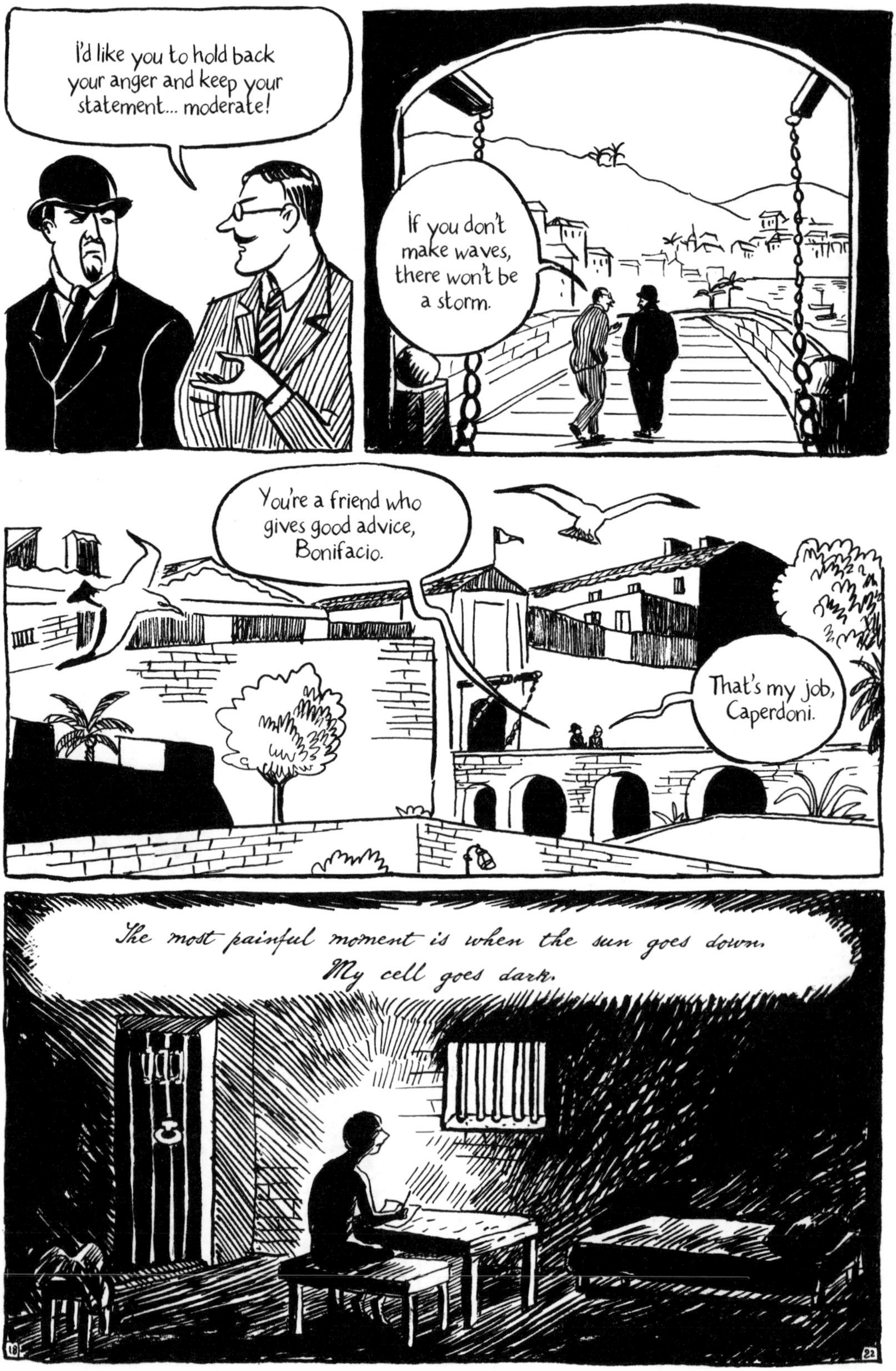
I'd like you to hold back your anger and keep your statement... moderate!
If you don't make waves, there won't be a storm.
You're a friend who gives good advice, Bonifacio.
That's my job, Caperdoni.
The most painful moment is when the sun goes down. My cell goes dark.

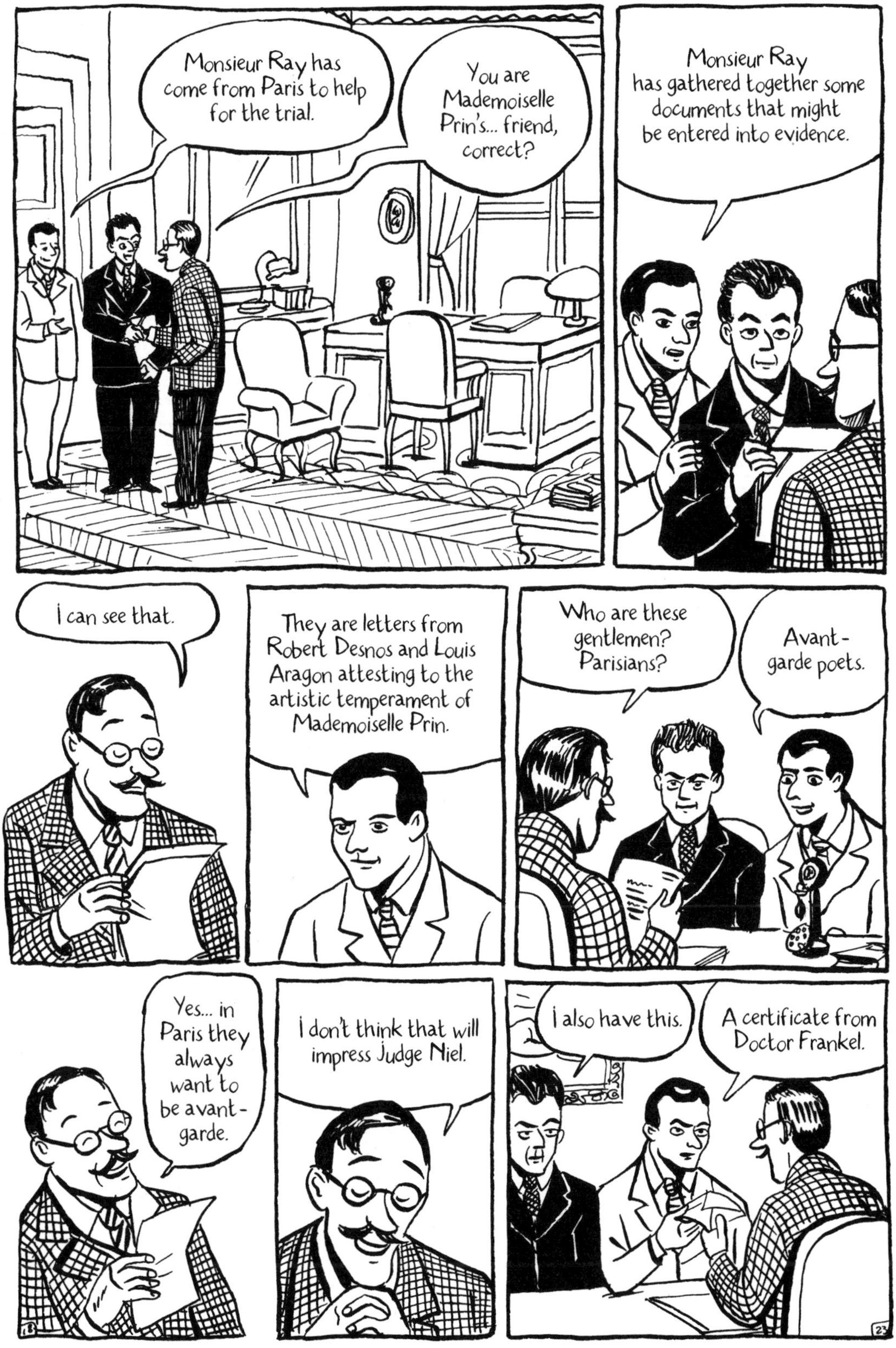

Monsieur Ray has come from Paris to help for the trial.
You are Mademoiselle Prin's... friend, correct?
Monsieur Ray has gathered together some documents that might be entered into evidence.
I can see that.
They are letters from Robert Desnos and Louis Aragon attesting to the artistic temperament of Mademoiselle Prin.
Who are these gentlemen? Parisians?
Avant-garde poets.
Yes... in Paris they always want to be avant-garde.
I don't think that will impress Judge Niel.
I also have this.
A certificate from Doctor Frankel.
18
23

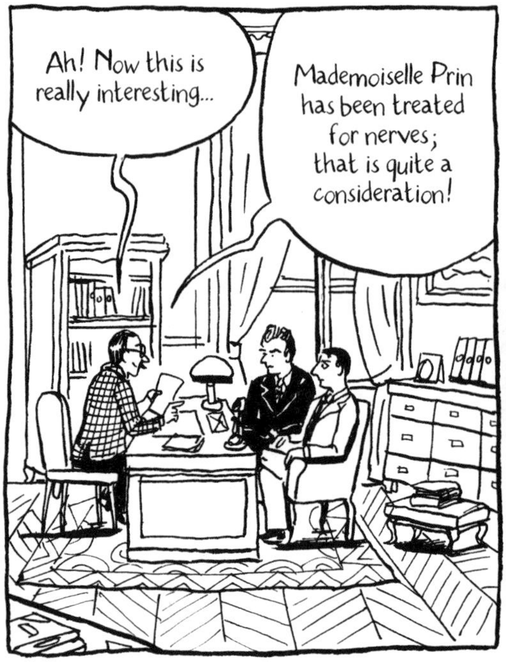
Ah! Now this is really interesting...
Mademoiselle Prin has been treated for nerves; that is quite a consideration!

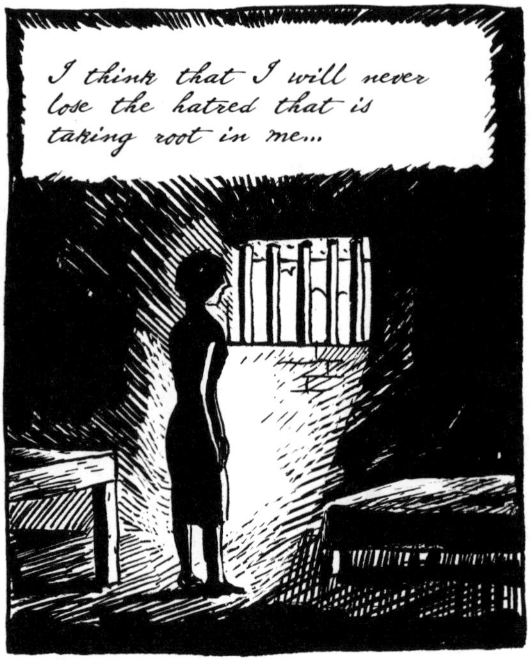
I think that I will never lose the hatred that is taking root in me...

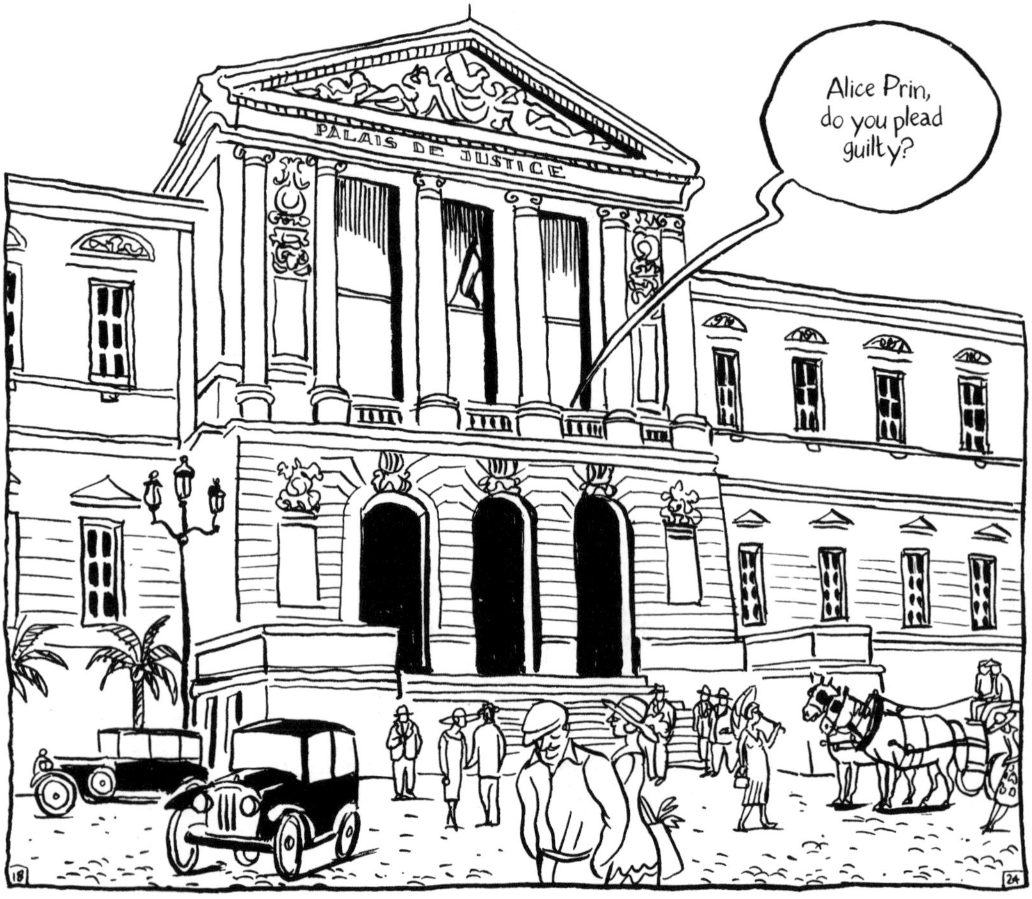
PALAIS DE JUSTICE
Alice Prin, do you plead guilty?
18
24

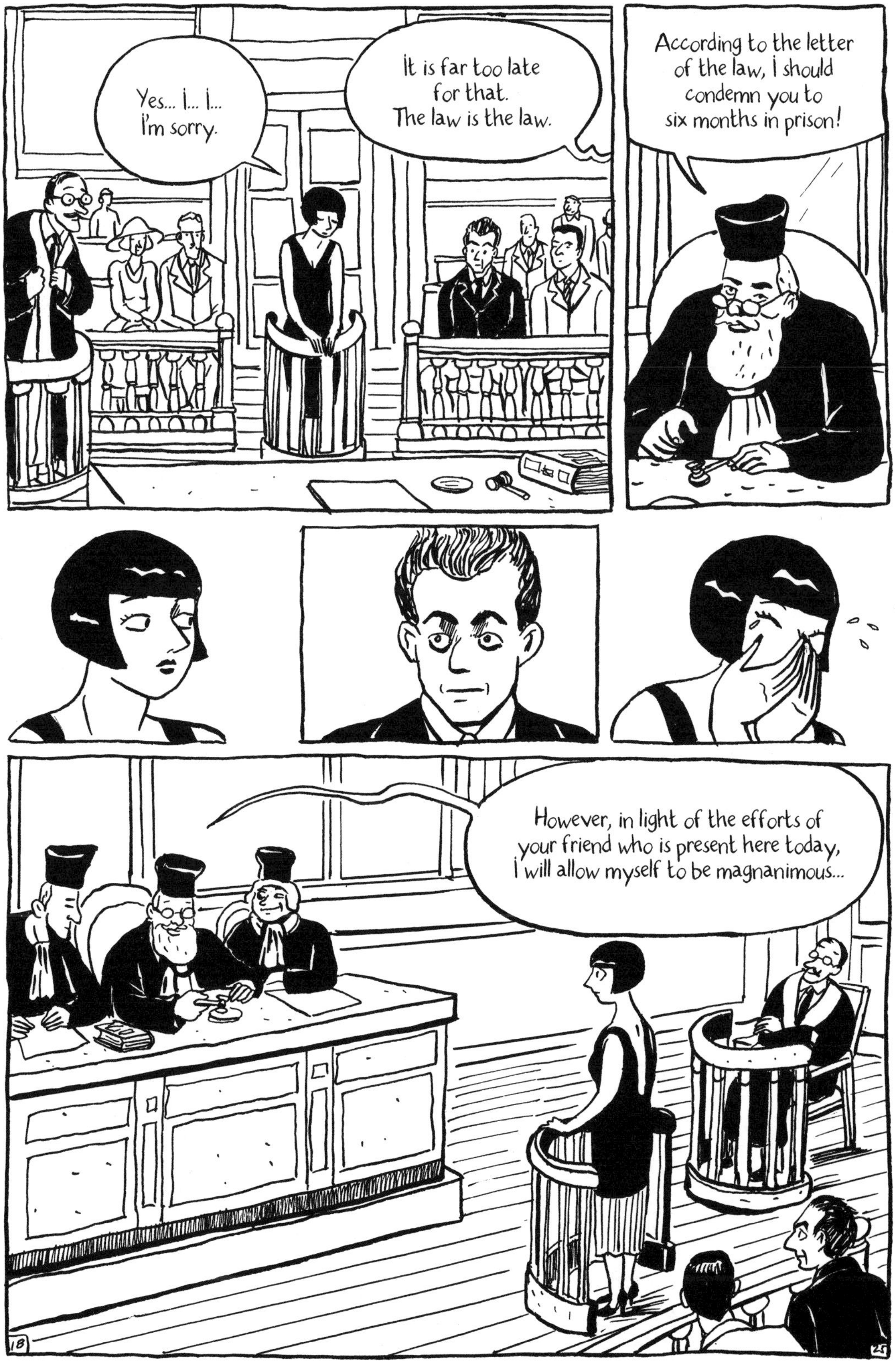
Yes... I... I...
I'm sorry.
It is far too late
for that.
The law is the law.
According to the letter
of the law, I should
condemn you to
six months in prison!
However, in light of the efforts of
your friend who is present here today,
I will allow myself to be magnanimous...
18
25

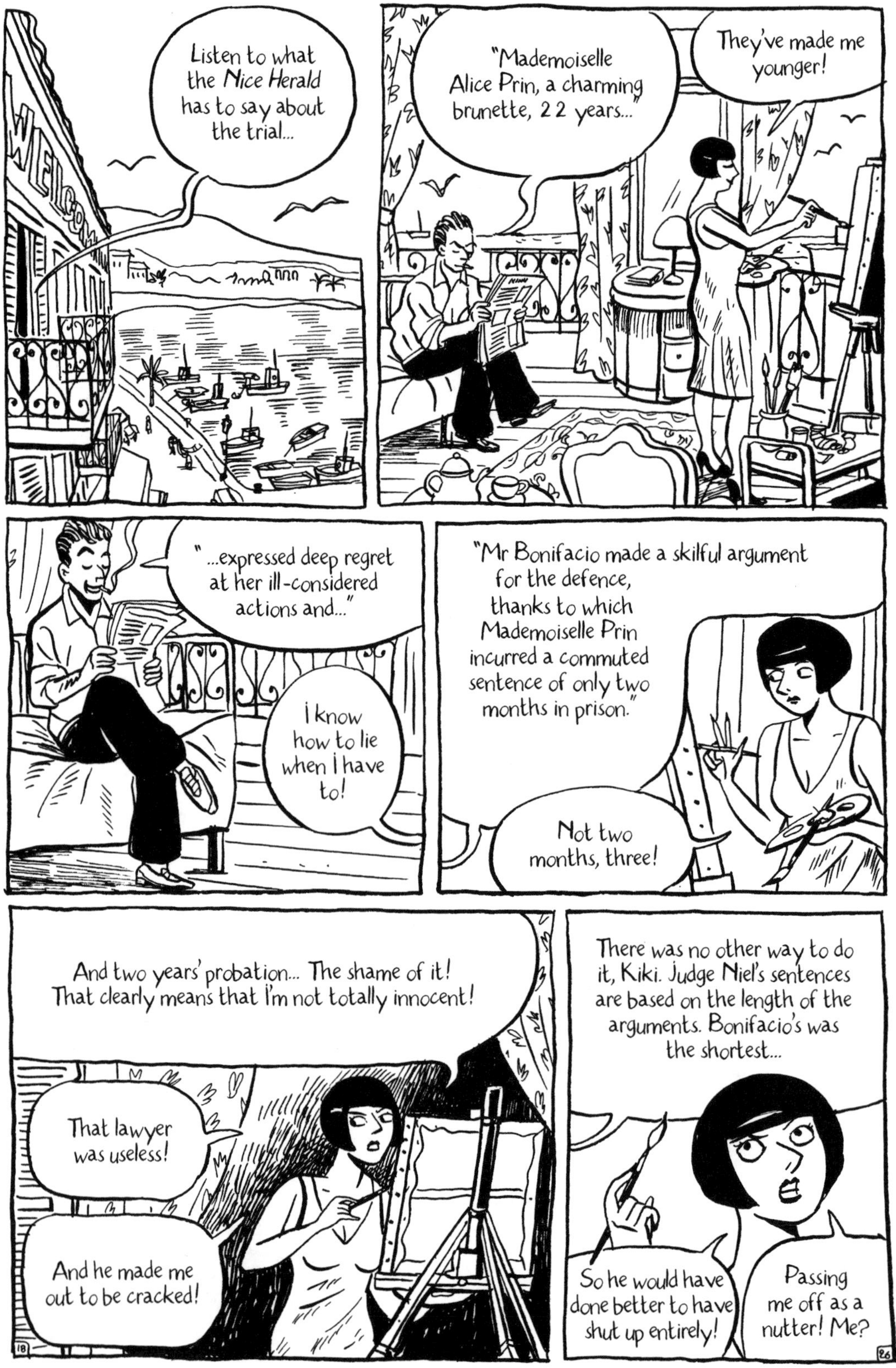
Listen to what the Nice Herald has to say about the trial...
WELCOME
"Mademoiselle Alice Prin, a charming brunette, 22 years..."
They've made me younger!
"...expressed deep regret at her ill-considered actions and..."
I know how to lie when I have to!
"Mr Bonifacio made a skilful argument for the defence, thanks to which Mademoiselle Prin incurred a commuted sentence of only two months in prison."
Not two months, three!
And two years' probation... The shame of it! That clearly means that I'm not totally innocent!
That lawyer was useless!
And he made me out to be cracked!
There was no other way to do it, Kiki. Judge Niel's sentences are based on the length of the arguments. Bonifacio's was the shortest...
So he would have done better to have shut up entirely!
Passing me off as a nutter! Me?

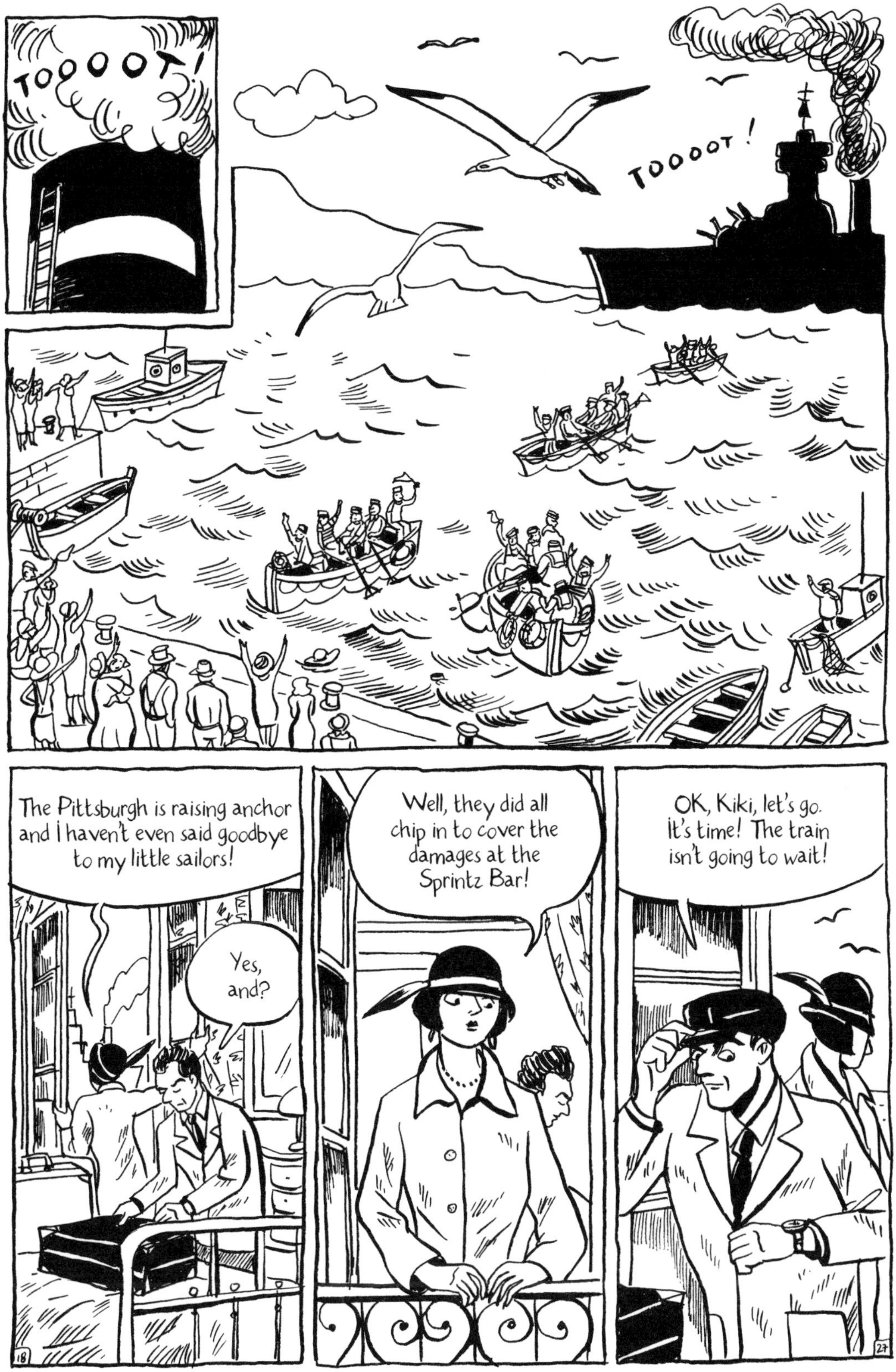
TOOOOT!
TOOOOT!
The Pittsburgh is raising anchor and I haven't even said goodbye to my little sailors!
Yes, and?
Well, they did all chip in to cover the damages at the Sprintz Bar!
OK, Kiki, let's go. It's time! The train isn't going to wait!

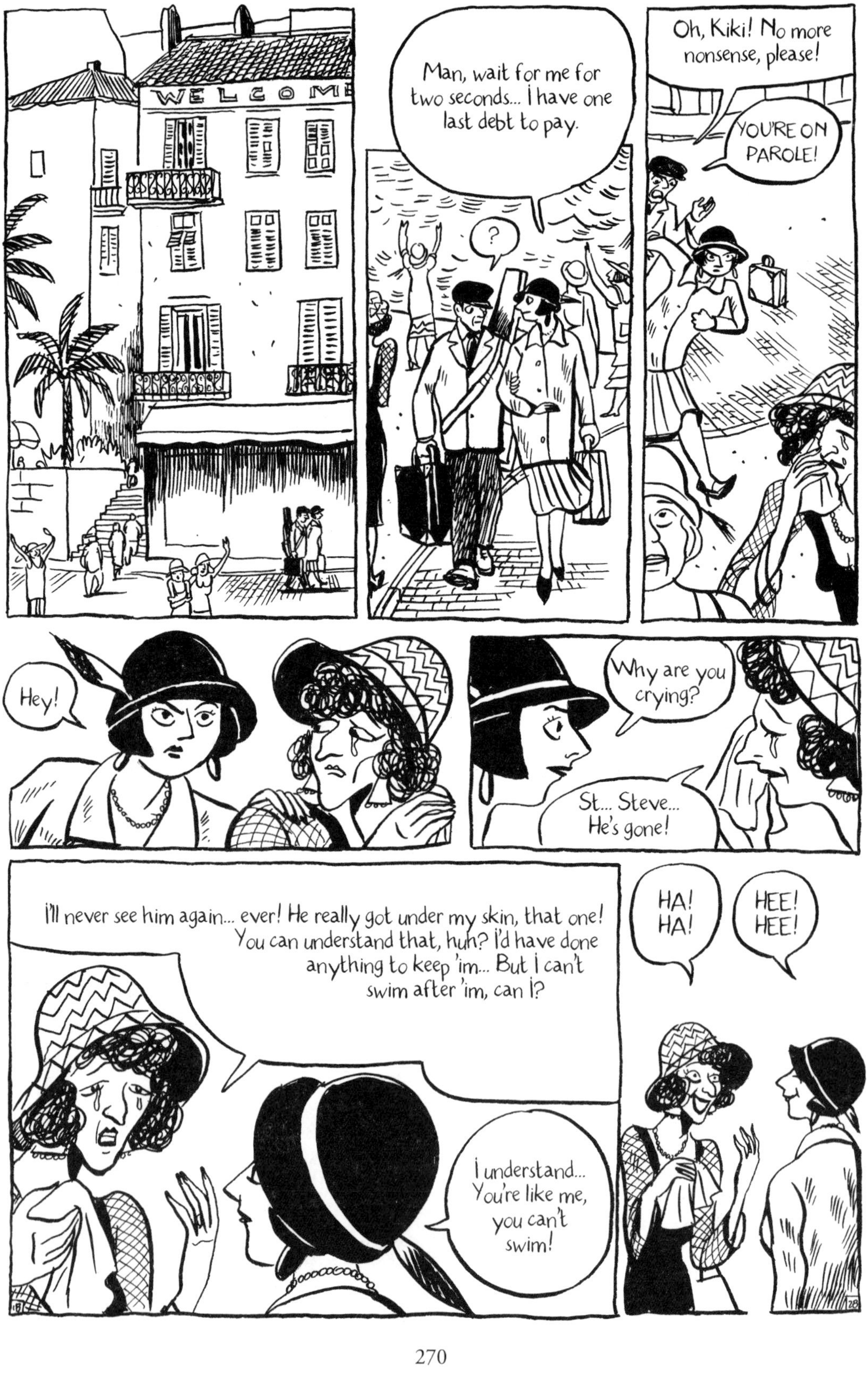
Man, wait for me for two seconds... I have one last debt to pay.
?
Oh, Kiki! No more nonsense, please!
YOU'RE ON PAROLE!
Hey!
Why are you crying?
St... Steve... He's gone!
I'll never see him again... ever! He really got under my skin, that one! You can understand that, huh? I'd have done anything to keep 'im... But I can't swim after 'im, can I?
I understand... You're like me, you can't swim!
HA! HA!
HEE! HEE!

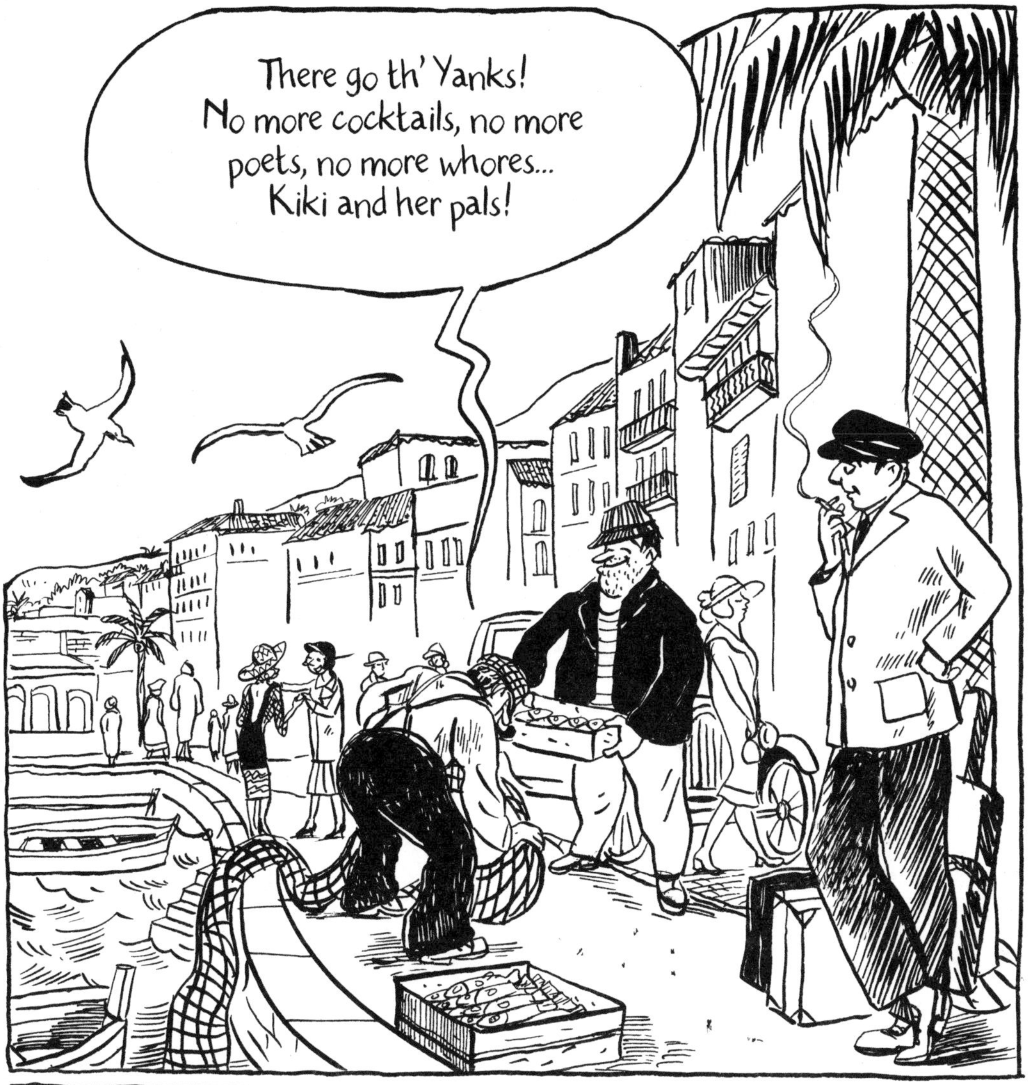
There go th' Yanks! No more cocktails, no more poets, no more whores... Kiki and her pals!

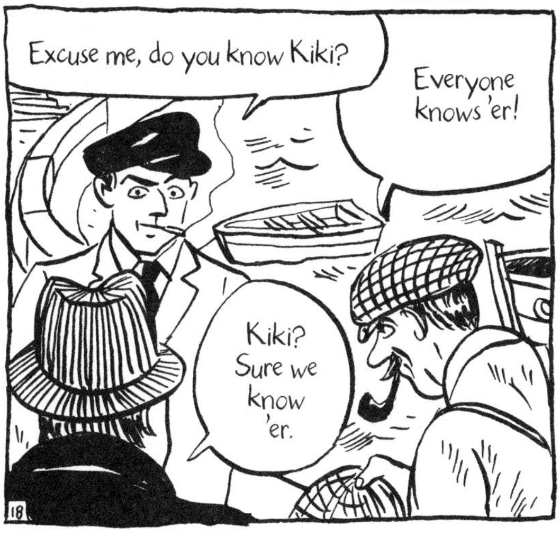
Excuse me, do you know Kiki?
Kiki? Sure we know 'er.
Everyone knows 'er!
18

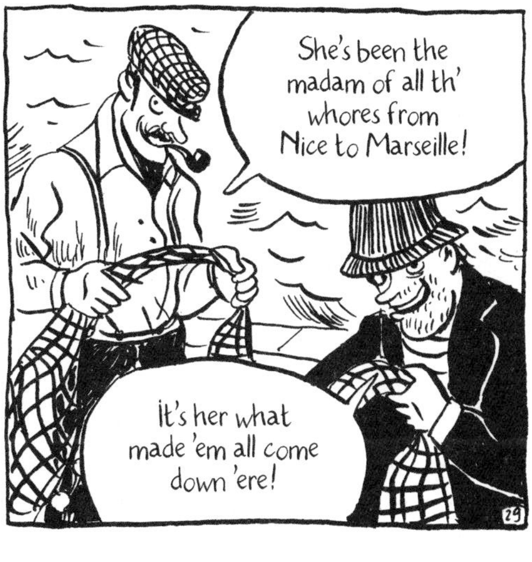
She's been the madam of all th' whores from Nice to Marseille!
It's her what made 'em all come down 'ere!
29

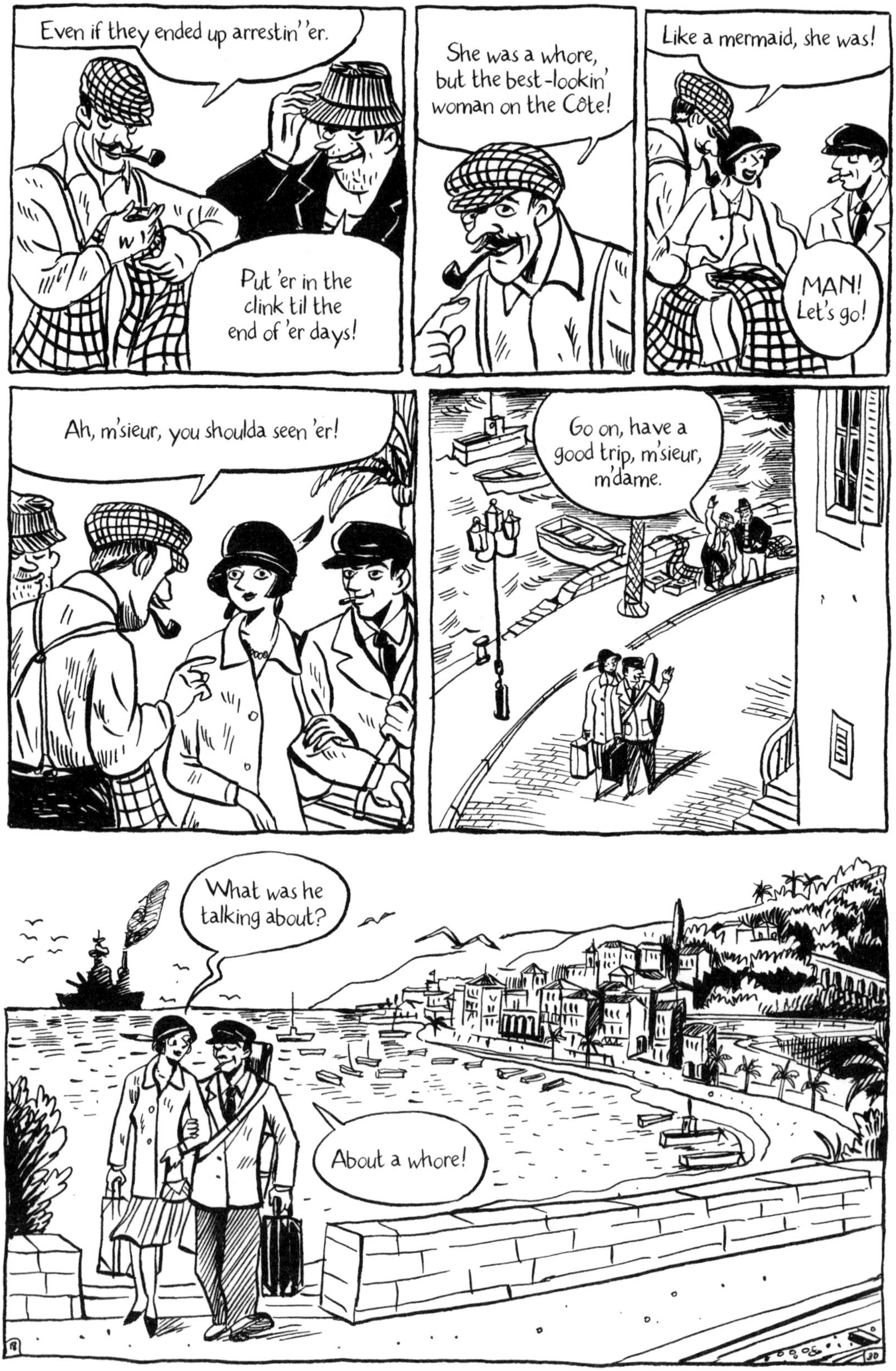
Even if they ended up arrestin' 'er.
Put 'er in the clink til the end of 'er days!
She was a whore, but the best-lookin' woman on the Côte!
Like a mermaid, she was!
MAN! Let's go!
Ah, m'sieur, you shoulda seen 'er!
Go on, have a good trip, m'sieur, m'dame.
What was he talking about?
About a whore!

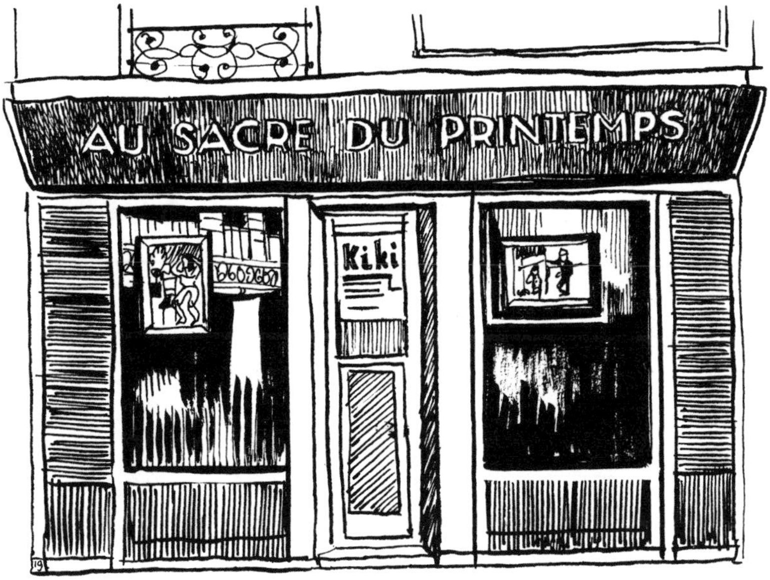
AU SACRE DU PRINTEMPS
Kiki

1927 - 5, rue du Cherche-Midi

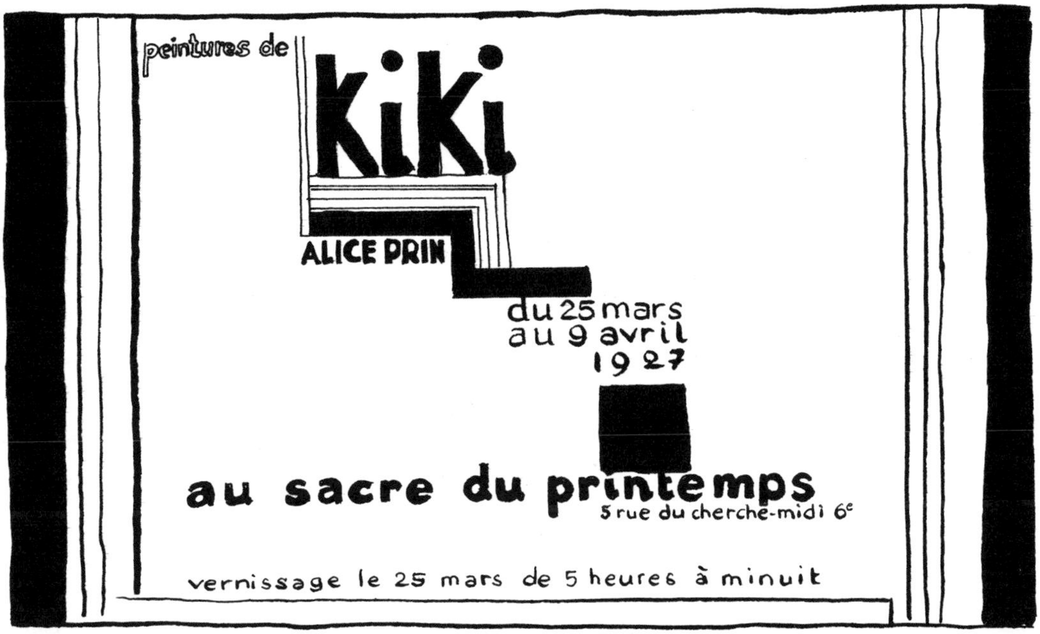
peintures de
KiKi
ALICE PRIN
du 25 mars
au 9 avril
1927
au sacre du printemps
5 rue du cherche-midi 6e
vernissage le 25 mars de 5 heures à minuit

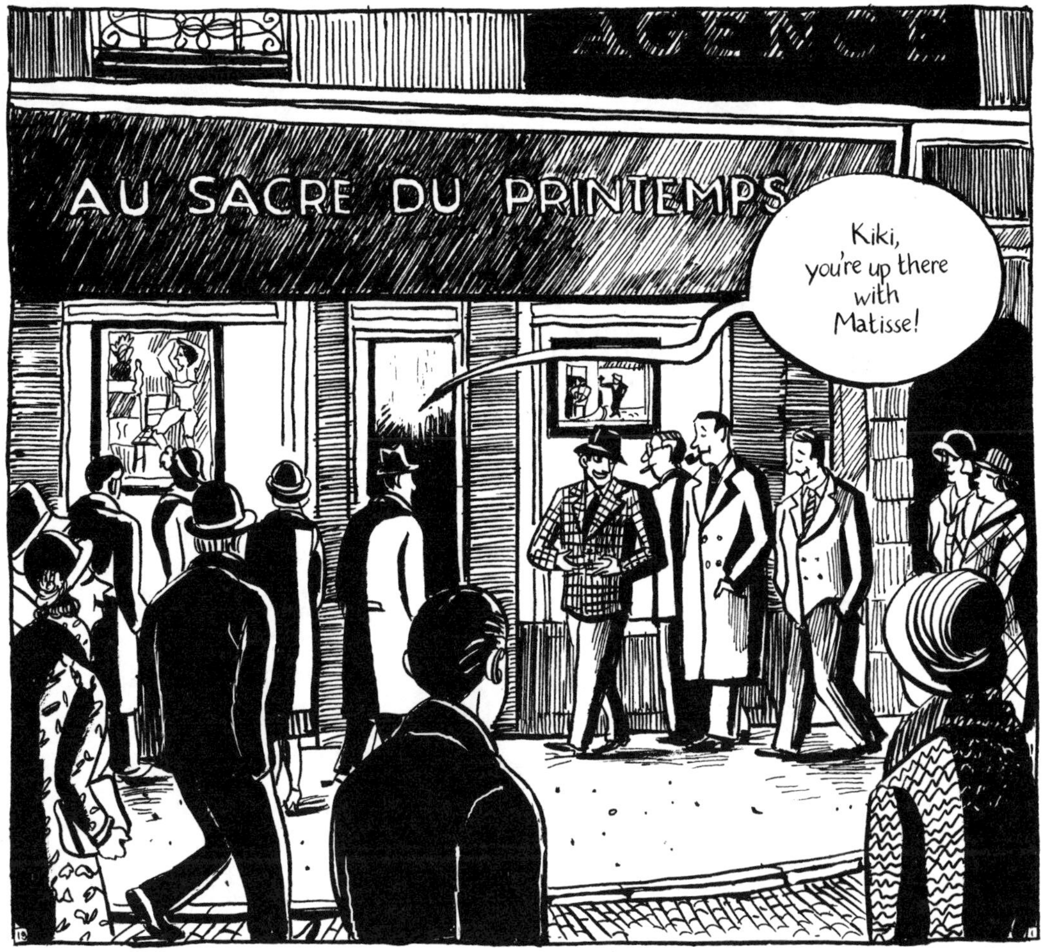
AGENCE
AU SACRE DU PRINTEMPS
Kiki, you're up there with Matisse!

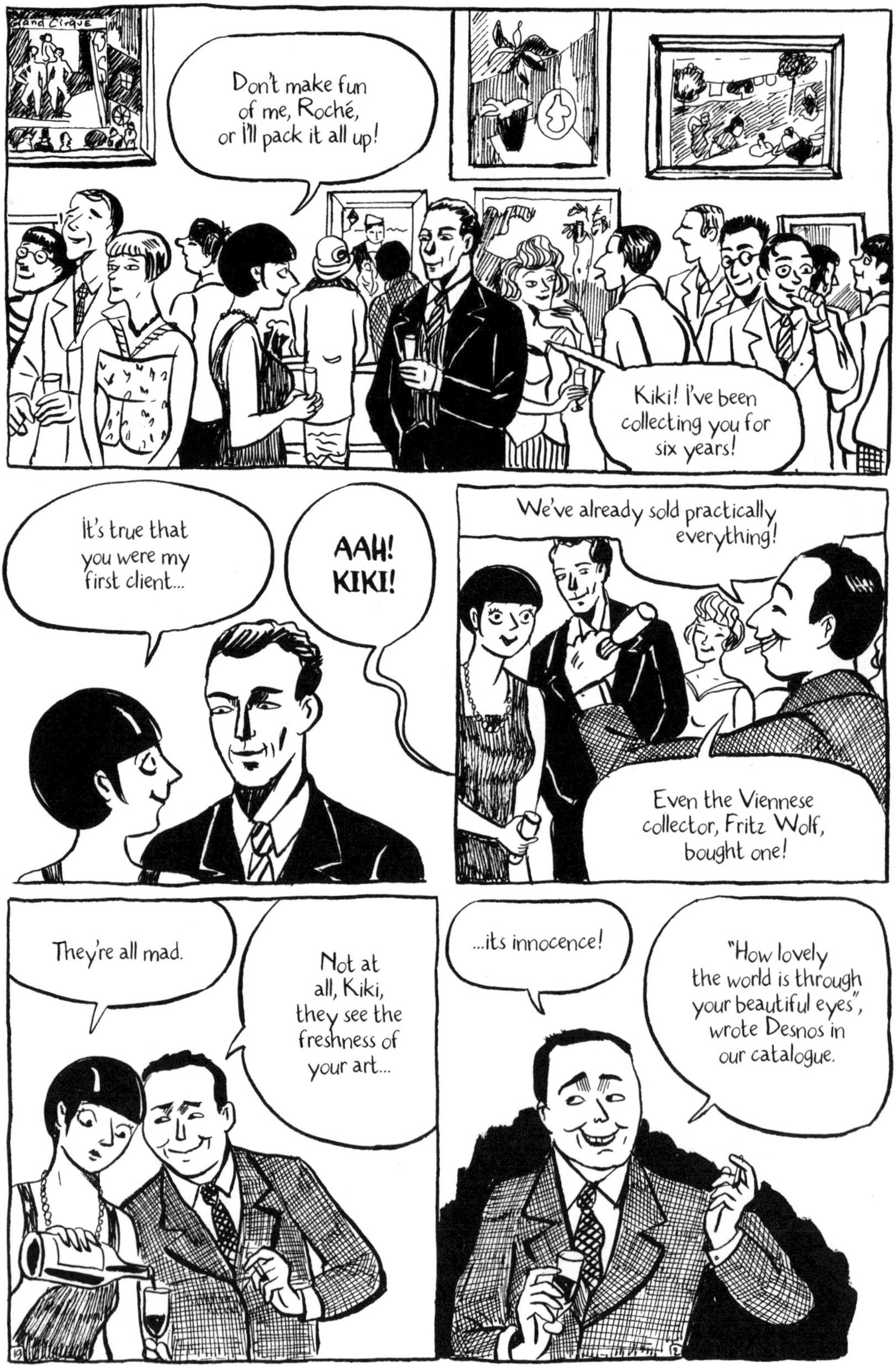
Grand Cirque
Don't make fun of me, Roché, or I'll pack it all up!
Kiki! I've been collecting you for six years!
It's true that you were my first client...
AAH! KIKI!
We've already sold practically everything!
Even the Viennese collector, Fritz Wolf, bought one!
They're all mad.
Not at all, Kiki, they see the freshness of your art...
...its innocence!
"How lovely the world is through your beautiful eyes", wrote Desnos in our catalogue.

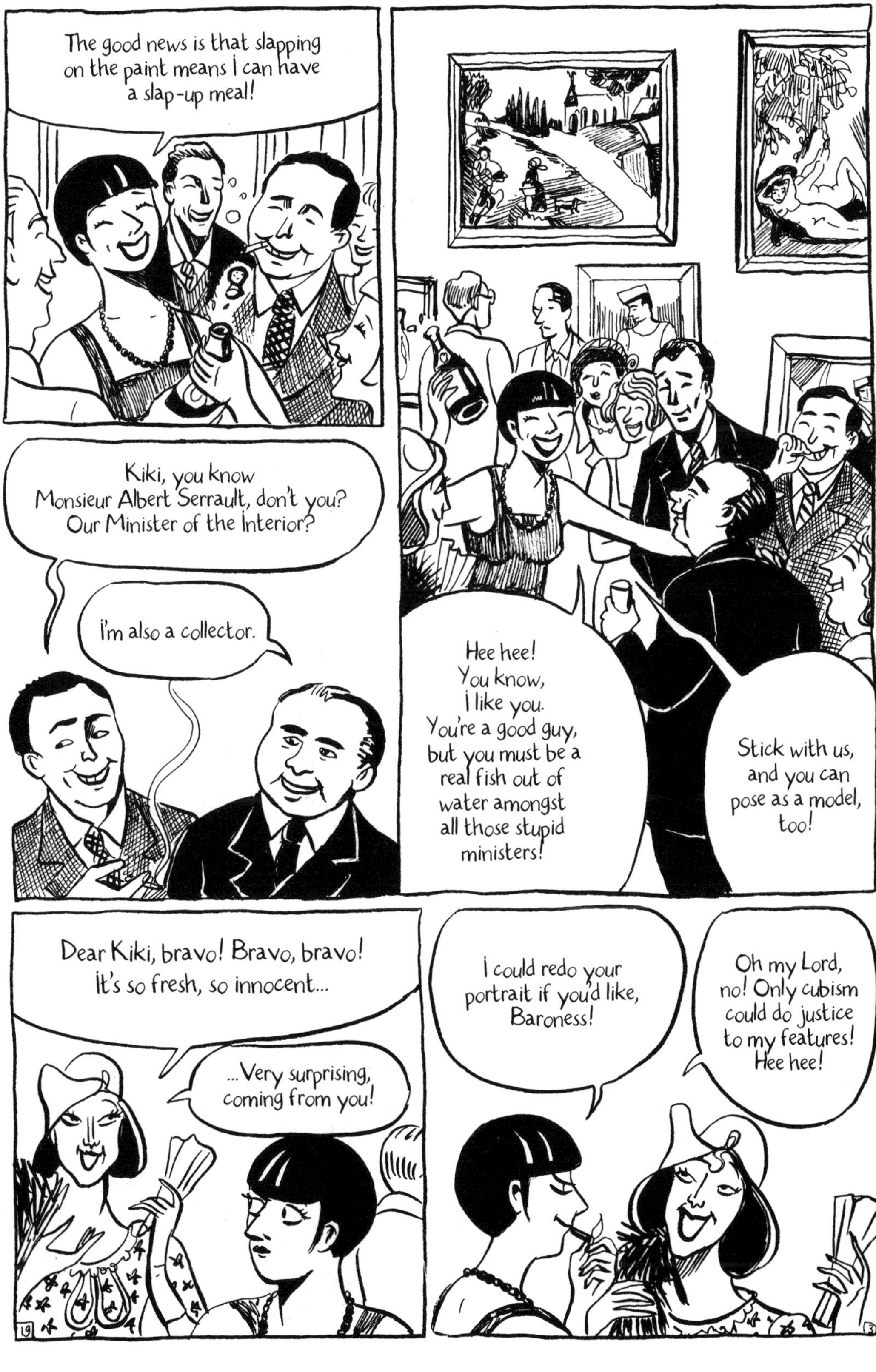
The good news is that slapping on the paint means I can have a slap-up meal!
Kiki, you know Monsieur Albert Serrault, don't you? Our Minister of the Interior?
I'm also a collector.
Hee hee! You know, I like you. You're a good guy, but you must be a real fish out of water amongst all those stupid ministers!
Stick with us, and you can pose as a model, too!
Dear Kiki, bravo! Bravo, bravo! It's so fresh, so innocent...
...Very surprising, coming from you!
I could redo your portrait if you'd like, Baroness!
Oh my Lord, no! Only cubism could do justice to my features! Hee hee!

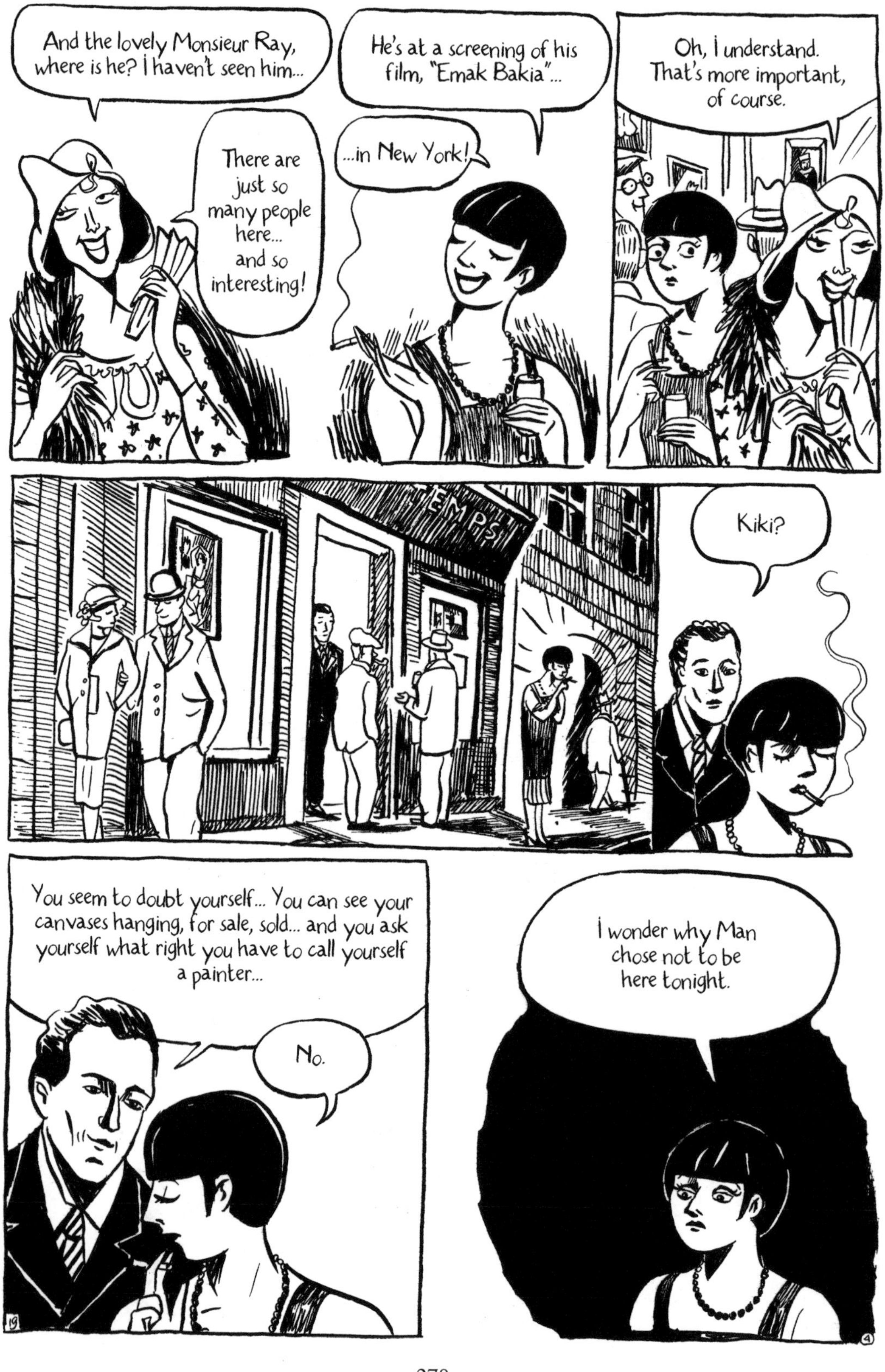
And the lovely Monsieur Ray, where is he? I haven't seen him...
There are just so many people here... and so interesting!
He's at a screening of his film, "Emak Bakia"...
...in New York!
Oh, I understand. That's more important, of course.
EMPS
Kiki?
You seem to doubt yourself... You can see your canvases hanging, for sale, sold... and you ask yourself what right you have to call yourself a painter...
No.
I wonder why Man chose not to be here tonight.

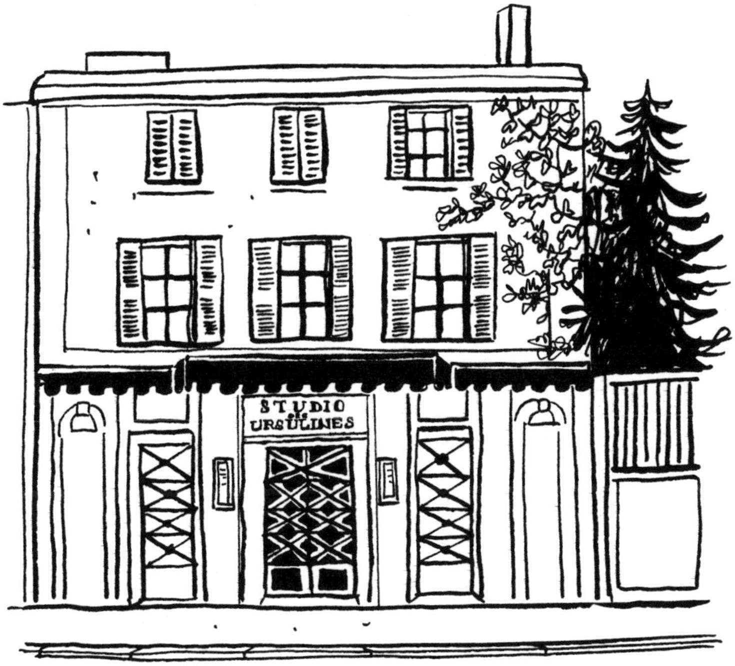
STUDIO
des
URSULINES

1928 - 10, rue des Ursulines

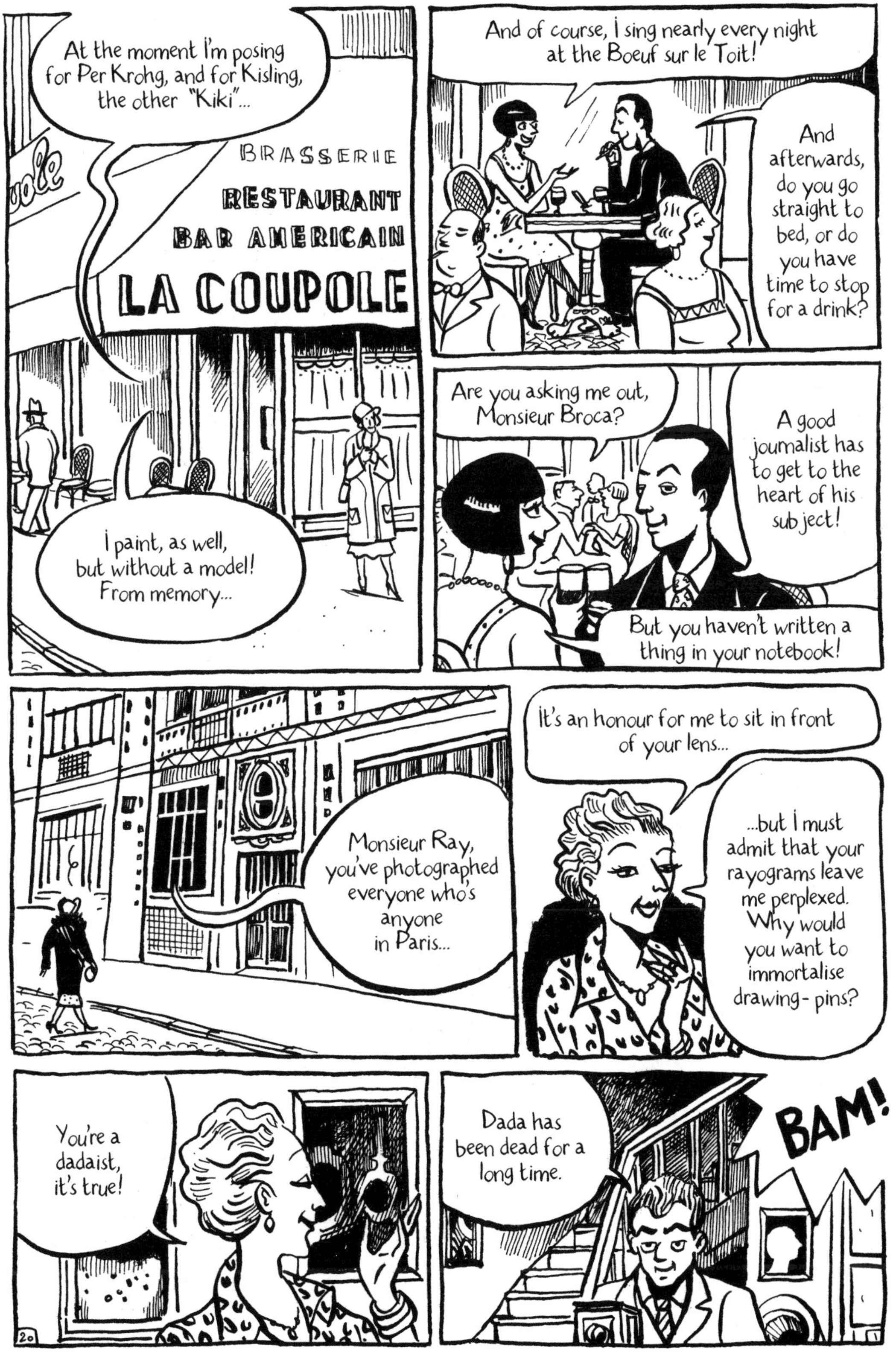
At the moment I'm posing for Per Krohg, and for Kisling, the other "Kiki"...
BRASSERIE
RESTAURANT
BAR AMERICAIN
LA COUPOLE
I paint, as well, but without a model! From memory...
And of course, I sing nearly every night at the Boeuf sur le Toit!
And afterwards, do you go straight to bed, or do you have time to stop for a drink?
Are you asking me out, Monsieur Broca?
A good journalist has to get to the heart of his subject!
But you haven't written a thing in your notebook!
Monsieur Ray, you've photographed everyone who's anyone in Paris...
It's an honour for me to sit in front of your lens...
...but I must admit that your rayograms leave me perplexed. Why would you want to immortalise drawing-pins?
You're a dadaist, it's true!
Dada has been dead for a long time.
BAM!

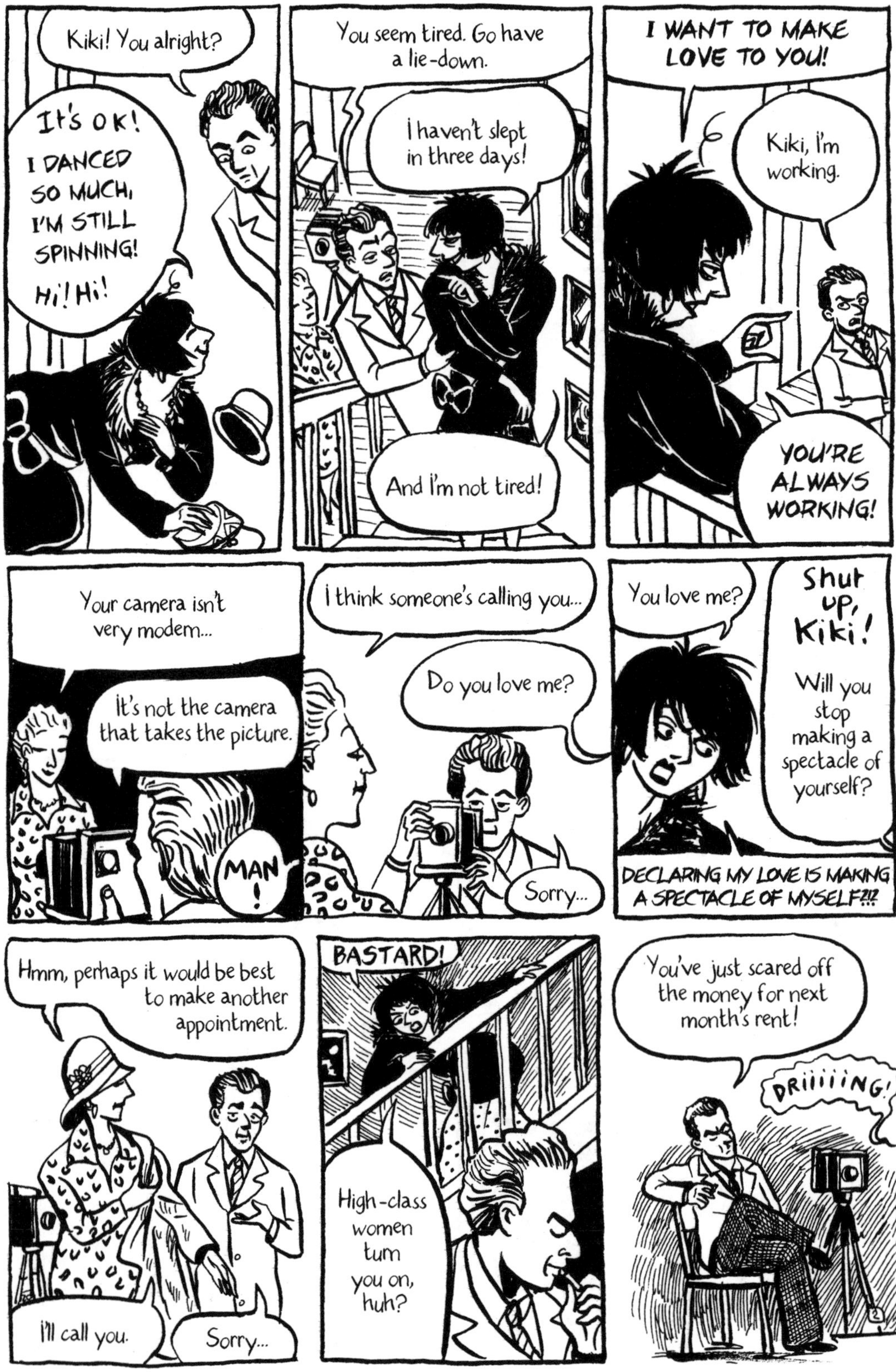
Kiki! You alright?
It's OK! I DANCED SO MUCH, I'M STILL SPINNING! Hi! Hi!
You seem tired. Go have a lie-down.
I haven't slept in three days!
And I'm not tired!
I WANT TO MAKE LOVE TO YOU!
Kiki, I'm working.
YOU'RE ALWAYS WORKING!
Your camera isn't very modern...
It's not the camera that takes the picture.
MAN!
I think someone's calling you...
Do you love me?
Sorry...
You love me?
Shut up, Kiki!
Will you stop making a spectacle of yourself?
DECLARING MY LOVE IS MAKING A SPECTACLE OF MYSELF?!?
Hmm, perhaps it would be best to make another appointment.
I'll call you.
Sorry...
BASTARD!
High-class women turn you on, huh?
You've just scared off the money for next month's rent!
DRIIIIING!

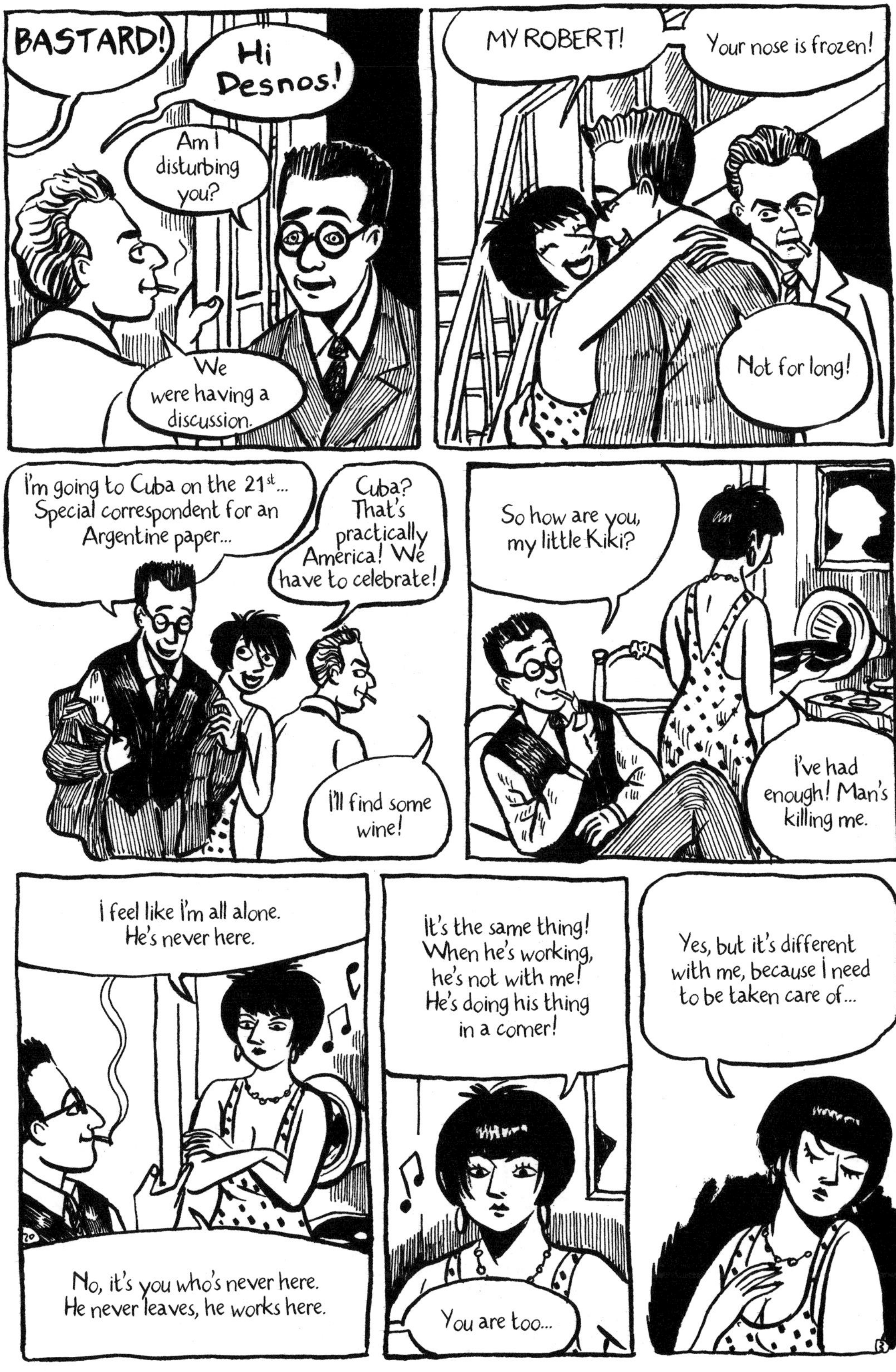
BASTARD!
Hi Desnos!
Am I disturbing you?
We were having a discussion.
MY ROBERT!
Your nose is frozen!
Not for long!
I'm going to Cuba on the 21st... Special correspondent for an Argentine paper...
Cuba? That's practically America! We have to celebrate!
I'll find some wine!
So how are you, my little Kiki?
I've had enough! Man's killing me.
I feel like I'm all alone. He's never here.
No, it's you who's never here. He never leaves, he works here.
It's the same thing! When he's working, he's not with me! He's doing his thing in a corner!
You are too...
Yes, but it's different with me, because I need to be taken care of...

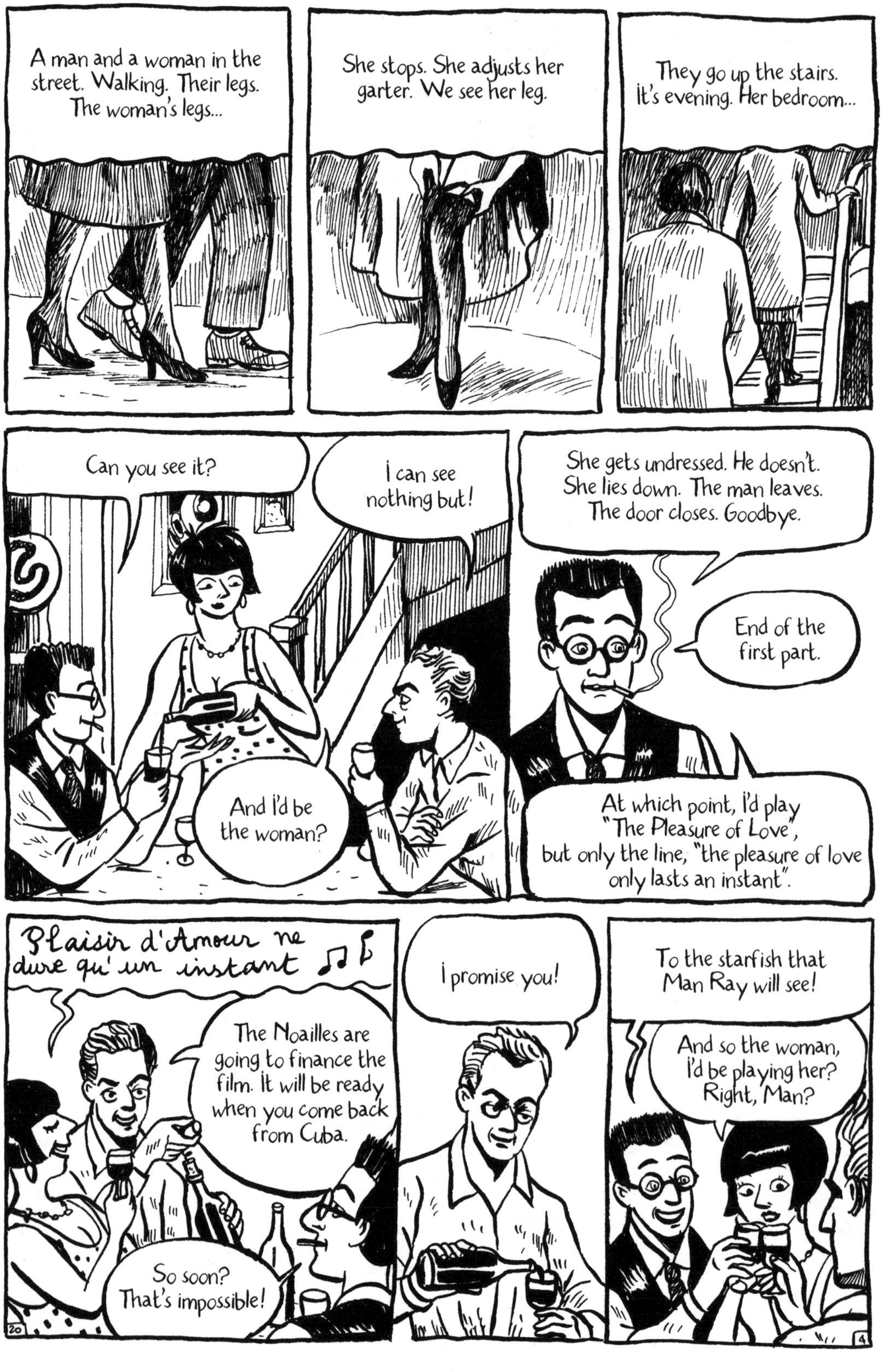
A man and a woman in the street. Walking. Their legs. The woman's legs...
She stops. She adjusts her garter. We see her leg.
They go up the stairs. It's evening. Her bedroom...
Can you see it?
I can see nothing but!
And I'd be the woman?
She gets undressed. He doesn't. She lies down. The man leaves. The door closes. Goodbye.
End of the first part.
At which point, I'd play "The Pleasure of Love", but only the line, "the pleasure of love only lasts an instant".
Plaisir d'Amour ne dure qu'un instant
The Noailles are going to finance the film. It will be ready when you come back from Cuba.
So soon? That's impossible!
I promise you!
To the starfish that Man Ray will see!
And so the woman, I'd be playing her? Right, Man?
20
4

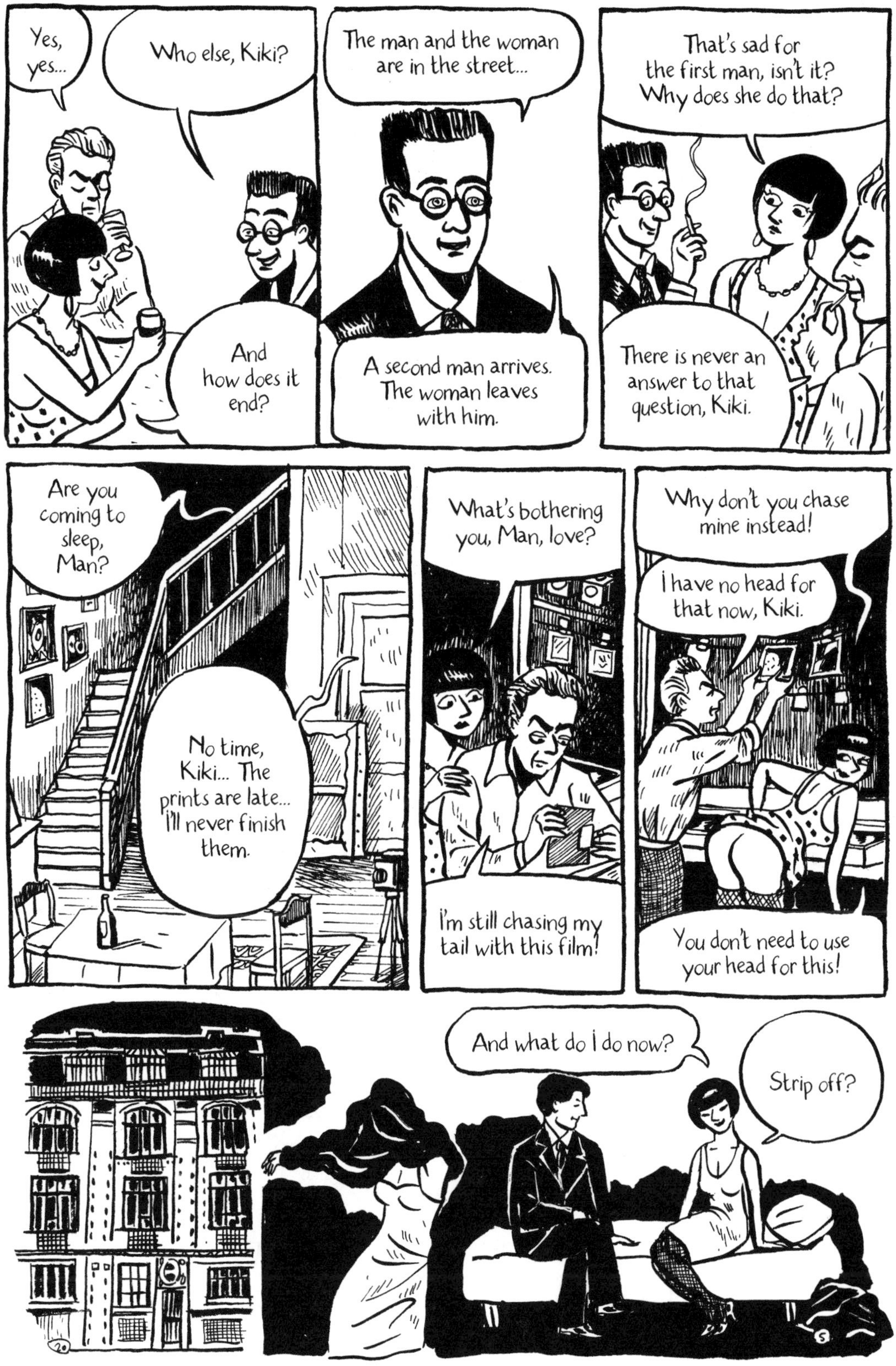
Yes, yes...
Who else, Kiki?
And how does it end?
The man and the woman are in the street...
A second man arrives. The woman leaves with him.
That's sad for the first man, isn't it? Why does she do that?
There is never an answer to that question, Kiki.
Are you coming to sleep, Man?
No time, Kiki... The prints are late... I'll never finish them.
What's bothering you, Man, love?
I'm still chasing my tail with this film!
Why don't you chase mine instead!
I have no head for that now, Kiki.
You don't need to use your head for this!
And what do I do now?
Strip off?

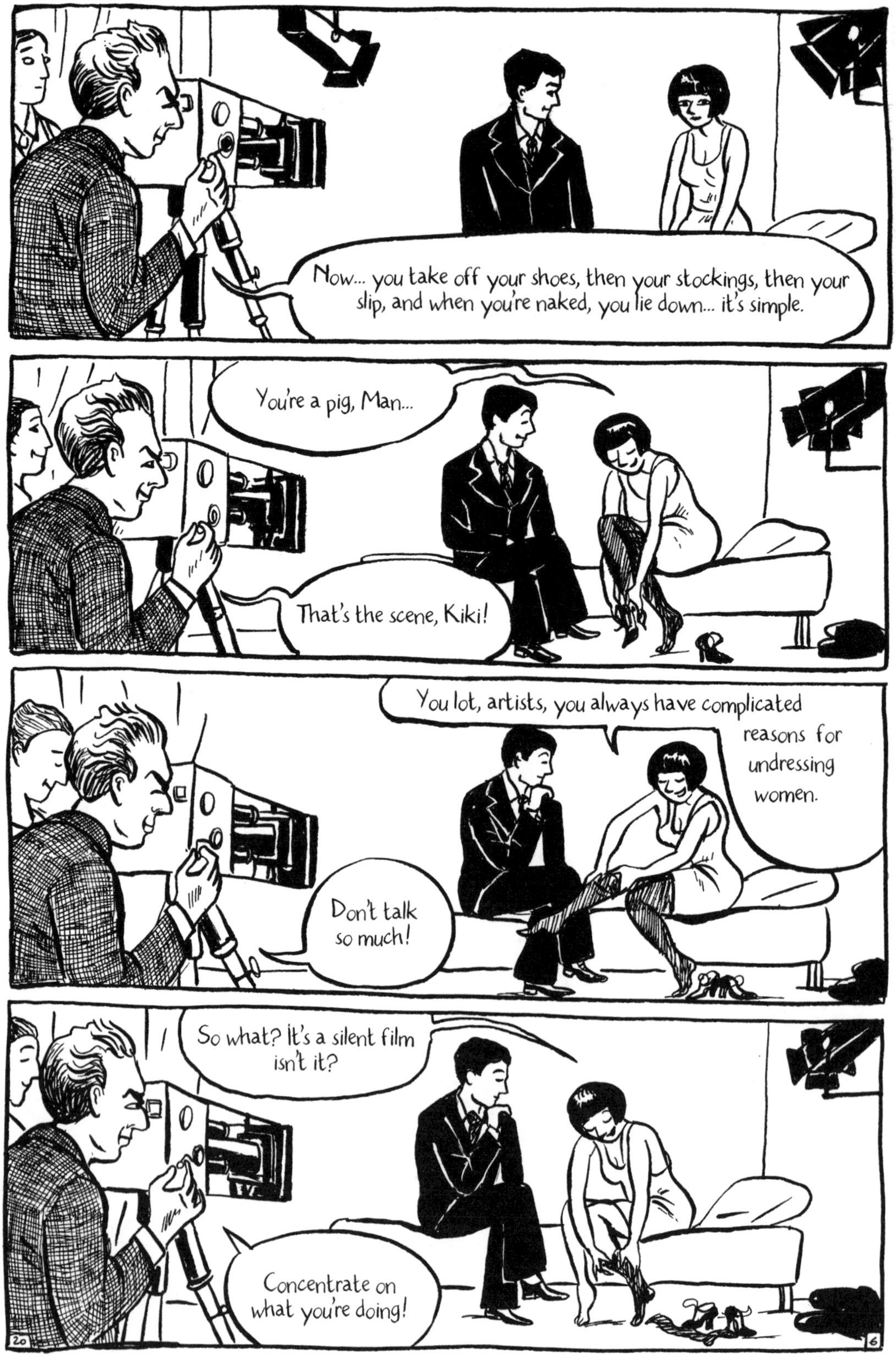
Now... you take off your shoes, then your stockings, then your slip, and when you're naked, you lie down... it's simple.
You're a pig, Man...
That's the scene, Kiki!
You lot, artists, you always have complicated reasons for undressing women.
Don't talk so much!
So what? It's a silent film isn't it?
Concentrate on what you're doing!

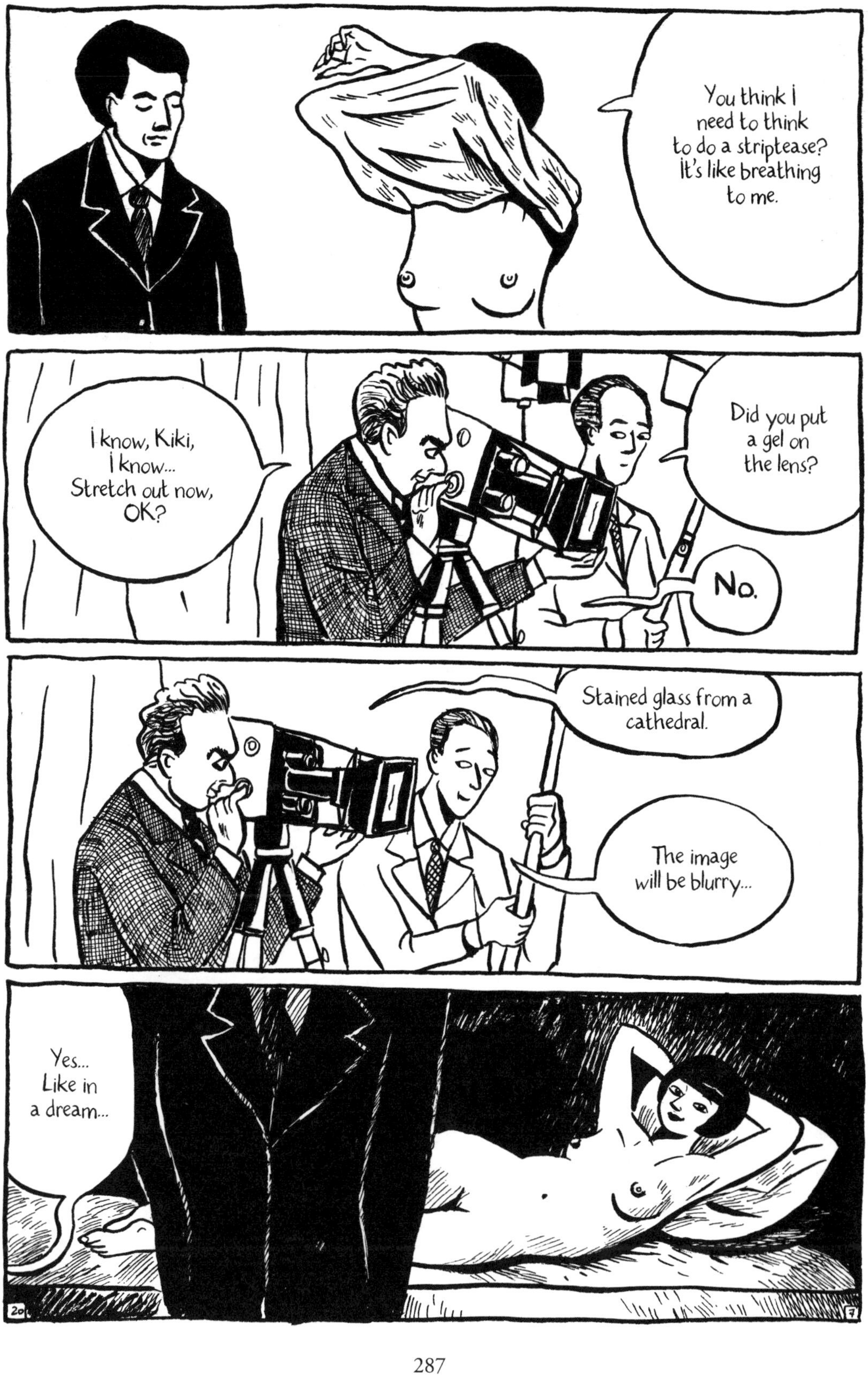
You think I need to think to do a striptease? It's like breathing to me.
I know, Kiki, I know... Stretch out now, OK?
Did you put a gel on the lens?
No.
Stained glass from a cathedral.
The image will be blurry...
Yes... Like in a dream...

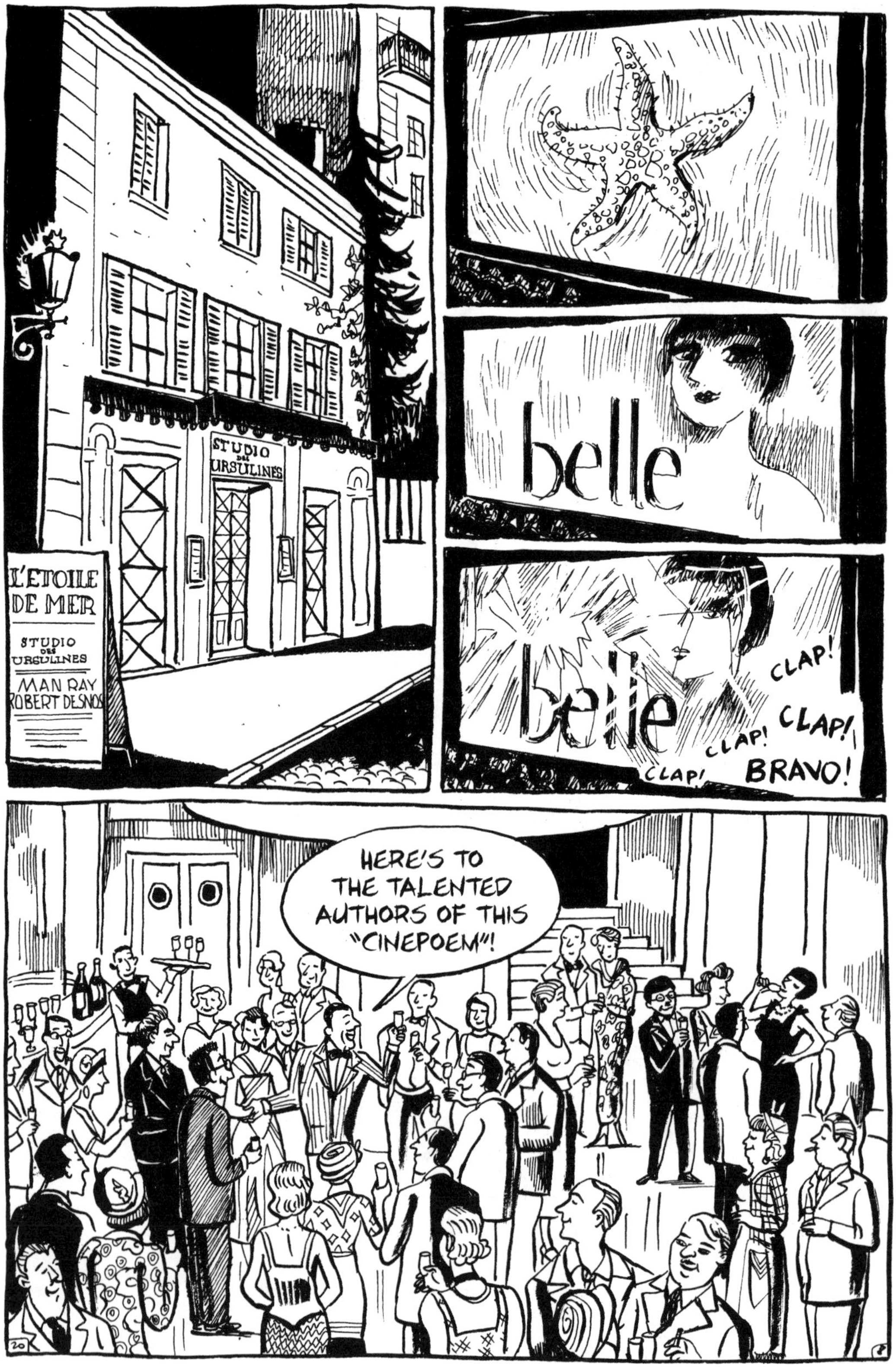
STUDIO DES URSULINES
L'ETOILE DE MER
STUDIO DES URSULINES
MAN RAY
ROBERT DESNOS
belle
belle
CLAP!
CLAP!
CLAP!
CLAP!
BRAVO!
HERE'S TO THE TALENTED AUTHORS OF THIS "CINEPOEM"!

I had bought a starfish at a junk shop on rue des Rosiers and I thought of it as being a physical incarnation of a lost love, a truly lost love...

I wrote this screenplay under the influence of that starfish, in the form of the apparitions and ghosts that Man Ray and I recognised as a poem – as simple as falling in love.

Tell me, Monsieur Ray, the close-up of a starfish, it's a woman's vagina, isn't it? A toothless vagina...

Man Ray isn't interested in artistic deformation, or a slavish reproduction of nature!

Light is as malleable as paint. So why not use the film like a painter uses a canvas?

Did they stick jam on the lens to film you?

Broca, really! It's surrealism!

At the end of the day, I prefer realism – to see you just as you are!

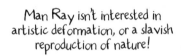

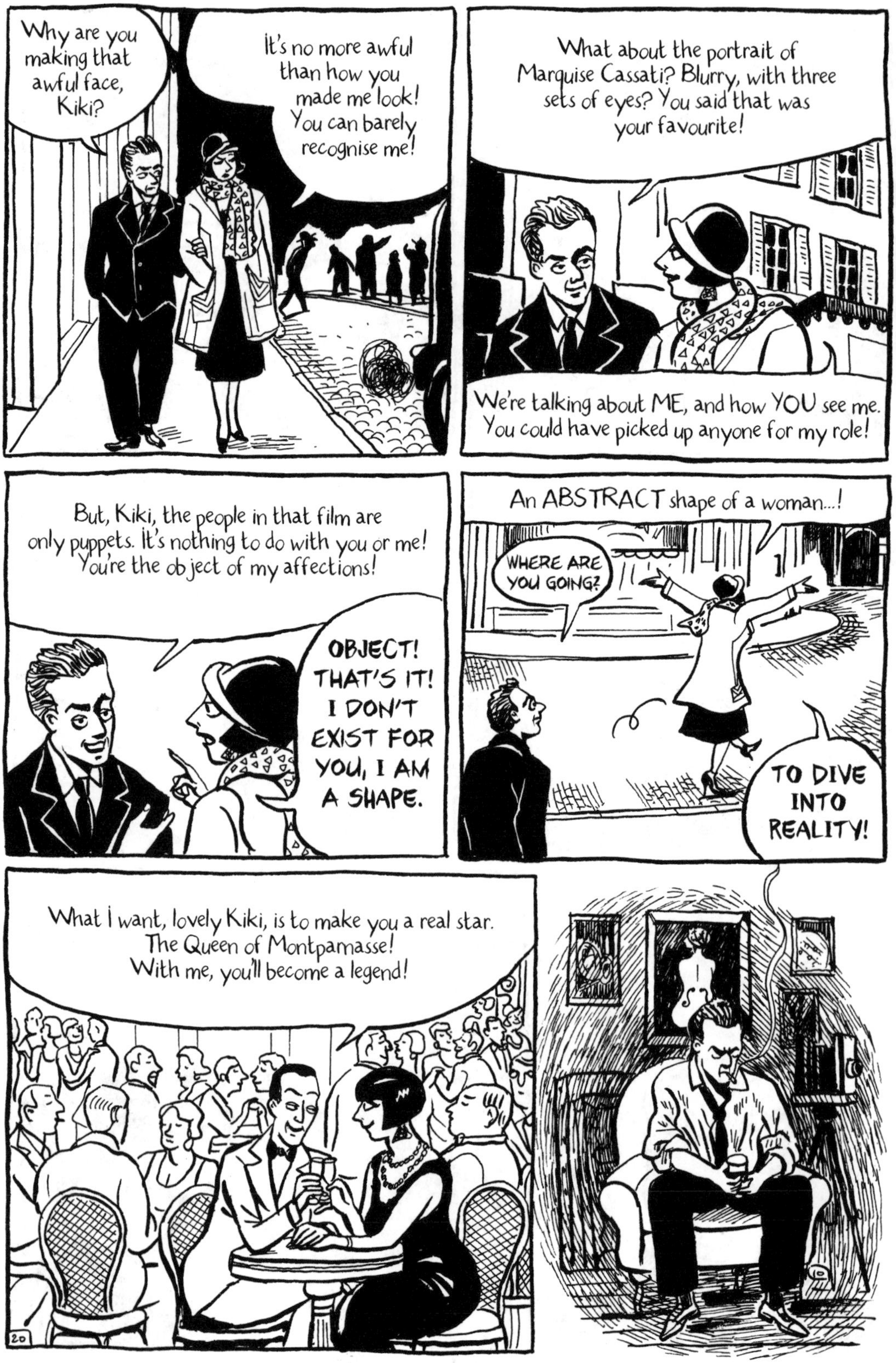
Why are you making that awful face, Kiki?
It's no more awful than how you made me look! You can barely recognise me!
What about the portrait of Marquise Cassati? Blurry, with three sets of eyes? You said that was your favourite!
We're talking about ME, and how YOU see me. You could have picked up anyone for my role!
But, Kiki, the people in that film are only puppets. It's nothing to do with you or me! You're the object of my affections!
OBJECT! THAT'S IT! I DON'T EXIST FOR YOU, I AM A SHAPE.
An ABSTRACT shape of a woman...!
WHERE ARE YOU GOING?
TO DIVE INTO REALITY!
What I want, lovely Kiki, is to make you a real star. The Queen of Montparnasse! With me, you'll become a legend!
20

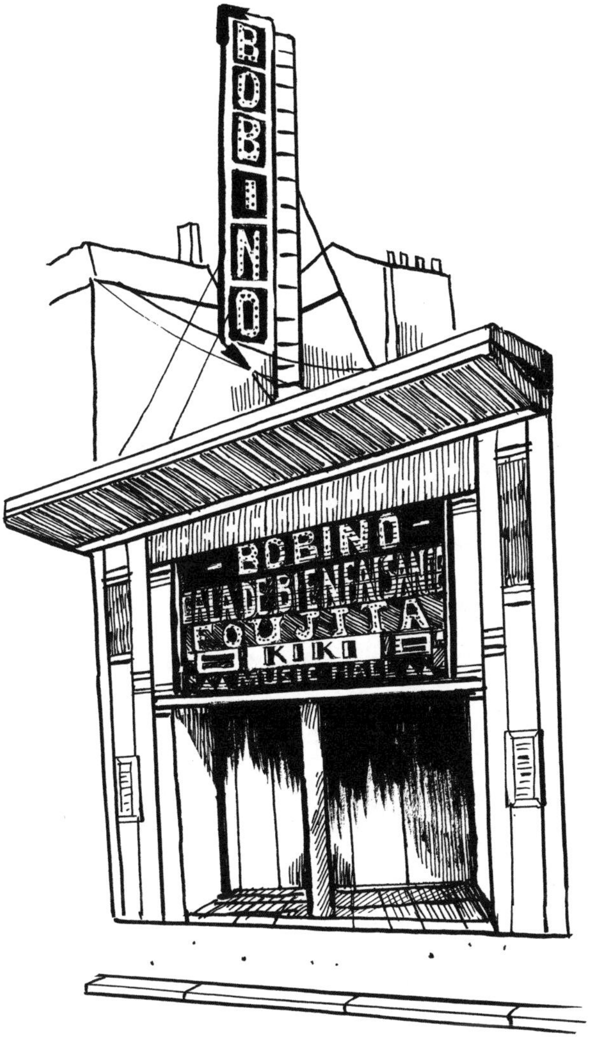
BOBINO
BOBINO
GALA DE BIENFAISANCE
FOUJITA
KIKI
MUSIC HALL

1929 - 20, rue de la Gaîté

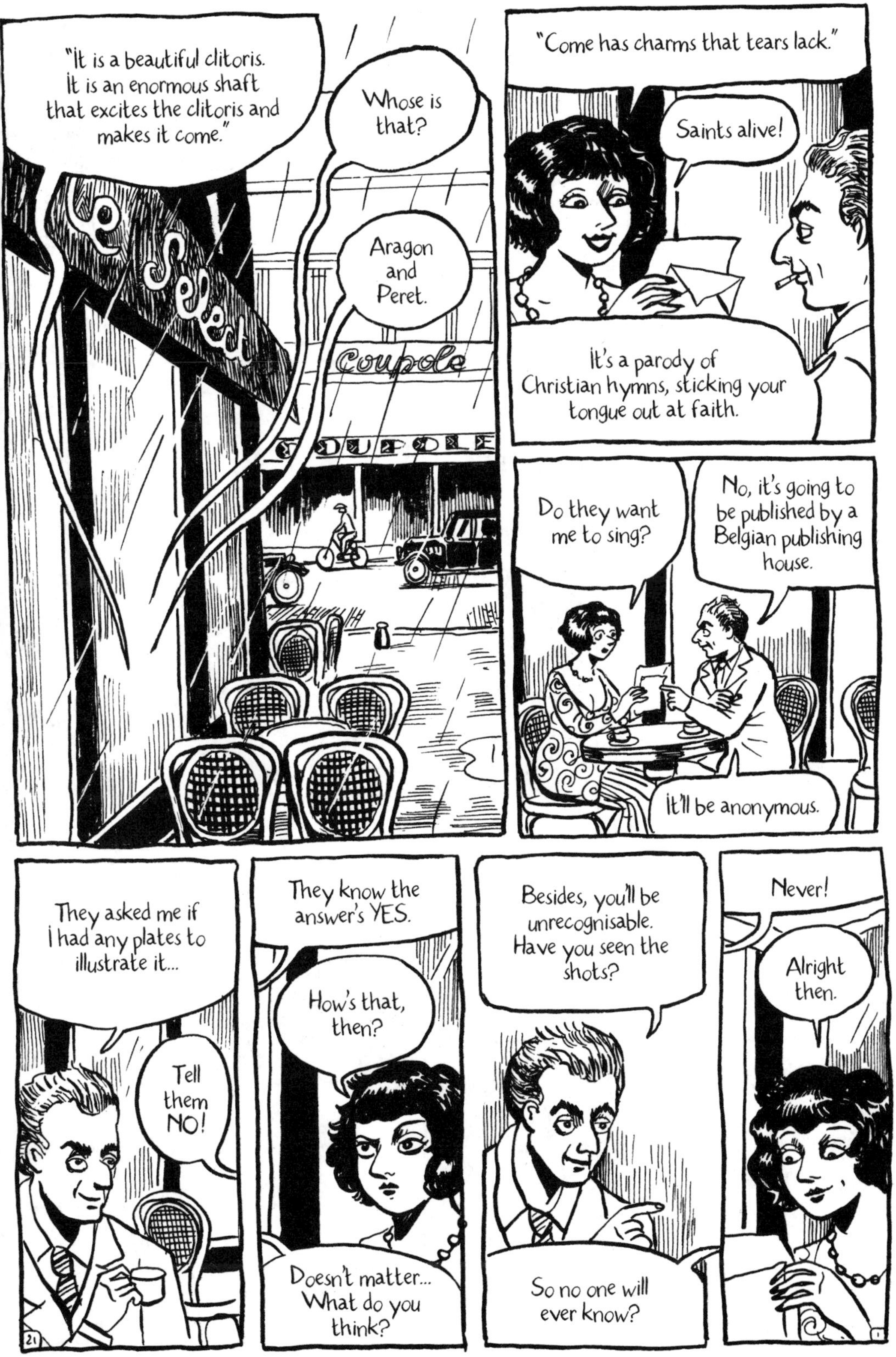
"It is a beautiful clitoris. It is an enormous shaft that excites the clitoris and makes it come."
Whose is that?
Aragon and Peret.
Le Select
Coupole
COUPOLE
"Come has charms that tears lack."
Saints alive!
It's a parody of Christian hymns, sticking your tongue out at faith.
Do they want me to sing?
No, it's going to be published by a Belgian publishing house.
It'll be anonymous.
They asked me if I had any plates to illustrate it...
Tell them NO!
They know the answer's YES.
How's that, then?
Doesn't matter... What do you think?
Besides, you'll be unrecognisable. Have you seen the shots?
So no one will ever know?
Never!
Alright then.

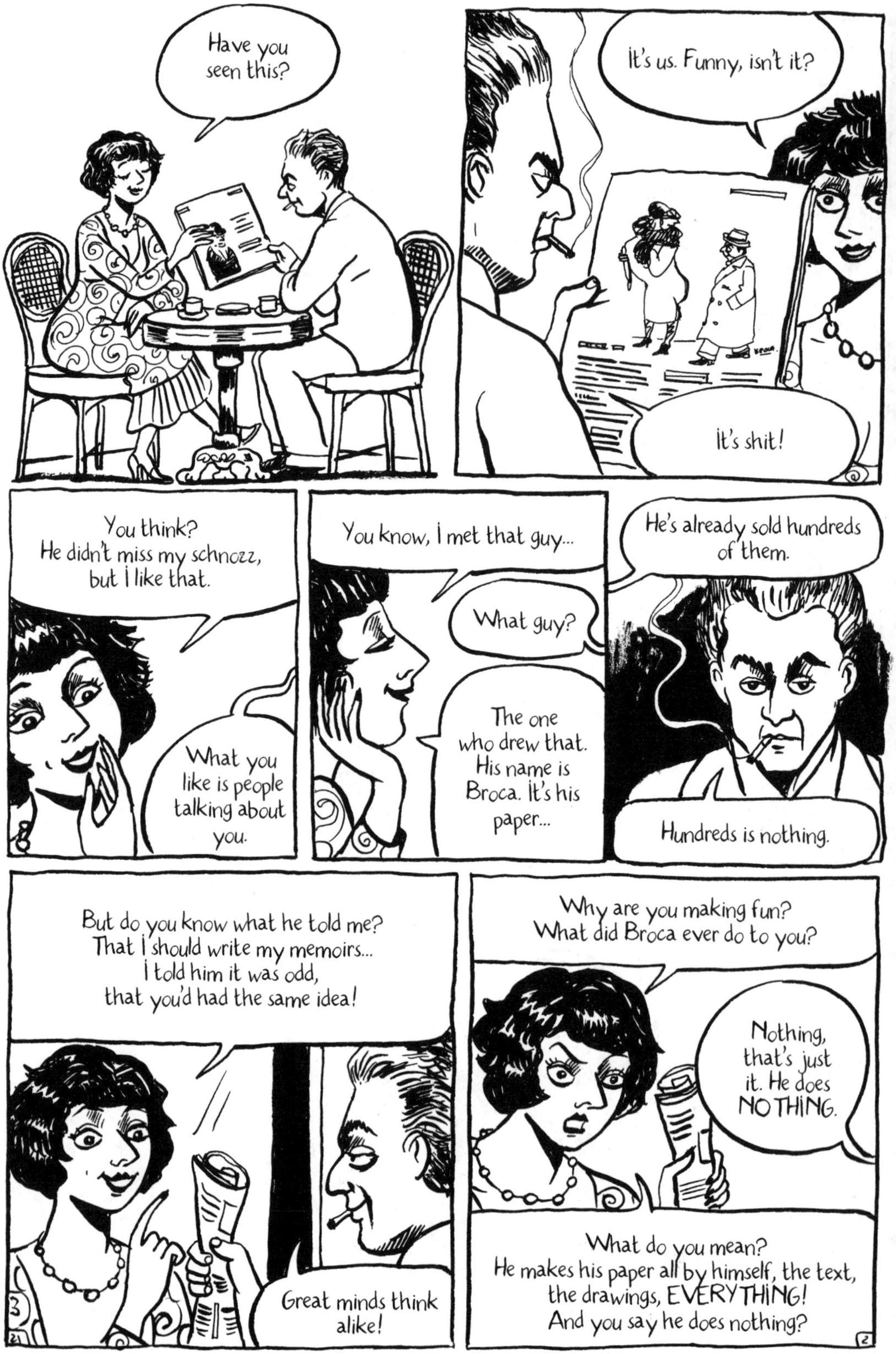
Have you seen this?
It's us. Funny, isn't it?
It's shit!
You think? He didn't miss my schnozz, but I like that.
What you like is people talking about you.
You know, I met that guy...
What guy?
The one who drew that. His name is Broca. It's his paper...
He's already sold hundreds of them.
Hundreds is nothing.
But do you know what he told me? That I should write my memoirs... I told him it was odd, that you'd had the same idea!
Great minds think alike!
Why are you making fun? What did Broca ever do to you?
Nothing, that's just it. He does NOTHING.
What do you mean? He makes his paper all by himself, the text, the drawings, EVERYTHING! And you say he does nothing?

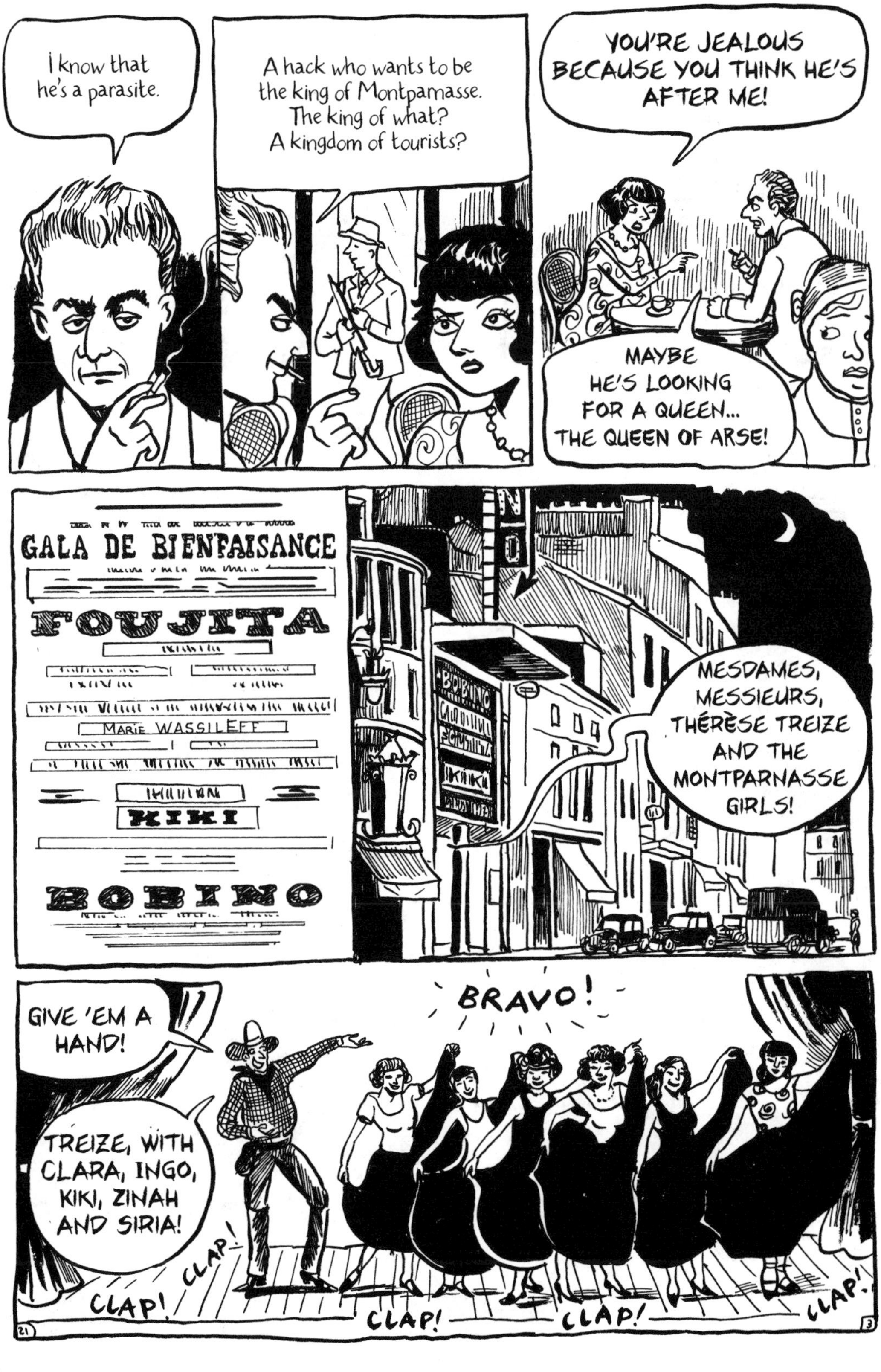

I know that he's a parasite.
A hack who wants to be the king of Montparnasse. The king of what? A kingdom of tourists?
YOU'RE JEALOUS BECAUSE YOU THINK HE'S AFTER ME!
MAYBE HE'S LOOKING FOR A QUEEN... THE QUEEN OF ARSE!
GALA DE BIENFAISANCE
FOUJITA
MARIE WASSILEFF
KIKI
BOBINO
MESDAMES, MESSIEURS, THÉRÈSE TREIZE AND THE MONTPARNASSE GIRLS!
GIVE 'EM A HAND!
BRAVO!
TREIZE, WITH CLARA, INGO, KIKI, ZINAH AND SIRIA!
CLAP! CLAP!
CLAP!
CLAP!
CLAP!

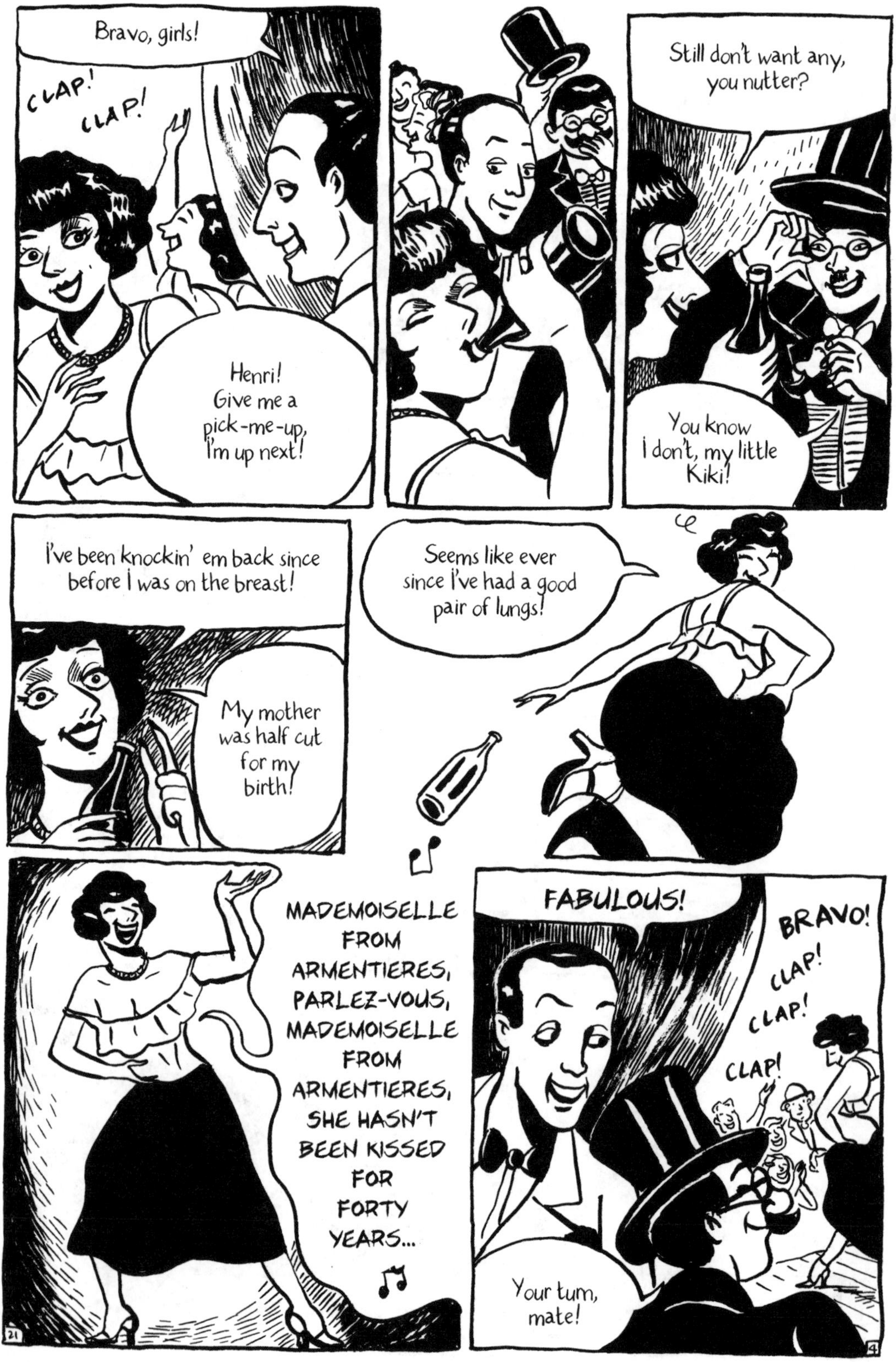
Bravo, girls!
CLAP!
CLAP!
Henri! Give me a pick-me-up, I'm up next!
Still don't want any, you nutter?
You know I don't, my little Kiki!
I've been knockin' em back since before I was on the breast!
My mother was half cut for my birth!
Seems like ever since I've had a good pair of lungs!
MADEMOISELLE FROM ARMENTIERES, PARLEZ-VOUS, MADEMOISELLE FROM ARMENTIERES, SHE HASN'T BEEN KISSED FOR FORTY YEARS...
FABULOUS!
BRAVO!
CLAP!
CLAP!
CLAP!
Your turn, mate!

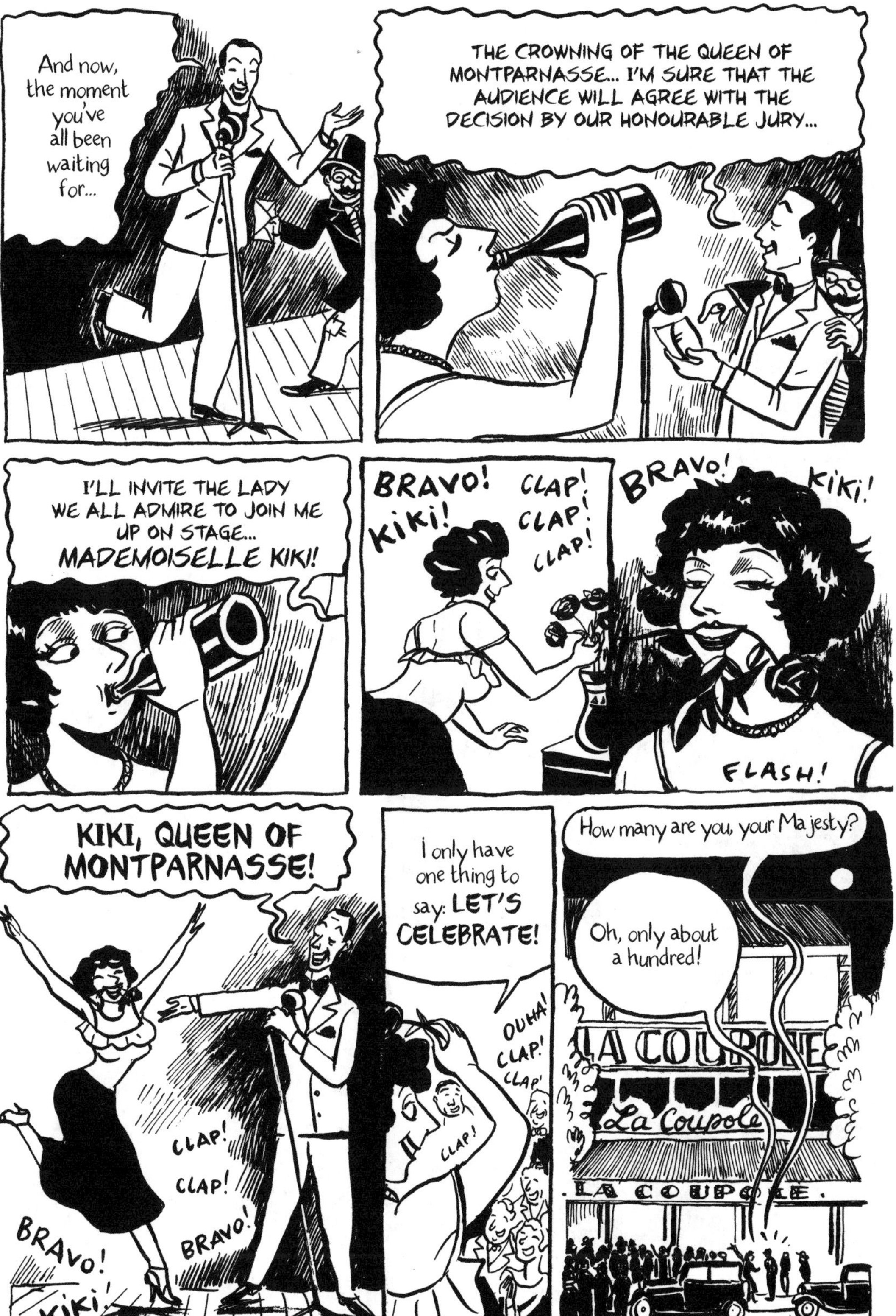

And now, the moment you've all been waiting for...
THE CROWNING OF THE QUEEN OF MONTPARNASSE... I'M SURE THAT THE AUDIENCE WILL AGREE WITH THE DECISION BY OUR HONOURABLE JURY...
I'LL INVITE THE LADY WE ALL ADMIRE TO JOIN ME UP ON STAGE... MADEMOISELLE KIKI!
BRAVO!
KIKI!
CLAP! CLAP! CLAP!
BRAVO!
KIKI!
FLASH!
KIKI, QUEEN OF MONTPARNASSE!
CLAP!
CLAP!
BRAVO!
BRAVO!
KIKI!
I only have one thing to say: LET'S CELEBRATE!
OUHA!
CLAP!
CLAP!
CLAP!
How many are you, your Majesty?
Oh, only about a hundred!
LA COUPOLE
La Coupole
LA COUPOLE.

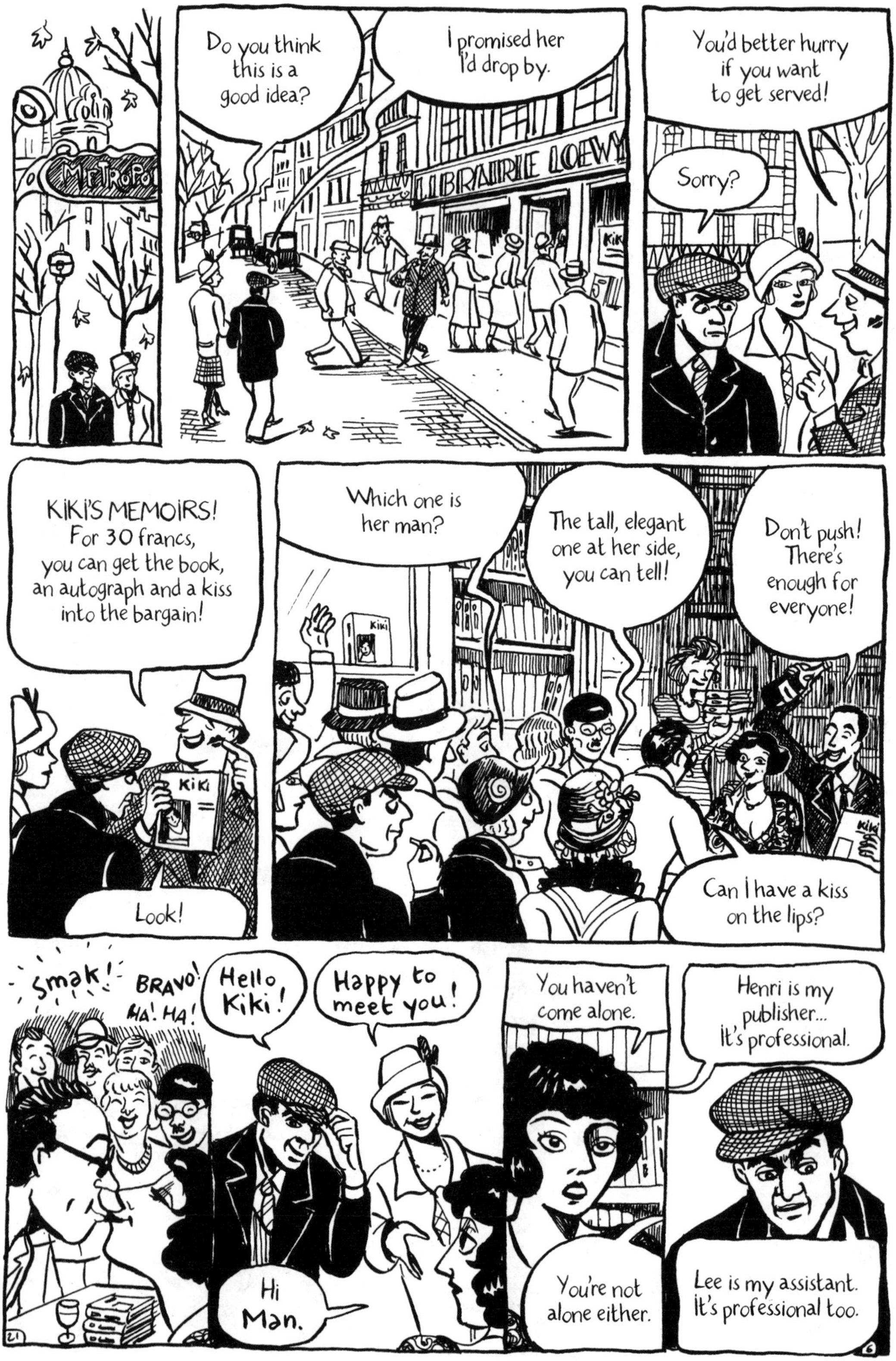
MéTROPO
Do you think this is a good idea?
I promised her I'd drop by.
LIBRAIRIE LOEWY
KIKI
You'd better hurry if you want to get served!
Sorry?
KIKI'S MEMOIRS! For 30 francs, you can get the book, an autograph and a kiss into the bargain!
KIKI
Look!
Which one is her man?
The tall, elegant one at her side, you can tell!
Don't push! There's enough for everyone!
KIKI
Can I have a kiss on the lips?
SMAK!
BRAVO! HA! HA!
Hello Kiki!
Happy to meet you!
Hi Man.
You haven't come alone.
Henri is my publisher... It's professional.
You're not alone either.
Lee is my assistant. It's professional too.

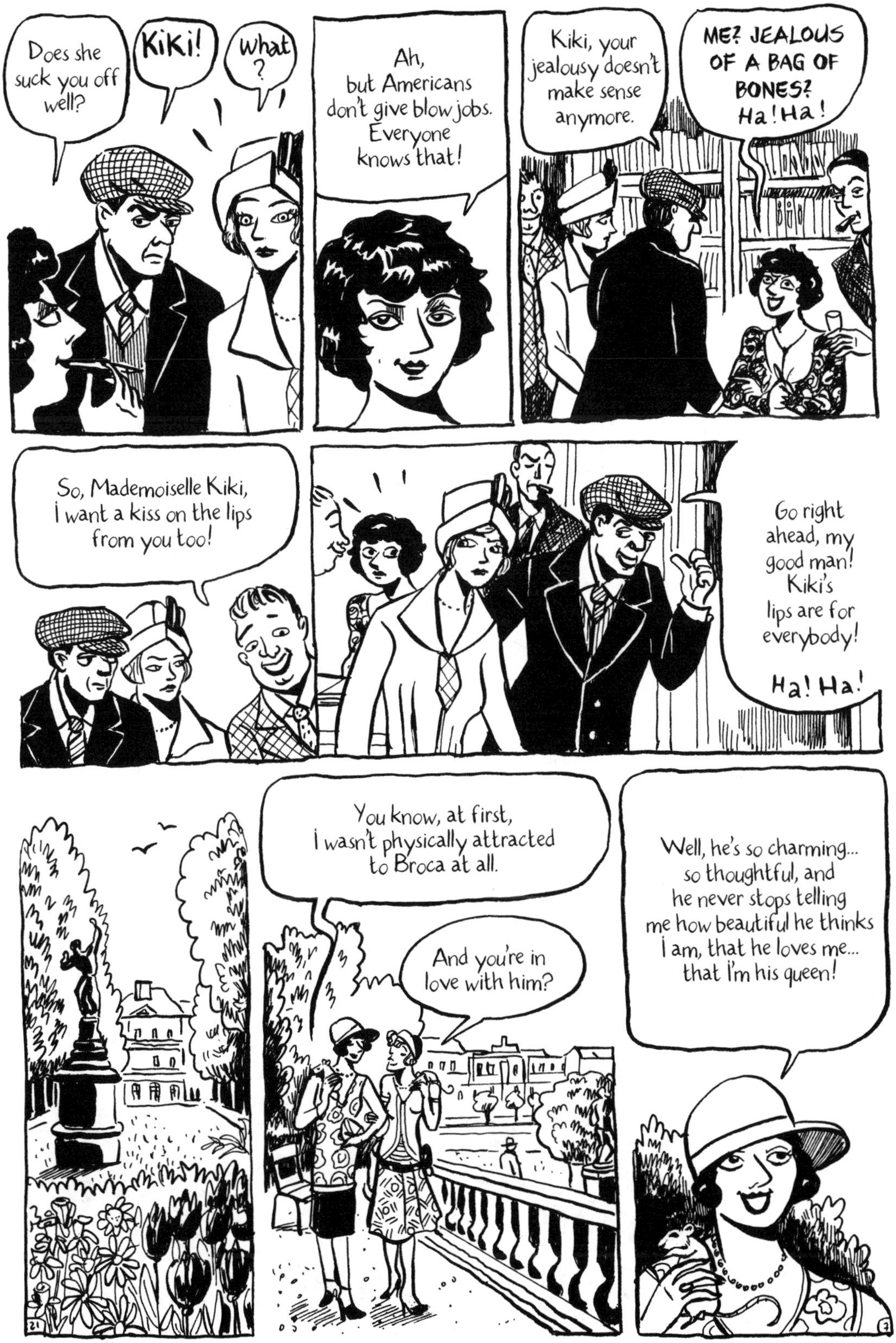
Does she suck you off well?
KiKi!
What?
Ah, but Americans don't give blow jobs. Everyone knows that!
Kiki, your jealousy doesn't make sense anymore.
ME? JEALOUS OF A BAG OF BONES? Ha! Ha!
So, Mademoiselle Kiki, I want a kiss on the lips from you too!
Go right ahead, my good man! Kiki's lips are for everybody!
Ha! Ha!
You know, at first, I wasn't physically attracted to Broca at all.
And you're in love with him?
Well, he's so charming... so thoughtful, and he never stops telling me how beautiful he thinks I am, that he loves me... that I'm his queen!

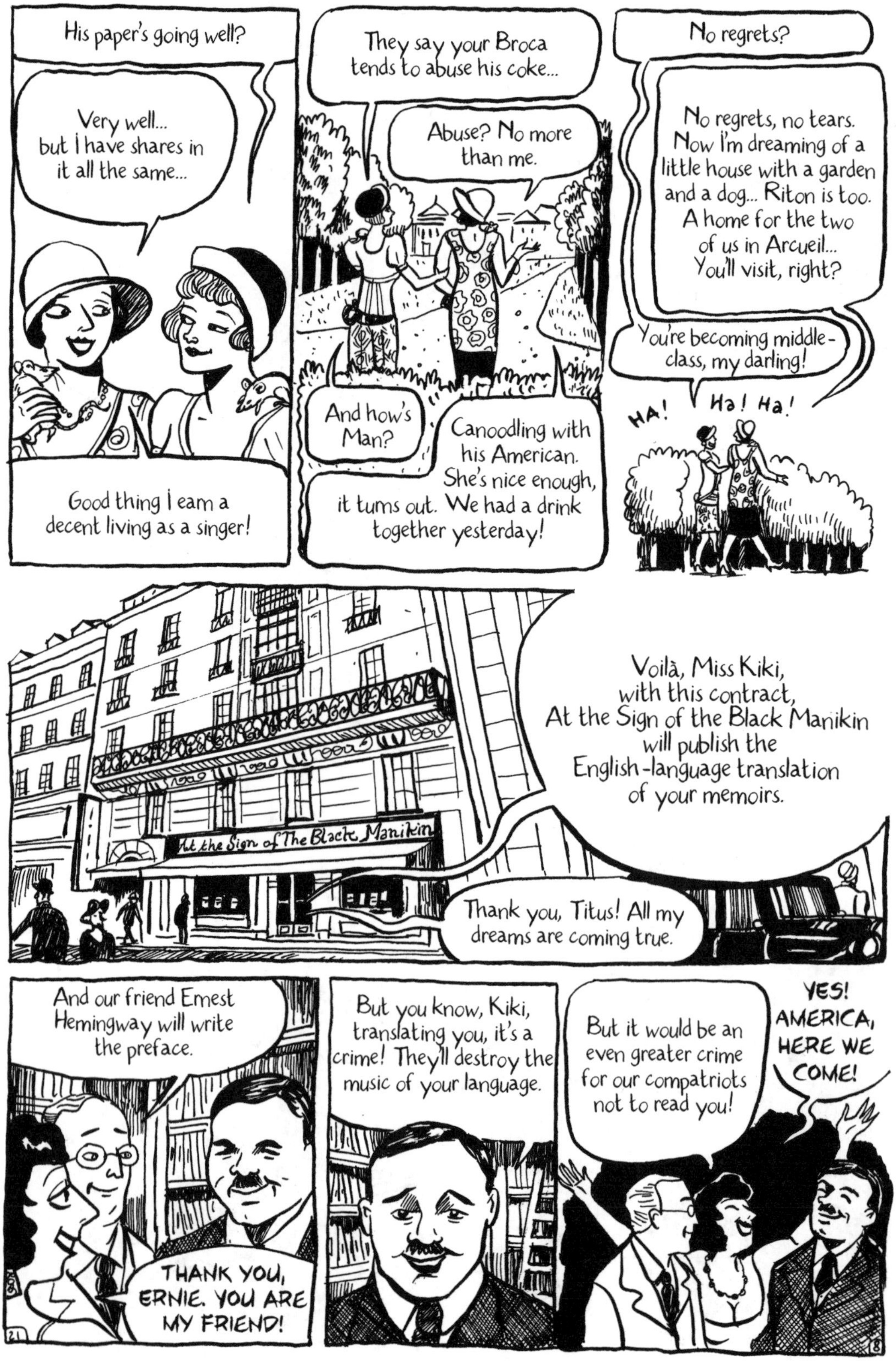
His paper's going well?
Very well... but I have shares in it all the same...
Good thing I earn a decent living as a singer!
They say your Broca tends to abuse his coke...
Abuse? No more than me.
And how's Man?
Canoodling with his American. She's nice enough, it turns out. We had a drink together yesterday!
No regrets?
No regrets, no tears. Now I'm dreaming of a little house with a garden and a dog... Riton is too. A home for the two of us in Arcueil... You'll visit, right?
You're becoming middle-class, my darling!
HA! Ha! Ha!
At the Sign of The Black Manikin
Voilà, Miss Kiki, with this contract, At the Sign of the Black Manikin will publish the English-language translation of your memoirs.
Thank you, Titus! All my dreams are coming true.
And our friend Ernest Hemingway will write the preface.
THANK YOU, ERNIE. YOU ARE MY FRIEND!
But you know, Kiki, translating you, it's a crime! They'll destroy the music of your language.
But it would be an even greater crime for our compatriots not to read you!
YES! AMERICA, HERE WE COME!

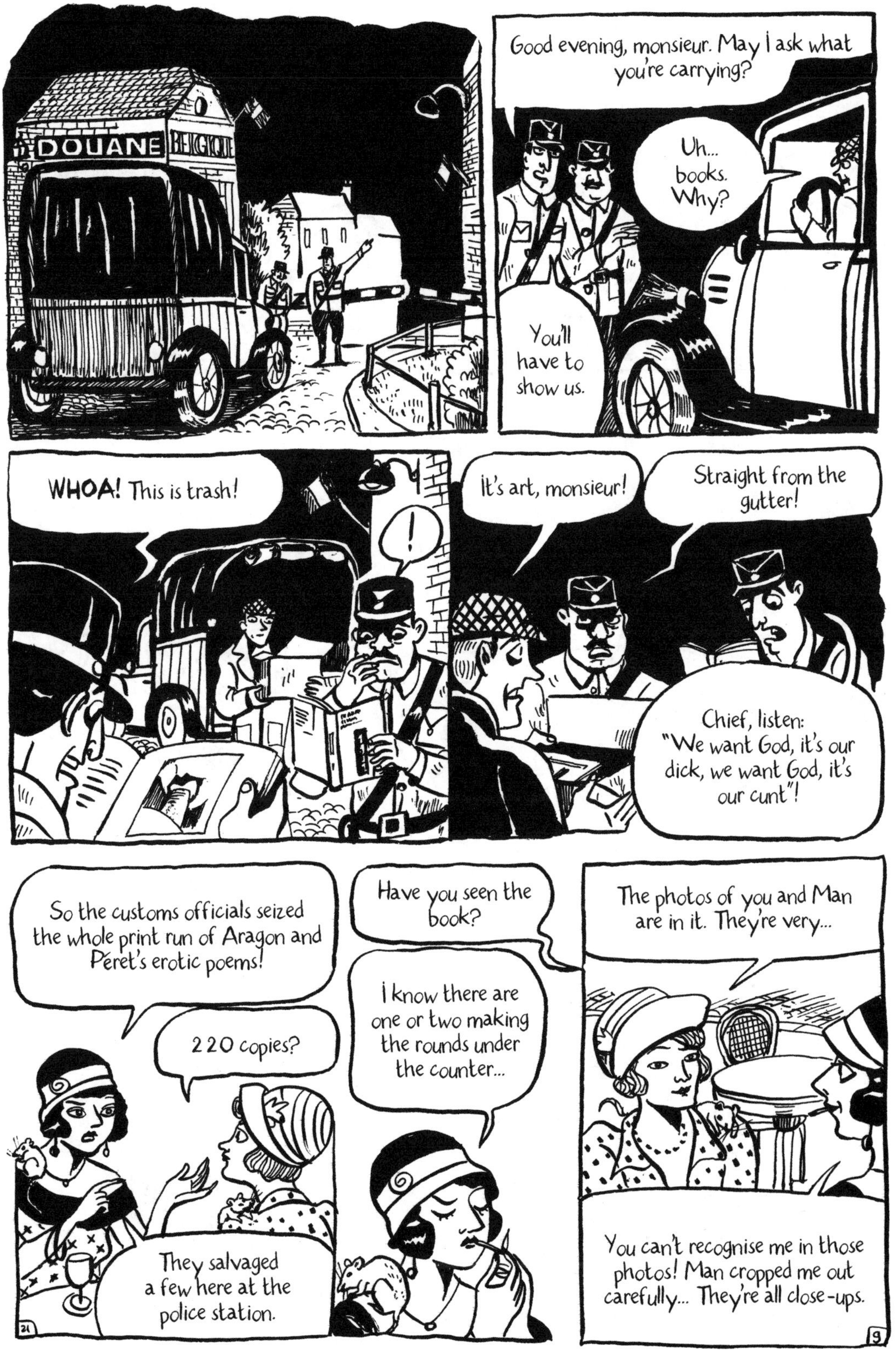
DOUANE
Good evening, monsieur. May I ask what you're carrying?
Uh... books. Why?
You'll have to show us.
WHOA! This is trash!
!
It's art, monsieur!
Straight from the gutter!
Chief, listen: "We want God, it's our dick, we want God, it's our cunt"!
So the customs officials seized the whole print run of Aragon and Péret's erotic poems!
220 copies?
They salvaged a few here at the police station.
Have you seen the book?
I know there are one or two making the rounds under the counter...
The photos of you and Man are in it. They're very...
You can't recognise me in those photos! Man cropped me out carefully... They're all close-ups.

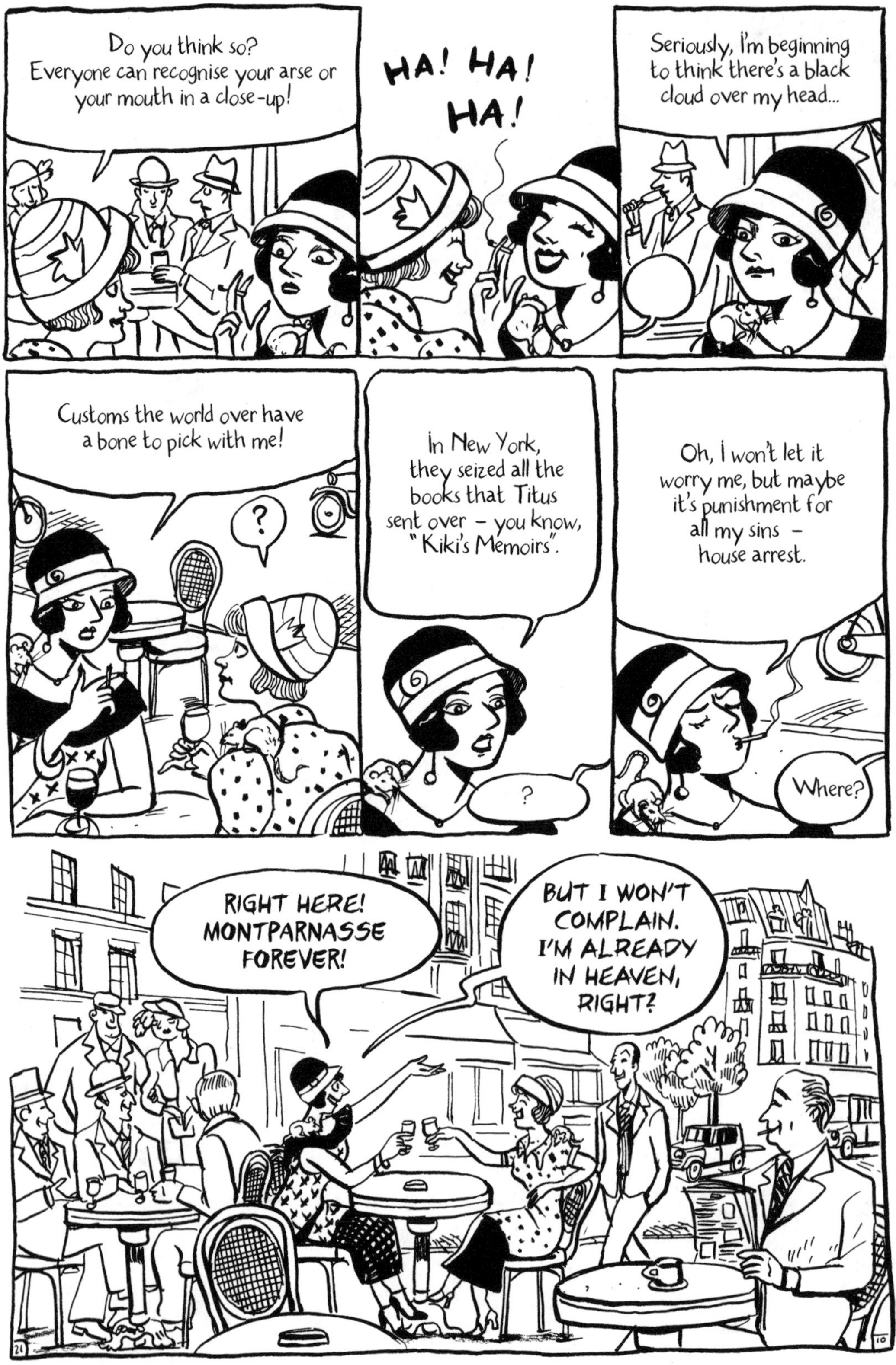
Do you think so? Everyone can recognise your arse or your mouth in a close-up!
HA! HA! HA!
Seriously, I'm beginning to think there's a black cloud over my head...
Customs the world over have a bone to pick with me!
?
In New York, they seized all the books that Titus sent over – you know, "Kiki's Memoirs".
?
Oh, I won't let it worry me, but maybe it's punishment for all my sins – house arrest.
Where?
RIGHT HERE! MONTPARNASSE FOREVER!
BUT I WON'T COMPLAIN. I'M ALREADY IN HEAVEN, RIGHT?

CENTRE HOSPITALIER SAINTE ANNE

1930 - 3, rue Cabanis

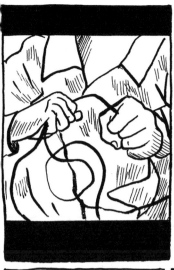

It looks like me, doesn't it?

Come on, we're going!

But... what about the film?

I CAN'T TAKE IT! I CAN'T TAKE IT ANY MORE!

Henri, are you not feeling any better? You look knackered!

Have a bit of blow, that'll wake you up!

I have to get back to the grindstone!

The Concerts Mayol is hardly next door... That's the problem with the suburbs...

BAM!

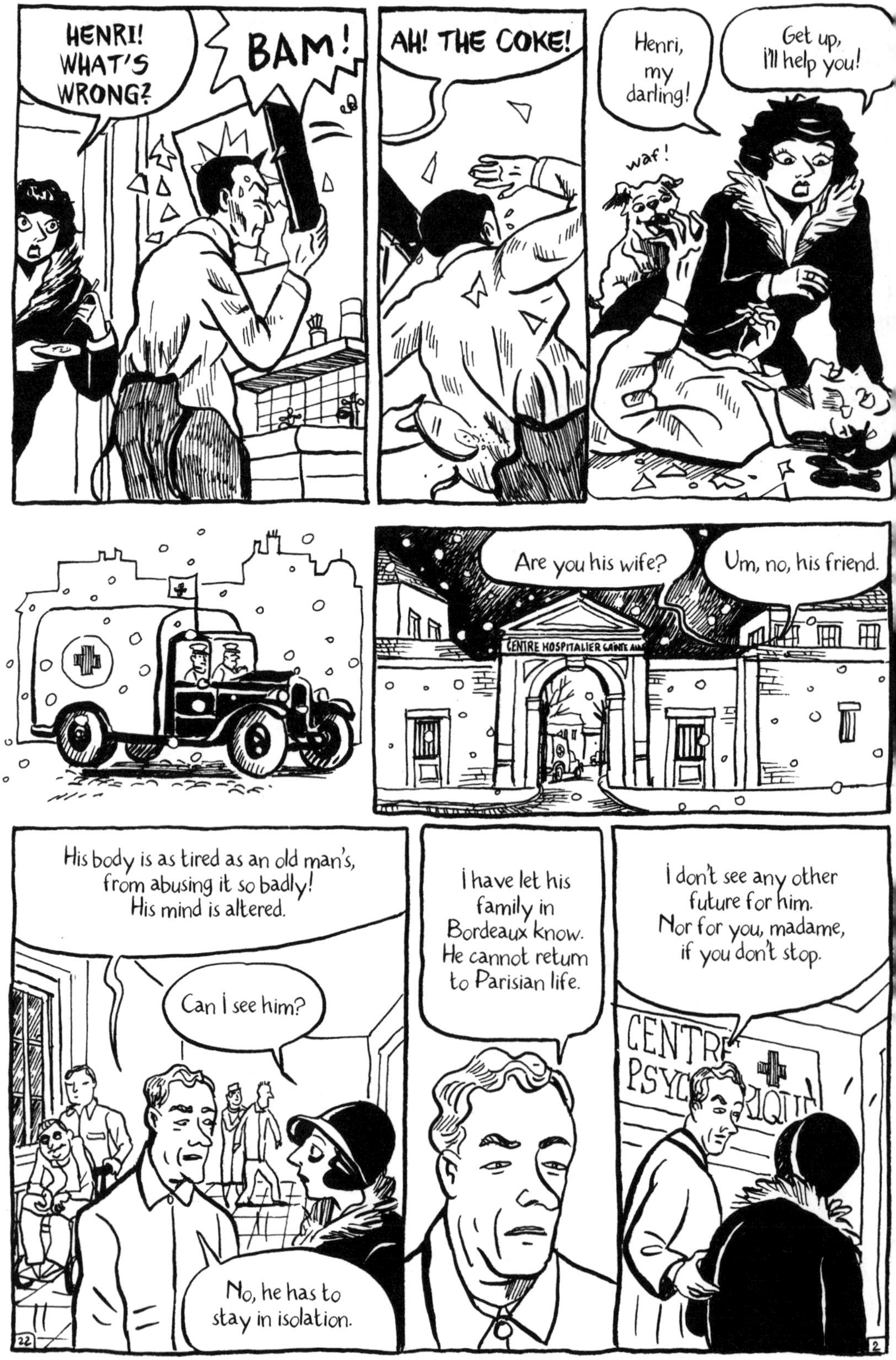

HENRI! WHAT'S WRONG?
BAM!
AH! THE COKE!
Henri, my darling!
Get up, I'll help you!
waf!
CENTRE HOSPITALIER
Are you his wife?
Um, no, his friend.
His body is as tired as an old man's, from abusing it so badly! His mind is altered.
Can I see him?
No, he has to stay in isolation.
I have let his family in Bordeaux know. He cannot return to Parisian life.
I don't see any other future for him. Nor for you, madame, if you don't stop.

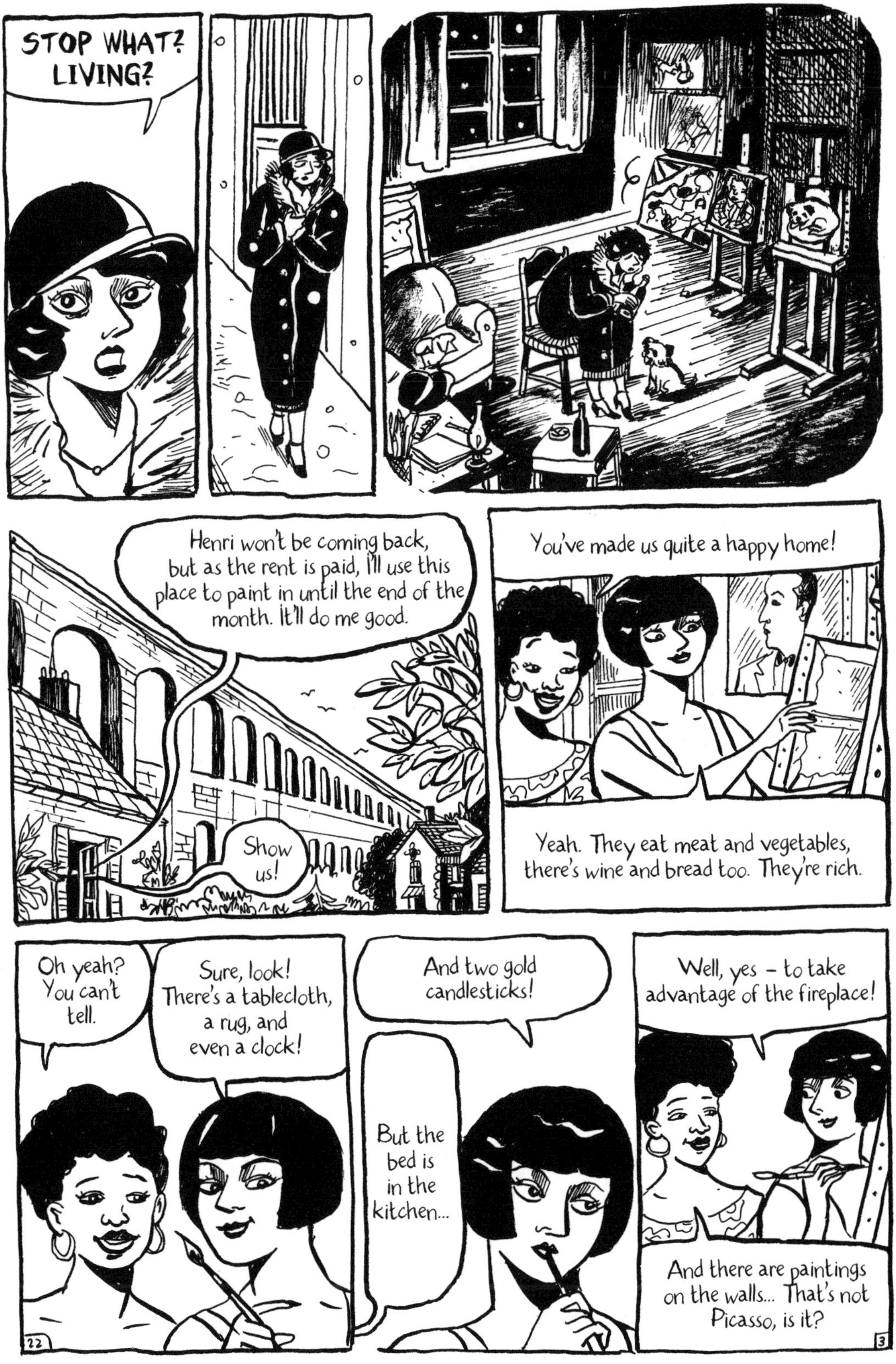

STOP WHAT? LIVING?
Henri won't be coming back, but as the rent is paid, I'll use this place to paint in until the end of the month. It'll do me good.
Show us!
You've made us quite a happy home!
Yeah. They eat meat and vegetables, there's wine and bread too. They're rich.
Oh yeah? You can't tell.
Sure, look! There's a tablecloth, a rug, and even a clock!
And two gold candlesticks!
But the bed is in the kitchen...
Well, yes – to take advantage of the fireplace!
And there are paintings on the walls... That's not Picasso, is it?
22
3

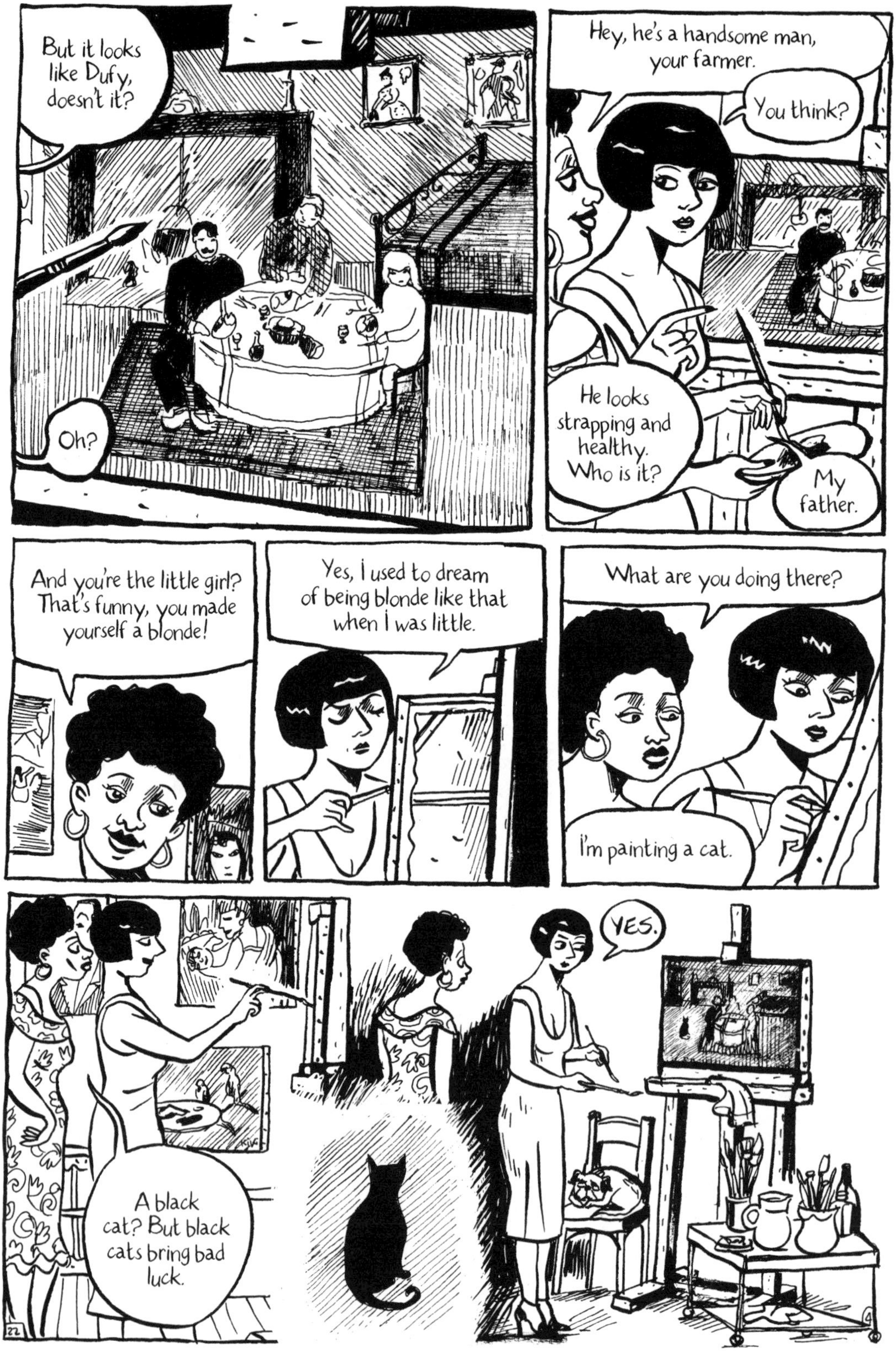
But it looks like Dufy, doesn't it?
Oh?
Hey, he's a handsome man, your farmer.
You think?
He looks strapping and healthy. Who is it?
My father.
And you're the little girl? That's funny, you made yourself a blonde!
Yes, I used to dream of being blonde like that when I was little.
What are you doing there?
I'm painting a cat.
A black cat? But black cats bring bad luck.
YES.

1931 - Saint-Tropez

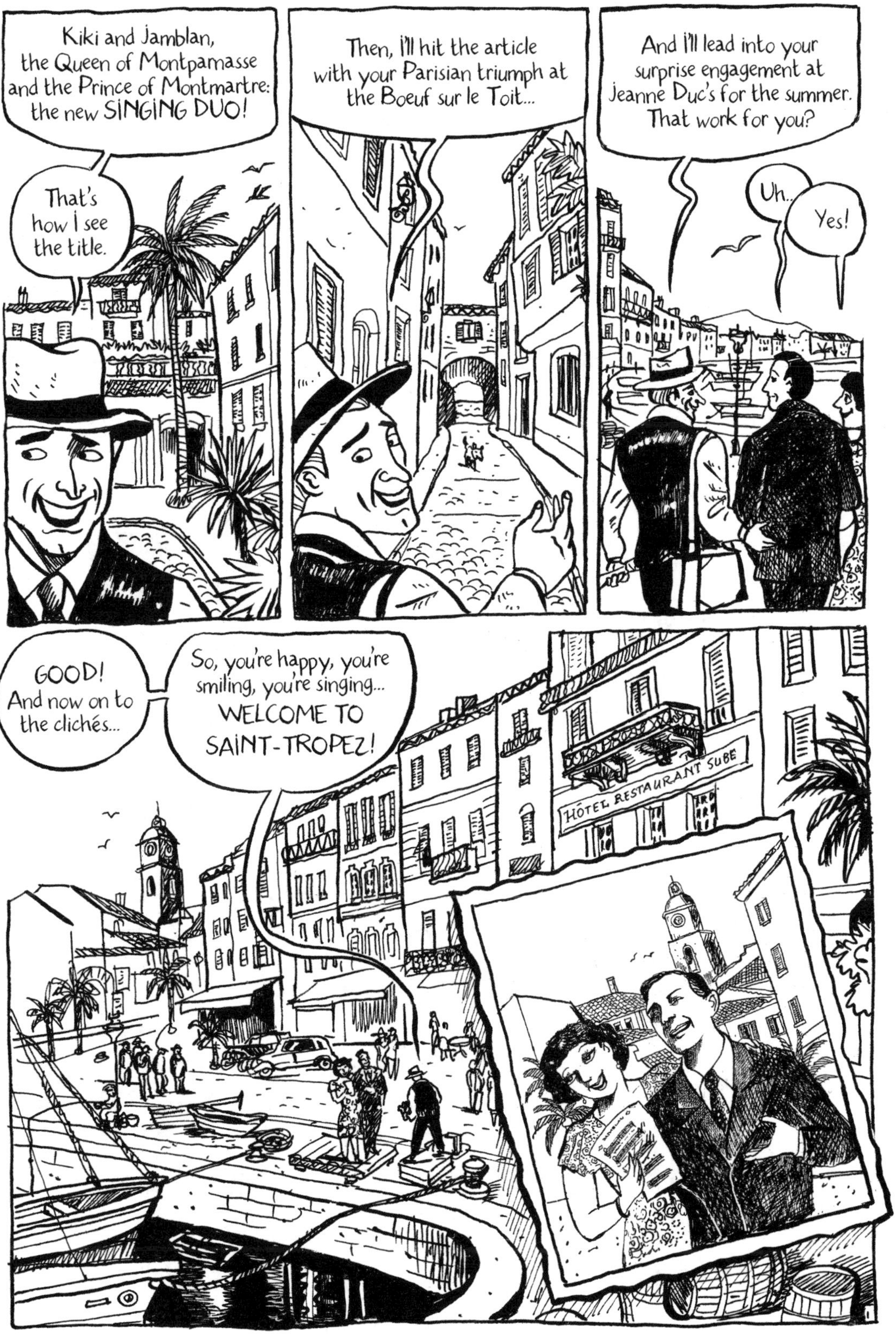
Kiki and Jamblan, the Queen of Montparnasse and the Prince of Montmartre: the new SINGING DUO!
That's how I see the title.
Then, I'll hit the article with your Parisian triumph at the Boeuf sur le Toit...
And I'll lead into your surprise engagement at Jeanne Duc's for the summer. That work for you?
Uh...
Yes!
GOOD! And now on to the clichés...
So, you're happy, you're smiling, you're singing... WELCOME TO SAINT-TROPEZ!
HÔTEL RESTAURANT SUBE

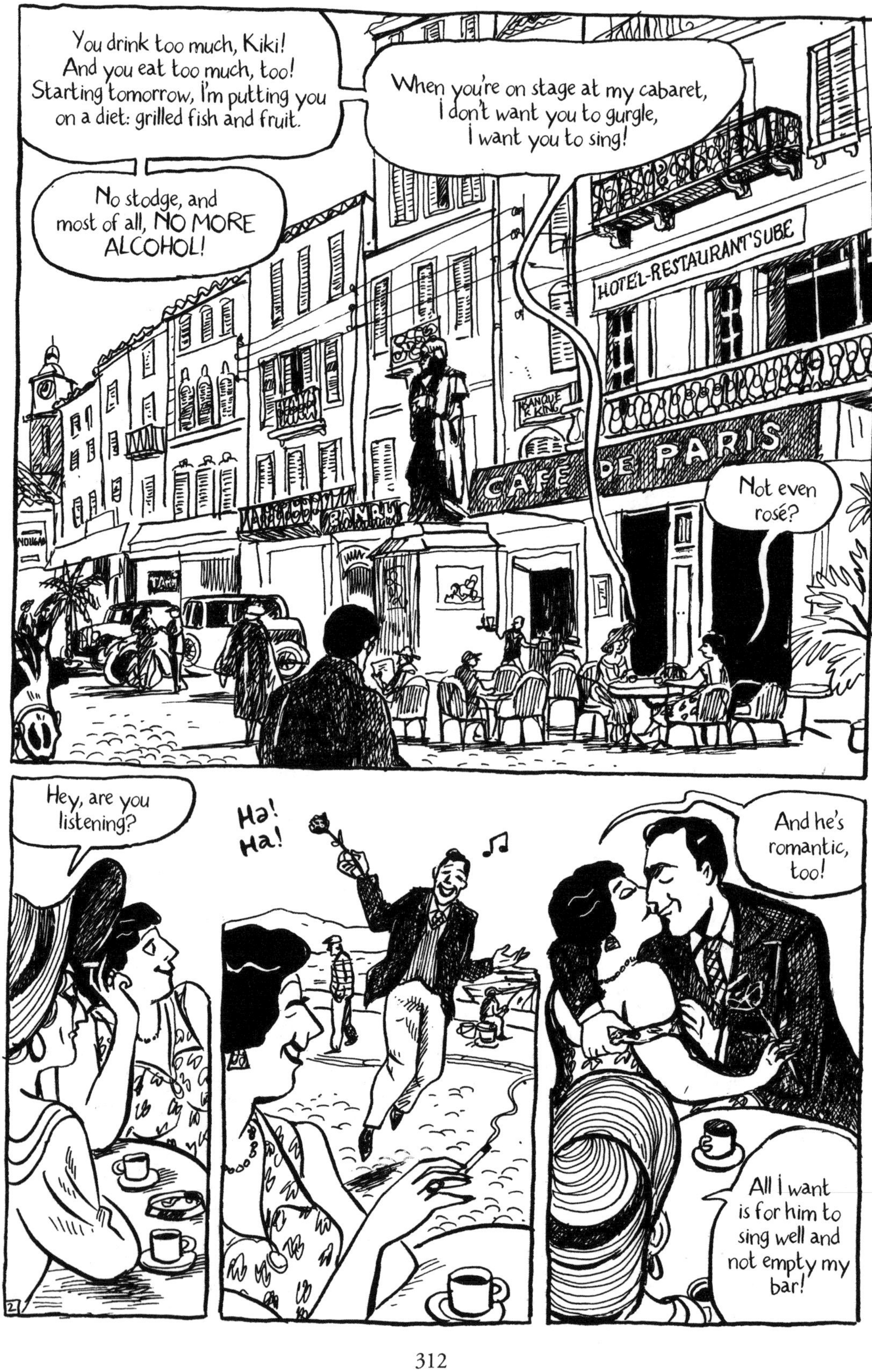
You drink too much, Kiki! And you eat too much, too! Starting tomorrow, I'm putting you on a diet: grilled fish and fruit.
No stodge, and most of all, NO MORE ALCOHOL!
When you're on stage at my cabaret, I don't want you to gurgle, I want you to sing!
HOTEL-RESTAURANT SUBE
CAFÉ DE PARIS
Not even rosé?
Hey, are you listening?
Ha! Ha!
And he's romantic, too!
All I want is for him to sing well and not empty my bar!

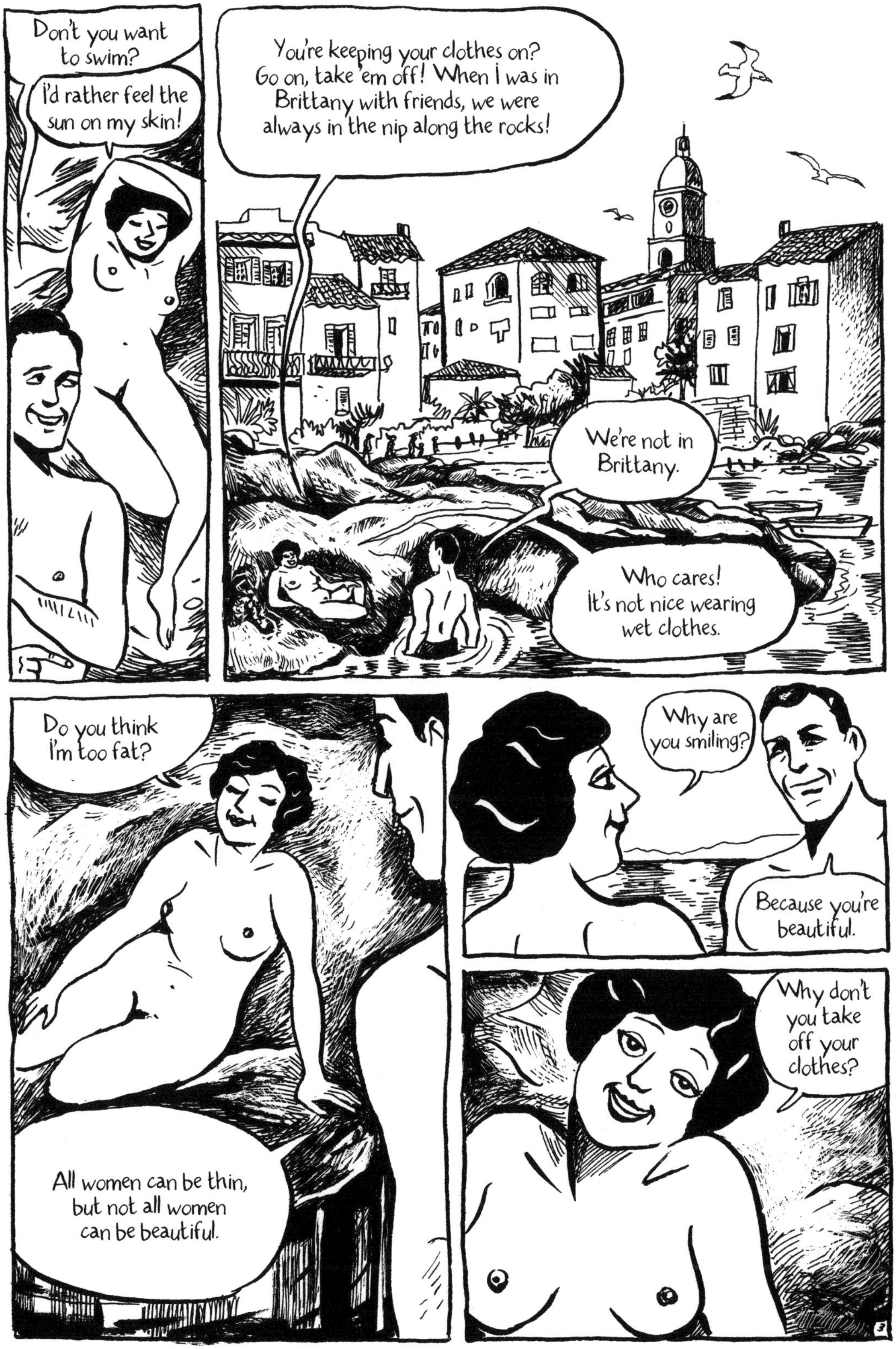
Don't you want to swim?
I'd rather feel the sun on my skin!
You're keeping your clothes on? Go on, take 'em off! When I was in Brittany with friends, we were always in the nip along the rocks!
We're not in Brittany.
Who cares! It's not nice wearing wet clothes.
Do you think I'm too fat?
All women can be thin, but not all women can be beautiful.
Why are you smiling?
Because you're beautiful.
Why don't you take off your clothes?

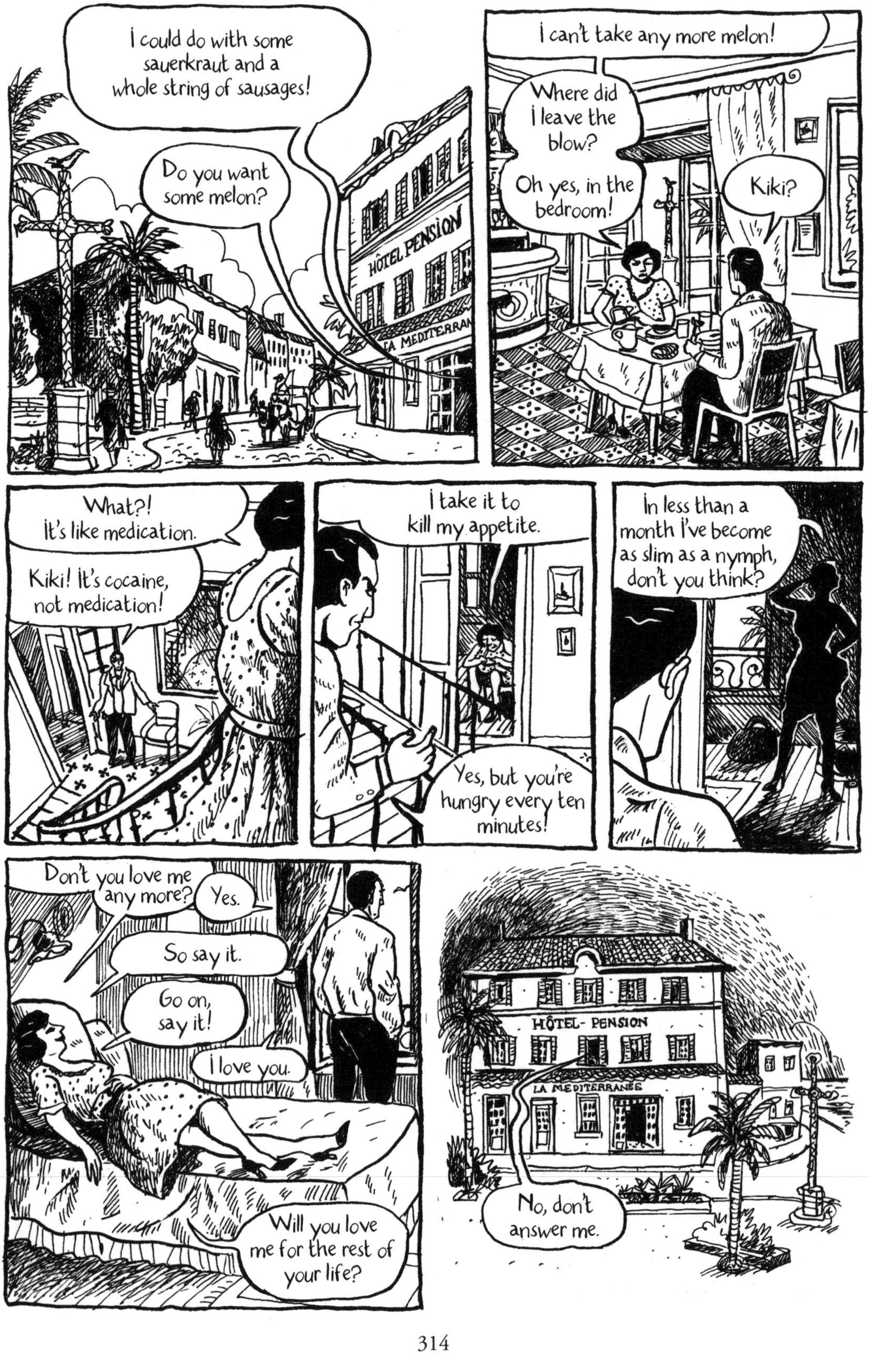
I could do with some sauerkraut and a whole string of sausages!
Do you want some melon?
HÔTEL PENSION
LA MEDITERRAN
I can't take any more melon!
Where did I leave the blow?
Oh yes, in the bedroom!
Kiki?
What?! It's like medication.
Kiki! It's cocaine, not medication!
I take it to kill my appetite.
Yes, but you're hungry every ten minutes!
In less than a month I've become as slim as a nymph, don't you think?
Don't you love me any more?
Yes.
So say it.
Go on, say it!
I love you.
Will you love me for the rest of your life?
HÔTEL- PENSION
LA MEDITERRANEE
No, don't answer me.

1932 - Berlin

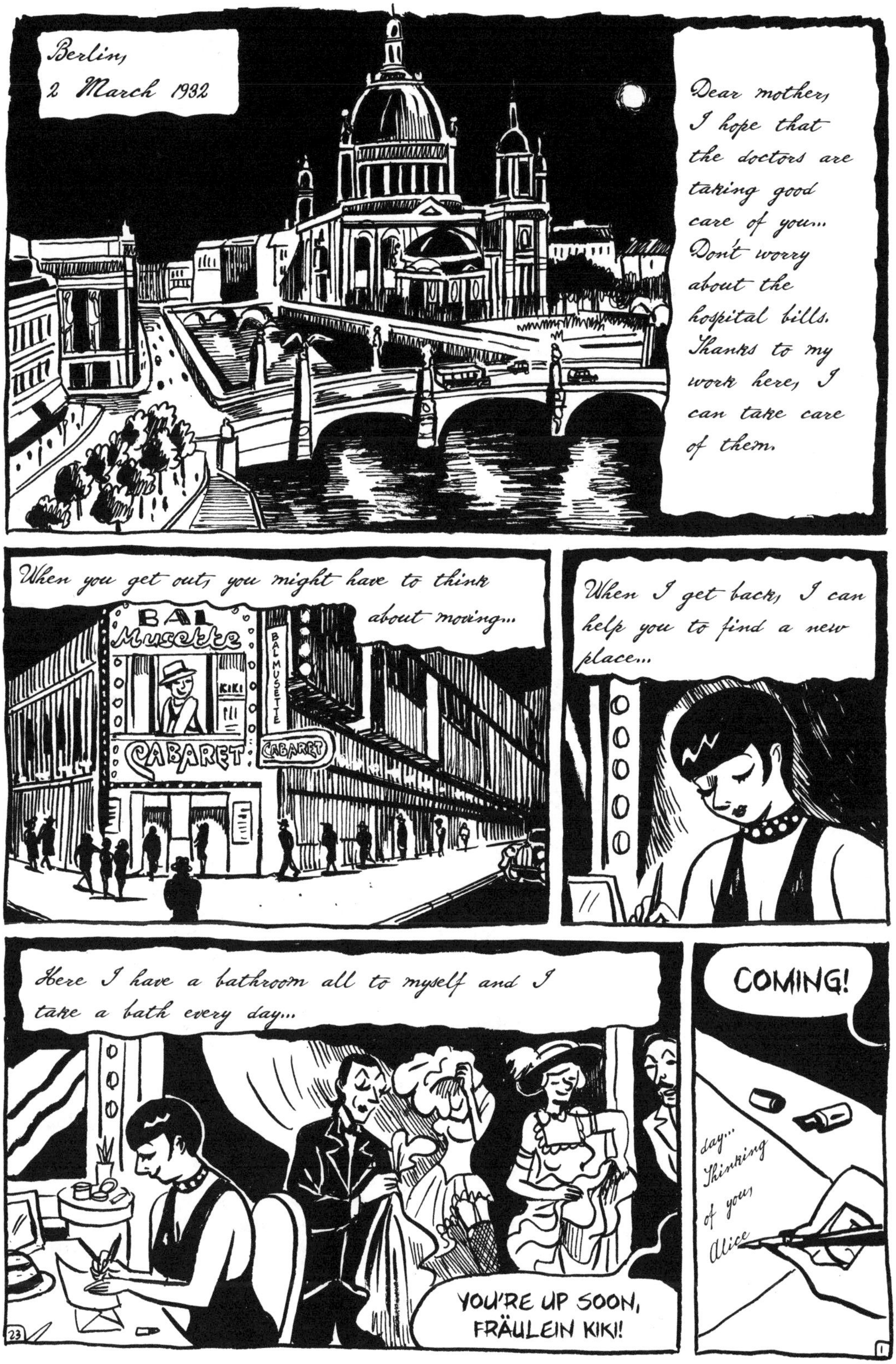
Berlin,
2 March 1932
Dear mother,
I hope that the doctors are taking good care of you... Don't worry about the hospital bills. Thanks to my work here, I can take care of them.
When you get out, you might have to think about moving...
BAL Musette
BAL MUSETTE
KIKI
CABARET
CABARET
When I get back, I can help you to find a new place...
Here I have a bathroom all to myself and I take a bath every day...
YOU'RE UP SOON, FRÄULEIN KIKI!
COMING!
day... Thinking of you,
Alice

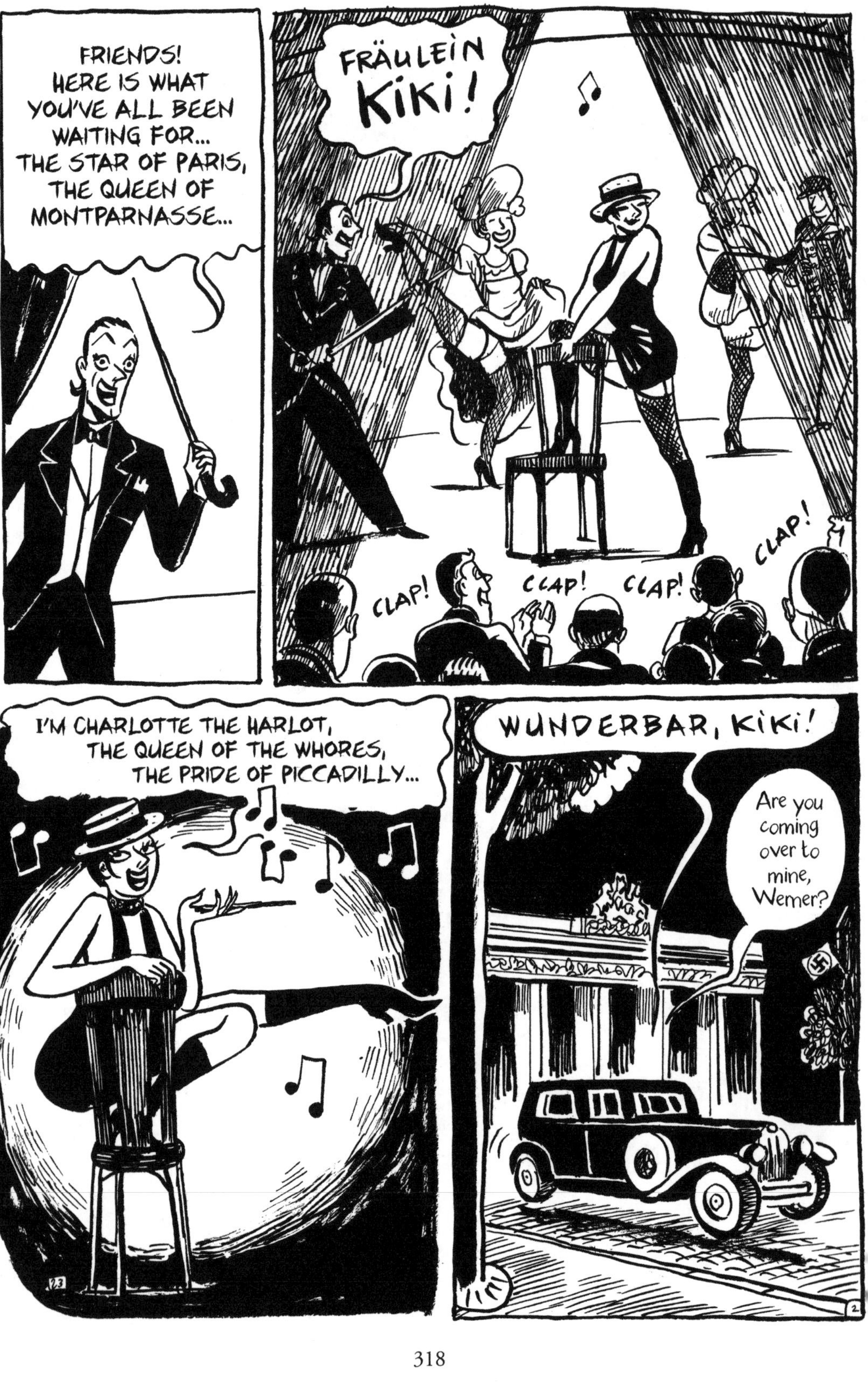

FRIENDS! HERE IS WHAT YOU'VE ALL BEEN WAITING FOR... THE STAR OF PARIS, THE QUEEN OF MONTPARNASSE...
FRÄULEIN KIKI!
CLAP!
CLAP!
CLAP!
CLAP!
I'M CHARLOTTE THE HARLOT, THE QUEEN OF THE WHORES, THE PRIDE OF PICCADILLY...
WUNDERBAR, KIKI!
Are you coming over to mine, Wemer?

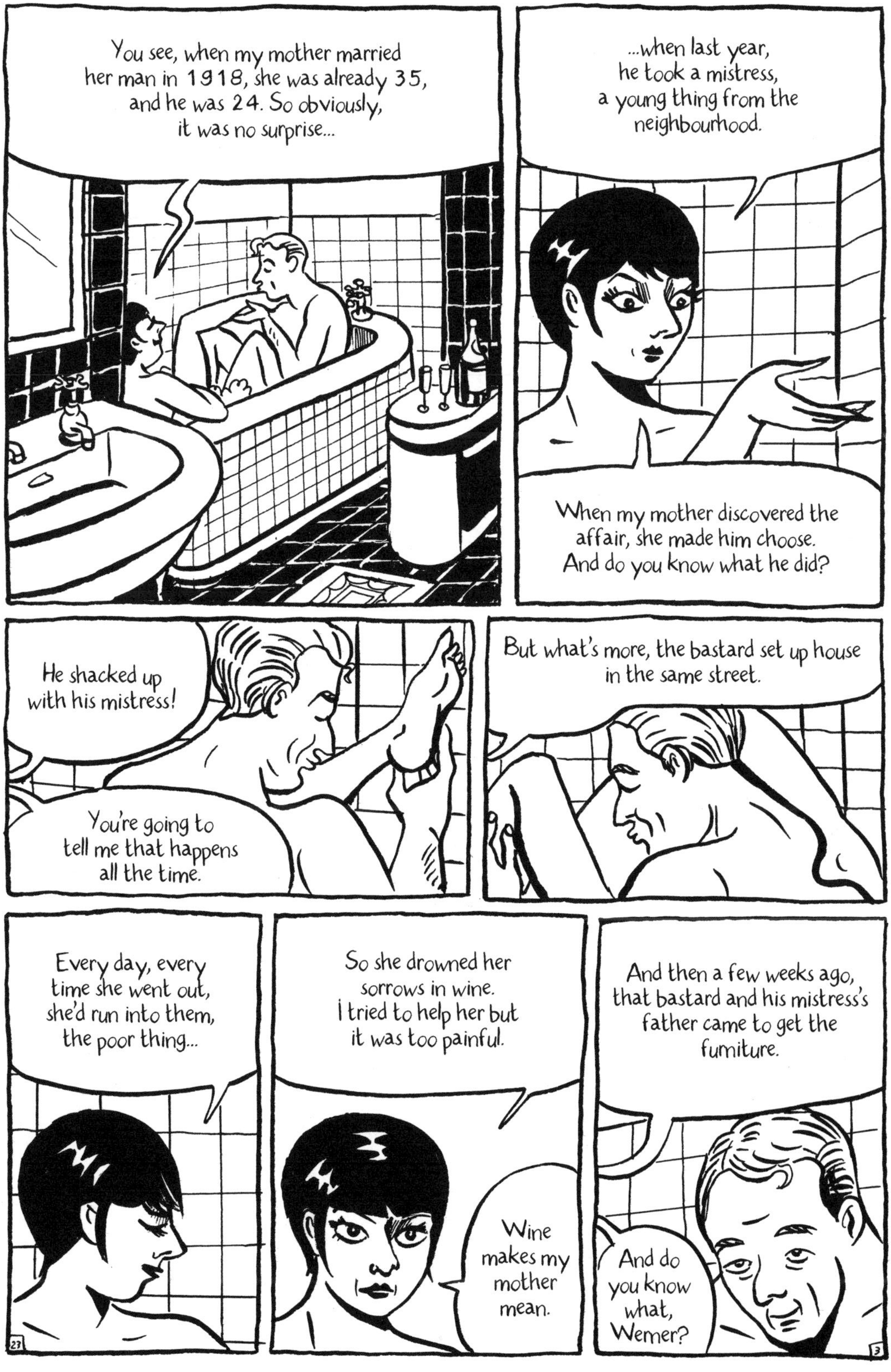
You see, when my mother married her man in 1918, she was already 35, and he was 24. So obviously, it was no surprise...
...when last year, he took a mistress, a young thing from the neighbourhood.
When my mother discovered the affair, she made him choose. And do you know what he did?
He shacked up with his mistress!
You're going to tell me that happens all the time.
But what's more, the bastard set up house in the same street.
Every day, every time she went out, she'd run into them, the poor thing...
So she drowned her sorrows in wine. I tried to help her but it was too painful.
Wine makes my mother mean.
And then a few weeks ago, that bastard and his mistress's father came to get the furniture.
And do you know what, Werner?

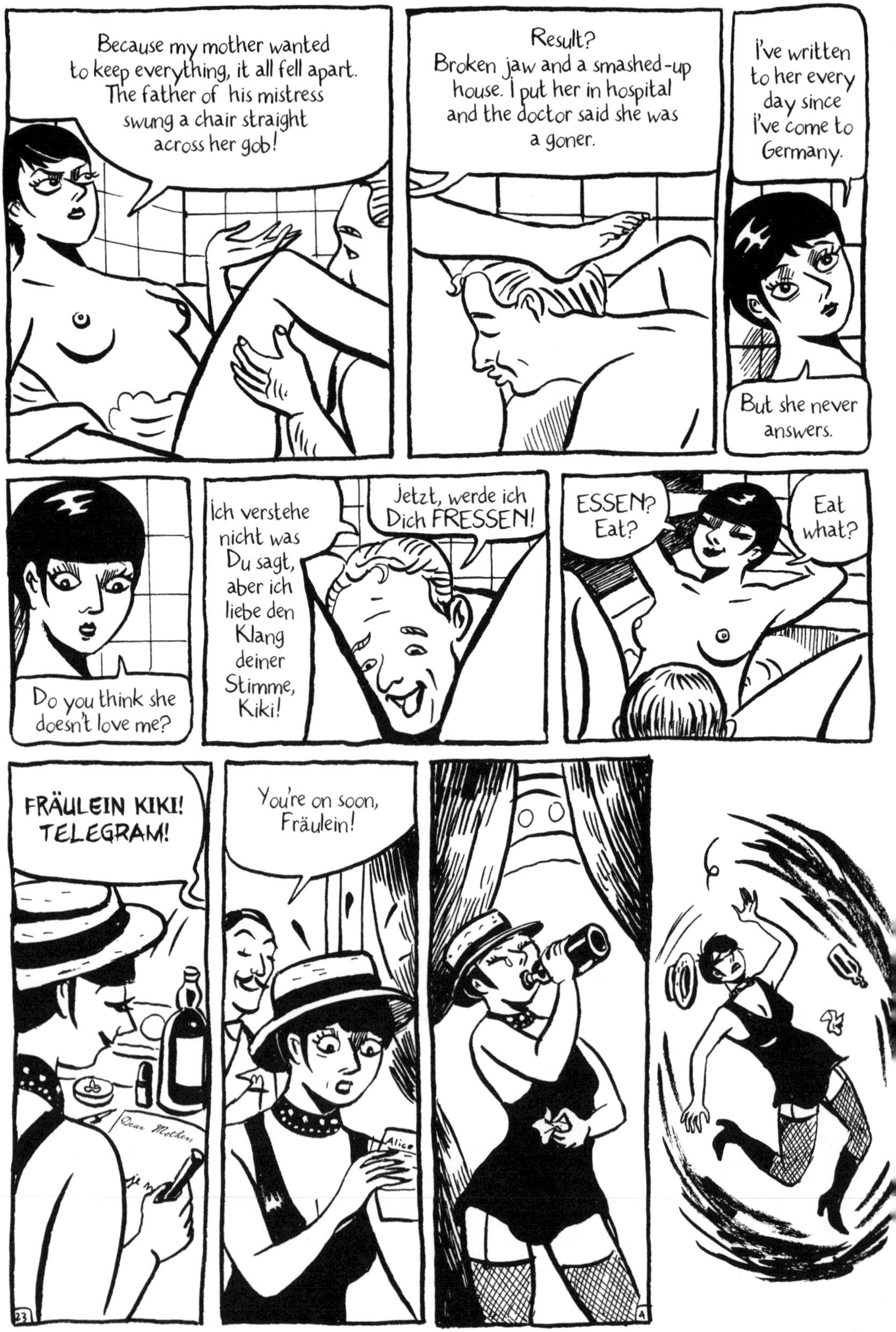
Because my mother wanted to keep everything, it all fell apart. The father of his mistress swung a chair straight across her gob!
Result? Broken jaw and a smashed-up house. I put her in hospital and the doctor said she was a goner.
I've written to her every day since I've come to Germany.
But she never answers.
Do you think she doesn't love me?
Ich verstehe nicht was Du sagt, aber ich liebe den Klang deiner Stimme, Kiki!
Jetzt, werde ich Dich FRESSEN!
ESSEN? Eat?
Eat what?
FRÄULEIN KIKI! TELEGRAM!
Dear Mother
You're on soon, Fräulein!
Alice

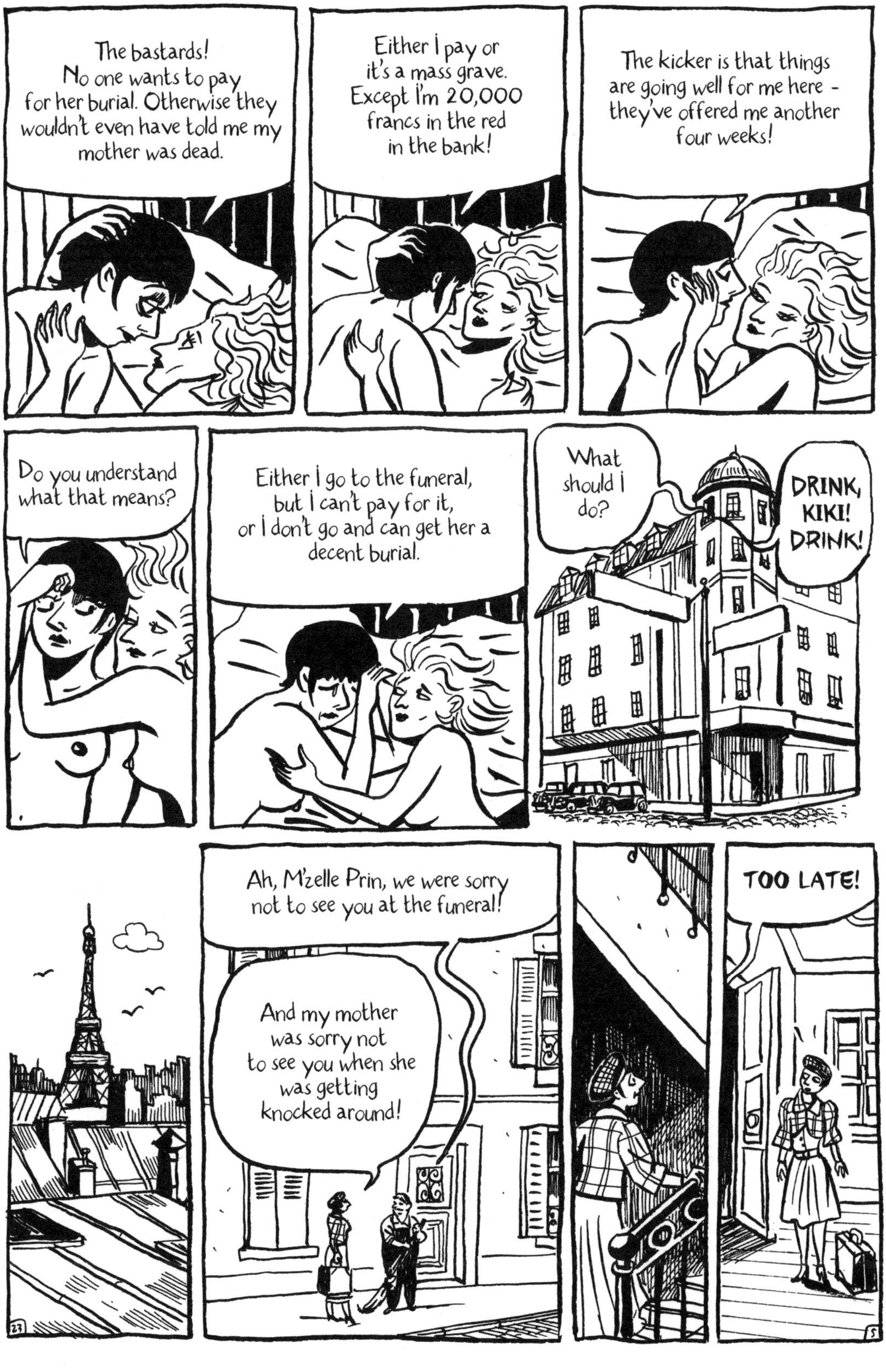

The bastards! No one wants to pay for her burial. Otherwise they wouldn't even have told me my mother was dead.
Either I pay or it's a mass grave. Except I'm 20,000 francs in the red in the bank!
The kicker is that things are going well for me here - they've offered me another four weeks!
Do you understand what that means?
Either I go to the funeral, but I can't pay for it, or I don't go and can get her a decent burial.
What should I do?
DRINK, KIKI! DRINK!
Ah, M'zelle Prin, we were sorry not to see you at the funeral!
And my mother was sorry not to see you when she was getting knocked around!
TOO LATE!

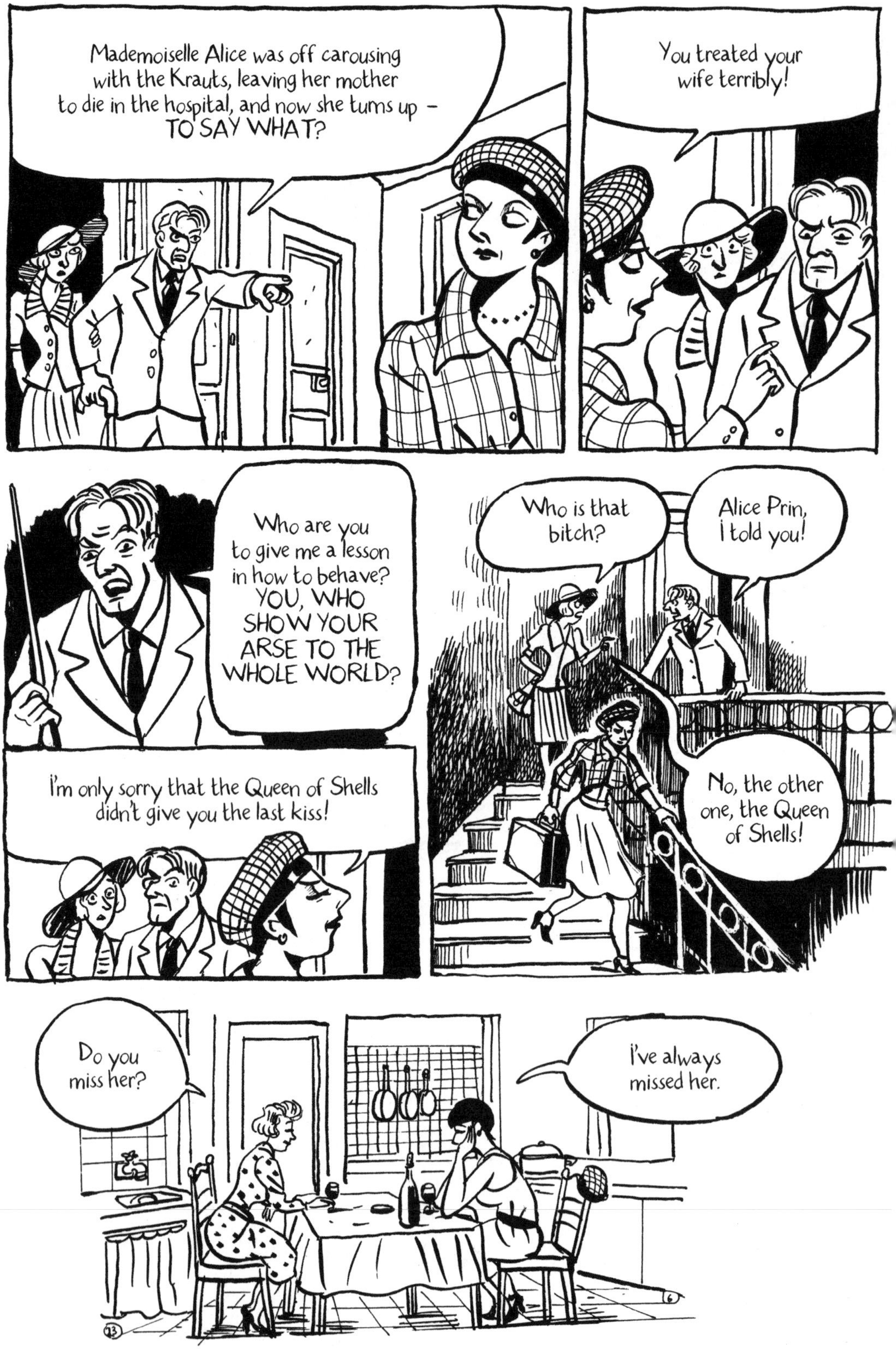

Mademoiselle Alice was off carousing with the Krauts, leaving her mother to die in the hospital, and now she turns up – TO SAY WHAT?
You treated your wife terribly!
Who are you to give me a lesson in how to behave? YOU, WHO SHOW YOUR ARSE TO THE WHOLE WORLD?
I'm only sorry that the Queen of Shells didn't give you the last kiss!
Who is that bitch?
Alice Prin, I told you!
No, the other one, the Queen of Shells!
Do you miss her?
I've always missed her.

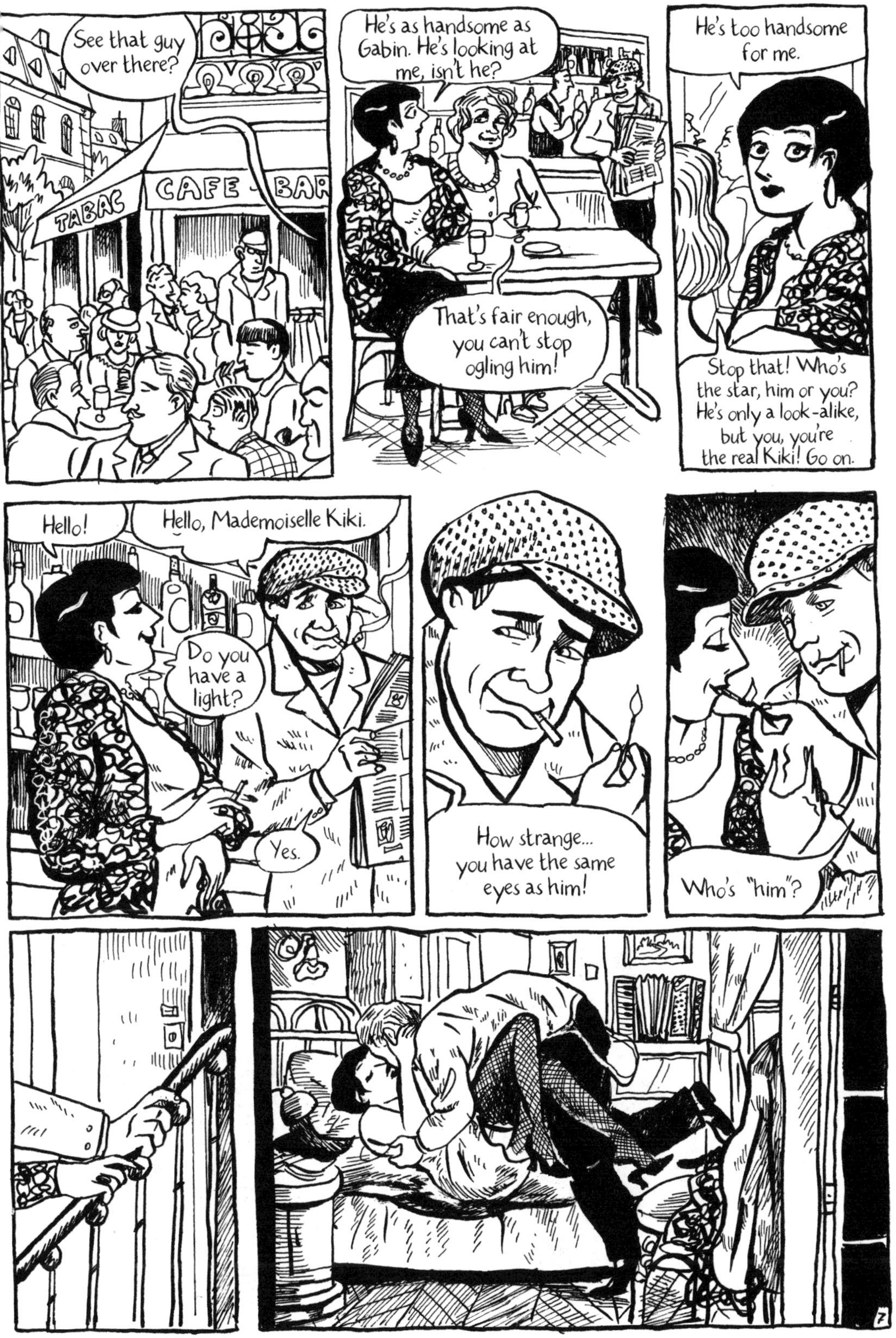

See that guy over there?
He's as handsome as Gabin. He's looking at me, isn't he?
That's fair enough, you can't stop ogling him!
He's too handsome for me.
Stop that! Who's the star, him or you? He's only a look-alike, but you, you're the real Kiki! Go on.
Hello!
Hello, Mademoiselle Kiki.
Do you have a light?
Yes.
How strange... you have the same eyes as him!
Who's "him"?

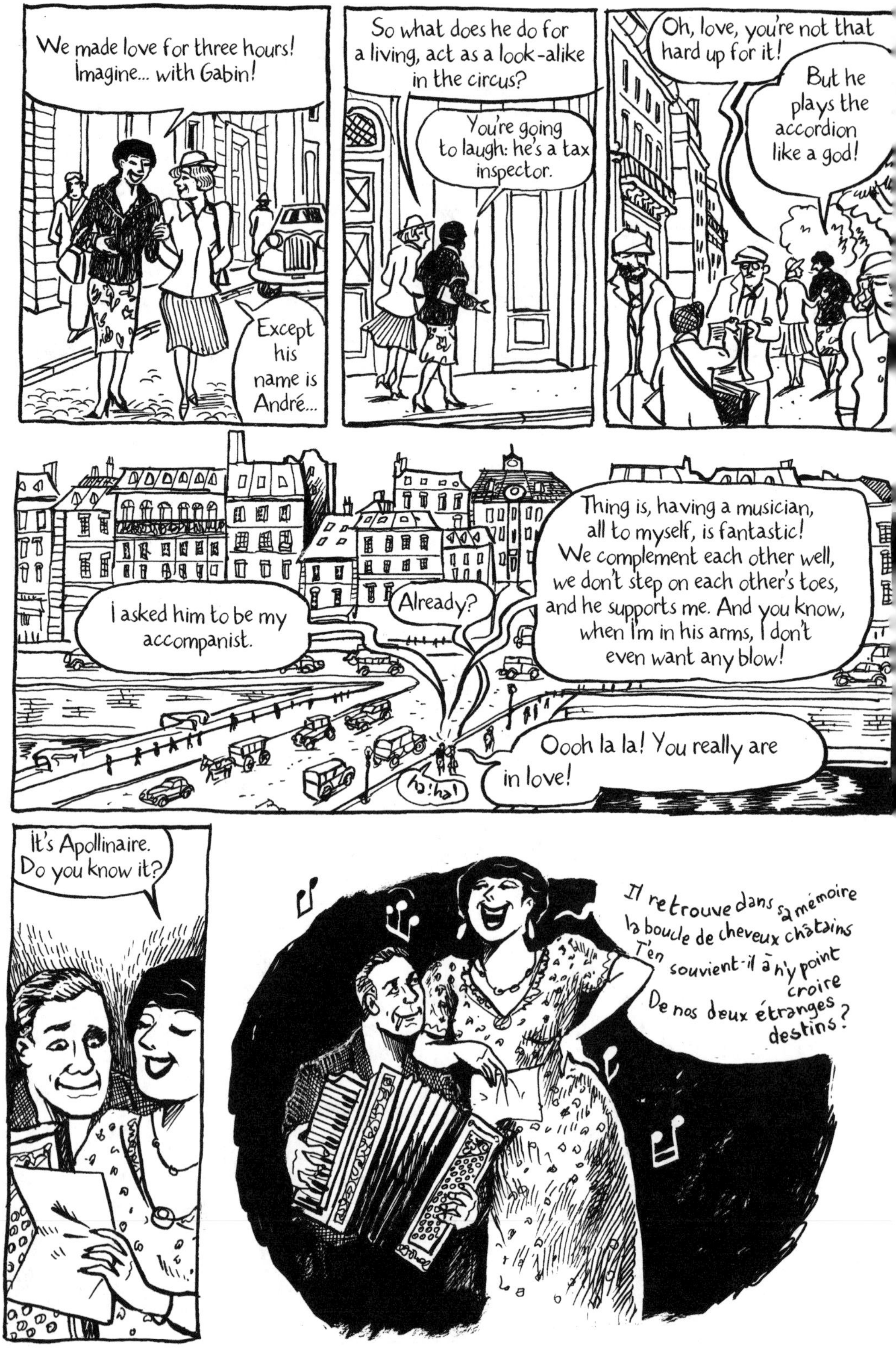
We made love for three hours! Imagine... with Gabin!
Except his name is André...
So what does he do for a living, act as a look-alike in the circus?
You're going to laugh: he's a tax inspector.
Oh, love, you're not that hard up for it!
But he plays the accordion like a god!
I asked him to be my accompanist.
Already?
Thing is, having a musician, all to myself, is fantastic! We complement each other well, we don't step on each other's toes, and he supports me. And you know, when I'm in his arms, I don't even want any blow!
Oooh la la! You really are in love!
ha! ha!
It's Apollinaire. Do you know it?
Il retrouve dans sa mémoire
la boucle de cheveux châtains
T'en souvient-il à n'y point croire
De nos deux étranges destins?

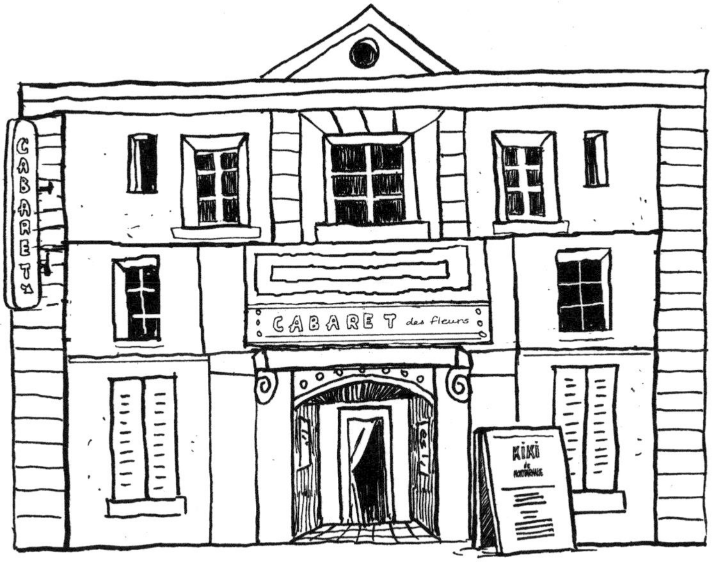
CABARET
CABARET des fleurs
KIKI

1934 - Cabaret Kiki

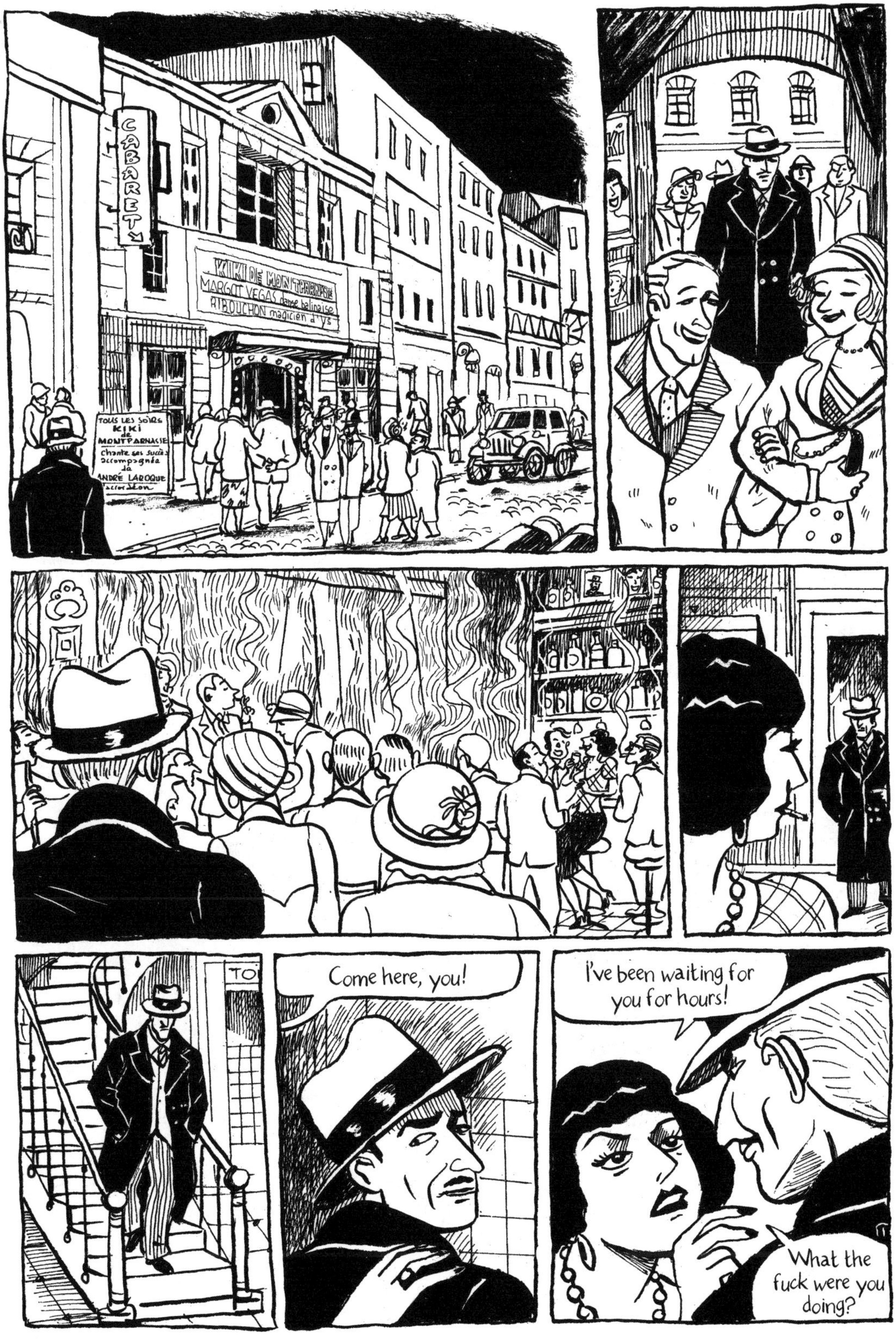
CABARET
KIKI DE MONTPARNASSE
MARGOT VEGAS danse balinaise
RIBOUCHON magicien d'ys
TOUS LES SOIRS
KIKI
de
MONTPARNASSE
chante ses succès
accompagnée
de
ANDRÉ LAROQUE
Come here, you!
I've been waiting for you for hours!
What the fuck were you doing?

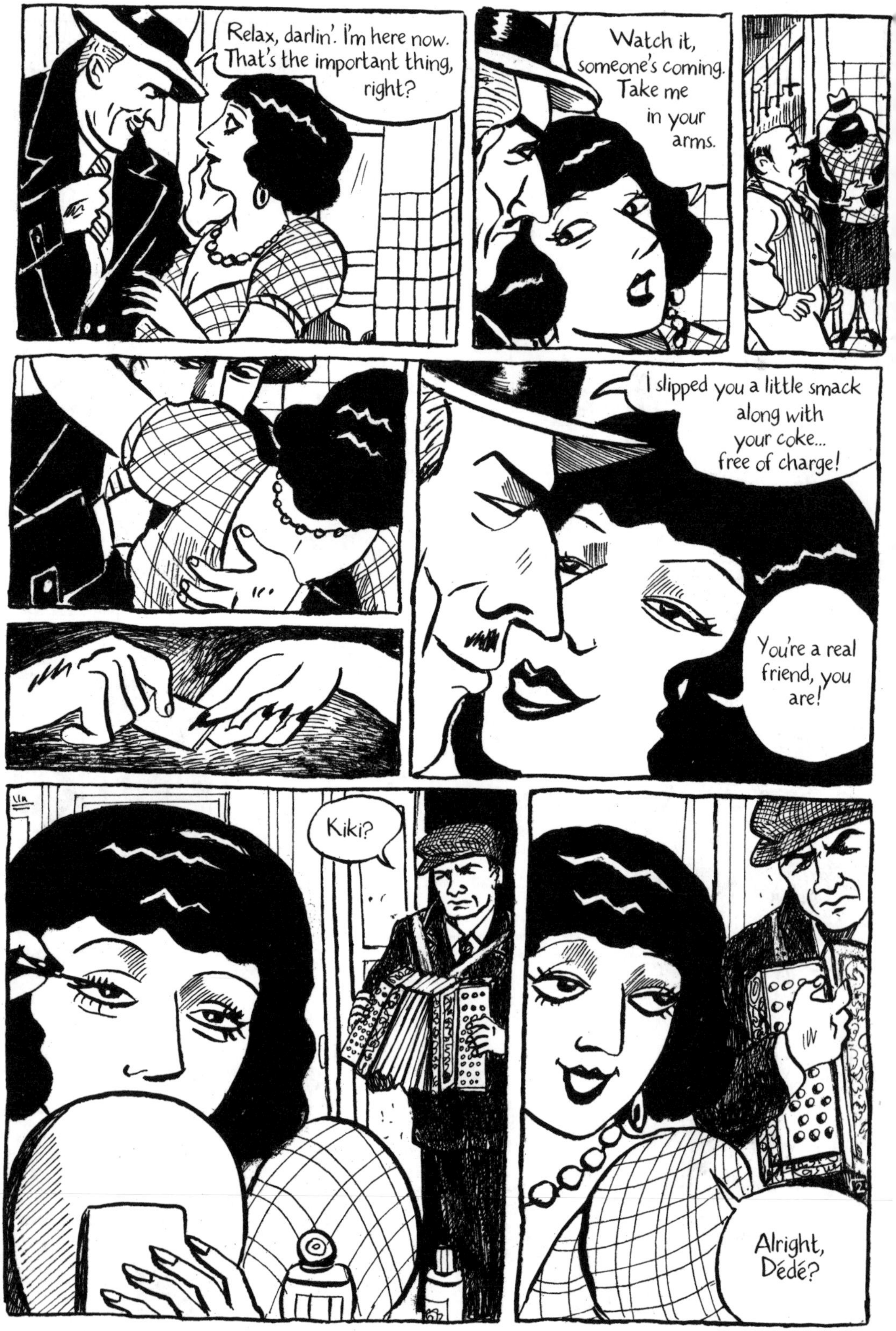

Relax, darlin'. I'm here now. That's the important thing, right?
Watch it, someone's coming. Take me in your arms.
I slipped you a little smack along with your coke... free of charge!
You're a real friend, you are!
Kiki?
Alright, Dédé?

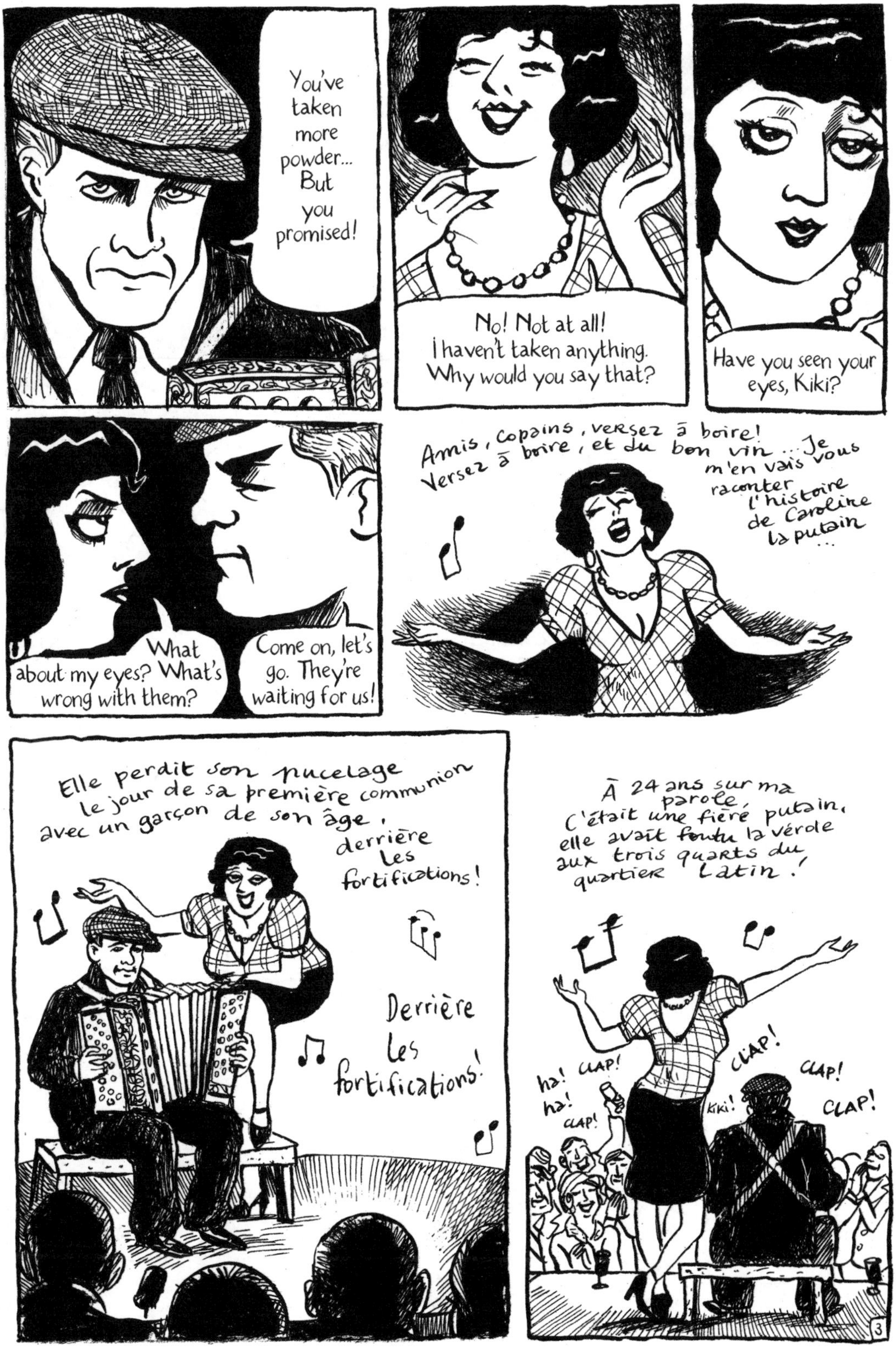
You've taken more powder... But you promised!
No! Not at all! I haven't taken anything. Why would you say that?
Have you seen your eyes, Kiki?
What about my eyes? What's wrong with them?
Come on, let's go. They're waiting for us!
Amis, copains, versez à boire! Versez à boire, et du bon vin... Je m'en vais vous raconter l'histoire de Caroline la putain...
Elle perdit son pucelage le jour de sa première communion avec un garçon de son âge, derrière les fortifications!
Derrière les fortifications!
À 24 ans sur ma parole, C'était une fière putain, elle avait foutu la vérole aux trois quarts du quartier Latin!
ha! ha!
CLAP!
CLAP!
KIKI!
CLAP!
CLAP!
CLAP!

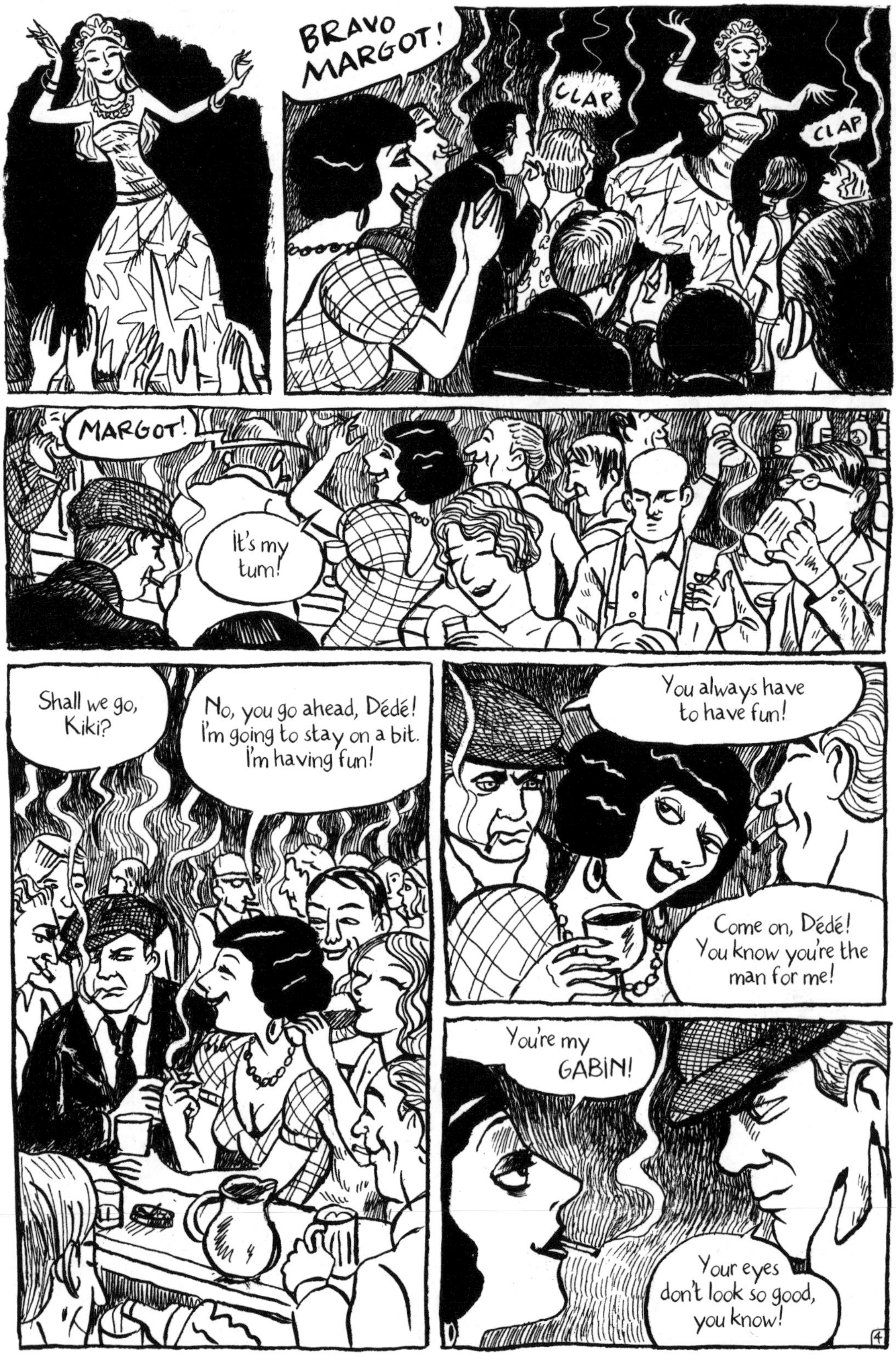
BRAVO MARGOT!
CLAP
CLAP
MARGOT!
It's my turn!
Shall we go, Kiki?
No, you go ahead, Dédé! I'm going to stay on a bit. I'm having fun!
You always have to have fun!
Come on, Dédé! You know you're the man for me!
You're my GABIN!
Your eyes don't look so good, you know!
4

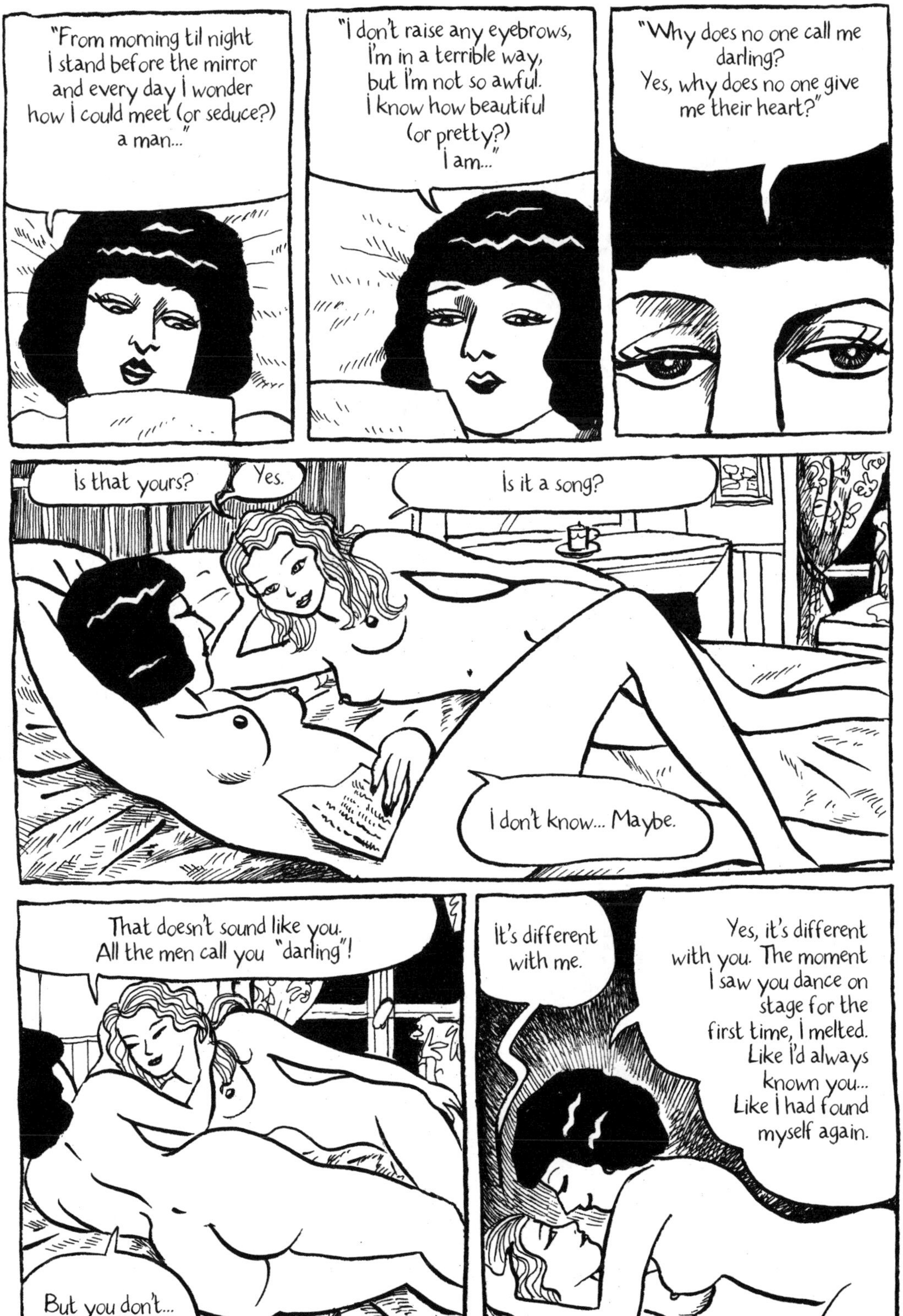
"From morning til night I stand before the mirror and every day I wonder how I could meet (or seduce?) a man..."
"I don't raise any eyebrows, I'm in a terrible way, but I'm not so awful. I know how beautiful (or pretty?) I am..."
"Why does no one call me darling? Yes, why does no one give me their heart?"
Is that yours?
Yes.
Is it a song?
I don't know... Maybe.
That doesn't sound like you. All the men call you "darling"!
But you don't...
It's different with me.
Yes, it's different with you. The moment I saw you dance on stage for the first time, I melted. Like I'd always known you... Like I had found myself again.
5

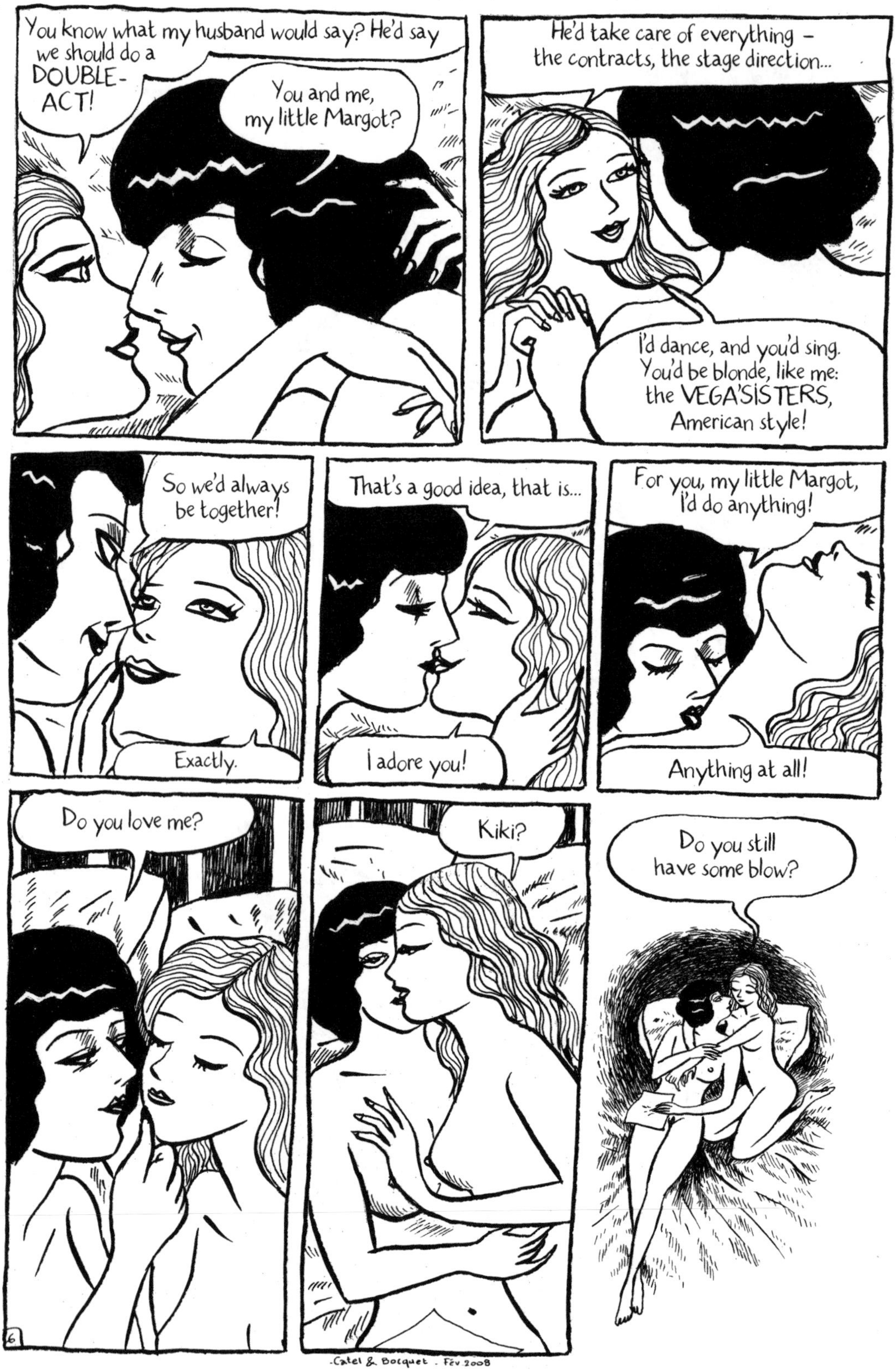
You know what my husband would say? He'd say we should do a DOUBLE-ACT!
You and me, my little Margot?
He'd take care of everything – the contracts, the stage direction...
I'd dance, and you'd sing. You'd be blonde, like me: the VEGA SISTERS, American style!
So we'd always be together!
Exactly.
That's a good idea, that is...
I adore you!
For you, my little Margot, I'd do anything!
Anything at all!
Do you love me?
Kiki?
Do you still have some blow?

-Catel & Bocquet . Fév 2008

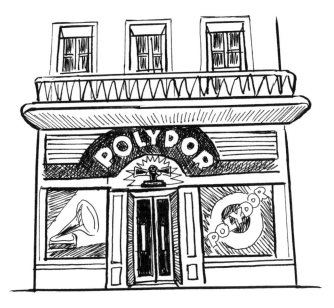

1939 - Studio Polydor, 4 rue de la Gare

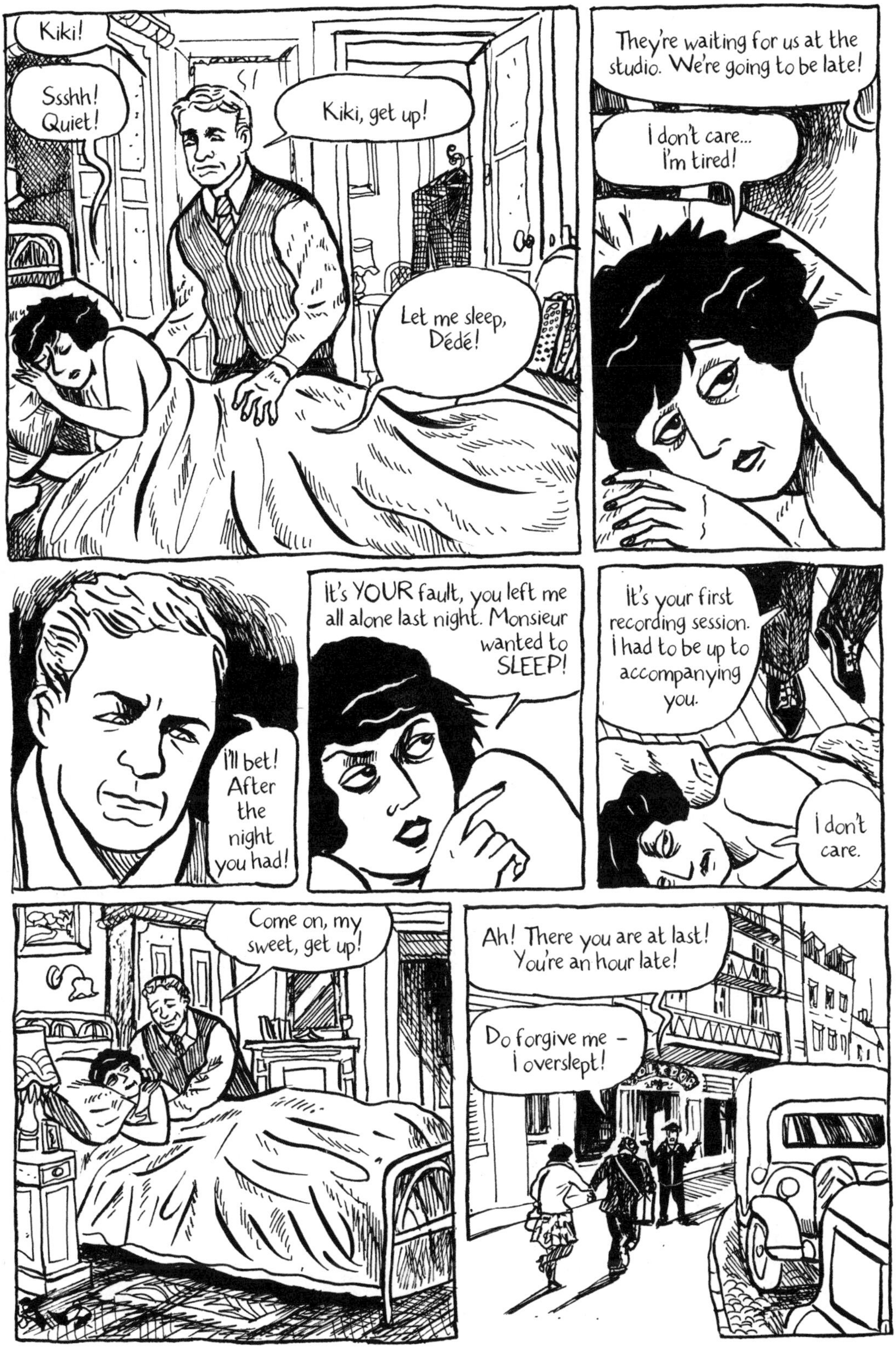

Kiki!
Ssshh! Quiet!
Kiki, get up!
Let me sleep, Dédé!
They're waiting for us at the studio. We're going to be late!
I don't care... I'm tired!
I'll bet! After the night you had!
It's YOUR fault, you left me all alone last night. Monsieur wanted to SLEEP!
It's your first recording session. I had to be up to accompanying you.
I don't care.
Come on, my sweet, get up!
Ah! There you are at last! You're an hour late!
Do forgive me – I overslept!

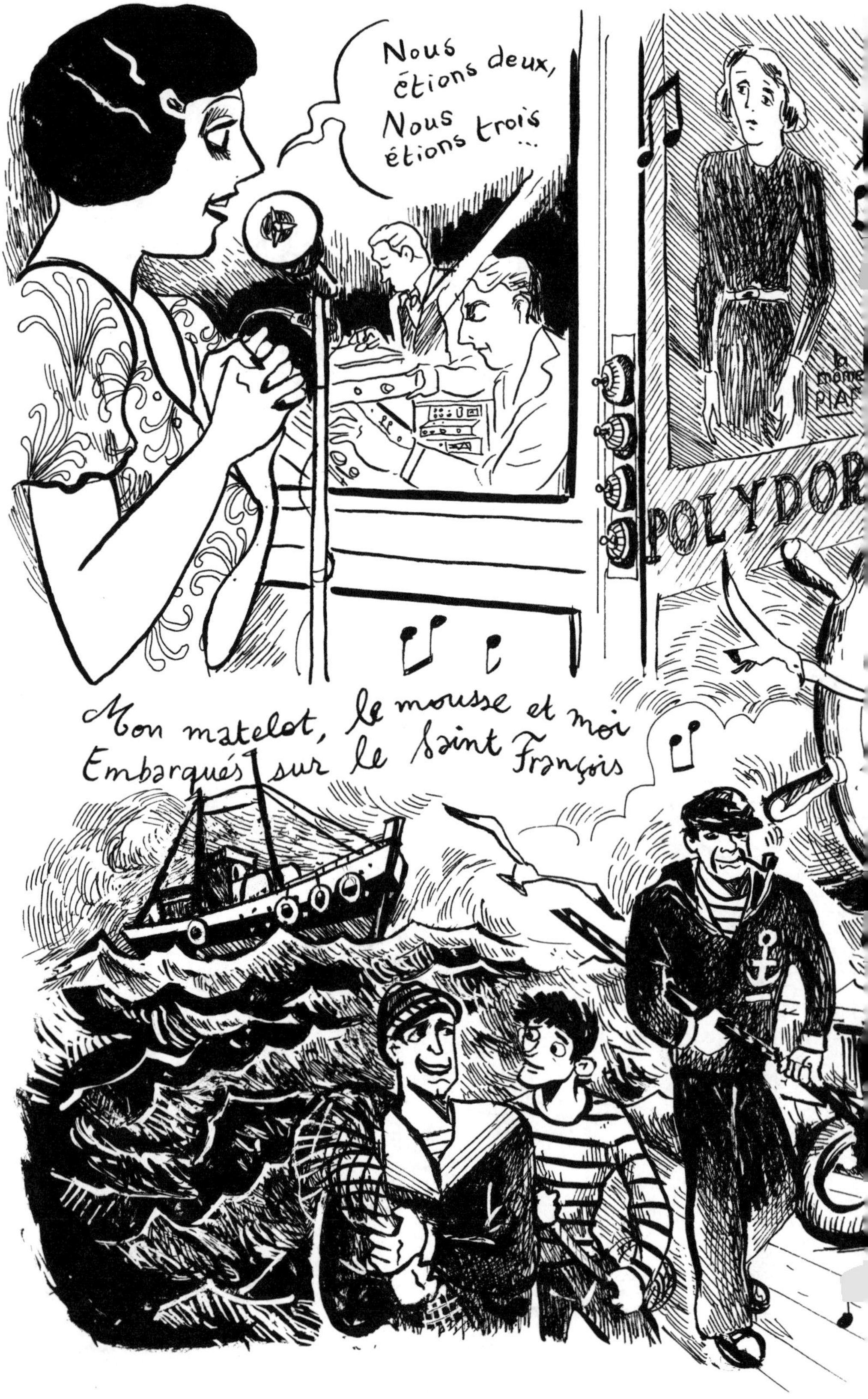
Nous étions deux, Nous étions trois ...
la mome PIAF
POLYDOR
Mon matelot, le mousse et moi
Embarqués sur le Saint François

ois marins de Groix
on tradéritra la la la
on tradéritra la lè-è-ē-re
PHONO DISC
Vint à venter de noroît
A faire céder votre mât!
Ce failli temps mollira pas
Je prends la barre
vas-y mon gars
POLYDOR
KiKi

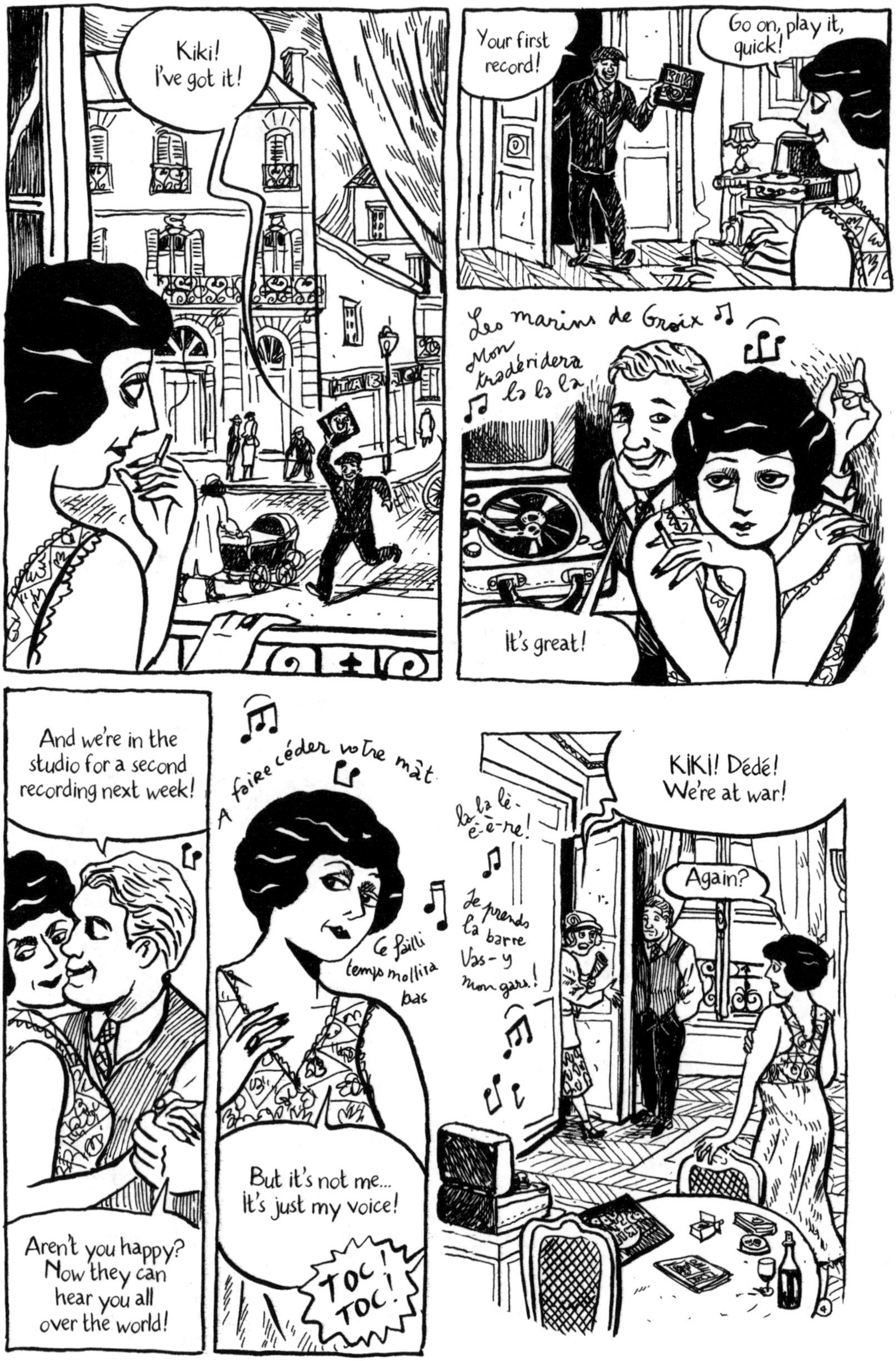
Kiki! I've got it!
Your first record!
Go on, play it, quick!
Les marins de Groix
Mon tradéridera la la la
It's great!
And we're in the studio for a second recording next week!
Aren't you happy? Now they can hear you all over the world!
A faire céder votre mât
Ce failli temps mollira bas
But it's not me... It's just my voice!
TOC! TOC!
la la lè-è-è-re!
Je prends la barre
Vas-y mon gars!
KiKi! Dédé! We're at war!
Again?

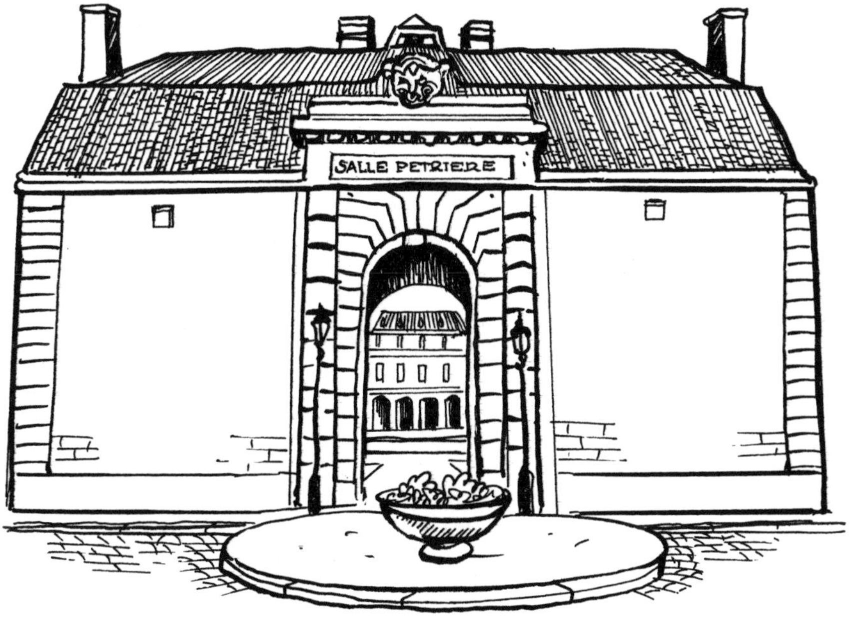
SALLE PETRIERE

1940 - 83 boulevard de l'Hôpital

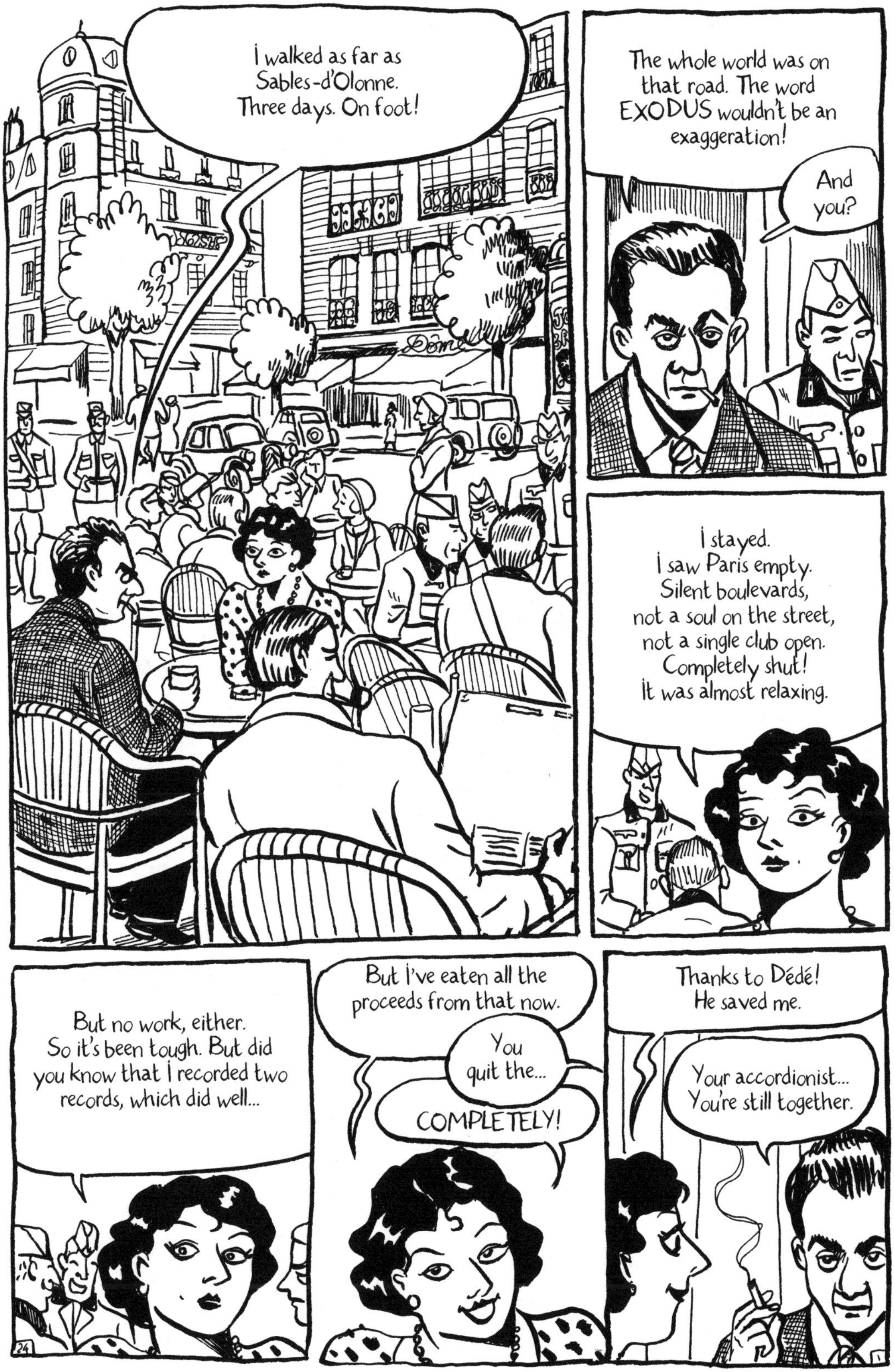
I walked as far as Sables-d'Olonne. Three days. On foot!
Dôme
The whole world was on that road. The word EXODUS wouldn't be an exaggeration!
And you?
I stayed. I saw Paris empty. Silent boulevards, not a soul on the street, not a single club open. Completely shut! It was almost relaxing.
But no work, either. So it's been tough. But did you know that I recorded two records, which did well...
But I've eaten all the proceeds from that now.
You quit the...
COMPLETELY!
Thanks to Dédé! He saved me.
Your accordionist... You're still together.

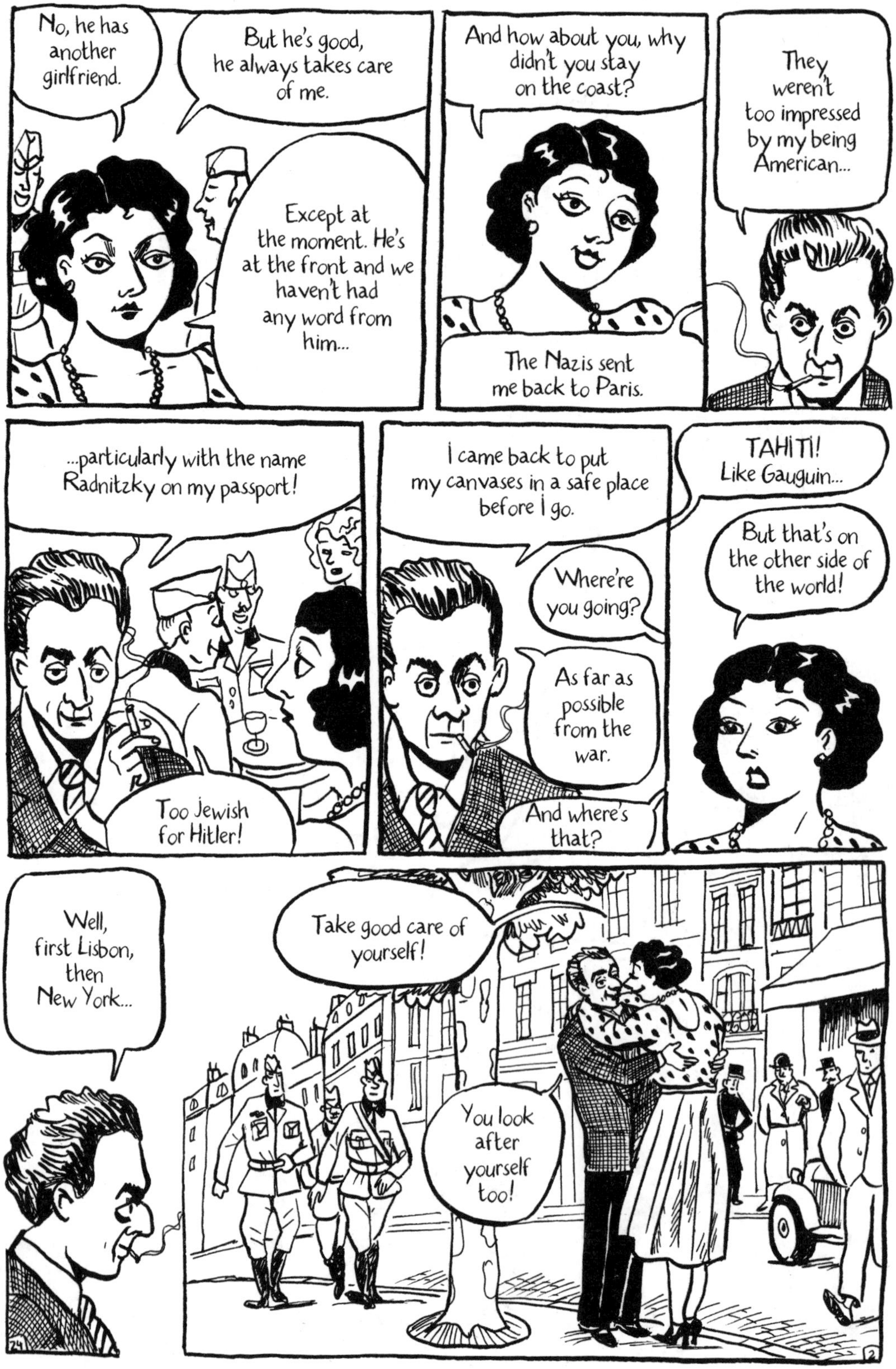
No, he has another girlfriend.
But he's good, he always takes care of me.
Except at the moment. He's at the front and we haven't had any word from him...
And how about you, why didn't you stay on the coast?
The Nazis sent me back to Paris.
They weren't too impressed by my being American...
...particularly with the name Radnitzky on my passport!
Too Jewish for Hitler!
I came back to put my canvases in a safe place before I go.
Where're you going?
As far as possible from the war.
And where's that?
TAHITI! Like Gauguin...
But that's on the other side of the world!
Well, first Lisbon, then New York...
Take good care of yourself!
You look after yourself too!

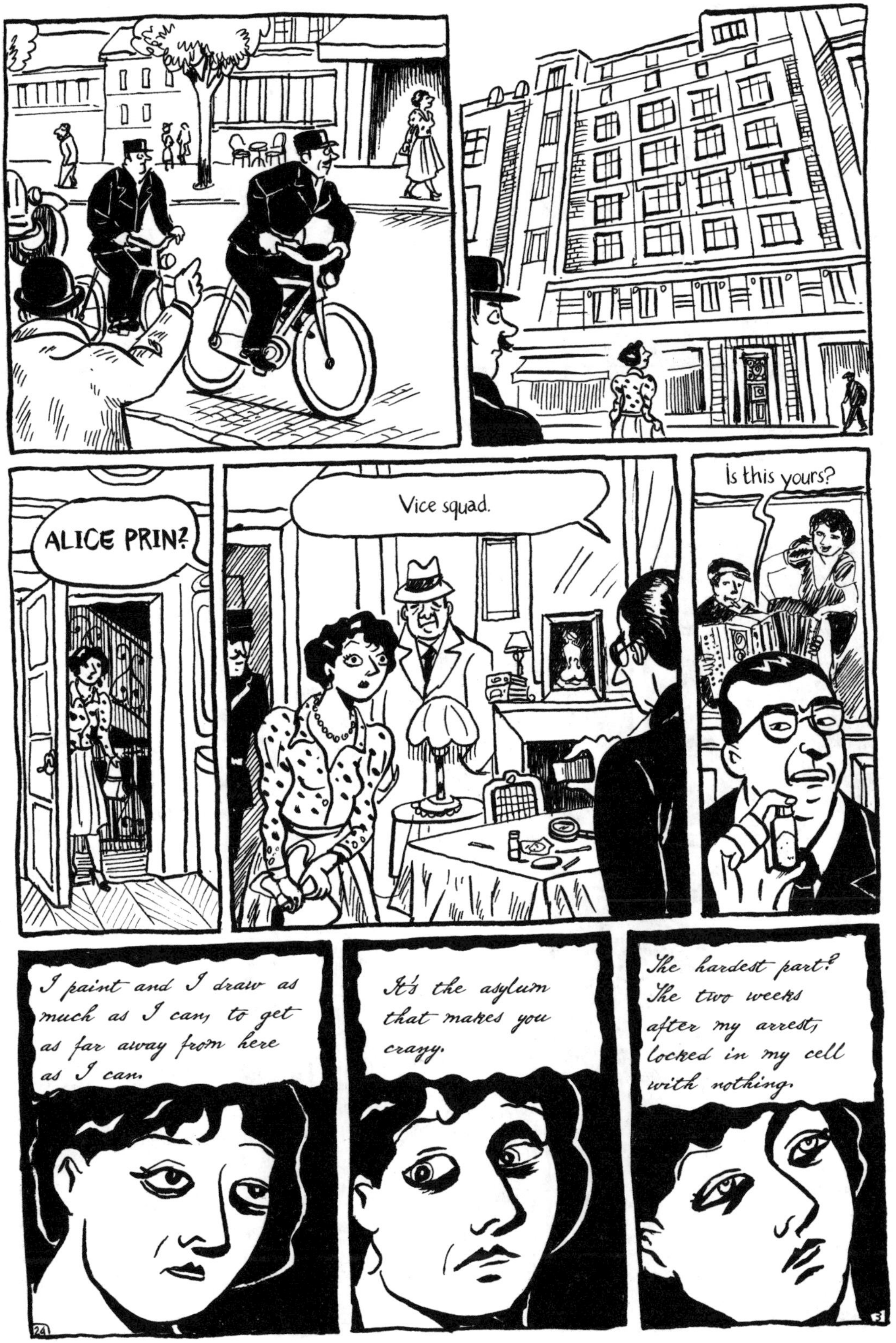
ALICE PRIN?
Vice squad.
Is this yours?
I paint and I draw as much as I can, to get as far away from here as I can.
It's the asylum that makes you crazy.
The hardest part? The two weeks after my arrest, locked in my cell with nothing.
24

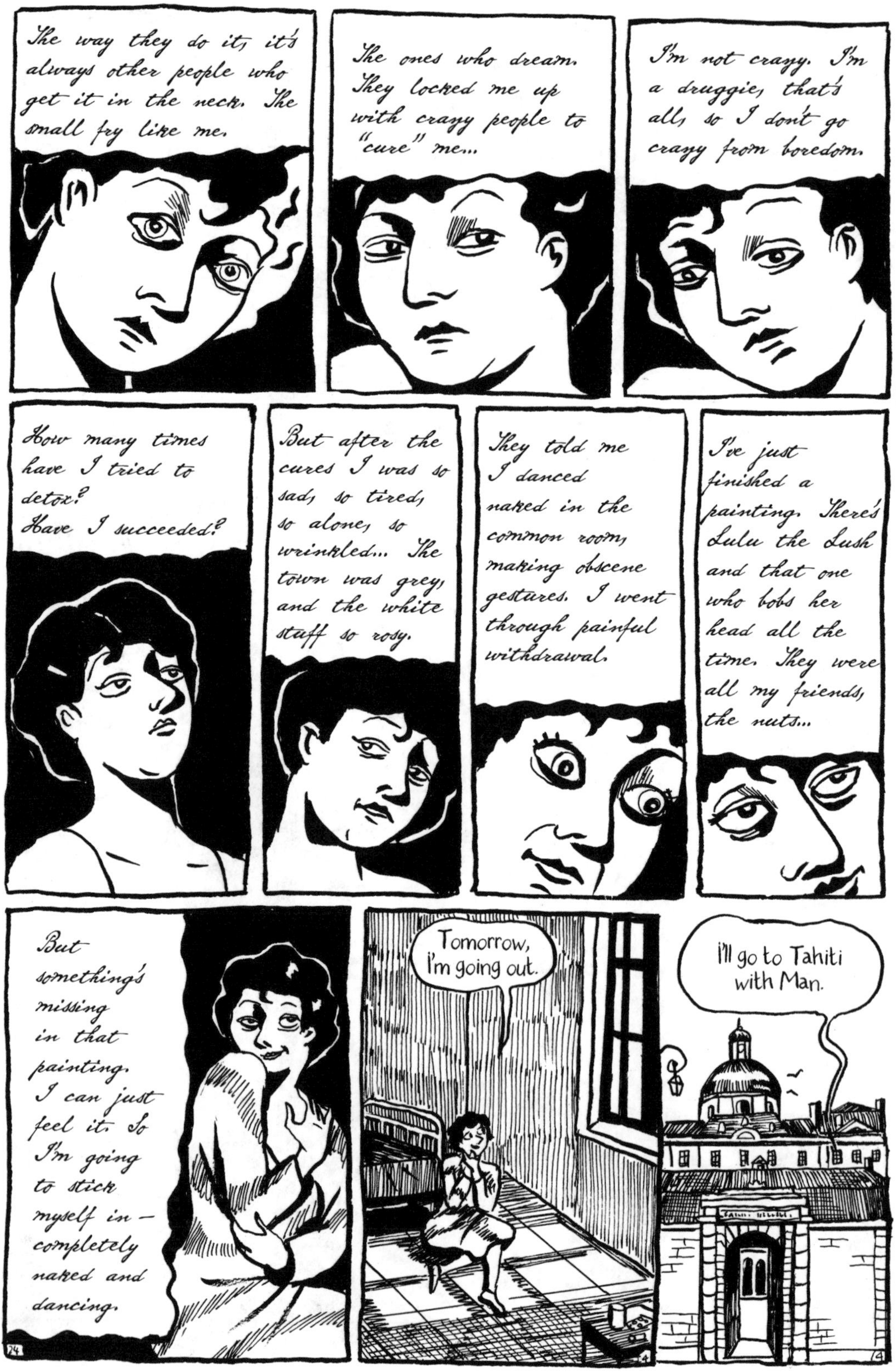
The way they do it, it's always other people who get it in the neck. The small fry like me.
The ones who dream. They locked me up with crazy people to "cure" me...
I'm not crazy. I'm a druggie, that's all, so I don't go crazy from boredom.
How many times have I tried to detox? Have I succeeded?
But after the cures I was so sad, so tired, so alone, so wrinkled... The town was grey, and the white staff so rosy.
They told me I danced naked in the common room, making obscene gestures. I went through painful withdrawal.
I've just finished a painting. There's Lulu the Lush and that one who bobs her head all the time. They were all my friends, the nuts...
But something's missing in that painting. I can just feel it. So I'm going to stick myself in – completely naked and dancing.
Tomorrow, I'm going out.
I'll go to Tahiti with Man.

1943 - L'Île Bouchard - La Commanderie

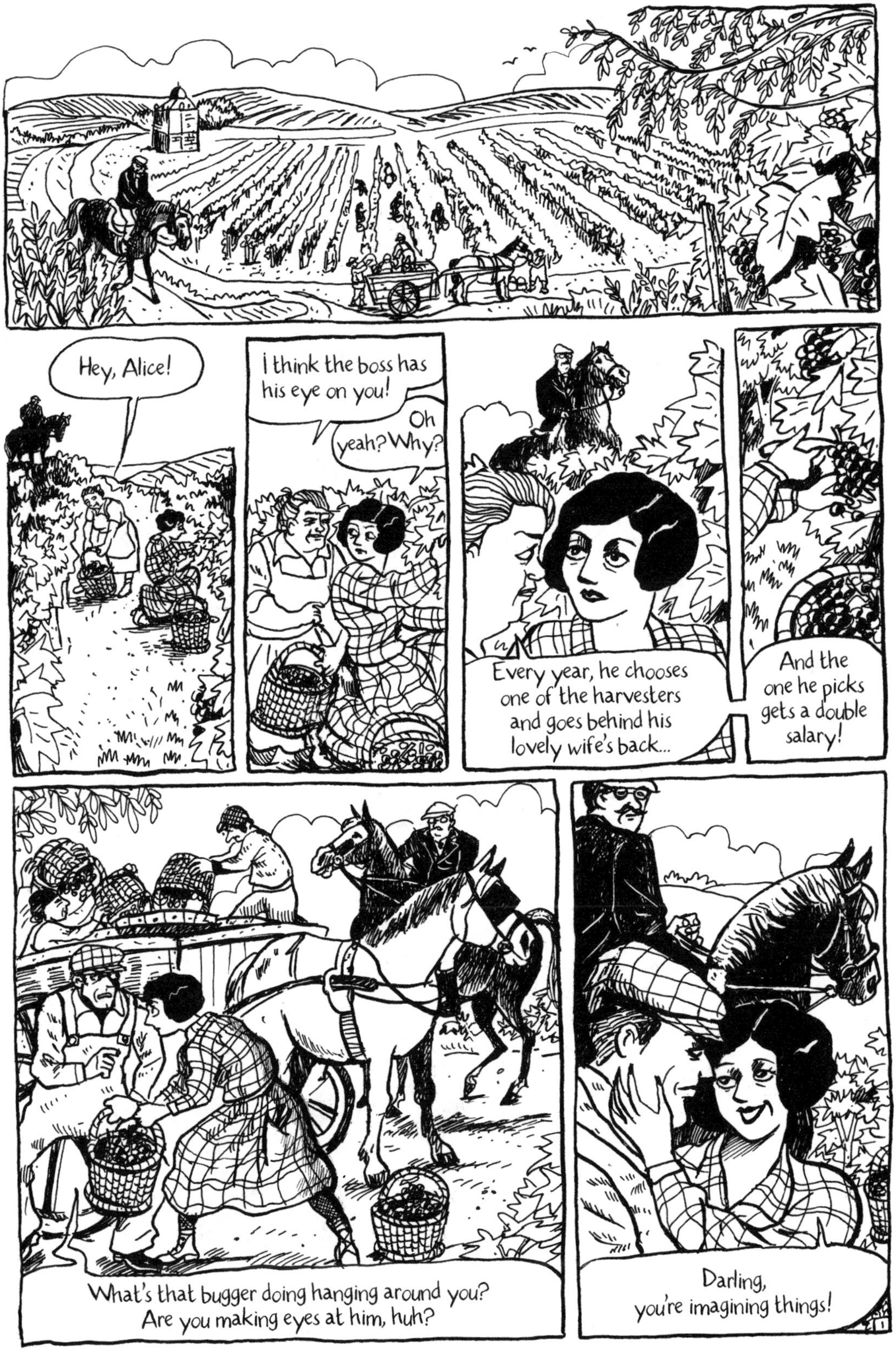
Hey, Alice!
I think the boss has his eye on you!
Oh yeah? Why?
Every year, he chooses one of the harvesters and goes behind his lovely wife's back...
And the one he picks gets a double salary!
What's that bugger doing hanging around you? Are you making eyes at him, huh?
Darling, you're imagining things!

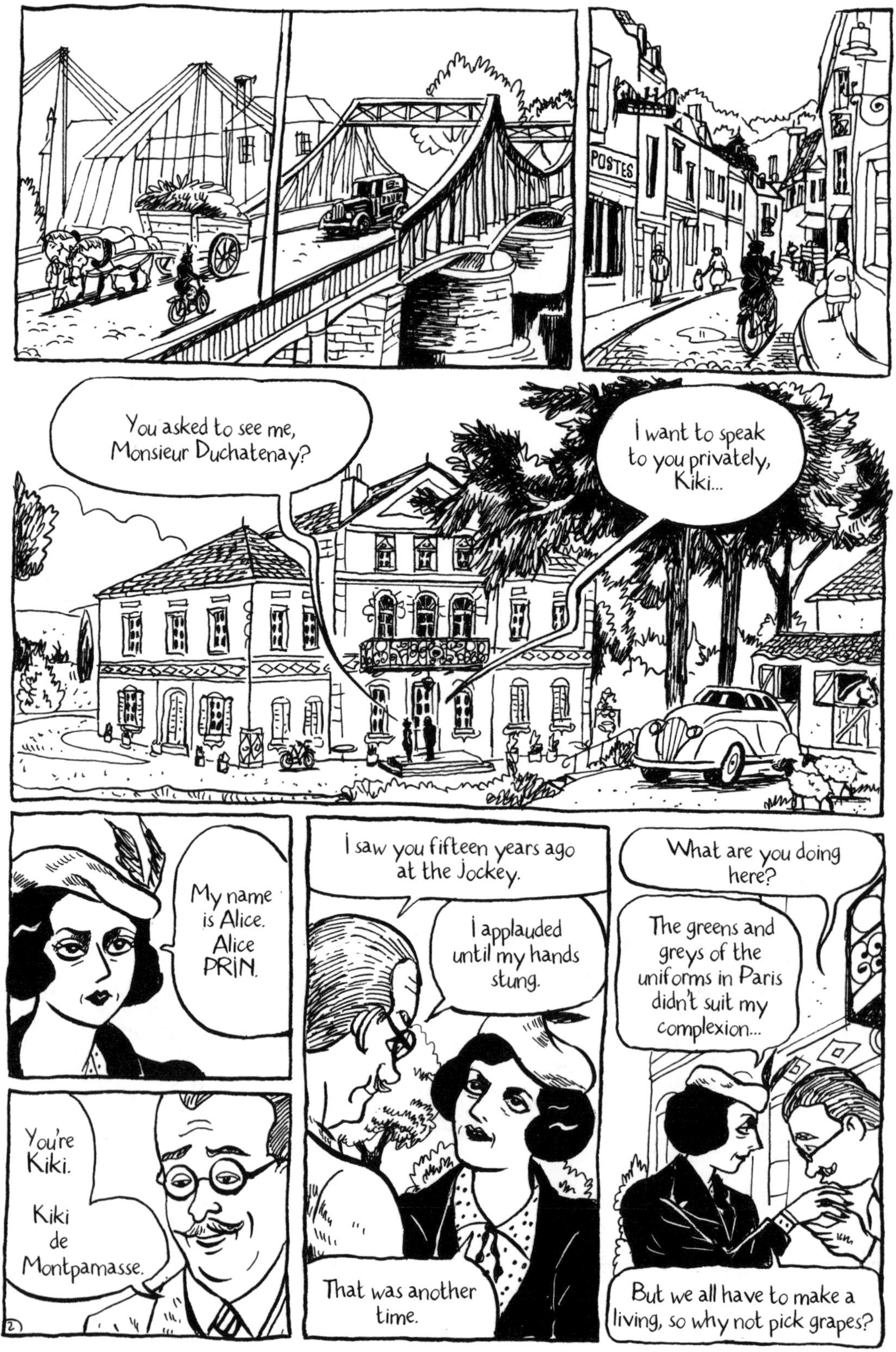
POSTES
You asked to see me, Monsieur Duchatenay?
I want to speak to you privately, Kiki...
My name is Alice. Alice PRIN.
You're Kiki.
Kiki de Montparnasse.
I saw you fifteen years ago at the Jockey.
I applauded until my hands stung.
That was another time.
What are you doing here?
The greens and greys of the uniforms in Paris didn't suit my complexion...
But we all have to make a living, so why not pick grapes?

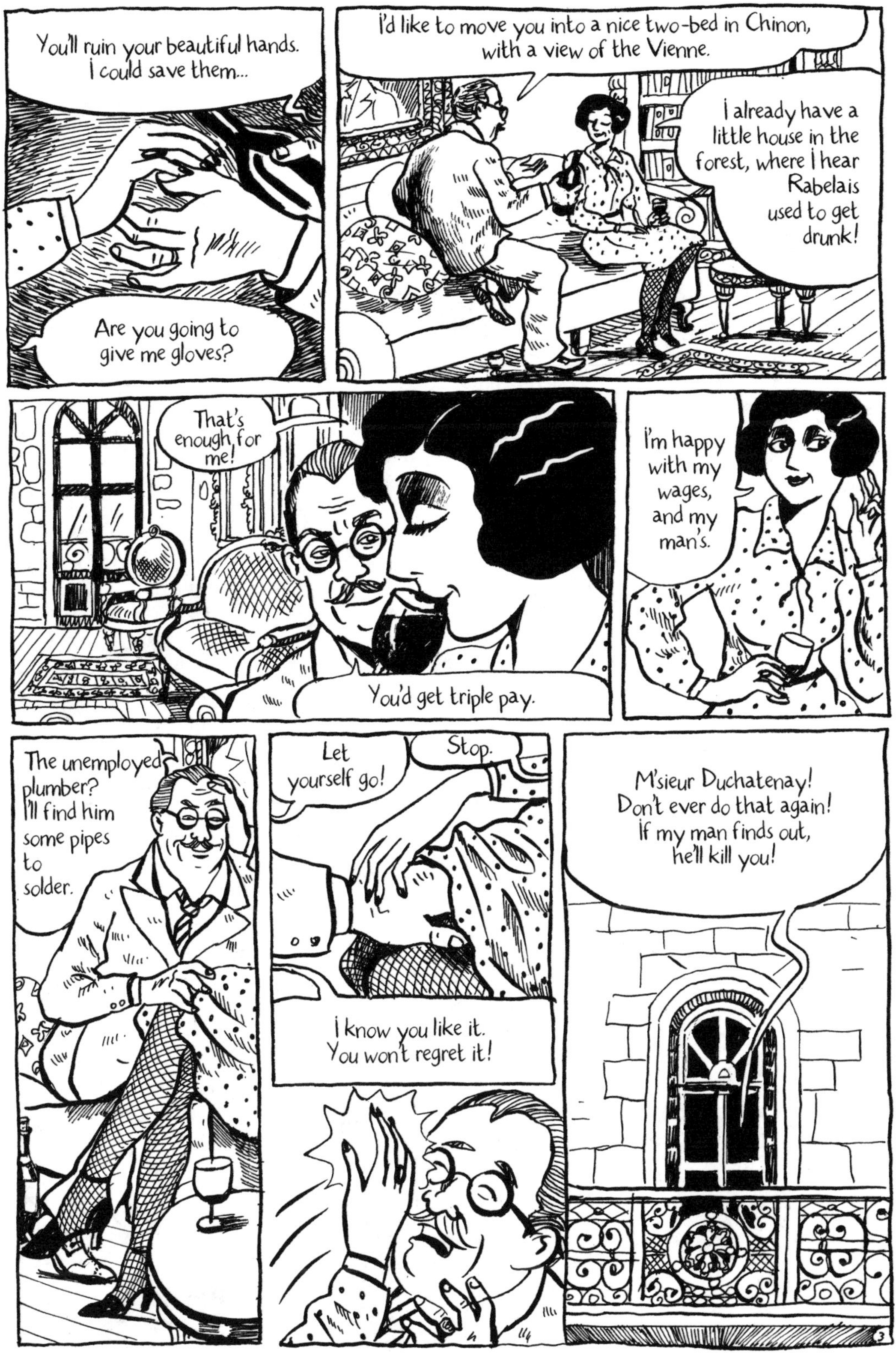
You'll ruin your beautiful hands. I could save them...
Are you going to give me gloves?
I'd like to move you into a nice two-bed in Chinon, with a view of the Vienne.
I already have a little house in the forest, where I hear Rabelais used to get drunk!
That's enough for me!
You'd get triple pay.
I'm happy with my wages, and my man's.
The unemployed plumber? I'll find him some pipes to solder.
Let yourself go!
Stop.
I know you like it. You won't regret it!
M'sieur Duchatenay! Don't ever do that again! If my man finds out, he'll kill you!
3

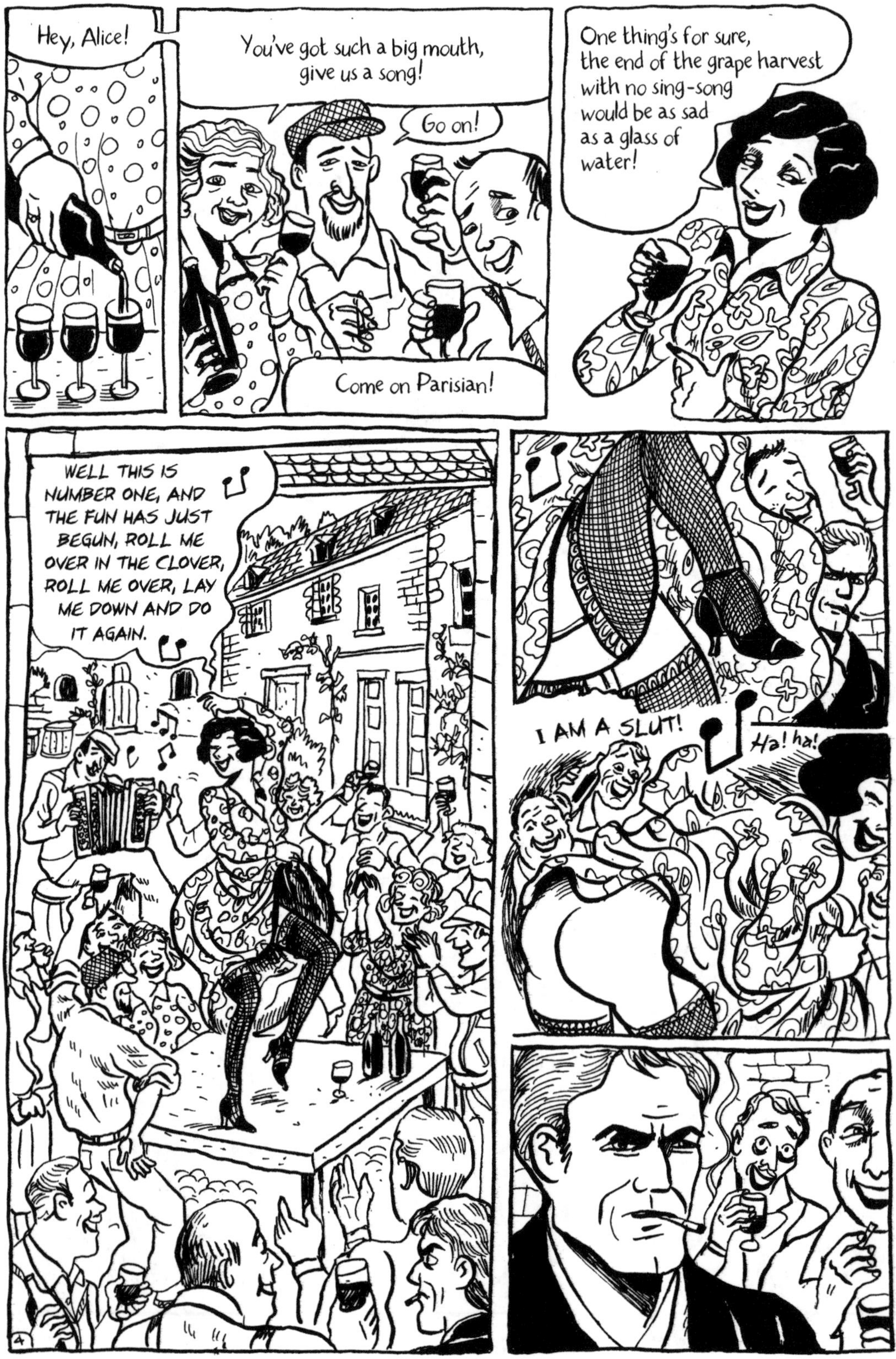
Hey, Alice!
You've got such a big mouth, give us a song!
Go on!
Come on Parisian!
One thing's for sure, the end of the grape harvest with no sing-song would be as sad as a glass of water!
WELL THIS IS NUMBER ONE, AND THE FUN HAS JUST BEGUN, ROLL ME OVER IN THE CLOVER, ROLL ME OVER, LAY ME DOWN AND DO IT AGAIN.
I AM A SLUT!
Ha! ha!

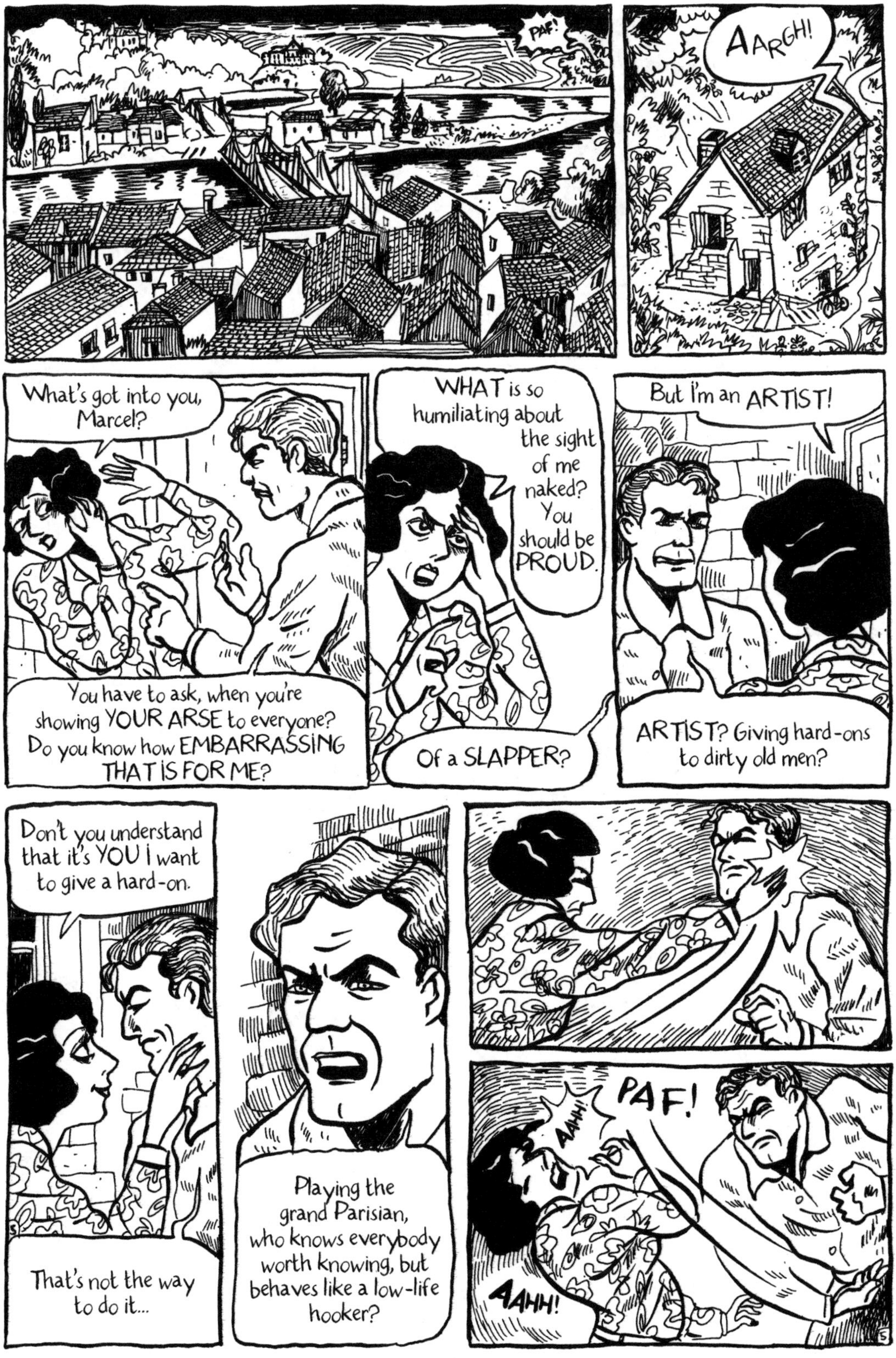
PAF!
AARGH!
What's got into you, Marcel?
You have to ask, when you're showing YOUR ARSE to everyone? Do you know how EMBARRASSING THAT IS FOR ME?
WHAT is so humiliating about the sight of me naked? You should be PROUD.
Of a SLAPPER?
But I'm an ARTIST!
ARTIST? Giving hard-ons to dirty old men?
Don't you understand that it's YOU I want to give a hard-on.
That's not the way to do it...
Playing the grand Parisian, who knows everybody worth knowing, but behaves like a low-life hooker?
PAF!
AAHH!
AAHH!

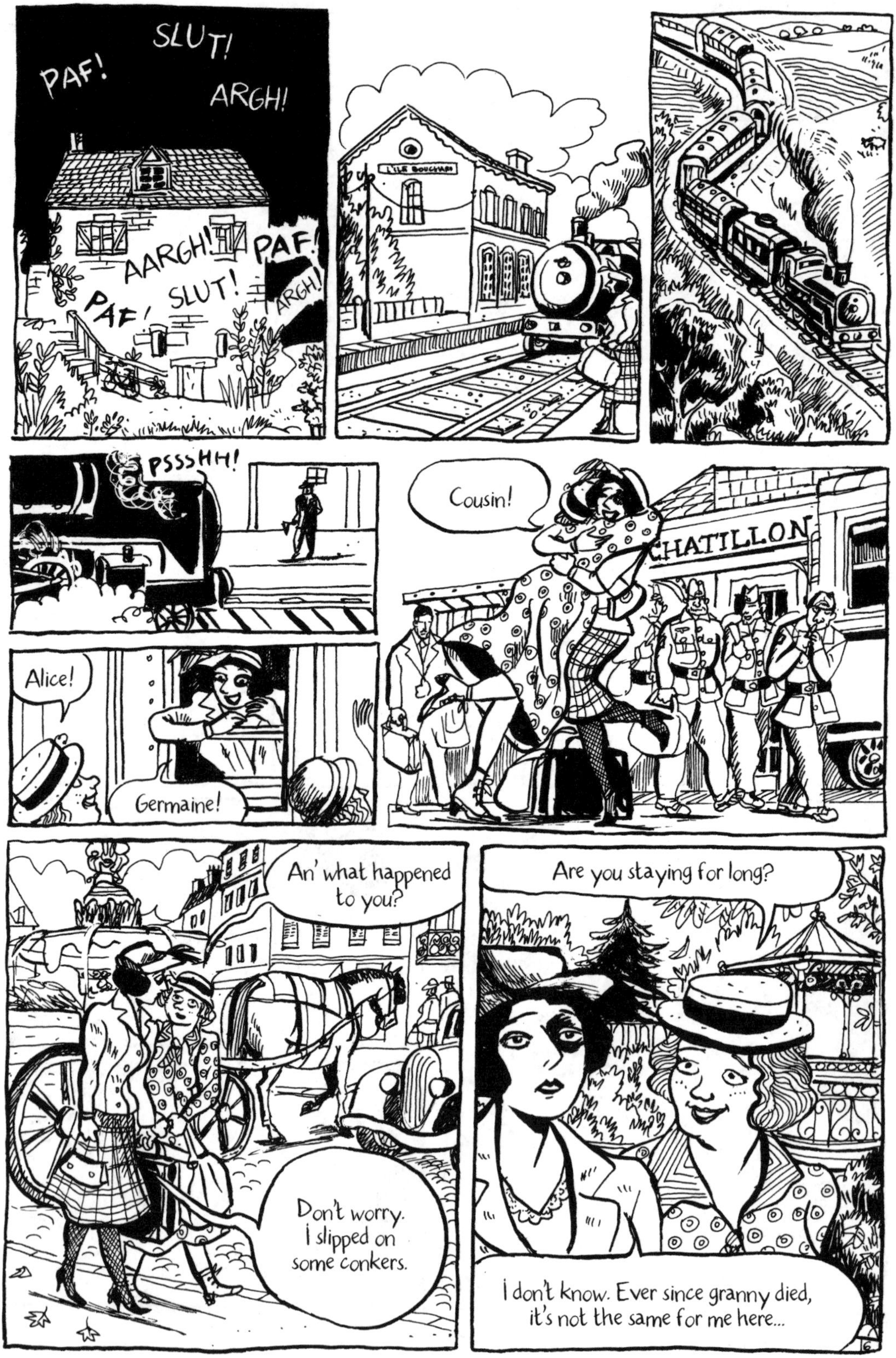
PAF!
SLUT!
ARGH!
AARGH!
PAF!
PAF!
SLUT!
ARGH!
L'ILE BOUCHARD
PSSSHH!
Alice!
Germaine!
Cousin!
CHATILLON
An' what happened to you?
Don't worry. I slipped on some conkers.
Are you staying for long?
I don't know. Ever since granny died, it's not the same for me here...

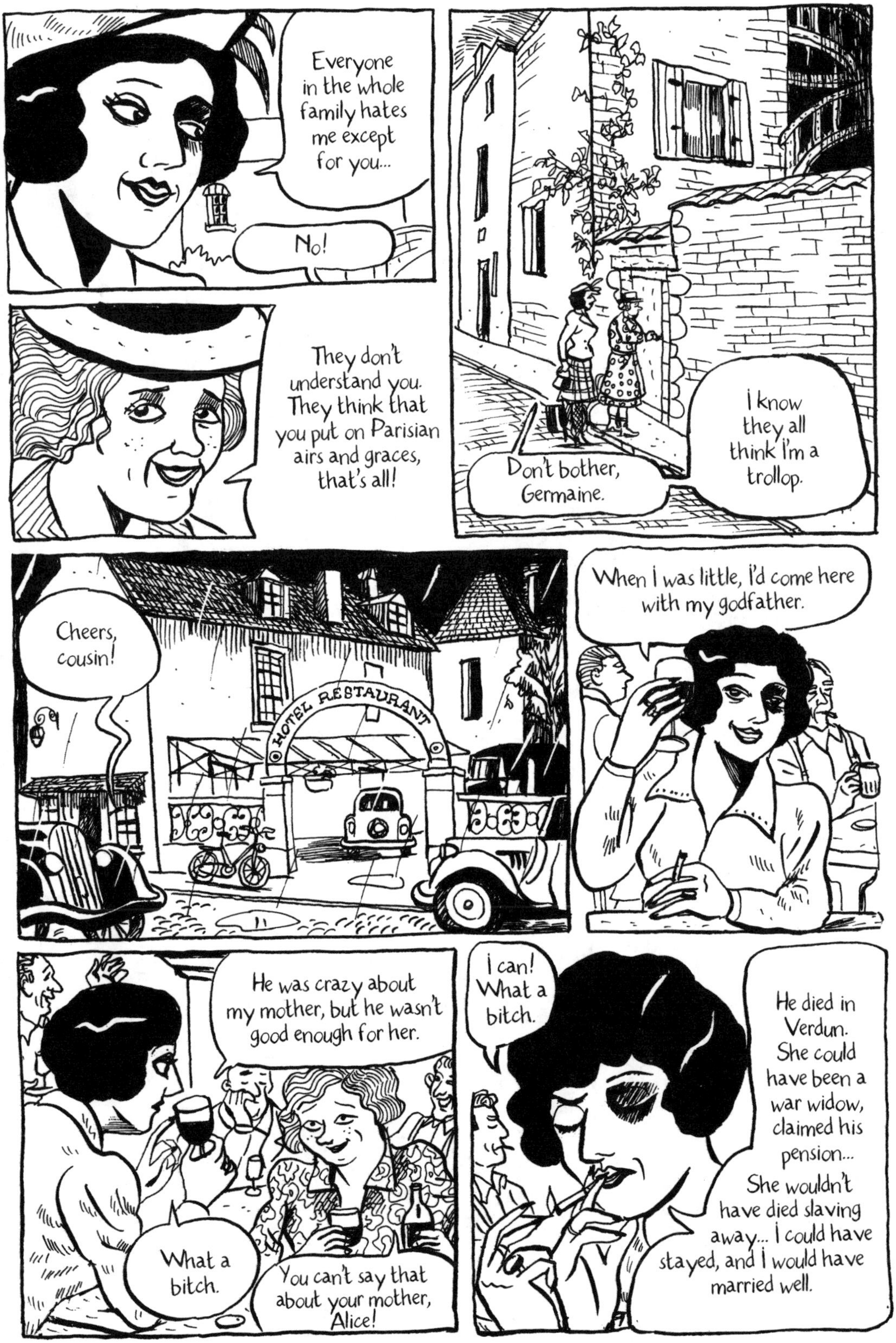
Everyone in the whole family hates me except for you...
No!
They don't understand you. They think that you put on Parisian airs and graces, that's all!
I know they all think I'm a trollop.
Don't bother, Germaine.
Cheers, cousin!
HOTEL RESTAURANT
When I was little, I'd come here with my godfather.
He was crazy about my mother, but he wasn't good enough for her.
What a bitch.
You can't say that about your mother, Alice!
I can! What a bitch.
He died in Verdun. She could have been a war widow, claimed his pension...
She wouldn't have died slaving away... I could have stayed, and I would have married well.

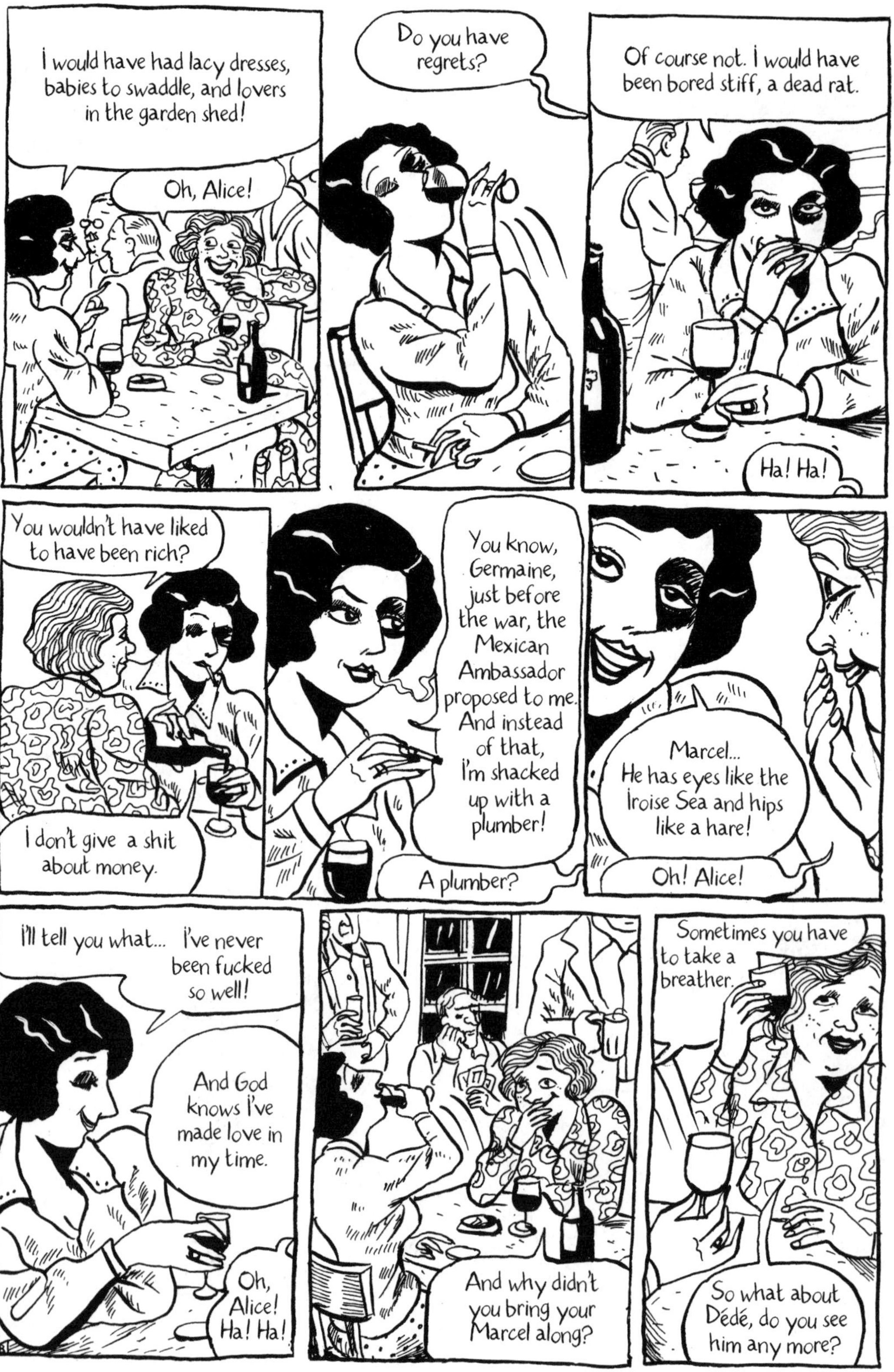
I would have had lacy dresses, babies to swaddle, and lovers in the garden shed!
Oh, Alice!
Do you have regrets?
Of course not. I would have been bored stiff, a dead rat.
Ha! Ha!
You wouldn't have liked to have been rich?
I don't give a shit about money.
You know, Germaine, just before the war, the Mexican Ambassador proposed to me. And instead of that, I'm shacked up with a plumber!
A plumber?
Marcel... He has eyes like the Iroise Sea and hips like a hare!
Oh! Alice!
I'll tell you what... I've never been fucked so well!
And God knows I've made love in my time.
Oh, Alice! Ha! Ha!
And why didn't you bring your Marcel along?
Sometimes you have to take a breather.
So what about Dédé, do you see him any more?

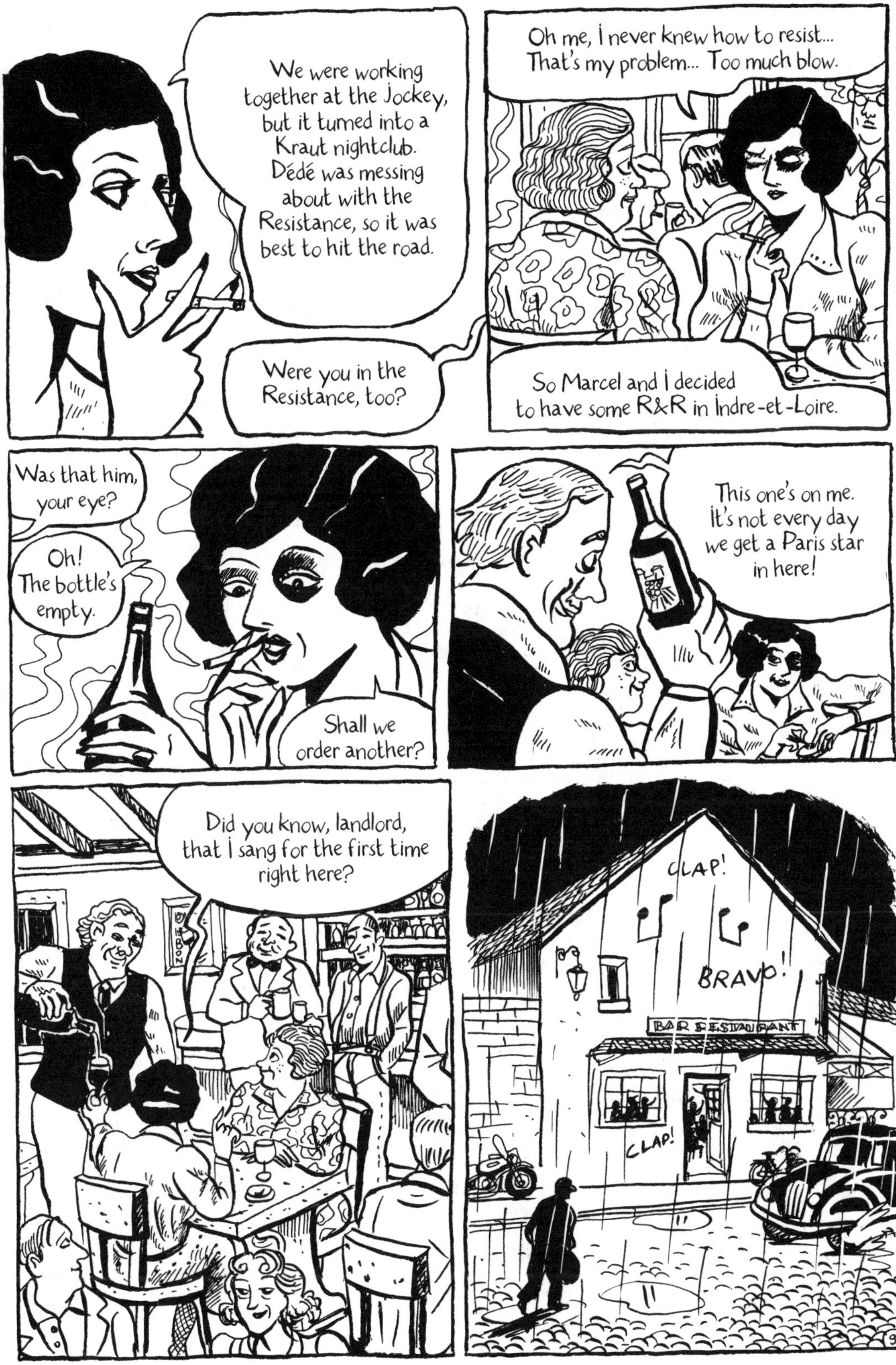
We were working together at the Jockey, but it turned into a Kraut nightclub. Dédé was messing about with the Resistance, so it was best to hit the road.
Were you in the Resistance, too?
Oh me, I never knew how to resist... That's my problem... Too much blow.
So Marcel and I decided to have some R&R in Indre-et-Loire.
Was that him, your eye?
Oh! The bottle's empty.
Shall we order another?
This one's on me. It's not every day we get a Paris star in here!
Did you know, landlord, that I sang for the first time right here?
CLAP!
BRAVO!
BAR RESTAURANT
CLAP!
9

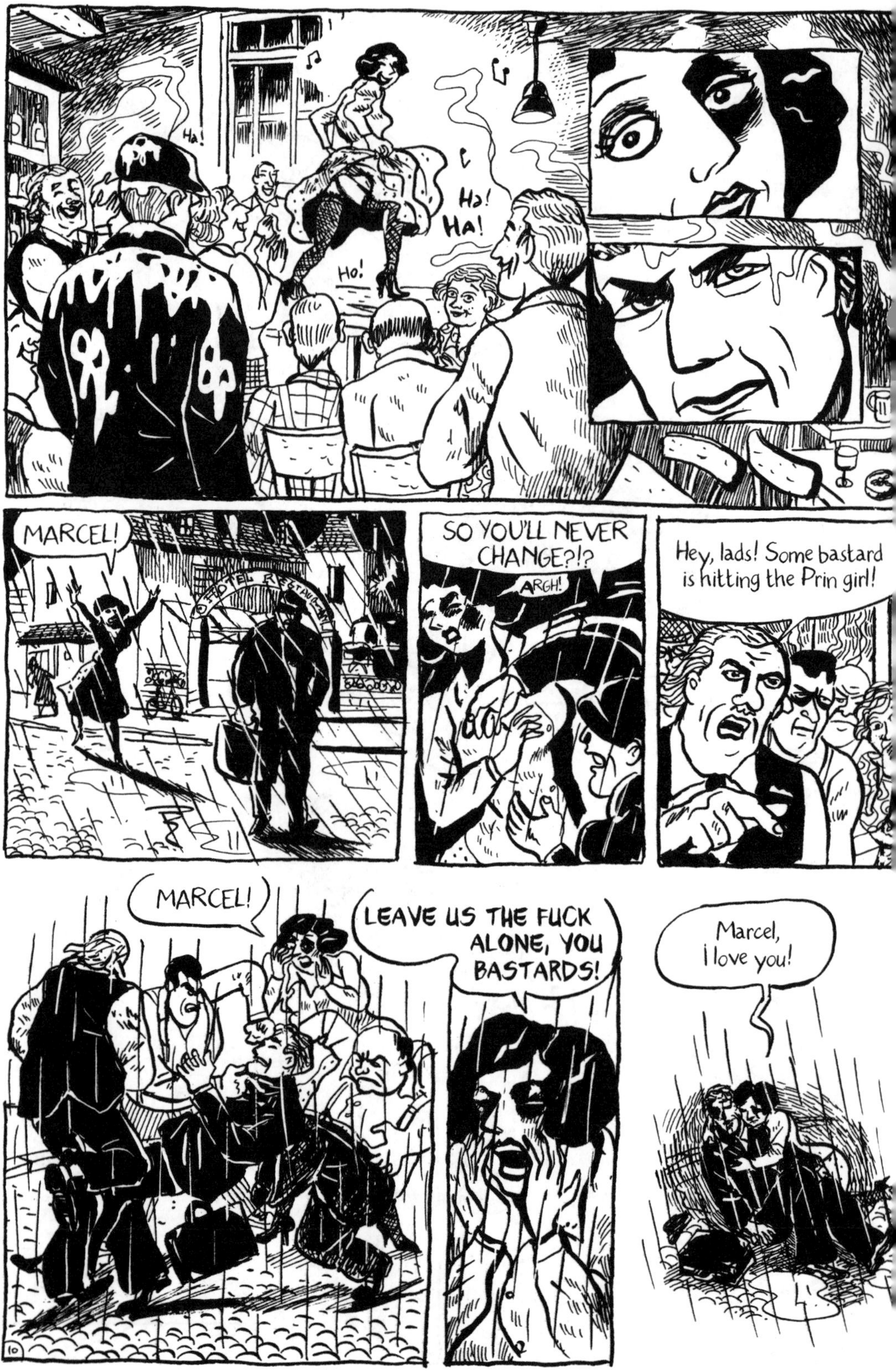
Ha!
Ha!
Ha!
Ho!
MARCEL!
SO YOU'LL NEVER CHANGE?!?
ARGH!
Hey, lads! Some bastard is hitting the Prin girl!
MARCEL!
LEAVE US THE FUCK ALONE, YOU BASTARDS!
Marcel, I love you!

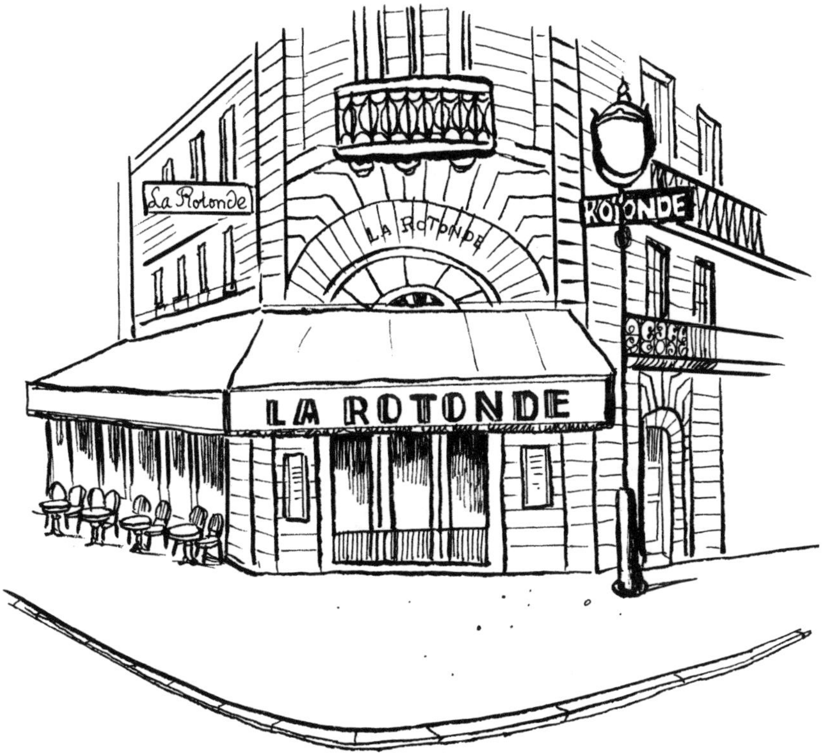
La Rotonde
LA ROTONDE
ROTONDE
LA ROTONDE

1951 - 105, boulevard du Montparnasse

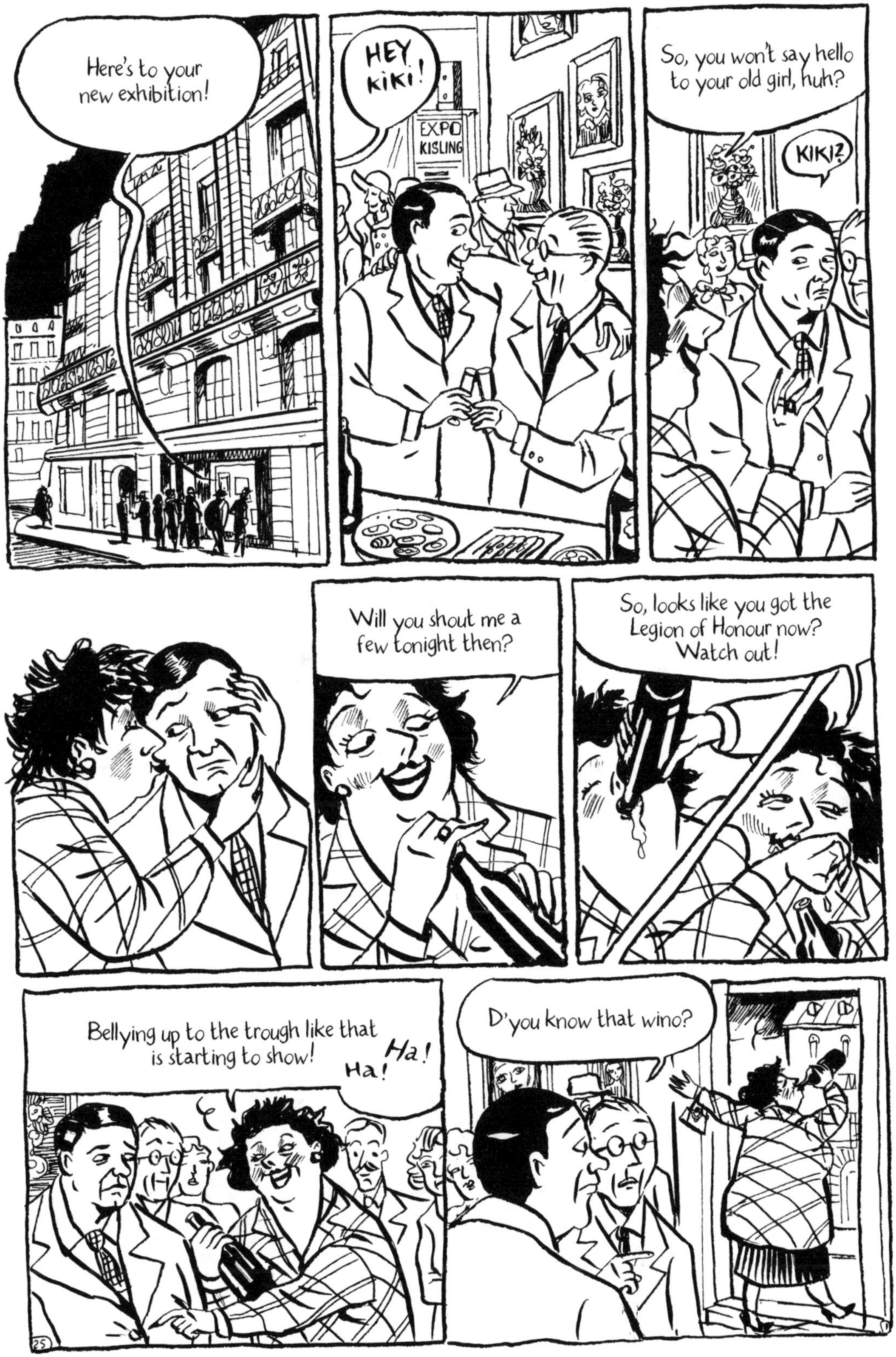
Here's to your new exhibition!
HEY KIKI!
EXPO KISLING
So, you won't say hello to your old girl, huh?
KIKI?
Will you shout me a few tonight then?
So, looks like you got the Legion of Honour now? Watch out!
Bellying up to the trough like that is starting to show!
Ha! Ha!
D'you know that wino?
25

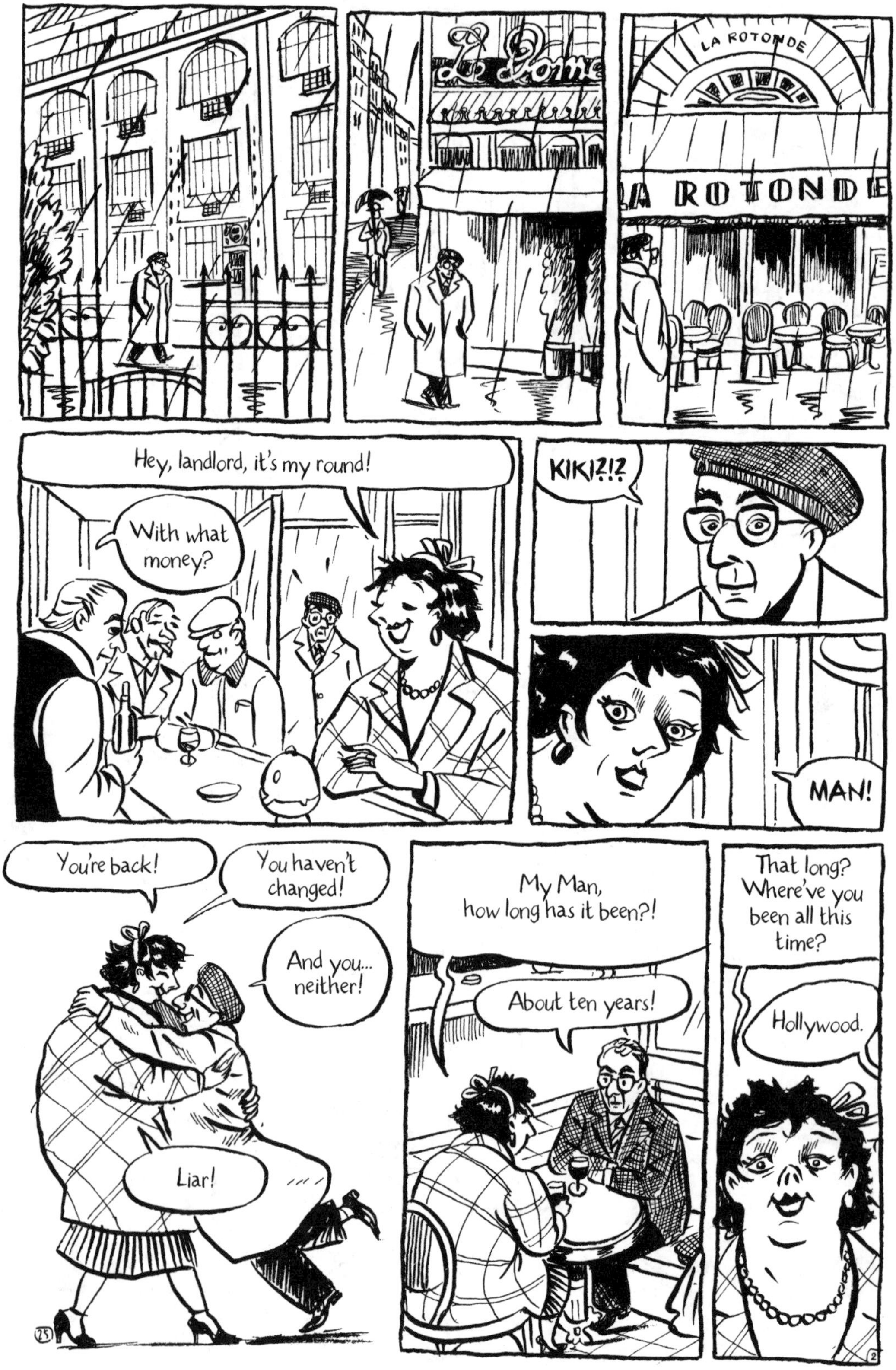

LA ROTONDE
LA ROTONDE
Hey, landlord, it's my round!
With what money?
KIKI?!?
MAN!
You're back!
You haven't changed!
And you... neither!
Liar!
My Man, how long has it been?!
About ten years!
That long? Where've you been all this time?
Hollywood.

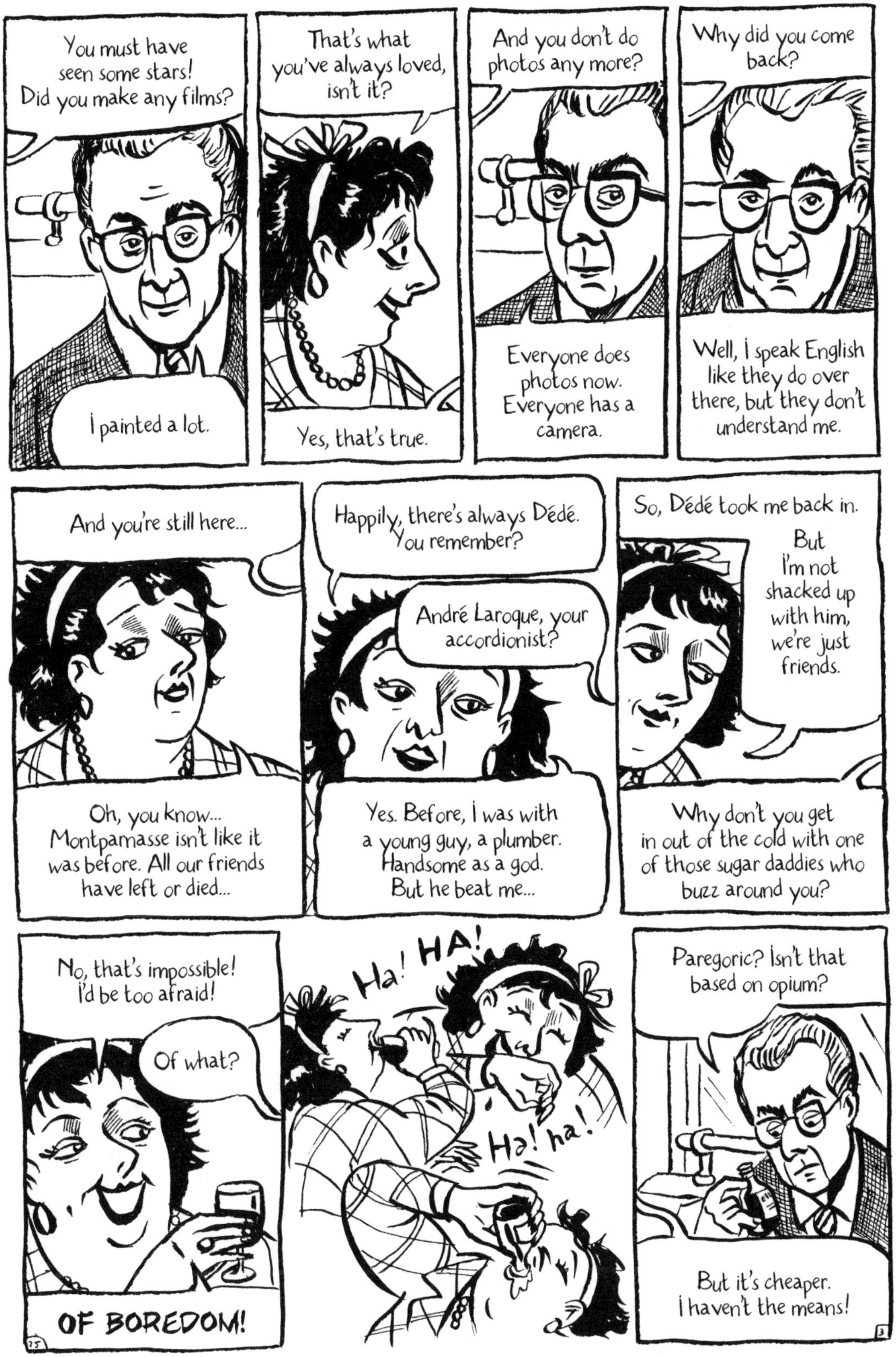
You must have seen some stars! Did you make any films?
I painted a lot.
That's what you've always loved, isn't it?
Yes, that's true.
And you don't do photos any more?
Everyone does photos now. Everyone has a camera.
Why did you come back?
Well, I speak English like they do over there, but they don't understand me.
And you're still here...
Oh, you know... Montparnasse isn't like it was before. All our friends have left or died...
Happily, there's always Dédé. You remember?
André Laroque, your accordionist?
Yes. Before, I was with a young guy, a plumber. Handsome as a god. But he beat me...
So, Dédé took me back in.
But I'm not shacked up with him, we're just friends.
Why don't you get in out of the cold with one of those sugar daddies who buzz around you?
No, that's impossible! I'd be too afraid!
Of what?
OF BOREDOM!
Ha! HA!
Ha! ha!
Paregoric? Isn't that based on opium?
But it's cheaper. I haven't the means!

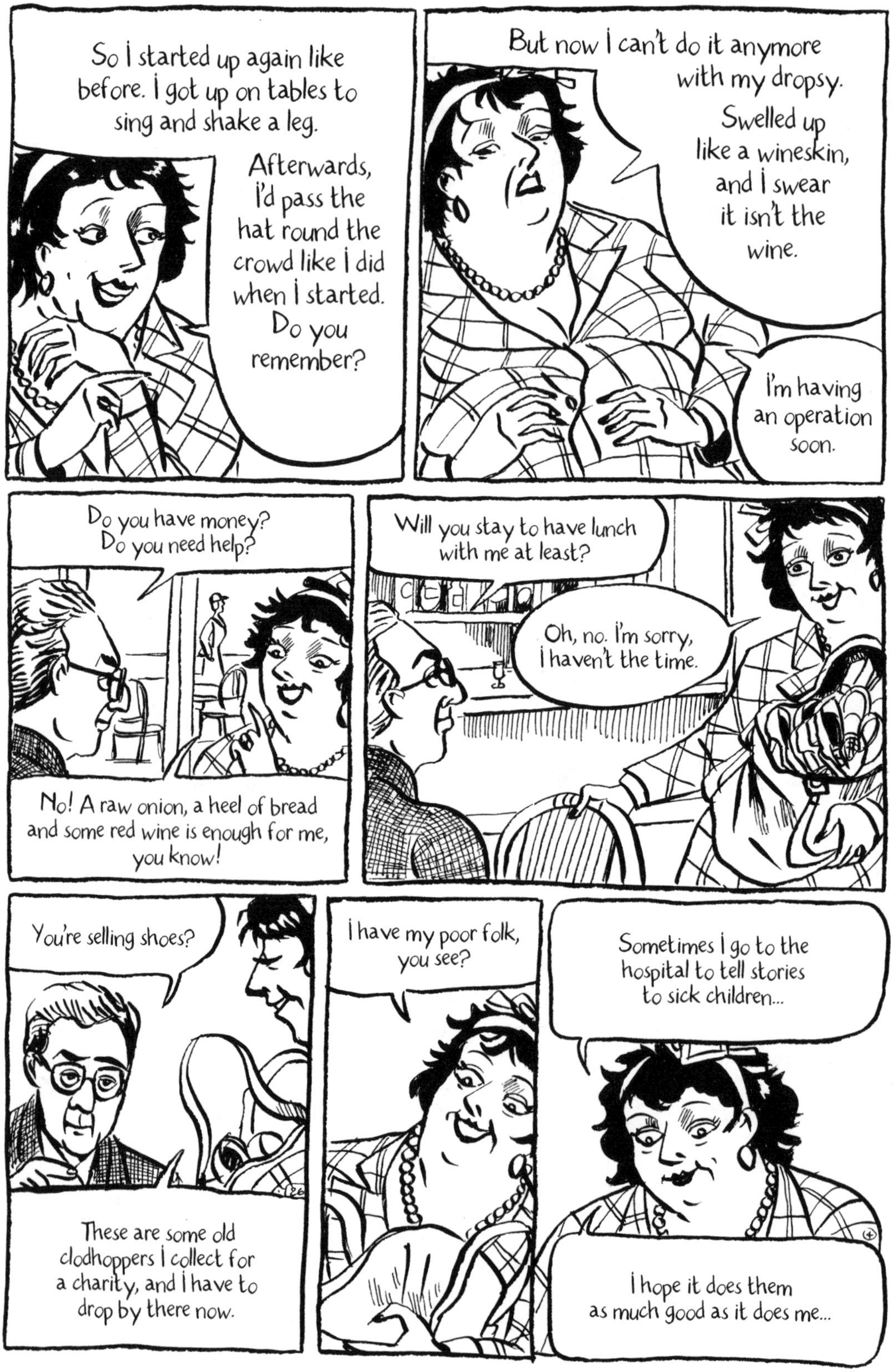

So I started up again like before. I got up on tables to sing and shake a leg.
Afterwards, I'd pass the hat round the crowd like I did when I started. Do you remember?
But now I can't do it anymore with my dropsy.
Swelled up like a wineskin, and I swear it isn't the wine.
I'm having an operation soon.
Do you have money? Do you need help?
No! A raw onion, a heel of bread and some red wine is enough for me, you know!
Will you stay to have lunch with me at least?
Oh, no. I'm sorry, I haven't the time.
You're selling shoes?
These are some old clodhoppers I collect for a charity, and I have to drop by there now.
I have my poor folk, you see?
Sometimes I go to the hospital to tell stories to sick children...
I hope it does them as much good as it does me...

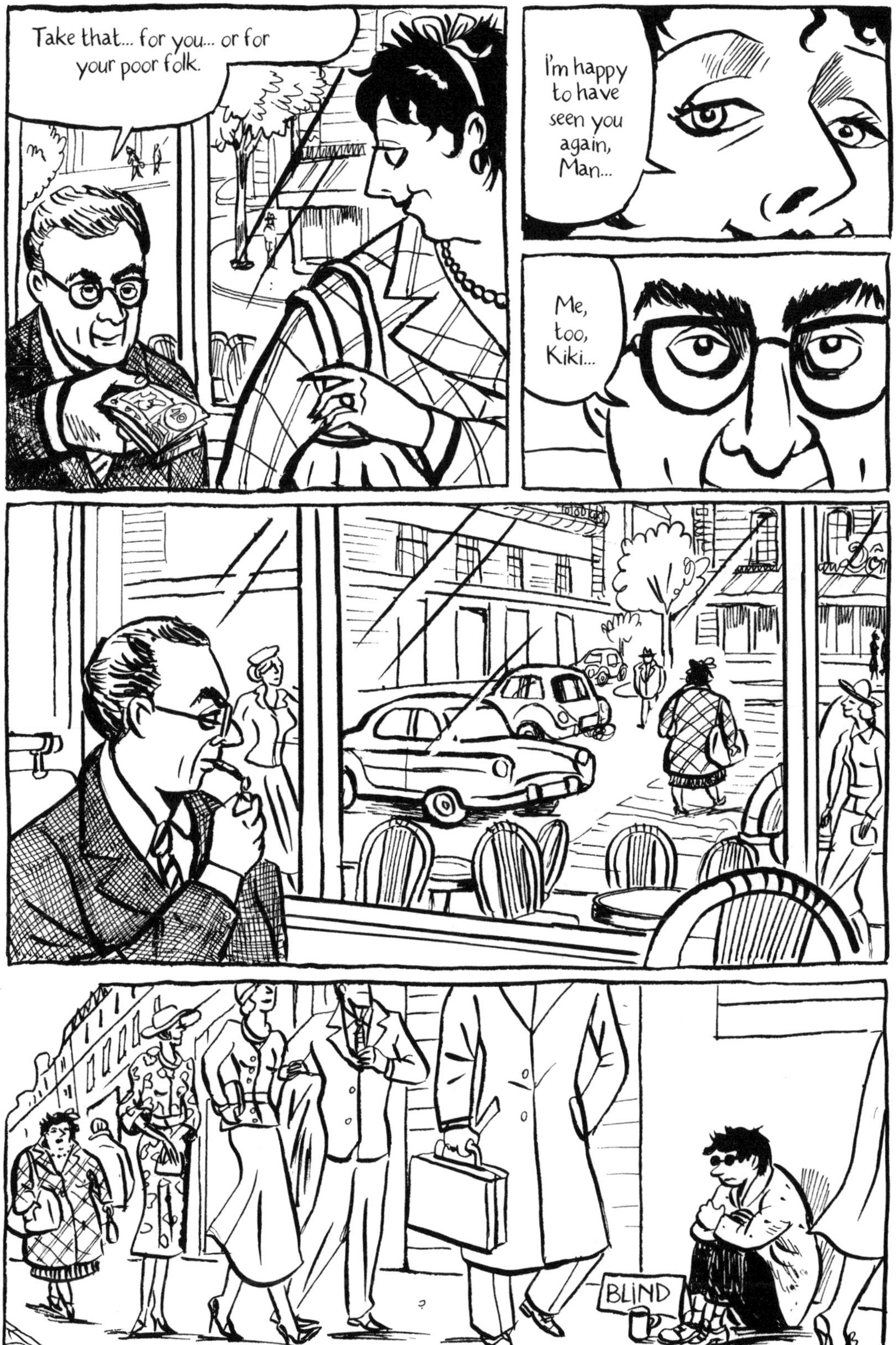
Take that... for you... or for your poor folk.
I'm happy to have seen you again, Man...
Me, too, Kiki...
BLIND

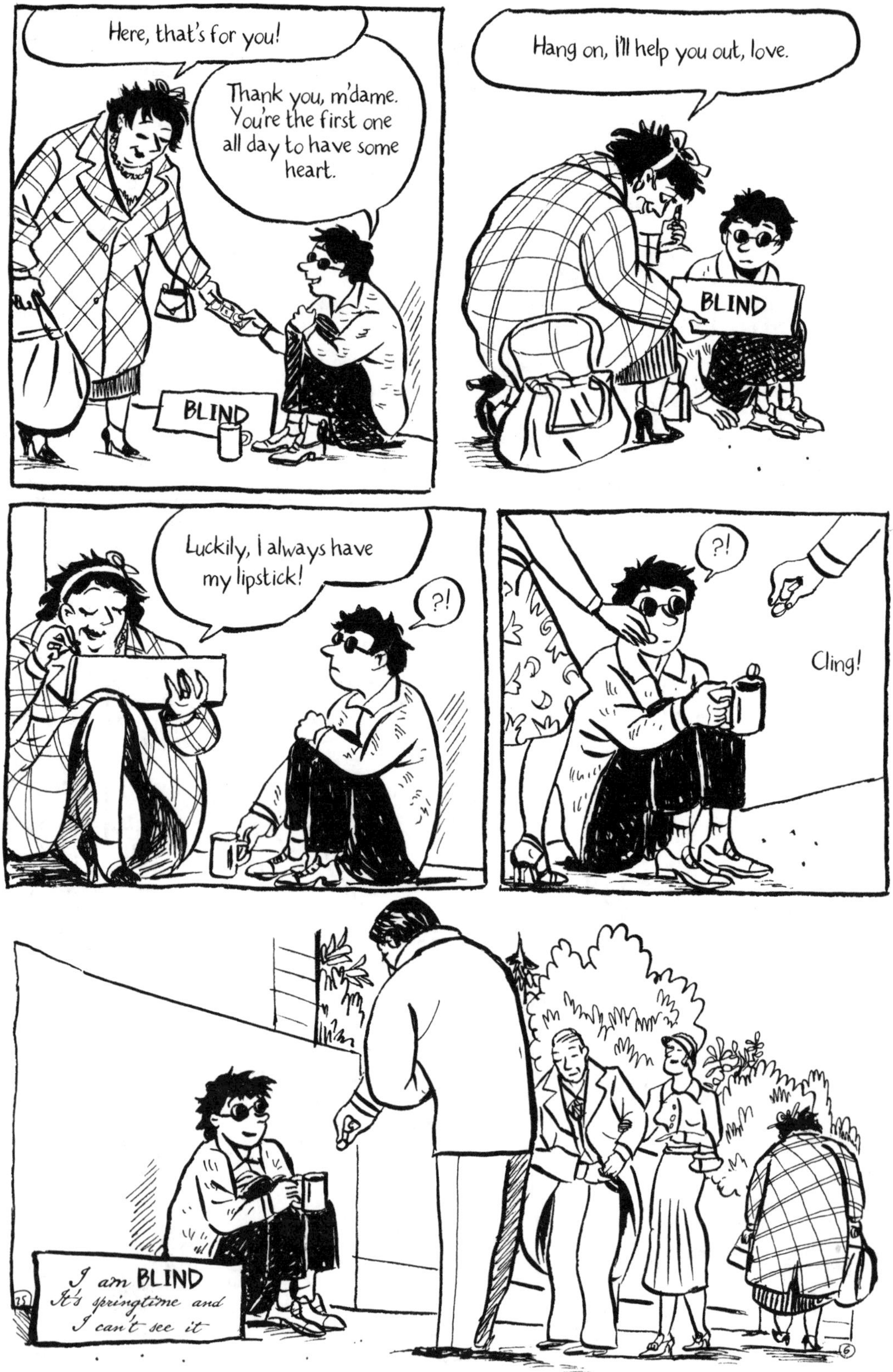

Here, that's for you!
Thank you, m'dame. You're the first one all day to have some heart.
BLIND
Hang on, I'll help you out, love.
BLIND
Luckily, I always have my lipstick!
?!
?!
Cling!
I am BLIND
It's springtime and
I can't see it

1953 - Cimetière de Thiais

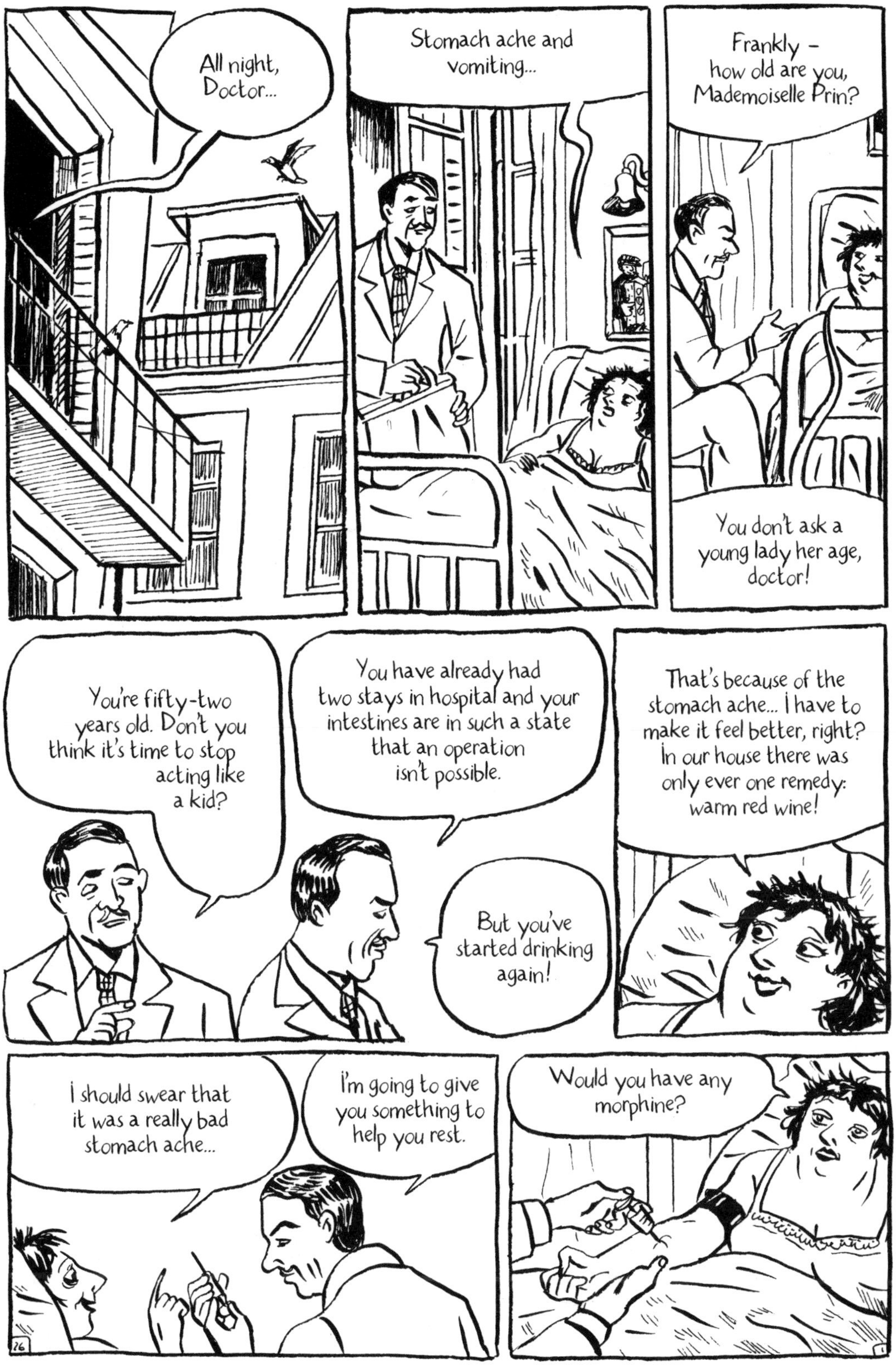
All night, Doctor...
Stomach ache and vomiting...
Frankly – how old are you, Mademoiselle Prin?
You don't ask a young lady her age, doctor!
You're fifty-two years old. Don't you think it's time to stop acting like a kid?
You have already had two stays in hospital and your intestines are in such a state that an operation isn't possible.
But you've started drinking again!
That's because of the stomach ache... I have to make it feel better, right? In our house there was only ever one remedy: warm red wine!
I should swear that it was a really bad stomach ache...
I'm going to give you something to help you rest.
Would you have any morphine?

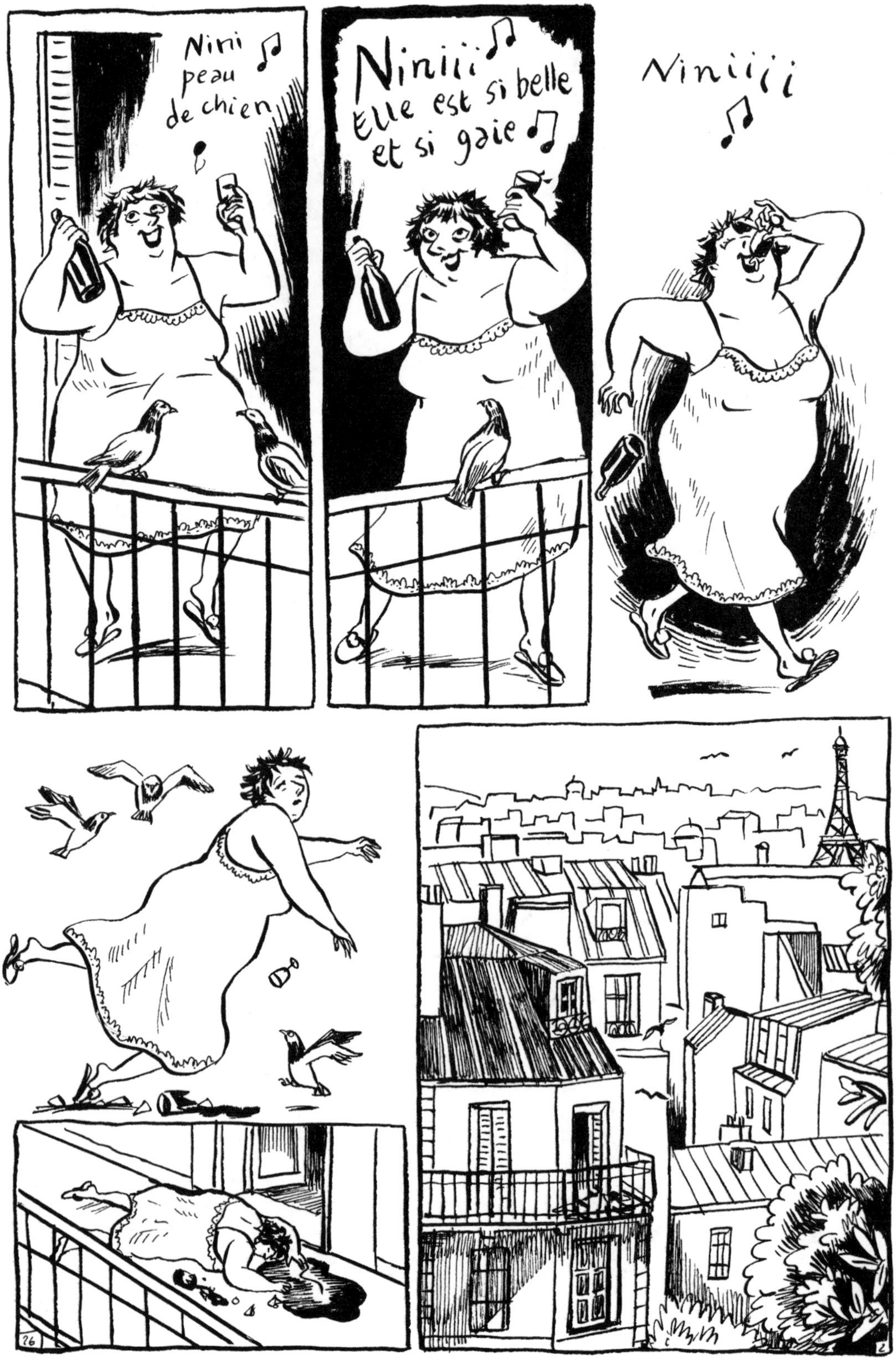
Niri peau de chien
Niniii Elle est si belle et si gaie
Niniiii
26

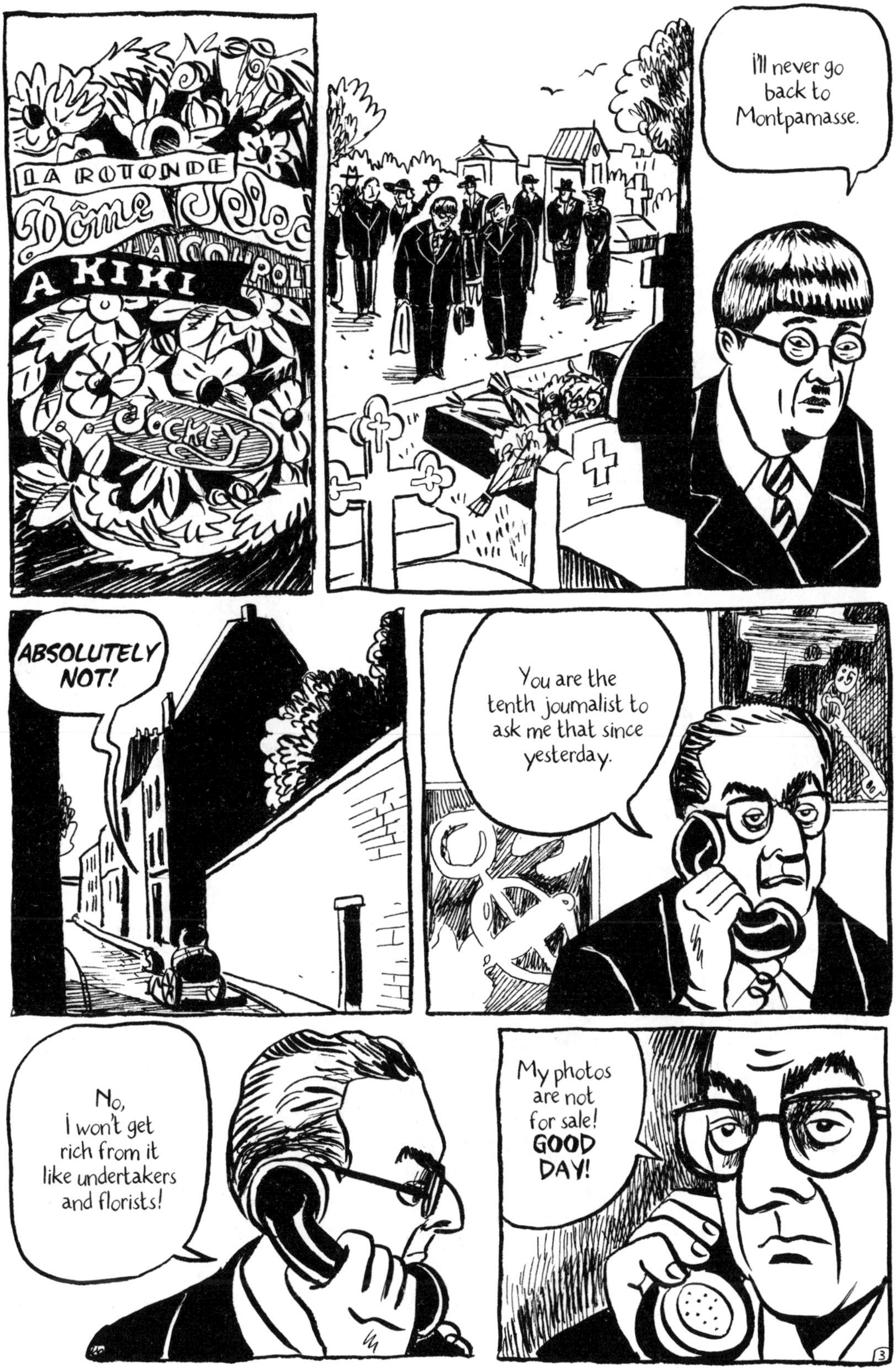
LA ROTONDE
Dôme
A KIKI
JOCKEY
I'll never go back to Montpamasse.
ABSOLUTELY NOT!
You are the tenth joumalist to ask me that since yesterday.
No, I won't get rich from it like undertakers and florists!
My photos are not for sale! GOOD DAY!
3

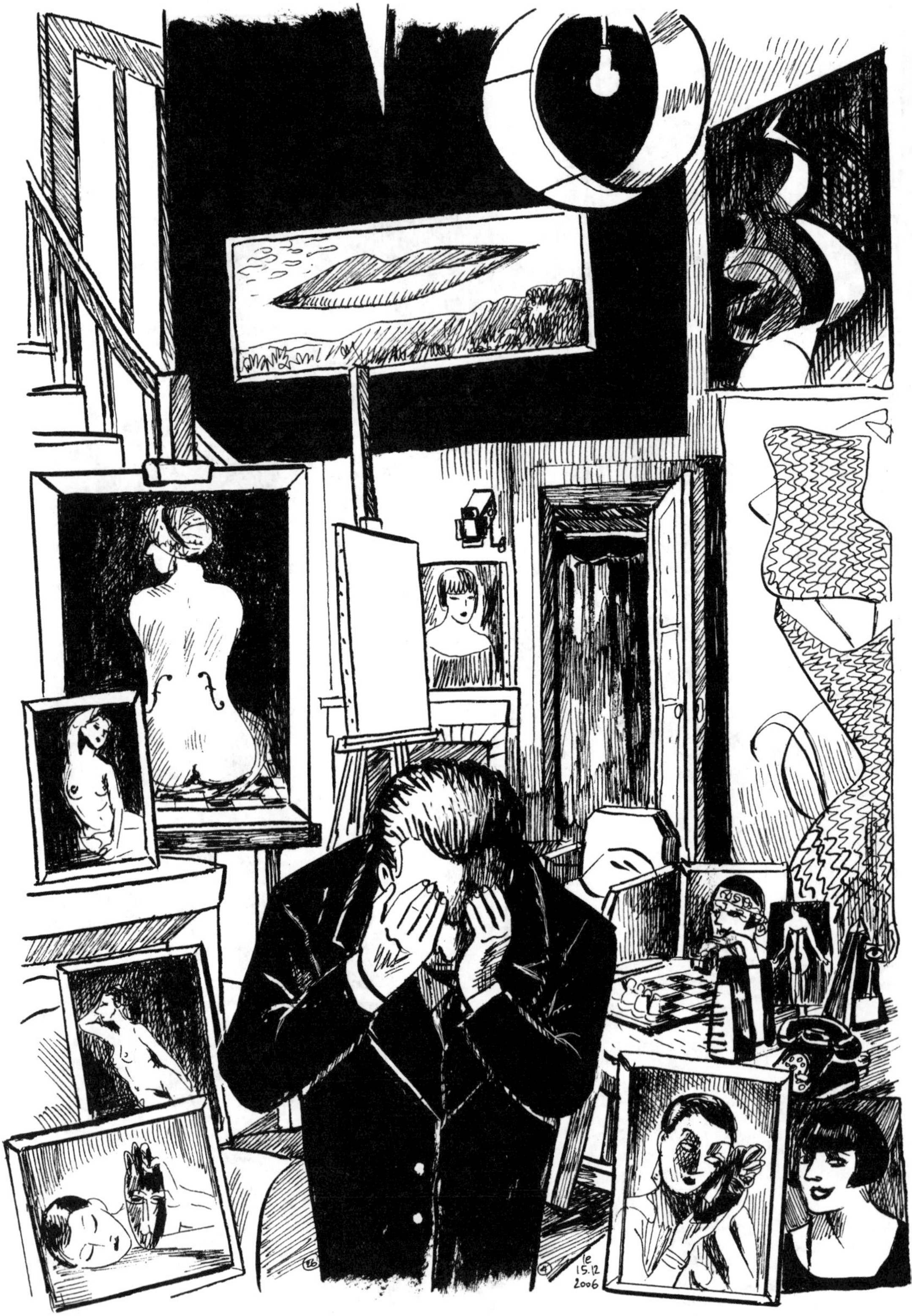
le
15.12
2006

CHRONOLOGY

Alice Prin - 1910.

2 October 1901

Alice Ernestine Prin is born at her grandmother's house at 9, rue de la Charme in Châtillon-sur-Seine. Her mother is listed as Marie Ernestine Prin, typographer, aged 19. Alice is her third child, after her first daughter was stillborn in September 1898, and her second, Maximillienne Alice, born in September 1899, died four months later. Maxime Legros, a wood and charcoal merchant, is presumed to be Alice's father. He lives on the same street with the daughter of a local farmer. This relationship is refuted by the descendants of Maxime Legros. When her mother leaves for Paris, little Alice is raised by her grandmother in rue du Cygne, along with her cousins, who have themselves been either orphaned or abandoned by their father.

Despite her love for the elder Marie Prin, Alice's childhood is miserable. She learns to drink and sing in bistrots with her godfather, a bootlegger. "You cannot know the sadness that invades the heart of a child who has no father, whose mother is far away, and whose only tenderness comes from a grandmother", Kiki would write in 1950.

1913

Alice leaves Châtillon to be with her mother in Paris, where she is working as a linotypist. They live at 12, rue Dulac, in the 16th arrondissement. Marie Prin sends her daughter to the school on rue de Vaugirard so that she can perfect her spelling. She plans for her to embrace a career as a linotypist.

1914

Marie Prin takes her daughter out of school. At first, Alice works as an apprentice bookbinder before starting at a factory "where we repair soldiers' shoes".

1916

Marie Prin falls in love with Noël Delecœuillerie, who has returned from the front wounded. Eleven years her junior, he would marry her in 1918.

1917

Alice is placed as a servant girl at a bakery. She objects to the poor treatment by the owner, who fires her. To make up for her loss of earnings, she poses for a sculptor for the first time. There follows a violent row with her mother. Alice finds herself on the street.

She lives by her wits, spending time with penniless artists-cum-pimps, discovers bohemian Montparnasse, and forms a relationship with the painter Soutine. Alice also meets painters Amedeo Modigliani and Maurice Utrillo in restaurant Chez Rosalie at 3, rue Campagne-Première. A Modigliani pencil portrait of Kiki dates from this time. Utrillo is also known to have used her as a model, and would come out of these sessions with simple landscapes.

1918

Alice falls in love with Polish painter Maurice Mendjisky, with whom she would live until 1922. It is Mendjisky who nicknames her "Kiki". She would model for many of the painter's works. That same year, the painter Kisling would notice Kiki at La Rotonde. She would be his model throughout the 1920s.

1921

Kiki poses for the Japanese painter, Foujita. Theirs would be a lifelong friendship.

December 1921

When Mendjisky leaves for the Côte d'Azur, Kiki meets the American painter and photographer Man Ray. In maids' quarters in rue de la Confamine, he takes his first pictures of the young woman. Shortly thereafter, they move in together on rue Delambre at the Hôtel des Écoles, room 27. From his arrival in Paris in July 1921, this close friend of Marcel Duchamp was immediately adopted by the members of the Dada group. At the beginning of December, his first exhibition under the aegis of the group is a financial failure; not a single work sells. However, Man Ray would make his money and, reluctantly, make his name from his work as a photographer. In addition to his revolutionary rayographs and his famous shots of Kiki, he would become the leading photographer of the interwar years. During their years living together, Man and Kiki spent time with artists, poets and writers who would pose in front of his lens, including Pablo Picasso, Jean Cocteau, Tristan Tzara, André Breton, Paul Eluard, Gertrude Stein, Henri Matisse, Fernand Léger, Francis Picabia, Pascin, Mina Loy, Djuna Barnes, Miró and Luis Buñuel.

10 January 1922

Kiki attends the opening of Boeuf sur le Toit at 28, rue Boissy d'Anglas. Named for a show by Cocteau and Milhaud, the bar would come to be the emblematic hotspot for the Roaring Twenties. The Paris in-crowd, artists and crowned heads all come. Man Ray's photos and Francis Picabia's canvases hang on the wall, including the famous *Oeil cacodylate*.

May 1922

First meeting with Henri-Pierre Roché, an art amateur who would encourage Kiki to paint.

Spring 1922

Man Ray's financial situation allows him to rent a studio at 31 bis, rue Campagne-Première. The bathroom is turned into a darkroom, and the loggia becomes the couple's bedroom.

14 July 1922

Thérèse Maure, aka "Treize", meets Kiki at La Rotonde. They become inseparable. "If something happens to either one of us, we share it, even if it's throwing a punch, or getting one!"

1922

Foujita's painting of Kiki, *Le Nu couché à la toile de Jouy*, is one of the hits of the Salon d'Automne.

June 1923

Marcel Duchamp returns from New York. Each night at about midnight, Treize, Kiki and Man meet him at the Dôme where he eats runny scrambled eggs before heading back home to work on tricky chess problems.

6 July 1923

The premiere of Man Ray's film, *La Retour à la raison* takes place at the Dada evening at the Coeur à Barbe at the Théâtre Michel on rue des Mathurins. Images of Kiki's chest appear in this first short black and white film, which is two minutes long. The second screening scheduled for the next day would not take place due to the scandal that night, which was orchestrated by Breton and his friends to break the Dadaist

Alice Prin dite Kiki - 1923-

ban. It wasn't until 1949 that *La Retour à la raison* reappeared on the big screen at the International Experimental and Poetic Film Festival in Knokke-le-Zoute on the Belgian–Dutch border.

14 July 1923
Man and Kiki go to Pascin's house to help with the fireworks and to celebrate.

End of July 1923
After an argument with Man Ray, Kiki takes the boat to New York. According to Man Ray's autobiography, Kiki leaves in the company of a couple of Americans who had decided to launch her film career. According to other witnesses, she accompanies an American journalist whose first name is Mike. She tried her luck at the Famous Players' studios, which would become Paramount, where Cecil B. DeMille was artistic director.

October 1923
The American studios were not interested in Kiki, and her lover leaves for Saint Louis. Man Ray pays for her return trip. A couple once again, they move into the hotel in rue Bréa.

November 1923
The Jockey opens. Situated at the corner of rue Campagne-Première and boulevard du Montparnasse, The Jockey is the top nightclub in the neighbourhood. It soon attracts all the night owls and artists in Paris. There could be found Foujita, Tzara, Cocteau, Pascin, Kisling, Ezra Pound, Jean Oberlé, André Warnot and the Russian actor Yvan Mosjoukine, who would be Kiki's lover.

Everyone does their party piece, dances or sings at The Jockey. One night, Kiki, tipsy, sings a bawdy song. It would become the number one attraction for the nightclub. She always starts her set with her signature tune, *Les Filles de Camaret*. Treize passes the hat and teaches Kiki to dance the French cancan. Sometimes, Kiki lifts her leg so high that everyone can see that she doesn't wear knickers.

16 February 1924
With the commission received for the purchase of a painting by Douanier Rousseau for an American collector, Henri-Pierre buys himself a watercolour painted by Kiki.

29 April 1924
Premiere of the film *La Galerie des Monstres* at the Artistic Cinéma on rue du Douai. Kiki plays herself in this feature-length film, at the heart of a troupe of performers touring in Spain. She appears in the credits by the name "Kiki Ray". Henri-Pierre Roché attends the screening and is full of praise for the young actress.

November 1924
Private screening of *Ballet Méchanique* by Fernand Léger and Dudley Murphy. The film is fifteen minutes long, and Kiki's face and features reappear regularly, surrounded by miscellaneous images. The "multiplied transformation" of Kiki is achieved with a system of lenses developed by Ezra Pound and Dudley Murphy. Several shots taken by the latter with Man Ray were integrated into the montage. According to researcher

William Moritz, the sequences that feature Kiki would have been shot by Man Ray himself. The film – today a classic of the avant-garde – was never screened publicly in Paris.

A study of a copy kept in Amsterdam reveals a subliminal, previously unpublished shot of Kiki nude.

June 1924
In the final edition of *Littérature*, André Breton publishes *Le Violon d'Ingres*, a photo collage by Man Ray made that same year. This portrait of Kiki would become the emblematic image of photographic surrealism.

October 1924
American Louis Wilson and his Dutch wife Yopi buy Le Dingo at 10, rue Delambre. It is in this bar that Ernest Hemingway and F. Scott Fitzgerald would meet for the first time. Like her friend Ernest, Kiki is a regular at Le Dingo. There she enjoys the company of American sailors. It is also frequented by the Fitzgeralds.

29 October 1924
Kiki's grandmother, Geneviève Eugénie Maria Prin, née Esprit, dies at the age of 76.

April 1925
On Cocteau's advice, Kiki moves into the Welcome Hotel on the port of Villefrance-sur-Mer. It is the only harbour deep enough to receive American warships.

Kiki likes to visit the sailors from the Pittsburgh, the flagship vessel. After an altercation with a publican, she is arrested for prostitution and thrown in prison. Man Ray and the surrealist Georges Malkine make great efforts to free her. Aragon and Desnos testify to her standing as an "artist". Kiki is released on 15 April, but with a suspended sentence.

1926
Man Ray photographs Kiki with a Baoulé tribal mask from the Ivory Coast. The study remained in his portfolio.

May 1926
While Man Ray is in Biarritz shooting *Emak Bakia*, Kiki and Treize move into the Raspail hotel at 232, boulevard Raspail.

23 November 1926
Private premiere of Man Ray's cinepoem, *Emak Bakia* – "Leave me alone" in Basque – at the Vieux Colombier. The seven-minute black and white film ends with Kiki's "double-awakening"; Man painted two pupils on her closed eyelids that would disappear when she slowly opened her eyes.

25 March 1927
Private viewing of Kiki's first painting exhibition Au Sacre du Printemps, 5 rue du Cherche-Midi. She follows photographer André Kertész who photographs her among his works. Twenty-seven of Kiki's paintings are exhibited. The catalogue text is written by Robert Desnos. The exhibition is a success.

The exhibition ends on 9 April. During this time, Man is in New York to present *Emak Bakia*.

8 June 1927
Marriage of Marcel Duchamp to Lydie Sarazin-Levassor. The wedding meal takes place in Brancusi's studio in impasse Ronsin, with the sculptor, his secretary and lover, Picabia and Germaine, Man Ray and Kiki.

20 December 1927
La Coupole opens. Three thousand invitations are sent. At midnight, 1,200 bottles of champagne are emptied. Kiki is among the crowd.

1928

Pierre Prévert and Marcel Duhamel direct the film *Paris-express* or *Souvenirs de Paris*. This stroll through a slipstream of pretty women shows Kiki and Treize on the terrace of the Dôme with Georges Malkine. Man Ray participates in some of the shooting.

13 May 1928

The first private screening of *L'Étoile de mer* at the Studio des Ursulines. Kiki is the main character in this fifteen-minute black and white film directed by Man Ray and written by Robert Desnos. Man Ray's first public success, this short film would be shown in Paris until 1931 as the opener for *La Zone* by Georges Lacombe, *A Girl in Every Port* by Howard Hawks, and then for *The Blue Angel* by Josef von Sternberg.

15 July 1928

One of the portraits of Kiki with an African mask taken two years earlier by Man Ray appears in issue three of the review *Variétés*. Titled *Noire et Blanche*, the photograph would become one of the most famous photographs by the American artist, along with *Le Violon d'Ingres*.

Early 1929

Underground publication of 1929, pornographic parodies of Christian hymns written by Louis Aragon and Benjamin Péret, illustrated by four Man Ray photographs representing the four seasons. In them, Man Ray and Kiki (who are unidentifiable) are making love. Printed in Belgium, the 215 copies of the edition were seized by French customs.

February 1929

Au Bal Nègre, the West Indian club launched by Desnos and Mado Anspach, hosts the Ubu Ball. Champagne flows and Kiki dances the cancan all night. The straps of her camisole keep sliding down, revealing her bosom to the crowd. All of Montparnasse is there, including Foujita, dressed as a prostitute. According to columnists, the Ubu Ball was the "last Montparnasse ball". Kiki would have been at all the previous famous balls of the decade, from the Bullier Ball to the Watteau Ball, through to the Quat'z'Arts balls thrown by the students of the École des Beaux-Arts.

Spring 1929

American sculptor Alexander Calder creates a portrait of Kiki out of wire in front of the Keystone news agency camera. Calder would create a second portrait of Kiki that would be exhibited with the first in 1931 in Paris.

15 April 1929

The first chapters of Kiki's memoirs are published in issue three of *Paris-Montparnasse*. The review, illustrated and written almost entirely by Henri Broca, is in large part funded by Kiki. A dozen issues would appear. Kiki would feature on the cover, as would her friends Kisling, Per Krohg, Foujita and Pascin.

It seems that during that spring Kiki had already left Man Ray for Hencri Broca, but regardless it was Man Ray and American editor Edward Titus, the husband of Éléna Rubinstein, who would encourage the young woman to take up writing her memoirs. It fell to Broca to push her to finish the manuscript.

During the same period, Kiki met the singer Jean Blanc. Together, they would sing at the new Bœuf sur le Toit on rue de Penthièvre.

2 May 1929

The "Paris-Montparnasse Dinners", started by Broca, take place once per month, presided over by a local personality. Kiki attends each of these banquets with Broca, and hosts the May dinner at Le Normandy restaurant. Foujita and Treize are of course in attendance.

30 May 1929

With Broca's backing, *Paris-Montparnasse* organises a charity gala at the Bobino music hall on rue de la Gaîté to benefit an emergency food fund for artists.

Pascin designed the programme cover. Foujita is billed as a clown act, Roland Toutain does acrobatics, Marie Vassilieff does Russian dances, Thérèse Maure takes up a French cancan with her "Montparnasse Girls" (including Kiki), Granowski the cowboy acts as MC, while the orchestra is composed of the musicians from the Jungle and the Lido. Kiki, of course, sings her risqué set. At the end of the show, Kiki is also elected "Queen of Montparnasse".

To celebrate her triumph, a hundred guests accompany the bohemian monarch to La Coupole.

June 1929

After the final show of the season for the Ballets Russes, Coco Chanel invites twenty-four guests to supper – all you can eat caviar. "Kiki, who had too much to drink, sang very obscene songs", notes Maurice Sachs in his journal.

25 July 1929

Souvenirs de Kiki is published by Henri Broca. The book benefits from a cover by Kisling and an introduction by Foujita. The text is illustrated with paintings and drawings by Kiki, but also by Man Ray's photographs and portraits by Foujita, Mayo, Hermine David and Per Krogh. These *Souvenirs*, augmented by additions to the American edition, would be republished in 1998 by Éditions Hazan by Billy Klüver and Julie Martin.

Déjeuner de famille, oil on canvas, Kiki, 1930

26 October 1929

Kiki signs her book at the Edouard Loewy bookshop on boulevard Raspail. For thirty francs, you can have the book, an autograph and a kiss from the author. The bookshop is packed.

December 1929

Kiki meets Russian filmmaker Serge Eisenstein, with Man Ray. She does his portrait, which is published in the cinema pages of *Paris-Montparnasse*. That same month, Kiki is invited to exhibit her paintings at the Trémois gallery, on avenue Rapp, along with Pascin, Hermine David, Per Krohg and Touchagues.

7 June 1930

In the midst of a large crowd, Kiki helps to bury her friend Pascin.

The painter had killed himself a few days previously. He had written "Adieu Lucy" in his own blood on a closet door. Per Krogh's wife, Lucy, was his last great love.

July 1930

The English-language edition of *Kiki's Memoirs* is published in Paris by Edward Titus at Black

Manikin Press. With additional new chapters, the work has a preface by Ernest Hemingway. It would be one of only two prefaces that the American novelist would agree to do in his entire career; the second would be for the memoirs of Jimmie Charters, the barman at the Dingo. For the launch, Kiki's paintings are exhibited in the window of Titus's bookshop, At the Sign of the Black Manikin, on rue Delambre. Copies of *Kiki's Memoirs* would be seized by American customs and the banned book would enter into American publishing history.

15 November 1930

Kiki exhibits at the Bernheim gallery on rue du faubourg Saint-Honoré. She then appears as a singer at La Jungle, 127, boulevard du Montparnasse, and from then on she lives in a villa in Arcueil with Henri Broca, whose mental health is wavering.

30 November 1930

Opening night of the *"Le Nu..."* review at the Concert Mayol. Kiki is the star of the *"Sailors' Songs"* set. It is her first appearance at a large popular venue.

December 1930

Broca's mental health becomes worrying to the point that Kiki has him committed to the Sainte-Anne hospital. She visits her lover regularly. After many months of committal, Broca returns to Montparnasse for a few months before the doctors send him to convalesce with his family in Bordeaux.

The caricaturist and journalist would pass away there in 1935, burned by his passion for Montparnasse.

1 January 1931

Film premiere of *Le Capitaine jaune* by Anders-Wilhelm Sandberg at the Gaumont-Palace. The cast includes Charles Vanel and Valéry

Inkijnoff. Kiki plays the role of a singer in a hole-in-the-wall in the old port of Marseille. The full-length film, a talkie, only played for one week.

Summer 1931

Kiki appears throughout the season with Jamblan at Jeanne Duc's in Saint-Tropez. At nearly 80 kilos, she has to stop abusing alcohol. To compensate, she delves into cocaine.

From this point on, she will continue to flirt dangerously with drugs.

September 1931

Kiki appears at the Océanic on rue du Montparnasse, again with Jamblan.

February–March 1932

Kiki agrees to appear at the Bal Musette, a large Berlin cabaret, by way of paying hospital bills for her now alcoholic mother. During her time in Germany, her mother dies.

Spring 1932

Kiki falls in love with André Laroque, who bears a striking resemblance to Jean Gabin. Dédé is a tax inspector, but also plays the accordion. The two appear together at the Cabaret des Fleurs on rue du Montparnasse, where the photographer Brassaï would immortalise them in his work.

1933

Anatole Litvak's film, *Cette vieille canaille*, comes out. Kiki plays a gang leader in a women's prison.

It is her last on-screen appearance.

Spring 1935

While still appearing at the Cabaret des Fleurs,

Kiki – 1936

Kiki falls in love with a young female dancer, Margot Vega, 22. She comes from the same region as Kiki, and like her, she never knew her father.

November 1935
At the suggestion of her husband, the blond Margot forms a duo with Kiki called "Les Vega Sisters". Kiki bleaches her hair for the occasion.

October 1936
As her success continues at the Cabaret des Fleurs, Kiki is urged by Dédé, her accompanyist, to go through drug rehabilitation. It would be her first attempt to end her addiction to drugs, but not her last.

Summer 1937
Kiki opens her own cabaret, Babel, in honour of the World Fair. A young singer, Charles Trenet, makes his debut there. Dédé Laroque, who is still around, plays accordion, alternating with a junkie pianist. The crazy atmosphere every night costs the owner money.
Kiki opts to give up her role as manager. Dédé

convinces her to take a detoxifying cure at a specialised institution. Only Desnos and his partner Youki are in on the secret; officially, Kiki is in Bourgogne.

1938
Nine years after the publication of her *Souvenirs*, Kiki takes up editing a new version. Written with the help of André Laroque on a typewriter belonging to the Revenue, the text would not be published during Kiki's lifetime.

Lou Mollgaard would use it as the basis for his biography of *Kiki: Reine de Montparnasse*, published by Robert Laffont in 1988. It would eventually be unearthed by the Serge Plantureux bookshop, who would entrust its publication to José Corti in 2005.

That same year, the patient Dédé finally left Kiki – but he didn't leave her for long. When Moysès hired Kiki at the Bœuf sur le Toit, then at rue Pierre-1er-de-Serbie, the accordionist would agree to accompany her for her three-month contract. In October, she sings at Gypsy's on rue Cujas.

July 1939
Kiki's first double-sided record comes out on the Polydor label.

Accompanied on the accordion by Laroque, Kiki sings "Les Marins de Groix" and "Le Retour du marin".

September 1939
Her accordionist is called up and Kiki has to give up her spot at Gypsy's. She tries to sing at the Jockey, but she doesn't get on well with the orchestra. Meanwhile, she has fallen back into the clutches of cocaine. She is arrested for possession of intoxicants over the winter. During her two weeks of detention, she is locked up again, this time in the Salpêtrière mental hospital; drug addicts were then considered to be mentally ill.

Early 1940

Kiki's second record comes out. Its two tracks, "La Volerie" and "Sur les marches du palais", were likely recorded before the Occupation.

March 1940

Kiki's third record comes out, with two tracks, "Là-haut sur la butte" and "Le Long de la Tamise", recorded with Laroque in 1939.

July 1940

Man Ray leaves France for the United States. Kiki and he would not see each other again until the early 1950s.

September 1941

A new love for Kiki: a blue-eyed plumber who beats her, but, she says, is divine in bed.

1942

The Jockey reopens. Kiki, unemployed, comes back to sing. Laroque, who has recently escaped Germany, finds work there.

The colours of the city quickly turn to field grey, and the new boss is suspected of being an informant for the Gestapo. Laroque, who has connections to the Resistance, decides to slip away. Kiki in turn leaves Paris. She moves in with her plumber on Île-Bouchard, near Chinon.

For the next two years, Kiki shares her time between Indre-et-Loire and Bourgogne.

1945

Kiki goes back to work at the Boeuf sur le Toit. At the same time, she escapes her lover's violence with Laroque's help.

Despite his partner's objections, the accordionist takes the former Queen of Montparnasse into his home on carrefour Vavin. André Laroque would keep an eye on Kiki until she died.

February 1946

Kiki is locked up for using forged prescriptions to obtain psychotropic substances. After a month of detention, she is released on parole. She is eventually sentenced to two months in prison with a suspended sentence.

1947

From then on, Kiki sings in a piano bar on rue Vavin, Chez Adrien. After her set, she would pass through the tables with a collection plate, and would finish her night in a nearby apartment, Le Printania. There she meets Raoul Dufy and Louis Armstrong.

July–August 1950

Eleven chapters of the unpublished version of Souvenirs de Kiki are published in Ici Paris and Ici Paris Hebdo under the title "Kiki vous parle sans pose". It mainly discusses her childhood.

Spring 1951

Man Ray returns to Paris. He bumps into Kiki by chance in Montparnasse. Since their last meeting, his one time muse has changed a great deal. Swollen by dropsy, alcoholism and drugs, she has lost her voice. She is living by her wits and on the generosity of old friends she meets in cafés. Her fall has been slow but steady. She no longer sees herself as a part of the art world.

23 March 1953

Alice Ernestine Prin, known as Kiki, dies in Paris. She is 52 years old. She is buried in the Thiais cemetery. Friends from her past, Treize, André Salmon and Foujita are the only ones present at her burial.

Biographical Notes

in order of appearance

CHAÏM SOUTINE

Born in 1893 in Smilovitchi, Belarus, Chaïm Soutine, the son of a tailor, grew up poor with his ten brothers and sisters. He studied fine art in Minsk and Vilnius before reaching Paris in 1912. Legend has it that on arriving at the Gare de l'Est, that he went straight to La Rotonde on foot.

When Kiki met Soutine, both were still penniless. The first time they met, on a harsh winter night, Soutine burned everything in his studio that he could light to warm the young girl. "From that day on, I liked Soutine" Kiki wrote ten years later. "We have been practically inseparable for some time."

In 1919, Soutine left Paris for Ceret in the Pyrenees. Zborowski, an art dealer, provided for his needs. The miracle took place four years later, in January 1923; the American collector Albert Barnes discovered Soutine's painting at Zborowski's and bought the whole body of his work for $3,000. Financial success had finally come. Soutine turned into a dandy, appearing in custom-made suits and ties. When he passed by the terraces of La Rotonde or the Dôme, he would avoid eye contact with anyone who might be looking for handouts – yet when he went up to the bar, he wouldn't hesitate to buy a round for his former comrades in misfortune.

In 1925, the artist completed several versions of his famous painting *Carcasse de boeuf*, inspired by Rembrandt's *Boeuf écorchéde*. Purchased at La Villette slaughterhouse, the meat decomposed rapidly, which alarmed the city health authorities. In future, in order to continue his work, the artist would inject formaldehyde into his models. "Painting must be vomited!" Soutine said to André Masson.

Despite his Jewish background, the artist refused to take refuge in the United States during the German occupation, and hid in Touraine with his last love, Marie-Berthe Aurenche, the ex-wife of Max Ernst.

Chaïm Soutine died of an ulcer in 1943.

AMEDEO MODIGLIANI

Amedeo Modigliani was born in 1884 in Livorno, Italy. After studying art in Florence and Venice, he arrived in Paris in 1906, aged 22. Initially he settled in Montmartre, and moved to Montparnasse in 1909, to the "laundry boat" La Ruche studios. As a result of his connection to Brancusi, Modigliani devoted himself primarily to sculpture.

Enriched by this experience, he returned to painting in the mid-1910s. In painting, his artistry was revealed. He would produce more than 350 paintings in his six remaining years.

At the end of the decade, Kiki approached Modigliani at Chez Rosalie, a restaurant on rue Campagne-Première. Rosalie Tobia, herself a former model of Italian origins, acts as a minder for her compatriot, feeding him in exchange for drawings. Sometimes, his friend Utrillo would come down from Montmartre to drink Chianti with him. Modigliani had a reputation for being a lush; women liked him, and he drank alcohol and took hashish. "It was very rare to see Modigliani sober," Kiki remembered. "The little money he earned was used to quench a burning thirst."

In the spring of 1917, the painter met Jeanne Hebuterne. She was 19 years old, studying painting and was a regular at La Rotonde. Foujita was said to have had an affair with her. Modigliani fell madly in love, much to the chagrin of the Hebuternes family, petty bourgeois Catholics who took a dim view of their daughter falling in love with a Jewish Italian painter. Jeanne left the family home and moved in with Amedeo. They had a daughter.

In January 1920, Modigliani became ill. His friends were either away or also bedridden. In the end, the painter was discovered unconscious in his frozen studio, Jeanne snuggled against him. He was hospitalised immediately, but died without regaining consciousness. Two days later, Jeanne, back at her parents' house, threw herself out of the window. She was nine months pregnant.

MOÏSE KISLING

Eldest son of tailor Wolf Kisling Brody, Moïse was born on 22 January 1891 in Krakow, Poland. His father died when he was nine years old, and the young Kisling joined the School of Fine Arts in his hometown six years later. As the sculpture course was full, he decided on painting. His teacher, an avid Francophile, advised him to take an apprenticeship in Paris. On his arrival in 1910, Kisling befriended Braque, Max Jacob, Andre Salmon and Modigliani, who would remain one of his closest friends. After a stay at the "laundry boat" in Montmartre, he moved to Ceret in the Pyrenees with Picasso, Gris and Max Jacob. On his return, he had his first exhibition at the Salon d'Automne. At number 3, rue Joseph-Bara, he rented a studio and an apartment. Pascin, Per Krohg Zborowski and Rembrandt Bugatti lived in the same building. His antics, *joie de vivre* and generosity soon made Kisling one of the leading lights of Montparnasse. In June 1914, he made headlines with his sabre duel against his compatriot, the painter Gottlieb. "A Matter of Honour" read the headline, but the history of art knows no more about it.

In 1914, when the Great War broke out, the artist immediately joined the Foreign Legion. A year later, at the Battle of Carency, he was wounded in the chest and was discharged. When he returned to Paris, he received a small windfall, bequeathed by an American friend of the Lafayette squadron who had been killed in combat. The inheritance was squandered in the months that followed. Previously, Moïse had met a student of fine arts, Renée, the daughter of the Commander of the Paris Republican Guard of Paris. Their marriage in 1917, remained a thing of legend in Montparnasse. "The orgy of my wedding lasted for three days and three nights. I don't really know any more." In 1920, Modigliani died. Kisling, who had worked with him in his studio in rue Bara for a long time, paid the funeral expenses. That year he painted his first portrait of Kiki. She would remain one of his favourite models throughout the decade. "He's a good – a very good – guy, very sensitive under his gruff exterior" she wrote later.

At that time, Kisling already had a good reputation as painter. His workshop was a famous meeting place. Writers, painters, sculptors, poets, journalists, actors, models – most of them penniless – gathered to drink, eat and dance to a phonograph. In 1922, the painter was the subject of a monograph, the first in a series dedicated to him. Two years later, Kisling finally became a French citizen. Meanwhile, Renée had given him two sons.

The 1930s saw the Kisling family stay more and more in the south of France. In 1933 he was made a Knight of the Legion of Honour. The "Montparnasse Success Story" celebrated his nomination at a banquet at La Coupole. Four years later, he started to build a villa in Sanary, Provence. The following year, he learned that the Germans had sentenced him to death for his anti-Nazi activities. When Germany's invasion of Poland was announced, the actor Raimu said, "We're still not going to fight for Polish Jews. Me, I say fuck the Polish Jews, my dear Kisling, don't you agree?" "I am a Polish Jew" Kisling replied. The actor didn't miss a beat: "Okay, so then I promise you we'll give the dirty Huns a fucking thrashing, with all our Polish Jew friends!"

After his discharge in 1940, Kisling went to Portugal and then made it to the United States. He stayed there throughout the war. When he returned to Paris, he found that his studio had been looted. From then on, the artist would continue his work in Provence. Immediately after the war, he would occasionally turn up at Chez Adrien, a piano bar in rue Vavin. Kiki still sang there, her beauty ruined by alcohol and drugs.

Moïse Kisling died on 29 April 1953 in Sanary from uremia.

FUJITA TSUGUHARU

In 1914, a Japanese man sat on the terrace of La Rotonde. He wore an old-fashioned tunic and a pair of sandals. He is "Foujita". He had been in Montparnasse for the past year to study painting.

Born 28 years earlier in Kumamoto, southern Japan, Fujita Tsuguharu lost his mother when he was four. When at the age of 12 he decided to devote himself to painting, his father, a medical officer in the army, approved of his choice and sent his son to the School of Fine Arts in Tokyo; in Japan, painting is an honourable profession. Despite a prestigious first commission, a portrait of the Emperor of Korea, his career was stagnating. He asked his father for permission to travel to France to perfect his art. The day after his arrival at Montparnasse, he was introduced to Picasso, who showed him his Henri Rousseau collection, whose simplistic style would have a lasting influence. Adopted by the Spanish painter, Foujita joined his circle and made ties with Apollinaire, Max Jacob and Braque. For several months, he visited Americans Raymond and Isadora Duncan, who advocated a return to the purity of the ancient Greeks. Foujita would dance in the woods in a toga...

His fringe cut straight across his forehead, his thick round glasses and his eccentric clothing made women notice him. Marcella, Gaby, Margaret, Margot, Loulou and the others taught him to sneak into the cinema, to practise French kissing, to buy cocaine and to use slang, but it was Fernande Barrey whom Foujita married in 1917. He fell deeply in love with the young painter at La Rotonde. She rejected him, but the next morning, he visited her and gave her a blouse he had sewn for her during the night. Fernande opened her icy studio to him – it was wartime and there was a coal shortage. She broke a chair and threw it in the fire to warm the place. Thirteen days later, they married. Foujita borrowed six francs from a waiter at La Rotonde to get the banns published.

Fernande believed in the talent of her "petit Japonais" who could now combine techniques from both the Western and Eastern traditions. She moved him into an old stable at the bottom of her building on rue Delambre and every day she courted the art dealers in vain. One day, caught out by the rain, she borrowed an umbrella from a dealer, Cheron. He had just refused the works of this unknown Japanese painter, but warily agreed to take two watercolours to sell. They sold the next day, and he wanted more – and fast. But he had taken neither Fernande's name nor address. A month later, he finally found her. He soon gave Foujita a contract for 450 francs per month. In return, the painter was to produce two pieces per day, eight francs per watercolour. With the funds, Fernande and Foujita paid for a trip south with Modigliani, Soutine and the poet and dealer Zborowski. They met Renoir, but, having failed to sell their works, the Montparnasse set had to return to Paris, leaving their luggage and canvases with their landlord.

Kiki was Foujita's favourite model. His *Nu couché à la toile de Jouy* marked the start of his success. From that point on, the Japanese painter's character marked him out as different in Montparnasse in the Roaring Twenties. Fernande and he went to all the parties and balls. But at midnight, the painter would go off to bed. This descendant of a samurai was disciplined. Every morning at sunrise, he was at his easel. Not Fernande. The day that he surprised his wife in the arms of his cousin Koyonaghi, Foujita bowed politely and left the marital home.

Lucie, a Belgian, was 20 when he met her at La Rotonde. They immediately locked themselves in a nearby hotel. They came out three days later; Lucy was henceforth called Youki – pink snow. Foujita led the high life with his new partner: townhouse in Montsouris, servants, a car and driver with a bronze of Rodin as a radiator cap. But in 1928, the tax man caught up with the successful painter. Both ruined, the relationship did not survive. Youki ran off with Robert Desnos, and Foujita, became infatuated with red-haired Mady "Panther" Dormans. He took her to Japan, but it would be a fatal journey. The Panther had been taken off cocaine too abruptly and fell into a coma and died without regaining consciousness.

Stuck in Japan during the war, Foujita returned to Paris in 1950. "I am back to stay." With his compatriot Kimyo, they became naturalized, baptized and settled in rue Campagne-Première. On the wall of his studio, he hung the *Nu couché à la toile de Jouy*, bought back from a collector. At Kiki's funeral, he was the only famous painter to walk behind the coffin. He was seen crying for the first time.

HENRI-PIERRE ROCHÉ

Born in Paris in 1879, Henri-Pierre Roché was educated at the School of Political Science. He planned for a career in diplomacy, but with no standing or money, he had to abandon his dream. In 1898, he enrolled at the Julian Academy where he studied painting. But again, he didn't stay with it, as he had insufficient talent to become a painter. He turned to writing, beginning a diary that he would continue for the rest of his life.

From the beginning of the century, Roché published in the top journals of the time such as *Le Mercure de France*. By his mid-teens, he had already befriended Braque, Picabia, Apollinaire and Picasso's lover Marie Laurencin, and met with the German writer Franz Hessel and his wife Helen Grund, who would become the two main characters in his future novel *Jules et Jim*. "He knew everybody and wanted everyone to know each other," noted Gertrude Stein whom, indeed, Roché introduced to Picasso.

In 1916, he was sent by the French government on an economic mission to the United States. In New York he saw Picabia, who was editing the journal *391*, and met Marcel Duchamp. With Duchamp, who would remain a firm friend known to Roché as "Victor" or "Totor", he founded *Blindman* magazine in 1917. But two avant-garde publications in New York was one too many. Picabia and Roché gambled their futures on a chess game. Roché lost, and *Blindman* was sunk.

Back in France, in addition to his work as an art critic, Roché took on the role of intermediary for the American collector John Quinn. He discovered and negotiated for him the purchase of works by Matisse, Derain, Dufy, De Chirico, Modigliani, Picasso, Rousseau and Brancusi.

The art lover took an interest in Man Ray from his early days in Paris. In July 1922, Quinn wrote: "I like Man Ray enough and have enough faith in his work to offer to lend him enough money for a large workshop with good photographic equipment.

He agreed, did so, is thriving and needed only half of the money I was offering him. Confidential." According to his journal, Roché met Kiki for the first time on 8 May 1922. It was he who encouraged her to paint and exhibit, even offering her his apartment for a small exhibition. In 1924, when he acquired a watercolour by Kiki, he noted in his journal, "Dinner with Man Ray, Kiki and Tzara. Bought a lovely watercolour, a super Matisse by Kiki."

Even though he refused to be considered a collector, Roché nonetheless acquired over the course of time works by Laurencin, Brancusi, Picasso, Duchamp, Braque, Modigliani and Dubuffet to name the best known. But it was in 1953 that he came to notoriety with the publication of his first novel, *Jules et Jim*, inspired by his relationship with the Hessel-Grunds. Henri-Pierre Roché was 74 years old. Three years later, he published his final work, *Les Deux Anglaises et le continent*.

That same year, a young film critic got in touch with him regarding a film adaptation of his first novel. He would write in *Arts*, "One of the most beautiful modern novels I know is *Jules et Jim*, which shows us two friends and their shared partner through a lifetime, who love each other with a tender love with almost no clashes thanks to a new aesthetic moral that is constantly being revised." François Truffaut wanted to base his first film on this unusual love story. A friendship formed between the two men, but Roché would never see Jeanne Moreau play the role of Kathe on the big screen. He died in April 1959.

MAN RAY

Emmanuel Rudnitzky was born in Philadelphia in 1890 to Jewish parents who had recently emigrated from Russia. He was seven years old when his family moved to Brooklyn where his father worked in a tailor's shop. The young Rudnitzky began to paint in 1908, and enrolled in an art school. Four years later, he took on the pseudonym Man Ray. He worked in an advertising agency, and later illustrated atlases at a publishing house to support himself. In 1913, he joined an avant-garde artist colony in Ridgefield, across from Manhattan. It was there that he would meet Frenchman Marcel Duchamp. Though his painting was initially inspired by cubism, Man Ray quickly set about trying abstract painting, sculpture, collage and photography. In 1921, he and Duchamp published the only issue of *New York Dada*. "Dada cannot live in New York," he wrote shortly thereafter to Tzara.

On 22 July, 1921, Man Ray arrived at the Gare Saint-Lazare where Marcel Duchamp was waiting for him. That day, he introduced his American friend to the Dadaist circle: Breton, Aragon, Eluard and Soupault. Soupault immediately offered to exhibit his work at Six bookshop. Six months later, Man would exhibit his paintings there. The catalogue was signed by Aragon, Breton, Eluard, Tzara, Arp, Ernst and Soupault, but not one canvas was sold. Abandoning his brushes, in early 1922 Man Ray turned to experimental photography and developed his famous rayographs – also called "rayographies" or "rayograms". With only a light source and photosensitive paper, he offered these chance images to Dada, described by Tzara as "a game of chess with the sun".

At the end of 1922, the publication of *Champs délicieux*, a collection of 12 of these images, made Man Ray one of the pillars of the movement.

Meanwhile, the American artist would meet Kiki, the favourite model of the painters of Montparnasse and its main source of photographic inspiration. During the seven years that their – often tumultuous, always passionate – relationship would last Man Ray would take pictures – from the rayograph to pornographic close-ups, everything from surrealist games to snapshots. If, in terms of painting, *À l'heure de l'observatoire, les amoureux,* featuring Lee Miller's lips, remains his most famous painting, two shots of Kiki undeniably placed Man Ray in the collective memory: *Le Violon d'Ingres* became a surrealist icon par excellence, and *Noir et Blanche*, in which Kiki's face rests perpendicular to a Baulé mask. However, in the 1920s, it was not his avant-garde studies that fed the artist, but rather his work as a portraitist and fashion photographer for *Harper's Bazaar*, *Vu* and *Vogue*. Aside from his Dadaist and later surrealist friends, the list of people immortalized by Man Ray's camera is a veritable who's who of the arts and literature of the interwar period: Dora Maar, Aldous Huxley, T. S. Eliot, Eisenstein, Nancy Cunard, Erik Satie, Max Ernst, Brancusi, Tanguy, Léger, Hemingway, Derain, Braque, Pascin, Matisse, Miró, Picasso, Cocteau, Dali, René Char, Magritte, De Chirico, Gertrude Stein, Picabia, Mina Loy, Djuna Barnes and Luis Buñuel.

Painting and photography were not the only two strings to the artist's bow. Man Ray became interested in cinema in 1923. The two minutes and forty-five seconds of his first film, *Rétour à la raison*, were screened at the Coeur à Barbe evening organized by Tzara, an evening that would see a physical divide – and blows – between Dadaists and future surrealists. Five years later, Man Ray's fourth film, *Étoile de mer* with a screenplay by Desnos and Kiki in the lead role, would be hailed by André Breton, the former leader of the artistic avant-garde worldwide. Unique in the annals of surrealism, Man Ray was the only person not to fall out with anyone else in the group. His friendship with Tzara, like those with Breton and Desnos would remain intact, despite the conflicts that faced the three men.

In 1929, when he realized that Kiki's liaison with Henri Broca was more than just a fling, he announced his romantic relationship with his assistant, Lee Miller. The young American, a former model for *Vogue* and future war photographer, would stay with her compatriot for three years before leaving him. A self-portrait entitled *Suicide* attests to the photographer's state of mind after the break-up.

In July 1940, the arrival of the Germans pushed the now famous photographer to cross the Atlantic. He took refuge in Hollywood. His major contribution to the film industry was his painted portrait of Ava Gardner for the film *Pandora*.

In 1951, Man Ray returned to Paris accompanied by the woman who would be his last great love, Juliet. He dedicated himself to painting and creating objects inspired by surrealism in a studio in rue Férou. He passed away in 1976 at the age of 86. His grave can be found in the Montparnasse Cemetery, a few hundred metres from the places that saw him become an artist.

MARIE VASSILIEFF

Born in Smolensk in 1884, Mary Vassilieff studied in St. Petersburg. After two trips to Paris and another to Munich where, with her hair cut short, she distributed revolutionary flyers, in 1907 she settled permanently in the French capital. A regular at La Rotonde, which had just opened, she became involved in the creation of the Russian Academy for young non-French-speaking artists. In 1912, she left the Academy, but continued her courses in her own workshop at 21, avenue du Maine, where Fernand Leger would give important lectures. She fell in love with a Moroccan officer who disappeared, leaving her a son.

With the war, starvation came to Montparnasse. In response, Mary Vassilieff organized a canteen in her art studio. At each meal, 45 people could eat for a nominal price. Considered a private club by the authorities, the canteen was not subjected to the curfew. Artists of all nationalities came together – Modigliani, Zadkine, Picasso, Ortiz de Zárate, Max Jacob, Cendrars, Braque and Gris enjoyed the convivial atmosphere of the place, where concerts were given every Saturday. Sometimes, the hostess would perform Cossack dances.

In December 1921, Mary Vassilieff introduced Kiki to Man Ray. Throughout the twenties, the small Russian woman made rag dolls painted by hand. When she went to The Jockey, she improvized traditional Russian dance numbers. In 1938, Kiki was said to admire her, while deploring their estrangement nine years before, when both women were nominated for the election of the Queen of Montparnasse. Kiki pipped her to the post; the Russian artist would never forgive her.

Today, impasse 21, avenue du Maine is one of the few vestiges of the old neighbourhood. Mary Vassilieff's studio now houses the Montparnasse Museum, which keeps the artistic memory and the spirit of the place alive.

PABLO PICASSO

Living in France near Montmartre since 1901, Pablo Picasso crossed the river in 1912. He was 31 years old and already known as a painter. It was his dealer, Kahnweiler, who moved him from boulevard Clichy to boulevard Raspail. In Montparnasse, the Spanish artist discovered the terraces of La Rotonde and the Dôme. In 1913, he moved into a new studio at 5 bis rue Schoelcher, with a view of the Montparnasse Cemetery.

A series of shots by Jean Cocteau on 12 August 1916 bears witness to the intermingling of neighbourhood personalities. Looking through the images, taken between La Rotonde and the Vavin metro stop, the poet snapped: Picasso and his mistress, the fashion model Pâquerette, Max Jacob, Moïse Kisling, Mary Vassilieff, Henri-Pierre Roché, Amedeo Modigliani, André Salmon and Ortiz de Zárate.

In 1922, when Man Ray photographed Picasso for the first time, he had already come back across the Seine to the right bank. He had left the bohemian areas for the chic neighbourhoods in 1918. At 23, rue la Boetie, he occupied two apartments: in one, he led a bourgeois life with Olga Kokhlova; in another, he set up his workshop. Later, Man Ray would say that he had visited Picasso a good deal in the 1920s. The Spaniard would also often visit the American in his studio in rue Campagne-Première. Picasso also attended the screening of Man Ray's first film during the evening at the Coeur à Barbe, the last Dada event, crashed by Breton and his cohort. The first issue of *La Révolution surréaliste* published a "construction" of Picasso's photographed by Man Ray. The friendship between the two men would last for decades.

Pablo Picasso died 8 April 1973 at the age of 91.

TRISTAN TZARA

Born on 16 April 1896 in Moinesti, Romania, Samuel Rosenstock was born into a wealthy Jewish family. Fond of French culture and influenced by the Symbolists, he published his first poems at age 16. The following year, he denied that they were his and invented the pseudonym Tristan Tzara, a Western phonetic spelling of the Romanian word for "earth". In 1915, he wanted to discover the world, but it was at war. Switzerland was neutral, and so Tzara joined his compatriot Marcel Janco in Zurich. In this city traditionally dedicated to banking, there was also a young population that objected to the war. In February 1916 German poet Hugo Ball opened the Cabaret Voltaire. Soon after, the two Romanians, along with Jean Arp from Alsace, Sophie Taueber from Switzerland and Huelsenbeck from Germany, joined in the creative fireworks. All of the arts were represented – poetry, dance, painting, music – to create what Ball termed "a whole work of art". The Cabaret Voltaire saw the birth of the Dada movement. Later, the founders of the movement would compete for ownership of the name. In the third issue of Dada, Tzara published the resounding Dada Manifesto of 1918.

"Dada means nothing ... After the carnage, we hold out hope for a purified humanity ... Everything we look at is false ... I am against systems; the most acceptable system is having no system on a point of principle ... We need strong works, straight, precise to the point of being impenetrable. Logic is complicated. Logic is always false ... the principle: 'Love thy neighbour' is hypocrisy. 'Know thyself' is utopian, but more acceptable because it contains the wickedness in it ... each man shouts, 'There is a great, destructive, negative job to be done. Sweep up, clean up.'"

In Paris, André Breton and his cohort were enflamed by this revolutionary text. They urged Tzara to bring the good word of Dada to Paris. Picabia took the young, monocled Romanian into his home. Through his eloquence, sense of showmanship and communication skills Tzara gathered around him all those who sought new meaning in art and writing since the great slaughter of 1914–18.

Aragon, Ribemont-Dessaigne, Eluard, Duchamp, Picabia, Soupault, Péret, Man Ray, even Cocteau followed suit, but, from 1924, the surrealist revolution would win out over Dada, and those who Breton dubbed "impostors, greedy for publicity". The violent opposition between the two leaders remains one of the pivotal episodes of the history of the artistic avant-garde during the early 20th century.

A close friend of Man Ray's, Tzara was present at the birth of his rayographs, wrote a preface for his first book and pushed him to make his first film, *La Retour à la raison*, which was screened during the Coeur à Barbe evening, the last major Dada event in 1923. The Romanian poet was also a close friend of Kiki's. It was a difficult friendship to manage when Breton's group broke away from that of the famous Dadaist. How could she have an aperitif on the terraces of Montparnasse with Desnos or Tzara when one was looking to give the other a punch in the face? Kiki and Treize devised all manner of tricks to prevent the two night owls from crossing.

Tzara was always a difficult character to grasp. Though he wrote every day in austere solitude, he was also a regular at the Boeuf sur le Toit and the costume balls of Montparnasse. He married a rich Swedish heiress he met at the Cigale bar, where one of his plays was put on, and went on to build a townhouse in Montmartre – but he was also a very active card-carrying member of the Communist Party. The whirlwind came to an end with the German occupation and Tzara became a member of the resistance.

The author of nearly 50 works, most of them poetry collections, Tzara's work was illustrated by Marcel Janco, Hans Arp, Picabia, Juan Gris, Marcoussis, Miró, Max Ernst, Tanguy, Kandinsky, Giacometti, Matisse, Picasso and André Masson. An African art enthusiast since his Cabaret Voltaire days, the poet went to Africa for the first time in 1962. He died the following year in Paris.

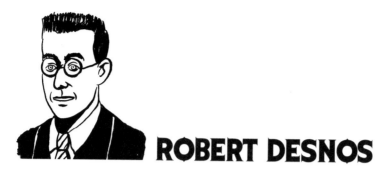

ROBERT DESNOS

Originally from Orne, Lucien Desnos was first a labourer at Les Halles market before becoming an important wholesaler in the "belly of Paris". As he rose into the middle classes he became the father, in 1900, to Robert-Pierre. Reader of the *Mystères de Paris* and of *Fantômas* from an early age, Robert inhaled the poems of Hugo, Nerval and Mallarmé. At 16, he decided to devote his life to writing; his father threw him out.

The young Desnos survived on odd jobs, and became friends with another young anarchist already working freelance, Henri Jeanson.

At 20, the apprentice poet signed up with the French Colonial Forces. The night before he was to leave for Morocco, he went to the Café Certà, where the Dadaists were holding court. The corporal in uniform was fascinated by Breton, "the human volcano". Back in Paris two years later, Desnos had a passion for jazz and revived the Breton group, breaking the divide with Dada. Surrealism was emerging. Desnos would be one of its most ardent devotees. In thrall to Breton, he participated in the "big sleeps" medium sessions. In a state of hypnotic trance, he composed "dream-poems" published in *Littérature*. The December 1922 issue contained the message that Rrose Sélavy (alias Marcel Duchamp) sent telepathically from New York. Kiki and Man Ray attended some of his performances. "The seances were miraculous even if they were rehearsed and learned by heart," Man Ray wrote 40 years later. In July 1923, Desnos participated alongside Breton in the brawl at the Coeur à Barbe that sounded the death knell of the Dada movement. But he had to survive. Through Jeanson, Desnos joined the team at the daily *Paris-Soir*. His professional writing would be severely criticized by his fellow surrealists and would precipitate his break away from Breton, whom he criticized for his commitment to the Communist Party and its stance against homosexuality. At the Boeuf sur le Toit, where he had been dragged by Jeanson, Desnos fell for singer Yvonne George. A multiple-drug addict, she led the reporter astray with opium, cocaine and heroin. His relationship with Yvonne George would inspire his novel published in 1943.

Le vin est tiré tells the cruel story of a man in the depths of his addiction who believes he has the power to join his beloved, lost in the artificial ecstasies. Yvonne, "the Star" was a close friend of Kiki's. During the 1920s, Robert thus became one of the confidantes of the future Queen of Montparnasse. He wrote the catalogue copy for her first painting exhibition. The following year, they would act together in *L'Étoile de mer*, Man Ray's film for which he wrote the screenplay. Later, her faithful friend would be suspected of having touched up the manuscript of her memoirs. In the final version of the memoirs, Kiki wrote of her "great friend", "Desnos is the guy you always see running! You'd think he's in a hurry to live!"

Yvonne died in 1930. Meanwhile, another woman came into Robert's life. He nicknamed her "the Mermaid"; everyone else knew her as Youki, Foujita's partner. Initially, the three were friends. The Japanese artist tattooed a mermaid on Youki's thigh, and a bear with a band of stars on the arm of the poet. Over time, their feelings changed; love set in without ever arousing jealousy. When in 1931, exhausted by the relentlessness of the French tax authorities, Foujita left without warning for South America along with the red-haired Madeleine, Robert and Youki were faced with a *fait accompli*. The following year, they moved in together in Saint-Germain-des-Prés and stayed together from that point forward.

The 1930s saw the poet turn to radio. He wrote his first big hit with *La Complainte de Fantômas*, performed by Antonin Artaud. On the back of this, he was soon creating radio advertisements. With this financial windfall, he forced himself to write poetry "so that my imagination can get some fresh air". During the German occupation, the journalist continued his career despite its detractors, including Céline who called him a "yid thinker". In 1942, after the Vel'd'Hiv round-up, Desnos entered the resistance and immediately joined the Action group. But in February 1944, the journalist and resister was arrested by the Gestapo. He was sent to Auschwitz, Buchenwald, Flöha and Flossenburg. While the Allies were crossing the Rhine, the poet was transferred to Czechoslovakia. He died of typhus in Terezin concentration camp on 8 June 1945 – one month after the end of the war. "I have always been, and will be to the end, a mad lover of freedom."

ANDRÉ BRETON

Born in 1896, André Breton grew up in the Parisian suburbs in a family of modest means. He developed a passion for poetry at a very young age, but entered medical school in 1914 due to family pressure. A few months later, he was drafted as a nurse.

In early 1918, Breton discovered the *Dada Manifesto*, published a month earlier by Tristan Tzara in Zurich. He admired the radical text immediately. He urged Tzara to join him. The friendship between the two men would last for two years. In 1921, when Breton organized the mock trial for writer Maurice Barrès, Tzara declared his mistrust of justice, including Dadaist justice. The next year, the Romanian poet declined Breton's invitation to participate in the Paris conference he was managing. In response, Breton condemned "the promoter of a movement that has come from Zurich". Tzara immediately accused him of xenophobia. Breton was humiliated to be thus confused with right-wing extremists, and a point of no return was reached. Soon after, he wrote *Après dada*, which put an end to his involvement in Dadaism. From then on, André Breton and his cohort would be known as surrealists – after a neologism invented by Guillaume Apollinaire. In 1924, the often contested leader of the movement would publish the *Surrealist Manifesto*, which defined it as: "pure psychic automatism through which we propose to express verbally, in writing, or by any other means, the real function of thought." Breton gathered together personalities as diverse as Louis Aragon, Paul Eluard, Philippe Soupault, Benjamin Péret, Max Ernst, Robert Desnos, Jacques Prévert, Salvador Dali and Léo Malet. But as the "excommunications" ordered by the "pope of surrealism" mounted, many of his lifelong friends turned against him. Man Ray was one of the few not to feel his wrath.

A Communist Party supporter in 1927, Breton would turn away from it eight years later. During the Nazi occupation, he found refuge in New York, and resumed his surrealist activities up in Paris in 1946. He died 20 years later, the embodiment of one of the most tumultuous intellectual scandals of the 20th century.

MARCEL DUCHAMP

Born in Blainville in 1887 to a family of artists, Marcel Duchamp put his name to his first painting when he was 15 years old. After a spell at the Julian Academy, and then at a printer's, he did drawings and illustrations for satirical journals. In New York in 1913, his *Nu descendant l'escalier no. 2* got him noticed. Escaping conscription for health reasons, Duchamp returned to the United States in 1915 and lived there until 1923.

His greatest work remains without a doubt *La Mariée mise à nu par ses célibataires*, also called *Le Grand Verre*. Duchamp would dedicate years to it, thinking and experimenting, publishing his notes in the form of facsimiles. Designed in 1912 and made between 1915 and 1923, the work would remain unfinished.

Soon after his arrival in New York, in the autumn of 1915, Duchamp coined the idea of the "ready-made" – a mass-produced object transformed into a work of art solely by the choice or intervention of the artist. Thus, this first "ready-made", a shovel purchased from a hardware store and immediately titled *In advance of a broken arm (after) Marcel Duchamp*. Duchamp created a scandal in 1917 with *Fountain*, a simple urinal signed with the pseudonym R. Mutt. In 1920, he created his female alter ego, Rrose Sélavy, immortalized by Man Ray's photographs.

The friendship between Man Ray and Marcel Duchamp dated from 1915, and would last a lifetime. Together, they created the magazine *New York dada* and, whenever the American headed to Paris, the Frenchman would give him a place to stay and introduce him to the avant-garde circle. During this period, Duchamp completed two works that were emblematic of the Dada movement, *L.H.O.O.Q.* and *Air de Paris*. The interwar period saw Duchamp follow his passion for visual experiences and chess. In the early 1940s, he left Paris again for New York. He died there in 1968.

In 2004, a British survey named *Fountain* as "the most influential work of art of the century".

TREIZE

Born in Paris in 1900, Thérèse Maure came from a middle-class family from Savoie. After finishing her school exams, she enrolled in a gymnastics class run by Georges Hébert. Healthy mind, healthy body was the ethos of this "college of female athletes". In a toga, the young Thérèse learned to box, throw the javelin and dance. She then became an instructor at the institution for many years. A Mexican dancer from Hébert's course introduced her to La Rotonde. She then decided to set up her own gymnastics class in Montparnasse. It was Robert Desnos, encountered on his return from Morocco in 1922, who gave her the nickname "Treize". In exchange, she taught him the art of kick-boxing. The two had a brief fling which turned to friendship.

That same year on 14 July at La Rotonde, she met up with a young woman with an infectious laugh – Kiki. They would become inseparable. "Treize and I are one and the same!" Kiki wrote in 1929. "If something happens to either one of us, we share it, even if it's throwing a punch, or getting one!"

In 1924, they went to Brittany together. The following year, they went to Villefranche-sur-Mer. Treize was accompanied by her lover, the painter Per Krohg, whose wife, Lucy, was having a passionate affair with Pascin, for whom she wouldn't leave Per and with whom she had a daughter. "Per Krohg ... helped by Treize ... spanks me to relax," wrote Kiki in her memoirs.

After Pascin's death, his passion for Lucy having driven him over the edge of despair, the split between Per and Lucy was final – as was his split with Treize. The young woman locked herself away for six weeks. Kiki brought her food and forced her to eat every day. When Per left for Oslo with the Scandinavian Ranghilde, Thérèse married Manuel Caño de Castro, a penniless painter of Spanish origin. Bit by bit, she broke away from Montparnasse and its sleepless nights, but she stayed in contact with Kiki. Treize would be at her friend's side until the end; she was one of the last to visit her in the hospital shortly before she passed away.

In the early 1980s, Thérèse Maure would be the main source of information for Billy Klüver and Julie Martin, and later Lou Mollgaard, for their biographies of Kiki.

IVAN MOSJOUKINE

Trained in the Russian theatre, Ivan Mosjoukine began acting for the screen in 1911. He was already famous in his home country when he emigrated in 1920 with part of the Ermolieff troupe. On arriving in France, the film producer founded the Albatros firm, the staff of which – actors, directors, screenwriters, set designers, costume designers, technicians – was largely made up of Russians. Albatros films were as well received artistically as they were commercially during the twenties. Films were still silent, and expressiveness and being photogenic were what got an actor noticed – so Ivan Mosjoukine quickly became a favourite of French audiences, then European ones. In 1923, the success of the film *Kean*, directed by Volkoff after Dumas, gave him a box office hit. He was then considered to be on a par with Rudolph Valentino. From then on, all the work by the Albatros studios in Montreuil centred around the man who was adored by the masses and cinema professionals alike. The actor played with Marcel L'Herbier and Jean Epstein. Louis Delluc wrote, "I admire Mosjoukine," and a young actor who debuted with him, Charles Vanel, would later say that the Russian was "the greatest". Mosjoukine eschewed the ordinary with his taste for fast cars, regular sessions in the bars of Montmartre or Montparnasse, and his conquests of women. It was in this context that he met Kiki. Treize would witness their brief and flamboyant love affair.

In Moscow, the Mosjoukine archives keep a unique vestige of this meeting: a dozen letters from Kiki. Written over a period of one month, they show the Frenchwoman's passion, which is clearly barely reciprocated by the Russian. In her last letters, Kiki complains about his silence and indifference.

Headhunted by Hollywood, Mosjoukine left France in 1927. On the other side of the Atlantic, he was first renamed Moskin, then Mosjukine. In the end, he made only one film, *The Hostage*, for Universal. He returned to Europe very soon after his failure in the US, the star realizing that his fame was fading. The advent of the talkies brought the downfall of an actor who could not speak French without a thick Russian accent.

Mosjoukine died in 1939, destitute and largely unknown.

JEAN COCTEAU

Jean Cocteau was born in Paris the same day as the Eiffel Tower was completed, on 5 July 1889. He grew up in the comfort of the family home, but the young boy was only nine years old when his father committed suicide with a bullet to the head. In 1909, aged 20, he published his first collection of poems, *La Lampe d'Aladin*. Over the next decade, the young man would come to spend time with Igor Stravinsky, Marcel Proust, André Gide and Roland Garros. Picasso brought him into the circle of Montparnasse artists, where he met Max Jacob, Kisling and Modigliani. Accompanied by Picasso, he also moved seamlessly into the avant-garde. With the painter, a troupe of Diaghilev's Russian dancers and the composer Erik Satie, in 1917 Cocteau created a "realist ballet", *Parade*. Apollinaire welcomed this first manifestation of the "New Spirit" with a word coined for the occasion: "sur-realism".

In 1919, Cocteau met a young poet, Raymond Radiguet, 16, for whom he became a mentor, protector and lover. That same year, he wrote to Tzara: "I will keep a close eye on all Dada efforts." The first subscriber to Dadaism, the poet quickly came into conflict with others among them. The Surrealists would make him their whipping boy. Yet much later, in 1930, Cocteau and Desnos reconciled over the body of the singer Yvonne George, their dear friend, and in 1937 Aragon would open the pages of the daily paper *Ce Soir* to him.

In 1922, shortly after his arrival in Paris, Man Ray photographed Cocteau. Kiki was there: "He had red, white and black woollen gloves." Through the 1920s, they see a great deal of each other. They shared sleepless nights at the Boeuf sur le Toit, the bar "launched" by the poet and named after his play of the same name. "He often came in the evening to listen to me at the Boeuf. His presence gave me more confidence," the singer would remember a few years later. It was also Cocteau who in 1925 introduced her to the virtues of the Welcome Hotel in Villefranche-sur-mer. There, on the Mediterranean coast, he was still trying to recover from the death of Radiguet some two years earlier.

Since then, he had plunged into opium and despair. "We met every night at the little hotel bar where we enjoyed ourselves watching the sailors and prostitutes," Kiki would say.

During those years, when Cocteau did the publicity for his books, he always sent a copy to "Man and Kiki Ray". Even though his pen seemed never to have been inspired by the painters' favourite model, Kiki produced a colour portrait of her friend Jean.

As the decades passed, Cocteau would turn his poetic talent to many things. He drew, painted, made films (*Le Sang d'un poète*, *L'Éternel Retour*, *La Belle et la Bête*, *Orphée*), and wrote poetry ("*Le Cap de Bonne Espérance*", "*Le Mystère de Jean l'oiseleur*"), theatre (*La Voix humaine*, *Les Parents terribles*), novels (*Thomas l'imposteur*, *Les Enfants terribles*) and autobiographical texts (*Opium*, *Portraits souvenirs*).

Jean Cocteau's life was a whirlwind of friendships and love affairs. In 1937 he got together with defeated boxer Al Brown and helped him to regain his title as World Champion. The same year, he discovered the young Jean Marais, who would become a new source of romantic inspiration. In 1940, he wrote *Le Bel Indifférent* for Édith Piaf and her lover, Paul Meurisse. In 1942, he officially took his leave of his friend Arno Breker, who was once Hitler's favourite sculptor. In 1943, he made Jean Genet famous and saved him from a life sentence in prison by declaring him "the greatest writer of our time". In 1944, the morning after the liberation of Paris, he joined Hemingway in the bar of the Ritz, which the writer had personally "liberated". In 1949, he was made a Knight of the Legion of Honour.

In 1953, when Kiki died, the protean poet – an avowed drug addict and assumed homosexual – entered the Académie française.

At noon on 11 October 1963, Jean Cocteau learnt of the death of Édith Piaf. "The boat has sunk," he declared. He died an hour later.

HENRI BROCA

The son of a strict professor of mathematics and the great-nephew of a famous doctor, Henri Broca would always be considered the black sheep of the family. After his initial theatrical and journalistic experiences in Bordeaux, the town where he grew up, the young Broca set off for Montparnasse in 1925. In 1928, he published *T'en fais pas! Viens à Montparnasse*, a collection of writing and caricatures. In February 1929, the caricaturist-cum-journalist launched the journal *Paris-Montparnasse*, the last issue of which would be printed in March 1930.

When Man Ray was shown a caricature of himself and Kiki as a couple, the American artist wrote across it, "This is shit – done by an asshole". The caricaturist in question was Broca. According to Man Ray, the romantic relationship between Kiki and Broca took shape during the editing of the model's memoirs, which the journalist published.

"Henri Broca impressed me with his astonishing qualities of intelligence, his unparalleled energy ... but the first time it struck me, there was no physical attraction on my end whatsoever. He is very charming and he has an incredible hold on me", Kiki would later write in the 1938 version of her *Souvenirs*.

On 30 May 1939, under the auspices of his journal, Broca organized the election of the Queen of Montparnasse at Bobino. Kiki was happy to be elected, and her title would never be challenged.

In 1938, Kiki would speak frankly of the end of their affair. High – according to Man Ray – or syphilitic – according to Lou Mollgaard – Henri Broca faded into dementia during the 1930s. Kiki had to have him committed. The doctors sent him back to his family in Bordeaux. Henri Broca died in 1935 without seeing Montparnasse again.

LEE MILLER

Born in Poughkeepsie, New York in 1907, Lee Miller was 19 years old when she was saved from being hit by a car by Condé Nast, the owner of *Vogue*. He hired her immediately as a model. Three years later, the young woman was in Paris. She wanted to learn photography and was introduced to Man Ray. "I am your new student," she said to him. "I don't have any students," the photographer responded. And I'm leaving tomorrow for Biarritz." "Me too!" she shamelessly replied. Lee and Man would stay together for three years, for work and love. Though she was at first aggressive towards the woman who had replaced her in the photographer's heart, Kiki would come to like her in the end.

In 1930, Cocteau chose Man's new model to play the role of a statue in his film, *Le Sang d'un poête*. The next year, the model fell in love with the Egyptian businessman Aziz Eloui Bey, whom she married and went to live with in Cairo. Man Ray was crushed, but a famous painting came out of the break-up. Man Ray would work for two years on *À l'heure de l'observatoire, les amoureux*, inspired by a trace of red lipstick left on his collar. As he worked, Lee's lips replaced Kiki's.

In 1937, Lee Miller came back to Paris and found her friends Eluard, Ernst, Picasso and Man Ray. She introduced the Englishman Roland Penrose to their fold. An art critic and future author of seminal works on Picasso and Man Ray, he would become her second husband.

In 1940, Lee took up her camera again. At first she specialized in fashion and portraits for *Vogue*, and in 1942 became a war photographer. She followed the Allies in Normandy and as far as Germany, helping in the liberation of the Buchenwald and Dachau camps.

In 1949, she moved with her husband to a farm in Sussex. She gave up photography to dedicate herself to gourmet cooking, and won culinary prizes. In 1966, Roland Penrose was knighted for services in promoting contemporary art.

Lady Lee, as she had come to be known, died of cancer in 1977.

ERNEST HEMINGWAY

Born in 1899, the American, Ernest Hemingway, discovered Europe during the First World War. He returned four years later and moved to Paris's Latin Quarter in January 1922. He was still a journalist, but he dreamt of literature. It was while on Parisian soil that he honed his concept of literature: "All you have to do is write one true sentence." In trying to put this principle into practice, he travelled across Europe as a press correspondent. After a trip across the Atlantic to hand in his resignation to the paper that employed him, Hemingway returned to France in 1924 resolved to dedicate himself exclusively to literature. The Paris-based literary journal *Transatlantic Review* published one of his short stories alongside another "upcoming writer", Tristan Tzara. At the Dingo Bar the following year, he would meet Scott Fitzgerald, the *enfant terrible* of American literature. The rivalry between the two men – fuelled by Hemingway – was the stuff of legend. It was during this period that the future Nobel prize winner would write his first novel of note, *The Sun Also Rises*.

Like the American novelist, Kiki was a regular at the Dingo. When she met Hemingway he was virtually unknown. In 1929, when he wrote the preface to the American edition of *Souvenirs de Kiki*, he had become a successful author thanks to *A Farewell to Arms*. In the preface, the writer remembers the Montparnasse he had known. On Kiki at the height of her powers, he wrote, "Having a fine face to start with she had made of it a work of art. She had a wonderfully beautiful body and a fine voice, a talking voice, not a singing voice, and she certainly dominated the era of Montparnasse more than Queen Victoria ever dominated the Victorian era." In the whole of his career, Hemingway would only agree to write two prefaces, first Kiki's, and then for Jimmie Charters, the former boxer who had become the barman at the Dingo.

In 1961, the author of *For Whom the Bell Tolls* and *The Snows of Kilimanjaro* took his own life with a shotgun. Three years later, the posthumous publication of the novelist's Parisian memoirs would reveal the innocence of his "lost generation" under the title *A Moveable Feast*.

JAMBLAN

Born in 1900 in Bressuire, Jean Blanvillain arrived in Paris 25 years later. He dedicated himself to poetry and caught the last of bohemian life on the hill of Montmartre. It was a simple side step from poetry to song for a man who wanted to live by his writing. Jamblan taught classes, recited poems and performed songs every night at L'Écu Terreux cabaret. Perhaps it was there that he met Kiki; Montmartre had always been her second-favourite neighbourhood. The Queen of Montparnasse and the handsome Montmartre singer were bound to meet. In the spring of 1929, Moyzès hired them to perform at Boeuf sur le Toit on rue de Penthièvre. Paul Morand, Rachilde et Jean Cocteau cheered them on. Kiki and Jamblan sang together for the entire summer of 1931 at Jeanne Duc's in Saint-Tropez. On their return, they appeared at the Océanic, a cabaret in Montparnasse. The next year, Kiki left for Berlin alone. Her addiction to "çakébon", as she called cocaine, had scared Jamblan off. In 1935, the singer came into new fame with *Ma Mie*, a standard of the late 1930s and part of the repertoires of Jean Sablon and Charles Trenet. Made famous in the wake of Lucienne and Suzy Solidor, Jamblan would never leave the musical scene. During the 1960s and 70s, his songs would still be sung by Jean Ferrat, the Jacques brothers, Patachou and Colette Renard.

Jamblan died at the age of 89 by falling down the stairs. He left behind an unfinished song in a trunk of mementos:

"Dis-moi l'amour, Kiki, comme tu l'aimes/Un peu naïf, assez coquin, toujours bohème / L'amour bien chaud, Kiki, par temps de glace / Quand le vent de noroît caressait Montparnasse/Les jours d'hiver où l'on ne voyait pas l'jour/Dis-moi l'amour, Kiki, comme à Saint-Trop'/Lorsque les Montparnos étaient déjà l'Europe/Et qu'il fallait parfois un jour entier/Pour aller de la mèr' Vachon à Sénéquier."

ANDRÉ LAROQUE

Kiki fell in love with Laroque because she thought he looked like film star Jean Gabin. André Laroque was a tax inspector, but he played the piano and the accordion well. Kiki made him her accompanyist. He would become her guardian angel.

Alice and André met in 1932 in a Parisian café. An officer's son from a middle-class family, Dédé dived into Paris nightlife with Kiki. The couple were immortalized by a photograph by Brassaï: Dédé poses with his accordion by Kiki's side and wears a flat cap like a farmer. That said, André was not a night owl, and he didn't tolerate his partner's excesses. He tried to subdue her, and to get her off of drugs; she would relent, and then she'd go right back. Her periods of indulgence would be followed by rehabilitation. To sing, she needed to alter her consciousness; without alcohol or çakébon (cocaine), partying had no meaning. For all that, their professional union spanned the 1930s, culminating in the release in 1939 of their first double-sided 78. They would release other albums on the Polydor label, but the Second World War sounded the death knell for Kiki's recording career. A soldier and, later, prisoner of war, Laroque escaped and took refuge in Paris. He was the barman at the Jockey, where Kiki sang. The atmosphere in the cabaret took on a distinctly field grey colour, and Laroque's work with the resistance made him wary, and he left Paris. Kiki did as well, but in another direction.

They met again after the war when, to escape beatings from a violent lover, Kiki took refuge at Dédé's. Another woman had meanwhile entered his life, but regardless, André Laroque would be his former mistress' protector, taking care of her until her final days. He would never manage to put a stop to the Queen of Montparnasse's fall.

BIBLIOGRAPHY

Albera, François. *Albatros, des Russes à Paris* (Éditions Mazzotta / Cinémathèque française).

Aragon, Louis, *Benjamin Péret & Man Ray. 1929* (Éditions Allia).

Baker, Carlos. *Histoire d'une vie* (Éditions Robert Laffont).

Baldwin, Neil. *Man Ray* (Éditions Plon).

Berger, Pierre. *Album Cocteau* (Éditions Gallimard).

Berger, Pierre. *Robert Desnos* (Éditions Seghers).

Brassaï. *Le Paris secret des années 30* (Éditions Gallimard).

Brassaï. *Conversations avec Picasso* (Éditions Gallimard).

Breton, André. *Oeuvres complètes* (Éditions Gallimard).

Breton, Simone. *Lettres à Denise Lévy, 1919-1929* (Éditions Joëlle Losfeld).

Buisson, Sylvie. *Foujita, le maître japonais de Montparnasse* (Éditions Musée de Montparnasse).

Buisson, Sylvie. *Les Ateliers de Pascin et de ses amis* (Éditions Musée de Montmartre).

Buot, François. *Tristan Tzara, l'homme qui inventa la révolution Dada* (Éditions Grasset).

Butor, Michel. *L'Atelier de Picasso. L'Alambic des formes* (Éditions Images modernes).

Calder, Alexander. *Autobiographie* (Éditions Maeght).

Calvocoressi, Richard. *Lee Miller, portraits d'une vie* (Éditions La Martinière).

Caracalla, Jean-Paul. *Montparnasse, l'âge d'or* (Éditions Denoël).

Chadwick, Whitney. *Les Femmes dans le mouvement surréaliste* (Éditions Thames & Hudson).

Cocteau, Jean. *Opium* (Éditions Le Livre de Poche).

Cocteau, Jean. *Romans, poésies, œuvres diverses* (Éditions Le Livre de Poche).

Collectif. *Les Années mémoire 1925/1929* (Éditions Larousse).

Collectif. *Les Années Montparnasse* (Éditions Contrejour / Le Monde).

Collectif. *Le Canton de l'Île-Bouchard* (Éditions Les Amis du Musée bouchardais).

Collectif. *Cocteau* (Éditions du Centre Pompidou).

Collectif. *Dada* (Éditions du Centre Pompidou).

Collectif. *Desnos, Foujita & Youki* (Éditions Des Cendres / Éditions Musée du Montparnasse).

Collectif. *Kisling, Centenaire (1891-1953)* (Éditions Galerie Daniel Malingue).

Collectif. *L'Œuvre et son accrochage* (Musée national d'Art moderne / Éditions du Centre Pompidou).

Collectif. *Man Ray, directeur de mauvais movies* (Éditions du Centre Pompidou).

Collectif. *La Ruche, centenaire d'une cité d'artistes* (Éditions Atlantica / Éditions Musée du Montparnasse).

Courrière, Yves. *Jacques Prévert* (Éditions Gallimard).

Crespelle, Jean-Paul. *Montparnasse vivant* (Éditions Hachette).

De Baecque, Antoine & Serge Toubiana. *François Truffaut* (Éditions Gallimard).

De L'écotais, Emmanuelle. *Man Ray* (Éditions Taschen).

De Saint-Pern, Dominique. *Les Amants du soleil noir* (Éditions Grasset).

Desanti, Dominique. *Robert Desnos, le roman d'une vie* (Éditions Mercure de France).

Desnos, Robert. *Nouvelles Hébrides et autres textes* (Éditions Gallimard).

Desnos, Youki. *Les Confidences de Youki* (Éditions Fayard).

Drot, Jean-Marie. *Les Heures chaudes de Montparnasse* (Éditions Hazan).

Duchamp, Marcel. *Duchamp du signe* (Éditions Flammarion).

Dumas, Marie-Claire. *Robert Desnos ou l'exploration des limites* (Éditions Klincksiek).

Eglington, Laurie. *Marcel Duchamp de retour en Amérique* (Éditions L'échoppe).

Gefen, Gérard. *Paris des artistes* (Éditions Le Chêne).

George-Michel, Michel. *Les Montparnos* (Éditions Del Duca).

Gindertael, R.V. *Modigliani et Montparnasse* (Éditions Tête de Feuilles).

Gossmann, Marlène. *Le Mythe de Kiki de Montparnasse* (Éditions Les Cahiers du Châtillonnais).

Hemingway, Ernest. *Paris est une fête* (Éditions Gallimard).

Hillion, Daniel. *La Mer s'affiche* (Éditions Ouest France).

Hodgson, Barbara. *Opium, histoire d'un paradis infernal* (Éditions Le Seuil).

Jouffroy, Alain. *La Vie réinventée* (Éditions Rocher).

Kiki. *Souvenirs* (Éditions Hazan).

Kiki. *Souvenirs retrouvés* (Éditions José Corti).

Klüver, Billy & Julie Martin. *Kiki de Montparnasse (1900-1930)* (Éditions Flammarion).

Kohner, Frédéric. *Kiki de Montparnasse* (Éditions Buchet/Chastel).

Kybalovà, Ludmila, Olga Herbenovà & Milena Lamarovà. *Encyclopédie illustrée du Costume et de la Mode* (Éditions Gründ Editions).

Lacôte, René. *Tristan Tzara* (Éditions Seghers).

Lanoux, Armand. *Paris 1925* (Éditions Robert Delpire).

Lesacher, Alain-François, Monique Sclaresky & Hervé Champollion. *Paris, hier et aujourd'hui* (Éditions Ouest-France).

Lipmann, Anthony. *Divinely Elegant, The World of Ernst Dryden* (Éditions Pavillon Michael Joseph).

Lottman, Herbert. *Man Ray à Montparnasse* (Éditions Hachette).

Mollgaard, Lou. *Kiki, reine de Montparnasse* (Éditions Robert Laffont).

Naumann, Francis. *Marcel Duchamp, l'art à l'ère de la reproduction mécanisée* (Éditions Hazan).

Naumann, Francis. *Marcel Janco se souvient de Dada* (Éditions L'échoppe).

Parisot, Christian. *Modigliani* (Éditions Canale Arte).

Passeron, René. *Encyclopédie du surréalisme* (Éditions Somogy).

Penrose, Antony. *Les Vies de Lee Miller* (Éditions Arléa/Seuil)

Penrose, Roland. *Man Ray* (Éditions Le Chêne).

Penrose, Roland. *Picasso* (Éditions Flammarion).

Poirier, René & Patrick Lehideux. *L'Automobile et son histoire* (Éditions Librairie Gründ).

Polizzoti, Mark. *André Breton* (Éditions Gallimard).

Rabaté, Marie-Rose & André Goldenberg. *Villefranche-sur-Mer, hier et aujourd'hui* (Éditions Vifa Serre).

Ray, Man. *Autoportrait* (Éditions Babel).

Ray, Man. *Ce que je suis et autres textes* (Éditions Hoëbeke).

Ravache, Martine & Brigitte Leblanc. *L'Album photo des Français de 1914 à nos jours* (Éditions Le Chêne).

Roché, Henri-Pierre. *Écrits sur l'art* (Éditions André Dimanche).

Sachs, Maurice. *Au temps du Boeuf sur le Toit* (Éditions Grasset).

Sers, Philippe. *Sur Dada* (Éditions Jacqueline Chambon).

Surirey, Gilles. *Chronique familiale d'Alice Prin* (Éditions Archives municipales de Châtillon-sur-Seine).

Steegmuller, Francis. *Cocteau* (Éditions Buchet / Chastel).

Thérond, Roger. *Surréalisme* (Éditions Le Chêne).

Touzot, Jean. *Jean Cocteau, qui êtes-vous?* (Éditions La Manufacture).

Vailland, Roger. *Chronique des Années folles à la Libération* (Éditions Buchet / Chastel).

Vieillevigne, Sylvie. *New York* (Éditions Flammarion).

Warnod, André. *Drôle d'époque. Souvenirs* (Éditions Fayard).

Warnod, Jeanine. *L'école de Paris* (Éditions Musée du Montparnasse/Arcadia Éditions).

Warnod, Jeanine. *La Ruche et Montparnasse* (Éditions Weber).

Wiéner, Jean. *Allegro Appassionato* (Éditions Belfond).

Zukor, Adolph. *Le public n'a jamais tort* (Éditions Corréa).

TABLE OF CONTENTS